EFFECTIVE TEACHING METHODS

EFFECTIVE TEACHING METHODS

4TH EDITION

Gary D. Borich
The University of Texas at Austin

Merrill
an imprint of Prentice Hall
Upper Saddle River, New Jersey   *Columbus, Ohio*

Library of Congress Cataloging-in-Publication Data

Borich, Gary D.
    Effective teaching methods/Gary D. Borich.— 4th ed.
        p.   cm.
    Includes bibliographical references (p.   ) and indexes.
    ISBN 0-13-936130-8
        1. Effective teaching. 2. Lesson planning—United States.
I. Title.
    LB1025.3.B67   2000
    371.102—dc21   99-34485
                                                                 CIP

Editor: Debra A. Stollenwerk
Developmental Editor: Linda Scharp McElhiney
Editorial Assistant: Penny S. Burleson
Production Editor: Mary Harlan
Copy Editor: Luanne Dreyer-Elliott
Design Coordinator: Diane C. Lorenzo
Photo Coordinator: Anthony Magnacca
Text Designer: STELLARViSIONs
Cover Designer: Brian Deep
Cover Photo: ©Unicorn Stock Photography
Production Manager: Pamela D. Bennett
Electronic Text Management: Marilyn Wilson Phelps, Karen L. Bretz, Melanie N. King
Illustrations: Christine Marrone
Director of Marketing: Kevin Flanagan
Marketing Manager: Meghan Shepherd
Marketing Coordinator: Krista Groshong

This book was set in Garamond by Prentice Hall and was printed and bound by R. R. Donnelley & Sons Company. The cover was printed by Phoenix Color Corp.

©2000, 1996 by Prentice-Hall, Inc.
Pearson Education
Upper Saddle River, New Jersey 07458

Earlier editions © 1992, 1988 by Macmillan Publishing Company.

Photo Credits: Scott Cunningham/Merrill: pp. 10, 27, 64, 110, 133, 171, 272, 324, 332, 347, 356, 370, 388; KS Studios/Merrill: pp. 141, 404; Mark Madden/Merrill: p. 427; Anthony Magnacca/Merrill: pp. 78, 82, 158, 196, 216, 222, 248, 257, 289, 308, 338, 400, 431, 436, 438, 458, 472; Barbara Schwartz/Merrill: pp. xx, 38, 57, 375; Anne Vega/Merrill: pp. 23, 48, 94, 185, 236, 255, 281, 316.

Printed in the United States of America

10 9 8 7 6 5 4 3

ISBN: 0-13-936130-8

Prentice-Hall International (UK) Limited, *London*
Prentice-Hall of Australia Pty. Limited, *Sydney*
Prentice-Hall of Canada, Inc., *Toronto*
Prentice-Hall Hispanoamericana, S. A., *Mexico*
Prentice-Hall of India Private Limited, *New Delhi*
Prentice-Hall of Japan, Inc., *Tokyo*
Prentice-Hall (Singapore) Pte. Ltd., *Singapore*
Editora Prentice-Hall do Brasil, Ltda., *Rio de Janeiro*

Preface

Microcomputers, competency testing for students and teachers, curriculum reform, new state and federal laws, multicultural classrooms, and new teacher certification and degree requirements are but a few of the factors changing the face of American schools and creating special challenges for you, the beginning teacher. This book has been written to help you prepare to meet these challenges and to discover the opportunities for professional growth and advancement they provide.

Goals of This Edition

To accomplish this, this fourth edition of *Effective Teaching Methods* has four simple goals. The first is to present effective teaching practices derived from a recent 25-year period of classroom research. In this research, different teaching practices were systematically studied for their effectiveness on learners. The results have made it possible to replace many age-old anecdotal suggestions for "good" teaching with modern, research-based teaching practices that are empirically related to positive outcomes in learners. How to use these teaching practices to become an effective teacher is a major focus of this book.

Second, this text describes these effective teaching practices in a friendly, conversational manner. The language of classrooms is informal, and there is no reason why a book about teachers in classrooms should not use the same language. Therefore, this book talks straight, avoiding complicated phrases, rambling discussions, or pseudoscholarly language. The idea behind each chapter is to get the point across quickly in a friendly and readable style.

The third goal of this book is practicality. Positive prescriptions for your classroom behavior show you how to engage students in the learning process, manage your classroom, and increase student achievement. This book not only tells *what* to do to obtain these results; it also shows *how* to obtain them, illustrating effective teaching practices with concrete examples and entertaining classroom dialogues.

The final goal of this book is to be realistic. Some of the literature on teaching is speculative. However, this book describes what real teachers do in real classrooms and which teaching practices are and are not effective in those classrooms. Nothing in this book is pie-in-the-sky theorizing about effective teaching, because most of what is presented results directly from years of research and observation of effective teaching practices in real classrooms.

These, then, are this book's four goals: to provide *research-based* effective teaching practices, presented in a *conversational style,* that are *practical* and *realistic.*

New to This Edition

Users of the earlier editions of this book will notice that many chapters have been revised due to the rapid pace of change occurring in nearly every aspect of teaching. These changes have resulted in a text that updates and extends the content in earlier editions.

Since publication of the last edition of this text, I have prepared a new and revised edition of a companion volume, *Observation Skills for Effective Teaching,* Third Edition (Borich, 1999, also from Merrill/Prentice Hall). This revised companion volume and workbook is intended to be used either in a preteaching observation experience or as an applications resource to the present volume. *Observation Skills for Effective Teaching* provides extensive examples, entertaining and instructional classroom dialogues, and practical observation and recording instruments keyed to and coordinated with the effective teaching methods presented in this text. Together, these texts provide the sequence of learning for the preservice and beginning teacher illustrated in the following figure.

Six levels of teacher training and development activities.

Observation Skills for Effective Teaching: 3rd ed.

STEP 6
Decision-making dialogues

STEP 5
Problem-solving activities

STEP 4
Classroom observation

Effective Teaching Methods: 4th ed.

STEP 3
Practice activities and exercises

STEP 2
Classroom dialogues and examples illustrating the method or technique

STEP 1
Structure and organization of a teaching method or technique

Special Features

Special features of this fourth edition include the following:

- A beginning chapter on who an effective teacher is and what an effective teacher does in the classroom (Chapter 1).
- A chapter on understanding the important role of individual differences and learner diversity—prior achievement, ability, learning style, culture and ethnicity, and home and family life—on student learning needs and classroom management (Chapter 2).
- A revised and expanded chapter on instructional goals and objectives that shows you how to assess the extent to which you are achieving thinking and problem-solving behaviors in your classroom (Chapter 3).
- Two chapters on teaching strategies that explain how to use direct instructional methods (such as explaining, lecturing, drill and practice, and recitation—Chapter 5) and indirect instructional methods (such as group discussion, collaboration, and discovery and problem-solving activities—Chapter 6).
- A chapter on teacher questioning that shows you how to raise questions at different levels of cognitive complexity and how to use probes and follow-up questions to promote higher-order thinking and problem-solving behavior (Chapter 7).
- A chapter on self-directed learning and how to use metacognitive techniques, teacher mediation, and the social dialogue of the classroom to help learners control, regulate, and take responsibility for their own learning (Chapter 8).
- A chapter on cooperative learning and the collaborative process for productively organizing and managing group and team activities that promote communication skills, self-esteem, and problem solving (Chapter 9).
- Two chapters on classroom management, including group development in the classroom (Chapter 10) and anticipatory management (Chapter 11).
- A chapter on evaluation of student achievement for measuring and interpreting student progress using teacher-made and standardized tests (Chapter 12).
- A chapter on performance assessment, which explains the concept of authentic assessment and how to construct and grade performance assessments, and a special extended discussion of student portfolios (Chapter 13).
- A revised and expanded *Bridges,* the student/instructor activity guide and assessment options (by Debra Bayles Martin) that accompanies *Effective Teaching Methods,* Fourth Edition.

For the Students

We also provide, specifically with you, the student, in mind:

- Classroom application questions at the beginning of each chapter that focus you on the key aspects of each chapter.
- End-of-chapter summaries that restate key concepts in an easy-to-follow outline format.
- End-of-chapter questions for discussion and practice, and keyed answers in Appendix B, with many additional applications in *Bridges: Activity Guide and Assessment Options*.
- A self-report survey instrument for measuring concerns about yourself, the teaching task, and your impact on students, to gauge your development and growth in the teaching profession (Chapter 1 and Appendix A).
- New procedures for organizing unit and lesson plans that let you graphically visualize the relationship between lessons and unit (Chapter 4).
- A Higher-Order Thinking and Problem-Solving Checklist to help you achieve a thinking curriculum in your classroom (Chapters 3, 8, 13, and Appendix C).

ACKNOWLEDGMENTS

Many individuals contributed to the preparation of this book. Not the least are the many professionals whose studies of classroom life have contributed to the effective teacher described in this text. The work of these professionals has made possible an integration and synthesis of effective teaching practices representing a variety of data sources and methodological perspectives. Although I accept responsibility for translations of research into practice that I have made, strengths the reader may see in this approach must be shared with the many individuals who made them possible.

I also wish to acknowledge those teachers who over the years have shared their insights about the teaching process with me. Among these have been teachers in the Austin, Texas, Independent School District, especially William B. Travis High School and Travis Heights Elementary School, who provided the opportunity to observe many of the effective teaching methods described herein. For their helpful reviews and contributions to the manuscript, I extend my gratitude to my good friend and colleague, Marty Tombari, and also to those who reviewed the text: Beatrice S. Fennimore, Indiana University of Pennsylvania; Margaret Ferrara, Central Connecticut State University; Michael James, Wichita State University; Barbara Kacer, Western Kentucky University; and Lynda Randall, California State University—Fullerton.

GDB
Austin, Texas

About the Author

Gary Borich grew up on the south side of Chicago, where he attended Mendel High School, and later taught in the public school system of Niles, Illinois. He received his Ph.D. from Indiana University, where he was director of evaluation at the Institute for Child Study under Nicholas J. Anastasiow. Dr. Borich is presently a member of the College of Education faculty at the University of Texas at Austin and a past member of the Board of Examiners of the National Council for the Accreditation of Teacher Education.

Dr. Borich's other books include *Clearly Outstanding: Making Each Day Count in Your Classroom; Becoming a Teacher: An Inquiring Dialogue for the Beginning Teacher; Observation Skills for Effective Teaching,* 3rd Edition; *Authentic Assessment in the Classroom* (with M. Tombari); *Educational Testing and Measurement,* 6th Edition (with T. Kubiszyn), and *Educational Psychology: A Contemporary Approach,* 2nd Edition (with M. Tombari).

Dr. Borich lives in Austin, Texas, with his wife, Kathy, and his two children, Brandy and Damon. His interests include pottery and training and riding Arabian horses.

Discover the Companion Website Accompanying This Book

THE PRENTICE HALL COMPANION WEBSITE: A VIRTUAL LEARNING ENVIRONMENT

Technology is a constantly growing and changing aspect of our field that is creating a need for content and resources. To address this emerging need, Prentice Hall has developed an online learning environment for students and professors alike—Companion Websites—to support our textbooks.

In creating a Companion Website, our goal is to build on and enhance what the textbook already offers. For this reason, the content for each user-friendly website is organized by chapter and provides the professor and student with a variety of meaningful resources. Common features of a Companion Website include:

For the Professor—
Every Companion Website integrates **Syllabus Manager**™, an online syllabus creation and management utility.

- **Syllabus Manager**™ provides you, the instructor, with an easy, step-by-step process to create and revise syllabi, with direct links into Companion Website and other online content, without having to learn HTML.
- Students may logon to your syllabus during any study session. All they need to know is the web address for the Companion Website and the password you've assigned to your syllabus.
- After you have created a syllabus using **Syllabus Manager**™, students may enter the syllabus for their course section from any point in the Companion Website.
- Class dates are highlighted in white and assignment due dates appear in blue. Clicking on a date, the student is shown the list of activities for the assignment. The activities for each assignment are linked directly to actual content, saving time for students.
- Adding assignments consists of clicking on the desired due date, then filling in the details of the assignment—name of the assignment, instructions, and whether or not it is a one-time or repeating assignment.
- In addition, links to other activities can be created easily. If the activity is online, a URL can be entered in the space provided, and it will be linked automatically in the final syllabus.
- Your completed syllabus is hosted on our servers, allowing convenient updates from any computer on the Internet. Changes you make to your syllabus are immediately available to your students at their next logon.

For the Student—

- **Chapter Objectives**—outline key concepts from the text
- **Interactive Self-quizzes**—complete with hints and automatic grading that provide immediate feedback for students. After students submit their answers for the interactive self-quizzes, the Companion Website **Results Reporter** computes a percentage grade, provides a graphic representation of how many questions were answered correctly and incorrectly, and gives a question by question analysis of the quiz. Students are given the option to send their quiz to up to four email addresses (professor, teaching assistant, study partner, etc.).
- **Message Board**—serves as a virtual bulletin board to post—or respond to—questions or comments to/from a national audience
- **Net Searches**—offer links by key terms from each chapter to related Internet content
- **Web Destinations**—links to www sites that relate to chapter content

To take advantage of these and other resources, please visit the *Effective Teaching Methods* Companion Website at

www.prenhall.com/borich

Brief Contents

Contents

CHAPTER 6

Indirect Instruction Strategies   196

CHAPTER 7

Questioning Strategies   236

EFFECTIVE TEACHING METHODS

1 The Effective Teacher

This chapter will help you answer the following questions:
1. What are some key effective teaching behaviors?
2. What are some behaviors that can help me perform the key teaching behaviors?
3. Why are multiple definitions of effective teaching necessary?
4. What are some important indicators of teaching effectiveness?
5. What are patterns of effective teaching behavior?

*W*hat is an effective teacher? How do I become one? How long does it take? These questions have been asked by every teacher, young or old. They are deceptively simple questions, for they have many different answers. Teaching is a complex and difficult task that demands extraordinary abilities. Despite decades of experience and research, one of the most difficult tasks in education today is defining an effective teacher.

This chapter offers no pat definitions of an effective teacher. Instead, the goal is to introduce you to practices used by effective teachers—practices related to positive outcomes in learners. These effective teaching practices do not tell the whole story of what an effective teacher is, but they do form an important foundation to help you understand the chapters that lie ahead and to help you become an effective teacher. Subsequent chapters blend these practices with other activities, such as writing of objectives, lesson planning, teaching strategies, questioning techniques, classroom management, and learner assessment. This will give you a rich and comprehensive picture of an effective teacher and, most importantly, help you become one.

WHAT IS AN EFFECTIVE TEACHER?

The Role-Model Definition

If you had grown up a century ago, you would have been able to answer "What is an effective teacher?" very simply: A good teacher was a good person—a role model who met the community ideal for a good citizen, good parent, and good employee. At that time, teachers were judged primarily on their goodness as people and only secondarily on their behavior in the classroom. They were expected to be honest, hardworking, generous, friendly, and considerate, and to demonstrate these qualities in their classrooms by being organized, disciplined, insightful, and committed. Practically speaking, this meant that to be effective, all a beginning teacher needed was King Solomon's wisdom, Sigmund Freud's insight, Albert Einstein's knowledge, and Florence Nightingale's dedication!

It soon became evident that this definition of an ideal teacher lacked clear, objective standards of performance that could be consistently applied to all teachers and that could be used to train future teachers.

The Psychological Characteristics Definition

The early role-model approach soon gave way to another, which attempted to identify the **psychological characteristics** of a good teacher: personality, attitude, experience, and aptitude/achievement. Table 1.1 lists some of these psychological characteristics. Because they have a certain intuitive appeal, it is worth noting why they have *not* been useful criteria for defining good teachers.

Personality.   Over the years, only a few personality measures have been developed that relate specifically to teaching. Because most personality measures have been designed to record behavior in clinical settings, much of what they measure has been of little help in identifying the positive or normal behaviors that may be needed to be an effective teacher. Consequently, the usefulness of many personality tests in

Table 1.1 Commonly studied teacher characteristics.

Personality	Attitude	Experience	Aptitude/Achievement
Permissiveness	Motivation to teach	Years of teaching experience	National Teachers Exam
Dogmatism	Attitude toward children	Experience in subject taught	Graduate Record Exam
Authoritarianism	Attitude toward teaching	Experience in grade level taught	Scholastic Aptitude Test
Achievement-motivation	Attitude toward authority	Workshops attended	1. verbal
Introversion-extroversion	Vocational interest	Graduate courses taken	2. quantitative
Abstractness-concreteness	Attitude toward self (self-concept)	Degrees held	Special ability tests, (e.g., reasoning ability, logical ability, verbal fluency)
Directness-indirectness	Attitude toward subject taught	Professional papers written	Grade-point average
Locus of control			1. overall
Anxiety			2. in major subject
1. general			Professional recommendations
2. teaching			Student evaluations of teaching effectiveness
			Student teaching evaluations

predicting a teacher's classroom behavior must be inferred from their more general success in the mental health field. Although certain interpersonal, emotional, and coping behaviors are believed to be required for effective teaching (Levis, 1987), personality tests have provided few insights into the positive social behavior that may be needed for effective teaching.

Attitude.   While attitude assessments may be either global (e.g., attitude toward the educational system and the teaching profession) or specific (e.g., attitude toward a particular task, child, or curriculum), most attempts to measure teacher attitude generally have failed to forecast what a teacher who has a particular attitude *actually does in the classroom.* Research generally has shown a low and nonsignificant correspondence between teacher attitude and classroom performance (Jackson, 1968; Walberg, 1986).

Therefore, the use of attitude data for measuring teacher effectiveness has had to rest on the *assumption* that attitudes are related to behaviors that are one or more steps removed from the actual teaching process, such as more organized lesson plans or better subject-matter preparation (Clark & Peterson, 1986; Kagan & Tippins, 1992). However, defining effective teaching in this manner always will be less direct and credible than observing actual classroom practices.

Experience.   You probably, at one time or another, provided biographical data about yourself when applying for a job. You may have found that a listing of your qualifications, such as years of experience, graduate credits earned, or hours of training defined your experience so broadly as not to be very predictive of what you could do on that specific job. Such descriptions typically do not describe experience relevant to performing the *day-to-day* tasks required in a specific context, such as classroom, grade level, or subject matter area. A teacher's experience with a *specific* grade level, curriculum, and type of learner is more relevant to actual classroom performance than general biographical data, which represents only a small portion of a teacher's qualification for a particular teaching assignment.

Aptitude and Achievement.   Like general experience, most aptitude and achievement data do not accurately predict classroom performance. Regardless of the fact that these measures often are used to predict student performance, a teacher's prior achievement seldom has correlated strongly with classroom performance—and here is why.

As an example of prior achievement, consider a teacher's college grades. Achieving good grades might indicate enthusiasm for teaching and a promise of good classroom performance. But standards set by training institutions require teachers to meet minimum levels of competence for certification. This is usually sufficient to make the small variations in grades among beginning teachers irrelevant to actual performance in the classroom.

To summarize, using psychological characteristics to define a good teacher represented an attempt to measure teacher behavior objectively. But these characteristics often were too remote from the teacher's day-to-day work in the classroom to meaningfully contribute to a definition of a good teacher. Most notably, these definitions excluded the most important and obvious measure of all for determining good teaching: *the performance of the students who are being taught.*

A New Direction

In the last three decades, a revolution has occurred in the definitions of good teaching. We have seen that defining good teachers by community ideals proved unrealistic. We also have seen how teachers' psychological characteristics proved to be poorly related to what teachers actually did in the classroom. This directed researchers to study the impact of specific teacher behaviors on the specific cognitive and affective behaviors of their students. The term *good teaching* changed to *effective teaching,* and the research focus shifted from exclusively studying teachers to include their effects on students. These new ways of studying classroom behavior have made the student and teacher–student interaction in the classroom the focus of modern definitions of effective teaching.

Linking Teacher Behavior with Student Performance.   During the 1970s and 1980s, researchers developed new methods for studying the interactive patterns of teachers and students. The goal was to discover which teacher behaviors promote desirable student performance. But before unveiling the findings of this research and their implications for effective teaching, let's see how the research was performed.

The Research Process.   To collect data on the classroom interaction of teachers and students, researchers often used instruments like those shown in Figures 1.1 to 1.3. These particular instruments, devised by Good and Brophy (1987, 1997) for their research on effective teaching, record observations of various student–teacher behaviors. Using the response form in Figure 1.2, the observer codes both student responses to questions and the teacher's reaction and feedback. For example, in the tenth interchange recorded on this form, a male student fails to answer a question (0), is criticized by the teacher for not answering (–), and then is given the answer by the teacher (Gives Ans.). Numbers for the interchanges are assigned as they occur, allowing the pattern of question-answer-feedback to be recorded over an entire class period.

In Figure 1.3 the observer codes the student performance being praised by the teacher (perseverance, progress, success, good thinking, etc.). Individual students are identified by assigning each a unique number. This form records not only the praise behavior of the teacher *in relation to* individual student behavior but also the overall pattern or sequence of action. For example, student 8 is praised three times in a row for "perseverance or effort."

With instruments such as these, a rich and varied picture of classroom activity can be captured over the course of a research study. Obviously, a single observation of a single class would produce too little data to reveal a consistent behavior pattern. However, multiple observation periods extending across different teachers, schools, and school districts can reveal consistent patterns of teacher–student interactions. These patterns of classroom behavior then can be related to student behaviors, such

Figure 1.1   Coding categories for question-answer-feedback sequences.

Symbol Label		Definition
Student Sex		
M	Male	The student answering the question is male.
F	Female	The student answering the question is female.
Student Response		
+	Right	The teacher accepts the student's response as correct or satisfactory.
±	Part right	The teacher considers the student's response to be only partially correct or to be correct but incomplete.
–	Wrong	The teacher considers the student's response to be incorrect.
0	No answer	The student makes no response or says he doesn't know (code student's answer here if teacher gives feedback reaction before he is able to respond).
Teacher Feedback Reaction		
++	Praise	Teacher praises student either in words ("fine," "good," "wonderful," "good thinking") or by expressing verbal affirmation in a notably warm, joyous, or excited manner.
+	Affirm	Teacher simply affirms that the student's response is correct (nods, repeats answer, says "Yes," "OK," etc.).
0	No reaction	Teacher makes no response whatever to student's response—he or she simply goes on to something else.
–	Negate	Teacher simply indicates that the student's response is incorrect (shakes head, says "No," "That's not right," "Hm-mm," etc.).
– –	Criticize	Teacher criticizes student, either in words ("You should know better than that," "That doesn't make any sense—you better pay close attention," etc.) or by expressing verbal negation in a frustrated, angry, or disgusted manner.
Gives Ans.	Teacher gives answer	Teacher provides the correct answer for the student.
Ask Other	Teacher asks another student	Teacher redirects the question, asking a different student to try to answer it.
Other Calls	Another student calls out answer	Another student calls out the correct answer, and the teacher acknowledges that it is correct.
Repeat	Repeats question	Teacher repeats the original question, either in its entirety or with a prompt ("Well?" "Do you know?" "What's the answer?").
Clue	Rephrase or clue	Teacher makes original question easier for student to answer by rephrasing it or by giving a clue.
New Ques.	New question	Teacher asks a new question (i.e., a question that calls for a different answer than the original question called for).

Source: From *Looking in Classrooms* (4th ed.), by T. Good and J. Brophy, 1987, New York: Addison-Wesley Longman. Copyright 1987 by Addison-Wesley Longman. Reprinted with permission.

Figure 1.2 Coding response form.

Stu. No.	Sex			Student Response									Teacher Feedback Reaction					
	M	F		+	±	−	0		+ +	+	0	−	− −	Gives Ans.	Ask Other	Other Calls	Repeat	Clue	New Ques.
1	-	√		√	-	-	-		-	√	-	-	-	—	—	—	—	—	—
2	√	-		√	-	-	-		-	√	-	-	-	—	—	—	—	—	—
3	√	-		-	-	-	√		-	-	-	-	-	—	—	—	—	√	—
4	√	-		√	-	-	-		√	-	-	-	-	—	—	—	—	—	—
5	√	-		√	-	-	-		-	√	-	-	-	—	—	—	—	—	—
6	-	√		-	-	√	-		-	-	-	-	√	—	—	—	—	—	√
7	√	-		√	-	-	-		√	-	-	-	-	—	—	—	—	—	—
8	√	-		√	-	-	-		-	-	√	-	-	—	—	—	—	—	—
9	√	-		√	-	-	-		-	-	√	-	-	—	—	—	—	—	—
10	√			-	-	-	√		-	-	-	-	√	√	—	—	—	—	—
11	-	-		-	-	-	-		-	-	-	-	-	—	—	—	—	—	—
12	-	-		-	-	-	-		-	-	-	-	-	—	—	—	—	—	—
13	-	-		-	-	-	-		-	-	-	-	-	—	—	—	—	—	—
14	-	-		-	-	-	-		-	-	-	-	-	—	—	—	—	—	—
15	-	-		-	-	-	-		-	-	-	-	-	—	—	—	—	—	—
-	-	-		-	-	-	-		-	-	-	-	-	—	—	—	—	—	—
-	-	-		-	-	-	-		-	-	-	-	-	—	—	—	—	—	—
-	-	-		-	-	-	-		-	-	-	-	-	—	—	—	—	—	—
-	-	-		-	-	-	-		-	-	-	-	-	—	—	—	—	—	—

Source: From *Looking in Classrooms* (4th ed.), by T. Good and J. Brophy, 1987, New York: Addison-Wesley Longman. Copyright 1987 by Addison-Wesley Longman. Reprinted with permission.

Figure 1.3   Coding form for measuring individual praise.

USE: Whenever the teacher praises an individual student
PURPOSE: To see what behaviors the teacher reinforces through praises, and to see how the teacher's praise is distributed among the students.

Behavior Categories	Student Number		Codes
1. Perserverence or effort; worked long or hard	14	1.	3
2. Progress (relative to the past) toward achievement	23	2.	3,4
3. Success (right answer, high score) achievement	6	3.	3
4. Good thinking, good suggestions, good guess, or nice try	18	4.	3
5. Imagination, creativity, originality	8	5.	1
6. Neatness, careful work	8	6.	1
7. Good or compliant behavior, follows rules, pays attention	8	7.	1
8. Thoughtfulness, courtesy, offering to share, prosocial behavior		8.	
9. Other (specify)		9.	
		10.	
		11.	
		12.	
		13.	
		14.	
		15.	
		16.	
		17.	
		18.	
		19.	
		20.	
		21.	
		22.	
		23.	
		24.	
		25.	

NOTES:

All answers occurred during social studies discussion

Was particularly concerned about #8, a low-achieving male

Source: From *Looking in Classrooms* (4th ed.), by T. Good and J. Brophy, 1987, New York: Addison-Wesley Longman. Copyright 1987 by Addison-Wesley Longman. Reprinted with permission.

as performance on end-of-year standardized achievement tests, specially prepared classroom tests, and performance and portfolio assessments to determine the effects of teacher–student interaction on student performance.

It was in this manner that **patterns of effective teaching** began to emerge in studies conducted by different researchers. As in all research, some studies provided contradictory results or found no relationships among certain types of classroom interactions and student outcomes. But many studies found patterns of interaction that consistently produced desirable student outcomes in the form of higher test scores, increased problem-solving skills, and improved learning skills.

Now that you know how the research was conducted, let's look at the teaching behaviors that researchers generally agree contribute to effective teaching.

FIVE KEY BEHAVIORS CONTRIBUTING TO EFFECTIVE TEACHING

Approximately 10 teacher behaviors show promising relationships to desirable student performance, primarily as measured by classroom assessments and standardized tests. Five of these behaviors have been consistently supported by research studies over the past three decades (Brophy, 1989; Brophy & Good, 1986; Dunkin & Biddle, 1974; Rosenshine, 1971; Teddlie & Stringfield, 1993; Walberg, 1986). Another five have had some support and appear logically related to effective teaching. The first five we will call **key behaviors,** because they are considered essential for effective teaching. The second five we will call **helping behaviors** that can be used in combinations to implement the key behaviors. The five key behaviors essential for effective teaching are

1. Lesson clarity
2. Instructional variety
3. Teacher task orientation
4. Engagement in the learning process
5. Student success rate

Lesson Clarity

This key behavior refers to how clear a presentation is to the class as indicated in the following examples:

Effective Teachers
- Make their points understandable.
- Explain concepts clearly so their students are able to follow in a logical step-by-step order.
- Have an oral delivery that is clear, audible, and free of distracting mannerisms.

Less Effective Teachers
- Use vague, ambiguous, or indefinite language: "might probably be," "tends to suggest," "could possibly happen."
- Use overly complicated sentences, such as "There are many important reasons for the start of World War II but some are more important than others, so let's start with those that are thought to be important but really aren't."
- Give directions that often result in student requests for clarification.

One result from research on teacher clarity is that teachers vary considerably on this behavior. Not all teachers are able to communicate clearly and directly to their students without wandering, speaking above students' levels of comprehension, or using speech patterns that impair their presentation's clarity (G. Brown & Wragg, 1993; J. T. Dillon, 1988a; Wilen, 1991).

If you teach with a high degree of clarity, you will spend less time going over material. Your questions will be answered correctly the first time, allowing more time for instruction. Clarity is a complex behavior because it is related to many other so-called cognitive behaviors, such as your organization of the content, lesson familiarity, and delivery strategies (whether you use a discussion, recitation, question-and-answer, or small-group format). Nevertheless, research shows that both the *cognitive* clarity and *oral* clarity of presentations vary substantially among teachers. This in turn produces differences in student performance on cognitive tests of achievement (Marx & Walsh, 1988). Table 1.2 summarizes some of the indicators of lesson clarity and teaching strategies you will learn about in this text, especially in Chapters 5 (direct instruction), 6 (indirect instruction), and 7 (questioning strategies).

Table 1.2 Indicators for clarity.

Being Clear (An effective teacher . . .)	Examples of Teaching Strategies
1. Informs learners of the lesson objective (e.g., describes what behaviors will be tested or required on future assignments as a result of the lesson).	Prepare a behavioral objective for the lesson at the desired level of complexity (e.g., knowledge, comprehension, etc.). Indicate to the learners at the start of the lesson in what ways the behavior will be used in the future.
2. Provides learners with an advance organizer (e.g., places lesson in perspective of past and/or future lessons).	Consult or prepare a unit plan to determine what task-relevant prior learning is required for this lesson and what task-relevant prior learning this lesson represents for future lessons. Begin the lesson by informing the learner that the content to be taught is part of this larger context.
3. Checks for task-relevant prior learning at beginning of the lesson (e.g., determines level of understanding of prerequisite facts or concepts and reteaches, if necessary).	Ask questions of students at the beginning of a lesson or check assignments regularly to determine if task-relevant prior knowledge has been acquired.
4. Gives directives slowly and distinctly (e.g., repeats directives when needed or divides them into smaller pieces).	Organize procedures for lengthy assignments in step-by-step order and give as handout as well as orally.
5. Knows ability levels and teaches at or slightly above learners' current level of functioning (e.g., knows learners' attention spans).	Determine ability level from standardized tests, previous assignments, and interests and retarget instruction accordingly.
6. Uses examples, illustrations, and demonstrations to explain and clarify (e.g., uses visuals to help interpret and reinforce main points).	Restate main points in at least one modality other than the one in which they were initially taught (e.g., visual vs. auditory).
7. Provides review or summary at end of each lesson.	Use key abstractions, repetition, or symbols to help students efficiently store and later recall content.

Instructional Variety

This key behavior refers to the variability or flexibility of delivery during the presentation of a lesson (Brophy & Good, 1986; Rohrkemper & Corno, 1988). One of the most effective ways of creating variety during instruction is to ask questions. As you will learn in Chapter 7, many different types of questions can be asked, and when integrated into the pacing and sequencing of a lesson, they create meaningful variation (Chuska, 1995; Wilen, 1991). Therefore, the effective teacher needs to know the art of asking questions and how to discriminate among different question formats—fact questions, process questions, convergent questions, and divergent questions. These question types will be introduced in Chapter 7 and expanded on in Chapter 8.

Another aspect of variety in teaching is perhaps the most obvious: the use of learning materials, equipment, displays, and space in your classroom. The physical texture and visual variety of your classroom can all contribute to instructional variety. This, in turn, influences student achievement on end-of-unit tests, performance assessments, and student engagement in the learning process. For example, some studies found the amount of disruptive behavior to be less in classrooms that had more varied activities and materials (Emmer, Evertson, Clements, & Worsham, 1997; Evertson, 1997). Other studies have shown variety to be related to student attention (Lysakowski & Walberg, 1981).

An important key behavior for effective teaching is the variability or flexibility of delivery during the presentation of a lesson.

Some ways to incorporate variety into your teaching will be presented in Chapter 5 (direct instruction), Chapter 6 (indirect instruction), and Chapter 9 (cooperative learning and the collaborative process). Table 1.3 summarizes some of the indicators of instructional variety and teaching strategies that will be covered in these chapters.

Teacher Task Orientation

Teacher task orientation is a key behavior that refers to how much classroom time the teacher devotes to the task of teaching an academic subject. The more time dedicated to the task of teaching a specific topic, the greater the opportunity students have to learn. Some task-related questions a teacher must answer are (1) How much time do I spend lecturing, asking questions, and encouraging students to inquire or think independently? (2) How much time do I spend organizing for teaching and getting my students ready to learn? And, (3) How much time do I spend assessing my learners' performance?

These questions pertain to how much material is presented, learned, and assessed, as opposed to how much time is delegated to procedural matters. All teachers need to prepare their students to learn and want them to enjoy learning.

Table 1.3 Indicators for variety.

Using Variety (An effective teacher . . .)	Examples of Teaching Strategies
1. Uses attention-gaining devices (e.g., begins with a challenging question, visual, or example).	Begin lesson with an activity in a modality that is different from last lesson or activity (e.g., change from listening to seeing).
2. Shows enthusiasm and animation through variation in eye contact, voice, and gestures (e.g., changes pitch and volume, moves about during transitions to new activity).	Change position at regular intervals (e.g., every 10 minutes). Change speed or volume to indicate that a change in content or activity has occurred.
3. Varies mode of presentation, (e.g., lectures, asks questions, then provides for independent practice [daily]).	Preestablish an order of daily activities that rotates cycles of seeing, listening, and doing.
4. Uses a mix of rewards and reinforcers (e.g., extra credit, verbal praise, independent study, etc. [weekly, monthly]).	Establish lists of rewards and expressions of verbal praise and choose among them randomly. Provide reasons for praise along with the expression of praise.
5. Incorporates student ideas or participation in some aspects of the instruction (e.g., uses indirect instruction or divergent questioning [weekly, monthly]).	Occasionally plan instruction in which student opinions are used to begin the lesson (e.g., "What would you do if . . . ").
6. Varies types of questions (e.g., divergent, convergent, [weekly] and probes (e.g., to clarify, to solicit, to redirect [daily]).	Match questions to the behavior and complexity of the lesson objective. Vary complexity of lesson objectives in accord with the unit plan.

However, most researchers agree that student performance has been higher in classrooms with teachers who spent the majority of their time teaching subject-specific content as opposed to devoting large amounts of time to the process and materials that may be needed to acquire the content. It follows that classrooms in which teacher–student interactions focus more on intellectual content that allows their students an opportunity to learn are more likely to have higher rates of achievement (Berliner & Biddle, 1995; Porter, 1993).

Also, teachers who are task oriented are highly conversant with topics that are likely to appear on performance assessments and end-of-year achievement tests. This is not to say that these teachers "teach to the test." Rather, their classroom instruction parallels the instructional goals and curriculum that guide the construction of assessments of student progress.

These topics are presented in Chapter 3, which prepares you to write lesson objectives, and Chapter 4, which shows you how to execute them in your classroom. Table 1.4 summarizes some of the indicators of teacher task orientation and teaching strategies that will be covered in these chapters.

Engagement in the Learning Process

Student engagement in the learning process is a key behavior that refers to the amount of time students devote to learning an academic subject. This is one of the most recently researched teacher behaviors related to student performance. It is related to a teacher's task orientation and to content coverage. A teacher's task orientation should provide students the greatest possible opportunity to learn the material to be assessed.

For example, Table 1.5 shows the results achieved in second-grade reading when the teacher's task orientation—or time teaching an academic subject—was increased over a 5-week period. Increasing the time devoted to this instructional objective from 4 minutes to 52 minutes a day, over an average of only 25 school days, yielded an increase of 27 percentile points (from 39 to 66) on a standardized achievement test. The researchers who recorded these data indicated that, although such large increases in instructional time might appear unusual, they actually were achieved by teachers in these elementary school classrooms.

Distinct from the amount of time you devote to teaching a topic is the time your students will be *actively engaged* in learning the material. This has been called the *engagement rate*. Engagement rate is the percentage of time devoted to learning when the student is actually *on task*, engaged with the instructional materials and benefiting from the activities being presented. Even though a teacher may be task oriented and may provide maximum content coverage, the students may be disengaged. This means that they are not actively thinking about, working with, or using what is being presented (Marx & Walsh, 1988; Savage, 1991).

Such disengagement can involve an emotional or mental detachment from the lesson that may or may not be obvious. When students jump out of their seats, talk, read a magazine, or leave for the restroom, they obviously are not engaged in

Table 1.4   Indicators for teacher task orientation.

Being Task Oriented (An effective teacher . . .)	Examples of Teaching Strategies
1. Develops unit and lesson plans that reflect the most relevant features of the curriculum guide or adopted text (e.g., each unit and lesson objective can be referenced back to curriculum guide or text).	Key each lesson to a unit plan, the curriculum guide, and the text to test its relevance. Confer with other teachers concerning the most relevant portions of the text and curriculum guide.
2. Handles administrative and clerical interruptions efficiently (e.g., visitors, announcements, collection of money, dispensing of materials and supplies) by anticipating and preorganizing some tasks and deferring others to noninstructional time.	Establish a 5- to 10-minute restriction on how much time per every hour of instruction you will devote to noninstructional tasks. Defer all other tasks to before or after the lesson.
3. Stops or prevents misbehavior with a minimum of class disruption (e.g., has preestablished academic and work rules to "protect" intrusions into instructional time).	Establish rules for the most common misbehaviors and post them conspicuously. Identify only the offender and offense during instructional time, deferring consequence to later.
4. Selects the most appropriate instructional model for the objectives being taught (e.g., primarily uses direct instruction for knowledge and comprehension objectives and indirect instruction for inquiry and problem-solving objectives).	Using your unit plan, curriculum guide, or adopted text, divide the content to be taught into (1) facts, rules, and action sequences, and (2) concepts, patterns, and abstractions. Generally, plan to use direct instruction for the former content and indirect instruction for the latter.
5. Builds to unit outcomes with clearly definable events (e.g., weekly and monthly review, feedback, and testing sessions).	Establish a schedule in which major classroom activities begin and end with clearly visible events (e.g., minor and major tests, and review and feedback sessions).

instruction. Students also can be disengaged in far more subtle ways, such as looking attentive while their thoughts are many miles away. An unpleasant fact of life is that a quarter of a class may be off task at any one time. Correcting this type of disengagement may be much more difficult, requiring changes in the structure of the task itself and the cognitive demands placed on the learner (N. Bennett & Desforges, 1988; Brophy, 1996; Doyle, 1983). Strategies for composing tasks and activities that elicit the active participation of your learners are presented in Chapters 5 through 9.

Several authors (Evertson, 1995; Tauber, 1990) have contributed useful suggestions for increasing learning time and, more importantly, student engagement. Their work, recently updated by Emmer et al. (1997), has provided the following suggestions for teachers to promote student engagement:

Table 1.5 Learning time and student achievement: Example from second-grade reading.

Reading Score at First Testing (October)		Student Engaged Time in Reading with High Success Rate		Estimated Reading Score, Second Testing (December)	
Raw Score (out of 100)	Percentile	Total Time Over 5 Weeks (Minutes)	Average Daily Time (Minutes)	Raw Score (out of 100)	Percentile
36	50	100	4	37	39
36	50	573	23	43	50
36	50	1300	52	52	66

Note: An average of 25 school days occurred between the first and the second testing.

Source: From Charles W. Fisher et al., *Teaching and Learning in the Elementary School: A summary of the Beginning Teacher Evaluation Study.* Beginning Teacher Evaluation Study Report VII-I. (San Francisco, CA: Far West Laboratory for Research and Development, 1978)

1. Set rules that let pupils attend to their personal and procedural needs without obtaining your permission each time.
2. Move around the room to monitor pupils' seatwork and to communicate your awareness of student progress.
3. Ensure that independent assignments are interesting, worthwhile, and easy enough to be completed by each pupil without your direction.
4. Minimize time-consuming activities such as giving directions and organizing the class for instruction by writing the daily schedule on the board. This will ensure that pupils know where to go and what to do.
5. Make abundant use of resources and activities that are at, or slightly above, a student's current level of understanding.
6. Avoid timing errors. Act to prevent misbehaviors from occurring or increasing in severity so they do not influence others in the class.

These teaching practices have also been found to be beneficial for small groups and independent seatwork (L. Anderson, Stevens, Prawat, & Nickerson, 1988). These and other more specific ways of increasing the engagement rates of students will be explored in Chapters 8 and 9. Table 1.6 summarizes some of the indicators of student engagement and teaching strategies that will be covered in these chapters.

Student Success Rate

Another key behavior, student success rate refers to the rate at which students understand and correctly complete exercises.

A crucial aspect of the research on task orientation and student engagement has been the level of difficulty of the material presented. In these studies, level of diffi-

Table 1.6 Indicators for engaging students in the learning process.

Engaging Students Effectively in the Learning Process (An effective teacher . . .)	Examples of Teaching Strategies
1. Elicits the desired behavior immediately after the instructional stimuli (e.g., provides exercise or workbook problems with which the desired behavior can be practiced).	Schedule practice exercises or questions to immediately follow each set of instructional stimuli.
2. Provides opportunities for feedback in a nonevaluative atmosphere (e.g., asks students to respond as a group or covertly the first time through).	Require covert responding or nonevaluative (e.g., group) feedback at the start of a guided practice session.
3. Uses individual and group activities (e.g., performance contracts, programmed texts, games and simulations, and learning centers as motivational aids) when needed.	Have individualized instructional materials available (e.g., remedial exercises or texts) for those who may need them.
4. Uses meaningful verbal praise to get and keep students actively participating in the learning process.	Maintain a warm and nurturing atmosphere by providing verbal praise and encouragement that is meaningful (e.g., explain why the answer was correct). Praise partially correct answers, with qualification.
5. Monitors seatwork and frequently checks progress during independent practice.	Limit contact with individual students during seatwork to about 30 seconds each, providing instructionally relevant answers. Circulate among entire class.

culty was measured by the rate at which students understood and correctly completed exercises. Three levels of difficulty are as follows:

- *High success:* The student understands the task and makes only occasional careless errors.
- *Moderate success:* The student has partial understanding but makes some substantive errors.
- *Low success:* The student does not understand the task at all.

Findings (Berliner, 1979) indicate that a teacher's task orientation (instructional time) and student engagement are closely related to student success rate, as shown in Figure 1.4. Instruction that produces a moderate-to-high success rate results in increased performance, because more content is covered at the learner's current level of understanding. This result was initially found for expository or didactic forms of instruction with which learners are taught basic academic skills most easily learned through practice and repetition (Rosenshine, 1986). But, more recent research has extended these findings to thinking skills instruction (Beyer, 1995) and project-based learning (Blumenfeld et al., 1991). Research has also shown that instruction that pro-

Figure 1.4 Levels of time.

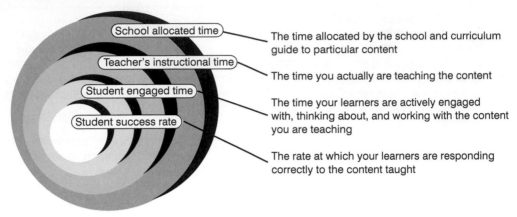

The time allocated by the school and curriculum guide to particular content

The time you actually are teaching the content

The time your learners are actively engaged with, thinking about, and working with the content you are teaching

The rate at which your learners are responding correctly to the content taught

motes low error rates (high success) can contribute to increased levels of student self-esteem and to positive attitudes toward the subject matter and the school (Slavin, 1991b).

The average student in a typical classroom spends about half of the time working on tasks that provide the opportunity for high success. But researchers have found that students who spend more than the average time in high-success activities have higher achievement, better retention, and more positive attitudes toward school. These findings have led to the suggestion that students should spend about 60 to 70 percent of their time on tasks that allow almost complete understanding of the material being taught with only occasional errors (Brophy & Evertson, 1976a, 1976b; Rosenshine, 1986).

Moderate-to-high success rates will produce mastery of the lesson content. But they also can provide the foundation for your students to apply learned knowledge in some practical way, such as thinking critically and independently. This has been the unique contribution of strategies for self-directed learning and learning to learn, which will be studied in Chapter 8. These strategies encourage learners to construct their own understandings and meanings from lesson content. They also encourage learners to reason, problem solve, and think critically about the content they are learning. By varying the complexity and variety of the tasks provided, such strategies provide opportunities for individual patterns of thinking to emerge through various forms of classroom discussion and dialogue (Duffy & Roehler, 1989; Rohrkemper & Corno, 1988). We will learn more about this approach to learning, called *constructivism,* in Chapters 6 and 8.

Many teachers devote insufficient time to this stage of learning, which is particularly crucial for attaining the goals of problem solving and critical thinking. A key behavior for the effective teacher is organizing and planning instruction that yields moderate-to-high success rates but then challenges the learner to go beyond the information given. You will discover ways to use moderate-to-high success rates to attain the goals of problem solving and critical thinking in Chapters 6 and 8. Table 1.7 sum-

Table 1.7 Indicators for student success.

Moderate-to-High Rates of Success (An effective teacher . . .)	Examples of Teaching Strategies
1. Establishes unit and lesson content that reflects prior learning (e.g., planning lesson sequences that consider task-relevant prior information).	Create a top-down unit plan in which all the lesson outcomes at the bottom of the hierarchy needed to achieve unit outcomes at the top of the hierarchy are identified. Arrange lessons in an order most logical to achieving unit outcomes.
2. Administers correctives immediately after initial response (e.g., shows model of correct answer and how to attain it after first crude response is given).	Provide for guided practice prior to independent practice, and provide means of self-checking (e.g., handout with correct answers) at intervals of practice.
3. Divides instructional stimuli into small chunks (e.g., establishes bite-size lessons that can be easily digested by learners at their current level of functioning).	Plan interdisciplinary thematic units to emphasize relationships and connections that are easily remembered.
4. Plans transitions to new material in easy to grasp steps (e.g., changes instructional stimuli according to a preestablished thematic pattern so that each new lesson is seen as an extension of previous lessons).	Extend unit-plan hierarchy downward to more specific lessons that are tied together above with a single unit theme and outcome.
5. Varies the pace at which stimuli are presented and continually builds toward a climax or key event.	Use review, feedback, and testing sessions to form intervals of increasing and decreasing intensity and expectation.

marizes some of the indicators of student success and teaching strategies that will be covered in these chapters.

Summary of Five Key Behaviors

The five key behaviors—lesson clarity, instructional variety, teacher task orientation, student engagement, and success rate—are essential for effective teaching. Classroom researchers undoubtedly will discover other effective teaching behaviors and attain a more thorough understanding of those already described. However, for the first time, research has provided a basis for better definitions of effective teaching and for training teachers. These five behaviors are the skeleton of the effective teacher, and the remainder of this text will construct the heart, mind, and body of the effective teacher.

You learned earlier that there can be no simple answer to the question What is an effective teacher? Many behaviors must be orchestrated into *patterns of behavior* for your teaching to be effective. The identification of only five behaviors makes teaching appear deceptively simple. However, as the following section will reveal, your success in implementing these five key behaviors in the classroom will be assisted by many other helping behaviors.

SOME HELPING BEHAVIORS RELATED TO EFFECTIVE TEACHING

To fill out our picture of an effective teacher, you also need to adopt other behaviors to help you implement the five key behaviors in your classroom. These behaviors can be thought of as helping behaviors for performing the five key behaviors.

Research findings for helping behaviors, although promising, are not as strong and consistent as those that identified the five key behaviors. The research has not identified explicitly how these behaviors should be used. This is why helping behaviors need to be employed *in the context of other behaviors* to be effective, making them catalysts rather than agents unto themselves. Among these helping behaviors are the following:

1. Using student ideas and contributions
2. Structuring
3. Questioning
4. Probing
5. Teacher affect

Use of Student Ideas and Contributions

Using student ideas and contributions is a behavior that includes acknowledging, modifying, applying, comparing, and summarizing student responses to promote the goals of a lesson and to encourage student participation. Note how any one of these activities (suggested by Flanders, 1970) could be used in achieving one or more of the five key behaviors:

- *Acknowledging:* Using the student's idea by repeating the nouns and logical connectives expressed by him or her (to increase lesson clarity).
- *Modifying:* Using the student's idea by rephrasing it or conceptualizing it in your words or another student's words (to create instructional variety).
- *Applying:* Using the student's idea to teach an inference or take the next step in a logical analysis of a problem (to increase success rate).
- *Comparing:* Taking a student's idea and drawing a relationship between it and ideas expressed earlier by the student or another student (to encourage engagement in the learning process).
- *Summarizing:* Using what was said by an individual student or a group of students as a recapitulation or review of concepts taught (to enhance task orientation).

More recently, the use of student ideas and contributions has been extended to reasoning, problem solving, and independent thinking. This has been achieved through **teacher-mediated dialogue** that helps learners restructure what is being learned using their own ideas, experiences, and thought patterns. Teacher-mediated dialogue asks the learner not just to respond to textual material, but to internalize its meaning by elaborating, extending, and commenting on it using the learner's own unique thoughts. In this manner, learners are encouraged to communicate the processes by which they are learning, thereby helping them to construct their own meanings and understandings of the content (Steffe & Gale, 1995). We will present strategies for constructivist teaching and teacher-mediated dialogue in Chapters 6 and 8.

Use of student ideas and contributions also can increase a student's engagement in the learning process. Thus, it has become a frequently used catalyst for helping achieve that key behavior (Emmer et al., 1997). Consider this brief instructional dialogue that uses student ideas to promote engagement:

Teacher: Tom, what is the formula for the Pythagorean theorem?
Tom: $c^2 = a^2 + b^2$.

At this point the teacher simply could have said "Good!" and gone on to the next question. Instead, this teacher continues:

Teacher: Let's show that on the board. Here is a triangle; now let's do exactly as Tom said. He said that squaring the altitude, which is a, and adding it to the square of the base, which is b, should give us the square of the hypotenuse, which is c. Carl, would you like to come up and show us how you would find the length of c, using the formula Tom just gave us?

Carl: Well, if a were equal to 3 and b equal to 4, the way I would solve this problem would be to add the squares of both of them together and then find the square root—that would be c.

Teacher: So, we square the 3, square the 4, add them together, and take the square root. This gives us 5, the length of the hypotenuse.

Which of the five ways of using student ideas are in this dialogue? First, by putting Tom's response graphically on the blackboard, this teacher *applied* Tom's answer by taking it to the next step, constructing a proof. Second, by repeating orally what Tom said, the teacher *acknowledged* to the entire class the value of Tom's contribution. And third, by having another student prove the correctness of Tom's response, a *summary* of the concept was provided. All this was accomplished from Tom's simple (and only) utterance. "$c^2 = a^2 + b^2$."

Research reveals that student ideas and contributions, especially when used in the context of the naturally occurring dialogue of the classroom, are more strongly and consistently related to student engagement than simply approving a student's answer with "Good!" (Good & Brophy, 1997, p. 146). The standard phrases we use to acknowledge and reward students ("correct," "good," "right") are so overused that they may not always convey the reward intended.

Although the use of student ideas looks simple, it takes skill and planning. Even when your response is unplanned, you should be prepared to seize opportunities to incorporate student ideas into your lesson.

Structuring

Teacher comments made for the purpose of organizing what is to come, or summarizing what has gone before, are called *structuring*. Used before an instructional activity or question, structuring serves as instructional scaffolding that assists learners in bridging the gap between what they are capable of doing on their own and what they are capable of doing with help from the teacher, thereby aiding their understanding and use of the material to be taught. Used at the conclusion of an instructional activity or question, structuring reinforces learned content and places it in proper relation to other content already taught. Both forms of structuring are related to student achievement and are effective catalysts for performing the five key behaviors (Rogoff, 1990; Rosenshine & Meister, 1992).

Typically, before- and after-structuring takes the following form:

Teacher: (At beginning of lesson) OK, now that we have studied how the pipefish change their color and movements to blend in with their surroundings, we will study how the pipefish gathers its food. Most important, we will learn how the pipefish grow and provide the means for other fish, like the kind we eat for food, to flourish deep below the ocean's surface.

Teacher: (At end of lesson) So, we have discovered that the pipefish protects itself by changing colors to blend in with plants on the ocean's floor and by swaying back and forth to fool its enemies. We might conclude from this that the pipefish evade rather than capture their natural enemies and feed close to the ocean's floor where they can't be noticed. Can you think of when this clever strategy might not work, making the pipefish prey to other fish deep below the ocean's surface? (Adapted from Palincsar & Brown, 1989.)

This sequence illustrates some of the many ways that you can use structuring. One way is to *signal* that a shift in direction or content is about to occur. A clear signal alerts students to the impending change. Without such a signal, students may confuse new content with old, missing the differences. Signals such as "Now that we have studied how the pipefish change their color and movements . . . we will learn . . . " help students switch gears and provide a perspective that makes new content more meaningful.

Another type of structuring uses *emphasis*. Can you find a point of emphasis in the previous dialogue? By using the phrase "most important," this teacher alerts students to the knowledge and understanding expected at the conclusion of this activity. This provides students with an organizer for what is to follow, called an *advance organizer.*

In this instance, the students are clued to consider the factors that extend beyond the color and movement of the pipefish to include how they grow and provide the means for other fish to flourish. This makes the teacher's final question more meaningful ("Can you think of when this clever strategy might not work, making the pipefish prey to other fish deep below the ocean's surface?"). The students have been clued that such a question might be raised and that generalizations beyond the concepts discussed will be expected. Phrases such as

Now this is important.
We will return to this point later.
Remember this.

are called *verbal markers*. They can emphasize your most important points.

In addition to verbal markers and advance organizers, the effective teacher organizes a lesson into an activity structure. An *activity structure* is a set of related tasks that differ in cognitive complexity and that to some degree may be placed under the control of the learner. Activity structures (Marx & Walsh, 1988; Rogoff, 1990) can be built in many ways (e.g., cooperatively, competitively, independently) to vary the demands they make on the learner and to give tempo and momentum to a lesson. For the effective teacher, they are an important means for engaging students in the learning process and moving them from simple recall of facts to the higher response levels that require reasoning, critical thinking, and problem-solving behavior.

The Art of Questioning

Questioning is another important helping behavior. Few other topics have been researched as much as the teacher's use of questions (G. Brown & Wragg, 1993; Risner, Skeel, & Nicholson, 1992; Wilen, 1991). One of the most important outcomes of research on questioning has been the distinction between *content* questions and *process* questions, which we will look at next.

Content Questions.   Teachers pose content questions to have the student deal directly with the content taught. An example is when a teacher asks a question to see if students can recall and understand specific material. The correct answer is known well in advance by the teacher. It also has been conveyed directly in class, in the text, or both. Few, if any, interpretations or alternative meanings of the question are possible.

Researchers have used various terms to describe content questions, such as the following:

Types of Content Questions
- *Direct:* The question requires no interpretation or alternative meanings. *Example:* "What is the meaning of the word *ancient* in the story just read?"
- *Lower-order:* The question requires the recall only of readily available facts, as opposed to generalizations and inferences. *Example:* "What was the mechanical breakthrough that gave the cotton gin superiority over all previous machines of its type?"
- *Convergent:* Different data sources lead to the same answer. *Example:* "What is one of the chemical elements in the air we breathe?"

- **Closed:** The question has no possible alternative answers or interpretations. *Example:* "What is the function of a CPU in a microcomputer?"
- **Fact:** The question requires the recall only of discrete pieces of well-
  accepted knowledge. *Example:* "What is the result of the number 47
  divided by 6?"

Some estimates have suggested that up to 80% of the questions teachers ask refer directly to specific content and have readily discernible and unambiguous correct answers (Gall, 1984; Risner et al., 1992). Perhaps even more important is the fact that approximately the same percentage of test items (and behavioral objectives) are written at the level of recall, knowledge, or fact (Tombari & Borich, 1999). Therefore, test items, behavioral objectives, and most instruction seem to emphasize readily known facts as they are presented in curriculum guides, workbooks, and texts.

The art of questioning will become one of your most important skills as a teacher. The variety you convey to your students will be determined in large measure by your flexible use of questions. Questions are rarely ends in themselves but rather a means of engaging students in the learning process by getting them to act on, work through, or think about the material presented.

Process Questions.   From the previous discussion, you can see why not all questions should be content questions. There are different purposes for which questions can be asked, with the intent of encouraging different mental processes. To problem solve, to guide, to arouse curiosity, to encourage creativity, to analyze, to synthesize, and to judge also are goals of instruction that should be reflected in your questioning strategies. For these goals, content is not an end itself but a means of achieving higher-order goals.

Researchers have used various terms to describe process questions, such as the following:

Types of Process Questions
- **Indirect:** The question has various possible interpretations and alternative meanings. *Example:* "What are some of the ways you have used the
  word *ancient?*"
- **Higher-order:** The question requires more complex mental processes
  than simple recall of facts (e.g., making generalizations and inferences).
  Example: "What were the effects of the invention of the cotton gin on
  attitudes in the North?"
- **Divergent:** Different data sources will lead to different correct answers.
  Example: "From what we know about the many forms of pollution today,
  what would be one of the first things we have to do to clean the air we
  breathe?
- **Open:** A single correct answer is not expected or even possible. *Example:*
  "How have recent advances in computer technology influenced your life?"

Constructivist teaching strategies emphasize the learner's direct experience and the dialogue of the classroom as instructional tools.

- *Concept:* The question requires the processes of abstraction, generalization, and inference. *Example:* Using examples of your own choosing, can you tell us some of the ways division and subtraction are similar?

Can you see the difference between this set of process questions and the list of content questions that preceded it? Notice that the process questions encourage more thinking and problem solving by requiring the learner to use personal sources of knowledge to actively construct her or his own interpretations and meanings rather than acquiring understanding by giving back knowledge already organized in the form in which it was told. As we saw earlier, this view of teaching and learning represents a movement in education called *constructivism*. **Constructivist teaching strategies** emphasize the learner's direct experience and the dialogue of the classroom as instructional tools while deemphasizing lecturing and telling (Steffe & Gale, 1995).

Process questions and the use of probes, our next helping behavior, are important aids in constructivist thinking and action in the classroom. We will have more to say about the role of direct experience and the use of constructivist strategies in the classroom in many of the chapters ahead, and especially in Chapters 6 and 8.

Probing

Another helping behavior is probing. *Probing* refers to teacher statements that encourage students to elaborate on an answer, either their own or another student's. Probing may take the form of a general question or can include other expressions that *elicit* clarification of an answer, *solicit* additional information about a response, or *redirect* a student's response in a more fruitful direction (Gage, 1976). Probing often is used to shift a discussion to some higher thought level.

Generally, student achievement is greatest when the eliciting, soliciting, and (if necessary) redirecting occur in cycles. This systematically leads the discussion to a higher level of complexity, as when interrelationships, generalizations, and problem solutions are being sought (J. Dillon, 1995). In this manner, you may begin a lesson with a simple fact question; then, by eliciting clarification of student responses, soliciting new information, or redirecting an answer, you can move to a higher level of questioning.

A typical cycle might occur in the following manner:

Teacher:	Bobby, what is a scientific experiment?
Bobby:	Well, it's when you test something.
Teacher:	But, what do you test? (elicit)
Bobby:	Mmm. Something you believe in and want to find out if it's really true.
Teacher:	What do you mean by that? (solicit)
Mary:	He means you make a prediction.
Teacher:	What's another word for *prediction*? (redirect)
Tom:	Hypothesis. You make a hypothesis, then go into the laboratory to see if it comes true.

Can you find the teacher's soliciting, eliciting, and redirecting behaviors in the remainder of the dialogue?

Teacher:	OK. So a scientist makes a prediction or hypothesis and follows up with an experiment to see if it can be made to come true. Then what?
Billy:	That's the end!
Teacher:	(No comment for 10 seconds; then . . .) Is the laboratory like the real world?
David:	The scientist tries to make it like the real world, but it's much smaller, like the greenhouse pictured in our book.
Teacher:	So what must the scientist do with the findings from the experiment, if they are to be useful? (No one answers, so the teacher continues.) If something important happens in my experiment, wouldn't I argue that what happened could also happen in the real world?
Bobby:	You mean, if it's true in a specific situation, it will also be true in a more general situation?

Betty Jo:	That's making a generalization.
Teacher:	Good. So we see that a scientific investigation usually ends with a generalization. Let's summarize. What three things does a scientific investigation require?
Class:	A prediction, an experiment, and a generalization.
Teacher:	Good work, class.

Notice that all of the ingredients in this teacher's lesson were provided by the class. The concepts of hypothesis, experiment, and generalization were never defined for the class. The students defined these concepts for themselves with only an occasional "OK" or "Good" to let them know they were on track. The teacher's role was limited to eliciting clarification, soliciting additional information, and redirection.

The purpose of this cycle of eliciting, soliciting, and redirection is to promote inquiry or independent discovery of the content of the lesson. Generally, *retention* of material learned has been greater from inquiry teaching than from formal lecturing methods (Paul, 1990).

Teacher Affect

Anyone who has ever been in a classroom where the teacher's presentation was lifeless, static, and without vocal variety can appreciate the commonsense value of affective behavior. However, unlike the behaviors discussed previously, affect cannot be captured in transcripts of teaching behavior or by classroom interaction instruments. Consequently, narrowly focused research instruments often miss a teacher's affective behavior, which may be apparent from a more holistic view of the classroom.

What the instruments miss, the students see clearly. Students are good perceivers of the emotions underlying a teacher's actions, and they often respond accordingly. A teacher who is excited about the subject being taught and shows it by facial expression, voice inflection, gesture, and general movement is more likely to hold the attention of students than one who does not exhibit these behaviors. This is true whether or not teachers consciously perceive these behaviors in themselves.

Students take their cues from such behavioral signs and lower or heighten their engagement with the lesson accordingly. Enthusiasm is an important aspect of a teacher's affect. *Enthusiasm* is the teacher's vigor, power, involvement, excitement, and interest during a classroom presentation. We all know that enthusiasm is contagious, but how is it so? Enthusiasm is conveyed to students in many ways, the most common being vocal inflection, gesture, eye contact, and animation. A teacher's enthusiasm was found to be related to student achievement (Bettencourt, Gillett, Gall, & Hull, 1983; Cabello & Terrell, 1994). It also is believed to be important in promoting student engagement in the learning process.

Obviously, no one can maintain a heightened state of enthusiasm for very long without becoming exhausted emotionally. Nor is this what is meant by enthusiasm. A proper level of enthusiasm is far more subtle, and perhaps that is why it has been so difficult to research. A proper level of enthusiasm involves a delicate balance of vocal inflection, gesturing, eye contact, and movement. It employs each of these behaviors in only moderate ways. *In combination,* these behaviors send to students a unified signal of vigor, involvement, and interest. It is the use of these behaviors in moderation and at the right times that conveys the desired message.

Timing and the ability to incorporate these behaviors into a consistent pattern make possible an unspoken behavioral dialogue with students that is every bit as important as your spoken words. Letting students know that you are ready to help by your warm and encouraging attitude is essential if your enthusiasm is to be taken as an honest and sincere expression of your true feelings.

THE COMPLEXITY OF TEACHING

The complexity and difficulty of learning to teach arise from the complexity of the varied decision-making contexts in which teaching must occur. Herein lies one of the major problems with earlier attempts to define effective teaching by describing ideal types or by describing a teacher's personality, attitude, experience, achievement, and aptitude. These attempts failed to consider that *different* teaching contexts require *different* teaching behaviors. Any single definition of effective teaching would be simplistic and inaccurate because of its insensitivity to the different learners, curricula, grade levels, and instructional materials with which teaching and learning must take place. It is the proper mix of key and helping behaviors in the context of your classroom that will come to define effective teaching for you. In the chapters ahead you will learn how to vary this mix accordingly, giving each key and helping behavior its proper emphasis within your grade, subject, learners, and curriculum.

Now let's turn to the importance of certain behaviors in several different teaching contexts.

TEACHING EFFECTIVELY WITH DIVERSE LEARNERS AND CONTENT

Researchers have uncovered behaviors of special importance to specific types of students and content. Two areas of findings having the most consistent results are

1. Teaching behaviors that positively affect learners of lower and higher socioeconomic status
2. Teaching behaviors that impact reading and mathematics

How Does Effective Teaching Differ When Learners Have a Variety of Socioeconomic Levels, Culture, and Ethnicity?

The phrase *socioeconomic status (SES)* can mean many different things, but generally it is an approximate index of one's income and education level. For the classroom researcher, the SES of students is determined directly by the income and education of their parents, or indirectly by the nature of the school the student attends.

Some schools are in impoverished areas where the overall income and education levels of the community are low, whereas other schools are located in more affluent communities. Many schools in impoverished areas qualify for special financial assistance from the federal government, based on the median income of their students' parents. Researchers consider these "Chapter I" schools to be those where the majority of students come from lower-SES homes and may be disadvantaged, and/or are "at risk" of school failure.

Because lower-SES and higher-SES students and schools are facts of life that are likely to exist for some time, classroom researchers have determined what teacher behaviors promote the most achievement in these two types of students. Bowers & Flinders (1991), Good & Brophy (1997), Hill (1989), and Kennedy (1991) provide suggestions for teaching these two student populations. Some important teaching behaviors to emphasize for these two groups are summarized in Table 1.8.

Notice in the table that, while each behavior is applicable to both lower and higher SES students, teacher affect is particularly important in lower-SES classrooms. Also, notice that some of these teaching behaviors received little or no mention in our preceding discussions, because those discussions applied to students generally. Four of the behaviors shown for lower-SES classrooms (student responses, overteaching/overlearning, classroom interaction, and individualization) can be seen as special ways of creating student engagement at high rates of success. This presents a particular challenge when teaching lower-SES students who may be at risk for school failure.

Also, frequently correcting wrong answers in the absence of support or encouragement could be construed as a personal criticism by some lower-SES students, who already may have a poor self-concept. Therefore, feedback that could be construed as criticism may need to occur in the context of a more supportive and

Effective teachers provide a warm and encouraging classroom climate by letting students know help is available.

Table 1.8   Important teaching behaviors for lower-SES and higher-SES students.

Helping Lower SES Populations Achieve Success

Teacher Affect	Provide a warm and encouraging classroom climate by letting students know help is available.
Student Responses	Encourage an initial response, however crude, before moving to the next student.
Content Organization	Present material in small pieces, with opportunity to practice what has been learned after each piece.
	Show how the pieces fit together and are to be applied before each new segment of instruction begins.
Classroom Instruction	Emphasize knowledge and applications before teaching patterns and abstractions. Present most concrete learnings first.
	Monitor each student's progress at regular intervals. Use progress charts to help record learner improvement.
	Help students who need help immediately. Use peer and cross-age tutors, if necessary.
	Minimize disruptions by maintaining structure and flow between activities. Organize and plan transitions in advance.
Individualization	Supplement standard curriculum with specialized materials to meet the needs of individual students. Use media, learning resources, and the personal experiences of the students to promote interest and attention.

Helping Higher SES Populations Achieve Success

Correcting	Check right answers by requiring extended reasoning.
Thinking and Decision Making	Pose questions that require associations, generalizations, and inferences. Encourage students to use this same level of questioning.
	Supplement curriculum with challenging material, some of which is slightly above students' current level of attainment.
	Assign homework and/or extended projects that require independent judgment, discovery, and problem solving using original sources of information obtained outside the classroom.
Classroom Interaction	Encourage student-to-student and student-to-teacher interactions in which learners take responsibility for evaluating their own learning.
Verbal Activities	Actively engage students in verbal questions and answers that go beyond text and workbook content.

Source: Based on Bowers and Flinders (1991), Good and Brophy (1997), Hill (1989), and Kennedy (1991).

encouraging environment than may be needed for the higher-SES learner (Cabello & Terrell, 1994).

Because much of the research on SES has been conducted in elementary classrooms, it is as yet uncertain to what extent these teaching behaviors apply to the secondary classroom. However, many of the learning characteristics of higher-SES and lower-SES students appear to be similar across these school contexts. Therefore, your success as a teacher in a predominantly lower-SES or higher-SES classroom may depend on your ability to vary the extent to which you emphasize the behaviors in Table 1.8.

How Does Effective Teaching Differ Across Content Areas?

Another set of findings pertains to the different teaching behaviors that distinguish reading from mathematics instruction (Brophy & Evertson, 1976a; Good & Grouws, 1979; Reynolds, 1989). Although not all teachers will teach either reading or mathematics, this set of findings may be generalized to some extent to other types of content that are similar in form and structure.

For example, social studies, history, and language instruction all have high reading content and share some of the same problem-solving features as reading. General science, biology, physics, and chemistry are similar to the science of mathematics in that concepts, principles, and laws all play a prominent role. Also, visual forms and symbolic expressions are at least as important to understanding science subjects as is the written word. Therefore, some cautious generalizations may be made about the teaching behaviors important for reading and *basic* mathematics instruction and for subjects similar to each.

Some important findings are summarized in Table 1.9. Notice the two different approaches implied by the behaviors listed. For *basic* mathematics instruction, a formal, direct approach appears to be most effective. This approach includes maintaining structure through close adherence to texts, workbooks, and application-oriented activities. It also maximizes instructional coverage by minimizing unstructured work that could diminish engaged learning time. On the other hand, reading instruction allows for a more interactive and indirect approach, using more classroom discussions and experience-oriented questions and answers.

These approaches, however, are not mutually exclusive. What the research shows is that, in general and over time, a more direct approach during basic mathematics instruction tends to result in greater student progress than would, say, the exclusive use of an inquiry approach. For reading, the reverse appears to be true: an exploratory, interactive approach that encourages the use of classroom dialogue and student ideas tends to result in greater student progress over time.

These different approaches represent *degrees of emphasis* and not exclusive strategies. Clearly, teaching the basics of mathematics will at times require an inquiry approach, just as reading sometimes requires a lecture or telling approach. More important than either of these approaches or the behaviors that represent them is the ability of the teacher to be flexible. The effective teacher senses when a change from one emphasis to another is necessary, regardless of the content being taught.

Table 1.9 Important teaching behaviors for reading and mathematics instruction.

<table>
<tr><td colspan="2" align="center">**Findings for Reading Instruction**</td></tr>
<tr><td>Instructional Activity</td><td>Spend sufficient time during reading instruction discussing, explaining, and questioning to stimulate cognitive processes and promote learner responding.</td></tr>
<tr><td>Interactive Technique</td><td>Use cues and questions that require every student to attempt a response during reading instruction.</td></tr>
<tr><td>Questions</td><td>Pose thought-provoking questions during reading instruction that require the student to predict, question, summarize, and clarify what has been read.</td></tr>
<tr><td colspan="2" align="center">**Findings For Basic Mathematics Instruction**</td></tr>
<tr><td>Instructional Materials</td><td>Use application- and experience-oriented activities and media during mathematics instruction to foster task persistence.</td></tr>
<tr><td>Instructional Content</td><td>Maximize coverage of instructional applications during mathematics instruction through the use of activity sheets, handouts, and problem sets at graduated levels of difficulty.</td></tr>
<tr><td>Instructional Organization</td><td>Emphasize full-class or small-group instruction during mathematics instruction. Limit unguided or independent work, especially when it may interfere with on-task behavior and learner persistence.</td></tr>
</table>

Source: Based on Reynolds (1989), Good & Grouws (1979), and Brophy and Evertson (1976b).

REVIEW OF SOME IMPORTANT TEACHER EFFECTIVENESS INDICATORS

If this chapter were reduced to simple advice to improve your teaching, the result would be a simplistic definition of an effective teacher. However, if you ask for some indicators of teaching effectiveness that have demonstrated importance in improving student achievement, the following list will help. These are some of the general indicators of effective teaching that are currently supported by the research literature. The following chapters use these indicators to introduce specific instructional practices that will help you create these same behaviors in your own classroom.

The effective teacher:

- Takes personal responsibility for students' learning and has ***positive expectations*** for every learner.
- ***Matches*** the difficulty of the lesson with the ability level of the students and ***varies*** the difficulty when necessary to attain moderate-to-high success.
- Gives students the ***opportunity to practice*** newly learned concepts and to receive timely feedback on their performance.
- ***Maximizes instructional time*** to increase content coverage and to give students the greatest opportunity to learn.
- Provides direction and control of student learning through ***questioning, structuring, and probing***.

- Uses a ***variety of instructional materials and verbal and visual aids*** to foster use of student ideas and engagement in the learning process.
- ***Elicits responses*** from students each time a question is asked before moving to the next student or question.
- Presents material in ***small steps*** with opportunities for practice.
- Encourages students to ***reason out*** and ***elaborate on*** the correct answer.
- Engages students in ***verbal questions and answers***.
- Uses naturally occurring ***classroom dialogue*** to get students to ***elaborate, extend, and comment on*** the content being learned.
- Gradually ***shifts some of the responsibility for learning to the students***—encouraging ***independent thinking, problem solving, and decision making***.
- ***Provides*** learners with ***mental strategies*** for organizing and learning the content being taught.

At this point, you might think that an effective teacher simply is one who has mastered all of the key behaviors and helping behaviors. But teaching involves more than a knowledge of how to perform individual behaviors. Much like an artist who blends color and texture into a painting to produce a coherent impression, so must the effective teacher blend individual behaviors to different degrees to promote student achievement. This requires orchestration and integration of the key and helping behaviors into meaningful patterns and rhythms that can achieve the goals of instruction within your classroom.

The truly effective teacher knows how to execute individual behaviors with a larger purpose in mind. This larger purpose requires placing behaviors side by side in ways that accumulate to create an effect greater than can be achieved by any single behavior or small set of them. This is why teaching involves a sense of timing, sequencing, and pacing that cannot be conveyed by any list of behaviors. The interrelationships among these behaviors, giving each its proper emphasis in the context of your classroom, are so important to the effective teacher. And, it is the combination of curriculum, learning objectives, instructional materials, and learners that provides the decision-making context for the proper connection.

YOUR TRANSITION TO THE REAL WORLD OF TEACHING

An important question for you as a prospective teacher is what type of knowledge and experiences will be needed to pass successfully into the real world of teaching. The chapters ahead will convey the types of knowledge you will need to move quickly up the hierarchy of knowledge and experiences that make an effective teacher. But, before learning about the tools and techniques that will help you progress up this hierarchy, you will want to determine your own concerns about teaching at this point in your career. Appendix A contains the Teacher Concerns

Checklist, a 45-item self-report instrument for assessing the stages of concern with which a teacher most strongly identifies. Using the Teacher Concerns Checklist, rank your own level of teaching concerns, and with the instructions provided, determine the concerns with which you identify most closely. Then return to this chapter and read further to learn more about this interesting facet of your growth and development as a teacher.

Stop now and complete the Teacher Concerns Checklist in Appendix A.

Now that you've ranked your most important teaching concerns, let's see what it means for your teaching. Your transition to the real world of teaching will usher in the first stage of teacher development, sometimes called the *survival stage* (Borich, 1993; Burden, 1986; Fuller, 1969; Ryan, 1992). The distinguishing feature of this first stage of teaching is that your **teaching concerns** and plans will focus on your own well-being more than on the teaching task or your learners. Bullough (1989) has described this stage as "the fight for one's professional life" (p. 16). During it, your concerns typically are focused on the following:

- Will my learners like me?
- Will they listen to what I say?
- What will parents and other teachers think of me?
- Will I do well when I'm being observed?

Typically, during this time, behavior management concerns become a major focus of your planning efforts. For most teachers, survival—or *self*—concerns—begin to diminish rapidly during the first months of teaching, but there is no precise time when they end. What signals their end is the transition to a new set of concerns and planning priorities. This new set of priorities focuses on how best to deliver instruction. Various labels have been used to describe this second stage, such as the mastery stage of teaching (Ryan, 1992), consolidation and exploration (Burden, 1986), and trial and error (Sacks & Harrington, 1982). Fuller (1969) described this stage as one marked by concerns about the teaching *task*.

At this stage you are beginning to feel confident that you can manage the day-to-day routines of the classroom and deal with a variety of behavior problems. You are at the point where you now can plan your lessons without an exclusive focus on managing your classroom. Your planning turns instead toward improving your teaching skills and achieving greater mastery over the content you are teaching.

Typically, your concerns during this stage are with the following:

- Where can I find good instructional materials?
- Will I have enough time to cover the content?
- Where can I get ideas for a learning center?
- What's the best way to teach writing skills?

The third and highest level of teacher planning is characterized by concerns that have less to do with management and lesson delivery and more with the impact of your teaching on learners. This stage of planning is sometimes referred to as the *impact* stage. At this stage you will naturally view learners as individuals and will be concerned that each of your students fulfills her or his potential to learn. At this time, your principal concerns will be the following:

- How can I increase my learners' feelings of accomplishment?
- How do I meet my learners' social and emotional needs?
- What is the best way to challenge my unmotivated learners?
- What skills do they need to best prepare them for the next grade?

Fuller (1969) speculated that concerns for *self, task,* and *impact* are the natural stages that most teachers pass through, representing a developmental growth pattern extending over months and even years of a teacher's career. Although some teachers may pass through these stages more quickly than others and at different levels of intensity, Fuller suggested that almost all teachers can be expected to move from one to another, with the most effective and experienced teachers expressing student-centered (impact) concerns at a high level of commitment.

Fuller's concerns theory has several other interesting implications. A teacher might return to an earlier stage of concern—move from a concern for students back to a concern for task as a result of having to teach a new grade or subject, or move from a concern for task back to a concern for self as a result of having to teach different and unfamiliar students. The second time spent in a stage might be expected to be shorter than the first. Finally, the three stages of concern need not be exclusive of one another. A teacher could have concerns predominately in one area while still having concerns at lesser levels of intensity in the other stages. Record your scores on the Teacher Concerns Checklist that you have just taken, and compare them with your scores at the end of this course to find out in what direction your concerns may have changed.

FINAL WORD

This chapter has presented some key and helping behaviors for becoming an effective teacher. These are not all of what the effective teacher is or does, but they are an important basis—perhaps the most valid basis—for beginning to understand the effective teacher. For us they will form the backbone and skeleton of an effective teacher. In the chapters ahead, we will assemble the remainder of this complex person called the effective teacher.

SUMMING UP

This chapter introduced you to definitions of effective teaching and key behaviors that help achieve it. Its main points follow:

1. Early definitions of effective teaching focused primarily on a teacher's goodness as a person and only secondarily on his or her behavior in the classroom.

2. The psychological characteristics of a teacher—personality, attitude, experience, achievement, and aptitude—do not relate strongly to the teacher's behavior in the classroom.

3. Most modern definitions of effective teaching identify patterns of teacher–student interac-

tion in the classroom that influence the cognitive and affective performance of students.

4. Classroom interaction analysis is a research methodology in which the verbal interaction patterns of teachers and students are systematically observed, recorded, and related to student performance.

5. Five key behaviors for effective teaching and some indicators pertaining to them are the following:
   - *Lesson clarity:* logical, step-by-step order, clear and audible delivery free of distracting mannerisms.
   - *Instructional variety:* variability in instructional materials, questioning, types of feedback, and teaching strategies.
   - *Task orientation:* achievement (content) orientation as opposed to process orientation, maximum content coverage, and time devoted to instruction.
   - *Student engagement:* limiting opportunities for distraction and getting students to work on, think through, and inquire about the content.
   - *Success rate:* 60% to 70% of time spent on tasks that afford moderate-to-high levels of success, especially during expository or didactic instruction.

6. Five helping behaviors for effective teaching and some indicators pertaining to them are the following:
   - *Use of student ideas and contributions:* Using student responses to foster the goals of the lesson, and getting students to elaborate on and extend learned content using their own ideas, experiences, and thought patterns.
   - *Structuring:* Providing advance organizers and mental strategies at the beginning of a lesson, and creating activity structures with varied demands.
   - *Questioning:* Using both content (direct) and process (indirect) questions to convey facts and to encourage inquiry and problem solving.
   - *Probing:* Eliciting clarification, soliciting additional information, and redirecting when needed.
   - *Enthusiasm:* Exhibiting vigor, involvement, excitement, and interest during classroom presentations through vocal inflection, gesturing, eye contact, and animation.

7. The key behaviors appear to be consistently effective across all or most teaching contexts.

8. Other teaching behaviors, such as use of student ideas and contributions, structuring, and questioning, may be more important with some learners and objectives than with others.

9. Effective teaching involves the orchestration and integration of key and helping behaviors into meaningful patterns to achieve specified goals.

FOR DISCUSSION AND PRACTICE

Questions marked with an asterisk are answered in Appendix B. See also *Bridges: An Activity Guide and Assessment Options,* which accompanies this text.

*1. In the following list, place the number 1 beside those indicators that most likely would appear in early definitions of effective teaching, based on the characteristics of a "good" person. Place the number 2 beside those indicators that most likely would appear in later definitions of effective teaching, based on the psychological characteristics of teachers. Place a check beside those indicators most likely to appear in modern definitions of effective teaching, based on the interaction patterns of teachers and students.

_____	Is always on time for work
_____	Is intelligent
_____	Stays after class to help students
_____	Works well with those in authority
_____	Has plenty of experience at his or her grade level
_____	Varies higher-level with lower-level questions
_____	Likes his or her job

_____ Uses attention-getting devices to engage students in the learning task

_____ Is open to criticism

_____ Shows vitality when presenting

_____ Has worked with difficult students before

_____ Always allows students to experience moderate-to-high levels of success

_____ Matches the class content closely with the curriculum guide

2. In your opinion, which of the following helping behaviors on the right would be *most* helpful in implementing the key behaviors on the left? More than a single helping behavior may be used for a given key behavior. Compare your results with those of another, and discuss the reasons for any differences.

Lesson clarity _____   1. Student ideas
Instructional variety _____   2. Structuring
Task orientation _____   3. Questioning
Engagement in the   4. Probing
   learning task _____   5. Enthusiasm
Success rate _____

*3. Using Table 1.8, identify one way in which you would try to achieve each of the following for *either* a predominately lower-SES classroom or a predominately higher-SES classroom: Individualization, teacher affect, thinking and decision making, and classroom interaction.

4. Which two teaching effectiveness behaviors would you emphasize if you were teaching fifth-grade mathematics? Which two would you emphasize when teaching fifth-grade reading? Justify your choices from the summary research tables in this chapter.

5. Indicate your perceived strengths in exhibiting the five key and five catalytic behaviors, using the following technique. First, notice the number assigned to each of the key behaviors.

1 lesson clarity

2 instructional variety

3 teacher task orientation

4 student engagement in the learning process

5 student success rate

Now, for each of the following rows of numbers listed, circle the number representing the key behavior in which you perceive yourself to have the greater strength.

1 versus 2   2 versus 4
1 versus 3   2 versus 5
1 versus 4   3 versus 4
1 versus 5   3 versus 5
2 versus 3   4 versus 5

Count up how many times you circled a 1, how many times you circled a 2, a 3, and so on, and place the frequencies on the following lines.

_____ 1
_____ 2
_____ 3
_____ 4
_____ 5

Your perceived greatest strength is the key behavior having the highest frequency. Your perceived least strength is the key behavior with the lowest frequency.

6. Repeat the paired comparison technique in the same manner for the five helping behaviors.

1 use of student ideas

2 structuring

3 questioning

4 probing

5 enthusiasm

1 versus 2   2 versus 4
1 versus 3   2 versus 5
1 versus 4   3 versus 4
1 versus 5   3 versus 5
2 versus 3   4 versus 5

_____ 1
_____ 2
_____ 3
_____ 4
_____ 5

7. Recall a particularly good teacher you had during your high school years—and a partic-

ularly poor one. Try to form a mental image of each one. Now rate each of them on the five key behaviors in the following list. Use 1 to indicate strength in that behavior, 2 to indicate average performance, and 3 to indicate weakness in that behavior. Are the behavioral profiles of the two teachers different? How?

Behavior	Teacher X (good)	Teacher Y (poor)
Lesson clarity	_____	_____
Instructional variety	_____	_____
Task orientation	_____	_____
Engagement in the learning process	_____	_____
Success rate	_____	_____

8. Now do the same for the five helping behaviors, using the same two teachers. Is the pattern the same? What differences in ratings, if any, do you find across key and helping for the same teacher? How would you account for any differences that occurred?

2 Understanding Your Students

This chapter will help you answer the following questions:

1. What is a reflective teacher?
2. How can I adapt my instruction to the needs and abilities of individual learners?
3. What are some of the ways I can use peer group membership to foster the goals of my instruction?
4. How can I help learners acquire a positive self-concept?
5. What are some ways I can promote family–school partnerships in my classroom?

Chapter 1 explained that teaching is not simply the transmission of knowledge from teacher to learner but rather is the interaction of teacher with learner. This chapter discusses the decisions you must make about whom you will teach. In subsequent chapters, we will consider the decisions you must make about what and how you will teach.

Not so long ago, students were viewed as empty vessels into which the teacher poured the contents of the day's lesson. Teachers perceived their task to be the skilled transmission of appropriate grade-level content as it appeared in texts, curriculum guides, workbooks, and the academic disciplines.

Contradictions arose from such a simplistic definition of teaching and learning. For example, this definition could not explain why some students get poor grades while others get good grades. Nor could it explain why some students want to learn while others do not even want to come to school; why some students do extra homework while others do none at all; or why some students have attitudes conducive to learning while others talk disparagingly about school.

These are just some of the individual differences existing in every classroom; they will influence the outcome of your teaching, regardless of how adept you may be at transmitting content. Adapting your teaching to individual differences will require that you make many decisions about your learners that cannot be reduced to simple formulas or rules. It will require that you become a **reflective teacher,** which means that you take the time to ask tough questions about the appropriateness and success of your teaching efforts. Reflective teachers are thoughtful and self-critical about their teaching. That is, they take the time necessary to adapt their lessons to their learners' needs, prior histories, and experiences, and to analyze and critique these lessons afterward.

To help adapt subject matter content to the world of their learners, reflective teachers use the direct experiences of their learners and their classroom interactions (questions, discussion, projects, cooperative activities) as instructional tools. By de-

emphasizing lecturing and telling, reflective teachers encourage their learners to use their own experiences to actively construct understandings that make sense to them. In other words, reflective teachers bridge the gap between teaching and learning by actively engaging students in their lessons and encouraging them to gradually accept greater responsibility for their own learning. In the chapters ahead, we will have more to say about how you can become a reflective teacher who adapts subject matter to the individual differences of learners and who uses direct experiences and the dialogue of the classroom to actively engage students in the learning process.

Becoming an effective teacher includes not only learning to be knowledgeable about content and how to teach it but also learning how to adjust both content and teaching practices to the individual differences among learners. This chapter contains some important facts about the psychology of learners that will help you understand and appreciate their individual differences.

WHY PAY ATTENTION TO INDIVIDUAL DIFFERENCES?

Any observer in any classroom quickly notices that schoolchildren vary in their experiences, socioeconomic status (SES), culture, language, and learning style. Differences in experience, SES, culture, language, and learning style influence what students learn (Banks, 1997; Dunn & Griggs, 1995). Of what consequence is such an obvious observation? After all, you must teach all the students assigned to you, regardless of their differences.

Two of the reasons for being aware of individual differences among learners in your classroom follow:

1. By recognizing individual differences, you can help your learners use their own experiences and learning histories to derive meaning and understanding from what you are teaching. With that knowledge, you will be better able to adapt your instructional methods to the individual learning needs of your students.
2. When counseling students and talking with parents about the achievement and behavior of your learners, you will be able to convey some of the reasons for what you are describing. Understanding your students' individual differences can provide perspective for parents, counselors, and other teachers when they wonder way Jared is not learning, why Anita learns without studying, or why Angela doesn't want to learn.

Researchers are discovering many content areas and individual differences for which adapting different instructional strategies to the strengths of learners has significantly improved their performance (Corno & Snow, 1986; Cronbach & Snow, 1977). For example, *student-centered discussions* have significantly improved the achievement of highly anxious students by providing a more informal, nurturing climate, while *teacher-centered lectures* have benefited the achievement of low-anxiety students by allowing for a more efficient and faster pace (Dowaliby & Schumer, 1973). The linguistic approach to the teaching of reading has resulted in higher vocabulary achievement for students *high* in auditory ability and who learn best by hearing, while the *whole-word* approach was more effective for students *low* in auditory ability and who learn best by seeing (Stallings & Keepes, 1970). Researchers have found that achievement can be increased when the instructional method favors the learners' natural modalities for learning (Cushner, McClelland & Safford, 1992; Messick, 1995).

Adaptive Teaching

The general approach to achieving a common instructional goal with learners whose individual differences, such as prior achievement, aptitude, or learning styles, differ widely is called **adaptive teaching.** Adaptive teaching techniques apply different instructional strategies to different groups of learners so that the natural diversity prevailing in the classroom does not prevent any learner from achieving success. Two approaches to adaptive teaching have been reported to be effective (Corno & Snow, 1986). They are the remediation approach and the compensatory approach.

The Remediation Approach.   The *remediation* approach provides the learner with the prerequisite knowledge, skill, or behavior needed to benefit from the planned instruction. For example, you might attempt to lower the anxiety of highly anxious students with a student-centered discussion before an important lecture, so that the lecture method could equally benefit all students. Or, you might teach listening skills to students low in auditory ability before using a linguistic approach to reading so that both groups could profit equally from the linguistic approach.

The remediation approach to adaptive teaching will be successful to the extent that the desired information, skill, or behavior can be taught within a reasonable period of time. When this is not possible or represents an inefficient use of classroom time, the compensatory approach to adaptive teaching can be taken.

The Compensatory Approach.   Using the *compensatory* approach, teachers choose an instructional method to circumvent or compensate for the lack of information, skills, or ability known to exist among learners. With this approach to adaptive teaching, teachers alter content presentation to circumvent a weakness and promote a strength. This is done by using alternate modalities (e.g., pictures vs. words) or by supplementing content with additional learning resources (games and simulations) and activities (group discussions, hands-on experiences). This may involve modifying the instructional technique to compensate for known deficiencies and to use known strengths. Techniques include the visual representation of content, using more flexible instructional presentations (films, pictures, illustrations), shifting to alternate instructional formats (self-paced texts, simulations, experience-oriented workbooks), or using authentic, performance-based assessment procedures that might require students to assemble a portfolio of their experiences, ideas, and products pertaining to a topic.

For example, students who are poor at reading comprehension and lack a technical math vocabulary might be taught a geometry unit supplemented with visual handouts. Portraying each theorem and axiom graphically emphasizes the visual modality. Other students having an adequate reading comprehension and vocabulary level might learn the same theorems and axioms exclusively from the text, thereby emphasizing verbal learning.

Benefits of Adaptive Teaching.

Notice that adaptive teaching goes beyond the simpler process of ability grouping, in which learners are divided into groups and then presented approximately the same material at different rates. Some research suggests that differences in academic performance between high and low achievers may actually *increase* with the use of ability grouping, creating a loss of self-esteem and motivation for the low group (Good & Stipek, 1983; Kerchoff, 1986; Slavin, 1991a).

Adaptive teaching, on the other hand, works to achieve success with all students, regardless of their individual differences. It does so either by remediation (building up the knowledge, skills, or abilities required to profit from the planned instruction) or by compensation (circumventing weaknesses by avoiding instructional methods/materials that rely on abilities that may be less well developed). Therefore, adaptive teaching requires an understanding of your students' learning abilities and the alternative instructional methods that can maximize their strongest receptive modalities (e.g., visual vs. auditory).

The chapters ahead provide a menu of such strategies from which to choose. Some of the most promising instructional alternatives in adaptive teaching include the following:

- Cooperative grouping versus whole class instruction
- Inductive versus expository presentation
- Rule–example versus example–rule ordering
- Inductive versus deductive presentation
- Teacher-centered versus student-centered presentation
- Direct versus indirect instruction
- Examples from experience versus examples from text
- Group phonics versus individualized phonics instruction
- Individual responses versus choral responses
- Subvocal responses versus vocal responses
- Self-regulated versus whole-group instruction
- Programmed versus conventional instruction

Each of these teaching methods or presentation styles has been found more effective for some types of learners than for others (Cronbach & Snow, 1977; Rohrkemper & Corno, 1988). The research literature and curriculum texts in your teaching area offer many examples of specific content areas in which a particular instructional method—in association with a particular student characteristic—has enhanced student performance. However, common sense and classroom experience will suggest many other ways in which you can alter teaching to fit the individual needs of your students. By knowing your students and having a variety of instructional methods available, you can adjust your instruction to the learning needs of your students with one of these two methods of adaptive teaching.

THE EFFECTS OF GENERAL INTELLIGENCE ON LEARNING

One thing everyone remembers about elementary school is how some students seemed to learn so easily, while others had to work so hard. In high school the range of student ability seemed even greater. In a practical sense, we associate the terms *smart, bright, ability to solve problems, learn quickly,* and *figure things out* with intelligence. Both in the classroom and in life, it seems that some have more abilities than others. This observation often has been a source of anxiety, concern, and jealousy among learners. Perhaps because the topic of intelligence can so easily elicit emotions like these, it is one of the most talked about and one of the least understood aspects of student behavior.

One of the greatest misunderstandings that some teachers, parents, and learners have about intelligence is that it is a single, unified dimension. Such a belief is often expressed by the use of word pairs such as *slow/fast* and *bright/dull* when referring to different kinds of learners. Unfortunately, these phrases indicate that a student is either fast *or* slow, either bright *or* dull; in fact, each of us, regardless of our intelligence, may be all of these at one time or another. On a particular task of a certain nature, you may appear to be slow, but given another task requiring different abilities, you may be fast. How do such vast differences occur within a single individual?

Everyone knows from personal experience in school, hobbies, sports, and interpersonal relationships that degree of intelligence depends on the *circumstances* and *conditions* under which the intelligence is exhibited. Observations such as these have led researchers to study and identify more than one kind of intelligence. This relatively new way of looking at intelligence has led to a better understanding of classic contradictions like why Carlos is good in vocabulary but not in spelling, why Angela is good in social studies but poor at reading maps, or why Tamara is good at analyzing the reasons behind historical events but not at memorizing the names and dates that go along with them. Each of these seemingly contradictory behaviors can be explained by the special abilities required by each task. These specific abilities, in which we all differ, are the most useful aspects of intelligence for understanding the learning behavior of your students.

Before turning to these specific abilities, you should be aware of some controversial issues about the use of general intelligence when discussing intelligence with parents, teachers, and school administrators. These issues often strongly divide individuals into two camps, known as the environmentalist position and the hereditarian position.

The Environmentalist Position

The *environmentalist* position criticizes the use of general IQ tests in the schools in the belief that they are culturally biased. Environmentalists believe that differences in IQ scores among groups such as African Americans, Hispanics, and Anglos can be attributed largely to social class or environmental differences. Environmentalists reason that some groups of students, particularly minorities, may come from impoverished home environments in which the verbal skills generally required to do well on intelligence tests are not practiced. Therefore, a significant part of minority-student scores on any IQ test represents the environment in which they grew up and not their true intelligence.

Environmentalists conclude and some research supports that the effect of home environment is at least as important as heredity in contributing to one's IQ (Bloom, 1981; Smilansky, 1979). This group believes that intelligence tests are biased in favor of the white middle class, who, it is believed, are able to provide their children with more intense patterns of verbal interaction, greater reinforcement for learning, more learning resources, and better physical health during the critical preschool years when cognitive growth is fastest.

The Hereditarian Position

The *hereditarian* position concludes that heredity rather than environment is the major factor determining intelligence. Hereditarians base their beliefs on the research and writings of Arthur Jensen (1969). They believe that not all children have the same potential for developing the same mental abilities. They contend that efforts such as compensatory education programs to make up for environmental disadvantages in the early elementary grades through remediation have limited success because the origin of the difference is genetic and not environmental (Herrnstein & Murray, 1994).

General versus Specific Intelligence

Common sense tells us there is some truth in both arguments. However, despite how parents, other teachers, and even your own students may feel, these positions are highly dependent on the notion of *general* intelligence. The arguments become less relevant in the context of specific abilities. General intelligence only moderately predicts school grades, whereas specific abilities tend to predict not only school grades but also more important real-life behaviors that school grades are supposed to represent (Tombari & Borich, 1999). For example, tests of general intelligence can not predict success as a salesperson, factory worker, carpenter, computer programmer, or teacher, because they measure few of the specific abilities required for success in these occupations.

If we think of school learning as a pie and IQ as a piece of it, we can ask the question: How large a piece of the classroom learning pie is taken up by IQ? Another way of asking this same question is: What percentage of school learning can be attributed to IQ and what percentage to other factors? Scarr (1981) indicates that many factors, in addition to IQ, will contribute to your learners' success: their motivation, support from parents, prior knowledge, health, use of learning strategies, emotional stability, and the quality of your teaching to name only some. Scarr classifies these factors under the term **social competence.** What percentage of school learning can be assigned to IQ and what percentage to all the other factors, Scarr's social competence? The answer, illustrated in Figure 2.1, is that only about 25% can be attributed to IQ; about 75% must be assigned to social competence. So, knowing your learners' *specific* strengths and altering your instructional goals and activities accordingly will contribute far more to your effective teaching than will categorizing your students' performances in ways that indicate only their *general* intelligence.

Figure 2.1 Factors contributing to school learning.

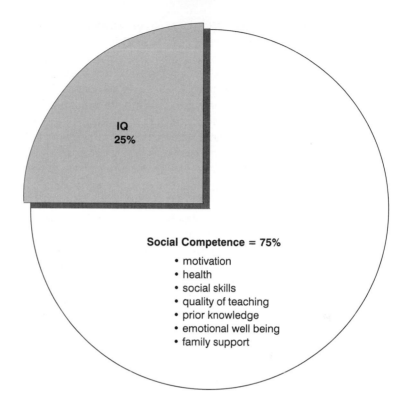

**IQ
25%**

Social Competence = 75%

- motivation
- health
- social skills
- quality of teaching
- prior knowledge
- emotional well being
- family support

THE EFFECTS OF SPECIFIC ABILITIES ON LEARNING

Specific definitions of intelligence and the behaviors they represent commonly are called *aptitudes.* As a teacher, you are unlikely to measure aptitudes in your classroom, but you need to know of their influence on the performance of your students. Your students may already have been aptitude-tested in a district-wide testing program, or you can ask the school counselor or psychologist to measure a specific aptitude to find the source of a specific learning problem. Your acquaintance with the division of general intelligence into specific aptitudes will help you see how a learner's abilities in specific areas can directly affect the degree of learning that takes place.

Multiple Intelligences

Some of the many specialized abilities that have been reliably measured include verbal comprehension, general reasoning, memory, use of numbers, psychomotor speed, spatial relations, and word fluency. This list of abilities resulted from the work of L. L. Thurstone (1947). Instead of reinforcing the idea of a single IQ score, Thurstone's work led to the development of seven different IQs, each measured by a separate test. In this manner the concept of general intelligence was divided into component parts; it had the obvious advantage that a specific score for a given part could be related to certain types of learning requirements.

Some learning activities require a high degree of memory, such as memorizing long lists of words in preparation for a spelling bee or a vocabulary test. Likewise, spatial relations, use of numbers, and general reasoning ability are essential for high levels of performance in mathematics. Such differences in aptitude are more useful than general intelligence in explaining to parents why Alexis can get excellent scores on math tests that emphasize number problems ($12 + 2 \times 6 =$) but poor scores on math tests that emphasize word problems (If Bob rows 4 mph against a current flowing 2 mph, how long will it take him to row 16 miles?). Such apparent contradictions become more understandable in the light of specific aptitudes.

Thurstone's (1947) dimensions were among the earliest, and other components of intelligence have been hypothesized. For example, H. Gardner and Hatch (1989) proposed eight different intelligences based on skills found in a modern technological society. The eight abilities identified by Gardner and Hatch, some representative individuals who would be expected to possess high levels of these abilities, and the things those individuals would be good at are identified in Table 2.1.

Campbell, Campbell and Dickinson (1996) and Lazear (1992) have developed instructional materials and modules to teach some of these abilities. The materials and methods developed by Campbell et al. (1996) and Lazear (1992) derive from the observation that many individuals who are successful in life do not score high in traditional indicators of ability, such as verbal or mathematical reasoning. Gardner and his associates (Gardner & Hatch, 1989) suggest that these individuals, to be successful, used other abilities, such as those in Table 2.1, to minimize their weaknesses in some areas and emphasize their strengths in others. Their theory may have particular relevance for teaching at-risk learners, some of whom may not learn from school in the traditional classroom setting using the traditional curriculum. These researchers reason that alternative forms of learning could tap into other dimensions of intelligence that in the traditional classroom may go unnoticed or underutilized.

Content area specialists have identified still other specific forms of intelligence nestled within those suggested by Thurstone (1947) and by Gardner and Hatch (1989). For example, content specialists in reading have identified no fewer than nine verbal comprehension factors, which indicate the ability to do the following:

- Know word meanings
- See contextual meaning
- See organization
- Follow thought patterns
- Find specifics
- Express ideas
- Draw inferences
- Identify literary devices
- Determine a writer's purpose

In other words, a learner's general performance in reading may be affected by any one or a combination of these specific abilities. This and similar lists point up an

Table 2.1   Gardner's multiple intelligences.

Dimension	Example	Things They Are Good At
Linguistic intelligence: Sensitivity to the meaning and order of words and the varied uses of language	Poet, journalist	Creative writing, humor/jokes, storytelling
Logical-mathematical intelligence: The ability to handle long chains of reasoning and to recognize patterns and order in the world	Scientist, mathematician	Outlining, graphic organizers, calculation
Musical intelligence: Sensitivity to pitch, melody, and tone	Composer, violinist	Rhythmic patterns, vocal sounds/tones, music performance
Spatial intelligence: The ability to perceive the visual world accurately, and to recreate, transform, or modify aspects of the world based on one's perceptions	Sculptor, navigator	Active imagination, patterns/designs, pictures
Bodily-kinesthetic intelligence: A fine-tuned ability to use the body and to handle objects	Dancer, athlete	Folk/creative dance, physical gestures, sports/games
Interpersonal intelligence: The ability to notice and make distinctions among others	Therapist, salesperson	Intuiting others' feelings, person-to-person communication, collaboration skills
Intrapersonal intelligence: Access to one's own "feeling life"	Self-aware individual	Silent reflection, thinking strategies, inventing
Naturalist intelligence: Observing, understanding, and organizing patterns in the natural environment	Molecular biologist, rock climber	Sensing, observing, nuturing

Source: Adapted from Campbell et al. (1996), Gardner and Hatch (1989), and Lazear (1992).

interesting and sometimes controversial aspect of intelligence: once abilities such as draw inferences, follow thought patterns, and find contextual meaning are defined, is it possible to *teach* these so-called components of intelligence?

Hereditarians say that intelligence is not teachable, but it seems logical that, with proper instruction, a learner could be taught to draw inferences, follow thought patterns, and find contextual meaning. As general components of intelligence, such as those defined by Thurstone (1947) and by Gardner and Hatch (1989) become divided into smaller and more specific aptitudes, the general concept of intelligence has become demystified. At least some elements of intelligence depend on achievement in certain areas that *can* be influenced by instruction. Therefore, another advantage of the multidimensional approach to intelligence is that some specific abilities once thought to be unalterable can be taught.

Sternberg's Theory of Intelligence

One of the most recent conceptions of specialized abilities comes from Sternberg (1994, 1995). Sternberg's work has been important in forming new definitions of intelligence that allow for intellectual traits, previously believed to be inherited and unalterable, to be improved through instruction. Further, Sternberg suggests not only that intelligence can be taught but also that the classroom is the logical place to teach it.

Let's look more closely at the theory from which this claim is made. Sternberg's theory of intelligence is called *triarchic* because it consists of three parts: (1) the individual's internal world, (2) how the individual acquires intelligence, and (3) the individual's external world.

The Individual's Internal World.   The first part of Sternberg's (1994, 1995) theory relates to the individual's internal world that governs thinking. Three kinds of mental processes occur, instrumental in planning (1) what things to do, (2) how to learn to do them, and (3) how to actually perform them. The first of these processes is used in planning, monitoring, and evaluating the performance of a task. In essence, this is an executive component that tells all other components of our intelligence what to do, like the boss who gives directions but who does none of the work. Hence, this component's role is purely administrative.

A second component of this internal world of intelligence governs behavior in actual task performance. This component controls the various strategies used in solving problems. For example, one strategy is to guide you to the most relevant details of a problem and steer you away from the irrelevant. Thus, individuals can become more or less intelligent by learning which details need attention and which to ignore.

Some aspects of the age-old concept of intelligence, once thought to be unalterable, now may be taught in the classroom.

A third component of this internal world of intelligence governs what previously acquired knowledge we bring to a problem. It is here that Sternberg's (1994, 1995) theory differs most from other concepts of intelligence. In his view, the innate and less alterable characteristics of memory, manipulating symbols, or mental speed are not particularly important to intelligence. Instead, he sees the *previously acquired knowledge* that one brings to problem solving as more important to thinking intelligently.

Sternberg (1994, 1995) points out that one of the biggest differences between experts and nonexperts in the real world is not the mental processes they use in performing a task, but their previously acquired knowledge. The task in expanding intelligence, or expertness, then, is to understand how experts acquire needed information when nonexperts seemingly fail to acquire it. This notion leads to the second part of Sternberg's triarchic theory.

How the Individual Acquires Intelligence. Sternberg (1994, 1995) proposes that intelligence is the ability to learn and to think using previously discovered patterns and relationships to solve new problems in unfamiliar contexts. By experiencing many novel tasks and conditions early in life, we discover the patterns and relationships that tell us how to solve new problems with which we may be totally unfamiliar. In other words, the greater our experience in facing unique and novel conditions, the more we grow and can adapt to the changing conditions around us. Sternberg suggests that confronting novel tasks and situations and learning to deal with them is one of the most important instructional goals in learning intelligent behavior. His writings provide many practical exercises and examples of how to become facile at learning to deal with novel tasks and situations that provide the patterns and relationships with which to enhance our intelligence.

The Individual's External World. The third part of Sternberg's theory relates intelligence to the external world of the individual. This is where an individual's intelligence shows most and can be altered quickest. This part of intelligence is governed by how well one learns to adapt to the environment (change his or her way of doing things to fit the world), to select from the environment (avoid unfamiliar things and choose familiar and comfortable ones), and to shape the environment (change it to fit a personal way of doing things). Thus, intelligent people *learn* to adapt, select, and shape their environment better and faster than do less intelligent people. Therefore, perhaps the most important aspect of Sternberg's theory is that intelligence results as much from how people learn to *cope* with the world around them as it results from the internal mental processes with which they are born (e.g., memory, symbol manipulation, mental speed).

This notion of coping is expressed by 20 characteristics that Sternberg (1994, 1995) suggests often impede intelligent behavior and, therefore, are often found in the unintelligent or the nonexpert:

- Lack of motivation
- Lack of impulse control
- Lack of perseverance

- Using the wrong abilities
- Inability to translate thought into action
- Lack of a product orientation
- Inability to complete tasks and to follow through
- Failure to initiate
- Fear of failure
- Procrastination
- Misattribution of blame
- Excessive self-pity
- Excessive dependency
- Wallowing in personal difficulties
- Distractibility and lack of concentration
- Spreading oneself too thin
- Inability to delay gratification
- Inability or unwillingness to see the forest for the trees
- Lack of balance between critical thinking and creative thinking
- Too little or too much self-confidence

According to Sternberg (1994, 1995), many aspects of intelligence can and should be taught and the classroom is the logical place to convey the attitudes and behaviors that can help learners avoid these impediments to intelligent behavior.

THE EFFECTS OF PRIOR ACHIEVEMENT ON LEARNING

Closely related to Sternberg's (1994, 1995) notion of intelligence are the prior knowledge and skills of your learners—specifically, their task-relevant knowledge and skills. *Task relevant* means those facts, skills, and understandings that must be taught if subsequent learning is to occur. Mastery of these behaviors makes possible future learning. Thus, their identification is important not only in planning instruction but also in accounting for why learning does not occur in some situations and for some students.

These task-relevant facts, skills, and understandings come in various shapes and sizes. In each content area, they are part of the logical progression of ideas with which a lesson is conveyed. For example, various orders of reasoning may be used—general-to-detailed, simple-to-complex, abstract-to-concrete, or conceptual-to-procedural. These logical progressions are **learning structures** that identify at each step those behaviors needed before new learning can take place (e.g., procedures must come before concepts, and simple facts must come before complex details). Many task-relevant prior learnings are embedded within these progressions. It is on these progressions that the final outcomes of a lesson or unit depend. This point is illustrated in Figure 2.2 for an instructional unit on government and Figure 2.3 for a unit on writing skills.

Notice that in Figure 2.2, the concepts of *presidential* and *parliamentary* would have to be learned before the concept of *a representative democracy* could be

Figure 2.2 Organization of content indicating a logical progression for a unit on government.

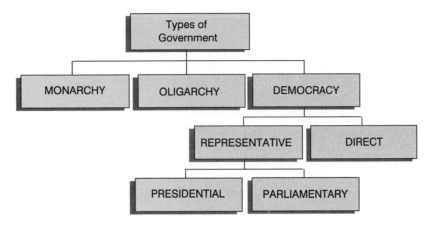

understood. And, the concepts of *monarchy, oligarchy,* and *democracy* would have to be learned before attaining an understanding of *types of government.* These **task-relevant prior achievements** provide a structure for learning that allows larger concepts, principles, and generalizations to be learned at the end of a lesson or unit. Notice that a breakdown in the flow of learning at almost any level would prevent learning from taking place at any subsequent level. Failure to attain concepts at higher levels in the instructional plan may not indicate a lack of ability but a failure to adequately attain task-relevant prior behaviors.

Figure 2.3 Organization of content indicating a logical progression for a unit on writing skills.

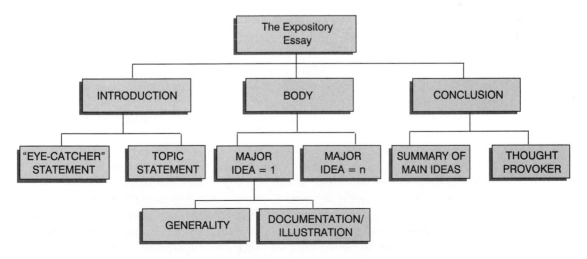

THE EFFECTS OF HOME AND FAMILY ON LEARNING

It is well known that a relationship exists between social class and educational achievement. Traditionally, students from lower-class and lower middle-class families have not performed as well on standardized achievement tests as have students from middle-class and upper-class families.

Researchers have studied the relationship among social class, race/ethnicity, and school achievement (Mansnerus, 1992; Sleeter & Grant, 1991). Their studies generally conclude that most differences in educational achievement occurring among racial and ethnic groups can be accounted for by social class, *even after the lower SES of minority groups is considered* (Gamoran, 1992; Levine & Havinghurst, 1984). In other words, if you know the SES of a group of students, you can predict their achievement with some accuracy. Information about their racial and ethnic group does little to improve the prediction. This indicates the powerful effect social class can have on the behavior of your students.

Why SES Is Important in Learning

It is now appropriate to ask "What is it about SES that creates differences in the classroom?" and "What can I, a teacher, do to lessen these differences?" Obviously, if SES plays a role in student achievement, it must stand for something more specific than income and the educational level of parents. Research shows that a number of more meaningful characteristics in which the home and family lives of higher- and lower-SES families differ are associated with income and educational level. These characteristics—which are indirect results of income and education—are thought to influence the achievement of schoolchildren.

One characteristic that seems to distinguish children of the lower class from those in the middle and upper socioeconomic class is that the latter are more likely to acquire knowledge of the world outside their home and neighborhood at an earlier age (Delgado-Gaitan, 1991; Lambert, 1991). Through greater access to books, magazines, social networks, cultural events, and others who have these learning resources, middle- and upper-class students develop their reading and speaking abilities more rapidly. This, in combination with parental teaching (which tends to use the formal or elaborated language that trains the child to think independently of the specific communication context), may give students in the middle and upper classes an advantage at the start of school. This contrasts with children who come from lower-class homes, which may emphasize obedience and conformity rather than independent thinking and may emphasize rote learning (memorization, recall of facts, etc.) rather than independent, self-directed learning (Christenson, Rounds, & Franklin, 1992; Grave, Weinstein, & Walberg, 1983; Leler, 1983).

Contributing to these differences is the fact that 70% of working-age mothers of disadvantaged students must work. In the last 30 years, the composition of the family has undergone a dramatic change. The traditional family unit is no longer the rule, but the exception. As recently as 1965, more than 60% of American families were traditional: a working father and a mother who kept the house and took care of the children. Only 10% of today's families represent the traditional family of past generations. Today's family is more likely to be a dual-career family, a single-parent family, a stepfamily, or a family that has moved an average of 14 times. All of these conditions affect the fabric of the family and the development of the school-age learners within it.

By some estimates, the majority of children now being born will live in a household where there is no adult 10 to 12 hours a day. Less time for parents to become involved in their child's education, more distracting lifestyles, and greater job and occupational stress can be expected to contribute to the growing numbers of disadvantaged learners. H. Levin (1986) has estimated that educationally disadvantaged youth comprise more than one third of all school-age children.

The Teacher's Role in Improving Achievement Among Lower-SES Students

The classroom is the logical place to begin the process of reducing some of the achievement differences that have been noted between lower- and middle/upper-SES students. Many formal interventions are trying to reduce the differences, from preschools to federally funded compensatory education programs. However, these interventions and programs are not likely to eliminate achievement differences among various groups of students who have highly divergent home and family lifestyles.

This leaves you, the classroom teacher, to deal with these differences as a daily fact of life. The general tendencies are clear: the home and family backgrounds of lower- and higher-SES students differentially prepare them for school. For the classroom teacher, the task becomes one of planning instruction around these differences in ways that reduce them as much as possible.

There are several ways to make the achievement differences between social classes in your classroom more easily altered by your instructional methods. One of these is your willingness to incorporate a variety of learning aids (such as audiovisuals, learning centers, and exploratory materials) into your lessons. This variety of materials encourages your learners to use their own experiences, past learnings, and preferred learning modalities in which to construct and demonstrate what they have learned. Thus, lesson variety can be an important resource for those who may benefit from alternative ways of learning.

Another way in which to reduce achievement differences due to social class is to have high expectations for all your students and to reward them for their accomplishments. Sufficiently high expectations and rewards for learning outside the classroom may not be equally available to all of your learners. Your role in providing high expectations, support, and encouragement in the classroom could be instrumental in bridging some of the differences in achievement among your learners.

Finally, as an effective teacher, you should provide learners the opportunity to express their own sense of what they know and to build connections or relationships among the ideas and facts being taught using their own experiences. It is important to encourage learners to construct and express understandings and meanings of their own in a form that is most comfortable to them. This has two important effects in helping you attain the instructional goals of your classroom: it promotes student engagement and interest in your subject while showing them that someone thinks they have something worthwhile to say.

Other ways you can reduce the differences among learners in your class include (Borich & Tombari, 1997, pp. 177–187) the following:

1. Organize learning and instruction around important ideas that your students already know something about.
2. Acknowledge the importance of your students' prior learning by having them compare what they know with what you are teaching.
3. Challenge the adequacy of your students' prior knowledge by designing lessons that create the opportunity for your students to resolve conflict and construct new meanings for themselves.
4. Provide some tasks that make students confront ambiguity and uncertainty by exploring problems that have multiple solutions in authentic, real-world contexts.
5. Teach students how to find their own approaches or systems for achieving educational goals.
6. Teach students that knowledge construction is a joint effort rather than a solitary search of knowledge or an exclusively teacher-controlled activity.
7. Assess a student's knowledge acquisition, and provide feedback during the lesson.

THE EFFECTS OF PERSONALITY ON LEARNING

Preceding sections discussed the potential influence on learning of students' general intelligence, specific aptitude, task-relevant prior achievement, and home life. In this section your students' personalities will be added to this equation.

When words such as *trustworthy, creative, independent, anxious, cheerful, authoritarian,* or *aggressive* are used to describe a student, they refer to an aspect of that student's personality. *Personality* is the integration of one's traits, motives, beliefs, and abilities, including emotional responses, character, and even values. The notion of personality is indeed broad and, according to some authors, even subsumes intelligence and specialized abilities. It is not necessary to take so broad a view of personality, because not every part of what is considered to be personality is applicable to classroom learning. On the other hand, several aspects of personality are so important to learning that learning probably could not occur without them. These aspects of personality are called traits.

Traits are enduring aspects of a person's behavior that are consistent across a variety of settings. Traits are not specific to subject matter content, grade level, or instructional objective, as are aptitude and achievement. However, this does not mean that variations in content, grade level, and objectives are unimportant to personality. In fact, many things within a classroom can trigger some personality traits and not others. Some parts of personalities lie dormant until stimulated to action by some particular perception of the world. This is the reason teachers often are dismayed to hear, for example, that an aggressive child in fifth-period social studies is shy and cooperative in someone else's seventh-period mathematics. It also is the reason that some students and teachers may never quite see eye to eye. Fortunately, such personality conflicts are rare, but they can be harmful to classroom rapport if left to smolder beneath the surface.

ERIKSON'S CRISES OF THE SCHOOL YEARS

Some psychologists believe that different personality traits dominate at certain periods of our lives. For example, Erikson (1968), who developed a theory on how we form our personalities, hypothesized eight different stages of personality growth between infancy and old age that he called crises. Three of these stages, shown in Figure 2.4, occur during the school years:

1. The crisis of accomplishment versus inferiority
2. The crisis of identity versus role confusion
3. The crisis of intimacy versus isolation

During the first crisis, of accomplishment versus inferiority, the student seeks ways of producing products or accomplishments that are respected by others. In this manner the child creates a feeling of worth to dispel feelings of inferiority or inadequacy that result from competing in a world where adults appear confident and competent. At first, such accomplishments may take the easiest course—being good at sports, being good in school, or being helpful at home. For the teacher this is a par-

Figure 2.4   Personal and social development during Erikson's three crises during the school years.

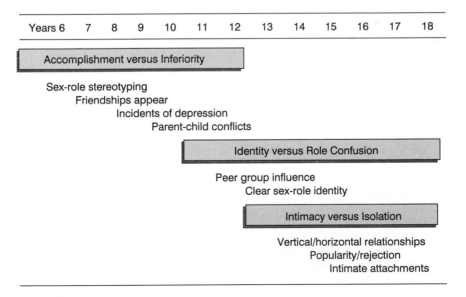

ticularly challenging time, because student engagement at high rates of success is needed to keep some feelings of worth focused in the classroom. Seeing that every student has some successful experiences in the classroom can be an important vehicle for helping students through this crisis.

Erikson's second crisis during the school years is precipitated by the student's need to understand oneself—to find his or her identity, "the real me." One's sex, race, ethnicity, religion, and physical attractiveness can play important roles in producing—or failing to produce—a consistent and acceptable self-image. This is a process of accepting oneself, as one truly is, apart from illusions, made-up images, and exaggerations.

Social psychologists believe that, in the process of finding and accepting oneself during this crisis, the individual must experience *recognition,* a sense of *control* over her or his environment, and *achievement.* Being a member of a group intensifies these needs. Social psychologists, such as Patricia and Richard Schmuck (Schmuck & Schmuck, 1992), urge teachers to recognize that groups help provide opportunities for recognition, control, and achievement and to use this heightened motivation to achieve academic goals. And they caution that classrooms that fail to satisfy these three basic needs may contain large numbers of learners who feel rejected, listless, and powerless, creating motivational and conduct problems within the classroom.

A task orientation in which the teacher plans to actively involve learners in ways they can express themselves and their uniqueness can help to meet these three basic needs. Some classroom activities that can provide your learners opportunities for recognition, control and achievement include

- Discussions
- Demonstrations and exhibits
- Cooperative activities
- Portfolios
- Project-based learning

The effective teacher not only understands and empathizes with the conflicting emotions of students at this stage but also provides the classroom structure needed to help resolve the crisis.

Erikson's third crisis during the school years is that of giving up part of one's identity to develop close and intimate relationships with others. For some, this stage may occur after the high school years, but for most, its roots are in high school. Forming relationships, especially with the opposite sex, may be one of the most important and traumatic experiences of school. For some students it may represent the only reason for coming to school. It is not unusual for students during this crisis to form emotional relationships with their teachers as well, especially when relationships with their peers are thwarted due to differences in maturity, attractiveness, interests, or physical size. There are no simple ways to deal with these emotions. Be aware of crushes, try to cushion their impact on the student, and try to channel the student's emotions productively.

Learning how to get along with teachers, parents, and classmates is one of the key developmental tasks learners must master to successfully resolve this crisis. Successful relationships with parents and teachers, referred to as **vertical relation-**

Successful relationships with peers, referred to as horizontal relationships, meet learners' needs for belonging and allow them to acquire and practice important social skills. These friendship patterns often are created through peer groups that exhibit strong commitments of loyalty, protection, and mutual benefit.

ships (Hartup, 1989), meet a learner's needs for safety, security, and protection. Successful relationships with peers, referred to as **horizontal relationships,** are of equal developmental significance for learners. They meet learners' needs for belonging and allow them to acquire and practice important social skills. Providing opportunities for learners to develop healthy relationships when they enter school helps them develop skills important in getting along with others, helping others, and establishing intimacy. The failure to experience healthy horizontal relationships and learn friendship-building attitudes and skills can have undesirable consequences. This failure is often described as *social rejection.*

Current research suggests that rejected children are more likely to be aggressive and disruptive in school (Hartup, 1989), experience intense feelings of loneliness (Cassidy & Asher, 1992), and suffer emotional disturbances in adolescence and adulthood (T. J. Dishon, Patterson, Stoolmiller, & Skinner, 1991). Nevertheless, researchers have shown that learners can be taught some of the social skills necessary to gain acceptance by peers. More importantly, by helping your learners construct their own well-functioning horizontal relationships, they will acquire friendship-building attitudes and skills that can have desirable consequences in your classroom.

Personality differences due to *anxiety, learning style,* and *self-concept* are important in all three of Erikson's crises of the school years. Let's see what the researchers have to say about them.

Anxiety

Everyone finds anxiety uncomfortable, if only because of its debilitating effect on getting things done. Anxiety makes even the simplest tasks seem difficult. One feels threatened, fearful of the unknown, and generally tense. Among your acquaintances, and perhaps within yourself, you have observed at least two types of anxiety. They are called state anxiety and trait anxiety.

State Anxiety.   **State anxiety** (Spielberger, 1966) is an experience of fear or threat related to a particular environmental situation. A common example is the anxiety felt before taking a test. This represents a state or condition that is *momentary* and produced by some specific stimulus in the environment (a test, a report card, a speech before the class, a first date). Levels of state anxiety vary with different environmental stimuli. However, given the right stimulus, this anxiety can occur at any time.

There is a positive side to state anxiety: some is necessary for learning. Without fearing the negative consequences of a failing grade, Mary may not do the studying required for a passing grade. Without some fear of injury in a poorly executed lab experiment, Damon may not be cautious enough to avoid the danger. Without fear of doing poorly in front of his peers, Billy may not organize his speech well enough to avoid embarrassment. Evaluation or assessment in the form of grades, report cards, and assignments are some of the ways the effective teacher provides the level of state anxiety necessary to motivate students.

Trait Anxiety.   A second type of anxiety is a general disposition to feel threatened by a wide range of conditions perceived to be harmful. This type of anxiety has been labeled **trait anxiety,** indicating its stability over time. No single stimulus, such as a grade or assignment, can be identified as the source of the anxiety. It results instead from many ill-defined sources. Unlike state anxiety, which all students experience to some degree, trait anxiety is a fairly stable characteristic of one's personality, with different individuals having different amounts.

High levels of trait anxiety seem to go with high motivation and the need to achieve. But, like state anxiety, extremely high levels of trait anxiety can be immobilizing, especially when the need to achieve is guided more by a fear of failure (shame, ridicule by peers, punishment from parents) rather than by a wish to do well. When fear of failure is the primary motive among high-anxiety students, they may complete more assignments with more accuracy, but they will complete them in a mechanical, perfunctory way, allowing for little more than the most obvious and expected learning outcomes.

Research shows that when motivation among high-anxiety students is guided more by a desire to do well (e.g., to produce a high-quality product, create something new and different, gain the respect of others, tackle the impossible) rather than by fear of failure, more work is accomplished toward a given goal in less time and in ways that engage students in discovery types of learning experiences that result in higher achievement (Covington & Omelich, 1987).

This suggests that one of your tasks as an effective teacher is to tailor the learning conditions of high-anxiety students. In the case of high trait anxiety, conveying a feeling of warmth, encouragement, and support before the assignment can turn fears of failure into more productive motives involving a desire to do well. Structuring the assignment in ways that provide for a *range of acceptable responses* serves to focus the high-anxiety student on an attainable end product and away from general fears of being unable to achieve an acceptable level of performance. As we will learn in Chapter 13, performance assessment and student portfolios also are excellent ways of accomplishing this goal.

Learning Style

A second aspect of personality that will influence your learners' achievement is their learning style. **Learning style** refers to the classroom or environmental conditions under which someone prefers to learn. Although there are a number of learning styles, the one most studied has been that identified with the characteristics of **field dependence** and **field independence.**

Field Dependence versus Field Independence.   Much has been written about how some learners are more global than analytic in how they approach learning (Franklin, 1992). Some researchers use the terms *holistic/visual* to describe global learners, and *verbal/analytic* to describe the opposite style or orientation (Tharp & Gallimore 1989). Still others (Hilliard, 1976) prefer the term *field sensitive* to refer to the holistic/visual learning style and the term *field insensitive* to refer to the verbal/analytic learning style. To what are these researchers referring?

Basically, these terms have come to refer to how people view the world. People who are field dependent see the world in terms of large, connected patterns. Looking at a volcano, for example, a field-dependent person would notice its overall shape, and the larger colors and topographical features that make it up. A field-independent person, on the other hand, would tend to notice the discrete parts of a scene. Thus, she might notice more the individual trees, the different rocks, the size of the caldera, where the caldera sits in relation to the rest of the structure, topographical features showing the extent of lava flow, and so on. To better understand what field dependence and field independence mean, and what these terms suggest about how different children learn, let's look at what some of the researchers say about them.

Franklin (1992) and Tharp (1989) believe that field dependence and independence are stable traits of individuals that affect different aspects of their lives, especially their approach to learning. Table 2.2 summarizes some of the characteristics associated with both types of learners. These researchers agree that the different personality characteristics or traits of field-dependent and -independent learners suggest that at least some learners think about and process information differently during classroom learning activities. Those authors suggest that each group would benefit from different instructional strategies, as suggested in Table 2.3.

Table 2.2 Field-dependent and field-independent learner characteristics.

Field-Dependent (Field-Sensitive) Learners	Field-Independent Learners
1. Perceives global aspects of concepts and materials.	1. Focuses on details of curriculum materials.
2. Personalizes curriculum—relates concepts to personal experience.	2. Focuses on facts and principles.
3. Seeks guidance and demonstrations from teacher.	3. Rarely seeks physical contact with teacher.
4. Seeks rewards that strengthen relationship with teacher.	4. Formal interactions with teacher are restricted to tasks at hand—seeks nonsocial rewards.
5. Prefers to work with others and is sensitive to their feelings and opinions.	5. Prefers to work alone.
6. Likes to cooperate.	6. Likes to compete.
7. Prefers organization provided by teacher.	7. Can organize information by him/herself.

Learning Style and Culture.   Educators have become interested in the relationship between learning style and culture. The work of several researchers has suggested that Native Americans, Hispanic Americans, and African Americans are more field-dependent than Anglo Americans and Asian Americans (C. Bennett, 1990; Cushner, McClelland, & Safford, 1992; Garcia, 1991; Hilliard, 1992; Tharp, 1989). These researchers advocate that teachers who work with these groups of learners use more field-dependent teaching styles.

These researchers have conducted studies to answer the question of how cultural groups differ in cognitive functioning. The reasoning underlying their studies is that different ethnic and cultural groups have different informal learning or socializa-

Table 2.3 Instructional strategies for field-dependent and field-independent learners.

Field-Dependent (Field-Sensitive) Learners	Field-Independent Learners
1. Display physical and verbal experiences of approval or warmth.	1. Be direct in interactions with learners; show content expertise.
2. Motivate by use of social and tangible rewards.	2. Motivate by use of nonsocial rewards such as grades.
3. Use cooperative learning strategies.	3. Use more mastery learning and errorless teaching strategies.
4. Use corrective feedback often.	4. Use corrective feedback only when necessary.
5. Allow interaction during learning.	5. Emphasize independent projects.
6. Structure lessons, projects, homework, etc.	6. Allow learners to develop their own structure.
7. Assume role of lecturer, demonstrator, checker, reinforcer, grader, materials designer.	7. Assume role of consultant, listener, negotiator, facilitator.

tion practices by which they teach their children the skills necessary to adapt successfully to their environment. These practices produce certain patterns of learning styles, which influence how these children learn in formal settings.

What evidence have these studies found that suggests that minority groups have different learning styles than Anglo Americans? While the evidence is sometimes inconsistent, in general, some evidence suggests that minority learners are more holistic/global/visual or field sensitive in their approach to learning than verbal/analytic or field independent. Shade (1982), Cohen (1969), and Hilliard (1976) present evidence suggesting that African American learners have a learning style emphasizing field-sensitive abilities as well as a preference for person-oriented classroom activities (cooperative learning and activities that focus on people and what they do, rather than on things or objects). Other researchers (Knight & Kagan, 1977; Ramirez & Castaneda, 1974) conclude that Mexican Americans are more field sensitive as a group than Anglo Americans. Those authors explain the higher relative performance of this group on measures of field sensitivity by pointing out that the childrearing practices of this group stress strong family ties and a respect and obedience to elders; experiences, the authors conclude, that lead to a more field-sensitive learning style.

Cultural Differences in Learning Styles: Some Cautions.   Is there sufficient justification to advocate field-sensitive teaching styles in classrooms with significant numbers of minority learners? Should teachers make greater use of instructional practices that emphasize cooperative learning, person and movement/action-oriented activities, visual/holistic learning, and so on when teaching significant numbers of African, Hispanic, or Native American learners? Before implementing culturally responsive teaching without qualification, keep in mind the following cautions:

1. *Beware of perpetuating stereotypes.* Grant (1991) cautions that cultural information such as that described previously may be used to "perpetuate ideas from the cultural deficit hypothesis that encourages teachers to believe that these students have deficits and negative differences and, therefore, are not as capable of learning as white students" (p. 245). Others (Weisner, Gallimore, & Jordan, 1988) claim that cultural explanations of differential achievement of minority groups often result in global and stereotypical descriptions of how minority cultures behave that exceed available evidence. Kendall (1983) argues that it is one thing to be aware of the potential effect of culture-specific learning and learning styles on classroom achievement but another to expect a child of a particular group to behave and to learn in a particular way.

2. *Note within-group differences.* Almost all studies of the learning style preferences of different minority groups have shown that differences within the cultural groups studied were as great as the differences between the cultural groups (Cushner et al., 1992; Henderson, 1980; Tharp, 1989). In other words, Native Americans, Hispanic Americans, African Americans, and Anglo Americans vary considerably on tests of field dependence and independence. Some Anglo Americans will be field dependent in their pattern of scores, and some Native Americans will be field independent. On the average, the groups may differ. But, around these averages are

ranges of considerable magnitude. Thus, using a field-dependent teaching style, even in a monocultural classroom, may fail to match the preferred learning style of at least some learners.

3. *Culturally responsive teaching may be more difficult in multicultural classrooms.* Culturally responsive teaching appears to be most efficient and practical in monocultural classrooms. In classrooms that are multicultural, it may be difficult, maybe impossible, to match the different learning styles of 30 or more children who may represent several different cultures.

4. *Culturally responsive concerns may take the focus away from "expert practice."* Educators such as Lindsley (1992) and Englemann and Carnine (1982) argue that, before assuming that differences in achievement are due to characteristics within the learner (e.g., learning style), factors external to the learner, such as ineffective teaching practices, should be ruled out. Also, the quality of instruction provided minority learners should be equivalent to that provided Anglo Americans. Majority- and minority-group learners should experience similar schooling in terms of resources, quality of teachers, expectations, expert practice in instruction, testing, and motivation techniques before teachers embrace specialized techniques specifically adapted to minorities. Although some evidence indicates that African American and Native American children improve in reading and math with culturally responsive teaching techniques (Franklin, 1992; Tharp, 1989), studies fail to indicate that expert instruction using traditional instructional methods could not have achieved the same or similar results.

Self-Concept

A third aspect of personality that will influence your learners' achievement is self-concept. **Self-concept** represents the beliefs, feelings, and attitudes we have about ourselves. Our self-concept grows out of interactions with *significant others,* such as parents, teachers, and peers. Significant others act as mirrors for our behavior. That is, they reflect the images we create of ourselves, sometimes in modified and revised form. When the image that is returned looks good, is acceptable to others, and is consistent with what we want it to be, a positive self-concept is formed. When the reflected image does not look good, is unacceptable to others, and is inconsistent with our beliefs about ourselves, a less favorable self-concept is formed.

The formation of self-concept is perhaps one of the most fascinating aspects of personality. It has captured the attention of many psychologists and researchers who have studied the relationship of self-concept to student achievement. The research thus far is sketchy and focuses only on certain grades and subjects. However, some evidence indicates that a positive self-concept may be moderately related to achievement (Beane, 1991; Hansford & Hattie, 1982; Walberg, 1986). This research has been taken as an encouraging sign that a student's concept of self can affect the extent to which he or she *becomes actively engaged in the process of learning,* and vice versa, even if it is not always strongly related to scores on tests of academic performance.

Does a positive self-concept promote achievement? Or does achievement promote a positive self-concept? We don't know. However, the intuitive value of having a positive self-concept is so pervasive in our culture that the order of the relationship may not be all that important. An increase in self-concept is believed to have positive results on behavior, either directly on school achievement or indirectly on one's ability to relate to others, to cope with the problems of daily life, and ultimately to succeed in a career or occupation.

Such important outcomes are not measured by tests of academic achievement. However, good performance on school tests might improve one's self-concept. This, in turn, could influence the other important life outcomes. This is reason enough for engaging students in the learning process at moderate-to-high rates of success: to provide a mirror with a positive image. While high rates of success are important for all students, they may be especially important to lower-SES students. These students have been found to have the poorest self-concepts, and their home life may provide few opportunities for improving them.

The crucial question asked by every student in the process of forming a self-concept is "How am I being perceived?" In the school environment, this reflected self-image is derived most often from direct, personal interaction with you, the teacher. As a teacher it will be your task to be sensitive to and to be understanding of the impact of the images you reflect to students by your words and deeds. You will not always want to reflect what your students believe about themselves. On the other hand, consider that any image you send back by interactions and performance evaluations may have implications far beyond the time when you deliver the message. The message you reflect may contribute to the ever-growing complement of data used by each of your students to form the self-concept they will "wear" for years to come. The secret to improving students' self-concepts lies in the process of finding and reflecting back to students the value of their unique talents.

THE EFFECTS OF THE PEER GROUP ON LEARNING

One of the most powerful but sometimes least noted influences on a student's behavior is the peer group. Often considered as the source of a hidden curriculum, the peer group can influence and even teach students how to behave in class, study for tests, and converse with teachers and school administrators, and it can contribute to the success or failure of performance in school in many other ways. From the play group in the elementary school to the teenage clique in high school, a student learns from peers how to behave in ways that are acceptable and that will establish status in the eyes of others. Establishing such status reflects group approval, which promotes a good self-concept.

The power of the peer group in influencing individual student behavior stems from the fact that it is the *voluntary* submission of one's will to some larger cause. Teachers and parents must sometimes beg, plead, punish, and reward to exact appropriate behavior from their students, sons, and daughters. But peer groups need not engage in any of these behaviors to obtain a high level of conformity to often unstated and abstract principles of behavior. Trendy school fashions, new slang words, places to "hang out," acceptable social mates, and respected forms of out-of-school activities are communicated and learned to perfection without lesson plans, texts, or even direct verbalization. Instead, these and other behaviors are transmitted by "salient others" and received by those who anxiously wish to maintain membership in or gain acceptance to a particular peer group.

Friendship patterns often are created through peer groups and sometimes are adhered to with strong commitments of loyalty, protection, and mutual benefit. These commitments can create individual peer cultures or even gangs within a school. Such cultures can rival the academic commitments made in the classroom and frequently supersede them in importance. Studying for a test or completing homework frequently may be sacrificed for the benefit of the peer group. Peer groups can form on the basis of many different individual differences, such as intelligence, achievement, personality, home life, physical appearance, and personal and social interests. But they commonly result from complex combinations of these that are not always discernible to outsiders and sometimes not even to those within the peer group (Hartup, 1989; Schmuck & Schmuck, 1992).

The importance of peer group characteristics in the classroom lies in the extent to which they can be used to promote behaviors that enhance a member's engage-

An important way to positively influence peer groups in your classroom is to conduct group discussions of class norms, describing what class members should and should not do to be socially acceptable, what you expect of them and what they should expect of each other.

ment in the learning process. Here are several approaches for constructively using peer relationships to foster classroom goals:

1. *Stress group work in which members are from different peer groups.* When forming work or cooperative groups, be sure group members represent different backgrounds and interests, which can bring different skills and talents to an assignment. When different types of individuals are assigned to work cooperatively, group behavior tends to follow a middle ground, discouraging extreme or disruptive behavior.

2. *Conduct a group discussion of class norms, describing what class members should and should not do to be socially acceptable.* Tell group members what you expect of them, and give some examples of what they might expect of others. Glasser (1990) suggests discussing with students ideas on how the class might be run, problems that may interfere with the group's performance, and needed rules and routines.

3. *Build group cohesiveness by promoting the attractiveness of each student to one another.* Provide opportunities for your students to know one another through one or more of the following: Construct a bulletin board around the theme of friendships; have students write a brief biography about themselves for all to read; publish a class directory that includes names, hobbies, jobs, and career aspirations; and have students bring something they have made or really care about (a toy, tool, model, etc.).

4. *Assign older or more mature students who are more likely to be respected as role models to interact with and help younger students in a peer tutoring situation.* Many schools have a formal peer tutoring program called *cross-age tutoring,* in which tutors may be chosen from higher grades, to help younger students who may be at risk, or discouraged learners. Research has shown that tutoring has been most successful when tutors have been trained and given explicit instruction on how to tutor.

THE EFFECTS OF THE SOCIAL CONTEXT ON LEARNING

Closely connected with the influence of the peer group on learning is the social context in which your learners live, play, and work. Among the most prominent sources of influence in this context will be your learners' family and its relationship to the school.

In 1990, the National Governors Conference for educational reform set forth a formidable agenda for educators. Their agenda, updated and approved by Congress in 1994, established the following goals to be achieved by the first decade of the twenty-first century (see the text and related strategies on the Web at http//inet.ed.gov/legislation/GOALS2000/TheAct/):

1. All children in America will start school ready to learn.
2. The high school graduation rate will increase to at least 90%.
3. American students will leave grades 4, 8, and 12 having demonstrated competency over challenging subject matter in the sciences and humanities.
4. The nation's teachers will have access to programs for professional development.

5. American students will be the best in the world in mathematics and science achievement.
6. Every adult American will be literate and will possess the knowledge and skills to compete in a global economy and exercise the rights and responsibilities of citizenship.
7. Every school in America will be free of drugs and violence and will offer a disciplined environment conducive to learning.
8. Every school will promote parental involvement and participation to promote the social, emotional, and academic growth of children.

A theme throughout the commentaries on the governors' agenda was the realization that schools would have to develop genuine partnerships with parents to achieve these goals. A singular focus on just teachers, parents, or administrators as the agents of reform would not produce the hoped-for results. Rather, only the active participation of parents, community groups, and educators in partnership with one another would bring about the desired objectives (Lambert, 1991).

When parents and teachers become partners, not only can student achievement increase but also parents learn about you and your school. Research confirms that coordination and collaboration between home and school improve learner achievement, attitude toward school, classroom conduct, and parent and teacher morale (Cochran & Dean, 1991). Establishing genuine partnerships with the parents and guardians of your learners is as essential a teacher practice as those that involve building a cohesive classroom climate, establishing a well-managed work environment, developing goals and objectives, conducting effective instruction, and assessing student performance.

The practice of parent involvement requires that you develop and strengthen throughout the school year "linking mechanisms" for parent participation and collaboration. **Family-school linking mechanisms** are opportunities for school and family involvement and may involve parent–teacher conferences, home visits, participation of teachers in community events, newsletters, phone calls, personal notes, volunteering as classroom aides, and the use of home-based curriculum materials. These efforts require more than just a handout sent home to parents at the beginning of the school year, an obligatory presentation during back-to-school night, or an occasional note home. The opportunities to develop and nurture linking mechanisms will be the culmination of your efforts to build a successful classroom workplace.

To assist in this process, Bronfenbrenner (1989) has urged us to view the family–school partnership from a **systems-ecological perspective.** Bronfenbrenner looks at the learner as a naturalist looks at nature—as an ecosystem. In the learner's ecosystem, the major systems include the family, school, and peer group.

One way to picture the learner's ecosystem is as a series of concentric circles, as shown in Figure 2.5. Each of these circles and their connections has a special term. The most central layer is called the *microsystem.* It includes all those settings where the child lives or spends significant portions of his or her time: the family, school, classroom, day care setting, playground, and job setting if the child is old enough. Bronfenbrenner (1989) refers to these settings as *subsystems.*

Figure 2.5   The child from a systems-ecological perspective.

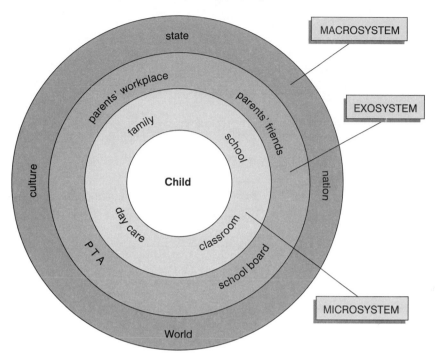

Each subsystem can be viewed within itself as a system. The school system is made up of subsystems that include teachers, administrators, support personnel, school board members, and learners. The family system includes a marital, parental, sibling, and often a grandparental subsystem. The peer system includes social friendships, academic friendships, and sports or hobby friendships.

The next layer of the system includes those subsystems the child does not directly experience but that affect the child because of the influence they exert on the microsystem. This layer is called the *exosystem*. It may include the parents' workplace, their friends, the PTA, the school board, and so on.

Finally, both microsystems and exosystems exist in a larger setting called the *macrosystem*. This system refers to the larger culture or society in which the micro- and exosystems function. Figure 2.6 indicates some of the relationships among these systems.

A systems-ecological perspective urges us to view a learner's behavior, not as a product of that individual alone, but as a product of the learner and the demands and forces operating within the systems of which the learner is a member. Family experiences and the culture of the family system influence school behavior and performance, which, in turn, affect the family system. School adjustment problems, which may be influenced by problems within the family may, in turn, exacerbate conditions within the family system itself. For example, the parent who never signs and

Figure 2.6 The child's ecosystem.

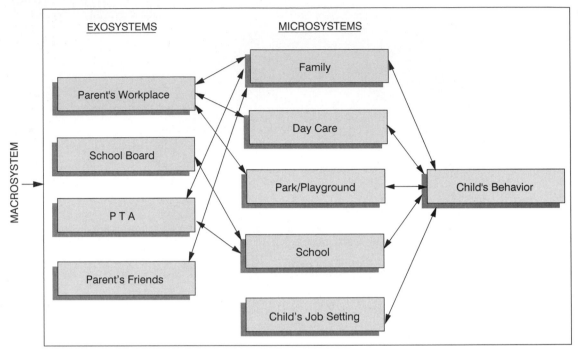

Source: From *The Developing Child,* 6th Edition by Helen Bee. Copyright © 1992 by HarperCollins College Publishers. Reprinted by permission of HarperCollins Publishers, Inc.

returns a note home may not be an uninterested and uninvolved parent—as might be assumed. Dynamics within the family system (e.g., other siblings who demand extensive care or adjustment to a new child) may explain the parents' apparent lack of involvement in their child's education.

Thus, when trying to understand the behavior of parents, teachers, and learners, the systems-ecological perspective recommends that we first ask ourselves "What forces within the family–school environment impel the person to act this way?" When the goal is to promote the academic and social development of the learner, the systems-ecological perspective focuses our most immediate concern on the family–school partnership.

Here are some guidelines for understanding and promoting family–school partnerships in your classroom.

1. *View the family from a systems-ecological perspective.* Avoid viewing the behavior of your learners or their mothers or fathers, as simply products of individual psychological forces. Instead, recognize that the family system is made up of several subsystems, including the *marital* subsystem, *parental* subsystem, the *sibling* subsystem, and *extrafamily* or exosystems such as grandparents and employers.

Changes in one subsystem inevitably bring about changes in the other. Asking parents to take greater responsibility for getting their child to bed earlier at night can result in an argument at home between husband and wife, punishment of the child, teasing by siblings, and concern and criticism by in-laws. Likewise, demands by school staff that parents do something at home to make the child complete homework inevitably reverberate throughout the entire family system. These effects may be so great as to preclude any change in parental behavior.

2. *Acknowledge changes in the American family.* Most families have two working parents. Research on teacher beliefs regarding families where both parents work shows that teachers believe that working parents are less involved with their children's education (Linney & Vernberg, 1983). However, a study conducted by Medrich, Roizen, Rubin, and Burkley (1982) concludes that working and nonworking mothers spend the same amount of time in child-related activities. Furthermore, their data show that children of working mothers are just as involved in extracurricular activities as are the children of nonworking mothers.

Single-parent families make up about 25% of the families of schoolchildren. Yet many teachers view this family pattern as an abnormality (Carlson, 1992). Joyce Epstein, a researcher at the Johns Hopkins Center for Research on Elementary and Middle Schools, reports that teachers have lower expectations for the achievement of children from single-parent families despite the fact that no data support this (Epstein, 1987). Some researchers suggest that the requirements in single-parent families for organization, schedules, routines, and division of responsibilities better prepare children to accept such structure in schools (Linney & Vernberg, 1983).

3. *View parent participation from an empowerment model rather than a deficit model.* Delgado-Gaitan (1991) and Valencia (1997) propose that we view parent participation as a process that involves giving parents both the power and the knowledge to deal with the school system. Typically, deficit model explanations have been offered for reasons why culturally different parents have not become involved with schools. These perspectives sometimes have portrayed parents as passive, incompetent, or unskilled. They propose that parents are unable to become involved in their children's education because they work long hours away from the home or are simply not interested. But, Delgado-Gaitan (1992) points out, when examined closely, research has shown that Hispanic families who speak a different language and have a different culture from that of the school do indeed care about their children and possess the capacity to advocate for them. This holds true for African Americans, Hispanic Americans, Native Americans, and other cultural and linguistic groups as well. The question is not *can* they become genuine partners with the school but *how* to empower them to do so.

4. *Recognize the unique needs of mothers and fathers when planning opportunities to involve parents.* Turnbull and Turnbull (1986) urge teachers to promote nonsexist views of parenting and parent involvement. They stress that teachers recognize the importance of mothers *and* fathers when designing home–school linkages. Encourage visiting opportunities for both parents, and develop flexible schedules to accommodate the working schedules of both parents. Send information about the children and schooling to both parents. Seek to promote teaching skills in

fathers as well as mothers. Finally, give consideration to the father's interests and needs when suggesting ways for parents to work with their children at home.

5. *Appreciate that parents are just like you—they experience periodic emotional, family, and economic problems.* Many parents may have personal, family, work, health, or other problems that remain hidden. Make a special effort to provide the benefit of the doubt, particularly when parents fail to respond in a timely manner to your requests. Carlson (1992) documents the overwhelming economic as well as divorce, custody, and career problems of single parents. Their failure to monitor their child's homework, or attendance, or tardiness to class may be due less to a lack of interest than to attempts to cope with day-to-day problems. When parents do not live up to your expectations, avoid trying to assign personal blame.

6. *Understand the variety of school–family linkages, and respect family preferences for different degrees of school participation.* As you are planning for parent involvement early in the school year, consider and evaluate the full range of ways in which parents can participate. These activities can be placed on a continuum anchored on one end by activities that involve parents as receivers of information (parent–teacher conference, notes home, classroom newsletter) and on the other end by activities that involve parents as active educational decision makers (school and classroom advisory councils, site-based management teams, tutoring).

Developing partnerships with the parents of your learners should be as much a focus of your planning for a new school year as your classroom rules, routines, instructional goals, and objectives. As the research suggests, your learners' achievement of academic goals, their adherence to rules and routines, and their attitudes and expectations about school can be enhanced by having parents as partners.

PLANNING TO ELIMINATE BIAS

Much of what has been said about individual differences suggests that planning to eliminate bias in classroom teaching can be one of the most significant aspects of becoming an effective teacher. Researchers recently have brought to our attention that, consciously or unconsciously, everyone has biases of one kind or another (Gage & Berliner, 1992). When applied in ways that affect only your own behavior and not that of others, we use the word *preference*. Biases, on the other hand, are not harmless; they can injure the personal growth and well-being of others and, if left unchecked, can significantly affect the growth and development of learners. Let's look at some of the ways you might show bias.

Biases in Labeling and Grouping

A particularly alarming case of bias was uncovered by Rist (1970) when he studied a single class of lower SES students from kindergarten through second grade. Rist observed that from the time these students entered kindergarten, they were divided into three groups—Tigers, Cardinals, and Clowns—each seated at a different table. Initial placement into these groups in kindergarten was made by the teacher according to SES, using information from registration forms and from interviews with mothers and social workers. The highest status children, called Tigers, were seated closest to the teacher and quickly labeled fast learners. The lowest status children, called Clowns, were farthest removed from the teacher and quickly were led to believe they were slow learners.

In reality, each of the three groups had a mixture of slow and fast learners; but the slow learners seated farthest from the teacher seldom got the opportunity to interact with her, while those closest to the teacher frequently received attention. Before long, the abilities of each group were taken as fact rather than as creations of the teacher, so much so that it was increasingly difficult for the Clowns to be considered other than slow by their teachers in the following grades.

At no time did the teacher seem to be aware that the arrangement was biased or that seating certain students consistently in the back of the room would reduce their contact with her. Thus, this teacher's bias became a self-fulfilling prophecy that extended even to subsequent grades and classes—all as a result of biased labeling during the early years of schooling.

Many other examples of teacher biases have been catalogued. For example, Good and Brophy (1997) summarize how teachers sometimes respond unequally to high and low achievers by communicating low expectations and thereby accepting, and unintentionally encouraging, a low level of performance among some students. They identified the following areas in which some teachers responded differently toward low and high achievers:

- Wait less time for low achievers to answer.
- Give low achievers the answer after their slightest hesitation.
- Praise marginal or inaccurate answers of low achievers.
- Criticize low achievers more frequently for having the wrong answer.
- Praise low achievers less when the right answer is given.
- Do not give feedback to low achievers as to why an answer is incorrect.
- Pay attention to (e.g., smile at) and call on low achievers less.
- Seat low achievers farther from the teacher.
- Allow low achievers to give up more.

Generally, these findings confirm that teachers usually do not compensate for differences between high and low achievers in allowing more response opportunities and more teacher contact for low achievers.

Biases in Interacting

Other types of bias can affect interactions with students. For example, Gage and Berliner (1992) identified several biased ways in which teachers interact with their students and then analyzed the extent to which experienced teachers actually exhibited these biases in their classrooms. Their biases included interacting with or calling on students disproportionately in these ways:

- Seated in front half of class versus seated in back half of class
- Nicer-looking students versus average-looking students
- More-able students versus less-able students
- Nonminority group members versus minority group members

Gage and Berliner (1992) calculated the number of student–teacher interactions that would be expected by chance for these classifications, and then from observation they determined the actual number of interactions that occurred. Somewhat surprisingly, their results indicate that *every* teacher showed some bias in these categories. In other words, every teacher favored at least one student classification over another by naming, calling on, requiring information from, and otherwise interacting with those in some classification disproportionally to those not in that classification.

Such biases may be meaningless over a single class period but can have significant and long-lasting emotional impact on students if continued throughout weeks, months, or the entire school year. The accumulated effect of systematic bias in a classroom is an open message to some students that they are less desirable and less worthy of attention than others, regardless of how unintentional the bias may be. The result of these biased messages is change in motivation, self-concept, and anxiety level of some students in ways that impede their development and learning.

Bias in the way a teacher interacts with students is undesirable in any form, but it is particularly distasteful when it pertains to students' ethnicity. Our nation and our educational system are based on the respect for individual differences of all types. This means that our classrooms become one of the most important showplaces of our democratic values. It is disturbing that researchers report frequent ethnic bias or cultural insensitivity during student–teacher interactions in mixed ethnic classrooms. Studies (D. Dillon, 1989; Tharp & Gallimore, 1989) point out that many actions of teachers diminish the classroom participation of minority students and/or build resentment because the teachers' actions are culturally incongruent.

Bowers and Flinders (1991) and Gage and Berliner (1992) provide the following suggestions for eliminating bias and increasing cultural sensitivity in the classroom:

1. Plan to spread your interactions as evenly as possible across student categories by deciding in advance which students to call on. Because the many classifications of potential bias are cumbersome to deal with, choose one or two bias categories you know or suspect you are most vulnerable to.

2. If you plan on giving special assignments to only some of your students, choose the students randomly. Place all of your students' names in a jar, and have one student draw the names of individuals needed for the special assignment. This protects you from inadvertently choosing the same students repeatedly and conveying the impression that you have pets.

3. Try consciously to pair opposites in what you believe to be a potential area of bias for you; for example, pair minority with nonminority, more able with less able, easy to work with and difficult to work with, and so on. In this manner,

when you are interacting with one member of the pair, you will be reminded to interact with the other. Occasionally change one member of the pair so that your pairing does not become obvious to the class.

4. When you discover a bias, plan a code to remind you of the bias and then embed it within your class notes, text, or lesson plan at appropriate intervals. For example, should you discover you systematically favor more able learners over less able learners, place a code on the margins of your exercise to remind you to choose a less able learner for the next response.

FINAL WORD

There is no question that your students' individual differences in intelligence, achievement, personality, home life, peer group, and social context can dramatically affect teaching methods and learning results. So, why place such diverse students in the same classroom? Would it not be more efficient to segregate students by intelligence and achievement level, personality type, degree of disadvantageness, or even according to the most advantageous peer group? The results of such grouping might be quite astounding, if it were tried.

It is difficult to imagine life in such a segregated environment, for we live, work, and play in a world that is complex and diverse. However, our forefathers seriously considered this very question. Their answer is in the first 10 amendments to the U.S. Constitution, known as the Bill of Rights, and in the Declaration of Independence, which gives every citizen the unqualified right to "life, liberty, and the pursuit of happiness." This constitutional guarantee specifically precludes any attempt to advance a single group at the expense of any other group. It even precludes segregating groups when "separate but equal" treatment is accorded them, because even the labeling of groups as different implies inequality, regardless of the motives for forming them.

These are important constitutional implications for the American classroom. They promote an environment that not only tolerates differences among individuals but also celebrates diversity in human potential. In a world complicated by such social and technological problems as pollution, disease, illiteracy, and congestion, we need divergent viewpoints, different abilities, and diverse values to address these problems. No single set of skills, attitudes, temperaments, personalities, or abilities can provide all that is needed to solve our problems. Your willingness to be flexible in your teaching can harness the diversity needed to solve these problems by adapting instruction to the strengths of your learners, by using different instructional approaches in teaching students of differing ethnic and racial backgrounds, and by promoting the family–school partnership. Above all, your teaching must emphasize the importance of all students working cooperatively with each other. In the chapters ahead, we will explore many ways of accomplishing these important goals.

SUMMING UP

This chapter introduced the diversity of students found in classrooms and how this diversity must be acknowledged in your teaching methods. Its main points were the following:

1. Early conceptions of teaching viewed students as empty vessels into which the teacher poured the content of the day's lesson. These conceptions failed to consider the effect of individual differences on learning.

2. A knowledge of the individual differences among learners is important (1) to adapt instructional methods to individual learning needs and (2) to understand and place in perspective the reasons behind the school performance of individual learners.

3. One misunderstanding that some teachers and parents have about intelligence, or IQ, is that it is a single, unified dimension.

4. Specific aptitudes or factors of intelligence are more predictive of success in school and specific occupations than is general intelligence.

5. Knowing your learners' specific strengths and weaknesses and altering instructional goals and methods accordingly will contribute to greater learning than will categorizing and teaching your students according to their general intelligence.

6. Task-relevant prior learning represents the facts, skills, and understandings that must be taught if subsequent learning is to occur. Mastery of task-relevant prior learning often is required for subsequent learning to take place.

7. An important characteristic that distinguishes lower-class children from middle-class and upper-class children is that the latter more rapidly acquire knowledge of the world outside their homes and neighborhoods.

8. Erikson's (1968) three crises during the school years are (1) accomplishment versus inferiority, (2) identity versus confusion, and (3) intimacy versus isolation.

9. State anxiety is a temporary condition produced by some specific stimulus in the environment, such as a test.

10. Some state anxiety is necessary for learning; grades, report cards, and assignments generally provide proper levels of state anxiety to motivate students to engage in the learning process.

11. Extreme levels of state anxiety can be avoided by putting in perspective the value (importance) of a specific assignment compared to other assignments and by clarifying its relative importance in the total context of assignments.

12. Trait anxiety is stable within individuals over time but varies among individuals. It is produced by a wide range of ill-defined conditions perceived by an individual to be harmful.

13. High levels of trait anxiety are associated with high motivation and a need to achieve, but extreme levels are associated with an intense fear of failure that dampens creativity and results in perfunctory, mechanical responses.

14. Extreme levels of trait anxiety sometimes can be avoided by making a range of alternative responses acceptable for a given assignment.

15. Learning style refers to the classroom or environmental conditions under which someone prefers to learn. One of the most frequently studied learning styles is field independence/dependence.

16. Research has shown that some learners tend to be field sensitive—or holistic/visual learners—while others tend to be less field sensitive—or verbal/analytic learners.

17. Before implementing instructional strategies to match students' learning styles, teachers should be cautious not to perpetuate stereotypes and ignore within-group differences.

18. Self-concept has only a modest relationship to school achievement but has a strong relationship to active engagement in the learning process and success in one's career or occupation. You can improve students' concept of self by finding and reflecting back to them the value of their unique talents.

19. Peer groups are an influential source of learner behavior both in and out of the classroom. Group work, group norms, group cohesiveness, and cross-age tutoring are

means of using peer group influence to foster instructional goals of the classroom.

20. Closely connected with the influence of peer group on learning is the social context in which your learners live, play, and work. Among the most prominent sources of influence in this context will be your learners' family and their relationship to the school.

21. Almost every teacher shows some type of bias in interacting with students. Bias may be avoided by

- Consciously spreading interactions across categories of students toward whom you have identified bias
- Randomly selecting students for special assignments
- Covertly pairing students who are opposite in your category of bias and then interacting with both members of the pair
- Coding class notes to remind yourself to call on students toward whom you may be biased

FOR DISCUSSION AND PRACTICE

Questions marked with an asterisk are answered in Appendix B. See also *Bridges: An Activity Guide and Assessment Options,* which accompanies this text.

*1. In what two ways might you use knowledge of the individual differences in your classroom to become a more effective teacher?

*2. Describe the environmentalist and hereditarian positions concerning the use of general IQ tests in schools. Devise a counterargument you could use in responding to an argument from an extremist in each camp.

*3. Explain the role that social competence is believed to play in school learning. If behaviors solely related to SES could be eliminated, how might differences in the tested IQ among subgroups of learners change?

*4. Identify some aptitudes or factors that are likely to be more predictive than general IQ of success in selected school subjects and occupations.

5. Give an example of a school subject in which you would not necessarily expect a high score on an aptitude test to predict a high score on a test of subject-matter achievement. How would you explain this result? What teaching strategies might you use to encourage this result in other subject matter areas?

6. Give an example of some task-relevant prior knowledge that might be required before each of the following instructional objectives could be taught successfully.

a. Adding two-digit numbers
b. Reading latitude and longitude from a map
c. Writing a four-sentence paragraph
d. Seeing an amoeba under a microscope
e. Correctly pronouncing a new two-syllable word
f. Understanding how the executive branch of government works
g. Playing 10 minutes of basketball without committing a foul
h. Responding correctly to a fire alarm
i. Solving the equation $c^2 = a^2 + b^2$
j. Punctuating two independent clauses

7. In thinking back to some of your own experiences in school, what might be some teaching practices that could be used to shrink differences in achievement due to SES?

*8. Identify one approach to teaching and assessment that might be used to improve the self-concept of lower-SES students.

*9. Which indicators do you think best represent state anxiety, and which best represent trait anxiety?

a. Looks scared and exhausted before a test
b. Becomes nervous whenever asked about where he lives
c. Continuously combs hair and puts on makeup
d. Has an incessant drive to get into college
e. Skips school whenever an oral presentation is required
f. Never fails to complete an extra-credit assignment

g. Always boasts and exaggerates about the number of girls he dates

h. Copies others' homework often

i. Wants to become the most respected athlete in the school

j. Never brings home papers that have received a grade lower than "A"

10. Think of two types of learners who have different learning style preferences. What different types of products would they likely submit to you for their portfolio assessment as evidence of their learning?

*11. Identify two methods for dealing with a disruptive peer group in your classroom. How might they be applied in a heterogeneous classroom?

12. Using specific examples in the life of a child that you have known, explain what is meant by a systems-ecological perspective.

*13. Gage and Berliner (1992) identify a number of ways in which your interactions with students can be biased. Name four, and then add one of your own that is not mentioned by Gage and Berliner. Why do you think the one you added is important? Can you think of an experience that you saw or encountered that made you add it to your list?

*14. Identify four procedures for reducing or eliminating the biases you may have when interacting with your students. Which would be the easiest to implement, and which would be the most difficult?

15. Explain in your own words what is meant by the family–school partnership. What are some things you can do to promote this partnership in your classroom?

3 Goals and Objectives

This chapter will help you answer the following questions:

1. Where do instructional goals come from?
2. What are some important educational goals for the year 2000?
3. Why do I need behavioral objectives?
4. What are the steps in writing a behavioral objective?
5. What types of cognitive, affective, and psychomotor behaviors will I want to teach in my classroom?

*C*hapters 1 and 2 introduced some behaviors expected of you as a teacher and some individual differences you can expect among your students. This chapter shows you how to organize your thinking about who, what, and how you will teach. First, let's consider the distinction among aims, goals, and objectives and their use in instructional planning.

AIMS, GOALS, AND OBJECTIVES

The words *aims, goals,* and *objectives* often are used interchangeably without recognizing their different, albeit related, meanings. Aims are general expressions of our values that give us a sense of direction. They are written broadly enough to be acceptable to large numbers of individuals, such as taxpayers, parents, or the American people. Goals are expressed from the learners' point of view and identify what your students will learn from your instruction. They energize and motivate students to become actively engaged in and committed to the learning process.

While aims and goals answer the question "Why am I teaching this?" they are not a satisfactory response to what or how you will teach on any given day. Aims and goals provide little direction as to what strategies to use to achieve them or when or even if they are met. A satisfactory answer to these questions requires that you prepare lesson **objectives,** which convey to your learners the *specific behavior* to be attained, the *conditions* under which the behavior must be demonstrated, and the *proficiency level* at which the behavior is to be performed. The examples in Table 3.1 show the distinctions among aims, goals, and objectives.

Several approaches have been formulated to help you prepare educational objectives. One approach comes from the work of Tyler (1974).

Table 3.1 The differences among aims, goals, and objectives.

Aims	Goals	Objectives
Express our values that give us a sense of direction	Identify what will be learned—energize and motivate	Convey the specific behavior to be attained, the conditions under which the behavior must be demonstrated, and the proficiency at which the behavior must be performed.
Examples:	**Examples:**	
1. Every citizen should be prepared to work in a technological world.	1. Students should understand the use of the microcomputer at home and work.	**Examples:**
2. Every adult should be functionally literate.	2. Students should be able to read and write well enough to become gainfully employed.	1. Students will, using their own choice of a microcomputer, produce an edited two-page manuscript free of errors in 15 minutes or less.
3. Every American should be able to vote as an informed citizen in a democracy.	3. Students should know how to choose a candidate and vote in an election.	2. Students will, at the end of the 12th grade, be able to write a 500-word essay with no more than two grammatical and punctuation errors.
		3. Students will, at the end of an eighth-grade unit on government, participate in a mock election by choosing a candidate and giving reasons for their choice.

Tyler's Goal Development Approach

The idea of an educational objective can be traced to the early part of the twentieth century, when Tyler (1934) first conceived of the need for goal-directed statements for teachers. He observed that teachers were concerned far more with the content of instruction (what to teach) than with what the student should be able to do with the content (i.e., whether it could be applied in some meaningful context).

Tyler's approach to generating educational objectives has had a major influence on curriculum development. Tyler believes that as society becomes more complex, there are more things for people to learn. But, the time to learn this ever-expanding amount of knowledge and skills may actually decrease in a technologically complex society. Consequently, educators must make informed choices about which goals are worth teaching.

Tyler identified five factors to consider when establishing priorities for what students should learn. First, goals must include

1. The subject matter we know enough about to teach (subject matter mastery)
2. Societal concerns, which represent what is valued in both the society at large and the local community
3. Student needs and interests and the abilities and knowledge they bring to school

Then, these goals must be refined to match

4. Your school's educational philosophy and your community's priorities
5. What instructional theory and research tells us can be taught

Goals are important because they tell your learners, their parents, and the community *why* you are teaching the lessons you have planned, which, then, energize and motivate them to become actively engaged in the learning process. Educational goals

- Provide direction for your unit and lesson planning.
- Communicate the importance of your instruction to parents and to the community.
- Energize your learners to higher levels of commitment and engagement in the learning process.

Tyler's approach to establishing educational goals is illustrated in Figure 3.1.

Figure 3.1 Tyler's considerations in goal selection.

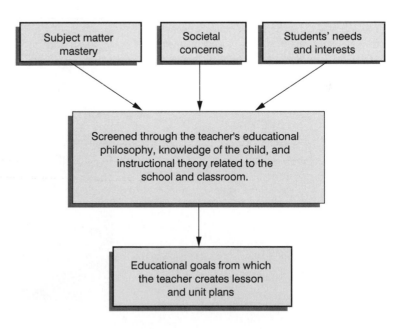

SOCIETAL GOALS FOR EDUCATION FOR THE YEAR 2000

In the past decade, several important developments have highlighted concerns about academic goals and how we measure them. In addition to the National Education Goals for the Year 2000, which we saw in Chapter 2, professional groups and associations have also become involved in establishing educational goals. Several of these groups and associations have reviewed comprehensive studies of the state of education in American elementary and secondary schools in an effort to set criteria by which to judge the adequacy of what students learn in their subject matter fields. Their reports include *Assessment Standards for School Mathematics,* by the National Council of Teachers of Mathematics (1995); *Benchmarks for Science Literacy,* by the American Association for the Advancement of Sciences (1993); *Expectations of Excellence: Curriculum Standards for Social Studies,* by the National Council for the Social Studies (1994); *National Science Education Standards,* by the National Research Council (1996); and *Standards for the English Language Arts,* by the National Council of Teachers of English (1996). Each of these reports has set forth new frameworks for curricula in its subject area.

These new standards suggest that instruction at all levels of schooling has been predominantly focused on memorization, drill, and workbook exercises. Their reports call for a commitment to developing a **thinking curriculum**, one that focuses on teaching learners how to think critically, reason, and problem solve in real-world contexts. They advocate that American schools adopt such a thinking curriculum and a performance-based examination system that would adequately mea-

An important recommendation for curriculum reform in the next decade is that learners should be better trained to work independently and to attain more high-level thinking, conceptual, and problem-solving skills.

sure complex cognitive skills (Loucks-Horsley et al., 1990; Parker, 1991; Mitchell, 1992; L. B. Resnick & Resnick, 1991; Tombari & Borich, 1999; Willoughby, 1990).

These new curriculum frameworks were stimulated in part by a disenchantment with the quality of public school education voiced by many segments of our society, including parents, taxpayers, legislators, business and military leaders, and some teacher groups. This disenchantment was not limited to matters of curriculum. It extended to the quality of teaching and teacher education (Council for Basic Education, 1996), leading in some cases to recommendations for teacher competency testing and new requirements for teacher certification. Each segment of society registered its own concerns, but together they expressed a consensus about what was wrong with American education and what to do about it.

For example, several reports agreed that our schools needed to strengthen curricula in math, science, English, foreign languages, and social studies. Also, high technology was represented by a call for higher levels of computer literacy, both as separate courses and as a tool integrated into the core disciplines. The reports called for renewed effort in teaching higher-order thinking skills, including the teaching of concepts, problem solving, and creativity (as opposed to rote memorization and parroting of facts, lists, names, and dates divorced from a larger problem-solving context).

Not surprisingly, all the reports recommended increasing both grading standards and the number of required core courses (as opposed to elective courses), especially at the secondary level. This recommendation went hand in hand with the suggestion that colleges raise their admission requirements by requiring more course work in core subjects, especially math and foreign languages. Most of the reports recommended increasing school hours and homework time. For example, one report suggested a minimum 7-hour school day (some schools have fewer than 6 hours) and a 200-day school year (many have a 180-day year). Time spent on noninstructional activities was to be reduced accordingly, as would administrative interruptions.

By taking a broad view of our educational establishment, these reports recommended the following goals:

- Students should be trained to live and function in a technological world.
- Students should possess minimum competencies in reading, writing, and mathematics.
- Students should possess higher-order thinking, conceptual, and problem-solving skills.
- Students should be required to enroll in all the core subjects each school year, to the extent of their abilities.
- Students should be trained to work independently and to complete assignments without direct supervision.
- Students should improve school attendance and stay in school longer each day and year.
- Students should be given more applications that require problem-solving skills and higher-order thinking skills.

The basis of these goals was the perception that our schools may have lost sight of their role in teaching students *how to think*. Traditionally, this was accomplished through the core curriculum (English, math, science, foreign languages, and social studies). However, with fewer advanced offerings in these areas and with additional time being spent in remedial and elective activities, the time devoted to teaching children how to think may have been insufficient. These reports suggested that schools should reverse this trend by requiring students to study both the core and more advanced content areas. Such instruction would require complex thinking skills, homework, higher assessment and grading standards, and performance assessments of what was learned. Mastering thinking skills, such as problem solving, decision making, and learning to make value judgments, was considered important because they are required both in the world of work and to gain admittance to advanced education and training opportunities (L. B. Resnick & Resnick, 1991).

Figure 3.2 illustrates the translation of aims and goals into objectives as a funneling or narrowing of focus in which the general aims of society, such as Goals for the Year 2000, are gradually translated through subject matter curricula into specific objectives for instruction.

Figure 3.2 The funneling of societal aims into instructional objectives.

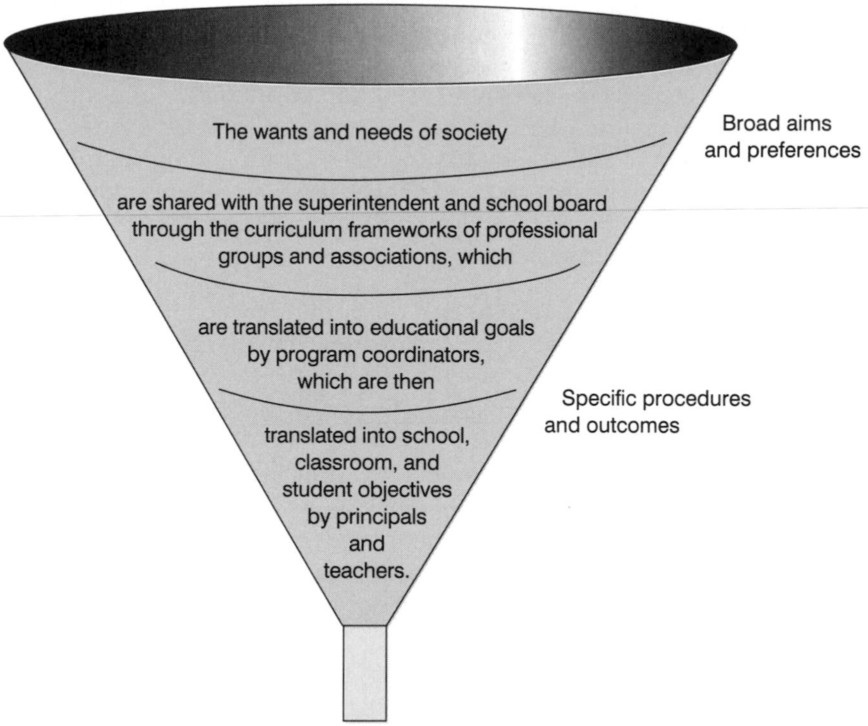

The wants and needs of society

Broad aims and preferences

are shared with the superintendent and school board through the curriculum frameworks of professional groups and associations, which

are translated into educational goals by program coordinators, which are then

Specific procedures and outcomes

translated into school, classroom, and student objectives by principals and teachers.

Source: From *Educational Testing and Measurement: Classroom Application and Practice* 6th Edition by Tom Kubiszyn and Gary Borich. Copyright © 2000 by Addison-Wesley Longman. Reprinted by permission.

THE PURPOSE OF OBJECTIVES

Objectives have two practical purposes. The first is to move goals toward classroom accomplishments by identifying the specific classroom strategies by which the goals can be achieved. The second is to express teaching strategies in a format that allows you to measure their effects on learners. A written statement that achieves these two purposes is called a **behavioral objective.**

What Does *Behavioral* Mean?

When the word *behavioral* precedes the word *objective,* learning is being defined as a change in *observable* behavior. Therefore, the writing of behavioral objectives requires that the behavior being addressed be observable and measurable (with a test, attitude survey, checklist, etc). Activities occurring in the seclusion of your learners' minds are not observable and thus cannot be the focus of a behavioral objective. Unobserved activities, such as the creation of mental images or rehearsing a response subvocally, can precede learning, but they *cannot constitute evidence that learning has occurred,* because they cannot be directly observed.

Further, the behavior of your learners must be observable over a period of time during which specific content, teaching strategies, and instructional materials have been used. This limits a behavioral objective to a time frame consistent with the logical divisions in school curricula, such as lessons, chapters, units, and grading periods. Feedback from behavioral objectives provides data for monitoring the consequence of your instructional strategy.

AN OVERVIEW OF BEHAVIORAL OBJECTIVES

The goal of this chapter is to show you how to prepare useful objectives as painlessly as possible. Simply put, writing behavioral objectives involves three steps:

1. Identify a specific goal that has an observable outcome (a learning outcome).
2. State the conditions under which learning can be expected to occur (e.g., with what materials, texts, and facilities and in what period of time).
3. Specify the criterion level—the amount of behavior that can be expected from the instruction under the specified conditions.

Before considering the actual written form of behavioral objectives, let's look at these three steps in more detail.

Specifying the Learning Outcomes

The first step in writing a behavioral objective is to identify an observable **learning outcome.** For an objective to be behavioral, it must be observable and measurable, so you can determine whether the behavior is present, partially present, or absent (Yelon, 1996). The key to identifying an observable outcome is your choice of words to describe it.

Word choice in writing behavioral objectives is important because the same word may have different meanings, depending on who is reading or hearing it. The endless puns heard in our culture are humorous illustrations of this: Does "well-rounded person" mean broadly educated or well fed? Words can express a concept not only accurately or inaccurately but also specifically or vaguely. It is vague usage that gives us the most trouble in writing behavioral objectives.

In a behavioral objective, learning outcomes must be expressed directly, concretely, and observably, unlike the way behaviors usually are described in the popular press, television, and even some textbooks. If you took these everyday sources as a guide for writing the behavioral expressions needed in the classroom, you would quickly find that they could not be easily observed and probably could not be measured, either. For example, we often hear these expressions as desirable goals:

Mentally healthy citizens

Well-rounded individuals

Self-actualized schoolchildren

Informed adults

Literate populace

But, what do *mentally healthy, well-rounded, self-actualized, informed,* and *literate* actually mean? If you asked a large number of individuals to define these terms, you would receive quite an assortment of responses. These diverse responses would have widely divergent implications for how to achieve each desired behavior and for observing its attainment. The reason, of course, is that the words are vague and open to many interpretations. Imagine the confusion such vagueness could cause in your classroom if your objective for the first grading period were simply to make the class *informed* about the content or to make them *high achievers.* Johnny's parents would have one interpretation of *informed,* and Betty's parents would have quite another. Let's hope they both don't show up on parent–teacher night! Also, you might mean one thing by *high achievers,* but your principal might mean another.

The point is that vague behavioral language quickly becomes a problem for those who are held accountable for bringing about the behavior in question. You can avoid this problem by writing behavioral outcomes in precise language that makes observation and measurement specific and noncontroversial.

One way to make your outcomes specific and noncontroversial is to choose behavioral expressions from a list of action verbs that have widely accepted meanings. These action verbs also allow easy identification of the operations necessary for displaying the behavior. For example, instead of expecting students to be informed or literate in a subject, expect them to

Differentiate between . . .

Identify outcomes of . . .

Solve a problem in . . .

Compare and contrast . . .

These action verbs describe what being *informed* or *literate* mean by stating specific, observable behaviors that the learner must perform. Although we have not yet indicated how well the learner must be able to perform these behaviors, we are now closer to the type of evidence that can be used to determine whether these objectives have been achieved.

Although a behavioral objective should include an action verb that specifies a learning outcome, not all action verbs are suitable for specifying learning outcomes. Some are better suited to specifying **learning activities.** Unfortunately, learning outcomes often are confused with learning activities. For example, which of the following examples represent learning *outcomes* and which represent learning *activities?*

1. The child will identify pictures of words that sound alike.
2. The child will demonstrate an appreciation of poetry.
3. The student will subtract one-digit numbers.
4. The student will show a knowledge of punctuation.
5. The student will practice the multiplication tables.
6. The student will sing "The Star-Spangled Banner."

In the first four objectives, the action words *identify, demonstrate, subtract,* and *show* all point to outcomes—end products of instructional units. However, the action word in the fifth example, *practice,* is only a learning activity; it is not an end in itself and only can work toward a learning outcome. The sixth objective is more ambiguous. Is *sing* an outcome or an activity? It is hard to say without more information. If the goal is to have a stage-frightened student sing in public, then it is a learning outcome. However, if singing is only practice for a later performance, it is a learning activity. Learning activities are important but only in relation to the specific learning outcomes, or end products, they are attempting to achieve. Without a learning outcome clearly in mind, there would be no way to determine the value of a learning activity for promoting desirable student outcomes.

The following examples differentiate between verbs used for learning outcomes and verbs used for learning activities:

Learning Outcomes (Ends)	Learning Activities (Means)
identify	study
recall	watch
list	listen
write	read

Behavioral objectives must include the end product, because you will use this end product in choosing your instructional procedures and evaluating whether you have achieved the desired result.

Identifying the Conditions

The second step in writing a behavioral objective is to identify the specific **conditions** under which learning will occur. If the observable learning outcome can be achieved only through use of particular materials, equipment, tools, or other resources, state these conditions in the objective. Here are some examples of objectives that state conditions:

- Using examples from short stories by John Steinbeck and Mark Twain, differentiate between naturalism and realism in American literature.
- Using the map of strategic resources handed out in class, identify the economic conditions in the South resulting from the Civil War.
- Using an electronic calculator, solve problems involving the addition of two-digit signed numbers.
- Using pictures of fourteenth- to eighteenth-century Gothic and Baroque European cathedrals, compare and contrast the styles of architecture.

If the conditions are obvious, they need not be specified. For example, it is not necessary to specify "Using a writing instrument and paper, write a short story." On the other hand, when conditions can focus learning in specific ways, eliminating some areas of study and including others, the statement of conditions can be critical to attaining the objective, and you should include it. For example, imagine that a student will be tested on the behavior indicated in the first objective in the preceding list but without the condition indicated. Differentiating naturalism from realism without reference to concrete examples in the writings of specific authors who represent these styles is likely to produce a more general, less structured response. If students are told the conditions, they can focus their studying on the precise behavior called for (e.g., applying learned distinctions to specific examples, as opposed to, say, memorizing a list of definitions).

Note also that without a statement of conditions to focus your instruction, your students may assume conditions different than you intend. In the absence of concrete examples, some students might prepare by studying the philosophical differences between the two styles of writing; others might focus on being able to apply their knowledge to examples in the literature. And, because objectives form the basis for tests, your tests might be more fair to some students than others, depending on the assumptions they make in the absence of stated conditions.

Notice in the other preceding examples that learning can take on different meanings, depending on whether students study and practice with or without the use of a map, electronic calculator, or pictures of fourteenth- to eighteenth-century cathedrals. Teaching and learning become more structured and resources more organized when you state conditions as part of your objectives. And, as we have seen, objectives that specify conditions of learning lead to tests that are fairer.

Conditional statements within a behavioral objective can be singular or multiple. It is possible, and sometimes necessary, to have two or even three conditional statements in an objective to focus the learning. Although too many conditions attached to an objective can narrow learning to irrelevant details, multiple conditions often are important adjuncts to improving the clarity of the behavior desired and the organization and preparation of instructional resources. Here are examples of multiple conditions, indicated by italics:

- Using a centigrade *thermometer,* measure the temperature of 2 liters of *water* at a depth of 25 centimeters.

- Using a *compass, ruler,* and *protractor,* draw three conic sections of different sizes and three triangles of different types.
- Using 4 grams of *sodium carbonate* and 4 grams of *sodium bicarbonate,* indicate their different reactions in H_2O.
- *Within 15 minutes* and using the *reference books* provided, write the formulae for wattage, voltage, amperage, and resistance.
- Using a *microcomputer* with word processing capability, correct the spelling and punctuation errors on a *two-page manuscript* in 20 minutes or less.

It is important not to add so many conditions that learning is reduced to trivial detail. It is also important to choose conditions that are realistic—that represent real-life circumstances your learners are likely to find in as well as out of the classroom. The idea behind stating conditions, especially multiple conditions, is not to complicate the behavior but rather to make it more natural and *close to the conditions under which the behavior will have to be performed in the real world* and in subsequent instruction. Always check the conditions specified to see if they are those under which the behavior is most likely to be performed outside the classroom or in subsequent instruction.

Stating Criterion Levels

The third step in writing a behavioral objective is to state the level of performance required to meet the objective. Specifying the outcome and conditions reveals the procedures necessary for the behavior to be observed. However, one important element is missing. *How much* of the behavior is required for you to consider the objective to be attained? This element of objective writing is the *criterion level.* It is the degree of performance desired or the **level of proficiency** that will satisfy you that the objective has been met.

Setting criterion levels is one of the most misunderstood aspects of objective writing. At the root of this misunderstanding is failure to recognize that criterion or proficiency levels are value judgments as to what performance level is required for adequately performing the behavior in some later setting. The mistaken assumption is often made that a single correct level of proficiency exists and that once established it must forever remain in its original form. At first, criterion levels should be taken as educated guesses. They should indicate the approximate degree of proficiency needed to adequately perform the behavior in the next grade, or in another instructional setting, or in the real world. Also, criterion levels should be adjusted periodically up or down to conform with how well your students are able to perform the behavior.

Often, criterion levels are set to establish a benchmark for testing whether an objective has been met, without recognizing that this level may not be relevant to subsequent learning tasks or instructional settings. To avoid this, always consider criterion levels to be adjustable and dependent on your evaluation of how well students can adequately use the behavior *at subsequent times* and *in contexts beyond your classroom.*

Criterion levels come in many sizes and shapes. For example, they can be stated in the following ways:

Number of items correct on a test

Number of consecutive items correct (or consecutive errorless performances)

Essential features included (as in an essay question or paper)

Completion within a prescribed time limit (where speed of performance is important)

Completion with a certain degree of accuracy

Recall the objective "Using short stories by John Steinbeck and Mark Twain, differentiate between naturalism and realism in American literature." Is a criterion stated? Remember, a criterion level establishes the degree of behavior required for the objective to be met. How would the teacher know if a student's written response to this objective has demonstrated a minimum level of differentiation? With only the information given, it would be difficult and arbitrary. Now, let's add a criterion to this objective:

- Using short stories by John Steinbeck and Mark Twain, differentiate between naturalism and realism by selecting four passages from each author that illustrate differences in these writing styles.

Now there is a basis for evaluating the objective. This particular criterion level requires considerable skill in applying learned information in different contexts and allows for flexibility in the range of responses that are acceptable. This type of objective is sometimes called an **expressive objective** (Eisner, 1969, 1998) because it allows for a variety of correct responses or for students to express themselves in a variety of forms for which there is no single correct answer. The amount of expressiveness in a response allowed by an objective is always a matter of degree. In other words, objectives can have more—or less—rigid criterion levels.

Consider another example:

- Using an electronic calculator, the student will solve problems involving the addition of two-digit signed numbers.

Is there a stated criterion level for this objective? No. There is no unambiguous basis for deciding whether Mary met the objective and Bobby did not. Now, add a criterion level:

- Using an electronic calculator, the student will correctly solve 8 of 10 problems involving the addition of two-digit signed numbers.

This objective now precisely identifies the minimum proficiency that must be observed to conclude that the desired behavior has been attained. Unlike the first objective, little flexibility is allowed in the required response. Notice that far less expression is possible in answering a question about mathematics than about literature; the former is more highly structured and more rigid in terms of possible responses. Notice also that this more structured approach to an acceptable response fits well with the nature of this particular objective, while the less structured approach fits well with the literature example.

Both of these objectives illustrate that the expressiveness of an objective is established by how you set an acceptable criterion. Also, the level of expressiveness that fits best often is a function of the objective itself—how many correct answers are possible. As a teacher, you control

1. Learning outcomes
2. Conditions
3. Criterion levels
   a. Proficiency level
   b. Level of expressiveness

Here are some of the earlier objectives with criterion levels added in brackets (or italicized where a criterion already was included):

- Using a centigrade thermometer, measure the temperature of 2 liters of water at a depth of 25 centimeters [to within 1 degree accuracy].
- Using a compass, ruler, and protractor, draw *three* conic sections of *different sizes* and *three* triangles of *different types.*
- Using 4 grams of sodium carbonate and 4 grams of sodium bicarbonate, indicate their different reactions with H_2O [by testing the alkalinity of the H_2O and reporting results in parts per million (PPM)].
- Within 15 minutes and using the reference books provided, find [and write correctly] the formulae for wattage, voltage, amperage, and resistance.
- Using a microcomputer with word processing capability, correct the spelling and punctuation errors for a two-page manuscript in *20 minutes* [with 100% accuracy].

These examples illustrate well-written behavioral objectives.

You have seen how to specify learning outcomes, state conditions for learning, and establish criterion levels. These are the three most important ingredients of well-written behavioral objectives. But, there is one more point to know about preparing objectives: Keep them simple.

Keeping Objectives Simple

Teachers often make the mistake of being too sophisticated in measuring learning outcomes. As a result, they resort to indirect or unnecessarily complex methods of measurement. If you want to know whether Johnny can write his name, ask him to write his name—but not while blindfolded! Resist the temptation to be tricky. Consider these examples:

- The student will show his or her ability to recall characters of the book *Tom Sawyer* by painting a picture of each.
- Discriminate between a telephone and television by drawing an electrical diagram of each.

- Demonstrate that you understand how to use an encyclopedia index by listing the page on which a given subject can be found in the *Encyclopaedia Britannica*.

In the first example, painting a picture surely would allow you to determine whether the students can recall the characters in *Tom Sawyer*, but is there an easier (and less time-consuming) way to measure recall? How about asking the students simply to list the characters? If the objective is to determine recall, listing is sufficient. For the second example, how about presenting students with two illustrations, one of a telephone, the other of a television, and simply ask them to tell (verbally or in writing) which is which?

The third example is on target. The task required is a simple and efficient way of measuring whether someone can use an encyclopedia index.

In this chapter you will begin writing objectives on your own. Be sure to include these three essential components in every objective you write: (1) observable learning outcome, (2) conditions, and (3) criterion level.

THE COGNITIVE, AFFECTIVE, AND PSYCHOMOTOR DOMAINS

You might have noticed that some of the example objectives shown earlier in this chapter have illustrated very different types of behavior. For example, compare the behaviors called for in these objectives:

- Using short stories by John Steinbeck and Mark Twain, differentiate between naturalism and realism by selecting four passages from each author that illustrate differences in these writing styles.
- Using a centigrade thermometer, measure the temperature of 2 liters of water at a depth of 25 centimeters to within 1 degree accuracy.

Common sense tells us that the behaviors called for require different patterns of preparation and study to attain. In the former objective, study and practice would focus on analysis—identifying the key aspects of naturalism and realism and explaining relationships between them, noting their similarities and differences and the application of these ideas to actual examples of the writings of a naturalist and a realist. Contrast this complicated process with how one might study to acquire the behavior in the second objective. Here the study and practice might consist simply of learning to accurately perceive distances between the markings on a centigrade scale. Such practice might be limited to training one's eyes to count spaces between the gradations and then assigning the appropriate number to represent temperature in degrees centigrade.

Note also the difference in study and preparation time required to achieve these two different objectives: the second could be learned in minutes, but the other might take hours, days, or even weeks. These different objectives represent only two examples of the variety of behavioral outcomes possible in your classroom.

Objectives can require vastly different levels not only of cognitive complexity but of affective and psychomotor complexity as well. The following section introduces behaviors at different levels of complexity for which behavioral objectives can be prepared. For convenience, these are organized into the following behaviors:

- **Cognitive** (development of intellectual abilities and skills)
- **Affective** (development of attitudes, beliefs, and values)
- **Psychomotor** (coordination of physical movements and performance)

The Cognitive Domain

Bloom, Englehart, Hill, Furst, and Krathwohl (1984) devised a method for categorizing objectives according to cognitive complexity. They delineate six levels of cognitive complexity, ranging from the knowledge level (least complex) to the evaluation level (most complex). As illustrated in Figure 3.3, Bloom et al. describe the levels as hierarchical; the higher-level objectives include, and are dependent on, lower-level cognitive skills. Thus, objectives at the evaluation level require more complex mental operations—higher cognitive skills—than objectives at the knowledge level.

Also, notice that higher-level objectives are more authentic than lower-level objectives. Let's consider what *authenticity* means.

So far in this chapter, you have seen a variety of skills and behaviors that children learn in school. Some of these require learners to acquire information by memorizing, for example, vocabulary, multiplication tables, dates of historical events, or the names of important persons. Other skills and behaviors involve learning action sequences or procedures to follow when, for example, using drawing materials, performing mathematical computations, operating a calculator, or practicing handwrit-

Figure 3.3 Taxonomy of educational objectives: Cognitive domain (Bloom et al., 1984).

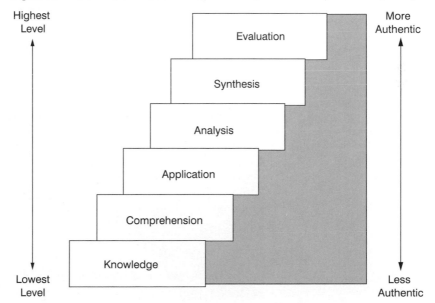

ing. In addition, you saw some example objectives in which students had to acquire concepts, rules, and generalizations that allowed them to understand what they read, to analyze, and to write an essay.

Some of these skills are best assessed with paper and pencil tests, as we will see in Chapter 12. But, skills requiring independent judgment, critical thinking, and decision making are best assessed with performance assessments. **Performance tests** measure a skill or behavior as it is used in the world outside your classroom.

Classroom assessment of learning, particularly beyond the early elementary grades, has been almost exclusively based on paper and pencil tests, which *indicate* rather than directly measure what children have learned (Gullickson & Ellwein, 1985). For example, you may measure an understanding of the scientific method, not by having learners plan, conduct, and evaluate an experiment (a direct measure), but by asking them to list the steps in conducting an experiment, write about the difference between an hypothesis and a theory, or choose the correct definition of a control group from a list of choices (all indirect assessment). Or, you may measure children's understanding of money, not by observing them buy food, pay for it, and get the correct change (direct assessment), but by asking them to recall how many pennies there are in a dollar or to write down how much change they would get back from a $10 bill if they paid $6.75 for a T-shirt (indirect assessment).

Indirect assessment of achievement and learning has obvious advantages, not the least of which is efficiency. It would be very time-consuming to directly measure all learning that goes on in a classroom. But, indirect assessment raises a problem:

Objectives requiring higher-level cognitive, affective, and psychomotor skills are more authentic behaviors because they are more likely to represent the types of performances required of your learners in the world in which they must live, work, and play.

How do you know your test is telling you if your learners can *apply* the skills and behaviors you are teaching? Authentic tests ask learners to display their skills and behaviors in a way that they would be displayed outside the classroom—in the real world. Authentic tests measure directly the skills and behaviors teachers and learners really care about. In other words, they ask the learners to do what was modeled, coached, and practiced during instruction as it would be done outside the classroom. If learners saw you demonstrate how to focus a microscope, were coached to do this, and practiced doing it, then an authentic assessment would ask them to focus a microscope rather than label the parts of the microscope on a diagram. If, on the other hand, your learners only needed to know the parts of a microscope so that they could read a story about the invention of the microscope—not use one—asking them to label the parts could be an authentic assessment.

Objectives requiring higher-level cognitive, affective, and psychomotor skills— those that most closely represent the thinking curriculum discussed in Chapter 3— are more **authentic behaviors** because they are more likely to represent the types of performances required of your learners in the world in which they must live, work, and play.

Now, let's look at how each behavior in the cognitive domain varies according to cognitive skill and authenticity. These behaviors are described next with examples of action verbs that represent them.

Knowledge. Objectives at the knowledge level require your students to remember or recall information such as facts, terminology, problem-solving strategies, and rules. Some action verbs that describe learning outcomes at the knowledge level are

define	list	recall
describe	match	recite
identify	name	select
label	outline	state

Here are example knowledge objectives that use these verbs:

- The student will recall the four major food groups, without error, by Friday.
- From memory, the student will match U.S. generals with their most famous battles, with 80% percent accuracy.

Comprehension. Objectives at the comprehension level require some degree of understanding. Students are expected to be able to change the form of a communication; translate; restate what has been read; see connections or relationships among parts of a communication (interpretation); or draw conclusions or see consequences from information (inference). Some action verbs that describe learning outcomes at the comprehension level are

convert	estimate	infer
defend	explain	paraphrase
discriminate	extend	predict
distinguish	generalize	summarize

Here are example comprehension objectives that use these verbs:

- By the end of the semester, the student will summarize the main events of a story in grammatically correct English.
- The student will discriminate between the *realists* and the *naturalists,* citing examples from the readings.

Application.   Objectives written at the application level require the student to use previously acquired information in a setting other than the one in which it was learned. Application objectives differ from comprehension objectives in that application requires the presentation of a problem in a different and often applied context. Thus, the student can rely on neither the *content* nor the *context* in which the original learning occurred to solve the problem. Some action verbs that describe learning outcomes at the application level are

change	modify	relate
compute	operate	solve
demonstrate	organize	transfer
develop	prepare	use

Here are example application objectives that use these or similar verbs:

- On Monday, the student will demonstrate for the class an application to real life of the law of conservation of energy.
- Given fractions not covered in class, the student will multiply them on paper with 85% accuracy.

Analysis.   Objectives written at the analysis level require the student to identify logical errors (e.g., point out a contradiction or an erroneous inference) or to differentiate among facts, opinions, assumptions, hypotheses, and conclusions. At the analysis level, students are expected to draw relationships among ideas and to compare and contrast. Some action verbs that describe learning outcomes at the analysis level are

break down	distinguish	point out
deduce	illustrate	relate
diagram	infer	separate out
differentiate	outline	subdivide

Here are example analysis objectives that use these verbs:

- Given a presidential speech, the student will be able to point out the positions that attack an individual rather than that individual's program.
- Given absurd statements (e.g., A man had flu twice. The first time it killed him. The second time he got well quickly.), the student will be able to point out the contradiction.

Synthesis.   Objectives written at the synthesis level require the student to produce something unique or original. At the synthesis level, students are expected to solve some unfamiliar problem in a unique way or to combine parts to form a unique or novel solution. Some action verbs that describe learning outcomes at the synthesis level are

categorize	create	formulate
compile	design	predict
compose	devise	produce

Here are example synthesis objectives that use these or similar verbs:

- Given a short story, the student will write a different but plausible ending.
- Given a problem to be solved, the student will design on paper a scientific experiment to address the problem.

Evaluation.   Objectives written at the evaluation level require the student to form judgments and make decisions about the value of methods, ideas, people, or products that have a specific purpose. Students are expected to state the bases for their judgments (e.g., the external criteria or principles they drew on to reach their conclusions). Some action verbs that describe learning outcomes at the evaluation level are

appraise	criticize	justify
compare	defend	support
contrast	judge	validate

Here are example evaluation objectives that use these verbs:

- Given a previously unread paragraph, the student will judge its value according to the five criteria discussed in class.
- Given a description of a country's economic system, the student will defend it, basing arguments on principles of democracy.

The Affective Domain

Another method of categorizing objectives was devised by Krathwohl, Bloom, and Masia (1964). This taxonomy delineates five levels of affective behavior ranging from the receiving level to the characterization level (see Figure 3.4). As in the cognitive domain, these levels are presumed to be hierarchical—higher-level objectives are assumed to include and be dependent on lower-level affective skills. As one moves up the hierarchy, more involvement, commitment, and reliance on one's self occurs, as opposed to having one's feelings, attitudes, and values dictated by others.

For each level of the affective domain—receiving, responding, valuing, organization, and characterization—the following sections contain examples of action verbs indicating each level.

Receiving.   Objectives at the receiving level require the student to be aware of, or to passively attend to, certain phenomena and stimuli. At this level students are expected simply to listen or be attentive. Some action verbs that describe outcomes at the receiving level are

Figure 3.4   Taxonomy of educational objectives: Affective domain (Kratwohl et al., 1964).

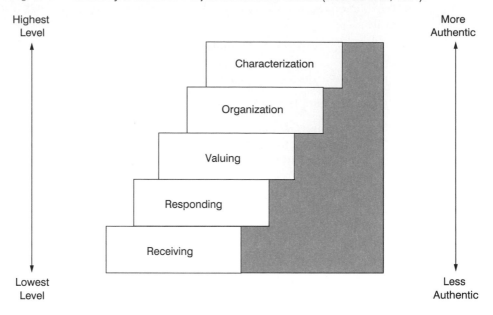

<table>
<tr><td>attend</td><td>discern</td><td>look</td></tr>
<tr><td>be aware</td><td>hear</td><td>notice</td></tr>
<tr><td>control</td><td>listen</td><td>share</td></tr>
</table>

Here are example receiving objectives that use these verbs:

- The student will be able to notice a change from small-group discussion to large-group lecture by following the lead of others in the class.
- The student will be able to listen to all of a Mozart concerto without leaving her or his seat.

Responding.   Objectives at the responding level require the student to comply with given expectations by attending or reacting to certain stimuli. Students are expected to obey, participate, or respond willingly when asked or directed to do something. Some action verbs that describe outcomes at the responding level are

<table>
<tr><td>applaud</td><td>follow</td><td>play</td></tr>
<tr><td>comply</td><td>obey</td><td>practice</td></tr>
<tr><td>discuss</td><td>participate</td><td>volunteer</td></tr>
</table>

Here are example responding objectives that use these verbs:

- The student will follow the directions given in the book without argument when asked to do so.
- The student will practice a musical instrument when asked to do so.

Valuing.   Objectives at the valuing level require the student to display behavior consistent with a single belief or attitude in situations where he or she is neither forced nor asked to comply. Students are expected to demonstrate a preference or display a high degree of certainty and conviction. Some action verbs that describe outcomes at the valuing level are

act	debate	help
argue	display	organize
convince	express	prefer

Here are example valuing objectives that use these verbs:

- The student will express an opinion about nuclear disarmament whenever national events raise the issue.
- The student will display an opinion about the elimination of pornography whenever discussing social issues.

Organization.   Objectives at the organization level require a commitment to a set of values. This level of the affective domain involves (1) forming a reason why one values certain things and not others and (2) making appropriate choices between things that are and are not valued. Students are expected to organize their likes and preferences into a value system and then decide which ones will be dominant. Some action verbs that describe outcomes at the organization level are

abstract	decide	select
balance	define	systematize
compare	formulate	theorize

Here are example organization objectives that use these verbs:

- The student will be able to compare alternatives to the death penalty and decide which ones are compatible with his or her beliefs.
- The student will be able to formulate the reasons why she or he supports civil rights legislation and will be able to identify legislation that does not support her or his beliefs.

Characterization.   Objectives at the characterization level require that all behavior displayed by the student be consistent with his or her values. At this level the student not only has acquired the behaviors at all previous levels but also has integrated his or her values into a system representing a complete and pervasive philosophy that never allows expressions that are out of character with these values. Evaluations of this level of behavior involve the extent to which the student has developed a consistent philosophy of life (e.g., exhibits respect for the worth and dignity of human beings in all situations). Some action verbs that describe outcomes at this level are

avoid	internalize	resist
display	manage	resolve
exhibit	require	revise

Some example objectives are

- The student will exhibit a helping and caring attitude toward students with disabilities by assisting with their mobility both in and out of classrooms.
- The student will display a scientific attitude by stating and then testing hypotheses whenever the choice of alternatives is unclear.

The Psychomotor Domain

A third method of categorizing objectives has been devised by Harrow (1972) and by Moore (1992). Harrow's taxonomy delineates five levels of psychomotor behavior ranging from the imitation level (least complex and least authentic) to the naturalization level (most complex and most authentic). Figure 3.5 illustrates the hierarchical arrangement of the psychomotor domain. These behaviors place primary emphasis on neuromuscular skills involving various degrees of physical dexterity. As behaviors in the taxonomy move from least to most complex and authentic, behavior changes from gross to fine motor skills.

Each of the levels—imitation, manipulation, precision, articulation, and naturalization—has different characteristics and is described in the following sections with examples of action verbs that represent each level.

Imitation.   Objectives at the imitation level require that the student be exposed to an observable action and then overtly imitate it, such as when an instructor demon-

Figure 3.5   Taxonomy of educational objectives: Psychomotor domain (Harrow, 1972).

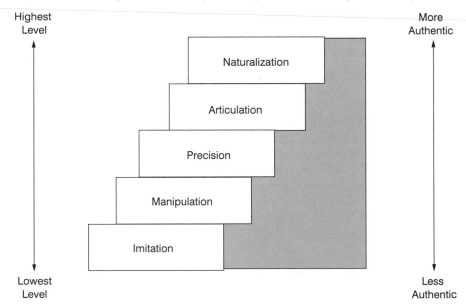

strates the use of a microscope by placing a slide on the specimen tray. Performance at this level usually lacks neuromuscular coordination (e.g., the slide may hit the side of the tray or be improperly aligned beneath the lens). Thus, the behavior generally is crude and imperfect. At this level students are expected to observe and be able to repeat (although imperfectly) the action being visually demonstrated. Some action verbs that describe outcomes at this level are

align	grasp	repeat
balance	hold	rest (on)
follow	place	step (here)

Here are example imitation objectives that use these or similar verbs:

- After being shown a safe method for heating a beaker of water to boiling temperature, the student will be able to repeat the action.
- After being shown a freehand drawing of a parallelogram, the student will be able to reproduce the drawing.

Manipulation.   Objectives at the manipulation level require the student to perform selected actions from written or verbal directions without the aid of a visual model or direct observation, as in the previous (imitation) level. Students are expected to complete the action from reading or listening to instructions, although the behavior still may be performed crudely and without neuromuscular coordination. Useful expressions to describe outcomes at the manipulation level are the same as at the imitation level, using the same action verbs, except they are performed from spoken or written instructions.

Here are example manipulation objectives:

- Based on the picture provided in the textbook, type a salutation to a prospective employer using the format shown.
- With the instructions on the handout in front of you, practice focusing your microscope until the outline of the specimen can be seen.

Precision.   Objectives at the precision level require the student to perform an action independent of either a visual model or a written set of directions. Proficiency in reproducing the action at this level reaches a higher level of refinement. Accuracy, proportion, balance, and exactness in performance accompany the action. Students are expected to reproduce the action with control and to reduce errors to a minimum. Expressions that describe outcomes at this level include performing the behavior

accurately	independently	with control
errorlessly	proficiently	with balance

Here are example precision objectives:

- The student will be able to accurately place the specimen on the microscope tray and use the high-power focus with proficiency as determined by the correct identification of three out of four easily recognizable objects.

- The student will be able to balance a light pen sufficiently to place it against the computer screen to identify misspelled words.

Articulation. Objectives at the articulation level require the student to display coordination of a series of related acts by establishing the appropriate sequence and performing the acts accurately, with control as well as with speed and timing. Expressions that describe outcomes at this level include performing the behaviors with

confidence	integration	speed
coordination	proportion	stability
harmony	smoothness	timing

Here are example articulation objectives:

- Students will be able to write all the letters of the alphabet, displaying the appropriate proportion between uppercase and lowercase, in 10 minutes.
- Students will be able to accurately complete 10 simple arithmetic problems on a hand-held electronic calculator quickly and smoothly within 90 seconds.

Naturalization. Objectives at the naturalization level require a high level of proficiency in the skill or performance being taught. At this level the behavior is performed with the least expenditure of energy and becomes routine, automatic, and spontaneous. Students are expected to repeat the behavior naturally and effortlessly time and again. Some expressions that describe this level of behavior are

automatically	professionally	with ease
effortlessly	routinely	with perfection
naturally	spontaneously	with poise

Here are example naturalization objectives:

- At the end of the semester, students will be able to write routinely all the letters of the alphabet and all the numbers up to 100 each time requested.
- After the first grading period, students will be able to automatically draw correct isosceles, equilateral, and right triangles, without the aid of a template, for each homework assignment that requires this task.

SOME MISUNDERSTANDINGS ABOUT BEHAVIORAL OBJECTIVES

Before beginning to write objectives, you should be aware of several misconceptions that have grown up around behaviors associated with the cognitive, affective, and psychomotor domains. These misconceptions are the understandable result of categorizing behaviors into many different levels, in the hopes of providing a practical tool that can be used across many different content areas. Following are some cautions to be mindful of when using behavioral objectives.

Are Some Behaviors More Desirable Than Others?

One misconception that often results from study of the cognitive, affective, and psychomotor domains is that simple behaviors, like the recall of facts and dates, are less desirable than more complex behaviors requiring the cognitive operations of analysis, synthesis, and decision making. However, the simple-to-complex ordering of behaviors within the cognitive, affective, and psychomotor domains do not imply desirability, because many lower-order behaviors must be learned before higher-order behaviors can be attempted.

Some teachers pride themselves on preparing objectives almost exclusively at the highest levels of cognitive complexity; they do not recognize that objectives at a lower order of complexity always will be required for some topics in order for students to achieve moderate-to-high rates of success for more complex behaviors. When task-relevant prior knowledge or skills necessary for acquiring more complex behaviors have not been taught, students may demonstrate high error rates and less active engagement in the learning process at the higher levels of behavioral complexity.

One of the most important uses of the taxonomies of behavior we have studied is to provide a menu of behaviors at different levels of complexity. As with any good diet, variety and proper proportion are the keys to good results.

What Is an Authentic Behavior?

Another misconception involves the meaning of the word *authentic*. The word *authentic* means relevant to the real world. If a learner would need to list the names of the presidents *in the real world*—on a job, at home, in a training program—that behavior could be measured authentically by asking the learner to repeat the names of the presidents, perhaps in the order in which they held office. Your measurement of this objective would be authentic because you are asking that the behavior be displayed in your classroom exactly as it would be performed outside. However, few occupations, courses, or programs of study will probably require your learners to recite the names of the presidents.

Knowledge (cognitive domain), receiving (affective domain), and imitation (psychomotor domain) are seldom sufficient in the world outside the classroom. Although they often are necessary in acquiring more complex behaviors, they seldom take on importance by themselves. Behaviors representing higher cognitive skills often do take on importance outside the classroom exactly as they are taught. Evaluation (cognitive domain), characterization (affective domain), and naturalization (psychomotor domain) are examples of such behaviors. Deciding what candidate to vote for, assuming the responsibility of an informed citizen, and being able to complete a voting ballot legibly are all authentic behaviors because they are *necessary performances in daily life*. Therefore, higher cognitive skills often are more authentic than lower cognitive skills because they represent more integrated behaviors necessary for living, working, and performing in the world outside your classroom. This is one of the best reasons for teaching higher cognitive skills *in* your classroom.

The behaviors and verb choices given previously for higher cognitive, affective, and psychomotor skills are by no means inclusive of all that's involved in authentic behavior. You may want to expand each definition to fit better with how you teach analysis, synthesis, and evaluation behavior in a particular content area and grade level. Or, you may be using a curriculum that defines these behaviors somewhat differently. The point is that you should be clear about what each authentic behavior entails by identifying what your learners must do to demonstrate the skill you wish to teach. To help you do this, you will find in Appendix C a Higher Order Thinking and Problem-Solving Checklist (Tombari & Borich, 1999) to help you select and prioritize some of the authentic behaviors you may want to teach and assess.

Are Less Complex Behaviors Easier to Teach?

Another misconception is that behaviors of less complexity are easier to teach than behaviors of greater complexity. This is an appealing argument because intuition and common sense indicate that this should be so. After all, complexity—especially cognitive complexity—often has been associated with greater difficulty, greater amounts of study time, and more extensive instructional resources.

Although simpler behaviors may be easier to teach some of the time, it can be just the opposite. For example, consider the elaborate study card and mnemonic system that might be needed to recall a portion of the periodic table of chemical elements, as opposed to the simple visual demonstration to teach its application. In this case, the so-called less complex behavior requires greater time and instructional resources. Also, whether a behavior is easier or harder to teach always will depend on the learning needs of the students.

These examples point out that errors of judgment can easily be made by automatically assuming that lower-order, less complex behaviors necessarily require little preparation, fewer instructional resources, and less teaching time than do higher-order, more complex behaviors. The ease with which a behavior can be taught is not synonymous with the level of the behavior in the taxonomy (i.e., lower or higher). These designations refer to the mental—or cognitive—operations *required of the student* and *not* the complexity of the activities *required of the teacher* to produce the behavior.

Are Cognitive, Affective, and Psychomotor Behaviors Mutually Exclusive?

Finally, categorizing behaviors into cognitive, affective, and psychomotor domains does not mean that behaviors listed in one domain are mutually exclusive of those listed in other domains. For example, it is not possible to think without having some feeling about what we are thinking or to feel or have a response without some cognition. Also, much thinking involves physical movements and bodily performances that require psychomotor skills and abilities. For example, conducting a laboratory experiment requires not only thought but pouring from one test tube to another, safely igniting a Bunsen burner, adjusting a microscope correctly, and so on. Legible handwriting requires neuromuscular coordination, timing, and control.

It is convenient for an objective to contain behavior from only one of the three domains at a time. But keep in mind that one or more behaviors from the other domains also may be required for the behavior to occur—for example, a good attitude about learning is required for the memorization of facts to occur. This is one of the best reasons for preparing objectives in all three domains: It is evidence of your awareness of the close and necessary relationship among cognitive, affective, and psychomotor behaviors. The following list will remind you of cautions when using and writing behavior objectives.

- Behaviors listed within the cognitive, affective, and psychomotor domains do not imply that some behaviors will be more or less desirable in your classroom than others.
- The word *authentic* means "relevant to the real world." Higher cognitive skills often are more authentic than lower cognitive skills because they represent more integrated behaviors necessary for living, working, and performing outside your classroom.
- Less complex behaviors within the cognitive, affective, and psychomotor domains do not imply that less teacher preparation, fewer instructional resources, or less teaching time will be required than for more complex behaviors.
- Although objectives usually contain behaviors from only one of the three domains, one or more behaviors from the other domains may also be required for the behavior to occur.

THE CULTURAL ROOTS OF OBJECTIVES

Finally, you should be prepared to have the source of your objectives questioned by parents, community members, and students. The technical process of writing objectives sometimes can obscure the reasons you are writing them because you were working so hard to produce objectives in the correct technical form. Some typical responses to parents about the source of objectives may include "from textbooks," "from curriculum guides," or "from department policies."

These answers are technically correct but miss the fundamental point, which is that objectives have roots much deeper than any single text, curriculum guide, or set of policies. These roots lie in the educational values we espouse as a nation. While parents, students, and other teachers may argue with the text used, the curriculum guide followed, or the department policies accepted, it is quite another thing to take exception to the values we share as a nation and that were created by many different interest groups over many years of thoughtful deliberation.

Texts, curricula, and policies are interpretations of these values shared at the broadest national level and translated into practice through goals and objectives. Texts, curriculum guides, and school district policies can no more create objectives than they can create values. Goals and their objectives, as we have seen earlier in this chapter, are carefully created to reflect our values from sources such as curriculum reform committees, state and national legislative mandates, and the professional associations to which you belong. This is why you must have a knowledge of these ultimate sources from which you have derived your objectives, or else you may continually be caught in the position of justifying a particular text, curriculum, or policy to parents, students, and peers—some of whom will always disagree with you. Reference to any one text, curriculum, or policy can never prove that your students should appreciate art or know how to solve an equation.

On the other hand, our *values,* as indicated by curriculum reform committees, state and national mandates, and professional associations, can provide appropriate and adequate justification for intended learning outcomes. Attention to these values as reported by the press, professional papers and books, curriculum committees, and national teacher groups is as important to teaching as the objectives you write.

SUMMING UP

This chapter introduced instructional objectives. Its main points were as follows:

1. Aims are expressions of societal values that provide a sense of direction but are broad enough to be accepted by large numbers of individuals.

2. Goals identify what will be learned from your instruction, energize and motivate.

3. Objectives have two purposes: (1) to tie general aims and goals to specific classroom strategies that will achieve those aims and goals and (2) to express teaching strategies in a format that allows you to measure their effects on your learners.

4. When the word *behavioral* precedes the word *objective,* the learning is being defined as a change in *observable* behavior that can be *measured* within a *specified period of time.*

5. The need for behavioral objectives stems from a natural preoccupation with concerns for self and task, sometimes to the exclusion of concerns for the impact on students.

6. Simply put, behavioral objectives do the following:
   - Focus instruction on a specific goal whose outcomes can be observed.
   - Identify the conditions under which learning can be expected to occur.
   - Specify the level or amount of behavior that can be expected from the instruction under the conditions specified.

7. Action verbs help operationalize the learning outcome expected from an objective and identify exactly what the learner must do to achieve the outcome.

8. The outcome specified in a behavioral objective should be expressed as an end (e.g., to identify, recall, list) and not as a means (e.g., to study, watch, listen).

9. If the observable learning outcome is to take place with particular materials, equipment, tools, or other resources, these conditions must be stated explicitly in the objective.

10. Conditional statements within a behavioral objective can be singular (one condition) or multiple (more than one condition).

11. Conditions should match those under which the behavior will be performed in the real world.

12. A proficiency level is the minimum degree of performance that will satisfy you that the objective has been met.

13. Proficiency levels represent value judgments, or educated guesses, as to what level of performance will be required for adequately performing the behavior in some later setting beyond your classroom.

14. The expressiveness of an objective refers to the amount of flexibility allowed in a response. Less expressive objectives may call for only a single right answer, whereas more expressive objectives allow for less structured

and more flexible responses. The expressiveness allowed is always a matter of degree.

15. "Complexity" of a behavior in the cognitive, affective, or psychomotor domain pertains to the operations required of the student to produce the behavior, not to the complexity of the teaching activities required.

16. Behaviors in the cognitive domain, from least to most complex, are knowledge, comprehension, application, analysis, synthesis, and evaluation.

17. Behaviors in the affective domain, from least to most complex, are receiving, responding, valuing, organization, and characterization.

18. Behaviors in the psychomotor domain, from least to most complex, are imitation, manipulation, precision, articulation, and naturalization.

19. Behavioral objectives have their roots in the educational values we espouse as a nation.

Texts, curricula, and department and school policies are interpretations of these values shared at the broadest national level and translated into practice through behavioral objectives.

20. Four important cautions in using the taxonomies of behavioral objectives are as follows:
    - No behavior specified is necessarily more or less desirable than any other.
    - Higher cognitive skills often are more authentic than lower cognitive skills.
    - Less complex behaviors are not necessarily easier to teach, less time-consuming, or dependent on fewer resources than are more complex behaviors.
    - Behavior in one domain may require achievement of one or more behaviors in other domains.

FOR DISCUSSION AND PRACTICE

Questions marked with an asterisk are answered in Appendix B. See also *Bridges: An Activity Guide and Assessment Options,* which accompanies this text.

*1. Distinguish aims from goals by placing an *a* to the left of each aim and a *g* to the left of each goal.

_____ Be able to live in a technological world.

_____ Know how to add, subtract, multiply, and divide.

_____ Appreciate the arts, both nationally and internationally.

_____ Know the historical reasons for World War II.

_____ Work together cooperatively.

_____ Know parliamentary procedure.

_____ Be able to read a popular magazine.

_____ Experience literature from around the world.

_____ Understand the rudiments of health and hygiene.

_____ Know how to swing a tennis racket.

2. Select one of the aims identified in the previous question, (1) translate it into a goal, and (2) translate that goal into an objective. Make sure your objective is responsive to the aim from which it was derived.

*3. Identify the two general purposes for preparing behavioral objectives. If you could choose only one of these purposes, which would be more important to you? Why?

*4. Explain what three things the word *behavioral* implies when it appears before the word *objectives.*

*5. Identify the three components of a well-written behavioral objective, and give one example of each component.

*6. Historically, why did the concept of behavioral objectives emerge?

*7. Why are action verbs necessary in translating goals such as *mentally healthy citizens, well-rounded individuals,* and *self-actualized schoolchildren* into behavioral outcomes?

*8. Distinguish learning outcomes (ends) from learning activities (means) by placing an O or A beside the following expressions:

_____ Working on a car radio
_____ Adding signed numbers correctly
_____ Practicing the violin
_____ Playing basketball
_____ Using a microscope
_____ Identifying an amoeba
_____ Naming the seven parts of speech
_____ Punctuating an essay correctly

*9. Define a *condition* in a behavioral objective. Give three examples.

*10. How can the specification of conditions help students study and prepare for tests?

*11. In trying to decide what condition(s) to include in a behavioral objective, what single most important consideration should guide your selection?

*12. What is the definition of *criterion level* in a behavioral objective? Give three examples.

13. Provide examples of two behavioral objectives that differ in the degree of expressiveness they allow.

*14. Group A contains objectives. Group B contains levels of cognitive behavior. Match the levels in group B with the most appropriate objective in group A. Group B levels can be used more than once.

Group A: Objectives:

_____ 1. Given a two-page essay, the student can distinguish the assumptions basic to the author's position.

_____ 2. The student will correctly spell the word *mountain*.

_____ 3. The student will convert the following English passage into Spanish.

_____ 4. The student will compose new pieces of prose and poetry

according to the classification system emphasized in class.

_____ 5. Given a sinking passenger ship with 19 of its 20 lifeboats destroyed, the captain will decide, based on his perceptions of their potential worth to society, who is to be placed on the last lifeboat.

Group B: Levels
a. knowledge
b. comprehension
c. application
d. analysis
e. synthesis
f. evaluation

15. Make up two objectives for each of the knowledge, comprehension, application, analysis, synthesis, and evaluation levels of the taxonomy of cognitive objectives. Select verbs for each level from the lists provided in the chapter. Try to make your objectives cover the same subject.

16. Exchange the objectives you have just written with a classmate. Have the classmate check each objective for (1) an observable behavior, (2) any special conditions under which the behavior must be displayed, and (3) a performance level considered sufficient to demonstrate mastery. Revise your objectives if necessary.

17. A parent calls to tell you that, after a long talk with her son, she disapproves of the objectives you have written for health education—particularly those referring to the anatomy of the human body—but which you have taken almost verbatim from the teachers' guide to the adopted textbook. Compose a response to this parent that shows your understanding of the roots of objectives and justifies your decision to teach these objectives.

4 Unit and Lesson Planning

This chapter will help you answer the following questions:

1. How do I use a curriculum guide to plan a lesson?
2. How do I make a unit plan?
3. How do I decide the level of behavioral complexity at which to begin a lesson?
4. How can my lessons provide for student diversity?
5. What is in a lesson plan?

*Y*ou are now ready to consider planning and its relationship to decisions you make in the classroom. Planning is the systematic process of deciding what and how your students should learn. Teachers make one such decision on the average of every 2 minutes while they are teaching, according to an estimate by Clark and Peterson (1986). However, these thinking "on your feet" decisions are only part of the decision-making process. Teachers also make many other decisions about the form and content of their instruction, such as how much lecturing, questioning, and discussing to do, how much material to cover in the allotted time, and how in-depth to make the instruction. In the previous chapter you saw the importance of goals and objectives in the planning process. Now, let's consider three other factors to the planning process: knowledge of the learner, knowledge of your subject matter, and knowledge of teaching methods.

TEACHER AS DECISION MAKER

Knowledge of Instructional Goals and Objectives

Chapter 3 noted that, before you can prepare a lesson, you must decide on instructional goals and objectives. These planning decisions are crucial for developing effective lesson plans, because they give structure to lesson planning and tie it to important sources of societal and professional values. Chapter 4 presents unit and lesson plans as tools for tying these values to the classroom and the school curriculum.

Knowledge of the Learner

Chapter 2 showed the importance of understanding learner needs. A review of six research studies on planning found that teachers spent more of their planning time on learner characteristics (an average of 43%) than on any other area (Clark & Peterson, 1986). Recall the major influences on student learning: ability and achievement, personality (including anxiety, learning style, and self-concept), peers, and home and family. These are windows through which you see special **learning needs.**

Planning with respect to learners includes consciously noting their characteristics in these areas and recognizing limitations of the traditional curriculum. Special learning needs require you to select content, materials, objectives, and methods that match your students' characteristics. An assessment of the needs of your students is instrumental in helping you organize, select, sequence, and allocate time to various topics of instruction.

Knowledge of Subject Matter

A second aspect of planning is knowledge of your academic discipline and grade level. As a student, you have spent much time and effort becoming knowledgeable in the subjects you will teach. You have observed and absorbed valuable information about how textbook authors, your instructors, and subject matter specialists *organize* concepts in your teaching area. This includes how parts relate to the whole, how content is prioritized, how transitions are made between topics, and which themes are major or minor. This **content organization**, as presented by subject matter specialists in instructional materials, texts, and curriculum guides, is used by teachers to make learning easier, more orderly, and more conducive to retention and later use. Deriving your content organization from these sources will be instrumental in helping you select, sequence, and allocate time to instruction.

Knowledge of Teaching Methods

A third input to the planning process is your knowledge of **teaching methods.** With this knowledge comes an awareness of different teaching strategies with which you can implement the key and helping behaviors introduced in Chapter 1. Also included under teaching methods are your decisions about the following:

- Appropriate pacing or tempo (the speed at which you introduce new material)
- Mode of presentation (lecture vs. group discussion)
- Class arrangement (small groups, full class, independent study)
- Classroom management (raise hand, speak out)

Your decisions about pacing, mode of presentation, class arrangement, and classroom management should work together to form a coherent whole from which you present individual lesson objectives.

Another aspect of your knowledge of teaching methods is your selection and use of teaching materials. Your decisions about textbooks and curriculum materials, workbooks, films, software, tests, and reference works are crucial to planning. Therefore, you will want to keep a record of the materials and media that may be useful in meeting instructional goals in your subject matter and grade level. As you gain experience in your content area or grade level through observation and student teaching, be sure to list texts, workbooks, and media, and, when possible, obtain copies of handouts, activity sheets, and assessment tools directed to your learners' ages and grade levels. This is an important part of the planning process.

Summary of Inputs to Planning

To recap, the four primary inputs to the planning process are the following:

1. Knowledge of goals and objectives
2. Knowledge of learner characteristics
3. Knowledge of subject matter
4. Knowledge of teaching methods

Shulman (1992) identifies four specific sources from which you may obtain knowledge about goals and objectives, learners, subject matter, and teaching methods: (1) *practical experiences,* such as classroom observation, student teaching, and regular teaching; (2) reading *case studies* about what more successful and less successful teachers have done; (3) reading *theoretical articles* about important ideas, conceptual systems, and paradigms for thinking about teaching; and (4) reading *empirical studies* about what the research says about your subject and how to teach it. Each of these is a valuable source for extending and updating your knowledge of learners, content, and teaching methods. The chapters ahead will present key findings from each of these four areas.

DECISION MAKING AND EXPERIENCE

As a beginning teacher, you probably regard your content and method knowledge as hard won during four long years of schooling. To be sure, it is—but you've only just begun. Your knowledge in content and methods will change with the *interaction* of book learning and classroom experience.

This change will result from what is called tacit, or personal, knowledge (Canning, 1991; Elbaz, 1983; Polanyi, 1958). **Tacit knowledge** represents what works, discovered over time and through experience. Through everyday experiences, such as observation, experience in schools, lesson planning, and student teaching, you will compile tacit knowledge that can guide your actions as effectively as knowledge from texts and formal instruction. This knowledge can add to the quality of your planning and decision making by bringing variety and flexibility to your lessons. Tacit knowledge can make your planning less rigid and over time add fresh insights to your personal teaching style.

Effective teachers reflect on their day-to-day experiences in the classroom and use them as yet another input to the planning process. Lesson plans that include your day-to-day experiences will give your teaching variety, flexibility, and creativity. Thus, we add this fifth input to the planning process, shown in Figure 4.1.

Figure 4.1 Inputs to the planning process.

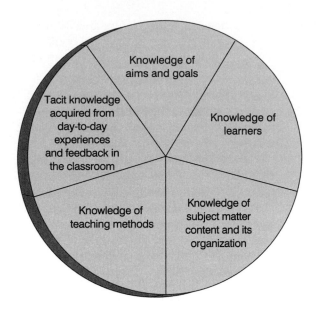

UNIT AND LESSON PLANS

The important process of unit and lesson planning begins with implementing the five planning inputs (Figure 4.1). This stage of the planning process takes a **system perspective,** meaning that your lessons will be part of a larger system of interrelated learning, called a *unit.*

The word *system* brings to mind phrases like *school system, mental health system,* and *legal system.* Schools, mental health services, and criminal justice agencies are supposed to work as systems. This means that their component parts are to interrelate and build toward some unified concept. For example, in a school system, discrete facts, skills, and understandings learned by the completion of sixth grade not only are important in themselves but also are important for successful completion of seventh grade. This, in turn, is important for completion of eighth grade, and so on through the educational system until the high school graduate has accumulated many of the facts, skills, and understandings necessary for adult living.

The strength of a system is that the whole is greater than the sum of its parts. But how can anything be more than the sum of its parts? Can a unit of instruction comprising individual lessons ever add up to anything more than the sum of the individual lessons? This sounds like getting something for nothing, a concept that does not ring true. But, if the system of individual lessons really does produce outcomes in learners that are greater than the sum of the outcomes of the individual lessons, then there must be a missing ingredient that we haven't mentioned.

That missing ingredient is *the relationship among the individual lessons.* This relationship must allow the outcome of one lesson to build on the outcomes of preceding lessons. Knowledge, skills, and understanding evolve gradually through the joint contribution of many lessons arranged to build more and more complex outcomes. It is this invisible but all-important relationship among the parts of a system, or instructional unit, that allows the unit outcomes to be greater than the sum of the lesson outcomes.

This does not mean that anything labeled a system or an instructional unit necessarily will achieve outcomes greater than the sum of its parts. If the relationship among parts of the system or instructional unit is not painstakingly planned to ensure that earlier lessons become building blocks for later lessons, a true system will not exist. Instead, only a mixture of bits and pieces bound together by some common unit title may exist, like the accumulation of miscellaneous items in an attic or in the glove compartment of your car. Nothing works in harmony with anything else to produce a coherent whole or a unified theme.

Of considerable importance is the relationship of your district's curriculum guide to your unit and lesson plans. *Units* generally extend over an instructional time period of 1 to 4 weeks. They usually correspond to well-defined topics or themes in the curriculum guide. *Lessons,* on the other hand, are considerably shorter, spanning a single class period or occasionally two or three periods. Because lessons are relatively short, they are harder to associate with a particular segment of a curriculum guide. This means that you can expect unit content to be fairly well structured and defined but lesson content to be much less detailed.

This is as it should be, because the arrangement of day-to-day content in the classroom must be flexible to meet individual student needs, your instructional preferences, and special priorities and initiatives in your school and community. So, although the overall picture at the unit level may be clear from the district's curriculum guide, at the lesson level, you must apply considerable independent thought, organization, and judgment. Figure 4.2 indicates the flow of teaching content from the state level to the classroom, illustrating the stages through which a curriculum framework is translated into unit and lesson plans.

MAKING PLANNING DECISIONS

Unit planning begins with an understanding of your goals, your students learning needs, the content you will teach, and the teaching methods available to you. Let's look closer at several types of decisions you will make pertaining to these inputs to the lesson planning process.

Goals

Curriculum guides at the grade, department, and school district level usually clearly specify what content must be covered in what period of time. But they may be far less clear about the specific behaviors that students are expected to acquire. For example, an excerpt from a curriculum guide for English language instruction might take this form:

Figure 4.2 Flow of teaching content from the state level to the classroom level.

State Curriculum Framework

- provides philosophy that guides curriculum implementation
- discusses progression of essential content taught from grade to grade; shows movement of student through increasingly complex material
- notes modifications of curriculum to special populations (e.g., at-risk, gifted, or bilingual learners, or learners with disabilities)

District Curriculum Guide

- provides content goals keyed to state framework
- enumerates appropriate teaching activities and assignment strategies
- gives outline for unit plans; lists and sequences topics
- reflects locally appropriate ways of achieving goals in content areas

Teacher's Unit and Lesson Plans

- describes how curriculum guide goals are implemented daily
- refers to topics to be covered, materials needed, activities to be used
- identifies evaluation strategies
- notes adaptions to special populations

Teacher's Grade Book

- records objectives mastered
- identifies need for reteaching and remediation
- provides progress indictators
- guides promotion/retention decisions

I. Writing concepts and skills. The student shall be provided opportunities to learn
    A. The composing process
    B. Descriptive, narrative, and expository paragraphs
    C. Multiple paragraph compositions
    D. Persuasive discourse
    E. Meanings and uses of colloquialism, slang, idiom, and jargon

Or for a life-science curriculum:

I. Life science. The student shall be provided the opportunity to learn
    A. Skills in acquiring data through the senses
    B. Classification skills in ordering and sequencing data
    C. Oral and written communication of data in appropriate form
    D. Concepts and skills of measurement using relationships and standards
    E. Drawing logical inferences, predicting outcomes, and forming generalized statements

Notice in these excerpts the specificity at which the content is identified (e.g., the composing process; descriptive, narrative, and expository paragraphs; multiple paragraph composition). In contrast, note the lack of clarity concerning the *level of behavioral complexity* to which the instruction should be directed. This is typical of many curriculum guides. Recalling the taxonomy of behavior in the cognitive domain (Chapter 3), you might ask the following questions:

- For which of these content areas will the simple *recall* of facts be sufficient?
- For which areas will *comprehension* of those facts be required?
- For which areas will *application* be expected of what the student comprehends?
- For which areas will higher-level outcomes be desired, involving *analysis, synthesis,* and *decision-making* skills?

Decisions made about goals often involve selecting (1) the level of behavioral complexity for which teachers will prepare an instructional unit or lesson and (2) the level at which teachers will expect student outcomes and test for them. The flexibility afforded by most curriculum guides in selecting the behavioral level to which instruction can be directed often is both purposeful and advantageous for you. For the curriculum guide to be adapted to the realities of your classroom, a wide latitude of expected outcomes must be possible. These depend on the unique behavioral characteristics of your students, the time you can devote to a specific topic, and the overall behavioral outcomes desired at the unit level.

Learners

Curriculum guides allow you the flexibility of adapting your instruction to the individual learning needs of your students. Chapter 2 presented several categories of individual differences that will be characteristic of students in your classroom. These included differences in ability, prior achievement, anxiety, self-concept, learning style, and home and family life. These factors can reflect entire classrooms as well as individuals. Other categories of learners—at-risk, bilingual, gifted, and learners with disabilities—add even greater diversity to the classroom. They may create the need for task-related subgroups that require instruction individually or time-limited ability groups, alternatives we will address in the chapters to come.

You will also want to remain flexible in choosing the level of behavioral complexity of your unit and lesson outcomes. For these decisions, the information you will need to match the complexity of your objectives to the needs of your learners will come from their in-class oral responses, practice exercises, performance assessments, homework, and tests. You will want to use these often to adjust the level of your instruction to your learners.

Content

Perhaps foremost in the mind of beginning teachers is the content to be taught. Your content decisions appear easy inasmuch as textbooks, workbooks, and curriculum guides may have been selected before your first day in the classroom. Indeed, as you saw in the excerpts from the curriculum guide, content often is designated in great detail. Textbooks and workbooks carry this detail one step further by offering activities and exercises that further define and expand the content in the curriculum guide. From this perspective it may appear as if all of the content has been handed to you, if not on a silver platter, then surely in readily accessible and highly organized tests, workbooks, and curriculum materials.

Although some teachers might wish this were true, most quickly realize that as many decisions must be made about content—what to teach—as about behavioral goals and learning needs. You will quickly come to realize that adopted texts, workbooks, and even detailed curriculum guides identify the content to be taught but do not select, organize, and sequence that content *according to the needs of your learners.* And increasingly, school districts are providing alternative texts and workbooks from which teachers can chose to better target specific populations of learners. For this task, you must select from among textbook and curriculum guide content and expand on it to strengthen the relationship between your behavioral goals and learner needs.

Thus, the content you present cannot be decided until you have determined your learners' characteristics and selected the level of behavioral complexity of your desired outcomes. Although textbook and curriculum guides indicate the content coverage to strive for, effective teachers know that they must *select from* this content for some behavioral goals and learners and *add to* this content for other goals and learners to engage them in the learning process at the *most appropriate level of behavioral complexity.*

Organization

Establishing relationships between lessons is one of the most important planning decisions you will make. How your lessons interrelate can even determine if and how well your learners achieve higher levels of cognitive, affective, and psychomotor behavior at the unit level. This, in turn, will determine how well your unit and lesson plans reflect a thinking curriculum.

The higher levels of behavior can rarely if ever be achieved in a single lesson. Thus, lessons must be placed within a unit (system) in which individual lessons build on previously taught behaviors to achieve these higher-order behaviors. This is why your structuring of content is so important to unit planning: without it, behavioral outcomes at the unit's end may be no different from the outcomes achieved at the completion of each single lesson. Unlike miscellaneous items in the attic or the glove compartment of your car, units must have a coherent, unified theme that rises above the cognitive, affective, and psychomotor complexity of any single lesson.

Thus far, this discussion has described sequencing of instruction, or relating lessons to one another, as a matter of personal preference. However, you should organize lesson content with both your goals and the learners in mind. For example, one reason for choosing a specific-to-general organization of instructional content might be to achieve outcomes at a higher level of behavioral complexity with poorly motivated learners. Your reason might be that, since the more difficult content will come at the conclusion of the unit, the most specific or concrete lesson content should be presented first. Thus, learners can more easily acquire the needed basics and achieve a higher level of interest before moving deeper into the topic. Or, the reason for choosing a particular series of lessons (e.g., on acid rain, new technologies, or heroic deeds) might be to show how several content areas can be brought together with a single theme for the purpose of solving a problem, thinking critically, and forming an independent judgment. In each case, the unit goal and needs of your learners will play an important role in selecting a particular organization. Thus, your decisions about unit structure will depend both on clearly stated goals and a knowledge of your learners.

VERTICAL AND LATERAL UNIT PLANNING

The following two sections will introduce unit plans and how to communicate them in a clear and orderly manner. The first approach to unit planning will show you how to plan and to teach knowledge and understanding vertically. **Vertical unit planning** is a method of developing units within a discipline in which the content to be taught is arranged hierarchically or in steps (e.g., from least to most complex, or from concrete to abstract) and presented in an order that ensures that all task-relevant prior knowledge required for subsequent lessons has been taught in previous lessons.

Following our discussion of vertical unit planning, we present a second means of communicating knowledge and understanding to your learners, called lateral planning. **Lateral unit planning** is often used for planning thematic units that integrate bodies of knowledge across disciplines or content areas to convey relationships, patterns, and abstractions that bind different aspects of our world together in some systematic way. Lateral unit plans move across the established boundaries of content areas to elicit problem solving, critical thinking, cooperative activity, and independent thought and action that emphasizes that the whole is greater than the sum of its parts. As you will see, both vertical and lateral unit planning are valuable tools for acquiring the skills of an effective teacher.

Disciplinary (Vertical) Thematic Unit Plans

An old Chinese proverb states, "A picture is worth a thousand words." This chapter applies this age-old idea to unit planning by showing how you can develop a unit plan by creating a visual blueprint of your thematic unit. This section shows you how to use a written and graphic format to express a unit plan within a discipline, subject matter, or content area.

While a visual device cannot substitute for a written description or outline of what you plan to teach, it is an effective means of organizing your thinking. Scientists, administrators, engineers, and business executives long have known the value of visuals in the form of flow charts, organization charts, blueprints, diagrams, and even doodles to convey the essence of a concept, if not the details. From the beginning, teachers have used this basic method, too. Pictures not only communicate the results of planning but are useful during that process to organize and revise a unit plan, and to see the big picture—or final outcome—you are working hard to achieve.

Although teaching parallels many other fields by using visual devices in planning, in many ways, teaching is a unique profession. Unlike business, education's product does not roll off an assembly line, and education does not build its product with the mathematical laws and physical substances used by the scientist and engineer. Consequently, your visual blueprints differ from those of others, but at the same time reflect the qualities that have made pictures so important to planning in these other professions. You already have been introduced to two of these qualities: the concept of *hierarchy*, which shows the relationship of parts to the whole (lessons to unit), and the concept of *task-relevant prior knowledge,* which shows the necessity for a certain lesson sequence (Walberg, 1991, p. 38). In vertical unit planning, both concepts are put to work in creating a visual picture of a unit; such a picture can both stimulate and organize your thoughts and communicate the results to others in an easy-to-follow graphic format.

Two simple rules are used in drawing a picture of a vertically planned unit. The first is to diagram how the unit goal is divided into specific lessons. The second is to show the sequence of these lessons and how their outcomes build on one another to achieve the unit goal. Let's look at these two rules.

Visualizing Specific Teaching Activities.   Our first rule simply uses boxes to visualize areas of content—or instructional goals—at various levels of generality. In other words, any goal at the unit level can be broken into its component parts at the lesson level. Those component parts represent everything that is important for attaining the goal. This idea is illustrated in Figure 4.3.

Notice that Figure 4.3 has three levels. For now, focus on the top and bottom levels. The top shows the unit's general intent, which is derived from the curriculum

Figure 4.3 Example of a hierarchy of reading content at different levels of specificity.

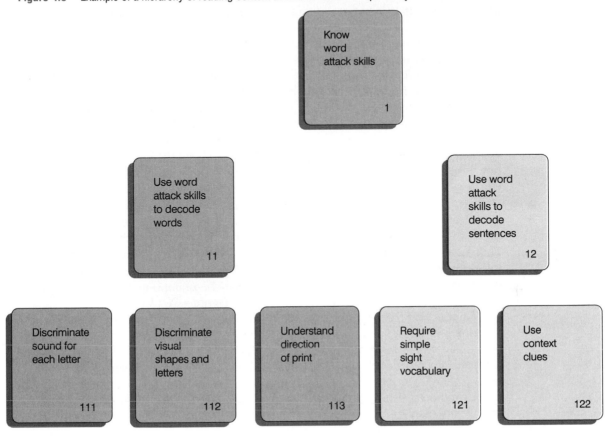

guide and adopted textbook, which in turn are based on societal, state, or locally stated goals. The bottom row shows content expressed at a level specific enough to prepare individual lessons.

This unit plan ends with bite-sized chunks that together exhaust the content specified at the higher levels. Just as in the story of Goldilocks and the three bears, the bottom of the unit plan hierarchy must end with the portion of content being served up as not too big and not too small but just right. How can you know whether you have achieved the right size and balance for a single lesson?

The second level of Figure 4.3 is a logical means of getting from the general unit goal to specific lesson content. It is an intermediate thinking process that produces the lower level of just-right-sized pieces. How many intermediate levels should you have? There is no magic number; this depends on how broadly the initial goal is stated and the number of steps needed to produce content in just the right amounts for individual lesson plans. Experience and judgment are the best guides, although logical divisions within the curriculum guide and text are helpful, too.

In some cases, the route from unit to lesson content can be very direct (two levels), while in other instances, several levels may have to be worked through before arriving at lesson-sized chunks. If you have trouble getting sufficiently specific for lesson-sized content, you may need to revise the unit goal by dividing it into two or more subgoals and beginning a new hierarchy from each subgoal. This was done in Figure 4.3, where the unit planner had to devise two units of instruction. Notice that this is done in the same way that you create an outline. This process of building a content hierarchy will guide you in making the important distinction between unit and lesson content and will prevent many false starts in lesson planning.

Visualizing the Sequence of Activities.   The second rule shows the sequence of lessons and how lesson outcomes build on one another to achieve a unit goal. This second rule, illustrated in Figure 4.4, shows the order of the individual lessons, when order is important. Notice that in Figure 4.4, we chose the first box from the second level (11) of the hierarchy in Figure 4.3 as our unit goal. The procedure is to indicate the intended unit outcome with an arrow extending from the right of this top box, as shown in Figure 4.4. The outcome of all the lessons derived from it, taken together, should be the same as this unit outcome. This will always be true, whether or not the sequence of your lessons is important. In some instances this sequence may be unimportant (Figure 4.5), while for others a partial sequence may be appropriate (Figure 4.6).

This second rule recognizes how previous lessons can *modify* or *constrain* the outcomes of subsequent lessons. It encourages you to use sequence, building on previously taught learning to provide increasingly more authentic and behaviorally complex outcomes at the unit level. This will be important if your unit plan is to promote a thinking curriculum. If lesson outcomes are unrelated, it is unlikely that your unit outcome will be at any higher a level of cognitive, affective, or psychomotor complexity than your individual lesson outcomes. As an effective teacher, you should

Figure 4.4   A unit plan showing a sequence of lessons.

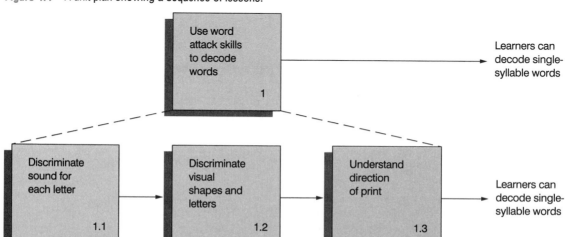

Figure 4.5 A unit plan without lesson sequence (Lessons 1.1, 1.2, and 1.3 can occur in any order).

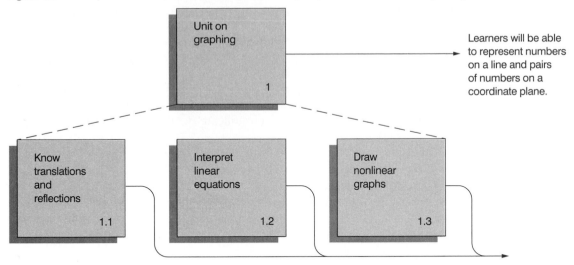

plan the interrelationships among lessons in a way that encourages higher-order behaviors to emerge at the unit level.

You can see that picturing your unit plan visually has several advantages. Seeing a lesson in context with other lessons that share the same purpose focuses your attention on the importance of task-relevant prior knowledge to lesson success. Recall that if learners have inadequately acquired (or not acquired) prerequisite knowledge and skills relevant to your lesson, some or most of your learners probably will not attain your les-

Figure 4.6 A unit plan with partial lesson sequence (Lesson 1.1 must precede Lesson 1.2).

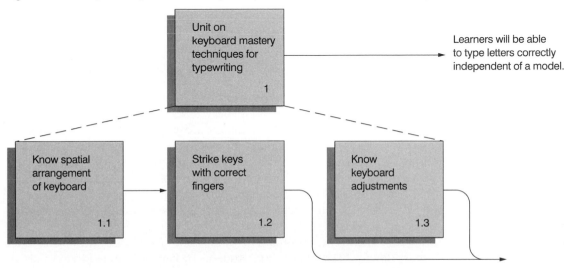

son objective. One purpose of seeing lessons within a unit plan is to determine whether you have provided all task-relevant prior knowledge required by each lesson. Because unit plans precede lesson plans, you can easily add overlooked lessons and objectives prerequisite to later lessons. You can draw your unit plans graphically, as shown in this chapter, using the word processing or graphics software on your personal computer.

The Written Unit Plan.   Planning units graphically will be helpful in organizing, sequencing, and arriving at bite-sized pieces of content at the lesson level. But, you will also need a description that will communicate details of the unit to others (and to remind yourself) at a later time.

One format for a written version of a unit plan appears in Figure 4.7. This format divides a written plan into its (1) main purpose, (2) behavioral objectives, (3) content, (4) procedures and activities, (5) instructional aids and resources, and (6) evaluation methods. To this written plan, attach your visual blueprint to indicate at a glance the organization, sequence, and sizing of the unit and to provide an introduction and overview of the written details. Together, they will give you a powerful tool for communicating your unit plans.

Finally, notice that in Figure 4.7 both objectives and individual learners progress from the lower levels of cognitive and psychomotor behavioral complexity (comprehension, application, imitation) to the higher levels (analysis, synthesis, precision). This illustrates how early lessons in a unit can be used as building blocks to attain higher levels of authenticity, helping to achieve a thinking curriculum (Kagan & Tippins, 1992).

Interdisciplinary (Lateral)Thematic Unit Plans

Results of recent research indicate that a unit in which many content areas are integrated can lead to high levels of thinking and meaningful learning, if the instructional techniques used involve students in interactive learning and higher order thinking (Aschlbacher, 1991; Richmond & Striley, 1994; Shavelson & Baxter, 1992).

An interdisciplinary thematic unit is a laterally planned unit of study in which topics are integrated to provide a focus on a specific theme (Martin, 1995; Martinello & Cook, 1994). This approach to learning helps students visualize connections. The principal aim of interdisciplinary instruction is to present learners with an opportunity to discover relationships and patterns that go beyond a specific discipline and that bind together different aspects of our world in some systematic way (McDonald & Czerniak, 1994). For example, interdisciplinary units often represent themes that can be related to several different subject matter areas at the same time, such as to English or reading, science, social studies, and the expressive arts. Effective interdisciplinary units also often require learners to conduct research that requires the cooperation of other learners and the independent use of materials. Interdisciplinary units provide opportunities for classroom dialogue in which learners are expected to reason critically, ask questions, make predictions, and, with the aid of the teacher, evaluate the appropriateness of their own responses.

For example, Roberts and Kellough (1996) describe one teacher who planned an interdisciplinary unit for her middle school students by having them read a story about

Figure 4.7   Example unit plan.

Grade: 10

Unit Topic: Pizza with Yeast Dough Crust

Course/Subject: Contemporary Home Economics

Approximate Time Required: One week

1. Main Purpose of the Unit: The purpose of this unit is to acquaint the students with the principles of making yeast dough by making pizza. The historical background, nutritional value, and variations of pizza will also be covered.
2. Behavioral Objectives
   The student will be able to:
   A. Describe the functions of each of the ingredients in yeast dough. (Cognitive-knowledge)
   B. Explain the steps in preparing yeast dough. (Cognitive-comprehension)
   C. Make a yeast dough for a pizza crust. (Cognitive-application and psychomotor-imitation)
   D. State briefly the history of pizza. (Cognitive-knowledge)
   E. Match the ingredients in pizza to the food groups they represent. (Cognitive-knowledge)
   F. Classify and give examples of different types of pizza. (Cognitive-analysis)
   G. Create and bake a pizza of their choice. (Cognitive-synthesis and psychomotor-precision)
3. Content Outline
   A. Essential ingredients in yeast dough
      (1) Flour
      (2) Yeast
      (3) Liquid
      (4) Sugar
      (5) Salt
   B. Non-essential ingredients
      (1) Fats
      (2) Eggs
      (3) Other, such as fruit and nuts
   C. Preparing yeast dough
      (1) Mixing
      (2) Kneading
      (3) Rising (fermenting)
      (4) Punching down
      (5) Shaping
      (6) Baking

   D. History of pizza
      (1) First pizza was from Naples.
      (2) Pizza is an Italian word meaning pie.
      (3) Originally eaten by the poor, pizza was also enjoyed by royalty.
      (4) Italian immigrants brought pizza to the United States in the late 1800s.
   E. Types of pizza
      (1) Neapolitan
      (2) Sicilian
      (3) Pizza Rustica
      (4) Pizza de Polenta
   F. Nutritional value of pizza
      (1) Nutritious meal or snack
      (2) Can contain all four food groups
      (3) One serving of cheese pizza contains:
         (a) Protein
         (b) Vitamins
         (c) Minerals
   G. Making a pizza
      (1) Prepare dough
      (2) Roll out dough
      (3) Transfer to pan
      (4) Spread sauce
      (5) Top as desired
      (6) Bake
4. Procedures and Activities
   A. Informal lecture
   B. Discussion
   C. Demonstration of mixing and kneading dough
   D. Filmstrip on pizza
   E. Education game (Pizzeria): Each time a student answers correctly a question about yeast dough or pizza, he gets a part of a paper pizza. The first to collect a complete pizza wins.
   F. Cooking lab
5. Instructional Aids or Resources
   A. Text: Guide to Modern Meals (Webster, McGraw-Hill, 1970)
   B. Filmstrip: Pizza, Pizza 10 minutes
   C. Pizza, Pizza booklets by Chef Boyardee
   D. Educational game (Pizzeria)
   E. Bake-it-easy Yeast Book by Fleischmann's Yeast
   F. Poster (showing different kinds of pizza from Pizza Hut)
6. Evaluation
   A. Unit test
   B. Lab performance

Source: From *Curriculum Planning: A Ten-Step Process* by W. Zenger and S. Zenger, 1982, Palo Alto, CA: R and E Research Associates. Copyright © 1982 by R and E Research Associates. Reprinted with permission.

a young boy who travels through time and journeys to a fantasy planet. As the boy struggles to adapt to his new culture, he experiences isolation, loneliness, domination, and imprisonment. To relate this story to several different disciplines based on their reading, the teacher planned a unit in which the following relationships were drawn between and within disciplines:

- *Related to English.* The students discussed changes in the novel's setting, the development of the plot, and the author's use of the literary device of foreshadowing.
- *Related to expressive arts.* The students made a model of the planet and a floor plan of some of the buildings, and designed a robot that was described in the story. They also staged a dramatic reenactment of a scene in the novel.
- *Related to science.* Some students studied the flora and fauna on the planet and compared it to the plants and animals of their own state, while others attempted to identify the chemical composition of the environment on the planet and identify a probable location for it in our solar system.
- *Related to social studies.* The students engaged in a map study of the planet, developed a government for the fantasy planet, compared the segregation practiced in the story with segregation elsewhere, compared the freedoms of the inhabitants on the planet with the freedoms in our own Bill of Rights, and discussed issues of prejudice and class structure.
- *Related to additional research.* The students studied popular research on dreams and experiments about the sleep of humans, which played a predominant role in the story.

Notice how the relationships and patterns across subject areas in this unit did not just happen. This teacher developed her unit from a carefully constructed list of interrelated themes that she could select from and add to when determining the areas of the curriculum to be taught. To prepare her unit plan, this teacher developed a list of possible themes, like those shown in Table 4.1. These thematic concepts, topics, and categories were mapped onto existing subject matter in her and other teachers' classrooms and brought to life through the interdisciplinary thematic unit.

Interdisciplinary units can help you achieve the following objectives:

1. Emphasize that the process of learning is sometimes best pursued as an interconnected whole rather than as a series of specific subjects.
2. Encourage students to work cooperatively in partnerships and small groups that focus on the social values of learning.
3. Teach students to be independent problem solvers and thinkers.
4. Assist students to develop their own individual interests and learning styles.
5. Help students find out what they need to know and what they need to learn rather than always expecting the teacher to give it to them.

A key component of thematic units is the varied structure of the instructional strategies used. Give students a variety of activities, materials, and learning strategies within each of the content areas to facilitate comprehension and create a desire to learn

Table 4.1 Theme development for interdisciplinary units.

Concepts	Topics	Categories
freedom	individual	autobiographies
cooperation	society	dreams
challenge	community	fantasies
conflict	relationships	tall tales
discovery	global concerns	experiences
culture	war	first-hand accounts
change	partnerships	
perseverance		

more about a topic. Have students work independently at times, but also collaborate in groups to read, pose and investigate problems, and complete projects. In this way, students interact and learn from each other. Your role is that of a facilitator of learning.

The Spectrum of Integrated Curricula.   Roberts and Kellough (1996) and Stevenson and Carr (1993) identify four ways you can implement integrated thematic teaching in your classroom, which represent different degrees of involvement:

Level 1.   At this level, you would use a thematic approach to relate content and material from various content areas during the same day. For example, the theme "Natural Disasters Cause Social Effects," could originate from the topics of weather normally taught within a science or geography lesson and the topic of community taught within a social studies lesson. You would convey the theme of this interdisciplinary lesson to learners at the beginning of the unit in the form of a question, such as "What necessary functions in a community are often disrupted after a natural disaster?" Encourage students to suggest adding other content and questions.

Level 2.   The next level of implementation requires you to consult with other teachers and agree on a common theme. Each teacher who decides to participate in the interdisciplinary unit teaches to that theme in his or her own classroom. In this manner students learn from a teacher in one classroom something that is related to what they are learning in another classroom. In the early elementary grades, a single teacher can perform this same function by referring back, say, during reading instruction, to a related concept in social studies, math, or science. Display on the bulletin board a list of themes developed beforehand based on interconnections among subject areas to remind both you and your learners to identify and discuss the connections and, then, have students create the connections with examples of their work.

Level 3.   At the third level, you and your students work together to form a list of common themes across subject areas. For example, in the later elementary and high school grades, you might give an assignment to search the table of contents of your text and those of other teachers for the topic of a thematic unit you might teach within your classroom. If other teachers agree on the theme developed, they, too, can be encouraged to mutually reinforce the connections identified in their classrooms, thereby providing momentum across disciplines for your thematic unit. This level of implementation is an effective way to initiate a team approach to your interdisciplinary teaching.

Level 4. At the fourth level, your students develop on their own a list of common themes or problems across disciplines. Your charge to students is to arrive at one or more themes in which a traditional subject, discipline, or content area would be inadequate for addressing a theme or resolving a problem. In other words, you instruct your students to find current, contemporary dilemmas, moral issues, and problems that defy solution in the context of any one or small number of traditionally defined subject areas. Students may therefore be challenged to raise such thorny problems as "How can we know when someone has really died?" requiring the simultaneous consideration of latest advances in the fields of medicine, religion, and philosophy, or "How can we rid our planet of life-threatening pollution?" possibly requiring your class to consider knowledge from general science, physics, and chemistry and from social studies, government, and the law. At this level, your students are playing the role of independent and socially responsible thinkers and you are playing the role of resource, guiding their thoughts and refocusing them when necessary in increasingly productive avenues for elaborating relationships, patterns, and abstractions for adult living.

Visualizing Your Interdisciplinary Unit. Because interdisciplinary units emphasize lateral knowledge, their graphic portrayal is different from disciplinary units, which emphasize vertical knowledge. The graphic technique you use for expressing lateral knowledge should allow for content to be woven in and out of lessons as the opportunity arises, without a predetermined sequence. Hence, a more free-form, or web type, visual format is required, sometimes called a concept map or thinking map (Buzan, 1994; Dochy & Alexander, 1995; Hyerle, 1995–1996). This type of format shows how content is *nestled* within other content, how different subject areas *share* a common theme, how a single theme is *threaded* through different content areas, or how one field of study is *immersed* in another. Thus, all important themes and issues in an interdisciplinary plan are shown simultaneously in association with one another. The rules for creating these types of graphic outlines or webs are as follows:

- Identify the single most essential theme or idea.
- Place this theme or idea in the center of your web.
- Use arrows or lines going outward from the main idea to show relationships with other, subordinate issues, topics, or content, which can become the topics of individual lessons.
- Label the arrows and all key concepts with code words or phrases to describe the relationships you have expressed.

Figures 4.8 and 4.9 provide examples of thematic webs for expressing an interdisciplinary thematic unit.

The Written Unit Plan. The written format for an interdisciplinary unit plan is the same as that for a disciplinary unit. Recall that a written unit is divided into its (1) main purpose, (2) behavioral objectives, (3) content, (4) procedures and activities, (5) instructional aids and resources, and (6) evaluation methods. An example of a written interdisciplinary plan appears in Figure 4.10. To this written plan attach the visual outline or web of your theme and its interrelationships.

Figure 4.8 Visual representation of the interdisciplinary unit theme "Adventures of Lewis and Clark."

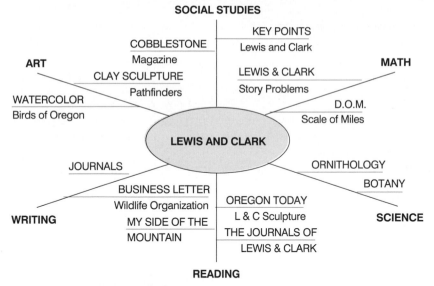

Source: From *The Classrooom of the 21st Century,* by S. Kovalik, 1994, Kent, WA: Books for Educators. Copyright © 1994 by S. Kovalik. Reprinted with permission.

Figure 4.9 Visual representation of the interdisciplinary unit theme "Dimensions of Time."

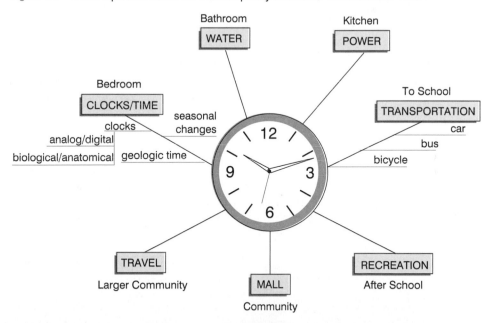

Source: From *ITI: The Model,* by S. Kovalik, 1994, Kent, WA: Books for Educators. Copyright © 1994 by S. Kovalik. Reprinted with permission.

Figure 4.10 Example interdisciplinary thematic unit.

Grade: 5

Unit Topic: Gold Rush

Course/Subject: Interdisciplinary

Approximate Time Required: One Month

1. **Main Purpose of the Unit**
   The purpose of this unit is to acquaint the students with the excitement, the hardships and the challenges of the nineteenth century gold rush.
2. **Behavioral Objectives**
   The student will be able to:
   A. *History/Social Science*—Give reasons why people came to California in the 1840s.
   B. *History/Social Science*—Describe the three routes the pioneers took to California.
   C. *History/Social Science*—Compare life in the United States in the 1840s to life in the United States now.
   D. *History/Social Science*—List supplies brought by the pioneers on the trip West.
   E. *Language Arts*—Write a journal entry to describe some of the hardships associated with the trip West.
   F. *Science*—Research and write a report on how gold is mined.
   G. *Math*—Weigh gold nuggets (painted rocks) and calculate their monetary value.
   H. *Art*—Design a prairie quilt pattern using fabric scraps.
3. **Content Outline**
   A. Reasons people came to California in the 1840s
      1. Gold
      2. Job opportunities
      3. Weather
   B. Supplies for the trip
      1. Tools
      2. Personal supplies
      3. Food
      4. Household items

C. Life on the trip West
   1. Weather conditions
   2. Roles of men, women, children
   3. Hazards of the trail
D. Life in California after arrival
   1. Inflated prices
   2. Staking a claim
   3. Striking it rich
   4. A typical day in the life of a miner
4. **Procedures and Activities**
   A. Read aloud
   B. Small-group reading
   C. Independent reading
   D. Discussion
   F. Journal entries
   G. Measurement
   H. Cooking
   I. Singing
5. **Instructional Aids and Resources**
   A. Literature selections
      1. *Patty Reed's Doll*
      2. *By the Great Horn Spoon*
      3. *If You Traveled West in a Covered Wagon*
      4. *Children of the Wild West*
      5. *Joshua's Westward Journal*
      6. *The Way West, Journal of a Pioneer Woman*
      7. *The Little House Cookbook*
   B. Items indicative of the period (if obtainable)
      1. Cast iron skillet
      2. Bonnet or leather hat
      3. Old tools
6. **Assessment/Evaluation**
   Develop a rubric to grade these.
   A. Essay—Choose one route that the pioneers took to get to California and describe the journey.
   B. Gold Rush Game Board—Design a board game detailing the trip to California. The winner arrives in California and strikes it rich!

(Written by Cynthia Kiel, teacher, Glendora, California.)

MAKING LESSON PLANS

Up to this point, we have emphasized the importance of choosing unit outcomes at a higher level of behavioral complexity than lesson outcomes in order to achieve a thinking curriculum. If you plan lessons without a higher-level unit outcome in mind, your students' attention will fall exclusively on each individual lesson without noticing the relationship among lessons. This relationship may appear deceptively unimportant until it becomes apparent that your lessons seem to pull students first in one direction (e.g., knowledge acquisition) and then abruptly in another (e.g., problem solving), without instruction to guide them in the transition. The result of such isolated lesson outcomes may well be confusion, anxiety, and distrust on the part of your students, regardless of how well you prepare each individual lesson and how effective they are in accomplishing their stated—but isolated—outcomes. Because outcomes at higher levels of behavioral complexity rarely can be attained within the time frame of a single lesson, they must be achieved in the context of unit plans.

Before you actually write a lesson plan, two preliminary considerations are necessary for your unit plan to flow smoothly: (1) determining where to start and (2) providing for learner diversity.

Determining Where to Start

Perhaps most perplexing to new teachers is deciding the level of behavioral complexity at which a lesson should begin. Do you always begin by teaching facts (instilling knowledge), or can you begin with activities at the application level or even at the synthesis and decision-making levels? Both alternatives are possible, but each makes different assumptions about the behavioral characteristics of your students and the interrelationship among your lessons.

Beginning a lesson or a sequence of lessons at the knowledge level (e.g., list, recall, recite, etc.) assumes that the topic you will be teaching is mostly new material. Such a lesson usually occurs at the beginning of a sequence that will progressively build this knowledge into more authentic behavior—perhaps ending at the application, synthesis, or evaluation level. When no task-relevant prior knowledge is required, the starting point for a lesson often is at the knowledge or comprehension level. When some task-relevant prior knowledge has been taught, lessons can begin at higher levels of behavioral complexity. Notice from the list of objectives in Figure 4.7 that each lesson having an outcome at a higher level of behavioral complexity is preceded by a lesson at some lower level. The behavioral complexity with which each lesson starts depends on the behavioral outcome of the lessons that preceded it.

As we have seen, unit plans should attempt to teach a range of behaviors that begin at a lower level and end with a higher level of behavioral complexity. Some units might begin at the application level and end at a higher level, if a previous unit has provided the task-relevant prior knowledge and understandings required. It also is possible to progress from one behavioral level to another within a single lesson. This may be increasingly difficult when lessons start at high levels of behavioral complexity, but it is possible and often desirable to move from knowledge to comprehension and on to application activities within a single lesson. This is illustrated in the flow of behaviors for the following third-grade social studies lesson:

Unit Title: Local, State, and National Geography

Lesson Title: Local Geography

Behaviors

- Student will know geographical location of community relative to state and nation (knowledge).
- Student will be able to describe physical features of community (comprehension).
- Student will be able to locate community on map and globe (application).
- Student will be able to discuss how the community is similar to and different from other communities (analysis).

In this lesson a comprehensive span of behaviors is required in a relatively brief time (a single lesson) by using objects already known to the students (their own community, map, globe) and by dovetailing one behavior into another so that each new activity is a continuation of the preceding one. When the teacher plans a transition across behavioral levels within a single lesson, the necessary question before each new level of complexity is, "Have I provided all the required task-relevant prior knowledge?" Only when you can answer "Yes" will the lesson be directed at the students' current level of understanding, and only then can students attain the unit objective.

Providing for Learner Diversity With Alternative Methods and New Technologies

A second consideration before writing a lesson plan is the extent to which the lesson provides for student diversity. Thus far, we have considered all the students within a class to be identical, sharing the same behavioral characteristics and task-relevant prior knowledge. Of course, diversity is the rule in any classroom.

Regardless of where you position the entry level of a lesson, some students will be above it and other students will be below it. Much of the work of unit and lesson planning is playing a game of averages in which you attempt to provide *most* of the instruction at the current level of functioning of *most* of the learners. Unless an entire course of study is individualized (sometimes the case with programmed and computer-assisted instruction curricula), most instruction must be directed at the "average" learner in your classroom.

However, some instructional methods and **tutorial and communication technologies** can supplement the game of averages. These methods and technologies share the following characteristics:

- Allow rapid movement within and across content, depending on the learners' success at any given time.

- Allow students the flexibility to proceed at their own pace and level of difficulty.
- Provide students immediate feedback as to the accuracy of their responses.
- Gradually shift the responsibility for learning from teacher to student.

Before you begin your lesson plan, decide on the extent to which methods and technologies for individualizing instruction are needed by the diversity of learning needs in your classroom. The following methods describe some of your options for individualizing instruction.

Task-Ability Grouping.   You can group your class for a specified period of time by the skills required to learn the material you are presenting. For example, more able readers can read ahead and work independently on advanced exercises while you direct your lesson to the average and less able readers. You can divide lesson plans, objectives, activities, materials, and tests into two or more appropriate parts, when learners exhibit noticeable strengths and weaknesses that cannot be bridged in a single lesson. The intent is to group learners homogeneously by learning skills relevant to a specific task or lesson, after which, you should consider regrouping.

Learning Centers.   Students tend to learn better when solving real-life problems. As a result, many schools are working to reorganize curriculum to support real-world problem solving and application (Boyer, 1993). One way to promote real-world problem solving and help individual learners apply what they have learned is through the

Learning centers containing media, supplemental resources, demonstration materials, and exercises can help individualize a lesson for those who may lack the prerequisite knowledge or skills required at the beginning of the lesson. The use of learning centers should be indicated in the lesson plan whenever applicable.

use of a learning center. Learning centers can individualize a lesson by providing resources for review and practice for those who may lack task-relevant prior knowledge or skills. When a learning center can contain media, supplemental resources, and/or practice exercises directly related to applying your lesson content, include it as an integral part of your lesson plan.

Review and Follow-Up Materials.   Some of your lessons will need to stimulate the recall of task-relevant prior knowledge. An oral summary, together with a supplementary handout on which individual learners may look up the required information, can bring some students to the required level while not boring others. The key to this procedure is to carefully prepare a *summary and review sheet* covering the critically needed prerequisite knowledge for the day's lesson. This lets you limit your review to the essentials and requires the least amount of time.

Instructional Games and Simulations.   Students who need an alternative or supplementary means of attaining your classroom objectives can use games and simulations either cooperatively or independently. Lessons may begin with whole-class instruction and, depending on interests and abilities, some students can be directed to instructional games and simulations to receive hands-on experiences that may remediate or enrich skills taught during full-class instruction (e.g., simulations across grade levels, see Grabe and Grabe, 1996; K. Jones, 1995; and Wood, 1992). Textbook publishers are increasingly providing computer simulations and practice-based instruction that teach and reteach basic skills relevant to your curriculum guide. Some of these curriculum supplements can be used by learners in cooperative groups.

Programmed Instruction.   Programmed instruction refers to written instructional materials that students work with by themselves at their own level and at their own pace. Programmed instruction materials typically break skills down into small subskills, such as might be identified in a learning hierarchy, through which students work in small steps. Questions and prompts along the way actively engage learners in formulating responses to which they are given immediate knowledge of whether they are correct, usually directly beneath or near the question or prompt. Programmed instruction has not been found to be more effective than more conventional methods, when it has been used as the sole source of new instruction (Bangert, Kulik, & Kulik, 1983; Slavin, 1993). However, when self-instructional materials have covered more familiar content and learners work in mixed ability learning teams in which teammates help each other (called Team Assisted Individualization), programmed materials have been effective in increasing achievement of all ability levels (Slavin, 1993).

Tutoring.   During **peer tutoring,** one student teaches another at the same grade and age level. During **cross-age tutoring,** the tutor is several years and grade levels above the learner receiving the instruction. Cross-age tutoring, generally, has been more effective than peer tutoring, owing to the fact that older students are more likely to be familiar with the material and are more likely to be respected as role models (Devin-Sheehan, Feldman, & Allen, 1976). Cross-age tutors should be separated by two or three grades. As with programmed instruction, tutoring has been most successful as an adjunct to regular instruction, usually in the form of providing greater amounts of instructional practice than could be provided in a whole-class or group setting. Tutoring has been most successful when tutors have been trained and given explicit instruction on how to tutor.

Computer-Assisted Instruction.   Computer-assisted instruction (CAI) provides many of the same practice opportunities of programmed instruction and tutors. CAI programs are now available at many different grade levels and content areas to give students practice, assess understanding, and provide remediation, if needed. The advantage of CAI over written programmed materials and tutors is that CAI programs can quickly assess the accuracy of student responses to practice activities and can change the sequence and difficulty of the activities to correspond with the learners' current level of understanding. In this manner, practice can be tailored to individual learners, depending on how well they respond at a certain level of difficulty. Students can spend more time on a particular topic or skill, or the program can return to an earlier sequence of instruction to review or reteach prerequisite learning. CAI also has the capability of providing color pictures, charts, and diagrams, which can motivate learners and enhance the authenticity of the practice experience. Most CAI is now presented to learners on personal computers in the classroom with software developed by publishers for the various grades and content areas in which instruction is being given. As with other individualized learning methods, CAI has been found most effective when providing practice opportunities for content already taught (Atkinson, 1984; Kulik & Kulik, 1984).

Interactive Videodiscs and CD-ROM.   Interactive videodiscs—or laser discs—are similar to the compact discs used for recording music. CD-ROM (compact disc—read-only memory) discs are similar to videodiscs but are smaller and can store more information. With their smaller size and greater information storage capacity, interactive videodiscs and CD-ROM share the same advantages over either written or CAI material. These new laser technologies can present to the learner *any combination* of text, diagrams, slides, maps, films, and animations on demand, thereby greatly increasing the flexibility of the recorded content over traditional programmed instruction. They can also hold different sound tracks, for example, one in English and another in Spanish. The learner can freeze frames indefinitely and locate any frame or sequence of frames on the disc almost instantaneously. And, unlike written texts or computer software (diskettes), they are sealed under a protective plastic surface through which light passes, making them nearly indestructible.

Because of these characteristics, interactive videodiscs and CD-ROM technology are particularly suited to simulating and modeling higher-order thinking skills and real-life experiences—such as laboratory experiments, physical motion, and even noises and sounds, which can make learning come alive. Interactive videodisc and CD-ROM technology therefore is quickly becoming the preferred medium for providing **interactive individualized practice activities.**

Fiber Optics/Telecommunications.   Fiber optics/telecommunications technology offers the most opportunities to stimulate the senses through multimedia, making the learning environment more fluid and personalized. Often referred to as the **living curriculum,** the combination of laser technology and telecommunications has many of the same features of interactive videodisc technology with the added advantage that the subject matter being studied no longer must reside on a videodisc inside a PC. Students may acquire information nearly instantaneously from communication superhighways, which can give the individual learner rapid access to human and textual resources across schools, geographical locations, and the world.

With the aid of a computer, learners create their own living curriculum with which to practice and apply the content learned. By selecting information networks and pathways that increasingly bring authentic detail and professional expertise to learners, responsibility for retaining and applying content passes gradually from the teacher to learners and to the world outside the classroom, encouraging cooperative ventures with other students, professionals, and resources. Once established, these information pathways provide students with many opportunities, among which are the following:

- Search beyond their local libraries; for example, browse through holdings on early flight in the Library of Congress, visually take a tour of a space station circling in space, or ask questions of a curator at the Air and Space Museum via electronic mail.
- Become more specialized and focused on current issues; for example, query a database being compiled by *The New York Times* on a fast-breaking story, scan a recent index of *Scientific American* for latest advances on gene splicing, or communicate via electronic mail with a researcher stationed in Antarctica.
- Cooperate with other learners at a distance to create class newspapers; for example, team up with students in another school, state, or nation to share news of mutual interest on acid rain, deforestation, or the global economy.
- Work with cross-age mentors outside their own school; for example, to explore connections between academic work and job opportunities or to see how principles and concepts are used at more advanced levels, such as in subsequent courses, in the workplace, or in different community contexts.

These methods and communication technologies are only some of the ways your lesson plans can provide for diverse learning needs among your students.

EVENTS OF INSTRUCTION

After you have determined where to start the lesson and how to provide for diverse learning needs, you are ready to start planning the lesson. At this time, you will specify the key events that occur during the lesson—and for which you are responsible.

Figure 4.11　Two related perspectives on events of instruction.

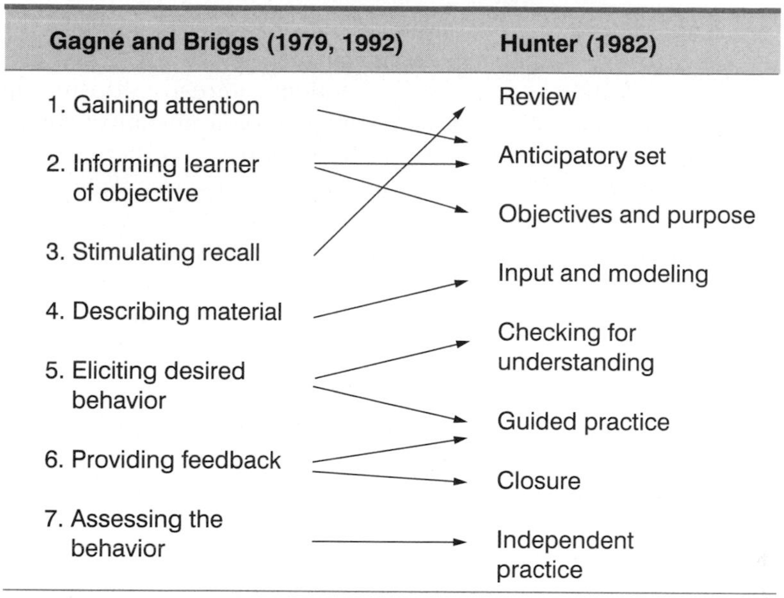

Gagné and Briggs (1979, 1992)	Hunter (1982)
1. Gaining attention	Review
2. Informing learner of objective	Anticipatory set
	Objectives and purpose
3. Stimulating recall	
4. Describing material	Input and modeling
5. Eliciting desired behavior	Checking for understanding
	Guided practice
6. Providing feedback	Closure
7. Assessing the behavior	Independent practice

By placing the responsibility on you for providing these events, we distinguish between teaching and learning. *Learning* refers to the internal events that go on inside your learners' heads. *Teaching* is the sum of the instructional activities you provide to influence what goes on in your learners' heads.

The sequence of steps you follow in lesson planning assumes that the instructional events you plan will influence learning. It is not unusual for teaching to be unrelated to learning, as when teachers teach and students listen, but nothing sinks in. The process of getting instructional events to sink in is one of planning instruction that fosters a close relationship between the external events of instruction and the internal events of learning, *actively engaging your learners in the learning process.*

You can achieve this tightly knit relationship between teaching and learning by considering seven instructional events suggested by R. Gagné and Briggs (1979, 1992).* These steps include the most relevant parts of other models of lesson preparation. For example, Hunter (1982) proposes a sequence of events, called the Mastery Learning Program, which is related to those of Gagné and Briggs (see Figure 4.11). Although not all of the events in either model are applicable to every lesson, they provide a basis—or menu—from which you can formulate many different lesson plans. Let's consider the types of instructional activity that each event entails and how you can relate them to the internal processes of learning.

---

* These steps also appear in slightly expanded form in R. Gagné and Briggs (1992).

1. Gaining Attention

Without your students' attention, little of your lesson will be heard, let alone actively engage your students in the learning process. Thus, each lesson plan begins with an instructional event to engage student interest, curiosity, and attention. In some classes this will mean raising their attention from almost complete disengagement to where their vision and hearing are receptive. In other classes this may mean raising their attention from an already receptive mode to a higher level of curiosity, interest, and attention. The intensity of your attention-gaining event will depend on the starting point of your learners. A fifth-period class that meets after lunch may require a more dramatic attention-getting event than will an eager first-period class. You will need to find the right event for gaining your students' attention.

One of the most common attention-gaining devices is to arouse curiosity. Often this can be accomplished by asking questions:

- Have you ever wondered how we got the word *horsepower*? Who would like to guess? (from a lesson on energy)
- Can anyone think of a popular automobile with the name of a Greek god? (from an introductory lesson on mythology)
- Have you ever wondered how some creatures can live both in the water and on land? (from a lesson on amphibious animals)

These questions, called *openers,* are designed not to have any single correct answer or even to accurately reflect the fine details of what is to follow. Instead they *amuse, stimulate, or even bewilder* students so that they become receptive to the content and questions that follow. Following are other thought-provoking openers:

- Why do some scientists think that traveling to the planets will make the space traveler younger? (from a lesson in physics)
- Why do we have the word i-t-s and another word i-t-apostrophe-s? (from a lesson in punctuation)
- Why is the dollar worth more today in Mexico than in Switzerland? (from a lesson in economics)
- Why do you think some eloquent lawyers become disliked by the juries they speak to? (from a lesson in public speaking)

Another useful technique for gaining students' attention is to present the following:

- An apparent *contradiction:*
  - Why do you think the Greek empire collapsed when it was at its strongest?
- Or a seeming *inconsistency* in real life:
  - Why do some lower forms of animal life live longer than human beings?
- Or something that at first appears to be *illogical:*
  - Why must something go backward every time something else goes forward?

For example, introducing a lesson in signed numbers by informing your learners that the multiplication of two negative numbers always results in a positive product may puzzle them, but it can arouse their curiosity about how two negatives could result in something positive. You could continue by explaining the mathematical rules behind this apparent contradiction.

Diagrams, pictures, illustrations, scale models, and films are other attention-getting aids. Use these devices to appeal to your learners' sense of vision while your oral presentation appeals to their sense of hearing. Graphics or visuals are particularly effective openers with students who are known to be more oriented and responsive to visual than auditory presentations. A visual opener can include samples of materials for the day's lesson so that students can touch them before the lesson begins. A visual opener also can show equipment you will use during the lesson (e.g., scales, meters).

2. Informing Learners of the Objective

Just because your learners have been turned on with some attention-getting device does not mean they will be tuned to the wavelength at which you present the lesson. Now you need to tell them the channel on which your lesson is being transmitted. The most effective way to focus your learners' receptivity is to inform them of the behavioral outcome they will be expected to attain by the end of the lesson. You can do this by telling them early in the lesson or unit how they will be examined or expected to show competence. For example, such expectations might be expressed in the following ways:

- Remember the four definitions of *power* that will be presented (science).
- Be able to express ownership orally in a sentence to the class (English).
- Identify correctly a mystery specimen of lower animal life using the microscope (life science).
- State your true feelings about laws dealing with the death penalty (social studies).

Such statements allow learners to know when they have attained the expected level of behavior and to become selective in how to use and remember the lesson information. If your students know they will be expected to recall four definitions of power at the end of your lesson on energy, then they know to focus their search, retrieval, and retention processes *during the lesson* on the definitions or categories of power you present.

Informing learners of your objective helps them organize their thinking in advance of the lesson by providing mental hooks on which to hang the key points. This activates the learning process and focuses your learners on obtaining the required behavioral outcome.

The key to the success of this instructional event is to communicate your objective clearly. Therefore, choose your words with your learners' vocabulary and language level in mind, and record what you tell them as a reminder in this second part of your lesson plan. The best way to communicate your objective is to provide examples of tasks that you expect your students to be able to perform after the lesson. This effectively translates the action verb associated with a level of behavioral complexity into some ways this behavior might be measured on tests, in class discussions, and in question-and-answer sessions.

For example, you might write on the blackboard the following examples of expected behavior at the beginning of a unit on lower forms of animal life, and then checkmark the ones that most apply at the start of each day's lesson:

__x__	Define an amoeba.
__x__	Draw the cellular structure of an amoeba.
_____	Explain the reproduction cycle of an amoeba.
_____	Using a microscope, properly distinguish an amoeba from other single-celled animals.

Notice that these behavioral outcomes range from recounting a fact to making decisions and judgments in a real biological environment. Without knowing in advance at which of these levels they are expected to perform, your learners will have no way of selecting and focusing their attention on those parts of the instruction leading to the desired behavior. This is not to say that they should ignore other aspects of the presentation, but students can now see the other aspects as tools or means for gaining the highest level of behavior required and not as ends in themselves.

3. Stimulating Recall of Prerequisite Learning

Before you can proceed with the new lesson content, one final preliminary instructional event is needed. Because learning cannot occur in a vacuum, the necessary task-relevant prior information must be retrieved and made ready for use. This calls for some method of reviewing, summarizing, restating, or otherwise stimulating the key concepts acquired in previous lessons. This information is instrumental for achieving the level of behavioral complexity intended in the present lesson.

For example, if your goal is to have learners use a microscope to properly distinguish an amoeba from other single-celled animals, it is clear that some previously acquired facts, concepts, and skills are relevant to this new task. Definitions of single-celled animals, unique characteristics of an amoeba that make it distinguishable from other one-celled animals, and skill in using the microscope are among the task-relevant prior knowledge that will influence your learners' attainment of this outcome.

Helping students retrieve earlier information requires condensing the key aspects into brief, easily understood form. Obviously, it is not practical to summarize all of it in a few minutes. You need to use thought-provoking and stimulating techniques to focus on sizable amounts of prior learning, but without reviewing all the content that was previously covered or that is needed for the new learning. Questions can help your students recall the most significant and memorable parts of earlier lessons:

- Do you remember why Johnny couldn't see the amoeba in the microscope? (it was on low magnification instead of high)
- Do you remember Betty Jo's humorous attempt to relate the reproduction cycle of an amoeba to that of human beings? (she had equated cell division with waking up one morning to find a new baby in the family)

Before the actual presentation of new content begins, the necessary task-relevant prior information must be retrieved and made ready for use. This can be accomplished by reviewing, summarizing, and restating, stimulating into action the key concepts acquired in previous lessons.

- Do you remember the three-color picture Bobby drew of the cellular structure of an amoeba? (everyone had commented on how lifelike the picture was)

Such questions help students retrieve task-relevant prior learning—not by summarizing that learning, but by tapping into a single *mental image* that recalls that learning. Once the image has been retrieved, students can turn it on and off at will to search for details that may be nestled within it, achieving still greater recall. Describing how to stimulate the recall of prerequisite learning, then, is the third entry in your lesson plan.

4. Presenting the Stimulus Material

Presenting the stimulus material will be the heart of your lesson plan. At first glance, this component may seem to require little explanation, but several important considerations for completing it often go unnoticed. These pertain to the authenticity, selectivity, and variety of your lesson presentation. Let's look closely at each of these.

Authenticity.   To teach a behavior that is authentic, your lesson must present content in a way in which it will be used by your learners on performance tests, in subsequent grades, and on the job. If your goal is to teach learners to use a microscope to identify single-celled animals, then teaching them to label the parts of a microscope would not be authentic. Although naming the parts may be a prerequisite skill and an important objective of an earlier lesson, it would not be sufficient to attaining the desired goal of this lesson. In other words, how you use a behavior in daily life must always be how you teach a behavior for it to be authentic.

You can make the behaviors you teach more authentic by changing the *irrelevant* aspects of what you are teaching as often as possible, and in as many different ways as possible, so that students learn which dimensions are irrelevant. This prevents learning an objective under only one condition but not under others that may be encountered in subsequent lessons, grades, and courses. Following are examples of changing the irrelevant aspects of a learning stimulus:

- In math, show both stacked format and line format:

$$\begin{array}{r} -2 \\ +5 \\ \hline \end{array} \text{ as well as } -2 + 5 =$$

- Introduce learners to examples of proper punctuation by using popular magazines and newspapers as well as the text and workbook (English or a foreign language).
- Show how the laws of electricity apply to lightning during a thunderstorm as well as to electrical circuitry in the laboratory (science).
- Relate rules of social behavior found among humans to those often found among animals (social studies).
- Compare the central processing unit in a microcomputer to the executive processes in the human brain (computer science).
- Show how the reasons for a particular war also can be applied to other conflicts hundreds of years earlier (history).

In each of these examples, the lesson designer is changing the irrelevant dimensions of the objective by applying key lesson ideas in different contexts. As a result, learners are more likely (1) to focus on correct mathematical operations and not the format of the problem, (2) to notice improper punctuation when it appears in a popular publication, (3) to understand the universality of physical laws governing electricity, (4) to not think that social behavior is a uniquely human phenomenon, (5) to not confuse the wonders of data processing with the hardware and equipment that only sometimes are needed to perform it, and (6) to understand that some reasons for conflict, war, and hostility are general as well as specific.

Selectivity.   A second consideration during this stage of lesson preparation is emphasizing the content most important to your lesson. Not everything in a chapter, workbook, film, lecture, or on the chalkboard will be of equal importance to the day's objective. Consequently, highlighting key aspects of the text and workbook at the *beginning* of the lesson will help students selectively review and retain the main points of your lesson. For example, focusing your learners' attention on the "six concepts on the bottom of page 50" or the "tables and figures at the end of Chapter 3" can help your learners place the day's lesson in the context of their curriculum and provide an anchor for future reference.

You will also want to highlight content *during* your lesson. Examples of such highlighting include verbally emphasizing the importance of certain events; telling students what to look for in a film (even stopping it to reinforce an idea, if need be); emphasizing key words on the chalkboard with underlining, circling, or color; and using verbal markers ("This is important"; "Notice the relevance of this"; "You'll need this information later"). These and other methods for selectively emphasizing key parts of your lesson will be taken up in later chapters, but remember to consider them at this stage of your lesson plan.

Variety.   A key behavior of the effective teacher is instructional variety. Gaining students' attention at the start of the lesson is one thing, but keeping their attention is quite another. Variety in the modalities of instruction (e.g., visual, oral, tactile) and instructional activity (large-group lecture, question and answer, small-group discussion) stimulates student thinking and interest. Shifting from visually dominated instruction to orally dominated instruction (or using both simultaneously) and breaking a lesson into several instructional activities (e.g., explanation followed by question and answer) are important.

Planning changes in modality and instructional activities presents the lesson in varied contexts, giving learners the opportunity to grasp material in several different ways, according to their individual learning styles. Such changes also give students the opportunity to see previously learned material used in different ways. This reinforces learned material better than simply restating it in the same mode and form. It also encourages learners to extend or expand material according to the new mode or procedure being used. For example, material learned in a lecture may be pushed to its limit in a question-and-answer period when the learner answers a question and finds out that previous understandings were partly incorrect due to the limited context in which they were learned. Quite apart from the well-known fact that instructional variety helps keep students attentive and actively engaged in the learning process, it also offers them a more memorable and conscious learning experience. Be sure to consider these and other methods of adding instructional variety to your lesson during this stage of your lesson plan.

5. Eliciting the Desired Behavior

After presentation of the stimulus material, provide your learners an opportunity to show whether they can perform the behaviors at the intended level of complexity. Learning cannot occur effectively in a passive environment—one that lacks activities to engage the learner in the learning process at moderate-to-high rates of success. Active engagement in the learning process at an appropriate level of difficulty must be a goal of every lesson, because without it little or no learning occurs.

Such engagement can be accomplished in many ways. It may even occur spontaneously as a result of getting your students' attention, informing them of the objectives, stimulating the recall of prerequisite learning, and presenting the stimulus material—but don't count on it! Active engagement, especially at an appropriate level of difficulty, is a slippery concept. If left to chance, it rarely occurs to the extent required for significant learning. While all of the instructional events presented thus far are required to actively engage your learners, they cannot guarantee engagement. Therefore, a fifth instructional event is needed; when added to a lesson plan it encourages and guides learners through a process that can be expected to produce the behavior intended.

This fifth event—eliciting the desired behavior—differs from the four preceding ones in that it seeks the individual's covert and personal engagement in the learning process. Each learner must be placed in a position of grappling in a trial-and-error fashion with summarizing, paraphrasing, applying, or solving a problem involving the lesson content. It is not important that the behavior be produced at this stage in a recognizable form, as long as the activity provided stimulates an *attempt to produce the intended behavior.* This activity encourages the learner to *organize a response* that meets the level of behavioral complexity stated when the student was informed of the objective.

The primary ways of staging this instructional event include workbooks, handouts, textbook study questions, verbal and written exercises, and questions that have students apply what was learned, if only in the privacy of their minds. The idea is to pose a classroom activity that encourages students to use the material in a nonevaluative atmosphere, as close in time as possible to presentation of new material. Sometimes such activities can be inserted throughout the lesson at the end of each new chunk of information, which also adds variety. In other instances, these activities occur near the end of presenting the new material.

Either way, the eliciting activity is brief, nonevaluative, and focused exclusively on posing a condition for which the learner must organize a response (e.g., a question, problem, or exercise). This response may be written, oral, or subvocal (students respond in their own minds). Eliciting activities can be as simple as your posing a question anywhere in a lesson, or as complex as a problem exercise completed in a workbook at lesson's end. The main attribute is that these activities be *nonevaluative,* to encourage a response unhampered by the anxiety and conservative response patterns that generally occur during testing. Rosenshine and Stevens (1986) suggest additional ways of eliciting the desired behavior:

- Prepare a large number of oral questions beforehand.
- Ask many brief questions on main points, on supplementary points, and on the process being taught. (Have students create their own questions.)
- Call on students whose hands are not raised in addition to those who volunteer.
- Ask students to summarize a rule or process in their own words.
- Have all students write their answers (on paper or the chalkboard) while you circulate.
- Have all students write their answers and check them with a neighbor (this is frequently used with older students).
- At the end of a lecture/discussion (especially with older students), write the main points on the chalkboard, and then have the class meet in groups to summarize the main points to each other.

6. Providing Feedback

The sixth instructional event is closely connected in time to the fifth event (eliciting the desired behavior). Eliciting the desired behavior promotes learning to the extent that learners come to understand the correctness of their responses. The response itself must be an individual attempt to recall, summarize, paraphrase, apply, or problem solve, but the feedback that immediately follows can be directed to the entire class. For example, you can anonymously report to the class an individual's correct answer or hold up several students' answers for comparison.

However, as stated, an eliciting activity's main attribute is that it is *nonevaluative.* At this stage of the learning process, it is important to respond to a wrong answer encouragingly, to maintain the nonevaluative flavor of the eliciting activity. Responses such as "That's a good try," "That's not quite what I'm looking for this time," or "Keep thinking" can switch the focus to more useful responses without penalizing students for responding.

Ways of confirming a correct response are to read aloud the correct answers from a workbook, or to provide a handout with the correct answers, or to provide a copy of the exercise with correct answers penciled in. You could use a transparency to pose the eliciting activity and then record volunteered answers. If students are working silently at their seats, you can walk about the room, using a simple nod and smile to indicate the correctness of an individual performance or to encourage the revision of a wrong response. This part of the lesson plan, then, should include the means by which feedback will be given learners about their responses. These and additional ways of providing feedback to individual students, small groups, and the entire class are summarized in Table 4.2.

7. Assessing the Behavior

You do not have to provide all your eliciting activities and feedback within a single instructional period. There are other ways to engage your students in the learning

Table 4.2   Some methods of providing feedback.

Individual Students	Small Groups	Class
Nod while walking past	Sit with group and discuss answers	Place answers on a transparency
Point to correct answer in workbook or text	Have one group critique another group's answers	Provide answers on a handout
Show student the answer key	Give each group the answer key when finished	Read answers aloud
Place check alongside incorrect answers	Assign one group member the task of checking the answers of other group members	Place answers on the chalkboard
Have students grade each others' papers by using the text, or assign references as a guide		Have selected students read their answers aloud
		Have students grade each others' papers as you give answers

process, to organize a response, and to create a product. These include tests and home-work problems that are returned the next day, or extended assignments that are returned days or weeks later (essays, research papers, and portfolios). However, tests, essays, term papers, and projects result from several individual lessons and therefore are considerably larger than the elicitation activities discussed thus far. These larger activi-ties are particularly valuable for eliciting more complex behavior than could be expected at the end of any single lesson and for evaluating how well behaviors are performed.

This final instructional event specifies what activity you will use to evaluate the behavior. As we have seen, eliciting activities can be immediate or delayed (an oral ques-tion vs. a research paper) and evaluative or nonevaluative. The fifth event described an immediate and nonevaluative eliciting activity. But for this instructional event—assessing the behavior—you will describe a *delayed* eliciting activity that is primarily *evaluative*.

Evaluative eliciting activities such as tests, research papers, graded homework and classroom performances, and student portfolios can be disadvantageous at ear-lier stages of learning because they limit risk-taking—or exploratory—behavior and their feedback lacks immediacy. Both of these factors can be counterproductive to learning when the instructional goal is to get learners to respond for the first time. Consequently, do not use a delayed eliciting activity to the exclusion of immediate and nonevaluative eliciting activities early in the lesson.

The means for completing this event can include the following:

Tests and quizzes	Oral presentations
Homework exercises	Extended essays
In-class workbook assignments	Research papers
Performance evaluations	Independent practice
Lab assignments	Portfolios

EXAMPLE LESSON PLANS

We are now ready to place these seven instructional events into a brief but effective lesson plan. To be both practical and effective, lesson plans must be short and yet provide all the ingredients needed to deliver the lesson. Following are some example plans on various subjects and grade levels that show how easy lesson planning can be when the task is organized by these seven instructional events. Let's review each of them with some examples.

Example Lesson Plan: Reading Skills

Unit Title: Reading: Word Attack Skills (Vertically Planned Unit)

Lesson Title: Sound Discrimination, Letters of the Alphabet—Lesson 2.1

The preceding titles indicate the general content of the lesson and its placement in a unit on word attack skills. The lesson identifier, 2.1, indicates that this lesson is the first one in Unit 2. It would appear on the graphic unit plan, as indicated in Figure 4.12.

Figure 4.12 The relationship of lessons, units, and a course or domain.

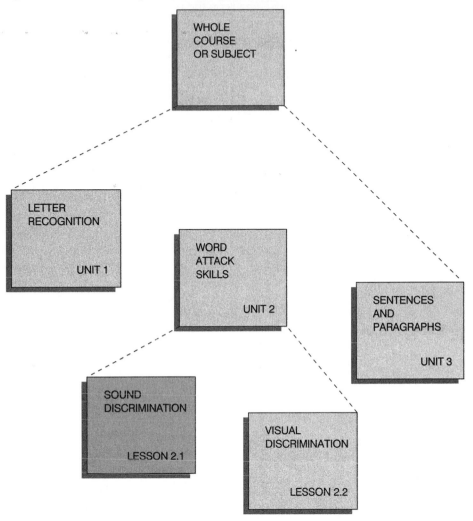

Next appears the elaboration of each of the seven instructional events for delivering this lesson to students:

1 Gaining attention Play an audiotape of a voice articulating the sounds.

This instructional event gains student attention and focuses them on what is to be presented. Whatever device or procedure you use should not only gain their attention but also motivate their continued concentration well into the lesson. Keep in mind that students, especially young ones, have trouble picking up subtle transitions in classroom activities. Often their attention is steadfastly on what has immediately preceded the lesson, and they are reluctant to change focus unless something new, interesting, or exciting is on the horizon.

Visual or auditory stimuli often are effective as attention-getters, because their ability to penetrate the senses exceeds that of more neutral stimuli like written words, verbal expressions, or pronouncements. Changing sensory modalities from listening to looking (or vice versa) often provides the incentive necessary to more selectively perceive and receive the message about to be communicated.

2 Informing the learner of the objective   When the tape is finished, indicate that at the end of the lesson students will be expected to repeat the vowel sounds out loud, independently of the tape.

This instructional event translates the behavioral objective for the lesson into a form that is meaningful to students. In this example, the transfer of information from one modality (listening) to another (speaking) is being sought, indicating that the objective for this lesson is written at the comprehension level of the cognitive domain. Your attention-getting device should be chosen to lead into the objective for the lesson. Simply clapping one's hands to gain attention, followed by the objective, would not be as effective as having the objective actually *contained within* the attention-getting procedure.

In this example, the audiotape was directly related to the lesson's content, allowing these two instructional events to work together to produce a unified theme, enhancing the learners' attention. Other simple but effective attention getters that easily can be made to reflect the lesson objective are a picture or chart, a question on the chalkboard, or a demonstration derived directly from lesson content.

3 Stimulating recall of prerequisite learning   Show how each vowel sound is produced by the correct positioning of the mouth and lips.

Identifying and successfully communicating task-relevant prior knowledge to students is critical to attaining the lesson objective. Unless you paraphrase, summarize, or otherwise review this information, at least some students will be unable to comprehend the information to be conveyed. Among the most frequent reasons that learners are unable to attain lesson outcomes is that they lack the needed skills and understandings of previously taught lessons necessary for subsequent learning to occur.

Prerequisite content must be recalled or stimulated into action for it to play a meaningful role in acquiring new learning. Most lessons require some previous facts, understandings, or skills, and these should be recalled and identified at this step of the lesson plan. You can achieve this by touching on the high points of this prior learning.

4 Presenting the stimulus material   Say each vowel sound, and then have the class repeat it twice, pointing to a chart of the position of the mouth and lips during the articulation of each vowel sound. Do the most commonly used vowels first.

You may feel that this is the heart of the lesson. You are partly right, except that there are six other hearts, each of which could entail as much effort in planning and instructional time as this event does. Beginning teachers tend to pack their lessons almost entirely with new stimulus material. They devote far less effort to gaining attention, to informing the learner of the objective, to recalling prerequisite learning, and to other instructional events that must follow the presentation of new material.

Obviously, the presentation of new material is indispensable, but it need not always encompass most (or even a large portion) of the lesson. The result of devoting a large portion of the lesson to new material, exclusive of the other instructional events, is that the lesson is likely to present content in pieces too big for learners to grasp. This often results in considerable reteaching during subsequent lessons and ultimately less content coverage at the end of a unit.

Although the presentation of new stimulus material is an important part of most lessons, it does not always have to compose the majority of instructional time. Just as the first three instructional events must come before the presentation of new material for this material to be meaningful, the next three instructional events will make clear that this new stimulus material must itself be a stimulus for something more to come.

5 Eliciting the desired behavior Have students silently practice forming correct mouth and lip positions for each vowel sound, following the pictures in their workbooks.

For this instructional event, the learner is given guidance in how to perform the behavior and an opportunity to practice it—two activities that must go hand in hand if learning is to occur. Eliciting the desired behavior for the first time without providing an opportunity to practice it diminishes the effect of this instructional event. The stimulus material described in the previous event should be presented in a form that affords the learner the opportunity to use the behavior repeatedly in a nonthreatening, nonevaluative environment. Grading or performance evaluations, therefore, should not be part of the performance being elicited in this instructional event, where spontaneity, freedom to make mistakes, and an opportunity for immediate feedback are the goals.

6 Providing feedback Randomly choose students to recite the vowel sounds; correct their errors to demonstrate to the class the desired sound.

Feedback should be given immediately after the eliciting activity. As short a time as possible between performance and feedback is one of the most essential elements of learning: the closer the correspondence between a performance and feedback, the more quickly learning will occur.

Your feedback can be part of the eliciting activity, or it can be a separate activity. In the previous example (the fifth instructional event), feedback was not provided and learners had no way of knowing the correctness of their behavior (mouth and lip movements). Pictures in the text guided their behavior, but because students could not see themselves performing the movements, they couldn't tell if they performed accurately. In this case, feedback would have to follow the eliciting activity, making this instructional event essential for learning. The previous eliciting activity, however, might have included feedback if, for example, students were asked to recite aloud the vowel sounds and the teacher determined the accuracy of their utterances. The correspondence of an eliciting activity and feedback is a matter of degree, but these two events should take place as closely in time as possible.

7 Assessing the behavior   The lesson objective is assessed as part of the unit test on word attack skills and from exercises completed in the workbook.

Few lesson objectives are assessed by individual lesson tests. Amounts of content larger than that contained in a single lesson usually are necessary to make tests efficient and practical. However, it is important to indicate which unit or subunit tests cover the lesson content and what means, other than formal tests (e.g., classroom performances, projects, and portfolios), you will use to grade the behaviors.

This entry on the lesson plan will remind you to include the lesson's content on subsequent tests or to find other means of checking learners' attainment of it. Some assessment method always should be designed into a lesson plan (tests, workbook exercises, homework, handouts, worksheets, oral responses, etc.). This information provides important feedback about students' readiness for new stimulus material and possible reasons for poor performance in later lessons for which the current material is prerequisite.

Example Lesson Plan: Literature and U.S. History

Unit Title: Gold Rush (Laterally Planned Unit)

Lesson Title: Westward Journals

Subject Areas: History/Social Science, Language Arts, Art (Written by Cynthia Kiel)

The preceding titles indicate the general content of the lesson and the unit of which it is a part. This lesson appears on an interdisciplinary unit plan as a lesson in reading or literature titled, "Westward Journals," as shown in Figure 4.13.

1 Gaining attention   Display items or pictures of items that pioneers may have brought with them on their trip West. These may include a diary, bonnet, old tools, *Bible*, and cast-iron skillet.

2 Informing the learner of the objective   Students will be expected to choose one of the routes to California and write a diary entry from the 1840s detailing a day on the trip. Students may be creative in their presentation of this product, choosing to design a diary, journal, or perhaps write their entry on a construction paper ship or wagon.

3 Stimulating recall of prerequisite learning   As a class, brainstorm on a large chart the main events learned about the trip West.

4 Presenting the stimulus material   Read excerpts from *The Way West, Journal of a Pioneer Woman,* by Amelia Stewart Knight, and *Joshua's Westward Journal,* by Joan Anderson. Lead a discussion of how each author details and summarizes events on the journey.

Figure 4.13 Visual representation of the interdisciplinary unit theme "Gold Rush," which includes the lesson "Westward Journals."

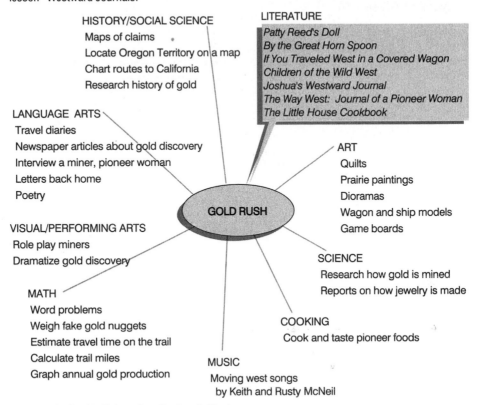

HISTORY/SOCIAL SCIENCE
Maps of claims
Locate Oregon Territory on a map
Chart routes to California
Research history of gold

LITERATURE
Patty Reed's Doll
By the Great Horn Spoon
If You Traveled West in a Covered Wagon
Children of the Wild West
Joshua's Westward Journal
The Way West: Journal of a Pioneer Woman
The Little House Cookbook

LANGUAGE ARTS
Travel diaries
Newspaper articles about gold discovery
Interview a miner, pioneer woman
Letters back home
Poetry

ART
Quilts
Prairie paintings
Dioramas
Wagon and ship models
Game boards

VISUAL/PERFORMING ARTS
Role play miners
Dramatize gold discovery

GOLD RUSH

SCIENCE
Research how gold is mined
Reports on how jewelry is made

MATH
Word problems
Weigh fake gold nuggets
Estimate travel time on the trail
Calculate trail miles
Graph annual gold production

COOKING
Cook and taste pioneer foods

MUSIC
Moving west songs
by Keith and Rusty McNeil

Developed by Cynthia Kiel, teacher, Glendora, California.

5 **Eliciting the desired behavior** Ask the students to pretend they are a child in a wagon train or aboard a ship on the trip West in the 1840s. Tell them to write a journal or diary about their experiences. Provide a variety of writing paper and construction paper, and invite creativity in designing their journal.

6 **Providing feedback** While the students are writing, periodically ask individuals to share an excerpt from their entries. Point out how the students are including items listed on the brainstorm chart made at the beginning of the lesson.

7 **Assessing the behavior** Design a rubric to grade the journal entries. Criteria may include adherence to factual events in 1840, descriptive language, and creativity.

Table 4.3 presents the *approximate* amount of time during a 50-minute class period that you might devote to each instructional event. Some periods will differ considerably

Table 4.3 Approximate distribution of instructional time across instructional events for a hypothetical 50-minute lesson.

Instructional Event	Ranges in Minutes	Ranges in Percentages of Time
Gaining attention	1–5	2–10
Informing learners of the objective	1–3	2–6
Stimulating recall of prerequisite learning	5–10	10–20
Presenting the stimulus material	10–20	20–40
Eliciting the desired behavior	10–20	20–40
Providing feedback	5–10	10–20
Assessing behavior	0–10	0–20

from these amounts of time, such as when the entire lesson is devoted to a review or when recall of prior learning and assessing behavior is not relevant to the day's lesson. Keep in mind that experience, familiarity with content, and common sense always are your best guides for the percentage of time to devote to each instructional event.

From Table 4.3 it is apparent that when you emphasize one instructional event, another must be deemphasized; tradeoffs always are necessary. Although every teacher would like to have more (sometimes less) time than allotted for an instructional period, decisions must be made that fit a lesson into the available time. Table 4.3 indicates some of the ways this might be done when planning a typical lesson.

The following lesson plans illustrate the seven instructional events in other content areas and grade levels.

Example Lesson Plan: United States History

Unit Title: United States History (Early Beginning Through Reconstruction)

Lesson Title: Causes of the Civil War—Lesson 2.3

1 Gaining attention   Show the following list of wars on a transparency:

French and Indian War, 1754–1769
Revolutionary War, 1775–1781
Civil War, 1861–1865
World War I, 1914–1918
World War II, 1941–1945
Korean War, 1950–1953
Vietnam War, 1965–1975

2 Informing the learner of the objective   Learners will be expected to know the causes of the Civil War and to show that those causes also can apply to at least one of the other wars listed on the transparency.

3 Stimulating recall of prerequisite learning   Briefly review the causes of both the French and Indian War and the Revolutionary War as covered in Lessons 2.1 and 2.2

4 Presenting the stimulus material   (a) Summarize major events leading to the Civil War: rise of sectionalism, labor-intensive economy, and lack of diversification. (b) Identify significant individuals during the Civil War and their roles: Lincoln, Lee, Davis, and Grant. (c) Describe four general causes of war and explain which are most relevant to the Civil War: economic (to profit), political (to control), social (to influence), and military (to protect).

5 Eliciting the desired behavior   Ask the class to identify which of the four causes is most relevant to the major events leading up to the Civil War.

6 Providing feedback   Ask for student answers and indicate plausibility of the volunteered responses.

7 Assessing the behavior   Assign as homework a one-page essay assessing the relative importance of the four causes for one of the wars listed on the transparency.

Example Lesson Plan: Language Arts

Unit Title   Writing Concepts and Skills

Lesson Title   Descriptive, Narrative, and Expository Paragraphs—Lesson 1.3

1 Gaining attention   Read examples of short descriptive, narrative, and expository paragraphs from Sunday's newspaper.

2 Informing the learner of the objective   Students will be able to discriminate among descriptive, narrative, and expository paragraphs from a list of written examples in the popular press.

3 Stimulating recall of prerequisite learning   Review the meanings of the words *description, narration,* and *exposition* as they are used in everyday language.

4 Presenting the stimulus material   Using a headline from Sunday's newspaper, give examples of how this story could be reported by description, narration, and exposition.

5 Eliciting the desired behavior   Take another front-page story from Sunday's newspaper, and ask students to write a paragraph relating the story in descriptive, narrative, or expository form, whichever they prefer.

6 Providing feedback   Call on individuals to read their paragraphs, checking each against the type of paragraph he or she intended to write.

7 Assessing the behavior   Provide multiple-choice examples of each form of writing on the unit test. Have students revise their paragraphs as needed and turn in as homework the following day.

Example Lesson Plan: Mathematics

Unit Title: Consumer Mathematics

Lesson Title: Operations and Properties of Ratio, Proportion, and Percentage—Lesson 3.3

1 Gaining attention   Display so all can see: (a) can of diet soft drink, (b) one-pound package of spaghetti, (c) box of breakfast cereal.

2 Informing the learner of the objective   Learners will be expected to know how to determine ratios, proportions, and percentages from the information on labels of popular food products.

3 Stimulating recall of prerequisite learning   Review the definitions of *ratio, proportion,* and *percentage* from the math workbook.

4 Presenting the stimulus material   Place the information from the soft-drink label on a transparency, and ask students to identify the percentage of sodium.

5 Eliciting the desired behavior   Write on the board the list of ingredients given on the cereal box; ask students to determine (1) the percentage of daily allowance of protein, (2) the proportion of daily allowance of vitamin A, and (3) the ratio of protein to carbohydrates.

6 Providing feedback   Using the information on the board, point to the correct answer for behaviors 1 and 2 and show how to find the appropriate numerator and denominator for behavior 3 (in step 5) from the ingredients on the label.

7 Assessing the behavior   Provide on the weekly quiz five problems covering ratios (two problems), proportions (two problems), and percentages (one problem) using labels from other consumer products.

Example Lesson Plan: Science

Unit Title: Manipulative Laboratory Skills

Lesson Title: Use of the Microscope—Lesson 1.1

1 Gaining attention   Show the first 5 minutes of a film about making a lens.

2 **Informing the learner of the objective**   Learners will be expected to be able to focus correctly a specimen of one-celled animal life, using both high and low magnification.

3 **Stimulating recall of prerequisite learning**   Review procedures for selecting a slide from the one-celled specimen collection and mounting it on the specimen tray of the microscope.

4 **Presenting the stimulus material**   Using a student in front of the class as a demonstrator, help position his or her posture and hands on the microscope. Gently bend body and hands until the correct posture results. Demonstrate the position of the eyes, and show clockwise and counterclockwise rotation of low and then high magnification adjustment.

5 **Eliciting the desired behavior**   Have each student obtain a specimen slide, mount it on a microscope, and focus on low magnification. Randomly check microscopes, correcting slide, positions, and focus as needed with student observing. Repeat for high magnification.

6 **Providing feedback**   The teacher has provided feedback in the context of the eliciting activity (step 5) to increase immediacy of the feedback. Also, refer students to the text for examples of focused and unfocused specimens.

7 **Assessing the behavior**   At the completion of the unit, the teacher will assess students during a practical lab exam requiring the correct mounting and identification of three unknown specimens using the microscope.

SUMMING UP

This chapter introduced you to unit and lesson planning. Its main points were as follows:

1. A unit of instruction may be thought of as a system; individual lessons within the unit are its component parts.
2. Four primary activities within the planning process are establishing instructional goals, identifying learner needs, and selecting and organizing content.
3. The two purposes of unit planning are (1) to convert generally stated activities and outcomes into specific objectives and lessons and (2) to provide a picture of long-term goals.
4. The concept of *hierarchy* tells us the relationship of parts to the whole (in this case, lessons to units) and the concept of *task-rel-*

evant prior knowledge tells us what must come before what in a sequence of events (lesson sequence). Systems thinking draws our attention to the relationship among parts of varying sizes to see what lessons make up what units.

5. Units can be planned vertically, emphasizing hierarchy of lesson content and task-relevant prior knowledge (sequence), or laterally, emphasizing themes that integrate bodies of knowledge across disciplines to convey relationships and patterns that bind different aspects of our world together.
6. In vertical planning, boxes illustrate areas of content, or instructional goals, at various levels of generality. Lines and arrows indicate

sequences among lessons and how outcomes of lessons build on one another to achieve a unit goal.

7. Three activities of vertical unit planning are as follows:
   • Classifying unit outcomes at a higher level of behavioral complexity than lesson outcomes by using one or more taxonomies of behavior.
   • Planning the instructional sequence so that the outcomes of previously taught lessons are instrumental in achieving the outcomes of subsequent lessons.
   • Rearranging or adding lesson content where necessary to provide task-relevant prior knowledge where needed.

8. In lateral planning, a central theme is identified, and lines or arrows are connected to it to indicate subordinate ideas for lesson content.

9. Three activities of lateral planning are the following:
   • Identify an interdisciplinary theme.
   • Integrate bodies of knowledge across disciplines.
   • Identify relationships and patterns that bind different aspects of our world together.

10. Before starting the preparation of a lesson plan, you must determine the behavioral complexity level of the lesson (e.g., knowledge, application, evaluation) and to what extent provisions for student diversity must accompany the lesson plan (e.g., time-limited ability grouping, peer tutoring, learning centers, specialized handouts, cooperative groups).

11. *Learning* refers to internal events in the heads of learners that result from external teaching events you provide. Hence, the words *teaching* and *learning* refer to two different but related sets of activities.

12. The following external events can be specified in a lesson plan:
   • Gain attention
   • Inform the learner of the objective
   • Stimulate recall of prerequisite learning
   • Present the stimulus material
   • Elicit the desired behavior
   • Provide feedback
   • Assess the behavior

13. Gaining attention involves gaining your students' interest in what you will present and getting them to switch to the appropriate modality for the coming lesson.

14. Informing learners of the objective involves informing them of the complexity of the behavior expected at the end of the lesson.

15. Stimulating recall of prerequisite learning is reviewing task-relevant prior information required by the lesson.

16. Presenting the stimulus material is delivering the desired content in a manner conducive to the modality in which it is to be received, using procedures that stimulate thought processing and maintain interest.

17. Eliciting the desired behavior gets learners to produce the intended behavior by organizing a response corresponding with the level of complexity of the stated objective.

18. Providing feedback tells the learner the accuracy of her or his elicited response in a nonthreatening, nonevaluative atmosphere.

19. Assessing the behavior evaluates the learner's performance with tests, homework, and extended assignments.

FOR DISCUSSION AND PRACTICE

Questions marked with an asterisk are answered in Appendix B. See also *Bridges: An Activity Guide and Assessment Options,* which accompanies this text.

*1. Identify the five inputs to the planning process from which the preparation of lesson plans proceeds. When would you consult each input in the design of a lesson or unit plan?

*2. How can a unit outcome be more than the sum of its individual lesson outcomes? Can you give an example using content for a specific unit in your subject matter area?

*3. Explain in your own words how the concepts of *hierarchy* and *task-relevant prior knowledge* are used in unit planning.

*4. How are the concepts of *hierarchy* and *task-relevant prior learning* related? Can you provide an example of a unit plan in which your knowledge of the hierarchy in which content is organized would help you determine task-relevant prior learning?

*5. Name the levels of behavioral complexity in each of the three domains (cognitive, affective, and psychomotor) that generally would be most suitable for a unit outcome.

*6. How are the boxes further down on a vertical unit plan different from the boxes higher up? Use the example you provided in Question 4 to illustrate your answer.

7. Vertically plan a three-lesson unit within a discipline in which the sequence of lessons is critical to achieving the outcome. Then, laterally plan a three-lesson interdisciplinary unit in which lesson sequence is unimportant. Be sure lesson outcomes for each unit reflect the unit outcome.

*8. Explain how a graphic unit plan for a vertical unit is different from a graphic unit plan for a lateral unit. In your own words, why must there be a difference?

*9. Identify some ways of providing for student diversity in the context of a lesson plan. Which do you believe will be most effective at your grade level or content area?

10. In your own words, how would you explain to another the distinction between *teaching* and *learning*? What examples might you use to illustrate the difference with respect to a learner in your classroom?

*11. Name the seven events of instruction that can be described in a lesson plan. Now, give an example of how you would implement each event for a lesson of your own choosing.

*12. Identify the instructional event(s) for which the key behavior of *instructional variety* would be most important.

*13. Identify the instructional event(s) for which the key behavior of *student success* would be most important.

*14. Identify the instructional event(s) for which the key behavior of *student engagement in the learning process* would be most important.

*15. Indicate how the instructional events of (1) providing feedback and (2) assessing behavior differ according to (a) the evaluative nature of the feedback provided and (b) the immediacy with which the feedback is given.

16. Following the form of the examples provided in this chapter, prepare a lesson plan for a topic in your major teaching area and another in your minor teaching area. Include the approximate number of minutes you expect to devote to each event out of a 50-minute class period.

5 Direct Instruction Strategies

This chapter will help you answer the following questions:

1. What is the direct instruction model?
2. How do I organize lesson content for direct instruction?
3. How can I encourage my learners to actively respond during direct instruction?
4. What are some ways of promoting the goals of direct instruction in a culturally diverse classroom?

T*he previous chapter presented seven instructional events that form the skeletal structure of a lesson plan:*

1. *Gaining attention*
2. *Informing the learner of the objective*
3. *Stimulating recall of prerequisite learning*
4. *Presenting the stimulus material*
5. *Eliciting the desired behavior*
6. *Providing feedback*
7. *Assessing the behavior*

To add flesh to this skeleton, this and subsequent chapters present different instructional strategies by which these seven events can be implemented. This chapter presents strategies for direct teaching that include explanations, examples, review, practice, and feedback in the context of a lecture-recitation format.

Have you ever wondered why some teachers are more interesting than others? This is an ageless phenomenon, well known to anyone who has spent time in school. Students cannot wait to attend the classes of some teachers but dread attending the classes of others. Interesting teachers often are described with phrases such as "is more organized," "has a better personality," and "is warmer and friendlier." Although these qualities may be present in teachers judged to be the most interesting, they are not the only reasons that a teacher can be interesting.

One of the most important factors in how interesting teachers are to their students is their use of the key behavior instructional variety. In a study of experienced and inexperienced teachers (Emmer, Evertson, & Anderson, 1980), experienced teachers who showed flexibility and variety in their instructional strategies were found to be more interesting than inexperienced teachers who had no knowledge of alternative teaching strategies.

Knowledge of a variety of instructional strategies and the flexibility to change them both within and among lessons are two of the greatest assets a teacher can have (Emmer et al., 1997). Without variety and flexibility to capture the interest and attention of students, it is unlikely that any other key behavior, however well executed, will have an effect on them. This chapter provides a variety of teaching strategies you can use to compose lesson plans and to create and maintain an atmosphere of interest and variety in your classroom using a direct instruction format.

CATEGORIES OF TEACHING AND LEARNING

Just as the carpenter, electrician, and plumber must select the proper tool for a specific task, you must select the proper instructional strategy for a learning outcome. To help determine your choice of strategies, here are two broad classifications of learning outcomes:

Type 1: Facts, rules, and action sequences

Type 2: Concepts, patterns, and abstractions

Type 1 outcomes often represent behaviors at lower levels of complexity in the cognitive, affective, and psychomotor domains. These include the knowledge, comprehension, and application levels of the cognitive domain; the awareness, responding, and valuing levels of the affective domain; and the imitation, manipulation, and precision levels of the psychomotor domain.

Type 2 outcomes, on the other hand, frequently represent behaviors at the higher levels of complexity in these domains. They include objectives at the analysis, synthesis, and evaluation levels of the cognitive domain; the organization and characterization levels of the affective domain; and the articulation and naturalization levels of the psychomotor domain. Examples of Type 1 and Type 2 outcomes are shown in Tables 5.1 and 5.2.

Table 5.1   Example Type 1 outcomes: Facts, rules, and action sequences.

Facts	Rules	Action Sequences
1. Recognize multiplication with two-digit numbers	Carrying with two-digit numbers	Multiplying to "1000"
2. Identify apostrophe "s"	Finding words with apostrophe "s"	Using apostrophe "s" in a sentence
3. Select multisyllable words from list	Pronouncing multisyllable words	Reading stories with multisyllable words
4. State chemical composition of water	Combining 2 parts hydrogen with 1 part oxygen	Writing the expression for water

Table 5.2 Example Type 2 outcomes: Concepts, patterns, and abstractions.

Concepts	Patterns	Abstractions
1. Positive and negative numbers	$-3 \, (-4) \, 11 =$ $10 \times (-6) =$	Signed numbers
2. Possessive form	Policeman's daughter Mrs. Burns's paper	Ownership
3. Vowels (v) and consonants (c)	cv order cvc order	Vowel/consonant blends
4. Element, atomic weight, and valence	H_2O	Molecular structure

These outcomes are two fairly broad distinctions and can overlap, but they are useful guides in selecting an instructional strategy to maximize learning. Some important differences between instructional goals requiring these two types of learning are shown in Table 5.3.

Notice across the left and right columns of Table 5.3 that two types of learning are being required. In the left column, Type 1 tasks require combining facts and rules at the knowledge and comprehension level into a sequence of actions that could be learned by observation, rote repetition, and practice. Students can learn the right answers by memorizing and practicing behaviors that you model.

In the right column, a quite different learning type is called for. The right answers are not so closely connected to facts, rules, or action sequences that can be memorized and practiced in some limited context. Something more is needed to help the learner go beyond the facts, rules, or sequences to create, synthesize, and ultimately identify and recognize an answer that cannot be easily modeled or memorized. The missing link involves learning an abstraction called a *concept*.

For example, to learn the *concept* of a frog involves learning the essential characteristics that make an organism a frog, as distinguished from closely similar animals (green chameleon). In other words, the learner needs to know not only the characteristics that all frogs have but also what characteristics distinguish frogs from other animals. If we classified frogs only on the characteristics of being green, having four legs, eating insects, and being amphibious, some turtles could be misidentified as frogs. Another category of knowledge must be learned that contains characteristics that separate frogs from similar animals (e.g., frogs have soft bodies, moist skin, strong hind limbs, and do not change color).

Figure 5.1 presents a diagram showing the information involved in learning the concept of *frog*. Notice that to properly classify a frog among other animals that may look like one, both *nonessential* and *essential* frog attributes need to be learned. The nonessential attributes can be learned only by studying nonexamples, thus allowing learners to eliminate characteristics that are not unique to frogs. Finally, as the learner gains more practice with both examples and nonexamples, the concept of a frog emerges as a tightly woven combination of characteristics. Now the learner

Table 5.3 Instructional objectives requiring Type 1 and Type 2 outcomes.

Type 1: Objectives Requiring Facts, Rules, and Sequences	Type 2: Objectives Requiring Concepts, Patterns, and Abstractions
1. IF Objective is to *recognize* multiplication to "1000" THEN TEACH the multiplication tables, and then have student *find examples*	BUT IF Objective is to *understand* multiplication of signed numbers THEN TEACH the concept of negative and positive numbers and *show how they are multiplied*
2. IF Objective is to *identify* the apostrophe "s" THEN TEACH words using the apostrophe "s", and then have student *find words denoting possession*	BUT IF Objective is to *express* ownership THEN TEACH the concept of the possessive form, and then have student *practice writing paragraphs* showing forms of possession
3. IF Objective is to *select* multisyllable words THEN TEACH how to *find each of the words* on a list, and then have student write words	BUT IF Objective is to *pronounce* vowel/consonant blends THEN TEACH vowels and consonants, and then have student *read story aloud*
4. IF Objective is to *state* the chemical composition of water THEN TEACH the symbol for 2 parts hydrogen and 1 part oxygen, and then have student *write the chemical composition of water*	BUT IF Objective is to *determine* the molecular structure of chemical substances THEN TEACH the concept of element, atomic weight, and valence, and then have student *practice balancing the atomic weights of chemical substances*

is able to disregard superficial characteristics such as color and to focus on characteristics that are unique to frogs. Given pictures of various toads, chameleons, turtles, snakes, and so on, the student learns to identify correctly those that are frogs.

At this point the learner has discovered at least some of the essential attributes of a frog and has formed an initial concept. Notice how different this teaching/learning process is from simply having Johnny repeat some recently memorized facts about frogs: "Frogs are green, have four legs, eat insects, and can swim." This response does not tell you whether Johnny has the grasped concept of a frog, or a pattern of which frogs are a part (e.g., amphibian), or even the most general and abstract frog characteristics (e.g., water life). Even if Johnny learns the considerably more complex task of how to care for frogs, he still has not learned the *concept* of a frog. He has grasped only how to arrange a constellation of facts into an action sequence.

Figure 5.1   Learning the concept of *frog*.

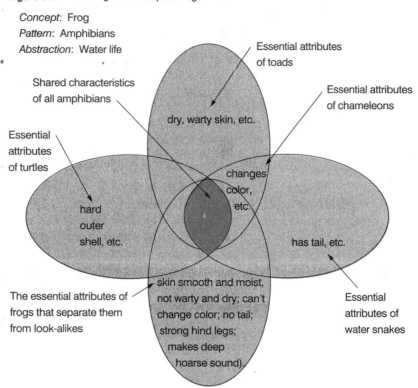

Concept: Frog
Pattern: Amphibians
Abstraction: Water life

Essential attributes
of toads

Shared characteristics
of all amphibians

Essential attributes
of chameleons

Essential
attributes
of turtles

dry, warty skin, etc.

changes
color,
etc.

hard
outer
shell, etc.

has tail, etc.

The essential attributes of
frogs that separate them
from look-alikes

skin smooth and moist,
not warty and dry; can't
change color; no tail;
strong hind legs;
makes deep
hoarse sound)

Essential
attributes of
water snakes

The preceding demonstrates how the processes used to learn facts, rules, and action sequences are different from those used to learn concepts, patterns, and abstractions. And just as different processes are involved in such learning, so are different instructional strategies needed to teach these outcomes. We most commonly teach facts, rules, and action sequences using strategies that emphasize *knowledge acquisition*. We most commonly teach concepts, patterns, and abstractions using strategies that emphasize *inquiry* or *problem solving*. These follow distinctions suggested by J. R. Anderson (1990) and E. Gagné, Yekovich, and Yekovich (1993), whose writings have highlighted the different instructional strategies required by these two types of learning.

Knowledge acquisition and inquiry are different types of learning outcomes, so each of them must be linked with the specific strategies most likely to produce them. This chapter presents a group of strategies for teaching knowledge acquisition involving facts, rules, and action sequences, called *direct instruction*. The next chapter presents strategies for teaching inquiry and problem-solving involving concepts, patterns, and abstractions, called *indirect instruction*. In subsequent chapters, both types of learning are combined to show how, together, they can build additional teaching strategies that help learners solve problems, think critically, and work cooperatively.

Figure 5.2   Some direct instruction functions.

1. Daily review, checking previous day's work, and reteaching (if necessary):
     Checking homework
     Reteaching areas where there were student errors
2. Presenting and structuring new content:
     Provide overview
     Proceed in small steps (if necessary), but at a rapid pace
     If necessary, give detailed or redundant instructions and explanations
     New skills are phased in while old skills are being measured
3. Guided student practice:
     High frequency of questions and overt student practice (from teacher and
       materials)
     Prompts are provided during initial learning (when appropriate)
     All students have a chance to respond and receive feedback
     Teacher *checks for understanding* by evaluating student responses
     Continue practice until student responses are firm
     Success rate of 80% or higher during initial learning
4. Feedback and correctives (and recycling of instruction, if necessary):
     Feedback to students, particularly when they are correct but hesitant
     Student errors provide feedback to the teacher that corrections and/or
       reteaching is necessary
     Corrections by simplifying question, giving clues, explaining or reviewing
       steps, or reteaching last steps
     When necessary, reteach using smaller steps
5. Independent practice so that student responses are firm and automatic:
     Seatwork
     Unitization and automaticity (practice to overlearning)
     Need for procedure to ensure student engagement during seatwork (i.e.,
       teacher or aide monitoring)
     95% correct or higher
6. Weekly and monthly reviews:
     Reteaching, if necessary

Source: From "Teaching Functions in Instructional Programs," by B. Rosenshine, 1983, *Elementary School Journal, 83,* p. 338. Reprinted by permission of the University of Chicago. Copyright © 1986 by the University of Chicago. All rights reserved.

WHEN IS DIRECT INSTRUCTION APPROPRIATE?

When direct instruction strategies are used for the proper purpose, with the appropriate content, and at the right time, they are important adjuncts to a teaching strategy menu. Most of these strategies are at their best when your purpose is to disseminate information not readily available from texts or workbooks in appropriately sized pieces. If such information were available, your students might well learn the mater-

ial fr᠁ ᵗʰ᠁ ᵗe sources independently, with only introductory or structuring com-
᠁ ed by you. However, when you must partition, subdivide, and translate
᠁ ᵃⁿᵈ workbook material into a more digestible form before it can be understood by your students, direct instruction is appropriate.

Another time for direct instruction strategies is when you wish to arouse or
heighten student interest. Students often fail to complete textbook readings and
exercises in the mistaken belief that the chapter is boring, is not worth their effort,
or presents material already learned. Your active participation in the presentation of
content can change such misperceptions by mixing interesting supplemental or
introductory information with the dry facts, by showing their application to future
schoolwork or world events, and by illustrating with questions and answers that the
material is neither easy nor previously mastered. Your direct involvement in presenting content provides the human element that may be necessary for learning to occur
in many of your students.

Finally, direct instruction strategies are indispensable for achieving content mastery and overlearning of fundamental facts, rules, and action sequences that may be
essential to subsequent learning (L. Anderson & Block, 1987; Good & Grouws, 1987;
Lindsley, 1992). The degree of **mastery learning** that occurs is directly related to the
time a student is actively engaged in the learning process. Therefore, efficient use of
class time and active student practice are important ingredients of mastery learning.

The two goals of mastery learning—efficient use of class time and active student
practice—are best achieved by an instructional sequence of review, presenting new
content, practice, feedback, and reteaching, as shown in Figure 5.3. These repetitive
cycles may compose nearly all of the time scheduled for a direct instruction lesson.
Many examples in this chapter illustrate this type of instructional sequence. When
the content to be taught represents task-relevant prior knowledge for subsequent
learning, a direct instruction format is the best insurance that this knowledge is
remembered and available for later use.

There also are times when direct instruction strategies are inappropriate. When
objectives other than learning facts, rules, and behavior sequences are desired,
direct instruction strategies become clumsy, less efficient, and often far less effective
than the inquiry or problem-solving strategies we will discuss in subsequent chapters. Teaching situations that need strategies other than direct instruction include (1)
presenting complex material having objectives at the analysis, synthesis, and evaluation levels of the cognitive domain and (2) presenting content that must be learned
gradually over a long period. Such material requires learner participation to heighten
a commitment to the learning process and to create the intellectual framework necessary for learning concepts and recognizing patterns. You can attain this learner participation through carefully crafted classroom dialogue, which will be illustrated in
Chapters 7 and 8.

Finally, when students have already mastered the fundamentals and task-relevant
prior knowledge required for more authentic outcomes at the problem-solving, critical thinking, and decision-making levels, direct instruction strategies can be inefficient and ineffective forms of instruction.

Figure 5.3 The direct instructional sequence for mastery learning.

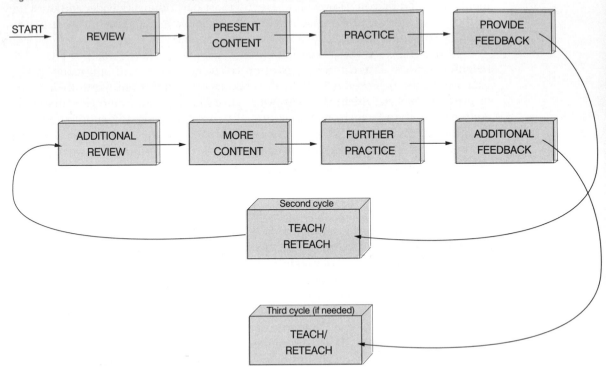

AN EXAMPLE OF DIRECT INSTRUCTION

To see what direct instruction looks like in the classroom, consider the following dialogue, in which the teacher begins a direct instruction sequence to teach the acquisition of facts, rules, and action sequences for forming and punctuating possessives. She begins by informing her students of the lesson's objective. As you read, note the italicized, bold, direct instruction functions from Figure 5.2.

Teacher:	Today we will learn how to avoid embarrassing errors such as this when forming and punctuating possessives (circles an incorrectly punctuated possessive in a newspaper headline). At the end of the period, I will give each of you several additional examples of errors taken from my collection of mistakes found in other newspapers and magazines. I'll ask you to make the proper corrections and report your changes to the class. Who knows what a possessive is? ***(Review and checking)***
Bobby:	It means you own something.
Teacher:	Yes, a possessive is a way of indicating ownership. It comes from the word *possession,* which means *something owned* or *something possessed.*

Forming possessives and punctuating them correctly can be difficult, as this newspaper example shows (points to paper again). Today I will give you two simple rules that will help you form possessives correctly. But first, to show ownership or possession, we must know who or what is doing the possessing.

Mary, can you recall the parts of speech from last week's lesson? (Mary hesitates, then nods.) What part of speech is most likely to own or possess something? *(Review and checking)*

Mary: Well, umm . . . I think . . . I think a noun can own something.

Teacher: Yes. A noun can own something. What is an example of a noun that owns something? Tommy.

Tommy: I don't know.

Teacher: Debbie.

Debbie: Not sure.

Teacher: Ricky.

Ricky: A student can own a pencil. The word *student* is a noun.

Teacher: Good. And who can remember our definition for a noun? *(Review and checking)*

Jim: It's a person, place, or thing.

Teacher: Good. Our first rule is: Use the possessive form whenever an *of* phrase can be substituted for a noun (teacher points to this rule written on board). *(Presenting and structuring)*. Let's look at some phrases on the board to see when to apply this rule. Johnny, what does the first one say? *(Guided student practice)*

Johnny: The daughter of the policeman.

Teacher: How else could we express the same idea of ownership?

Mary: We could say "the policeman's daughter."

Teacher: And, we could say "the policeman's daughter" because I can substitute a phrase starting with *of* and ending with policeman for the noun *policeman*. Notice how easily I could switch the placement of *policeman* and *daughter* by using the connecting word *of.* Whenever this can be done, you can form a possessive by adding an *apostrophe s* to the noun following *of. (Presenting and structuring)*

Now we have the phrase (writes on board) *policeman's daughter* (points to the apostrophe). Betty, what about our next example, *holiday of three days* (pointing to board)? *(Guided student practice)*

Betty: We could say "three days' holiday."

Teacher: Come up and write that on the board just the way it should be printed in the school paper. (Mary writes *three day's holiday.*)

Would anyone want to change anything?

Susan: I'm not sure, but I think I would put the apostrophe after the *s* in *days*.

Teacher: You're right *(Feedback)*, which leads to our second rule: If the word for which we are denoting ownership is a plural ending with *s*, place an apostrophe after the *s*. But if the word is a name—called a proper noun—ending with *s,* place an apostrophe *and* an *s* after the *s.* This is an important rule to remember, because it accounts for many of the mistakes that are made in forming possessives. As I write this rule on the board, copy down these two rules for use later. ***(Presenting and structuring)*** (Finishes writing second rule on board.) Now let's take a moment to convert each of the phrases on the overhead to the possessive form. Write down your answer to the first one. When I see all heads up again, I will write the correct answer. ***(Guided student practice)*** (All heads are up.) Good. Now watch how I change this first one to the possessive form; pay particular attention to where I place the apostrophe, then check your answer with mine. (Converts *delay of a month* to *month's delay.*) Any problems? ***(Checking)*** (Pauses for any response.) OK, do the next one.

(After all heads are up, teacher converts *home of Jenkins* to *Jenkins's home.*) Any problems? (Johnny looks distressed.) ***(Checking)***

Teacher:	Johnny, what did you write?
Johnny:	*J-E-N-K-I-N apostrophe S.*
Teacher:	What is the man's name, Johnny?
Johnny:	Jenkins.
Teacher:	Look at what you wrote for the second rule. What does it say? ***(Feedback and corrective)***
Johnny:	Add an apostrophe and an *s* after the *s* when the word is a name that already ends in an *s.* Oh, I get it. His name already has the *s,* so it would be *s apostrophe s.* That's the mistake you showed us in the headline, isn't it?
Teacher:	Now you've got it. Let's continue. (Proceeds with the following in the same manner: *speech of the President* to *President's speech, the television set of Mr. Burns* to *Mr. Burns's television set, pastimes of boys* to *boys' pastimes.*) Now open your workbooks to the exercise on page 87.
	Starting with the first row, let's go around the room and hear your possessives for each of the sentences listed. Spell aloud the word indicating ownership, so we can tell if you've placed the apostrophe in the right place. Debbie . . . (looking at "wings of geese") ***(Guided student practice)***
Debbie:	geeses wings . . . spelled *W-I-N-G-S apostrophe.*
Teacher:	That's not correct. What word is doing the possessing? ***(Feedback and corrective)***
Debbie:	The geese, so it must be *G-E-E-S-E apostrophe S.*
Teacher:	Good. ***(Feedback)*** Next.

Now, let's look at our six direct instruction functions in Figure 5.2 as they relate to the preceding dialogue.

DAILY REVIEW AND CHECKING THE PREVIOUS DAY'S WORK

The first ingredient in direct instruction (Figure 5.2), **daily review and checking** emphasizes the relationship between lessons so that students remember previous knowledge and see new knowledge as a logical extension of content already mastered. Notice that early in the example lesson the definition of a noun was brought into the presentation. This provided review of task-relevant prior knowledge needed for the day's lesson.

It also provided students with a sense of wholeness and continuity, assuring them that what was to follow was not isolated knowledge unrelated to past lessons. This is particularly important for securing the engagement of students who do not have appropriate levels of task-relevant prior knowledge or who may be overly anxious about having to master yet another piece of unfamiliar content.

Review and checking at the beginning of a lesson also are the most efficient and timely ways of finding out if your students have mastered task-relevant prior knowledge sufficiently to begin a new lesson; if not, you may reteach the missing content, as shown in Figure 5.2.

You might think that beginning a lesson by checking previously learned task-relevant knowledge is a common practice. Yet, many teachers fail to begin a lesson in

A major purpose of daily review and checking is to emphasize the relationship between lessons and to provide students with a sense of wholeness and continuity, assuring them that what is to follow is a logical extension of content already mastered.

this fashion. This is unfortunate, because daily review and checking at the beginning of a lesson is easy to accomplish:

1. Have students correct each other's homework at the beginning of class.
2. Have students identify especially difficult homework problems in a question-and-answer format.
3. Sample the understanding of a few students who probably are good indicators of the range of knowledge possessed by the entire class.
4. Explicitly review the task-relevant information that is necessary for the day's lesson.

Dahllof and Lundgren (1970) proposed the use of a *steering group* of low achievers as a particularly effective way of determining the extent to which review and reteaching may be needed. An expanded notion of the steering group is a small number of low, average, and high performers who can be queried at the start of class on the task-relevant prior knowledge needed for the day's lesson. When high performers miss a large proportion of answers, this warns you that extensive reteaching for the entire class is necessary. When high performers answer questions correctly but average performers do not, some reteaching should be undertaken before the start of the lesson. And, finally, if most of the high and average performers answer the questions correctly but most of the low performers do not, you will need to use individualized materials, supplemental readings, summary and review sheets, or tutorial arrangements and communication technologies. This ensures that large amounts of class time are not devoted to review and reteaching that may benefit only a small number of students.

Such strategies for daily review and checking, especially when used with a carefully selected steering group, are indispensable for warning you that previous instruction was over the heads of some or most of your students and, therefore, that additional review and reteaching are necessary.

PRESENTING AND STRUCTURING

The second step in the direct instruction model consists of **presenting and structuring** new content. One of the primary ingredients of the model is presenting material in small steps. Lessons must be served up in small portions that are consistent with the previous knowledge, ability level, and experience levels of your students. Likewise, the content *within* the lessons must be partitioned and subdivided to organize it into small bits. No portion can be too large, or you will lose your students' attention.

The key is to focus the material on one idea at a time and to present it so that learners master one point before the teacher introduces the next point. This is most easily accomplished by dividing a lesson into easily recognizable subparts, rules, or categories. It is no coincidence that the strategy of divide and conquer is as appropriate in the classroom as in military battles. Just like any great warrior, you can derive much benefit from it.

Remember that the subdivisions you use can be your own; they need not always follow those provided by the text, workbook, or curriculum guide. There is an important difference between content divisions used in books and content divisions needed in teaching: Content divisions in texts, workbooks, and curriculum guides generally are created for the purpose of communicating *content intended to be read,* not for the purpose of presenting *content that must be explained orally* to learners within the time frame of a specific lesson. Consequently, published divisions like chapter titles, subheadings, or Roman numerals in outlines sometimes are too broad to form bite-sized pieces that students can easily digest within a single lesson.

Unfortunately, many beginning teachers stick tenaciously to these formal headings without realizing either the volume of content that falls within them or the time it takes to orally explain, illustrate, and practice this content. The truth is that you are not discarding content by creating new organizational divisions; you only are breaking content into smaller steps suitable for presentation in a single period. You can create your own subdivisions consisting of rules ("here are some rules to follow"), steps ("we will do this, then that"), or practices ("here is the first of five things we will cover"). These subdivisions preorganize your instruction into bite-sized pieces and, most importantly, communicate this organization to your students.

Chapter 2 (Figures 2.2 and 2.3) illustrated the importance of structuring content in ways that are meaningful to students (e.g., general to detailed, simple to complex). Following are some additional ways of structuring content that are particularly relevant to direct instruction. These are the part–whole, sequential, combinatorial, and comparative methods.

Part–Whole Relationships

A part–whole organizational format introduces the topic in its most general form ("What is a possessive?") and then divides the topic into easy-to-distinguish subdivisions (Rule 1, Rule 2). This creates subdivisions that are easily digested and presents them in ways that always relate back to the whole. Students should always be aware of the part being covered at any particular time ("This is Rule 2") and its relationship to the whole ("This leads to our second rule for denoting ownership"). Use verbal markers to alert students that a transition is under way ("This is Rule 1," "Here is the first part," "This is the last example of this type; now let's move to the next type").

This type of organization creates bite-sized chunks; it helps students organize and see what is being taught and informs them of what portion they are studying. Part–whole organization is illustrated in Figure 5.4.

Sequential Relationships

Another way of structuring content is by sequential ordering; you teach the content according to the way in which the facts, rules, or sequences to be learned occur in the real world. Students may already have a feel for sequential ordering from practical experience.

In algebra, for example, equations are solved by first multiplying, then dividing, then adding, and finally subtracting. This order of operations must occur for a solution to be correct. A sequentially structured lesson, therefore, might introduce the

Figure 5.4 Structuring a lesson by identifying part–whole relationships.

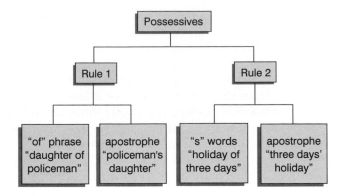

manipulation of signed numbers in the order multiplication-division-addition-subtraction, which reinforces the way equations must actually be solved, making the skill and behavior you are teaching more authentic. In other words, you would complete all examples used in teaching signed-number multiplication before introducing any examples about division, thereby teaching the correct sequence as well as the intended content. Sequential ordering is illustrated in Figure 5.5.

Combinatorial Relationships

A third way you can structure lesson content is to bring together in a single format various elements or dimensions that influence the use of facts, rules, and sequences. This allows an overall framework to direct the order of content by showing the logic of some combinations of facts, rules, and sequences and the illogic of other combinations.

Figure 5.5 Structuring a lesson by identifying sequential relationships.

$$y = a - b + \frac{cd}{e}$$

1. First, let's determine cd when

   $c = -1, d = 2$

   $c = 0, d = -4$

   $c = 2, d = -3$

2. Next, let's determine $\frac{cd}{e}$ when

   $cd = -2, e = -2$

   $cd = 0, e = 1$

   $cd = -6, e = 4$

3. Now, let's determine $b + \frac{cd}{e}$ when

   $b = 1, \frac{cd}{e} = 1$

   $b = -2, \frac{cd}{e} = 0$

   $b = 2, \frac{cd}{e} = -1.5$

4. Finally, let's determine $a - b + \frac{cd}{e}$ when

   $a = 10, b + \frac{cd}{e} = 2$

   $a = 7, b + \frac{cd}{e} = -3$

   $a = 5, b + \frac{cd}{e} = .5$

For example, in teaching a direct instruction lesson in social studies, you might develop a scheme to reveal the relationship between marketable products and the various means of transporting them to market. You could draw an organizational chart (Figure 5.6) to structure the content. You could show the chart to your students, and then teach all the relevant facts (e.g., relative weights of products), rules (the heavier the product, the more efficient the transportation system must be), and action sequences (first analyze the product's size and weight, then choose the best location). The shaded cells in Figure 5.6 identify the *combinations,* or dimensions of content, that are most relevant to the lesson objectives.

Comparative Relationships

In comparative structuring of content, you place different pieces of content side by side so that learners can compare and contrast them. Placing facts, rules, and sequences side by side across two or more categories enables students to observe their similarities and differences. For example, you might want to compare and contrast governmental aspects of the United States and England. You could order the instruction according to the format shown in Figure 5.7. Then you could teach the relevant facts (economic systems), politics (type of government), and source of laws (U.S. Constitution vs. legal codes) by moving first across the chart and then down. The chart structures content in advance, and students can easily see the structure and content to be covered.

Figure 5.6 Structuring a lesson by identifying combinatorial relationships.

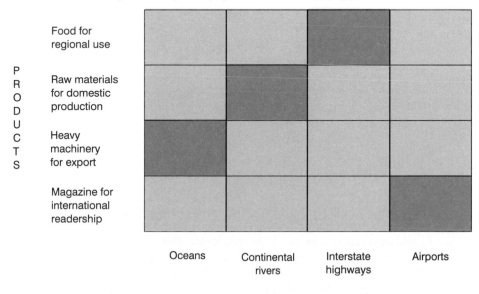

Food for regional use

P R O D U C T S

Raw materials for domestic production

Heavy machinery for export

Magazine for international readership

Oceans   Continental rivers   Interstate highways   Airports

TRANSPORTATION SYSTEMS

Figure 5.7 Structuring a relationship by identifying comparative relationships.

Points of Comparison	U.S.	England
Economics	Capitalism	Capitalism
Politics	Representative democracy	Parliamentary democracy
Source of laws	U.S. Constitution	English legal codes
Representative body	Congress	Parliament

Using the Methods

Whether you use one structuring method or a combination to organize a lesson, remember to divide the content into bite-sized pieces. To the extent that these structuring techniques divide larger units of content into smaller and more meaningful units, they will have served an important purpose.

Finally, note how the teacher in our classroom dialogue combined rules and examples in organizing and presenting the content. She always presented the rule first and then followed with one or more examples. Note also that after some examples illustrating the rule, she repeated it—either by having students write the rule after seeing it on the board, or by having a student repeat it to the class. Learning a rule in one sensory modality (e.g., seeing it on the board) and then recreating it in a different sensory modality (e.g., writing or speaking it) generally promotes greater learning and retention than seeing the rule only once or reproducing it in the same modality in which it was learned.

Giving a rule, then an example of the rule, followed by repetition of the rule is called the *rule-example-rule order*. It generally is more effective than simply giving the rule and then an example (rule-example order), or giving an example followed by the rule.

GUIDED STUDENT PRACTICE

The third step in the direct instruction model is **guided student practice.** Recall from the structure of a lesson plan that presentation of stimulus material is followed by eliciting practice in the desired behavior. This section presents several ways of accomplishing this in the context of the direct instruction model. These elicitations are teacher guided, providing students with guided practice that you organize and direct.

Recall the important ingredients for eliciting a student response. One is to elicit the response in as nonevaluative an atmosphere as possible; this frees students to risk creating responses about which they may be unsure but from which they can begin to build a correct response. Any response, however crude or incorrect, can be the basis for learning if it is followed by proper feedback and correctives.

A second ingredient for eliciting a student response is the use of covert responses. This not only ensures a nonthreatening environment but also encourages student engagement in the learning task with the least expenditure of your time and effort. In the preceding example dialogue, by having students privately write their responses before seeing the correct answers on the overhead, the teacher guided each student to formulate a response; it was not necessary to call on each of them. She guided the students into responding by encouraging, and later rewarding, their covert responses.

An equally important aspect of eliciting a desired response is to check for student understanding. When necessary, prompt to convert wrong answers to right ones. In the example dialogue, the teacher stopped after every item to see if there were problems and prompted students to create correct answers when necessary. Prompting is an important part of eliciting the desired behavior, because it strengthens and builds the learners' confidence by encouraging them to use some aspects of the answer that have already been given in formulating the correct response (E. Gagné et al., 1993). In the example dialogue, Johnny was encouraged to *rethink* his response, to *focus* consciously on the specific part of the problem causing the error, and to *remember* the rule that will prevent such errors in the future.

Prompting

During direct instruction the effective teacher often provides prompts, hints, and other types of supplementary instructional stimuli to help learners make the correct response. You can use three categories of prompts to shape the correct performance of your learners: verbal prompts, gestural prompts, and physical prompts.

Verbal Prompts.   **Verbal prompts** can be cues, reminders, or instructions to learners that help them perform correctly the skill you are teaching. For example, saying to a first-grade learner as he is writing, "Leave a space between words," reminds him what you previously said about neat handwriting. Or saying, "First adjust the object lens," to a learner while she is looking at a microscope slide, prompts her as she is learning how to use a microscope. Verbal prompts help guide the learner to connect performances and prevent mistakes and frustration.

Gestural Prompts.   **Gestural prompts** model or demonstrate for learners a particular skill you want them to perform. For example, if as the teacher above, you were to point to the fine adjustment knob on the microscope and make a turning gesture with your hand, you would be prompting, or reminding, the student to perform this step of the process. Gestural prompts are particularly helpful when you anticipate that the learner may make a mistake. You can use gestural prompts routinely to remind learners how to fold a piece of paper, how to grasp a pair of scissors, how to raise their hand before asking a question, or how to hold a pen properly when writing.

Physical Prompts.   Some learners may lack the fine muscle control to follow a demonstration and imitate the action being modeled. For example, you might verbally describe how to form the letter *a* and demonstrate this for the learner, and the learner may still be unable to write *a* correctly. In such a case, you might use your hand to guide the learner's hand as he writes. This is called a physical prompt. With a **physical prompt,** you use *hand-over-hand* assistance to guide the learner to the correct performance. You can routinely use physical prompts to assist learners with handwriting, cutting out shapes, tying shoelaces, correctly holding a dissecting tool, or performing a complex dance routine.

Least-to-Most Intrusive Prompting.   Many educators recommend that you use the least intrusive prompt first when guiding a learner's performance. Verbal prompts are the least intrusive, while physical prompts are the most intrusive (Cooper, Heron, & Heward, 1987). Thus, it would be more appropriate, first, to say, "Don't forget the fine adjustment!" when guiding a learner in the use of a microscope than to take the learner's hand and physically assist her. The reasoning behind using a least-to-most intrusive order is that verbal prompts are easier to remove or fade than are physical prompts. Learners who are dependent on physical prompts to perform correctly will find it more difficult to demonstrate a skill independently of the teacher and to acquire authentic behavior.

Full-Class Prompting.   You can also check for understanding and prompt for correct responses using the full class. The example dialogue showed one approach: The teacher asked all the students to respond privately at the same time and then encouraged them to ask for individual help ("Any problems?").

Another approach is to call on students whether or not their hands are raised, thereby seeking opportunities to prompt and correct wrong answers. One version of this is called *ordered turns,* in which you systematically go through the class and expect students to respond when their turn arrives. When groups are small, this approach is more effective in producing student achievement gains than randomly calling on students (L. Anderson et al., 1982; Brophy & Evertson, 1976a). But, generally, the ordered turns method is less efficient than selecting students to respond during full-class instruction (L. Anderson et al., 1982).

Yet another approach is to have students write out answers to be checked and perhaps corrected by a classmate. Finally, you can develop questions beforehand to test for the most common errors. Check student responses for accuracy and prompt when necessary. This approach has the advantage of assuming that not everyone understands or has the correct answer when no responses are received. Researchers have found this approach to be particularly effective in increasing student achievement (McKenzie, 1979; Singer & Donlon, 1982).

Modeling

Modeling is a teaching activity that involves demonstrating to learners what you want them to do or think.

When used correctly, modeling can assist learners to acquire a variety of intellectual and social skills more effortlessly and efficiently than with verbal, gestural, or physical prompts alone. Modeling is particularly effective for younger learners who may not be able to follow complex verbal explanations, for visually dominant learners who may need to see how something is done before they can actually do it, and for communicating mental strategies for problem solving to all ages of learners.

Bandura and his colleagues have studied how and why we learn from models (Bandura, 1986; Zimmerman, 1989). Their research on modeling is referred to as *social learning theory,* and it attempts to explain how people learn from observing other people. From their work we know that children not only can learn attitudes, values, and standards of behavior from observing adults and peers but may also learn physical and intellectual skills.

Some of this learning takes place by directly imitating what a teacher is doing, while other learning takes place by inferring why the model is acting a certain way, or what type of person the model is. For example, learners acquire certain values about the importance of learning, caring for others, doing work neatly, or respect for other cultures by observing how their parents, friends, and teachers actually behave in the real world, and then inferring from their observations how they, too, should behave. Although teachers model all the time, we know that some forms of modeling are better than others. Zimmerman (1989) found that teachers who were taught the practice of modeling were far more effective at helping young children to learn than teachers who were not.

Modeling is a direct teaching activity that allows students to imitate from demonstration or infer from observation the behavior to be learned. Four psychological processes need to occur for your learners to benefit from modeling:

1. Attention
2. Retention
3. Production
4. Motivation

Let's take a closer look at these to discover how students learn from what they see.

Attention.   Demonstrations are only of value if learners are looking and/or listening to them. In other words, without attention there can be no imitation or observational learning. The previous section highlighted the importance of gaining a learner's attention. Modeling requires that you not only gain your learners' attention but that you retain it throughout the lesson. Bandura (1977) found that learners hold their attention better under the following conditions:

1. The model is someone who is respected as an expert in his or her field.
2. The model is demonstrating something that has functional value to the learner. Learners pay little attention to those things for which they see no immediate relevance.
3. The demonstration is simplified by subdividing it into component parts and presented in a clearly discernible step-by-step fashion.

Retention. Teachers model because they want their learners to be able to repeat their same actions when they are no longer present. For example, teachers typically model when they demonstrate how to add a column of numbers, sound out a word, or evaluate a short essay. But, the transfer of these actions will only occur if learners remember what they saw or heard. Demonstrations from which imitation is to occur must be planned with the goal of retention in mind.

Learners are more likely to remember the following types of demonstrations:

1. Demonstrations linked to previous skills or ideas that they have already learned. The more meaningful the demonstration, the more likely it will be retained. ("Remember how yesterday we added one-digit numbers in a column? Well, today we will use the same procedure on numbers that have two or more digits.")
2. Demonstrations that include concise labels, vivid images, code words, or visual mnemonics (to be discussed in Chapter 8), which help learners hold new learning in memory. ("Look at how I hold my lips when I pronounce this next word.")
3. Demonstrations that are immediately rehearsed. This rehearsal can be overt, as when the teacher asks learners to say or do something immediately following the demonstration, or covert. Covert rehearsal occurs when the learner visualizes or mentally creates an image of what the teacher demonstrated. ("Now, everyone read the next passage to themselves, repeating silently the sequence of steps I just demonstrated.")

Production. The third component of the modeling process occurs when learners actually do what the teacher demonstrated. In this stage of the process, the mental images or verbal codes learners retained in memory direct their actual performance. Learners recall these images or codes by the practice situation the teacher creates and by the verbal cues given. Having been evoked, these images guide the actual performance of what was learned during the demonstration.

Learners are more likely to produce what they saw under the following conditions:

1. Production closely follows the retention phase. ("OK, now that you've practiced remembering the correct sequence of steps I demonstrated, let's use them to interpret the meaning of the following passage.")
2. The practice situation contains cues or stimuli that evoke the retained mental images or verbal codes. ("This next word requires you to position your lips exactly as you saw me do in the last example.")
3. The performance immediately follows mental rehearsal. ("Let's switch to several new examples that you haven't seen before.")

The production phase increases the likelihood that images of the demonstration learners have remembered will guide the production of newly acquired behavior. In addition, this phase allows the teacher to observe learners and give feedback on how well they have mastered the behavior. Giving learners information about the correctness of their actions—without expressing negativity or dissatisfaction—has been shown to increase the likelihood of a correct performance (Vasta, 1976).

Motivation.   The final stage of the process of learning through modeling occurs when learners experience desirable outcomes following their performance. Desirable outcomes usually take the form of some type of teacher praise, which motivates learners to want to imitate at some future time what they have seen. Learners are less likely to repeat the actions of a model if they have experienced punishing or unsatisfying consequences following their initial attempts to imitate the model.

On the other hand, learners are more likely to repeat the actions of a model both immediately and to transfer it to new situations over time when the following occur:

1. Praise and encouragement rather than criticism immediately follow performance. ("Your answer is partly correct; think some more about what we've just discussed," as opposed to, "Your answer is wrong. You're not listening again.")
2. The praise is directed at specific aspects of the performance. ("I like how you left enough space between your words," as opposed to, "That's neat.")
3. Directions rather than corrections follow incorrect performance. ("Remember, the first step is to generate a hypothesis," as opposed to, "You don't state the research design before you generate a hypothesis!")

FEEDBACK AND CORRECTIVES

The next ingredient in the direct instruction model is provision of **feedback and correctives.** You need strategies for handling right and wrong answers. Based on several studies, Rosenshine (1983) identified four broad categories of student response: (1) correct, quick, and firm; (2) correct but hesitant; (3) incorrect due to carelessness; and (4) incorrect due to lack of knowledge. These are described next, with some direct instruction strategies for handling them.

Correct, Quick, and Firm

The student response that teachers strive most to inspire is *correct, quick, and firm.* Such a response most frequently occurs during the latter stages of a lesson or unit, but it can occur almost anytime during a lesson or unit if you have divided the content into bite-sized portions. A moderate-to-high percentage of correct, quick, and firm responses is important if students are to become actively engaged in the learning process. Not every response from every student must be a correct one, but *for most learning that involves knowledge acquisition, make the steps between successive portions of your lesson small enough to produce approximately 60% to 80% correct answers in a practice and feedback session* (N. Bennett, Desforges, Cockburn, & Wilkinson, 1981; Brophy & Evertson, 1976b; Lindsley, 1991).

This research suggests that your best response to a correct, quick, and firm student response is to ask another question of the same student. This increases the potential for feedback or, if time does not permit, to move on quickly to another question and student. Keep the lesson moving quickly, involving as many students as possible in the practice exercise, and covering as many stimulus problems as possible. Once 60% to 80% right answers are produced, you will have created a rhythm and momentum that heighten student attention and engagement and provide for a high level of task orientation. The brisk pace of right answers also will help minimize irrelevant student responses and classroom distractions.

Correct But Hesitant

The second student response is *correct but hesitant.* This type frequently occurs in a practice and feedback session at the beginning or middle of a lesson. Positive feedback to the student who supplies a correct but hesitant response is essential. The first feedback to provide in this instance is a positive, reinforcing statement, such as "good," or "that's correct," because the correct but hesitant response is more likely to be remembered when linked to a warm reply. This helps the student advance into the correct, quick, and firm category when next responding to the same type of problem.

Affirmative replies, however, seldom effect significant change on a subsequent problem of the same type unless the teacher addresses the reasons behind the hesitant response. Although discovering the precise reason for a hesitant response is desirable, it takes time. A quick restatement of the facts, rules, or steps needed to obtain the right answer often accomplishes the same end more efficiently. This restatement not only aids the student who is giving the correct but hesitant response, but also helps reduce subsequent wrong answers or hesitant responses among other students who hear the restatement.

Incorrect Because of Carelessness

The third student response is *incorrect because of carelessness.* As many as 20% of student responses fall into this category, depending on the time of day and the students' level of fatigue and inattentiveness. When this occurs, and you feel that they really know the correct response, you may be tempted to scold, admonish, or even verbally punish students for responding thoughtlessly (e.g., "I'm ashamed of you," "That's a dumb mistake," "I thought you were brighter than that"). However, resist this temptation, no matter how justified it seems. Nothing is more frustrating than to repress genuine emotions, but researchers and experienced teachers agree that you do more harm than good if you react emotionally to this type of problem.

Verbal punishment rarely teaches students to avoid careless mistakes. Further, experience shows that the rhythm and momentum built and maintained through a brisk and lively pace can easily be broken by such off-task attention to an individual student. Emotional reaction rarely has a positive effect, so the best procedure is to acknowledge that the answer is wrong and to move immediately to the next student for the correct response. By doing so, you will make a point to the careless student that he or she lost the opportunity for a correct response and the praise that goes with it.

Incorrect Because of Lack of Knowledge

Perhaps the most challenging response is *incorrect because of a lack of knowledge.* Such errors typically occur, sometimes in large numbers, during the initial stages of a lesson or unit. It is better to provide hints, probe, or change the question or stimulus to a simpler one that engages the student in finding the correct response than to simply give the student the correct response. After all, the goal is not to get the correct answer from the student but to *engage the learner in the process by which the right answer can be found.*

In the example lesson, the teacher tried to focus Johnny on the *apostrophe s* he had missed at the end of the proper noun *Jenkins* and to restate the rule concerning formation of possessives in words ending in *s.* Likewise, the teacher probed Debbie after her wrong answer by asking, "What word is doing the possessing?" Each of these instances led to the right answer without actually telling the student the right answer. When your strategy channels a student's thoughts to produce the right answer without your actually giving it, you provide a framework for producing a correct response in all subsequent similar problems.

Strategies for Incorrect Responses

The most common strategies for incorrect responses are the following:

1. Review key facts or rules needed for a correct solution.
2. Explain the steps used to reach a correct solution.
3. Prompt with clues or hints representing a partially correct answer.
4. Take a different but similar problem, and guide the student to the correct answer.

Such strategies used with one student benefit all the rest by clarifying information that they may have learned only partially. Because this type of corrective feedback is used with individual students, its effects on the entire class will be evidenced by an increasing percentage of correct responses. Reviewing, reexplaining, and prompting are effective until approximately 80% of the students respond correctly. After that point, make the correctives briefer, eventually guiding students who are making incorrect responses to helpful exercises in the text or to remedial exercises (N. Bennett & Desforges, 1988).

Finally, note that when you use the direct instruction model for teaching facts, rules, and sequences, you should not allow an incorrect answer to go undetected or uncorrected. Respond to every wrong answer with one or more of the preceding strategies. Leaving an answer uncorrected due to inattentiveness or distraction signals students who do know the answer that paying attention and active responding are not to be taken seriously.

Lindsley (1992) and R. V. Hall, Delguardi, Greenwood, and Thurston (1982) make a useful distinction between active and passive responding. **Active responding** includes orally responding to a question, writing out the correct answer, calculating an answer, or physically making a response (e.g., focusing a microscope), and so on. **Passive responding** includes listening to the teacher's answer, reading about the correct answer, or listening to classmates recite the right answer.

Greenwood, Delguardi, and Hall (1984) report that nearly half of a learner's day is involved in passive responding. This is unfortunate because their research also demonstrates a strong relationship between learner achievement and active responding. These researchers urge you to plan your lessons so that learners spend *about 75% of their time engaged in active responding.*

A second finding of their research is that correct responses are more likely when you design your practice material to elicit correct responses 60% to 80% of the time. Many teachers purposefully design materials for learner practice to be overly challenging, that is, with a strong likelihood that many learners will make mistakes. Researchers have demonstrated that learners acquire basic facts and skills faster when their opportunities for practice result in high rates of success (Lindsley, 1991).

In summary, when providing feedback and corrections:

- Give directions that focus on the response you want learners to make.
- Design instructional materials both for initial learning and practice so that learners can produce correct answers 60% to 80% of the time.
- Select activities to engage your learners in active responding about 75% of the time.

INDEPENDENT PRACTICE

The fifth ingredient in direct instruction is the opportunity for **independent practice**. Once you have successfully elicited the behavior, provided feedback, and administered correctives, students need the opportunity to practice the behavior independently. Often this is the time when facts and rules come together to form action sequences. For example, learning to drive a car requires a knowledge of terminology and rules. But until the knowledge and rules are put together, meaningful learning cannot occur.

Independent practice provides the opportunity in a carefully controlled and organized environment to make a meaningful whole out of the bits and pieces. Facts and rules must come together under your guidance and example in ways that (1) force simultaneous consideration of all the individual units of a problem and (2) connect the units into a single harmonious sequence of action. Learning theorists call these two processes *unitization* and *automaticity* (La Berge & Samuels, 1974).

Notice the manner in which these two processes were required in the example lesson. The individual units were the definition of a possessive (a fact) and two statements about forming possessives (Rules 1 and 2). The lesson connected these units into a single harmonious sequence of action in two ways. First was the exercise with which the example ends, in which the teacher directed students to a workbook to provide independent practice opportunity. The workbook sentences should contain possessives similar to those found in any newspaper, magazine, or school essay. Second was the teacher's intention to provide examples of real mistakes occurring in

During independent practice, the teacher circulates around the classroom, scanning written responses, prompting for alternative answers, and reminding students of necessary facts or rules, being careful to keep interchanges short so that the work of as many students as possible can be checked.

newspapers and magazines for additional practice at the end of the lesson. Figure 5.8 traces the steps a student might take in combining the facts and rules into an action sequence for one sentence in the workbook.

The preceding direct instruction dialogue demonstrated that the meaningful *application* of knowledge requires knowledge that is highly familiar to the learner and rich in examples and associations learned from detailed and redundant practice. In this sense, less complex levels of behavior almost always are required for more complex forms of learning to occur. It is important that facts and rules not be left dangling but be practiced with detailed and redundant examples that create more complex forms of learning, such as action sequences.

Figure 5.8 Steps involved in translating the following sentence into correct possessive form: "In Mrs. Jones paper, there was an article about a friend of Robert."

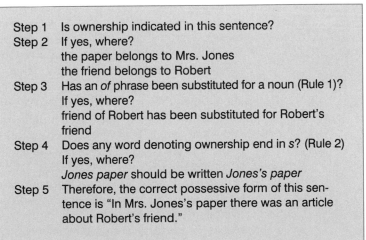

Step 1	Is ownership indicated in this sentence?
Step 2	If yes, where?
	the paper belongs to Mrs. Jones
	the friend belongs to Robert
Step 3	Has an *of* phrase been substituted for a noun (Rule 1)? If yes, where?
	friend of Robert has been substituted for Robert's friend
Step 4	Does any word denoting ownership end in *s*? (Rule 2) If yes, where?
	Jones paper should be written *Jones's paper*
Step 5	Therefore, the correct possessive form of this sentence is "In Mrs. Jones's paper there was an article about Robert's friend."

In the preceding dialogue, the teacher's examples of errors from newspapers and magazines provided students an opportunity to form action sequences from the facts and rules they learned. These real-life examples further increased the authenticity of their learning. In your own classroom, make opportunities for practice increasingly resemble applications in the real world until the examples you provide are indistinguishable from those outside the classroom. Using clippings from actual newspapers and magazines was this teacher's way of doing so.

The purpose of providing opportunities for all types of independent practice is to develop automatic responses in students, so they no longer need to recall each individual unit of content but can use all the units simultaneously. Thus, the goal of the example lesson was "to write a sentence using possessives correctly" and not "to recite Rule 1 and Rule 2." As we have seen, automaticity is reached through mastery of the units that make up a complete response and sufficient practice in composing these pieces into a complete action sequence. Your goal is to schedule sufficient opportunities for independent practice to allow students' individual responses to become composed and automatic.

Regardless of the type of practice activity used, you should keep in mind several guidelines for promoting effective practice:

- *Students should understand the reason for practice.*   Practice often turns into busywork, which can create boredom, frustration, and noncompliance. Learners should approach classroom practice with the same enthusiasm that an Olympic athlete pursues laps in the pool or on the track. This is more likely to occur if (1) you make known to learners the purpose of the practice ("We will need to be proficient at solving these problems in order to go on to our next activity"), and (2) practice occurs during as well as after new learning ("Let's stop right here, so you can try some of these problems yourselves").

- *Effective practice is delivered in a manner that is brief, nonevaluative, and supportive.*   Practice involves more than simply saying, "OK. Take out your books, turn to page 78, and answer questions 1, 3, 7, and 9. You have 20 minutes." Rather, your introduction to a practice activity should accomplish three objectives: (1) Inform the learners that they are going to practice something they are capable of succeeding at ("You've done part of this before, so this shouldn't be much different"); (2) dispel anxiety about doing the task through the use of nonevaluative and nonthreatening language ("You've got part of it right, Anita. Now, think some more and you'll have it"); and (3) let the learners know that you will be around to monitor their work and support their efforts ("I will be around to help, so let me know if you have a problem").

- *Practice should be designed to ensure success.*   Practice makes perfect only when those practicing are doing so correctly. If your learners are making many math, punctuation, or problem-solving mistakes, practice is making imperfect. Design your practice to produce as few errors as possible. For example, you should develop worksheets to ensure that most learners complete correctly at least 60% to 80% of the problems.

- *Practice should be arranged to allow students to receive feedback.* As we learned earlier in our discussion of modeling, feedback exerts a powerful effect on learning. Develop procedures and routines for rapid checking of work so that learners know as soon as possible how well they are performing. Using peers to correct one another's practice is an efficient way to give feedback. Also, having answer sheets handy so that learners can check their own work can be a simple and effective means of providing feedback.
- *Practice should have the qualities of progress, challenge, and variety.* Kounin (1970) found that the key to preventing learners from becoming bored was to design practice opportunities so that learners actually see that they are making progress. ("Don't forget to check your answers with the key on the board.") In addition, introduce practice in a challenging and enthusiastic manner. ("This will really test your understanding with some new and interesting kinds of problems.") Finally, practice exercises should include a variety of examples and situations.

You should perform the following activities to ensure that students become actively engaged in the practice you provide:

1. **Direct** the class through the first independent practice item. This gives the scheduled seatwork a definite beginning, and students who are unclear about the assignment can ask questions without distracting others. This also provides a mental model for attaining a correct answer, which students can use in subsequent problems.

2. **Schedule** seatwork as soon as possible after the eliciting and feedback exercises. This helps students understand that independent practice is relevant to the guided practice provided earlier. If you do not provide opportunities for independent practice immediately but provide them on a later day, students likely will make a high number of requests for information; this will lead you inefficiently to repeat key portions of the previous day's lesson. As with all forms of learning, *practice should follow the time of learning as soon as possible* for maximum recall and understanding.

3. **Circulate** around the classroom while students are engaged in independent practice, to provide feedback, ask questions, and give brief explanations (Emmer et al., 1997). Spend circulation time equally across most of your students—don't concentrate on a small number of them. Try to average 30 seconds or less per student (if you average 30 seconds per student, and have 30 students, that consumes 15 minutes of class time). Minimize your scanning of written responses, prompting for alternative answers, or reminding students of facts and rules so as not to reduce your time available for monitoring the work of other students. Monitoring student responses during independent seatwork can be an important direct instruction function if you keep contacts short and focused on specific issues for which a brief explanation is adequate.

WEEKLY AND MONTHLY REVIEWS

The sixth and final direct instruction function involves conducting **weekly and monthly reviews**. Periodic review ensures that you have taught all task-relevant information needed for future lessons and that you have identified areas that require the reteaching of key facts, rules, and sequences. Without periodic review, you have no way of knowing whether direct instruction has been successful in teaching the required facts, rules, and sequences.

Periodic review has long been a part of almost every instructional strategy. In the context of direct instruction, however, periodic review and the recycling of instruction take on added importance because of the brisk pace at which direct instruction is conducted. You usually establish the proper pace by noting the approximate percentage of errors occurring during guided practice and feedback; 60% to 80% correct responses indicate a satisfactory pace.

Weekly and monthly reviews also help determine whether the pace is right or whether to adjust it before covering too much content (Cooper et al., 1987; Englemann, 1991). When student responses in weekly and monthly reviews are correct, quick, and firm about 95% of the time, the pace is adequate. Independent practice and homework should raise the percentage of correct responses from approximately 60% to 80% during guided practice and feedback to approximately 95% on weekly and monthly reviews. If results are below these levels—and especially if they are substantially below—your pace is too fast and some reteaching of facts, rules, and sequences may be necessary, especially if they are prerequisite to later learning.

Another obvious advantage of weekly and monthly reviews is that they strengthen correct but hesitant responses. Reviewing facts, rules, and sequences that are the basis of task-relevant prior understandings for later lessons will give some learners a second chance to grasp material that they missed or only partially learned the first time around. These reviews often are welcomed by students; it is a chance to go over material that they may have missed, that was difficult to learn the first time through, and that may be covered on unit tests.

Finally, a regular weekly review (not a review "every so often") is the key to performing this direct instruction function. The weekly review is intended to build momentum. Momentum results from gradually increasing the coverage and depth of the weekly reviews until it is time for a comprehensive monthly review (Posner, 1987). The objective is to create a review cycle that rises and falls in about a month. The low point of this cycle occurs at the start of a direct instruction unit, when only 1 week's material need be reviewed. The weekly reviews then become increasingly comprehensive until a major monthly review restates and checks for understanding of all the previous month's learning. Momentum is built by targeting greater and greater amounts of instruction for review. This is done in gradual stages so that students are not overwhelmed with unfamiliar review content and so they always know what will be covered in the next review.

Following is a lesson plan for direct instruction based on the dialogue about possessives presented in this chapter.

Example Direct Instruction Lesson Plan: Grammar

Unit Title: Punctuation

Lesson Title: Forming and Punctuating Possessives

1 Gaining attention   Display October school newspaper with punctuation error in head-line. Point to error.

2 Informing the learner of the objective   At the end of the period, students will be able to find mistakes in the newspapers (on file under "Punctuation") and make the necessary changes.

3 Stimulating recall of prerequisite learning   Review the part of speech most likely to own or possess something by asking for the definition of a noun.

4 Presenting the stimulus material   Present two rules of possession: Rule 1. Use the possessive form whenever an *of* phrase can be substituted for a noun. Rule 2. For words that are plurals ending in *s*, place an apostrophe after the *s*. But for proper nouns ending in *s*, place an *apostrophe s* after the *s*. Write rules on board.

5 Eliciting the desired behavior   Display the following examples on a transparency, and ask students to convert them to the possessive form one at a time:

Delay of a month   Speech of the President
Home of Jenkins   The television set of Mr. Burns

(See Smith, G. [1995]. *Understanding Grammar*. New York: City Press, pp. 101–103 for other examples.)

6 Providing feedback   Write the correct possessive form on the transparency as students finish each example. Wait for students to finish (all heads up) before providing the answer for the next example. Probe for complete understanding by asking for the rule.

7 Assessing the behavior   Use the exercise on page 87 of the workbook to assess student understanding and to provide additional practice. Use ordered recitation until about 90% correct responses are attained. Place 10 possessives on the unit test requiring the application of Rule 1 and Rule 2. Use examples in G. Smith (1995), pp. 101–103.

OTHER FORMS OF DIRECT INSTRUCTION

So far, direct instruction has been discussed as though it occurs only in a lecture-recitation format. This is perhaps the most popular format for direct instruction but is by no means the only one. Other ways of executing the direct instruction model (either independent of the lecture-recitation format or in association with it) include computer-assisted instruction, peer and cross-age tutoring, various kinds of audiolingual and communication tools (e.g., recorded lessons for learning to read in the early grades), and the use of the computer as an information provider.

Some of these approaches have been creatively programmed to include all, or almost all, of the six direct instruction functions (checking, presenting and structuring, guided student practice, feedback and correctives, independent practice, and periodic review). Research demonstrates that some of these alternatives to the lecture-recitation format have succeeded with certain types of content and students (Atkinson, 1984; Kulik & Kulik, 1984). However, because these alternative approaches are much less under your control than is the lecture-recitation format you create, you should carefully consider their applicability to your specific instructional goals and students. Although programmed instruction, computer-assisted instructional software, and various drill and practice media, such as described in Chapter 4, often are associated with the direct instruction model, their treatment of the intended content may be far from direct. Therefore, whenever using these formats and associated courseware, be sure to preview both their method and content for close adherence to the six functions of the direct instruction model.

Finally, programmed instruction, computer-assisted instruction software, specialized media, and information and communication technologies follow a direct instruction model most closely when they are programmed for basic academic skills. This is where the direct instruction format can be of most benefit in increasing student achievement (Lindsley, 1991, 1992). At the same time, it can relieve you of the sometimes arduous chore of providing individualized remedial instruction to a small number of students. Building a library of individualized courseware that covers the basic skills most frequently needed in your grade level and content area will be an important goal for your classroom.

PROMOTING THE GOALS OF DIRECT INSTRUCTION IN THE CULTURALLY DIVERSE CLASSROOM

We have seen that a task-oriented teacher maximizes content coverage and gives students the greatest opportunity to learn. Likewise, students who are involved in, acting on, and otherwise thinking about the material being presented have the greatest opportunity to learn. The key to bringing these two important dimensions of effective teaching together—task orientation and student engagement—rests with how you interact with your students to invoke a willingness to respond and apply what they have been learning. In classrooms where the range of individual and cultural differences is great, student engagement in the learning process during direct instruction can be a major challenge to achieving performance outcomes.

One facet of research dealing with cultural diversity and student engagement has focused on differences in fluency and oral expression among learners during lecture-recitation. For example, Kendon (1981) has studied how student fluency or quickness to respond can be influenced by nurturing and expressive qualities of the teacher. The implication of these findings is that student hesitancy in responding and becoming engaged in the learning process may, for some cultural groups, be more a function of the attitude and cultural style of the teacher than of student ability. Douglas (1975) has shown that student engagement is, in part, an expression of the interactive process between student and teacher. Specifically, her research has found that body posture, language, and eye contact form a pattern of *metacommunication* that is recognized by the learner—and acted on according to the message being conveyed, intentionally or not. For example, a formal body posture and questions posed in an expressionless voice, without eye contact, may not invoke a commitment to respond. In other words, teachers must convey a sense of caring about the learner before engagement can take place. Engagement techniques alone (e.g., presenting and structuring, guiding student practice, and providing feedback and corrections) will not be sufficient to actively engage students in the learning process unless these techniques are accompanied by the appropriate metacommunication expressing nurturance and caring. Bowers and Flinders (1991) suggest some of the ways teachers can promote student engagement by conveying a sense of nurturance and caring:

- Use appropriate examples to clarify concepts and model performance. "Let me give you an example that will help you see the relationship."
- Accept the student's way of understanding new concepts. "That's an interesting answer. Would you like to tell us how you arrived at it?"
- Reduce feelings of competitiveness. "Today, those who wish can work with a partner on the practice exercise."
- Increase opportunities for social reinforcement. "If you like, you can ask someone sitting nearby how they worked the problem."
- Facilitate group achievement. "When you're finished with your work, you might join another group to help them solve the problem."
- Use and expect culturally appropriate eye contact with students. "Amanda, I'm going to sit down next to you and watch you work the first problem."
- Recognize longer pauses and slower tempo. "Take your time. I'll wait for you to think of an answer."
- Respond to unique or different questions during a response. "You're asking about something else. Let me give you that answer, then we'll go back to the first question."
- Balance compliments and reinforcement equally. "Let's not forget, both Angel and Damon got the right answer but in different ways."

Although much still needs to be known about cultural diversity and student engagement during direct instruction, one thing is clear: Students of any culture are more likely to engage expressively in the learning process in an atmosphere that (1) emphasizes the importance of unique learner responses, (2) reduces feelings of individual competitiveness, (3) promotes a multisensory learning environment, (4) encourages social reinforcement and peer interaction, and (5) conveys a sense of nurturance and caring.

SUMMING UP

This chapter introduced you to direct instruction strategies. Its main points were as follows:

1. Two broad classifications of learning are facts, rules, and action sequences (Type 1) and concepts, patterns, and abstractions (Type 2).

2. Type 1 outcomes generally represent behaviors at the lower levels of complexity in the cognitive, affective, and psychomotor domains; Type 2 outcomes frequently represent behaviors at the higher levels of complexity in these domains.

3. Type 1 teaching activities require combining facts and rules at the knowledge and comprehension level into a sequence of actions that can be learned through observation, rote repetition, and practice. Type 1 outcomes have "right answers" that can be learned by memorization and practice.

4. Type 2 teaching activities go beyond facts, rules, and sequences to help the learner create, synthesize, identify, and recognize an answer that cannot be easily modeled or memorized. Type 2 outcomes may have many "right answers" that contain criterial attributes forming a concept or pattern.

5. The learning of facts, rules, and action sequences are most commonly taught with teaching strategies that emphasize knowledge acquisition; the learning of concepts, patterns, and abstractions are most commonly taught with teaching strategies that emphasize inquiry or problem solving.

6. The acquisition of facts, rules, and action sequences is most efficiently achieved through a process known as the *direct instruction model.* This model is primarily teacher centered; facts, rules, and action sequences are passed on to students in a lecture-recitation format involving large amounts of teacher talk, questions and answers, review and practice, and the immediate correction of student errors.

7. The direct instruction model is characterized by full-class (as opposed to small-group) instruction; by the organization of learning based on questions posed by you; by the provision of detailed and redundant practice; by the presentation of material so that learners master one new fact, rule, or sequence before the teacher presents the next; and by the formal arrangement of the classroom to maximize drill and practice.

8. Direct instruction is most appropriate when content in texts and workbooks does not appear in appropriately sized pieces, when your active involvement in the teaching process is necessary to arouse or heighten student interest, and when the content to be taught represents task-relevant prior knowledge for subsequent learning.

9. Techniques for daily review and checking include the following:
   - Have students identify difficult homework problems in a question-and-answer format.
   - Sample the understanding of a few students who are likely to represent the class.
   - Explicitly review task-relevant prior learning required for the day's lesson.

10. Techniques for presenting and structuring new content include the following:
    - Establish part–whole relationships.
    - Identify sequential relationships.
    - Find combinatorial relationships.
    - Draw comparative relationships.

11. Techniques for guiding student practice include the following:
    - Ask students to respond privately and then be singled out for help.
    - Call on students to respond whether or not their hands are raised.
    - Prepare questions beforehand, and randomly ask students to respond.

12. Providing appropriate feedback and correctives involves knowing how to respond to answers that are (1) correct, quick, and firm; (2) correct but hesitant; (3) incorrect but careless; and (4) incorrect due to lack of knowledge.

13. For a correct, quick, and firm response, acknowledge the correct response and either ask another question of the same student or quickly move on to another student.

14. For a correct but hesitant response, provide a reinforcing statement and quickly restate the facts, rules, or steps needed for the right answer.

15. For a correct but careless response, indicate that the response is incorrect and quickly move to the next student without further comment.

16. For an incorrect response that is not due to carelessness but to a lack of knowledge, engage the student in finding the correct response with hints, probes, or a related but simpler question.

17. For most learning involving knowledge acquisition, the steps between successive portions of your lesson should be made small enough to produce approximately 60% to 80% correct answers in a practice and feedback session.

18. Reviewing, reexplaining, and prompting are effective until approximately 80% of your students respond correctly, after which correctives should be made briefer or students should be guided to individualized learning materials.

19. Design independent practice so that the learner puts together facts and rules to form action sequences that increasingly resemble applications in the real world. Make opportunities for independent practice as soon after the time of learning as possible.

20. Pace instruction so that student responses to questions posed in weekly and monthly reviews are correct, quick, and firm about 95% of the time.

21. Use independent practice and homework to raise the percentage of correct responses from approximately 60% to 80% during guided practice and feedback to approximately 95% on weekly and monthly reviews.

22. Student engagement in the culturally diverse classroom is promoted by accepting unique learner responses, reducing competitiveness, promoting peer interaction, and conveying a sense of nurturance and caring.

FOR DISCUSSION AND PRACTICE

Questions marked with an asterisk are answered in Appendix B. See also *Bridges: An Activity Guide and Assessment Options,* which accompanies this text.

*1. Identify the learning outcomes associated with Type 1 and Type 2 teaching strategies. To what levels of behavior in the cognitive domain does each type of learning apply?

*2. What type of learning outcomes are elicited by instructional strategies that emphasize knowledge acquisition? What type of learning outcomes are elicited by instructional strategies that emphasize inquiry or problem solving?

*3. If you were to describe the direct instruction model, what instructional characteristics would you associate with it?

*4. Provide some examples of action verbs in the cognitive, affective, and psychomotor domains that describe the type of outcomes expected from the direct instructional model. Which outcomes to you think would be hardest to achieve?

*5. For what instructional goals is the direct instruction model most appropriate? Can you think of any others not cited in the chapter?

*6. During direct instruction, what would be some of the ways you might review and check the previous day's work? Which do you feel would be the most appropriate for your classroom?

*7. After identifying the four techniques for structuring content, provide an example of each in a subject you will be teaching. Which do you think most naturally fits the way your subject matter is organized?

*8. Identify the order in which rules and examples of the rules should be given to promote the greatest amount of comprehension and retention of content. Illustrate a rule–example sequence with content from your major teaching area.

*9. Explain why providing guided student practice in a nonevaluative atmosphere is important for learning to occur. What would you do to encourage a reluctant student to make a first crude response?

*10. During direct instruction, how is prompting used to help a student achieve the correct response? Choose a topic, and create an example of a prompt you would give a student after a wrong or partially wrong response. Indicate both the student's incorrect answer and your response.

*11. What are four different degrees at which a student response may vary in its correctness? Create a teacher response that you think is appropriate to each of the four degrees.

12. The following second-grade student responses were received by a teacher after asking the question, "What does 5 plus 3 equal?"

Brooke: It could be 8.
Juan: 9.
Jason: 53.
Ashley: 8.

Role play an appropriate teacher prompt that moves each student closer to the right or more confident answer.

13. The following tenth-grade student responses were received by a teacher who asked, "What was one of the underlying reasons for the Civil War?"

Tahnee: The South wanted the land owned by the North.
Akim: I read somewhere it was religious persecution.
Ken: Well, let me think . . . it had something to do with slavery.
Tracy: The economics of the South.

Role play an appropriate teacher prompt that moves each student closer to the right or more confident answer.

*14. What are four strategies for responding to an incorrect response cited in this chapter? Think of at least one other, and give an example of how you would use it.

*15. What approximate percentage of correct answers should you work toward in a practice and feedback session? How you would change your instructional approach if only 30% of your student responses were correct in a practice and feedback session.

*16. What is the primary purpose of independent practice in direct instruction? Choose a lesson in your teaching area, and show how you would use independent practice to fulfill this purpose. How would you vary the independent practice if more time and opportunity for practice became available?

*17. When circulating around the room to monitor independent practice, what would be some of the ways you could make your monitoring time more efficient?

*18. Approximately what percentage of student responses during weekly and monthly review sessions should be correct, quick, and firm? What percentage would prompt you to reconsider your teaching approach to this content?

*19. Describe a cycle of weekly and monthly review that you would like to implement in your classroom. Indicate how the sequence of review activities you have described can engage students in the learning process by creating rising and falling action, heightening student interest, and building momentum.

20. What metacommunication techniques might be used in a culturally diverse classroom to promote engagement during instruction? With examples, illustrate how some might be more culturally appropriate than others.

6 Indirect Instruction Strategies

This chapter will help you answer the following questions:

1. What is the indirect instruction model?
2. What are constructivist strategies for teaching?
3. How does direct instruction differ from indirect instruction?
4. What teacher behaviors are required for indirect instruction?
5. What are some ways of promoting the goals of indirect instruction in a culturally diverse classroom?

*Chapter 5 introduced you to direct instruction for teaching facts, rules, and action sequences. Now we will consider strategies using the **indirect instruction model** for teaching concepts, patterns, and abstractions.*

Inquiry, problem solving, and discovery learning each are different forms of the more general concept of indirect instruction. Indirect instruction is an approach to teaching and learning in which (1) the learning process is inquiry, (2) the result is discovery, and (3) the learning context is a problem.

These three ideas of inquiry, discovery, and problem solving are brought together in special ways in the indirect model of teaching and learning. This chapter presents instructional strategies you can use to compose your own indirect teaching approach.

It is the third 6 weeks of the fall semester, and Tim Robbins is teaching a unit on fractions to his fourth-grade class.* During the first 12 weeks of the year, all fourth graders learned about numbers and number theory. They covered such topics as odd, even, positive, and negative numbers. The fourth graders are also familiar with such numerical concepts as multiples, factors, and the base 10 system for writing numbers.

On the day we observe Mr. Robbins, he is teaching a lesson about equivalent fractions as different ways of representing the same amount. During the preceding four lessons, his learners have studied about fractions as quantities and learned how fractions that look different (e.g., ½, ¾) actually represent the same amount. The present lesson is intended to reinforce this idea.

Mr. Robbins begins the lesson with a quick review of the previous lesson. On the overhead projector, he shows pictures of objects such as pies and loaves of bread divided to represent different fractions of the whole. In rapid-fire fashion, his learn-

---

*Adapted from *Educational Psychology: A Contemporary Approach* (pp. 174–176), by G. Borich and M. Tombari, 1997, New York: Longman.

Figure 6.1 Mr. Robbins's chart for teaching fractions.

$\frac{1}{4}$ x $\frac{25}{25}$	$\frac{25}{100}$	.25
$\frac{1}{2}$ x $\frac{}{50}$	$\frac{}{100}$	.
$\frac{1}{5}$ x	$\frac{}{100}$	.
$\frac{2}{5}$	$\frac{}{100}$	.
$\frac{3}{4}$	$\frac{}{100}$	.
$\frac{5}{4}$	$\frac{}{100}$	.
$\frac{3}{2}$	$\frac{}{100}$	.

ers call out the fractions. He then projects a chart with undivided whole objects and has learners come up and divide them into halves, thirds, fourths, and so on while other learners do the same on worksheets. Each learner gets immediate feedback on his or her answers.

Next, he signals the class to clear their desks except for a pencil and draws their attention to a large, brightly colored chart hanging from the front blackboard. (The chart is shown in Figure 6.1.)

He passes out a similar dittoed chart to the students. Mr. Robbins explains that for each row the students are to complete the fraction with a denominator of 100 that equals the fraction in the row. Then, they are to fill in the third square with the decimal equivalent of that fraction.

Mr. Robbins first models how to do this. He demonstrates (pointing out that they have already learned this) how to make an equivalent fraction by multiplying the original fraction by a fraction that equals 1. He works several examples to be sure that his students have the concept and copy the examples onto their chart.

He then calls on several students to come to the front of the room and demonstrate several more examples for the class. Mr. Robbins has the students state as they work, for the class to hear, how they are solving the problems. He checks that the rest of the class correctly fills in the chart at their desks.

Finally, he breaks the class into small groups and directs them to fill out the remainder of the chart. He provides each group with a key to immediately check their responses when finished. As the learners busily engage in their seatwork, Mr. Robbins moves from group to group, checking, giving feedback, correcting, or praising as needed.

Mr. Robbins has designed this lesson to show that fractions that look different can be equal in order to point out the relationship of decimals and fractions and to use this as a foundation for teaching the relationships between dollars, decimals, and fractions in a subsequent lesson.

In the classroom next door to Mr. Robbins, Kay Greer also is teaching a unit on fractional equivalents.*

As the lesson begins, Mrs. Greer asks Denisha to tell the class what she said yesterday about fractions. "A fraction like ½ isn't a number," she asserts, "because it isn't on the number line," Denisha points to the number line running along the top of the front blackboard. "See! There's no ½. Just 1, 2, 3, 4, . . . like that!"

"Well, class, let's think about what Denisha says. Let me give you a problem, and we'll study it and, then, maybe come to some conclusion about if a fraction is a number." She turns on the overhead and projects the following for all to see:

A boy has four loaves of bread that he bought at the local supermarket. He has eight friends, and he wants each friend to get an equal part of the bread. How much bread should he give each of his friends?

Mrs. Greer draws the four loaves on the overhead and watches as the children, arranged in six groups of five children, copy the drawings into the notebook. She walks around the classroom, occasionally prompting groups with the question "How much bread is each one going to get?"

The children argue among themselves: "You can't do it!" "There isn't enough bread!" "How many slices are in each loaf?" After about 10 minutes Mrs. Greer asks, "Does anyone need more time to work on this? How many are ready to discuss?"

A few raise their hands. The rest are busy drawing and redrawing loaves of bread, sketching lines across them. Several minutes go by, and Mrs. Greer says, "OK, would someone like to show their solution?"

Frank raises his hand, walks to the overhead, and draws his solution. "I'm not sure it's right," he hedges. Frank draws four loaves of bread and divides each loaf into eight slices.

---

*Adapted from "Teaching Mathematics for Understanding: What Do Teachers Need to Know About Subject Matter?" by D. L. Ball, in *Teaching Academic Subjects to Diverse Learners* (pp. 67–69), edited by M. L. Kennedy, 1991, New York: Teachers College Press.

He looks up and announces to the class, "Each friend gets four slices!"

"That's wrong!" challenges Rosa. "Each friend gets two slices, see!" She walks to the overhead, draws four loaves of bread, and divides each loaf into four slices. "Each friend gets two slices," she asserts, pointing to the equal portions.

"Why not just give each friend half a loaf?" asks Albert.

"Come up here and draw your solution," says Mrs. Greer. Albert walks up to the overhead and sketches his proposal to the class. "Can you write the number that each gets?" she asks. Albert writes the number "1/2" on the board.

"Well, Albert's and Rosa's slices are bigger than mine," protests Frank.

"Frank," asks Mrs. Greer, "why not write the number that shows how much of the bread your eight friends get? Albert's number is ½. How much is one slice as Albert sees it?" she asks the class.

"One-eighth," proposes Cal.

"Can you write that?" inquires Mrs. Greer. Cal comes up to the overhead and writes ⅛ next to Frank's drawing.

As children write different numbers for their solutions, Mrs. Greer asks, "Well, how can we have three different numbers for each of these solutions? We have one-half, two-fourths, four-eighths," pointing to the different quantities and fractions on the overhead.

After several moments of silence, several hands shoot up, and one by one the children give explanations for the seeming discrepancy.

The lesson continues in this vein until 5 minutes before the bell. Mrs. Greer reviews what was concluded and sets the goal for the next lesson on fractions.

Now, let's compare the lessons of Mrs. Greer and Mr. Robbins. Both lessons had the same goal: to help learners understand the concepts of quantity and equivalence pertaining to fractions. But, they have designed two very different lessons to achieve this same end!

You may have noticed that the direct instruction approach has heavily influenced Mr. Robbins's lesson. He designed his lesson to elicit a minimum of mistakes. His activities elicit practice of correct responses followed by immediate feedback. For Mr. Robbins, learning involves correct responding, which is best accomplished by a teacher-directed or teacher-centered lesson.

Mrs. Greer, on the other hand, has a more indirect approach to learning. She is less focused on correct, rapid responses than on thought processes involving reflection, problem solving, analysis, and inquiry. Her lesson takes into consideration that her learners already have information and beliefs about fractions that may or may not be correct.

She wants to expose misconceptions and challenge learners to acquire new, more accurate perceptions through their own powers of reasoning. She carefully avoids providing answers. Her objective is to help learners understand fractions by influencing the cognitive processes by which they can elicit correct responses. Let's look at some of the cognitive processes around which she planned her lesson.

THE COGNITIVE PROCESSES OF LEARNING

Cognitive psychologists have identified three essential conditions for meaningful learning (R. E. Mayer, 1987): reception, availability, and activation. The *reception* and *availability* conditions are met when teachers focus their learners' attention on a problem and provide them with an anticipatory set or advance organizer (Glover & Corkill, 1990). Teachers fulfill the *activation* condition by modeling the inquiry process and by skilled questioning techniques. As learners develop greater skill at inquiry and problem solving, the teacher gradually fades assistance and allows learners to assume more and more responsibility for their own learning.

Supporting this approach to learning and instruction is a movement called **constructivism.** Constructivist lessons are designed and sequenced to encourage learners to use their own experiences to actively construct meaning that makes sense to them rather than to acquire understanding through exposure to a format organized by the teacher (Steffe & Gale, 1995).

Constructivists believe that knowledge results from the individual constructing reality from her or his own perspective. Learning occurs when the learner creates new rules and hypotheses to explain what is being observed. The need to create new rules and formulate hypotheses is stimulated by classroom dialogue, problem-solving exercises, and individual projects and assignments that create discrepancies—or an imbalance—between old knowledge and new observations. Teachers use direct experience (Piaget, 1977), project-based learning (Blumenfeld et al., 1991), and social interaction (Vygotsky, 1962) to restore the balance, while deemphasizing the role of lecturing and telling. Recent subject matter advances in reading, writing, mathematics, and social studies have followed constructivist thinking and the indirect instructional strategies that support it (T. Duffy & Jonassen, 1992). Let's look at some of these indirect instructional strategies that have followed constructivist thinking.

Reading

For most of the twentieth century, reading curricula have taught the skills of decoding, blending, sequencing, finding main ideas, and so on outside the context of reading itself. These skills were usually practiced with contrived stories written in basal readers. Constructivist-influenced reading curricula now teach basic reading skills with a balanced approach, such as through the reading of literature while engaged in a search for meaning. Learners often work in small groups, cooperatively reading to one another and asking and answering questions based on extended reading assignments. Fact-oriented worksheets are deemphasized.

Writing

Constructivist-oriented approaches to writing instruction provide a problem-solving context by focusing learners' attention on the importance of communication. They practice writing skills not in isolation but while working on writing activities that require learners to communicate ideas meaningfully to real audiences. From their very earliest attempts at writing, learners realize that someone will read what they write. Thus, what they write must be understandable. Writing instruction, then, involves a process of developing initial drafts, revising, and polishing.

Mathematics

Authentic problems, such as the one presented in the dialogue with Mrs. Greer at the beginning of this chapter, are the focus of constructivist approaches to math instruction. In such approaches we see little time spent on the rote drill and practice of individual math skills. Rather, students are taught within a problem-solving or application context from the very beginning. The teacher attempts to have learners become actively involved in exploring, predicting, reasoning, and conjecturing.

Social Studies

Constructivist approaches to social studies have the goal of helping learners acquire a rich network of understandings around a limited number of topics. Parker (1991) advocates that the K–12 social studies curriculum should focus on five essential learnings: the democratic process, cultural diversity, economic development, global perspectives, and participatory citizenship. The blending of these critical elements within a single curriculum requires a constructivist view of teaching and learning that promotes the following:

1. In-depth study—the sustained examination of a limited number of important topics
2. Higher-order challenge—the design of curriculum and instruction that requires students to gather and use information in nonroutine applications
3. Authentic assessment—pointing students' schoolwork toward performance-oriented exhibitions of learning

These subject matter advances assume that students construct their own understanding of skills and knowledge rather than having it told or given to them by the teacher. Therefore, lesson plans are expected to have the following characteristics:

1. Present instructional activities in the form of problems for students to solve.
2. Develop and refine students' answers to problems from the point of view and experience of the student.
3. Acknowledge the social nature of learning by encouraging the interaction of teacher with students and students with one another.

Another goal of constructivist teaching is to present **integrated bodies of knowledge.** Integrated units and lessons stress the connections between ideas and the logical coherence of interrelated topics (Calfee, 1986; Rosenshine, 1986), as shown in Figure 6.2 for the social studies curriculum suggested by Parker (1991). The role of the constructivist approach is to present authentic problems using the interaction and naturally occurring dialogue of the classroom to foster integrated bodies of knowledge. Let's see how this is done using the indirect model of instruction.

Figure 6.2 Five essential learnings spiral upward through each grade to form an integrated body of knowledge.

Source: From *Renewing the Social Studies Curriculum* (p. 2), by W. Parker, 1991, Alexandria, VA: Association for Supervision and Curriculum Development. Copyright 1991 by Association for Supervision and Curriculum Development. Reprinted with permission.

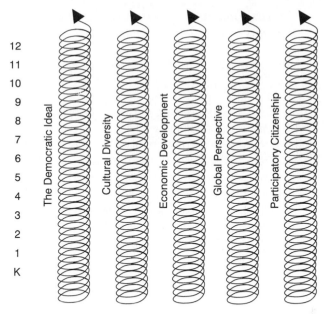

History - Geography - Civics

COMPARING DIRECT AND INDIRECT INSTRUCTION

Because direct instruction strategies are best suited for the teaching of facts, rules, and action sequences, it should be no surprise to learn that indirect instruction strategies are best suited for teaching concepts, patterns, and abstractions.

When you present instructional stimuli to your learners in the form of content, materials, objects, and events and ask them to go beyond the information given to make conclusions and generalizations or find a pattern of relationships, you are using the indirect model of instruction. *Indirect* means that the learner acquires a behavior indirectly by transforming—or constructing—the stimulus material into a meaningful response or behavior that differs from both (1) the content used to present the learning and (2) any previous response given by the student. Because the learner can add to the content and rearrange it to be more meaningful, the elicited response or behavior can take many different forms. In contrast to direct instruction outcomes, there is rarely a single, best answer when using the indirect model of instruction. Instead, the learner is guided to an answer that goes beyond the specific problem or content presented.

You might wonder why, if direct instruction is so effective teaching many facts, rules, or action sequences, it is not used all the time. The answer is that not all desired outcomes call for responses that resemble the stimulus material. Direct instruction is limited to (1) learning units of the stimulus material so they can be remembered and (2) composing parts of the stimulus material into a whole, so a rapid and automatic response can occur. As noted in Chapter 5, these two cognitive processes are called *unitization* and *automaticity*.

Learning at the lower levels of the cognitive, affective, and psychomotor domains places heavy reliance on these two processes. Both can be placed into action by stimulus material that closely resembles the desired response (e.g., "Look at this word and then say it," "Watch me form a possessive and then you do the next one," "Read the instructions, then focus the microscope.") The desired response need not go much beyond what is provided. The task for the learner is simply to produce a response that mirrors the form and content of the stimulus. A great deal of instruction involves behavior that requires only unitization and automaticity. For this, the direct instruction model is most efficient and effective.

Real-world activities often involve analysis, synthesis, and decision-making behaviors in the cognitive domain, organization and characterization behaviors in the affective domain, and articulation and naturalization behaviors in the psychomotor domain. This complicates instruction, because these behaviors are not learned by memorizing the parts and reassembling them into a whole rapidly and automatically, as are behaviors at lower levels of complexity. Instead, they must be constructed by the learner's own attempts to use personal experiences and past learnings to bring meaning to—and make sense out of—the stimulus material. While lower-level behaviors are required to attain more complex behaviors, much more is needed by both teacher and learners before higher-level behaviors can be learned. As you will see in this chapter, the teaching of higher-level behaviors requires a different set of instructional strategies.

EXAMPLES OF CONCEPTS, PATTERNS, AND ABSTRACTIONS

Before describing the strategies that allow your learners to acquire higher-level behaviors, let's consider some examples of topics that require complex behavior to master:

- Concept of a quadratic equation (algebra)
- Process of acculturation (social studies)
- Meaning of *contact sports* (physical education)
- Workings of a democracy (government)
- Playing a concerto (music)
- Demonstration of photosynthesis (biology)
- Understanding the law of conservation of energy (general science)

Learning these topics requires not just facts, rules, and action sequences but much more: *concepts, processes, meanings,* and *understandings.* If you teach just the facts, rules, and action sequences about quadratic equations—"Here is the *definition,*" "Here are the *rules* for solving them," or "Follow this *sequence* of steps"—your students may never learn the concept that binds together quadratic equations of different forms or how to use these equations in a new or novel situation. Instead, your students must learn to add to, rearrange, and elaborate on the stimulus material you present, using more complex cognitive processes. Let's consider how this is done.

Recall from Chapter 5 (Table 5.3) the distinction between Type 1 and Type 2 behaviors. Type 1 behaviors become Type 2 behaviors by using facts, rules, and sequences to form concepts. Notice what would be required, for example, if students tried to learn the concept of *frog* in the same way they acquired facts, rules, and action sequences about a frog.

First, students would have to commit to memory all possible instances of frogs (of which there may be hundreds). Trying to retain hundreds of frog images *in the same form they were presented* would quickly overburden students' memories. Second, even after committing many types of frogs to memory, learners could confuse frogs with similar animals. This is because the memorization process does not include the characteristics that exclude other animals from being frogs (e.g., a hard shell, dry skin, color changes, tail).

The process of generalization and discrimination, if planned for in the presentation of your lesson, can help students overcome both of these problems. **Generalization** helps them respond in a similar manner to stimuli that differ, thereby increasing the range of instances to which particular facts, rules, and sequences apply (e.g., to all types of frogs). In addition, **discrimination** selectively restricts this range by eliminating things that appear to match the student's concept (e.g., a chameleon) but that differ from it in critical dimensions (e.g., has a tail).

Generalization and discrimination help students classify visually different stimuli into the same category, based on *criterial attributes*. Criterial attributes act as magnets, drawing together all instances of the same type without requiring the learner to memorize all possible instances. As a concept (frog) becomes combined with other concepts to form larger patterns (amphibians), patterns of increasing complexity are produced. Figure 6.3 shows a hierarchy of concepts, patterns, and abstractions typically found in a science curriculum.

It is apparent that your role as teacher and your organization of stimulus material need to be different for the learning of concepts, patterns, and abstractions. For outcomes at higher levels of behavioral complexity, the stimulus material cannot contain all possible instances of the concept being learned. However, it must provide the appropriate associations or generalizations necessary to distinguish the most important dimensions—the criterial attributes.

The indirect instruction model uses instructional strategies that encourage the cognitive processes required both to form concepts and to combine concepts into larger patterns and abstractions. Figure 6.4 shows some of the **indirect instruction functions** performed by a teacher using this model.

You can see from Figure 6.4 that indirect instruction is more complex than direct instruction. Classroom activities are less teacher centered. This brings student ideas and experiences into the lesson and lets students begin evaluating their own responses. Because the behaviors are more complex, so too are your teaching strategies. To build toward outcomes that may require either advance organization or inductive and/or deductive reasoning, extended forms of reasoning and questioning are required. Teachers can use a variety of examples and group discussions to accomplish this.

Figure 6.3 A hierarchy of abstraction representing possible units of instruction in a science curriculum.

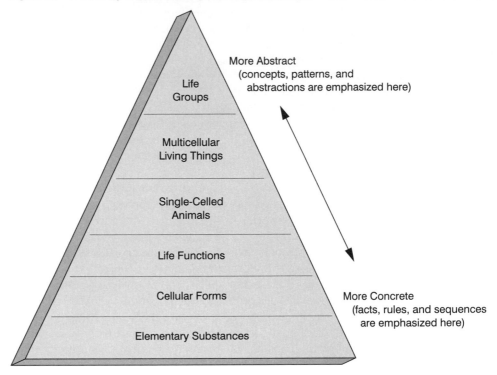

The indirect instruction functions in Figure 6.4 and the teaching behaviors that compose them are among the teaching functions having the highest correlation with positive student attitudes (Fielding, Kameenui, & Gerstein, 1983). These also are the teaching functions thought to be most useful in providing behaviors that students will use in their adult lives (Mitchell, 1992; Tombari & Borich, 1999).

AN EXAMPLE OF INDIRECT INSTRUCTION

Now let's examine a dialogue of indirect instruction and compare it to the dialogue of direct instruction in Chapter 5. The objective this time is Type 2 outcomes, not Type 1 outcomes. This dialogue reflects some facts, rules, and sequences that were taught previously, but the ultimate goal is the formation of concepts, patterns, and abstractions. As you read, note the italicized, bold, indirect instruction functions from Figure 6.4.

This lesson is a glimpse into a government class where a lesson on different economic systems is in progress. The teacher gets the students' attention by asking if anyone knows what system of government in the world is undergoing the most change. Marty raises his hand.

Figure 6.4   Some indirect instruction functions.

1. *Content Organization:* Providing advance organizers that serve as "pegs" on which students
   • Hang key points
   • Focus learning in most productive areas
2. *Conceptual movement:* Induction and deduction using
   • Selected events to establish general concepts and patterns (induction)
   • Principles and generalizations that apply to specific events (deduction)
3. *Examples and nonexamples*
   • Introducing critical attributes that promote accurate generalizations
   • Gradually expanding a set of examples
   • Heightening discrimination with noncritical attributes
4. *Questions:* Raising questions that
   • Guide the search and discovery process
   • Present contradictions
   • Probe for deeper understanding
   • Point the discussion in new directions
   • Pass responsibility for learning to the student
5. *Learner experience* (Using student ideas): Encouraging students to
   • Use references from their own experience
   • Use examples to seek clarification
   • Draw parallels and associations
6. *Student self-evaluation*
   • Asking students to evaluate the appropriateness of their own responses
   • Providing cues, questions, and hints that call attention to inappropriate responses
7. *Discussion:* Promoting classroom dialogue that encourages students to
   • examine alternatives
   • judge solutions
   • make predictions
   • discover generalizations that encourage critical thinking

Teacher:	Marty.
Marty:	I think it's communism, because the Soviet Union broke up, and Russia instituted democratic reforms.
Teacher:	That's right. And because this change will probably continue to affect all our lives in the years ahead, it may be a good idea to know what communism is and why those who live under it want to change it. To get us started, let me ask if anyone knows where the phrase "government of the people, by the people, for the people" comes from. (Rena raises her hand.) Rena?
Rena:	From Lincoln's Gettysburg Address . . . I think near the end.

Teacher:	That's right. Most nations have similar statements that express the basic principles on which their laws, customs, and economics are based. Today, we will study three systems by which nations can guide, control, and operate their economies. The three systems we will study are *capitalism, socialism,* and *communism.* They often are confused with the political systems that tend to be associated with them. A political system not only influences the economic system of a country but also guides individual behavior in many other areas, such as what is taught in schools, the relationship between church and state, how people are chosen for or elected to political office, what jobs people can have, and what newspapers can print. ***(Content organization)***
	For example, in the United States, we have an economic system that is based on the principles of capitalism—or private ownership of capital—but a political system that is based on the principle of democracy—or rule by the people. These two sets of principles are not the same, and in the next few days, you will see how they sometimes work in harmony and sometimes create contradictions that require changes in an economic system, like those occurring today in some formerly communist economies. ***(Content organization)***
	Today we will cover only systems dealing with the ownership of goods and services in different countries—that is, just the economic systems. Later I will ask you to distinguish these from political systems. Who would like to start by telling us what the word *capitalism* means? ***(Questions)***
Robert:	It means making money.
Teacher:	What else, Robert?
Robert:	Owning land . . . I think.
Teacher:	Not only land, but . . . ***(Probes for deeper understanding)***
Robert:	Owning anything.
Teacher:	The word *capital* means tangible goods or possessions. Is a house tangible? ***(Conceptual movement: Deduction)***
Betty:	Yes.
Teacher:	Is a friendship tangible?
Betty:	Yes.
Teacher:	What about that, Mark? ***(Asks student to self-evaluate)***
Mark:	I don't think so.
Teacher:	Why?
Mark:	You can't touch it.
Teacher:	Right. You can touch a person who is a friend but not the friendship. Besides, you can't own or possess a person. . . . So, what would be a good definition of *tangible goods?*
Betty:	Something you own and can touch or see.
Teacher:	Not bad. Let me list some things on the board, and you tell me whether they could be called capital. (Writes the list) ***(Examples and nonexamples)***

car

stocks and bonds

religion

information

clothes

vacation

OK. Who would like to say which of these are *capital?* (Ricky raises his hand.) *(Conceptual movement: Deduction)*

Ricky: Car and clothes are the only two I see.

Barbara: I'd add stocks and bonds. They say you own a piece of something, although maybe not the whole thing.

Teacher: Could you see or touch it? *(Questions)*

Barbara: Yes, if you went to see the place or thing you owned a part of.

Teacher: Good. What about a vacation? Did that give anyone trouble?

Mickey: Well, you can own it . . . I mean you pay for it, and you can see yourself having a good time. (The class laughs.)

Teacher: That may be true, so let's add one last condition to our definition of capital. You must be able to own it, see or touch it, and it must be *durable*—or least for a reasonable period of time. So now, how would you define *capitalism?* **(Conceptual movement: Induction)**

Sue: An economic system that allows you to have capital—or to own tangible goods that last for a reasonable period of time. And, I suppose, sell the goods, if you wanted.

Teacher: Very good. Many different countries across the world have this form of economic system. Just to see if you've got the idea, who can name three countries, besides our own, that allow the ownership of tangible goods? *(Learner experience)*

Joe: Japan, Germany, and Canada.

Teacher: Good. In all these countries, capital, in the form of tangible goods, can be owned by individuals.

This dialogue illustrates one variation of the indirect model of instruction. Notice that this lesson used the naturally occurring dialogue of the classroom to encourage learners to bring their own experiences and past learnings to the topic rather than to acquire an understanding by having it presented to them in an already organized form. This lesson required learners to build an understanding of the topic collectively under the guidance of the teacher using one another's predictions, hypotheses, and experiences. Figure 6.4 summarized some of the teaching functions used in indirect instruction. Remembering these functions, let's consider the extent to which this example lesson contains key aspects of indirect instruction.

ADVANCE ORGANIZERS

Comparing the dialogues for direct and indirect instruction, what differences do you notice? Obviously, they differ in complexity. This is not by chance, because teaching more complex behaviors takes more time and planning. The extensive planning needed for higher-order learning is one of the most overlooked aspects of indirect instruction. With more expansive and complex content, the lesson must be introduced with a framework or structure that organizes the content into meaningful parts *even before the content is presented*. This is the first element of planning for indirect instruction—organizing the content in advance.

One way of providing this framework is to use advance organizers (Ausubel, 1968; Glover & Corkill, 1990; Luiten, Ames, & Aerson, 1980). An advance organizer gives learners a *conceptual preview* of what is to come and helps prepare them to store, label, and package the content for retention and later use. In a sense, an advance organizer is a treelike structure with main limbs that act as pegs, or place holders, for the branches that are yet to come. Without these limbs on which to hang content, important distinctions can easily become blurred or lost.

For example, the lesson dialogue began with an introduction about coverage of the day's lesson. To set the stage, the teacher introduced two abstractions (economic systems and political systems), each comprising a complex network of concepts (taxes, ownership, goods, services, etc.). At the beginning of the lesson, he alerted students to the reason for drawing such an early distinction between a political and an economic system ("*capitalism, socialism,* and *communism* . . . often are confused with the political systems"; "Today we will cover only . . . *economic* systems. Later I will ask you to distinguish these from political systems.") Figure 6.5 represents a graphic representation of an advance organizer that this teacher might have used to open the lesson

Advance organizers, especially at the higher levels of behavioral complexity, are rarely single words or phrases that enlighten students when merely uttered. Instead, they are concepts woven into the lesson fabric to provide an overview of the day's work *and all topics to which it will subsequently relate*. Advance organizers can be presented orally or as charts and diagrams, as seen in Figure 6.4. Following are example advance organizing activities provided at the beginning of a lesson:

- Showing a chart that illustrates the skeletal evolution of humans before explaining the skeletal relationships among forms of animal life (biology).
- Drawing examples of right, equilateral, and isosceles triangles before introducing the concept of a right triangle (plane geometry).
- Discussing the origins of the Civil War before describing its major battles (American history).
- Describing what is meant by a *figure of speech* before introducing the concepts of *metaphor* and *simile* (English).
- Listening to examples of both vowels and consonants before teaching the vowel sounds (reading).
- Showing and explaining the origins of the periodic table of elements before introducing any of the individual elements (chemistry).

Figure 6.5 An advance organizer for a unit on government.

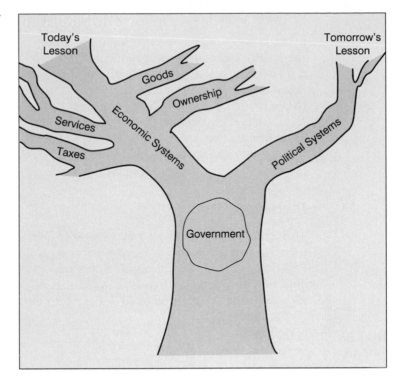

Notice that each of these examples presents a general concept into which fits the specific concept that is the subject of the day's lesson. This is not accomplished by reviewing earlier content, which often is confused with the idea of an advance organizer. Instead, it is done by creating a conceptual structure—skeletal evolution, various triangular shapes, Civil War origins, figures of speech, the alphabet, an organized system of chemical elements—into which you can place not only the content to be taught but also the content for related lessons.

Therefore, these advance organizers set the groundwork for focusing the lesson topic. They prevent every lesson from being seen as something entirely new. Finally, they integrate related concepts into larger and larger patterns and abstractions that later become more authentic unit outcomes (evolution of man, triangular shapes, determinants of civil war, figures of speech). An advance organizer identifies the highest level of behavior resulting from a lesson sequence and to which the outcome of the present day's lesson will contribute. In the example, this higher-level outcome was to distinguish between economic and political systems, a distinction organized in advance by the teacher's introductory remarks.

Methods that are particularly suited for structuring content and composing advance organizers for indirect instruction are the *problem-centered, decision-making,* and *network* approaches for organizing content.

Problem Centered

A problem-centered approach identifies and provides students in advance with all the steps required to solve a particular problem. This approach begins by observing a specific event and concludes with how or why it occurred. For example, you might begin a general science lesson by demonstrating that liquid cannot be removed through a straw from a tightly sealed bottle. The question "Why does this happen?" establishes the problem. You then might give your students a problem-solving sequence like the one shown in Figure 6.6. Such a chart and its sequence of events become the advance organizer for the lesson. Each of its steps provides an organizational branch for a particular part of the lesson.

Decision Making

This same problem can also be organized hierarchically by showing the internal branching, or steps, that you must follow to arrive at a conclusion. While the problem-centered approach establishes the steps to be followed, the decision-making approach focuses on *alternative paths* that might be followed—or decisions that must be made—in exploring and discovering new information about a topic.

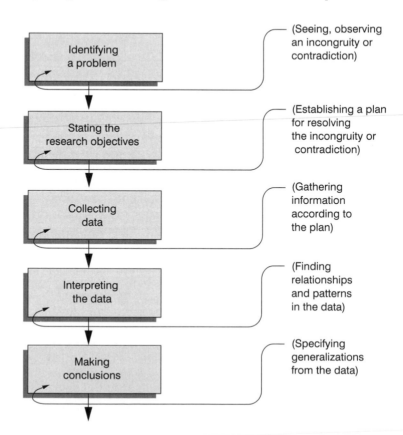

Figure 6.6   Structuring a lesson using a problem-centered approach.

Figure 6.7 shows how the decision-making approach can be applied to the science question just posed. Although the students don't know at what level of the hierarchy the experiment will end, they could be shown the entire list of possible alternatives. This form of advance organizer is a particularly effective attention getter when you are asking students to contribute branches to the hierarchy and allowing them to trace the results of their inquiry as each decision point is reached (as indicated by the solid lines).

Networking

Networking is a third type of organization often helpful for organizing and communicating the structure of a lesson in advance. Networking illustrates relationships among the data, materials, objects, and events that students must consider to solve a problem. When different aspects of a problem are to be considered in relation to each other, as in Figure 6.8, a picture of the network of relationships becomes the advance organizer. The triangular network in Figure 6.8 is particularly important to

Figure 6.7 Structuring a lesson using a decision-making approach.

Why doesn't the liquid flow through the straw?

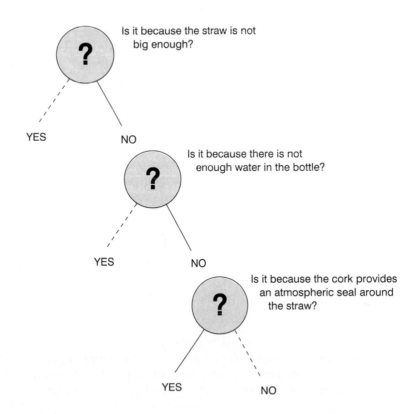

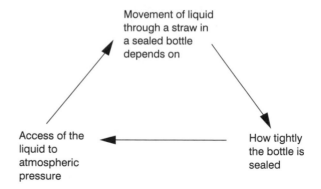

Figure 6.8 Structuring a lesson using a network approach.

the goals of the example science lesson, because it is the *relationship among several events* that may provide the best solution to this problem.

Each of these structuring methods—problem centered, decision making, networking—is a useful advance organizer when you communicate it to students in advance and when you tie key steps, decisions, or relationships back to the advance organizer as they occur in the lesson. To the extent these structuring devices can provide the branches on which subsequent content can be placed, they serve a useful purpose as advance organizers.

CONCEPTUAL MOVEMENT—INDUCTIVE AND DEDUCTIVE

Inductive Reasoning

Inductive reasoning is a thinking process used when a set of data is presented and students are asked to draw a conclusion, make a generalization, or develop a pattern of relationships from the data (Tamir, 1995). It is a process in which students observe specific facts and then generalize them to other circumstances. Much of our everyday thinking proceeds in this manner. For example:

1. We notice that rain-slick roads are causing accidents on the way to school, so we reduce speed at all subsequent intersections.
2. We get an unsatisfactory grade on a chemistry exam, so we study 6 extra hours a week for the rest of the semester in all our subjects.
3. We see a close friend suffer from the effects of drug abuse, so we volunteer to disseminate information about substance abuse to all our acquaintances.
4. We get a math teacher who is cold and unfriendly, so we decide never to enroll in a math course again.

What these instances have in common is that they started with a specific observation of a limited set of data and ended with a generalization in a much broader context. Between the beginning and end of each sequence was an interpretation of observed events and the projection of this interpretation to all similar circumstances.

Deductive Reasoning

Deductive reasoning proceeds from principles or generalizations to their application in specific instances. Deductive thinking includes testing generalizations to see if they hold in specific cases. Typically, a laboratory experiment in the sciences follows the deductive method. In these fields the experimenter often begins with a theory or hypothesis about what should happen and then tests it with an experiment to see if it accurately predicts. If it does, the generalization with which the experiment began is true, at least under the conditions of the experiment. The following steps are frequently used in deductive thinking:

1. State a theory or generalization to be tested.
2. Form a hypothesis in the form of a prediction.
3. Observe or collect data to test the hypothesis.
4. Analyze and interpret the data to determine if the prediction is true, at least some of the time.
5. Conclude whether the generalization held true in the specific context in which it was tested.

Deductive methods are familiar in everyday life. For example, consider the four examples of inductive thinking listed previously to see how much change is required for them to become examples of deductive thinking. Here are the examples again—this time illustrating deduction:

1. We believe that rain-slick roads are the prime contributor to traffic accidents at intersections. We make observations one rainy morning on the way to school and find that, indeed, more accidents have occurred at intersections than usual—our prediction that wet roads cause accidents at intersections is confirmed.
2. We believe that studying 6 extra hours a week will *not* substantially raise our grades. We study 6 extra hours and find that our grades have gone up—our prediction that extra studying will not influence our grades is *not* confirmed.
3. We believe that drug abuse can be detrimental to one's physical and emotional well-being. We observe and find physical and emotional effects of drug abuse in everyone that has admitted to using them—our prediction that drug abuse and physical and emotional impairment are related has been confirmed.
4. We believe that we could never like a subject if it is taught by a cold and unfriendly teacher, regardless of how good we are in it. We think back and remember that we had just such a teacher in high school, who taught math. We observe that we have always done everything possible to avoid a math course—our prediction that we could never like a subject taught by a cold and unfriendly teacher has been shown to be accurate.

These examples have in common the fact that they begin with a general statement of belief—a theory or hypothesis—and end with some conclusion based on an observation that tested the truth of the initial statement. Of course, we could be wrong, even though in some instances the prediction *appeared* to be true (e.g., you might have no problem liking sports despite the fact that you once had a cold and unfriendly gym teacher). As you might expect, deductive logic has been most closely associated with the scientific method.

Applying Induction and Deduction

Both induction and deduction are important methods for teaching concepts, patterns, and abstractions. One application for such teaching is to move into progressively deeper levels of subject complexity, using inductive and deductive methods and occasionally changing from one to the other:

- Greater levels of complexity are achieved using the *inductive* process when specific examples or events introduced earlier are later linked to other examples or events to create concepts and generalizations.
- Greater levels of complexity are achieved using the *deductive* process when generalizations and patterns introduced earlier in the lesson are later applied to specific instances, testing the adequacy of the generalizations.

Many forms of investigation and laboratory experiments follow the deductive method in which the student begins with a prediction about what should happen in a specific instance and then conducts an investigation to see if the prediction comes true.

In the earlier example of the government lesson about economic systems, consider how these two processes were employed. Using deduction, the teacher built a definition of *tangible goods* and tested it with a specific example: "Is a house tangible?" Notice how the examples increased not only in number, but also in abstraction (e.g., stocks and bonds). Also, he provided both examples and nonexamples to round out the definition of tangible goods in a capitalist system and to fine tune the concept. In other words, tangible goods could exist at different levels of abstraction, but some abstractions (e.g., friendships, vacation) could not qualify as tangible goods. This teacher also skillfully used the inductive process, beginning with specific examples (making money and owning land) and increasingly broadening the examples to form a generalization (tangible goods that last for a reasonable length of time).

Also notice that a brief venture into deduction ended the teacher's introduction to capitalism. By asking students to name three countries that fit the concept of capitalism, he made them find specific instances that fit the general concept. He also asked whether the general notion of ownership of tangible goods could be applied to the real world using the student's own experience, and it could, thereby testing the credibility of the more general concept of tangible goods.

Note that, although the concept of capitalism was understood by most students at the end of the first part of the lesson as an economic system that allows the ownership of tangible goods that last, it was a rather crude interpretation that would fail many subsequent tests. For example, citizens of most socialist and communist countries own tangible goods that last a reasonable period of time (e.g., a wristwatch, a tie, a set of dinnerware). Recall that this crude version of the concept of capitalism emerged even after providing carefully planned examples and nonexamples. This means that the teacher's job was not over at the end of the lesson. Further *conceptual movement* must be made to fine tune this concept, producing more accurate discriminations to be applied to the concept of capitalism.

This is what could occur in subsequent portions of the lesson, in which the teacher can move students from the ownership of tangible goods as their working definition of an economic system to a definition including the following five different elements:

1. The *degree* to which
2. goods and services
3. that all value
4. and see as essential for daily living
5. are owned by a government

The teacher, using questions and examples, can redefine the initial concept until it expands to include a greater number of attributes, thereby making it more accurate. The teaching of concepts, patterns, and abstractions with the indirect instructional model is patterned around the inductive and deductive movement of concepts wherein you process initially crude and overly restrictive concepts into more expansive and accurate abstractions. Table 6.1 illustrates the different steps involved in inductive versus deductive teaching.

Table 6.1   A comparison of steps in inductive versus deductive teaching.

Teaching Inductively	Teaching Deductively
1. Teacher presents specific data from which a generalization is to be drawn.	1. Teacher introduces the generalization to be learned.
2. Each student is allowed uninterrupted time to observe or study the data that illustrates the generalization.	2. Teacher reviews the task-relevant prior facts, rules, and action sequences needed to form the generalization.
3. Students are shown additional examples and then nonexamples containing the generalization.	3. Students raise a question, pose an hypothesis, or make a prediction thought to be contained in the generalization.
4. Student attention is guided first to the critical (relevant) aspects of the data containing the generalization and then to its noncritical (irrelevant) aspects.	4. Data, events, materials, or objects are gathered and observed to test the prediction.
5. A generalization is made that can distinguish the examples from nonexamples.	5. Results of the test are analyzed and a conclusion is made as to whether the prediction is supported by the data, events, materials, or objects that were observed.
	6. The starting generalization is refined or revised in accordance with the observations.

Source: From *Renewing the Social Studies Curriculum,* by W. Parker, 1991, Alexandria, VA: Association for Supervision and Curriculum Development. Copyright 1991 by Association for Supervision and Curriculum Development. Reprinted with permission.

USING EXAMPLES AND NONEXAMPLES

Both inductive and deductive methods help in concept teaching. Recalling our previous examples, one generalization was made after seeing several accidents: "accidents tend to occur at intersections on rainy days." Is there a concept, pattern, or abstraction here? Are there also facts, rules, and sequences?

There is no question that facts had to be known to form this generalization—facts about cars, streets, rain, and intersections. Rules also had to be present, such as "don't accelerate quickly on wet pavement," "slow down at intersections," and "a red light means stop." And, of course, sequences of actions had to be understood, such as "watch for intersections, look for signs, slow down, brake gently."

However, the intended generalization cannot be derived from these facts, rules, and sequences alone. Why? Because they are not sufficiently separated from specific examples to be applied appropriately in all circumstances. For example, you may learn the rule "stop at red lights" to perfection, but until you have seen examples of when to modify the rule (e.g., when an emergency vehicle with flashing lights is behind you), you do not have the complete concept of a red light—only the rule.

To learn concepts, your learners will need to go beyond the acquisition of facts, rules, and sequences to be able to distinguish examples from nonexamples (R. Mayer & Wittrock, 1996). Observing examples and nonexamples—when studying 6 extra hours pays off and when it does not, when disseminating drug abuse literature is likely to help and when it is not, when a cold and unfriendly teacher is likely to adversely affect your performance in a subject and when not—allows you to grasp *concepts. Examples* represent the concept being taught by including all of the attributes essential for recognizing that concept as a member of some larger class. *Nonexamples* fail to represent the concept being taught by purposely not including one or more of the attributes essential for recognizing it as a member of some larger class. Therefore, the third element for the teaching of concepts, patterns, and abstractions is the use of both examples and nonexamples that define the **criterial and noncriterial attributes** of a concept that are needed for producing accurate generalizations (Figure 6.4).

As another example, consider the concept that private ownership of goods and services under socialism is more limited than under capitalism. How would this teacher develop this concept, moving from a definition of capitalism to a discussion of socialism? The teacher would have to make clear that ownership in the context of different economic systems is always a matter of degree. That is, the system determines not only *what* is owned by a government but *how much* and therefore is unavailable for private ownership. Accordingly, the teacher might arrange the next set of interchanges to bring out these specific points.

Teacher:	What types of things could a group of people, say the size of a nation, agree on that would be absolutely essential for everyone's existence?
Ronnie:	Food.
Teacher:	Good. What else?
Billy:	A hospital.
Teacher:	Very good.
Sue:	Highways.
Teacher:	OK. Any others?
Ricky:	If they couldn't agree on the importance of cars for everyone, then they would have to agree on some form of public transportation, like buses, trains, or planes.
Teacher:	Yes, they would, wouldn't they? These examples show one of the purposes of a socialist economic system—that is, to control and make available to everyone as many things as possible that (a) everyone values equally and (b) everyone needs for everyday existence.

The teacher redirected the discussion by having students think about things that "a group of people, say the size of a nation, could agree on that would be absolutely essential for everyone's existence"—thereby encouraging students to broaden their earlier definitions. The question generated some examples for beginning to discriminate between capitalism and socialism that would need further discussion. (Some highways and forests are owned by both capitalist and socialist governments.) This is not an easy distinction from a student's point of view. The teacher helped the students understand the concepts by using specific strategies:

1. Providing more than a single example.
2. Using examples that vary in ways that are important to the concept being defined (e.g., house is tangible, stocks and bonds are abstract, but both are instances of tangible goods).
3. Including nonexamples of the concept that nonetheless possess important dimensions of the concept (e.g., a vacation can be bought or owned but is not an example of a tangible good).
4. Explaining why nonexamples are nonexamples, even though they may share some of the same characteristics as examples (e.g., a vacation is not durable).

THE USE OF QUESTIONS TO GUIDE SEARCH AND DISCOVERY

Guiding the search-and-discovery process with questions is the fourth indirect instruction function.

One difference you may have noticed between the direct and indirect instruction dialogues is *the way* in which the teachers asked questions. In the direct dialogue, the questions were specific and to the point, aimed at eliciting a single right answer. But in the indirect dialogue, questions steered the students to seek and discover the answer with minimum assistance from the teacher. In direct instruction, answering questions is how students show what they know (exhibit their level of understanding) so that you may provide clues, hints, and probes. In indirect instruction, your questions guide students into discovering new dimensions of a problem or ways of resolving a dilemma.

The indirect instruction dialogue included several questions that guided the search-and-discovery process. The purpose of this teacher's questions was to focus students' attention and to promote the widest possible discussion of the topic from the students' point of view. In this manner the class begins with everyone being able to participate, regardless of their task-relevant prior knowledge. By accepting almost any answer at the beginning, this teacher can use student responses to formulate subsequent questions and begin the process of shaping more accurate responses.

The point of using questioning strategies in indirect instruction, then, is not to arrive at the correct answer in the quickest and most efficient manner. The point is to stimulate a process that not only forms successively more correct answers but also forms those answers using a personal search-and-discovery process chosen by the learner and guided by the teacher. For example, the teacher followed up Robert's response that capitalism means "making money" with the phrase, " . . . what else?" and followed Robert's next response ("owning land") with a leading response ("not only land but . . . "), encouraging Robert to broaden his answer.

By beginning with a broad question such as "What does the word *capitalism* mean to you?" this teacher could have been confronted just as easily with the task of narrowing, not broadening, Robert's first response. In the next interchange, this problem actually occurs, because Robert replies that capitalism means "owning anything." Now the job is to narrow or limit his response, which is accomplished by presenting the first criterial attribute of the concept of capitalism, tangible goods.

You can see that a single guided question in the context of indirect instruction is seldom useful in itself. Questions must dovetail into other questions that continually refocus the response (e.g., broaden, then narrow, then broaden slightly again) and keep the search going. The process is much like focusing a camera, because rarely is the camera initially set at the right focus for the subject. Similarly, we could not expect Robert's first response to perfectly represent the concept of capitalism. Just as one begins focusing the camera in the appropriate direction, often passing the point at which the subject is in focus, so also the teacher's follow-up probe led Robert to over-shoot the mark and respond with too broad a response (e.g., owning anything). The teacher acknowledged the error and slightly narrowed Robert's response by noting that "The word *capitalism* means tangible goods or possessions."

Questions also can be used in the search-and-discovery process to do the following:

- *Present contradictions to be resolved*—"Who owns the highways under capitalism?"
- *Probe for deeper, more thorough responses*—"So, what would be a good definition of tangible goods?"
- *Extend the discussion to new areas*—"What things could a group of people, say the size of a nation, agree are absolutely essential for everyone's existence?"
- *Pass responsibility back to the class*—"Good question. Who knows the answer to who pays for services provided under a socialist system?"

Questions like these guide students to increasingly better responses through a search-and-discovery process. This process is one of the most useful for forming concepts and abstractions and for recognizing patterns. The back-and-forth focusing of student responses often is required to attain the appropriate level of generalization.

LEARNER EXPERIENCE (USE OF STUDENT IDEAS)

The Changing View

Until recently, the use of student ideas was considered the centerpiece of indirect instruction. Using student ideas meant incorporating student experiences, points of view, feelings, and problems into the lesson by making the student the primary point of reference. A completely student-oriented lesson might be initiated by asking students what problems they were having with the content; these problems would become the focus of the lesson. This approach was intended to heighten student interest, to organize subject content around student problems, to tailor feedback to individual students, and to encourage positive attitudes and feelings toward the subject.

This is where early attempts to use student ideas sometimes went astray. The goals of incorporating student ideas into the lesson in an open discussion format often became the end itself, rather than the means by which learning could be accomplished. Unfortunately, many forms of problem solving, inquiry, and discovery

Small-group discussions often require the teachers to become a moderator, visiting each group periodically to answer questions, review and summarize, redirect group work, provide new or more accurate information, and achieve consensus.

learning were thought to be synonymous with open, freewheeling discussions that began and ended with student-determined ideas and content.

The position of this text, like that of recent research, is that while heightening student interest, selecting content based on student problems, and increasing affect are important goals, they are best achieved in a carefully crafted teacher–student dialogue that promotes higher-order thinking. These goals can and should be achieved in the context of classroom dialogue that encourages students to make references to, use examples from, and draw parallels and associations with their own experience. Therefore, in the indirect instruction model, use of student ideas is the means of attaining essential concepts, patterns, and abstractions.

Productively Using Student Ideas

So, how can teachers productively use student ideas in the context of indirect instruction? In this context, you can use student ideas in the following ways:

- Encourage students to use *examples* and *references* from their own experience, from which they can construct their own meanings from text.
- Share mental strategies by which the students can learn more easily and efficiently.
- Ask students to seek clarification of and to draw *parallels* to and *associations* from things they already know.
- Encourage understanding and retention of ideas by relating them to the students' own sphere of *interests, concerns,* and *problems.*

For examples of these uses, recall again the dialogue about economic systems. By asking students to name three other countries that follow a capitalistic economic system, the teacher elicited examples and references from the learners' experience.

Perhaps more important than the questions themselves was the way in which the teacher incorporated student responses into the lesson. By asking what the word *capitalism* "means to you," this teacher was asking students to express themselves by using parallels and associations they already understood—perhaps by having a job, or by recalling a conversation about occupations, or by remembering television images of life in Eastern Europe. Parallels and associations such as these are likely to be vastly different among students. This is desirable, both for heightening student interest and involvement and for exposing the students to a variety of responses, many of which may be appropriate instances of the concept to be learned.

A third way to incorporate student ideas into your lesson is to allow students to respond using their own interests, concerns, and problems. Student interests—and especially individual choices affecting future assignments—can be important motivators for ensuring active student involvement in subsequent assignments that may be lengthy and time-consuming.

Finally, notice that even within the context of these examples the instruction remained *content centered.* The instruction allowed students to participate in determining the *form* in which learning occurred but not the *substance* of what was learned. This substance usually is determined by the curriculum guide and textbook. Our example dialogue, therefore, contrasts with what is called *student-centered learning,* which allows students to select both the form and substance. This is sometimes associated with *unguided discovery learning,* wherein the goal is to maintain high levels of student interest, accomplished largely by selecting content based on student problems or interests and by providing individually tailored feedback.

Sometimes unguided discovery learning is desired in the context of independently conducted experiments, projects, portfolios, research papers, and demonstrations, where the topic may be selected by the student. However, even when unguided discovery learning is desired, the content still must fit within the confines of the curriculum. Therefore, whether your approach is the guided use of student ideas (as in this example) or unguided (as in research assignments), some preorganization and structure always will be necessary before you solicit and use student ideas.

STUDENT SELF-EVALUATION

The sixth ingredient of indirect instruction is to engage students in evaluating their own responses and thereby taking responsibility for their own learning. Because there are many right answers when teaching concepts, patterns, and abstractions, it is virtually impossible for you to judge them all. In direct instruction, nearly all instances of the learned facts, rules, or action sequences likely to be encountered can be learned during guided and independent practice. But, because specifying all possible instances of a concept is neither possible nor efficient, you must use indirect instruction to have students look critically at their own responses.

You can encourage self-evaluation by gradually giving control of the evaluation function to students and by letting them provide reasons for their answers so that you and other students can suggest needed changes. Recall that early in the dialogue, the teacher let the students know that some of the responsibility for determining appropriate answers would fall on them. After writing a list on the board, he said, "OK. Who would like to say which of these are *capital?*" The message is received when Ricky responds and Barbara modifies Ricky's response:

Ricky: Car and clothes are the only two I see.
Barbara: I'd add stocks and bonds. They say you own a piece of something, although maybe not the whole thing.

Even after Barbara's efforts to correct Ricky's response, the teacher still does not supply an answer but instead keeps the evaluation of the previous responses going by responding with, "Could you see or touch it?"

The goal here was to create a student dialogue focused on the appropriateness of previous answers. The success of this self-evaluation strategy is most readily seen in the sequence of dialogue that occurs between students and teacher. This strategy promotes a student-to-student-back-to-teacher interchange, as opposed to the more familiar teacher-to-student-back-to-teacher interchange. The teacher's role is to maintain the momentum by offering hints or focusing statements that students can use to evaluate their previous responses.

In the process of these exchanges, students learn the reasons for their answers in slow, measured steps. By allowing partially correct answers to become the bases for more accurate ones, this teacher is showing the class how to modify incorrect and partially correct answers into better ones. Especially for the learning of concepts, patterns, and abstractions that involve more than a single criterial attribute, these layers of refinement, gradually built up by student interchange, help the students develop a level of generalization.

Of course, there is no reason why such interchanges must be limited in size. Three, four, or even five successive exchanges among students before control returns to the teacher can work in circumstances that need less guidance and structuring. Classes of students who are more able or who have considerable knowledge of the content can sustain protracted exchanges without going so far astray that you need to restructure.

USE OF GROUP DISCUSSION

When student-to-student-to-teacher exchanges grow into long interactions among large numbers of students, a **group discussion** has begun. In these discussions, you may intervene only occasionally to review and summarize main points, or you may schedule periodic interaction to evaluate the group's progress and to redirect if necessary.

Group discussions can be useful for encouraging critical thinking, for engaging learners in the learning process, and for promoting the "reasoning together" that is necessary in a democratic society (J. Dillon, 1995; Krabbe & Polivka, 1990). Because group discussion helps students think critically—examine alternatives, judge solutions, make predictions, and discover generalizations—it is yet another approach to teaching concepts, patterns, and abstractions. It is the seventh and last indirect instruction function in Figure 6.4.

When your objective is to teach well-established concepts, patterns, or abstractions that already are structured in the text or workbook, a lecture-recitation may be more efficient and effective than a discussion. This might be the case with topics requiring little personal opinion and judgment, in which agreement about the topic may be so high as to preclude the controversy needed to promote discussion.

But sometimes you may prefer a group discussion to a lecture-recitation. When concepts, patterns, and abstractions have a less formal structure and are treated minimally in the text or workbook, then the lack of consensus can make a discussion rewarding. Examples of such topics are: Would photosynthesis be useful in space? How much aggression do you think it takes to start a war? In what ways can the legislative branch of government be influenced by the executive branch? Topics that are not formally structured by the text and for which a high degree of consensus does not yet exist make good candidates for discussion sessions for building, expanding, and refining concepts, patterns, and abstractions.

During the discussion, you are the moderator. Your tasks include the following:

1. *Orient the students to the objective of the discussion.*   "Today we will discuss when a nation should decide to go to war. Specifically, we will discuss the meaning of the concept of aggression as it has occurred in history. In the context of wars between nations, your job at the end of the discussion will be to arrive at a generalization that could help a president decide if sufficient aggression has occurred to warrant going to war."

2. *Provide new or more accurate information where needed.* "It is not correct to assume that World War II started with the bombing of Pearl Harbor. Many events occurred earlier on the European continent that some nations considered to be aggression."

3. *Review, summarize, or put together opinions and facts into a meaningful relationship.* "Bobby, Mary, and Billy, you seem to be arguing that the forcible entry of one nation into the territory of another nation constitutes aggression, while the rest of the class seems to be saying that undermining the economy of another nation also can constitute aggression."

4. *Adjust the flow of information and ideas to be most productive to the goals of the lesson.* "Mark, you seem to have extended our definition of aggression to include criticizing the government of another nation through political means, such as shortwave media broadcasts, speeches at the United Nations, and so forth. But that fits better the idea of a cold war, and we are trying to study some of the instances of aggression that might have started World War II."

5. *Combine ideas and promote compromise to arrive at an appropriate consensus.* "We seem to have two definitions of aggression—one dealing with the forcible entry of one nation into the territory of another and another that has to do with undermining a nation's economy. Could we combine these two ideas by saying that anything that threatens either a nation's people or its prosperity, or both, could be considered aggression?"

Group discussion can take several different forms. *Large-group discussions* in which all members of the class participate are the most familiar. Large groups can be difficult to handle, because discipline and management problems occur easily when numerous learners are interacting in student exchanges that you interrupt only occasionally. The moderating functions just listed allow you to control and redirect the discussion as necessary without overly restricting the flow of ideas. During a large group discussion, you should frequently perform one or more of these moderating functions. The frequency will vary with the topic and students, but the greater the consensus, the fewer the students, and the higher their ability to grasp the concepts and abstractions to be learned, *the more you can relinquish authority to the group* (Oser, 1986).

Small-group discussions of 5 to 10 students also are useful for teaching concepts, patterns, and abstractions (E. Cohen, 1994). When multiple topics must be discussed within the same lesson and time does not permit full-class discussion of the topics in sequential order, try using two, three, or four small groups simultaneously. You have three tasks here: (1) to form groups whose members can work together, (2) to distribute students with diverse learning needs across groups, and (3) to move among the groups as moderator. Stopping the groups periodically, either to inform the entire class of important insights discovered by a group or to apply moderating functions across groups, will help keep the groups close together and maintain your control and authority.

Another group format for indirect instruction is to have students work in pairs or teams. This can be effective when the discussion entails writing (e.g., a summary report), looking up information (in the text, encyclopedia, etc.), or preparing materials (chart, diagram, graph, etc.) (Johnson, Johnson, & Holubec, 1994; Slavin, 1990b). In the **pair** or **team discussion** arrangement, your role as moderator increases in proportion to the number of pairs or teams, so only brief interchanges with each may be possible.

The pair or team approach works best when the task is highly structured, when some consensus about the topic already exists, and when the orienting instructions fully define each member's role (e.g., student A searches for the information, student B writes a summary description of what is found, and both students read the summary for final agreement). Pairs or teams frequently become highly task oriented, so pairing or teaming tends to be most productive when discussion objectives go beyond just an oral report and include a product to be delivered to the class.

Following is a lesson plan for this indirect instruction lesson, following the written format provided in Chapter 4.

Example Indirect Instruction Lesson Plan: Social Studies

Unit Title: Economic Systems

Lesson Title: Comparisons and Contrasts Among Capitalist, Socialist, and Communist Economies

1 Gaining attention   Ask if anyone knows where the phrase "government of the people, by the people, for the people" comes from, to establish the idea that the principles and rules by which a country is governed also influence its economic system.

2 Informing the learner of the objective   This session: To relate economic systems to the ownership of goods and services in different countries. Next session: To be able to distinguish economic systems from political systems and to show why the communist economic system is changing.

3 Stimulating recall of prerequisite learning   Ask for a definition of capitalism, and then refine with questioning and probing of the definition given. Continue probing until students arrive at a definition of capitalism as "an economic system that allows the ownership of tangible goods that last for a reasonable period of time." Check understanding by asking for three countries (other than ours) that have capitalist economies.

4 Presenting the stimulus material   A: Ask what the word *socialism* means. Refine the definition by questioning and probing until a definition is arrived at that defines socialism as "an economic system that allows the government to control and make available to everyone as many things as possible that (1) everyone values equally and

that (2) are seen as essential for everyday existence." Have students compare capitalism and socialism by degree of ownership of public services and degree of taxes paid under each system.

B: Ask what the word *communism* means, and establish its relationship to the idea of *community.* Refine the definition, using the concept of degree of ownership by questioning and probing until the students arrive at still more examples of things owned and controlled by the government under communism.

5 Eliciting the desired behavior   *A:* Use questions to encourage the identification of public services most commonly owned under socialism, for example, hospitals, trains, and communication systems. Some types of farms and industries will also be accepted when their relation to the public good is understood.

B: Use questions to encourage the identification of those public services most commonly owned under communism, for example, food supply, housing, and industries. Emphasize those services and goods that are different from those identified under socialism.

C: Use questions to identify the amount and types of things owned by the government across the three systems, to establish the concept that differences among the systems are a matter of degree of ownership and degree of taxation.

6 Providing feedback   Pose questions in a manner that encourages the student to evaluate his or her own response and those of other students. Probe until student responses approximate an acceptable answer. On the blackboard, place side by side those goods and services the students have identified as likely to be owned by the government in all three systems and those likely to be owned uniquely by any one or combination of systems. You may wish to make a distinction between these goods and services and the personal items that students may have mentioned, such as clothes or household goods, which cannot be used to distinguish economic systems.

7 Assessing the behavior   After completion of a research paper describing three countries of the students' own choosing, each of which represents a different economic system, grade students on their comprehension of the concepts of (1) degree of ownership and (2) degree of taxation as discussed by L. Rugherford (1995) *Economics in a Modern World,* Columbus, OH: Intex.

COMPARISON OF DIRECT AND INDIRECT INSTRUCTION

The direct and indirect instruction models were presented in separate chapters because each includes distinctive teaching strategies. As you have seen, the models have two different purposes:

- The direct model is best suited to the teaching of facts, rules, and action sequences and provides six teaching functions for doing so: daily review and checking, presenting and structuring new content, guided student practice, feedback and correctives, independent practice, and weekly and monthly reviews.

- The indirect model is best suited for the teaching of concepts, patterns, and abstractions and provides seven teaching functions for doing so: advance organization of content, inductive and deductive conceptual movement, use of examples and nonexamples, use of questions to guide search and discovery, use of student ideas, student self-evaluation, and group discussion.

Neither model should be used to the exclusion of the other. Many times the two models can be effectively interwoven in a single lesson, as when a small number of facts, rules, or action sequences must be acquired before introducing a concept, pattern, or abstraction.

Let us now place the direct and indirect models of instruction side by side for comparison. Table 6.2 presents teaching events you can employ using both models.

Table 6.2 Some example events under the direct and indirect models of instruction.

Direct Instruction	Indirect Instruction
Objective: To teach facts, rules, and action sequences	Objective: To teach concepts, patterns, and abstractions
Teacher begins the lesson with a review of the previous day's work.	Teacher begins the lesson with advance organizers that provide an overall picture and that allow for concept expansion.
Teacher presents new content in small steps with explanations and examples.	Teacher focuses student responses using induction and/or deduction to refine and focus generalizations.
Teacher provides an opportunity for guided practice on a small number of sample problems. Prompts and models when necessary to attain 60–80% accuracy.	Teacher presents examples and nonexamples of the generalization, identifying critical and noncritical attributes.
Teacher provides feedback and corrections according to whether the answer was correct, quick, and firm; correct, but hesitant; careless; or incorrect.	Teacher draws additional examples from students' own experiences, interests, and problems.
Teacher provides an opportunity for independent practice with seatwork. Strives for automatic responses that are 95% correct or higher.	Teacher uses questions to guide discovery and articulation of the generalization.
Teacher provides weekly and monthly (cumulative) reviews and reteaches unlearned content.	Teacher involves students in evaluating their own responses.
	Teacher promotes and moderates discussion to firm up and extend generalizations when necessary.

Under direct instruction, the objective is rapid attainment of facts, rules, and action sequences. Content is divided into small, easily learned steps through a lecture format involving brief explanations, examples, practice, and feedback. Both guided and independent practice, under tight control of the teacher, help ensure that students are actively engaged in the learning process at high rates of success. Everything that is not learned is revealed in weekly and monthly reviews and retaught as needed.

Under indirect instruction, the objective is to engage students in inquiry to eventually develop concepts in the form of patterns or abstractions. Here the teacher prepares for the complexity of the lesson by providing an overall framework into which the day's lesson is placed, allowing room for expansion of concepts. Initially crude and inaccurate responses are gradually refined through inductive and deductive movement, focusing the generalization to the desired degree. To do this, both examples and nonexamples (some drawn from the students' interests and experiences) are used to separate criterial from noncriterial attributes. Throughout, the teacher uses questions that guide students to discover the generalization and to evaluate their own responses. When the concepts are relatively unstructured and have moderate-to-low degrees of consensus, discussion groups may replace a more teacher-controlled format; in this case, the teacher becomes a moderator.

PROMOTING THE GOALS OF INDIRECT INSTRUCTION IN THE CULTURALLY DIVERSE CLASSROOM

One of the most recent developments in the area of cultural diversity and indirect instruction involves the concept of social framing. **Social framing** refers to the context in which a message, such as a lesson, is received and understood. Tannen (1986) defines a frame as a taken-for-granted context that delimits the sources from which meaning can be derived. When a teacher announces, "Today's lesson will expect you to know the differences between *capitalism, socialism,* and *communism,*" the teacher has implicitly set a frame for the lesson that conveys to learners what they are expected to learn. Recent research has examined how best to frame a lesson so that learners can derive understanding from the content presented, or how to alter the frame of a lesson so that it will be more understandable to cultural or ethnic groups that may be accustomed to an alternate frame. For example, Michaels and Collins (1984) report an example of an Anglo teacher who framed a story with linear, topic-centered patterns (e.g., "Today I will read you a series of events that happened in the lives of three characters"), while her African American students framed the task according to topic-associating patterns (e.g., "She's going to tell us the kinds of things that can happen to people"). While one group primarily looked for a sequential list of events that unfolded from the beginning to end of the story, the other group made notes about the events and the memories they evoked. Thus, frames that are ambiguous or less appropriate to one group than another can alter how and what content is learned.

Bowers and Flinders (1991) make a case for understanding the context in which different cultures expect information to be transmitted that is particularly relevant during indirect instruction. They recommend that the teacher (1) present content from the frame most dominant to the classroom; (2) make explicit what the frame—context—is through which learners must see the content (e.g., as facts to be learned, skills to be performed, or concepts to think about); and/or (3) negotiate, when necessary, the frame with students at the start of the lesson.

Bowers and Flinders (1991) suggest three ways of establishing a frame at the start of a lesson that encourage students to respond in like manner. These approaches involve self-disclosure, humor, and dialogue:

- *Self-disclosure* involves being open about your feelings and emotions that lead up to the lesson. "I've been struggling to make this topic meaningful, and here's what I've come up with." This will encourage similar statements of self-disclosure from students, which can be used to frame the lesson.
- *Humor* at the start of a lesson establishes a flexible, spontaneous, expressive mood from which frames can become established. "Here's a funny thing that happened to me that's connected to what we're going to study today" will encourage students to share other personal episodes that can be used to provide a context for the lesson.
- *Dialogue* involves the back-and-forth discussion of lesson content involving random and simultaneous responding. Here every student can expect to be heard, and the teacher expresses lesson content idiosyncratically in the words of the learners. The teacher uses the responses of students to further structure and elaborate lesson content.

Each of these framing techniques is believed to enhance student engagement during indirect instruction across cultural and ethnic groups, some of whom can be expected to be less responsive to the traditional frames of prepackaged lesson plans and textbooks.

A FINAL WORD

This chapter and the preceding one presented a variety of teaching strategies. When used with the appropriate content and purpose, these strategies can significantly improve your teaching effectiveness. Although both the direct and indirect models of instruction are significant contributions to teaching and learning, neither should exclusively dominate your instructional style. It would be unfortunate if you exemplified only the direct model or the indirect model, because the original purpose of introducing these models is to *increase the variety* of instructional strategies at your disposal.

These models and their strategies provide a variety of instructional tools that you can mix in many combinations to match your particular objectives and students. Just as different entrées have prominent and equal places on a menu, so do the direct and indirect models have prominent and equal places in your classroom.

The underlying point of these two chapters is that you should alternately employ the direct and indirect models to create tantalizing combinations of educational flavors for your students. Your own objectives are the best guide to what combination from the menu you will serve on any given day. In the chapters ahead, we will extend this basic menu to provide still greater variety in the teaching methods at your command.

SUMMING UP

This chapter introduced you to indirect instruction strategies. Its main points were as follows:

1. Indirect instruction is an approach to teaching and learning in which the process of learning is *inquiry,* the result is *discovery,* and the learning context is a *problem.*

2. In indirect instruction, the learner acquires information by transforming stimulus material into a response that is different (1) from the stimulus used to present the learning and (2) from any previous response emitted by the student.

3. During indirect instruction, the learner acquires concepts, patterns, and abstractions through the processes of generalization and discrimination, which require the learner to rearrange and elaborate on the stimulus material.

4. The generalization process helps the learner respond in a similar manner to different stimuli, thereby increasing the range of instances to which particular facts, rules, and sequences apply.

5. The process of discrimination selectively restricts the acceptable range of instances by eliminating things that may look like the concept but that differ from it on critical dimensions.

6. The processes of generalization and discrimination together help students classify different-appearing stimuli into the same categories on the basis of criterial attributes. Criterial attributes act as magnets, drawing together all instances of a concept without the learner having to see or memorize all instances of it.

7. The indirect instruction model provides instructional strategies that encourage the processes of generalization and discrimina-

tion for the purpose of forming concepts, patterns, and abstractions.

8. The following are the instructional functions of the indirect model:
   - Use of advance organizers
   - Conceptual movement—inductive and deductive
   - Use of examples and nonexamples
   - Use of questions to guide search and discovery
   - Use of student ideas
   - Student self-evaluation
   - Use of group discussion

9. An advance organizer gives learners a conceptual preview of what is to come and helps them store, label, and package content for retention and later use.

10. Three approaches to composing advance organizers are the problem-centered approach, the decision-making (hierarchical) approach, and the networking approach.

11. Induction starts with a specific observation of a limited set of data and ends with a generalization about a much broader context.

12. Deduction proceeds from principles or generalizations to their application in specific contexts.

13. Providing examples and nonexamples helps define the criterial and noncriterial attributes needed for making accurate generalizations.

14. Using examples and nonexamples correctly includes the following steps:
    - Providing more than a single example
    - Using examples that vary in ways that are irrelevant to the concept being defined
    - Using nonexamples that also include relevant dimensions of the concept
    - Explaining why nonexamples have some of the same characteristics as examples

15. In indirect instruction, the role of questions is to guide students into discovering new dimensions of a problem or new ways of resolving a dilemma.

16. Some uses of questions during indirect instruction include the following:
    • Refocusing
    • Presenting contradictions to be resolved
    • Probing for deeper, more thorough responses
    • Extending the discussion to new areas
    • Passing responsibility to the class

17. Student ideas can be used to heighten student interest, to organize subject content around student problems, to tailor feedback to fit individual students, and to encourage positive attitudes toward the subject. Because these goals should not become ends unto themselves, you must plan and structure the use of student ideas to promote reasoning, problem solving, and critical thinking.

18. Student-centered learning, sometimes called unguided discovery learning, allows the student to select both the form and substance of the learning experience. This is appropriate in the context of independently conducted experiments, research projects, science fair projects, and demonstrations. However, pre-organization and guidance always are necessary to ensure that the use of student ideas fits within the prescribed curriculum.

19. Self-evaluation of student responses occurs during indirect instruction when you give students the opportunity to reason their answers so that you and other students can suggest needed changes. Students can most easily conduct self-evaluation in the context of student-to-student-to-teacher exchanges, wherein you encourage students to comment on and consider the accuracy of their own and each others' responses.

20. A group discussion involves student exchanges with successive interactions among large numbers of students. During these exchanges, you may intervene only occasionally to review and summarize, or you may schedule periodic interaction to evaluate each group's progress and to redirect when necessary.

21. The best topics for discussion include those that are not formally structured by texts and workbooks and for which a high degree of consensus among your students does not yet exist.

22. Your moderating functions during discussion include the following:
    • Orient students to the objective of the discussion.
    • Provide new or more accurate information that may be needed.
    • Review, summarize, and relate opinions and facts.
    • Redirect the flow of information and ideas back to the objective of the discussion.

23. The greater the group consensus, the fewer the students in the group, and the higher their ability to grasp concepts and abstractions, then the more you can relinquish authority to the group.

24. Teachers generally use direct and indirect instruction together, and you should not adopt one model to the exclusion of the other. Each contains a set of functions that can compose an efficient and effective method for the teaching of facts, rules, and sequences or concepts, patterns, and abstractions.

FOR DISCUSSION AND PRACTICE

Questions marked with an asterisk are answered in Appendix B. See also *Bridges: An Activity Guide and Assessment Options,* which accompanies this text.

*1. What three learning concepts are brought together in the indirect model of instruction?

Provide a content example in which all three come together.

*2. What types of behavioral outcomes are the (1) direct and (2) indirect instructional models most effective in achieving?

*3. How would you explain where the word *indirect* comes from in the *indirect instruction* *model?* Can you provide an example to illustrate your point?

*4. Why can't direct instruction be used all the time? Give an example in which it would clearly not be appropriate.

*5. Explain in your own words what is meant by the words *unitization* and *automaticity*. Give an example of a single learning task that requires both these processes.

*6. Explain in your own words what is meant by the words *generalization* and *discrimination*. Give an example of a single learning task that requires both these processes.

*7. Identify which of the following learning tasks require only facts, rules, or action sequences (Type 1) and which, in addition, require concepts, patterns, and abstractions (Type 2):
  a. Naming the presidents
  b. Selecting the best speech
  c. Shifting the gearshift in a car
  d. Writing an essay
  e. Describing the main theme in George Orwell's *1984*
  f. Hitting a tennis ball
  g. Winning a tennis match
  h. Inventing a new soft drink
  i. Reciting the vowel sounds
  j. Becoming an effective teacher

*8. Describe two problems that would result if a concept or abstraction had to be learned using only the cognitive processes of unitization and automaticity by which facts, rules, and sequences are acquired.

9. Prepare a 2-minute introduction to a lesson of your own choosing that provides your students with an advance organizer.

10. Provide one example each of an advance organizer using the problem-centered, decision-making, and networking approaches.

*11. In your own words, define *inductive* and *deductive* reasoning. Give an example of each, using content from your teaching area.

*12. Identify the five steps to deductive reasoning commonly applied in the laboratory. With what teaching content would you consider using these steps?

13. For each of the following, show with specific examples how the concept might be taught both inductively and deductively. Pay particu-

lar attention to whether your instruction should begin or end with a generalization.
  • Democracy
  • Freedom
  • Education
  • Effective teaching
  • Parenting

*14. For the concept of *effective teaching,* identify five criterial attributes and five noncriterial attributes. Then, using what you have written, write a paragraph explaining what effective teaching is.

*15. Identify four ways in which examples and nonexamples can be used in the teaching of concepts. Show how they can be applied with a topic you will be teaching.

*16. Using what you have learned in this and the previous chapter, distinguish the different purposes for asking questions in the (1) direct and (2) indirect model of instruction.

*17. Besides refocusing, what other types of questions can be used in the search-and-discovery process? Choose a lesson topic, and provide an example of each of these.

*18. What type of learning might be represented by discussions that begin and end with student-determined ideas and content? How is this different from the use of student ideas in the context of the indirect instruction model?

*19. What are three ways student ideas might be incorporated into an indirect instruction lesson? Show how they would apply to a lesson you might teach.

*20. Why is student self-evaluation more important in the indirect model of instruction than in the direct model of instruction? What's a way you could promote student self-evaluation in your classroom?

*21. What are five moderating responsibilities of the teacher during group discussion? Which do you feel would be most important for the age students you will be teaching?

*22. For which of the following teaching objectives might you use the direct model of instruction, and for which might you use the indirect model? Teaching your class to do the following:
  a. Sing
  b. Use a microscope properly

c. Appreciate Milton's *Paradise Lost*
d. Become aware of the pollutants around us
e. Solve an equation with two unknowns
f. Read at grade level
g. Type at the rate of 25 words per minute
h. Write an original short story
i. Build a winning science fair project
j. Distinguish war from aggression

Are there any for which you might use both models?

23. Provide an example of social framing using a topic with which you are familiar. Use quotes to indicate the exact words a teacher might use to convey this frame to students at the beginning of class.

7 Questioning Strategies

This chapter will help you answer the following questions:

1. What is an effective question?
2. How are different types of questions classified?
3. What is a question-asking sequence?
4. How do I ask questions at different levels of cognitive complexity?
5. How do I ask questions that promote thinking and problem solving?

n the classroom dialogues of previous chapters, you saw the important role of questions in the effective teacher's menu. This is no coincidence, because most exchanges between teachers and students involve questions in some form. This chapter explores the definition of a question, the varied ways questions can be asked, and the types of questions that you should ask more frequently than others.

Also discussed is the closely related topic of probes. Like questions, probes are effective catalysts for performing the five key behaviors of (1) lesson clarity, (2) instructional variety, (3) task orientation, (4) student engagement in the learning process, and (5) student success. Subsequent chapters extend these questioning techniques, showing how you can use them to form other types of teaching strategies.

WHAT IS A QUESTION?

In the context of a lively and fast-paced exchange in a classroom, questions are not always obvious. As observed by G. Brown and Wragg (1993), students routinely report difficulty in distinguishing some types of questions in the context of a classroom dialogue—and even whether a question has been asked. For example, imagine hearing these two questions:

Raise your hand if you know the answer.

Aren't you going to *answer the question?*

The first is expressed in command form (italics), yet it contains an implicit question. The second sounds like a question, yet contains an implicit command. Will your students perceive both of these statements as questions? Will they both evoke the same response?

Voice inflection is another source of confusion; it can indicate a question even when sentence syntax does not. For example, imagine hearing the following two sentences spoken with the emphasis shown:

You *said* the President can have two terms in office?

The President can have *two* terms in office?

The proper voice inflection can turn almost any sentence into a question, whether you intend it or not. In addition, a real question can be perceived as a rhetorical question because of inflection and word choice:

We all have done our homework today, *haven't we?*

Whether this is intended as a question or not, it is certain that all who failed to complete their homework will assume the question to be rhetorical.

Effective questions are ones for which students actively compose a response and thereby become engaged in the learning process (Chuska, 1995; Wilen, 1991). The previous examples show that effective questions depend on more than just words. Their effectiveness also depends on *voice inflection, word emphasis, word choice,* and the *context* in which the question is raised. Questions can be raised in many ways, and each way can determine whether the question is perceived by your students, and how.

In this chapter any oral statement or gesture intended to evoke a student response is considered to be a question. And if it evokes a response that actively engages a student in the learning process, it is an *effective question*. With this distinction in mind, let us now explore many ways of asking questions that actively engage students in the learning process.

What Consumes 80% of Class Time?

In almost any classroom at any time, you can observe a sequence of events in which the teacher structures the content to be discussed, solicits a student response, and then reacts to the response. These activities performed in sequence are the most common behaviors in any classroom. They were first described by Bellack, Kliebard, Hyman, and Smith (1966) as the following chain of events:

1. The teacher provides structure, briefly formulating the topic or issue to be discussed.
2. The teacher solicits a response or asks a question of one or more students.
3. The student responds or answers the question.
4. The teacher reacts to the student's answer.

The teacher behaviors in this chain of events compose the activities of **structuring, soliciting,** and **reacting.** At the heart of this chain is soliciting, or question-asking behavior. Questions are the tool for bridging the gap between your presentation of content and the student's understanding of it. The purpose of using questions must not be lost among the many *forms* and *varieties* of questions presented in this chapter. Like all the ingredients of direct and indirect instruction, questions are tools to encourage students to think about and act on the material you have structured.

The centerpiece of this chain—soliciting or questioning—is so prevalent that as many as 100 questions per class hour may be asked in the typical elementary and secondary classroom (G. Brown & Edmondson, 1984). Gall (1984) notes that sometimes as much as 80% of all school time can be devoted to questions and answers. This enormous concentration on a single strategy attests both to its convenience and to its perceived effectiveness. But, as noted, not all questions are *effective* questions. That is, not all questions actively engage students in the learning process.

Are We Asking the Right Questions?

Some research data indeed show that not all questions actively engage students in the learning process. Early studies estimated that 70% to 80% of all questions require the simple recall of facts, while only 20% to 30% require the higher-level thought processes of clarifying, expanding, generalizing, and making inferences (Corey, 1940; Haynes, 1935). Evidently little has changed since these early studies. Recent work in the United States and England indicates that, of every five questions asked, about three require data recall, one is managerial, and only one requires higher-level thought processes (Atwood & Wilen, 1991; G. Brown & Wragg, 1993; Wilen, 1991).

This lopsided proportion of recall questions to thought questions is alarming. Behaviors most frequently required in adult life, at work, and in advanced training— those at the higher levels of cognitive complexity involving analysis, synthesis, and evaluation—seem to be the least-emphasized behaviors in the classroom (Glover & Corkill, 1990; Risner, Skeel & Nicholson, 1992).

WHAT ARE THE PURPOSES OF QUESTIONS?

It would be easy to classify all questions as either lower-order (requiring the recall of information) or higher-order (requiring clarification, expansion, generalization, and inference). But such a broad distinction would ignore the many specific purposes for which questions are used. Most reasons for asking questions can be classified into the following general categories:

1. *Interest getting and attention getting:* "If you could go to the moon, what would be the first thing you would notice?"
2. *Diagnosing and checking:* "Does anyone know the meaning of the Latin word *via?*"
3. *Recall of specific facts or information:* "Who can name each of the main characters in *The Adventures of Huckleberry Finn?*"
4. *Managerial:* "Did you ask my permission?"
5. *Encourage higher-level thought processes:* "Putting together all that we learned, what household products exhibit characteristics associated with the element sodium?"

6. *Structure and redirect learning:* "Now that we've covered the narrative form, who can tell me what an expository sentence is?"
7. *Allow expression of affect:* "What did you like about *Of Mice and Men?*"

Most of the questions in these categories have the purpose of shaping or setting up the learner's response. In this sense, a well-formulated question serves as an advance organizer, providing the framework for the response that is to follow.

WHAT ARE CONVERGENT AND DIVERGENT QUESTIONS?

Questions can be narrow or broad, encouraging either a specific, limited response or a general, expansive one. A question that limits an answer to a single or small number of responses is called a **convergent** (or *direct* or *closed*) **question.** For such questions, the learner has previously read or heard the answer and so has only to recall certain facts.

Convergent questions set up the learner to respond in a limited, restrictive manner: "Does anyone know the meaning of the Latin word *via?*" "Who can name the main characters in *The Adventures of Huckleberry Finn?*" The answers to these questions are easily judged right or wrong. Many convergent, or closed, questions are used in direct instruction. As mentioned, up to 80% of all questions may be of this type.

Another type of question encourages a general or open response. This is the **divergent,** or *indirect,* **question.** It has no single best answer, but it can have wrong answers. This is perhaps the most misunderstood aspect of a divergent question. Not just any answer will be correct, even in the case of divergent questions raised for the purpose of allowing students to express their feelings. If Johnny is asked what he liked about *Of Mice and Men* and says "Nothing," or "The happy ending," then either Johnny has not read the book or he needs help in better understanding the events that took place. A passive or accepting response on your part to answers like these is inappropriate, regardless of your intent to allow an open response.

You can expect far more diverse responses from divergent questions than from convergent questions—which may explain why only 20% of all questions are divergent. It always will be easier to determine the right or wrong answer to a convergent question than it will be to sift through the range of acceptable responses to a divergent question. Even so, it is your responsibility to identify inappropriate responses, to follow them up, and to bring them back into the acceptable range. Thus, you often will need to follow up divergent questions with more detail, new information, or encouragement. In this sense, divergent questions become a rich source of lively, spontaneous follow-up material that can make your teaching fresh and interesting.

Note that the same question can be convergent under one set of circumstances and divergent under another. Suppose you ask a student to *decide* or *evaluate,* according to a set of criteria, which household products exhibit characteristics of the element sodium. If the student only recalls products from a previously memorized list, then the question is convergent. But if the student has never seen such a list and must analyze the physical properties of products for the first time, then the question is divergent.

Convergent questions also can inadvertently turn into divergent questions. When the answer to a question thought to involve simple recall ("Does anyone know the meaning of the Latin word *via?*") has never been seen before, and the student arrives at the right answer through generalization and inductive reasoning (e.g., by thinking about the meaning of the English word *viaduct* or the phrase "via route 35"), then the question is divergent.

A convergent question in one context may be a divergent question in another and vice versa. The question "What do you think of disarmament?" may require the use of evaluation skills by eighth graders but only the recall of facts by twelfth graders who have just finished memorizing the details of the Strategic Arms Limitation Treaty. Also, both of the questions "What do you think about disarmament?" and "What do you think about the Dallas Cowboys?" may require some analysis, synthesis, or decision making, but for most of your students, disarmament will require a higher level of thought than will the Dallas Cowboys. As has been shown, effective questions depend on more than just words—they depend on the *context* of the discussion in which the question is raised, *voice inflection, word emphasis,* and *word choice.*

What Research Exists on Convergent Versus Divergent Questions?

Classroom researchers have studied the effects on student achievement of convergent and divergent questions (J. Dillon, 1990; Gall, 1984). Remember that far more convergent questions are raised in classrooms than divergent questions; the ratio is about 4:1. Most rationales for using higher-level, divergent-type questions include promotion of thinking, formation of concepts and abstractions, encouragement of analysis-synthesis-evaluation, and so on. But interestingly, research has not clearly substantiated that the use of higher-level questions is related to gains in student achievement—at least not as measured by tests of *standardized* achievement.

Although some studies report modest improvements in achievement scores with the use of divergent questioning strategies, others have not. Some studies even report larger achievement gains with convergent questioning than with divergent questioning strategies. Although these studies found a large imbalance in favor of convergent questions, four important factors must be considered when looking at their results:

1. Tests of achievement—and particularly tests of *standardized* achievement—employ multiple-choice items that generally test for behaviors at lower levels of cognitive complexity. Therefore, the achievement measures in these studies may have been unable to detect increases in behaviors at the higher levels of cognitive complexity, increases that might have resulted from the use of divergent questions.

2. The diversity of responses normally expected from divergent questions, and the added time needed to build on and follow up on responses, may prohibit large amounts of class time from being devoted to higher-order questioning. Because less instructional time often is devoted to divergent questioning than to convergent

questioning, some study results may simply reflect the imbalance in instructional time, not their relative effectiveness.

3. The content best suited for teaching more complex behaviors may constitute only a small amount of the content in existing texts, workbooks, and curriculum guides. Although this is changing as a result of constructivist views on teaching and learning, much of the typical curricula in math, science, English, and even the social sciences emphasize facts and understandings at the knowledge and comprehension level. This may be because such achievements are the most easily measured and because needed improvements can be identified from standardized tests. Until larger portions of curricula are *written to encourage or require higher-level thought processes,* the time teachers actually devote to these behaviors may not increase.

4. Thinking and problem-solving behaviors most closely associated with divergent questions may take much longer to become noticeable in the behavior of learners than less complex behaviors. Less complex behaviors (learning to form possessives, memorizing Latin roots, knowing multiplication tables) are quickly elicited with convergent questioning strategies and are readily detected with fill-in, matching, or multiple-choice exams at the end of a lesson or unit. But more complex and authentic behaviors (learning to distinguish economic systems from political systems, learning to analyze household products for their chemical components, recognizing forms of quadratic equations) may take a unit, a grading period, or even longer to build to a measurable outcome. This time span is beyond that of most, if not all, of the studies that have compared the effects of convergent and divergent strategies on school achievement.

Thus, the seeming imbalance in the use and effectiveness of divergent and convergent questioning strategies may have little to do with the strategies themselves. Because factual recall always will be required for higher-order thought processes, numerous convergent questions always will be a necessary precondition for achieving higher-level behaviors. Also, because more instructional time is needed for higher-order questioning to be used effectively, the consistent use of moderate amounts of divergent questions may be more effective than intense but brief episodes of divergent questioning. The most appropriate *convergent/divergent* question ratio may be about 70:30 in classrooms where lesson content emphasizes lower levels of behavioral complexity, to about 60:40 in classrooms where lesson content emphasizes higher levels.

It is important to note that many of the same studies that fail to link higher-order questioning with increases in school achievement indicate that higher-order questioning tends to encourage students to use higher thought processes in composing a response. Research (J. T. Dillon, 1988b) suggests that teachers who ask questions requiring analysis, synthesis, and evaluation elicit these behaviors from students more frequently than teachers who use fewer higher-level questions.

Therefore, these higher-level thought processes seem desirable, regardless of whether their effects show up on immediate tests of achievement. The effects of higher-level questioning on the thinking process may justify applying higher-level questions consistently at moderate rates over extended periods.

WHO ARE THE TARGETS OF QUESTIONS?

Research by G. Brown and Wragg (1993) and G. Brown and Edmondson (1984) suggests that questions at various levels of cognitive complexity can be directed to individuals, to groups, or to the entire class. Occasionally posing questions over the heads of some learners and under the heads of others will keep all students alert and engaged in the learning process.

In more homogeneously grouped classes, questions can be spread across individuals, groups, and the full class but crafted to fit the cognitive complexity most appropriate for the learners being taught. For example, a general question can be composed requiring less or more cognitive complexity and prerequisite knowledge, as illustrated in the following examples:

Less Complex	**More Complex**
"Tell me, Johnny, if you sat down to breakfast, what things at the breakfast table would most likely contain the element sodium?"	"Mary, what are some forms of the element sodium in our universe?"
"After the death of Lenny in *Of Mice and Men,* what happens to the other main character?"	"What would be an example of an anticlimax in *Of Mice and Men?*"
"After thinking about the words *photo* and *synthesis,* who wants to guess what *photosynthesis* means?"	"Who can tell me how photosynthesis supports plant life?"
"Ted, if we have the equation $10 = 2/x'$ do we find x by multiplying or dividing?"	"Rich, can you solve this problem for $x?$ $10 = 2/x'$"

Notice that these examples vary not only in cognitive complexity but also in how they are framed, or phrased. More advance organizers, hints, and clues will be more appropriate for some types of learners than for others (Michaels & Collins, 1984).

One way of framing questions for heterogeneous classes is to design them so different responses at various levels of complexity will be correct. You can accept less complex responses as being just as correct as more complex answers, if they match the level of the question being asked. Although a response from some learners may not be as complete, you can evaluate the response in terms of the behavioral complexity required by the question and the student's ability to respond to it. Therefore, the elaboration given and depth of understanding required may be less for one type of learner than for another. Table 7.1 suggests specific questioning strategies.

Table 7.1 Characteristics of more and less complex questions.

More Complex Questions	Less Complex Questions
Require the student to generalize the content to new problems	Require the student to recall task-relevant prior knowledge
Stymie, mystify, and challenge in ways that do not have predetermined answers	Use specific and concrete examples, settings, and objects with which students are familiar
Are delivered in the context of an investigation or problem that is broader than the question itself	Use a step-by-step approach, where each question is narrower than the preceding one
Ask students to go deeper, clarify, and provide additional justification or reasons for the answers they provide	Rephrase or reiterate the answers to previous questions
Use more abstract concepts by asking students to see how their answers may apply across settings or objects	Suggest one or two probable answers that lead students in the right direction
Are part of a sequence of questions that builds to higher and more complex concepts, patterns, and abstractions	Are placed in the context of a game (e.g., 20 questions) with points and rewards

WHAT SEQUENCES OF QUESTIONS ARE USED?

Questions also can vary according to the sequence in which they are used. Recall that the most basic **question sequence** involves structuring, soliciting, and reacting. However, many variations are possible. Studies by Wilen (1991), G. Brown and Edmondson (1984), and B. Smith and Meux (1970) note that one of the most popular sequences employs divergent questions that lead to convergent questions. They report that many teachers begin the structuring-soliciting-reacting process by starting with an open question that leads to further structuring, and then to subsequent questions that involve recall or simple deduction.

This general-to-specific approach can take several twists and turns. For example, in the following dialogue, the teacher begins by encouraging speculative responses and then narrows to a question requiring simple deduction:

Teacher: What do astronauts wear on the moon?
Students: Spacesuits.
Teacher: So what element in our atmosphere must *not* be in the atmosphere on the moon?

It is the same approach when a teacher poses a problem, asks several simple recall questions, and then reformulates the question to narrow the problem still further:

Teacher:	If the Alaskan Eskimos originally came from Siberia on the Asian continent, how do you suppose they got to Alaska?
Students:	(No response.)
Teacher:	We studied the Bering Strait, which separates North America from Asia. How wide is the water between these two continents at their closest point?
Student:	About 60 miles. The Little and Big Diomede Islands are in between.
Teacher:	If this expanse of water were completely frozen, which some scientists believe it was years ago, how might Asians have come to the North American continent?

In many studies reviewed by Redfield and Rousseau (1981), teachers frequently employed this type of funneling: adding conditions of increasing specificity to a question. However, no evidence indicates that one sequencing strategy is any more effective in promoting student achievement than any other. The specific sequence should depend on the behavioral objectives, the instructional content being taught, and the ability level of the students.

Other types of questioning sequences that teachers can implement in a cycle of structuring, soliciting, and reacting, suggested by Hunkins (1989) and G. Brown and Edmondson (1984), are illustrated in Table 7.2. With the appropriate objectives, content, and students, all offer useful additions to your teaching menu.

WHAT LEVELS OF QUESTIONS ARE USED?

As we have seen, as an effective teacher, you must be able to formulate divergent and convergent questions, to target questions to specific types of learners, and to arrange questions in meaningful sequences. You also must be able to formulate questions at different levels of cognitive complexity.

One of the best-known systems for classifying questions according to cognitive complexity is the taxonomy of objectives in the cognitive domain that was presented in Chapter 3. This system has the advantage of going beyond the simple recall-versus-thought dichotomy frequently used in the research cited previously. Not all recall questions should deal with the lowest and most mundane forms of learning (e.g., recall of names, dates, facts), and not all thought questions should deal with the highest and most superlative forms of learning (e.g., discovery, insight, judgment). A continuum of question complexity that fills the space between these ends of the scale is a useful addition to the art of asking questions.

Recall that the cognitive-domain taxonomy contains six levels of behavioral complexity:

Table 7.2 Some sequences of questions.

Type		Description
Extending	——————	A string of questions of the same type and on the same topic
Extending and lifting		Initial questions request examples and instances of the same type, followed by a leap to a different type of question; a common sequence is likely to be recall, simple deduction and descriptions leading to reasons, hypothesis
Funneling		Begins with open question and proceeds to narrow down to simple deductions and recall or to reasons and problem solving
Sowing and reaping		Problem posed, open questions asked, followed by more specific questions and restatement of initial problem
Step-by-step up		A sequence of questions moving systematically from recall to problem solving, evaluation or open ended
Step-by-step down		Begins with evaluation questions and moves systematically through problem solving towards direct recall
Nose-dive		Begins with evaluation and problem solving and then moves straight to simple recall

Source: From "Asking Questions" by G. Brown and R. Edmondson, in *Classroom Teaching Skills* (pp. 97–119), edited by E. Wragg. Copyright © 1984 by Nichols Publishing Company. Adapted by permission of Nichols Publishing Company.

- Knowledge
- Comprehension
- Application
- Analysis
- Synthesis
- Evaluation

Table 7.3 identifies the types of student behaviors associated with each level. Look at each level to get a feel for the question-asking strategies that go along with it.

Knowledge

Recall from Chapter 3 that knowledge objectives require the student to recall, describe, define, or recognize facts that already have been committed to memory. Some action verbs you can use to formulate questions at the knowledge level follow:

Table 7.3 A question classification scheme.

Level of Behavioral Complexity	Expected Student Behavior	Instructional Processes	Key Words
Knowledge (remembering)	Student is able to remember or recall information and recognize facts, terminology, and rules.	repetition memorization	define describe identify
Comprehension (understanding)	Student is able to change the form of a communication by translating and rephrasing what has been read or spoken.	explanation illustration	summarize paraphrase rephrase
Application (transferring)	Student is able to apply the information learned to a context different than the one in which it was learned.	practice transfer	apply use employ
Analysis (relating)	Student is able to break a problem down into its component parts and to draw relationships among the parts.	induction deduction	relate distinguish differentiate
Synthesis (creating)	Student is able to combine parts to form a unique or novel solution to a problem.	divergence generalization	formulate compose produce
Evaluation (judging)	Student is able to make decisions about the value or worth of methods, ideas, people, or products according to expressed criteria.	discrimination inference	appraise decide justify

define	list
describe	name
identify	recite

Sample questions are

- What is the definition of capitalism?
- How many digits are needed to make the number 12?
- Can you recite the first rule for forming possessives?
- What is the definition of a *straight line?*

Notice that each of these questions can be answered correctly simply by recalling previously memorized facts. They do not require understanding of what was memorized or the ability to use the learned facts in a problem-solving context. However, when facts are linked to other forms of knowledge, such as those in subsequent lessons and units, they become steppingstones for gradually increasing the

Knowledge questions require recalling previously memorized facts. They do not require that the student understand what was memorized or be able to use the facts in a problem-solving context, for which higher-level questions will be needed.

behavioral complexity of teaching outcomes. To avoid the overuse or disconnected use of questions at the knowledge level, ask yourself: Do the facts required by my questions represent task-relevant prior knowledge for subsequent learning?

If your answer is no, you might consider assigning text, workbook, or supplemental material that contains the facts, instead of incorporating them into your question-asking behavior. If your answer is yes, then determine in what ways learners will use the facts in subsequent lessons, and raise questions that eventually will help form more complex behaviors.

Your students may *not* need the ability to recite the names of the presidents, the Declaration of Independence, or the elements in the periodic table, because these facts may not be task-relevant prior knowledge for more complex behavioral outcomes. On the other hand, it is likely that your learners *will* need to recite the multiplication tables, the parts of speech, and the rules for adding, subtracting, multiplying, and dividing signed numbers, for these will be used countless times in completing exercises and solving problems at more complex behavioral levels.

Always take time to ask yourself: Are the facts that I am about to teach task-relevant prior knowledge for subsequent lessons? By doing so, you will avoid knowledge questions that may be trivial or irrelevant.

Comprehension

Comprehension questions require some level of understanding of facts the student has committed to memory. Responses to these questions should show that the learner can explain, summarize, or elaborate on the facts that have been learned. Some action verbs you can use in formulating questions at the comprehension level follow:

convert	paraphrase
explain	rephrase
extend	summarize

Sample questions are

- Can you, in your own words, explain the concept of capitalism?
- How many units are there in the number 12?
- In converting a possessive back to the nonpossessive form, what must be rephrased so that the first rule applies?
- What steps are required to draw a straight line?

In responding to each of these questions, the student acts on previously learned material by changing it from the form in which it was first learned. For example, the teacher asks not for the definition of capitalism, but "in your own words, explain the concept of capitalism." This requires translation or conversion of the original definition (the teacher's) into another (the student's).

There is an important step in moving from knowledge-level questions to comprehension-level questions. Knowledge-level questions require no cognitive processing—thinking—at the time of response, but comprehension-level questions do. In the former case, the learner actually may think about the material only once, at the time it was originally learned. In the latter case, the learner must actively think about the content twice: once when the facts are memorized and again when they must be composed into a response in a different form. Although fact questions must logically precede comprehension questions, comprehension questions are superior to knowledge questions by encouraging long-term retention, understanding, and eventual use of the learned material in authentic contexts.

Application

Application questions extend facts and understanding to the next level of authenticity. They go beyond memorization and translation of facts. Application questions require the student to apply facts to a problem, context, or environment that is different from the one in which the information was learned. Thus, the student can rely on neither the original context nor the original content to solve the problem.

Some action verbs you can use in formulating questions at the application level are

apply	operate
demonstrate	solve
employ	use

Sample questions are

- What countries from among those listed do you believe have a capitalist economic system?
- Can you show me 12 pencils?
- Consider the first rule for forming possessives; who can apply it to the errors in the following newspaper article?
- Can you draw for me a straight line between these two points?

Your job in application questions is to present your learners with a context or problem different from that in which they learned the material. Application questions encourage the transfer of newly learned material to a new and different environment.

Application questions require two related cognitive processes: (1) the simultaneous recall and consideration of all the individual units (facts) pertaining to the question and (2) the composing of units into a single harmonious sequence wherein the response becomes rapid and automatic. Application questions ask students to compose previously learned responses under conditions approximating some real-world problem. You can see that action sequences require two precedents: learned facts and understandings acquired via knowledge and comprehension questions *and* the use of previously learned facts and rules in new contexts. The number and quality of your application questions will determine how rapid and automatic your learners' action sequences become.

The number of application questions you ask may be less important than your *consistency* in asking them. Many beginning teachers inappropriately believe that application questions should be reserved for the end of a unit or even the end of a grading period. But, as you have seen, they are essential whenever a rapid, automatic response involving facts or rules is desired, or when an action sequence is the lesson goal.

The quality of your application questions will be determined largely by how much you change the problem, context, or environment in which the students learned the facts or rules. If your change is too small, transfer of learning to an expanded context will not occur, and your "parrots" will recite facts and rules from the earlier context. On the other hand, if your change is too great, the new context may require a response beyond the grasp of most of your learners. The key is to raise application questions that require the transfer of learning to new problems or contexts only after you have taught all the task-relevant facts and rules. The easiest way to accomplish this is to change the context only a bit at first and then gradually shift to more unfamiliar contexts.

Analysis

Questions at the analysis level require the student to break a problem into its component parts and to draw relationships among the parts. Some purposes of questions at the analysis level are to identify logical errors; to differentiate among facts, opinions, and assumptions; to derive conclusions; and to find inferences or generalizations—in short, to discover the reasons behind the information given.

Some action verbs you can use in formulating questions at the analysis level are

break down	point out
differentiate	relate
distinguish	support

Sample questions are

- What factors distinguish capitalism from socialism?
- Which of the boxes do not contain 12 things?
- In what ways can you differentiate Rule 1 possessive errors from Rule 2 possessive errors in the following essay?
- Which of the following pictures represents a straight line?

Analysis questions tend to promote behaviors in the form of concepts, patterns, and abstractions. They generally are the most elementary form of the inquiry or problem-solving process, which is most closely associated with the functions of indirect instruction. You may consider analysis questions to be the start of the inquiry or problem-solving process, and the beginning of a change from direct to indirect instructional strategies.

Observe that the majority of the questions lack the single best answer so common in the teaching of facts, rules, and action sequences. Consequently, you will encounter and evaluate a much broader range of responses at the analysis level. You may not anticipate all the varied responses you will receive (some in fact may be surprising). If you cannot prepare for all possible responses (which is very likely at the higher levels of behavioral complexity), then you should prepare yourself psychologically for the diverse responses that analysis questions generate. Preparing yourself psychologically may mean simply shifting your classroom to a less rigid, more deliberate, and slower-paced climate to give yourself some time to evaluate responses on the spot. It also may help to admit to yourself that some of the responses you hear may never have been heard before.

Synthesis

Questions at the synthesis level ask the student to produce something unique or original—to design a solution, compose a response, or predict an outcome to a problem for which the student has never before seen, read, or heard a response. This behavior level often is associated with *directed* creativity in which not all responses are equally acceptable. The facts, rules, action sequences, and any analysis questions that have gone before will define the limits and directions of the synthesis requested.

Some action verbs you can use in formulating questions at the synthesis level are

compare	formulate
create	predict
devise	produce

Sample questions are

- What would an economic system be like that combines the main features of capitalism and socialism?
- What new numbers can you make by adding by 12s?
- How could you write a paragraph showing possession without using any possessives?
- How would you make a straight line without using a ruler?

This illustrates that even more diversity in answers can be expected with synthesis questions than with analysis questions. Such openness is apparent at the analysis level, but it is even more pronounced at the synthesis level. Therefore, your preparation for diversity is critical to how your students receive your synthesis questions.

A question asking for ways to identify undiscovered elements other than by using the periodic table opens up many possible responses. Some may not be acceptable ("consult an astrologer"), but others will be ("analyze minerals from the moon and other planets"). Accept all reasonable answers, even though your own solutions may be limited to one or two efficient, practical, accurate solutions. Efficiency, practicality, and accuracy might be built from student responses, but you cannot initially expect it of them.

Another characteristic of higher-level questions is that they are likely to generate multiple responses. Multiple-response questions actively encourage diverse responses and are used to build increasingly more appropriate answers. Table 8.2 shows different types of questioning sequences, several of which are capable of molding student responses to be either more expansive or more restrictive than the original. You can use diverse responses to synthesis questions to draw out and direct creativity without restricting or narrowing the question itself, as the following dialogue illustrates:

Teacher:	In what ways other than from the periodic table might we predict the undiscovered elements?
Bobby:	We could go to the moon and see if there are some elements there we don't have.
Betty:	We could dig down to the center of the earth and see if we find any of the missing elements.
Ricky:	We could study debris from meteorites—if we can find any.
Teacher:	Those are all good answers. But what if those excursions to the moon, to the center of the earth, or to find meteorites were too costly and time-consuming? How might we use the elements we already have here on earth to find some new ones?
Betty:	Oh! Maybe we could try experimenting with the elements we do have to see if we can make new ones out of them.

This simple exchange illustrates a funneling strategy: broad, expansive answers are accepted and then are followed up with a narrower question on the next round. In this manner, the diverse multiple responses that typically result from synthesis and other higher-level questions can be used to direct creative responses into gradually more structured avenues of inquiry, thereby contributing to critical thinking.

Evaluation

Questions at this highest level of behavioral complexity require the student to form judgments and make decisions using stated criteria. These criteria may be subjective (when a personal set of values is used in making a decision) or objective (when scientific evidence or procedures are used in evaluating something). In both cases, however, it is important that the criteria to be expressed be clearly understood—although not necessarily valued—by others.

Some action verbs you can use in formulating questions at the evaluation level are

appraise	defend
assess	judge
decide	justify

Sample questions are

* Using evidence of your own choosing, do capitalist or socialist countries have a higher standard of living?
* Which of the following numbers contain multiples of 12?
* Using Rules 1 and 2 for forming possessives and assigning one point for each correct usage, what grade would you give the following student essay?
* Given the following lines, which are curved and which are straight?

Evaluation questions have the distinct quality of confronting the learner with authentic problems much as they appear in the real world, as indicated by the list of higher-order thinking and problem-solving behaviors in Appendix C. Because decisions and judgments are prime ingredients of adult life, it is essential that classroom experiences link learners to the world in which they will live, regardless of their age or maturity.

Unfortunately, evaluation questions often are reserved for the end of a unit. Even more misguided is the notion that evaluation questions are more suited to junior high and high school than to elementary grades. Both misconceptions have reduced the impact of evaluation questions on learners. If learners are to cope with real-world problems, they must learn to do so starting at the earliest grades and throughout their schooling. Therefore, your ability to ask evaluation questions that can bring the world to your learners *at their own level of knowledge and experience* is one of the most valued abilities that you, the effective teacher, can have.

This ability, however, does not come easily. To be sure, all characteristics of the previously discussed higher-order questions—diversity of responses, opportunities for open-ended or divergent questioning, and multiple responses—are present in evaluation questions. But criteria must be applied to these in deciding the appropriateness of a solution. Notice in the preceding examples that the criteria (or their source) are identified: "using evidence of your own choosing," "if accuracy was your sole criterion," "using Rules 1 and 2," "given the graphs." The more specific your criteria, and the better your learners know them, the more actively engaged they will become in answering the question.

It is important to note that evaluation questions can be either convergent or divergent. When you ask "Is the equation $2 + 2 = 4$ correct?" you are asking an evaluation question for which only a single, narrow, correct response is possible. Here, the student's engagement in the learning process may be limited to simply conjuring up a memorized portion of the addition table. This evaluation question has far fewer implications for training learners to judge, to make decisions, and to think critically than one that asks, "What kinds of goods and services would be owned by a government under a socialist economic system that would not be owned by a government under a capitalist economic system?" Your fundamental criteria for evaluation questions are decisions and judgments as they are made in the real world.

Summary of Question Types

You now know the levels of questions that can be asked of learners and some factors to consider in selecting the appropriate question type. To summarize:

- Type 1 behaviors (those calling for the acquisition of facts, rules, and action sequences) generally are most efficiently taught with convergent questions that have a single best answer (or a small number of easily definable answers). Type 1 behaviors are most effectively learned with a direct instruction model that focuses convergent questions at the knowledge, comprehension, and application levels of behavioral complexity.
- Type 2 behaviors (those calling for the acquisition of concepts, patterns, and abstractions) generally are most efficiently taught with divergent questions, for which many different answers may be appropriate. Type 2 behaviors are most effectively learned with an indirect instruction model that poses divergent questions at the analysis, synthesis, and evaluation levels of behavioral complexity.

Now that you are acquainted with these broad distinctions among types of questions, we turn to several specific techniques that can help you deliver these questions to your students with ease and perfection.

HOW ARE PROBES USED?

A **probe** is a question that immediately follows a student's response to a question for the following purposes:

- Eliciting clarification of the student's response
- Soliciting new information to extend or build on the student's response
- Redirecting or restructuring the student's response in a more productive direction

Probes follow questions and are used to clarify a student's response, solicit new information, or redirect a response in a more productive direction.

Use probes that *elicit clarification* to have students rephrase or reword a response so you can determine its appropriateness or correctness. **Eliciting** probes, such as "Could you say that in another way?" or "How would that answer apply in the case of _____?" induce learners to show more of what they know, thereby exposing exactly what they understand (Dann, 1995). The brief and vague responses often given in the context of a fast-paced and lively classroom discussion can mask partially correct answers or answers that are correct but for the wrong reason. When you are unsure how much understanding underlies a correct response, slow the pace with a probe for clarification.

Use probes that **solicit** new information following a response that is at least partially correct or that indicates an acceptable level of understanding. This time you are using the probe to push the learner's response to a more complex level (e.g., "Now that you've decided the laboratory is the best environment for discovering new elements, what kind of experiments would you conduct in this laboratory?" or "Now that you've taken the square root of that number, how could you use the same idea to take its cube root?").

This type of probe builds higher and higher plateaus of understanding by using the previous response as a steppingstone to greater expectations and more complete responses. This involves treating incomplete responses as part of the next higher-level response—not as wrong answers. The key to probing for new information is to make your follow-up question only a small extension of your previous question; otherwise, the leap will be too great and the learner will be stymied by what appears to be an entirely new question. This type of probe, therefore, requires much the same process for finding the right answer as does the previously correct question, only this time applied to a different and more complex problem.

Use probes to *redirect the flow* of ideas instead of using awkward and often punishing responses such as "You're on the wrong track," "That's not relevant," or

"You're not getting the idea." Probes for **redirecting** responses into a more productive area can accomplish the needed shift less abruptly and more positively, to avoid discouraging students from venturing another response. A probe that accomplishes this purpose moves the discussion sideways, setting a new condition for a subsequent response that does not negate a previous response.

Probing to redirect or restructure a discussion can be a smooth and effortless way of getting learners back on track. Notice in the following example how the teacher blends the use of all three types of probes in the context of a single discussion:

Teacher:	What do we call the grid system by which we can identify the location of any place on the globe? (To begin the questioning.)
Bobby:	Latitude and longitude.
Teacher:	Good. What does longitude mean? (To solicit new information.)
Bobby:	It's the grid lines on the globe that . . . go up and down.
Teacher:	What do you mean by *up and down?* (To elicit clarification.)
Bobby:	They extend north and south at equal intervals.
Teacher:	OK. Now tell me, where do they begin? (To solicit new information.)
Bobby:	Well, I think they begin wherever it's midnight and end where it's almost midnight again.
Teacher:	Let's think about that for a minute. Wouldn't that mean the point of origin would always be changing according to where it happened to be midnight? (To redirect.)
Bobby:	Yes, so the grids must start at some fixed point.
Teacher:	Anybody know where they begin? (To solicit new information.)
Sue:	Our book says the first one marked *0* starts at a place called Greenwich, England.
Teacher:	How can a grid that runs continuously north and south around the globe *start* anyplace, Sue? (To elicit clarification.)
Sue:	I meant to say that it *runs through* Greenwich, England.
Teacher:	Good. Now let's return to Bobby's point about time. If we have a fixed line of longitude, marked *0,* how might we use it to establish time? (To solicit new information.)
Bobby:	Now I remember. Midnight at the *0* longitude—or in Greenwich, England—is called *0* hours. Starting from there, there are timelines drawn around the world, so that when it's midnight at the first timeline, it will be one o'clock back at Greenwich, England; and when it's midnight at the next timeline, it will be two o'clock back at Greenwich, England, and so on.
Teacher:	What does that mean? (To elicit clarification.)
Bobby:	Each line equals 1 hour—so . . . so there must be 24 of them!
Teacher:	It should be no surprise to learn that time determined in reference to the *0* grid of longitude is called Greenwich Mean Time.

HOW SHOULD YOU USE WAIT TIME?

An important consideration during questioning and probing is how long to wait before initiating another question. Sometimes your "wait time" can be as effective in contributing to the desired response as the question or probe itself, especially when you give students time to thoughtfully compose their answers. Wait times that are either too short or too long can be detrimental and, when too long, they also waste valuable instructional time. Obviously, wait time will be longer when students are weighing alternative responses (which often occurs during indirect instruction) than it will when their responses must be correct, quick, and firm (which often occurs during direct instruction).

Rowe (1986, 1987) distinguishes two different wait times. **Wait-time 1** refers to the amount of time a teacher gives a learner to respond when first asked a question. Classrooms with short wait-time 1s do not give learners much time to think before answering the question. In these classrooms, the teacher is repeating the question, or calling on another learner to answer the same question after only a 2- or 3-second period of silence.

Wait-time 2 refers to the interval of time after a learner's first response until the teacher or other students affirm or negate the answer and the teacher then moves on. Teachers with long wait-time 2s wait several seconds before asking a follow-up question, correcting the answer, or otherwise commenting on what the learner said,

Wait-time 1 refers to the amount of time a teacher gives a learner to respond to a question. Classrooms with short wait-time 1s do not give learners sufficient time to think before answering the question.

giving that learner and others time to rethink, extend, or modify a response. Classrooms with short wait-time 2s are characterized by frequent interruptions of learners before they finish answering.

The following dialogue illustrates wait-time 1 and wait-time 2:

Teacher: From our discussion yesterday about volcanos, can anyone tell us what a caldera is?

(Wait-time 1: The teacher gives students time to think about the question and read nonverbal cues indicating the possible need for a probe—especially important for divergent and higher order questions.)

Nelda: I remember. It's the crater formed by the collapse of the central part of the volcano. I'm not sure, but I think it's used to vent all the steam and gases that spew out.

(Wait-time 2: The teacher waits for other students or Nelda to think about and affirm or negate what was said—especially important for responses that are hesitant or only partially correct.)

. . . Yes, that's it, now I remember the picture in the text with all the smoke coming out of it.

Martin: She's right. That's how we drew on the board. Everyone remember?

Teacher: And, what else did the picture on the board show?

Rowe (1986) and Tobin (1987) have found that increasing either wait time has the following effects on learner responses:

- Learners give longer answers to questions.
- Learners volunteer more responses.
- There are fewer unanswered questions.
- Learners are more certain of their answers.
- Learners are more willing to give speculative answers.
- The frequency of learner questions increases.

Generally, you should wait *at least 3 seconds* before asking another question, or repeating the previous question, or calling on another student. During indirect instruction, when divergent questions may require thinking through and weighing alternatives, up to *15 seconds* of wait time may be appropriate.

These research findings provide impressive testimony to the important effect that wait time can have on your learners' responses. If only a single piece of advice were given to beginning teachers concerning wait time, it would be *slow down, and pause longer between questions and answers than what at first feels comfortable.*

Finally, remember that questions are a principal means of engaging students in the learning process by getting them to think through and problem solve with the material you are presenting. Following are suggestions for using questions to promote your learners' thinking and problem solving:

- *Plan in advance the type of questions you will ask.* Although talk-show hosts make it appear as if their questions are spontaneous and unrehearsed, this seldom is the case. In reality, ad-libbing and spontaneity can lead to as much dead time on the air as they can in your classroom. The type of questions you select, their level of difficulty, and the sequence in which you ask them should be based on your lesson objectives.

- *Deliver questions in a style that is concise, clear, and to the point.* Effective oral questions are like effective writing; every word should be needed. Pose questions in the same natural conversational language you would use with any close friend.

- *Allow time for students to think: Wait-time 1.* Research on question asking points to the fact that many teachers do not allow learners sufficient time to answer a question before calling on someone else or moving to the next question. Gage and Berliner (1992) and Rowe (1986, 1987) report that, on the average, teachers wait only about 1 second for learners to respond. These researchers recommend that you increase wait time to 3 to 4 seconds for lower-level questions and as much as 15 seconds for higher-level questions.

- *Keep the students in suspense.* First, deliver the question, then mention the student's name. Similarly, randomly select the students you want to answer your questions. You want your learners to anticipate that they can be called on at any time. This both increases accountability and maintains attention and alertness (Kounin, 1970).

- *Give students sufficient time to complete their response before redirecting the question or probing: Wait-time 2.* Wait-time 2 is the time you wait following a student answer before probing for deeper understanding or redirecting the question when the answer is incomplete or wrong. Teachers who are making a deliberate effort to maintain lesson momentum will often interrupt before a learner is finished responding. Some cultural and ethnic groups have a different wait-time 2 than others. Tharp and Gallimore (1989) relate that in certain cultures a long wait-time 2 makes the teacher appear disinterested in the lesson, while in other cultures, this is a sign of respect for the speaker.

- *Provide immediate feedback to the learner.* Correct answers should be acknowledged and followed by either encouragement, elaborations on the response, further probing, or moving on to another question. The important point is to communicate to the learner that you heard and evaluated the answer. Often learners (unbeknown to the teacher) perceive that their answers have been ignored. Incorrect, incomplete, or inadequate answers should be followed by probes or redirection of the question to another student. Research suggests that learners of different achievement levels and social class benefit from different redirecting and probing techniques.

ARE QUESTIONING TECHNIQUES CULTURE SPECIFIC?

Sociolinguistics is the study of how cultural groups differ in the courtesies and conventions of language rather than in the grammatical structure of what is said. Sociolinguistics examines the **culture-specific questioning** rules that govern social conversation: with whom to speak, in what manner, when to pause, when to ask and answer questions, how to interrupt a speaker. Sociolinguists study, for example, aspects of communication as revealed by the average length of utterances, time between utterances, speech rhythms, and rules for when, how, and about what people converse with each other. Among these aspects of communication, the most frequently studied are *wait time, rhythm, participation structure, and language*.

Wait Time

Tharp (1989) reports that different cultures often have different wait times. Navajo children, for example, are raised in a culture that allows longer responses (wait-time 2) than Anglo children. Some studies show that Navajo children speak in longer sentences and volunteer more answers when given more time to respond. On the other hand, Tharp reports that in Hawaiian culture interruptions are a sign of interest in the speaker and in what she is saying. Conversely, long wait-time 2s suggest to Hawaiian learners that the speaker is uninterested or bored with the conversation. Other studies of Hispanic and African American learners appear to suggest that optimal wait times are culture and even context specific (Hill, 1989). Although specific prescriptions cannot be made from this research, it does suggest that teachers must determine the way they pose a question and the wait time between questions and answers within the cultural context and learning history of their learners.

Rhythm

Conversational rhythm pertains to the tempo, inflections, and speed of conversations between two speakers as they converse. Young (1970) and Piestrup (1973) have observed that African American children and their mothers converse with one another using rapid rhythms and a "contest" style of interaction. Mothers encourage their children to be assertive. Directions for household chores and the children's responses to these directions take on an almost debate-like tone with the mother directing or calling and the children responding. Franklin (1992) suggests that this style of interaction creates a high-energy, fast-paced home environment that contrasts with the low-energy, slow-paced environment of the typical classroom.

Franklin speculates that this contrast between the pace of conversation at home and in school may be one reason why some African American children may be inappropriately referred for behavior problems in the classroom. Similarly, M. G. Anderson (1992) states that many Anglo teachers overreact to the conversational style of African American adolescents, which may explain the disproportionate referral of these children to programs for learners with behavior disorders. Anderson recommends that teachers allow African American learners to use in the classroom the conversational style they bring from home. This would include speaking more rhythmically, with greater variation in intonation, and engaging in more fast-paced verbal interplay.

Participation Structure

The typical classroom conversation occurs in a one-to-one, question–answer type participation structure or format. A teacher looks directly at a child, asks him or her a question, and waits for an answer before making a follow-up response. Tharp and Gallimore (1989) observe that such a participation structure results in very little participation by Hawaiian or Navajo children.

For children both at home and in the community, the typical participation structure when adults are present involves a relatively small group of children together with an encouraging, participating, but nondirective adult in an informal setting. For example, when the classroom participation structures were based on those found in their cultures, both Hawaiian and Navajo children, who rarely participated in classroom discussions or question–answer formats, became surprisingly verbal (Watson-Gegeo & Boggs, 1977).

Sociolinguists point out that children are more comfortable in classrooms where the sociolinguistic patterns (wait times, rhythms, participation structures, etc.) are compatible with those of their home and community. Bartz and Levine (1978) and Lein (1975) point out that often schools view African American or Hispanic migrant children as nonverbal. Yet, when observed in familiar home or neighborhood environments, they use vibrant, expressive, and creative language patterns. Those researchers observe that the sociolinguistic patterns of the typical American classroom make certain minority group learners uncomfortable. This, in turn, causes those students to participate less in class, in ways Anglo American teachers view as deficient or inappropriate, and to achieve less.

Language

Since much questioning is conducted in the formal language of the classroom, you should know your learners' language abilities. Approximately 5 million students—about 10% of the school-age population—have a primary language other than English. For some, English is their dominant language in the receptive mode (listening, reading), while for others, English may be their dominant language in the expressive mode (talking, writing).

It is not unusual to find bilingual learners who choose, for example, Spanish as their dominant means of speaking but English as their dominant means of listening. This allows you to speak and be understood in English even though at least some of the learners' communications to you might be in Spanish. Knowing your learners' language achievement will provide more opportunities to engage all your students in the learning process. If a learner does not use English as his or her dominant language, either in the expressive or receptive mode, and you do not speak that language, you can

1. Emphasize other forms of communication including the visual, kinesthetic, and tactile modalities to supplement your teaching objectives, thus bringing a multi-sensory approach to your teaching.

2. Be sensitive to cultural differences. For example, frequent meaningful praise and encouragement can set the stage for learning more efficiently than the repeated recitation of rules and warnings, which may not be fully understood by some of your learners.

3. Evaluate the reading level and format of the materials you use. When selecting or adapting materials, you may find a Spanish version of comparable content and reading level. After a trial period, evaluate the materials again and adjust the reading level accordingly.

4. Don't confuse language proficiency with subject matter achievement or ability. Research by Hakuta, Ferdman, and Diaz (1987) indicates that bilingual children, in comparison to monolingual children, show superior performance on tests of analytical reasoning, concept formation, and cognitive flexibility. Other research shows that learners who are fluent in two or more languages have a better knowledge of language structure and detail, understand that words are arbitrary symbols for other words and actions, and can better detect grammatical errors in written and spoken communication (Galambos & Goldin-Meadow, 1990). It is also important to note that some have suggested that children from economically impoverished areas who speak a nonstandard form of English (e.g., Black English) may suffer impaired cognitive development as a result (Bereiter & Englemann, 1966; Hess & Shipman, 1965). This hypothesis has been conclusively refuted (Dillard, 1972; Henderson, Swanson, & Zimmerman, 1974). We now know that *all* languages, including dialects and other forms of nonstandard English, are equally complex and equally capable of being used for learning and problem solving. Linguists have demonstrated that languages cannot be ranked in terms of intellectual sophistication. Consequently, intellectual impairment or slow cognitive development cannot result from the primary language a learner speaks, regardless of how nonstandard that language is.

WHAT ARE COMMON PROBLEMS IN USING QUESTIONS?

Based on classroom observations of the question-asking behavior of beginning teachers, here are some of the most frequently observed problems to watch for and suggested remedies.

Do You Use Complex, Ambiguous, or Double Questions?

One of the most common question-asking problems of beginning teachers is the use of the complex, ambiguous, or double question. This is a question that is so long and complicated that students easily lose track of the main idea by the time it is completed. Sometimes, a teacher will unknowingly pack two (or even more) questions within its complicated structure.

Because such questions are delivered orally and are not written, students have no way of rereading the question to gain its full intent. It is unfortunate that these questions sometimes are so complicated that even the teacher cannot repeat the question precisely when requested, thus providing different versions of the same question. Consider the following three examples of needlessly complex questions and their simpler but equally effective revisions.

Example 1

Complex form: "We all know what the three branches of government are, but where did they come from, how were they devised, and in what manner do they relate?"

This question is actually three questions in one and requires too long a response if each point in the question were responded to individually. In addition, the first two questions may be redundant—or are they?—while the third is sufficiently vague to bewilder most students. Finally, what if some students do not know or cannot recall the three branches of government? For those students, everything that follows is irrelevant, opening the door to boredom and off-task behavior.

Simpler form: "Recall that there are three branches of government: the executive, judicial, and legislative. What governmental functions are assigned to each by the Constitution?"

Example 2

Complex form: "How do single-celled animals propagate themselves and divide up to create similar animal life that looks like themselves?"

If you were to ask this question, you can be sure that some of your students would ask you to repeat the question, in which case you might not remember your own complex wording. This question fails to get to the point quickly and appears to ask the same thing three times: how do single-celled animals propagate . . . divide up . . . create similar animal life? This redundancy could easily be mistaken for three separate questions by students struggling to understand single-celled reproduction at an elementary level. State your questions only one way and rephrase later, if need be, when students know that it is the same question being rephrased.

Simpler form: "By what process do single-celled animals reproduce?"

Example 3

Complex form: "What do you think about the Civil War, or the Vietnam War, or war in general?"

Depending on what part of this question a student wants to hear, you may get noticeably different answers. The intention was to raise a question that would provide enough options to get almost any student involved in composing a response; but, unless you intend only to start a controversy, the range of responses will probably be so broad that moving to the next substantive point may be impossible. This question may leave students arguing feverishly for the entire period without being able to focus on the real purpose for raising the question in the first place (e.g., as an introduction to the Civil War, or to unpopular wars, or to the concept of war). This question is too broad, too open, and too divergent to be of practical value for framing a day's lesson.

Simpler form: "What are the factors that you believe would justify a war among groups within the same nation?"

Here are basic rules for avoiding complex, ambiguous, or double questions:

1. Focus each question on only one idea.
2. State the main idea only once.
3. Use concrete language.
4. State the question in as few words as possible.

Do You Accept Only the Answers You Expect?

Another common mistake of beginning teachers is to rely almost exclusively on the answer they expect. Recall the discussion in Chapter 2 regarding the bias that teachers sometimes have about whom they call on and interact with in classroom exchanges. Biases can extend to favorite answers as well as to favorite students. When teaching new content, which frequently is the case during your first year, you naturally strive to become more secure and confident by limiting answers to those with which you are most familiar. Your first reaction will be to discourage responses at the edge of what you consider to be the appropriate range. This range is directly related to the openness of your questions. Open questions encourage diversity, and it is this diversity that often catches the beginning teacher off guard and forces an expansive question into a limited one. Note in the following dialogue how this teacher's posture is changed by the nature of the response:

Teacher:	OK, today we will study the European settlers who came to America, and why they came here. Why did they come to America?
Student 1:	To farm.
Teacher:	No, not to farm.
Student 2:	To build houses and churches.
Teacher:	No, that's not right either.

If this exchange were to continue for very long, it no doubt would turn off many students, if only because they know that these responses cannot be entirely wrong even if they are not what the teacher wants. What does the teacher want? Probably, the desired answer is that the early Americans came because of religious persecution in their European communities. The last student's response, "to build houses and churches," was a perfect opportunity for a probe that simply asked "Why churches?"

Unfortunately, this teacher missed that opportunity in favor of waiting for the exact response, because this teacher was unable or unwilling to *build on existing responses*. This teacher may have a long wait, in which case valuable instructional time will be lost by calling on student after student in the hope that the only acceptable answer will eventually emerge.

Answers that are just what you are looking for are always desirable, but remember that partially correct answers and even unusual and unexpected ones can become effective additions to the discussion through the use of probes. The solution to this problem is to use probes and build gradually toward your targeted responses.

Why Are You Asking This Question?

Perhaps the most serious error of all in question asking is not being certain of why you are asking a question. Remember, questions are tools that support the teaching and learning processes. Your first decision in using questions is to determine whether your lesson is teaching facts, rules, and action sequences or concepts, patterns, and abstractions. If the former is your goal, convergent questions at the knowledge, comprehension, or application levels probably are the ones to ask. If the latter is your goal, then divergent questions at the analysis, synthesis, or evaluation levels usually are the questions to ask. This decision strategy is summarized in Figure 7.1.

Figure 7.1   A decision tree for deciding on the types of questions to ask.

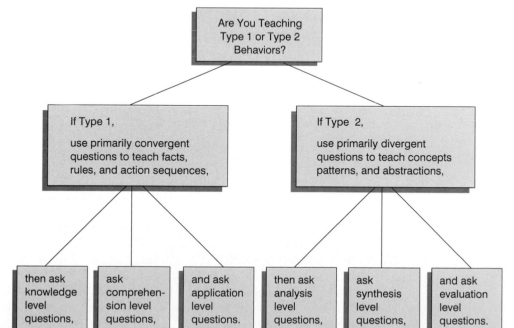

If you have not determined where you are on Figure 7.1, you are likely to ask the wrong type of question, and your questions will lack logical sequence. They may jump from convergent to divergent and move back and forth from simple recall of facts to the acquisition of concepts and patterns. Your students will find your questions disconcerting, because your ideas will not be linked by any common thread (at least, not by one that they can follow), and you will be seen as vague or lacking the ability to connect content in meaningful ways. Therefore, it is important that you decide in advance where your questioning strategy is going and then move toward this goal by choosing appropriate questions and levels of behavioral complexity.

Finally, it is important to note that just because your goal may be Type 1 or Type 2 behaviors, this does not mean that you cannot vary your questioning strategy across the levels shown on Figure 7.1. Questions should vary within types of learning (e.g., from knowledge to application or from analysis to synthesis) and across types of learning (e.g., from application to analysis). It is important to keep in mind your ultimate goal for the lesson and to choose the best combination of questions to reach that goal.

Do You Answer the Question Yourself?

Another common problem with beginning teachers is posing a question, and then answering it yourself. Sometimes a student begins a response but is cut off, only to hear the remainder of the response supplied by the teacher:

Teacher:　　So, who was the president who freed the slaves?
Student:　　Abraham—
Teacher:　　Lincoln! Yes, that's right.

Sometimes the reverse occurs: a student begins a response that the teacher knows is wrong and then is cut off by the teacher, who gives the correct response:

Teacher:　　So, who was the president who freed the slaves?
Student:　　George—
Teacher:　　No, no! It was Abraham Lincoln.

Needless to say, both outcomes demoralize the student, who either is deprived of the chance to completely give a right answer or is shown to have a response so incorrect that it is not even worth hearing in its entirety. Neither of these outcomes may be intended, but this is how your students will see it.

Your job is to use student responses to build to other more complex outcomes. Probes to elicit new information, to go beyond an already-correct answer, or to provide hints and clues after a wrong answer are particularly useful, because they extend to your students the right to give a full and deliberate response, right or wrong.

Teachers who frequently interrupt student responses because of a desire for perfect answers, a dominant personality, or talkativeness, may ultimately produce frustrated learners who never learn to give full and thoughtful responses or to participate voluntarily.

Do You Use Questions as Punishment?

Our final problem, and perhaps the most difficult, is the use—or rather, abuse—of questions to punish or to put a student on the defensive. Being asked a question can be a punishment as well as a reward. For example, questions can be used as punishment in the following ways:

1. A student who forgot to do the homework is deliberately asked a question from that homework.
2. A student who never volunteers is always asked a question.
3. A student gives a wrong response and then is asked an even harder question.
4. A student who disrupts the class is asked a question for which the answer cannot possibly be known.
5. A student who gives a careless response is asked four questions in a row.

Nearly every teacher has, at one time or another, used questions in one or more of these ways. Interestingly, some teachers do not always see these uses as punishment. Regardless of intent, however, such questions *are* punishment in that they (1) are unlikely to engage the student actively in meaningful learning and (2) leave the student with a poorer self-image, less confidence, and more anxiety (perhaps anger) than before the question. These are behaviors that can only impede the learning process and that, therefore, have no place in your repertoire of questioning strategies. Each of the student-centered problems reflected in the preceding examples could have been handled more effectively, perhaps by doing the following:

1. Make a list of students who don't do homework.
2. Give example questions beforehand to students who never volunteer.
3. Give another try and provide hints and clues to students who give wrong responses until they give partially correct answers.
4. Give disciplinary sanctions or reprimands to students who disrupt class.
5. Pass quickly to another student after receiving a careless answer.

Ample means are available for dealing with misbehavior, and such means are far more effective than using questions. Questions are *instructional tools* that should be prized and protected for their chosen purpose. To misuse them or to use them for any other purpose may affect how your students will perceive your questions ("Did I get the hard question because she thinks I'm smart or because I'm being punished?"). Such conflicts can drain students of the energy and concentration needed to answer your questions and may forever cast doubts on your motives.

The other side of questions is that they can be implicit rewards when used correctly. The opportunity to shine, to know and display the correct answer in front of others, and to be tested and get an approving grade are rewarding experiences for any learner. Consequently, every learner, regardless of ability level or knowledge of a correct response, should periodically experience these emotions.

Don't ignore students who have difficulty responding, and don't accept wrong answers. Instead, occasionally try a broader criterion than correct/incorrect to help all students share in the emotional and intellectual rewards of answering questions. For example, try rewarding the most novel, most futuristic, most practical, and most thought-provoking answers along with the most accurate response. This will let every learner share in the challenge and excitement of questions. Questions are another tool to add to your teaching menu. Because of their almost endless variety, they may well be the most flexible tool on your menu.

SUMMING UP

This chapter introduced you to questioning strategies. Its main points were as follows:

1. An effective question is one for which students actively compose a response and thereby become engaged in the learning process.

2. An effective question depends on voice inflection, word emphasis, word choice, and the context in which it is raised.

3. The three most commonly observed teacher behaviors in the classroom are structuring, soliciting, and reacting.

4. Soliciting—or question-asking behavior—encourages students to act on and think about the structured material as quickly as possible after it has been presented.

5. It has been estimated that 70% to 80% of all questions require the simple recall of facts, but only 20% to 30% require clarifying, expanding, generalizing, and the making of inferences. In other words, as few as one of every five questions may require higher-level thought processes, even though behaviors at the higher levels of cognitive complexity are among those most frequently required in adult life, at work, and in advanced training.

6. Common purposes for asking questions include the following:
   • Getting interest and attention
   • Diagnosing and checking
   • Recalling specific facts or information
   • Managerial
   • Encouraging higher-level thought processes

   • Structuring and redirecting learning
   • Allowing expression of affect

7. A question that limits possible responses to one or a small number is called a *convergent, direct,* or *closed* question. This type of question teaches the learner to respond in a limited, restrictive manner.

8. A question that has many right answers or a broad range of acceptable responses is called a *divergent* question. Divergent questions, however, can have wrong answers.

9. The same question can be convergent under one set of circumstances and divergent under another, as when so-called creative answers to a divergent question have been memorized from a list.

10. Research has not established that the use of higher-order questions is related to improved performance on standardized achievement tests. However, higher-order questions have been found to elicit analysis, synthesis, and evaluation skills, which are among the skills most sought in adult life.

11. Questions can be specifically worded for cognitive complexity as well as directed to individuals, groups, or the entire class.

12. Questions may be used in the context of many different sequences, such as funneling, where increasingly specific conditions are added to an original question, narrowing it to one requiring simple deduction.

13. In addition to being divergent, convergent, and targeted to specific types of learners,

questions can be formulated at different levels of cognitive complexity that comprise the knowledge, comprehension, application, analysis, synthesis, and evaluation levels of the cognitive domain.

14. Knowledge questions ask the learner to recall, describe, define, or recognize facts that already have been committed to memory.

15. Comprehension questions ask the learner to explain, summarize, or elaborate on previously learned facts.

16. Application questions ask the learner to go beyond the memorization of facts and their translation and to use previously acquired facts and understandings in a new and different environment.

17. Analysis questions ask the learner to break a problem into its component parts and to draw relationships among the parts.

18. Synthesis questions ask the learner to design or produce a unique or unusual response to an unfamiliar problem.

19. Evaluation questions ask the learner to form judgments and make decisions, using stated criteria for determining the adequacy of the response.

20. A *probe* is a question that immediately follows a student's response to a question; its purpose is to elicit clarification, to solicit new information, or to redirect or restructure a student's response.

21. The key to probing for new information is to make the follow-up question only a small extension of the previous question.

22. The time you wait before initiating another question or turning to another student may be as important in actively engaging the learner in the learning process as the question itself. Teachers should observe a wait time of at least 3 seconds before asking another question, repeating the previous question, or calling on another student.

23. Longer wait times have been associated with longer responses, greater numbers of voluntary responses, greater behavioral complexity of the response, greater frequency of student questions, and increased confidence in responding.

24. Avoid problems commonly observed in the question-asking behavior of beginning teachers:

   • Do not raise overly complex or ambiguous questions that may require several different answers.

   • Be prepared to expect correct but unusual answers, especially when raising divergent questions.

   • Always establish beforehand why you are asking a particular question. Know the complexity of behavior you may expect as a result of the question.

   • Never supply the correct answer to your own questions without first probing. Never prevent a student from completing a response to a question, even if incorrect. Use partially correct or wrong answers as a platform for eliciting clarification, soliciting new information, or redirecting.

   • Never use questions as a form of embarrassment or punishment. Such misuse of questions rarely changes misbehavior, and questions are academic tools that should be prized and protected for their chosen purpose. To misuse them or to use them for any other purpose may affect how your students will perceive your questions.

FOR DISCUSSION AND PRACTICE

Questions marked with an asterisk are answered in Appendix B. See also *Bridges: An Activity Guide and Assessment Options,* which accompanies this text.

*1. What is the definition of an *effective question* as used in this chapter? Pose a question that you believe represents this definition.

*2. Identify the chain of events that forms the most frequently observed cycle of teacher–student interaction. For a topic you will be teaching, show how this chain of events would unfold using actual teacher and student dialogue.

*3. Approximately what percentage of all school time may be devoted to questions and answers? What is your opinion as to why this percentage is so high?

*4. Approximately what percentage of questions asked require simple recall of facts, and approximately what percentage require clarifying, expanding, generalizing, and the making of inferences? What is your opinion as to why the latter percentage is so low?

*5. What are seven specific purposes for asking questions. Give an example of each with content you will be teaching.

*6. In your own words, what is a convergent question and what is a divergent question? How do they differ with respect to right answers? How are they the same with respect to wrong answers?

7. Using the same question content, give an example of both a convergent and a divergent question.

*8. Under what circumstances might a divergent question such as "What propulsion systems might airplanes use in the year 2050?" actually function as a convergent question?

*9. Explain under what circumstances a convergent question such as, "What is 2 multiplied by 4?" might actually function as a divergent question.

*10. According to research, how does the asking of higher-order questions affect (1) a learner's standardized achievement score and (2) a learner's use of analysis, synthesis, and evaluation skills in thinking through a problem?

11. Compose a question that is more cognitively complex and another that is less cognitively complex. How do these two questions differ in cues, hints, and advance organizers?

12. Write a brief classroom dialogue of teacher questions and student responses illustrating the funneling of student responses.

13. Using Table 7.2 as a guide, compose a sequence of related questions that extend and lift student responses.

14. Using the same content as in question 13, prepare one question that elicits the appropriate level of behavioral complexity at each level of the cognitive domain—knowledge, comprehension, application, analysis, synthesis, and evaluation.

15. In the context of a brief classroom dialogue, provide one example each of questions that (1) elicit clarification, (2) solicit new information, and (3) redirect or restructure a student's response. In which order did these occur?

*16. What is meant by the phrase *wait time?* Generally speaking, why should beginning teachers work to increase their wait time?

*17. Identify and give an example of the five most troublesome question-asking problems for the beginning teacher. Which fault do you feel most likely to make?

18. What is sociolinguistics, and why is this area of study important in a culturally diverse classroom? Can you think of one sociolinguistic finding that will be important to you in your classroom?

8 Self-Directed Learning

This chapter will help you answer the following questions:

1. What teaching behaviors are required for self-directed learning?
2. How can my learners explore content through classroom dialogue?
3. How do I get learners to accept responsibility for their own learning?
4. What are some cognitive learning strategies that can help my learners retain, order, and comprehend new information?
5. How can I engage my learners in problem-based learning?
6. How can I promote the goals of self-directed learning in a culturally diverse classroom?

n this chapter on self-directed learning, you will study an important method for engaging your students in the learning process. Here you will learn how to teach learners to go beyond the content given—to think critically, reason, and problem-solve—using a self-directed approach to learning. You will see how to use self-directed strategies to actively engage your students in the learning process and to help them acquire the reasoning, critical thinking, and problem-solving skills required in today's complex society.

SELF-DIRECTED LEARNING

Much of today's classroom learning is focused on activities by which the learner acquires facts, rules, and action sequences. The majority of lessons require outcomes only at the lower levels of behavioral complexity: knowledge, comprehension, and application. This may explain why some national studies of the state of education in the United States (National Governors Association, in Lambert 1991; National Commission on Excellence in Education, 1983) found many students unable to think independently of the teacher or to go beyond the content in their texts and workbooks. These reports suggest that the manner in which most schooling occurs may not be teaching students to become aware of their own learning, to think critically, and to derive their own patterns of thought and meaning from the content presented, as suggested by the higher-order thinking and problem-solving behaviors in Appendix C (Beyer, 1995; Hester, 1994; Walberg, 1991).

Self-directed learning is an approach to teaching *and* learning that actively engages students in the learning process to acquire outcomes at the higher levels of behavioral complexity. Self-directed learning helps students construct their own understanding and meaning and helps them to reason, problem solve, and think critically about the content (Rallis, Rossman, Phlegar, & Abeille, 1995).

Self-directed learning requires you to perform several unique teaching functions:

1. Provide information about when and how to use mental strategies for learning.
2. Explicitly illustrate how to use these strategies to think through solutions to real-world problems.
3. Encourage your learners to become actively involved in the subject matter by going beyond the information given, to restructure it in their own way of thinking and prior understanding.
4. Gradually shift the responsibility for learning to your students through practice exercises, question-and-answer dialogues, and/or discussions that engage them in increasingly complex thought patterns.

Consider the following excerpt, which illustrates how some of these teaching functions might be accomplished in a typical lesson:

Teacher: (A poem is written on the board; teacher reads it to class:)
Man is but a mortal fool
When it's hot, he wants it cool
When it's cool, he wants it hot
He's always wanting what is not.

Today, I want to illustrate some ways to understand a poem like the one I've just read. This may seem like a simple poem, but its author put a lot of care and meaning into each one of its words. Now, let me give you an approach to studying poems like these and gaining from them the meaning intended by their authors. First, let's identify the key words in this poem. Bobby, what do you think are some of the most important ones?

Bobby: Well, I'd say the word *man* because it's the first.

Teacher: Any others? (Still looking at Bobby.)

Bobby: Not that I can see.

Teacher: Anita?

Anita: The words *hot* and *cool* have to be important, because they appear twice and they rhyme with the last words of the first and last lines.

Teacher: Any other key words? Rick?

Rick: Well, I think a *mortal fool* is supposed to be telling us something, but I don't know what.

Teacher: Good. So, now we've identified some words we think are especially important for understanding this poem. Why don't we look up in the dictionary the meanings of any of these words we don't know or are unsure of. That will be our second step. Ted, look up the word *mortal* for us, while we begin work on our third step. The third step is to paraphrase what you think this author is saying. Susan, can you paraphrase what he is saying?

Susan:	I think he's saying we're always changing our minds, and that's why we look so stupid sometimes.
Teacher:	We are all human, so we certainly change our minds a lot, don't we? Rhonda looks like she wants to say something. Rhonda?
Rhonda:	Well, I'd say it's not that we're stupid that we change our minds, but that it's just part of who we are—we can't help wanting what we can't have.
Teacher:	So, you've added a little something to Susan's interpretation. What do you think, Susan? Do you agree?
Susan:	Yeah, we're not stupid; we're just mortals.
Teacher:	Chris, do you want to add anything?
Chris:	I'd say that we're not stupid at all. That to really enjoy something, we must have experienced its opposite—otherwise we wouldn't know how good it is.
Teacher:	Now, that brings us to our fourth and last step. Let's try to relate what Chris just said to our own experience. Anyone ready? Bobby?
Bobby:	I agree with Chris, because I remember thinking how much I welcomed winter because of how hot it was last summer.
Teacher:	(Marcia is waving her hand.) Marcia, what do you have to say about this?
Marcia:	But, now that it's winter, I can't wait for the cold weather to end, so I can go swimming again. (Class nods in agreement.)
Teacher:	It looks as though Chris was right. We sometimes have to see both sides of something—hot/cold, good/bad, light/dark—to fully appreciate it. Now, Ted, what did you find for *mortal* in the dictionary?
Ted:	It says "having caused or being about to cause death," "subject to death," and "marked by vulnerability."
Teacher:	Which of those do you think best fits the use of *mortal fool* in our poem?
Ted:	Well, hmm . . . the last one, because it kind of goes with what we have been saying about how we choose one thing and then another . . . like when we get too cold, dream of summer, and then when summer comes, think it's too hot.
Teacher:	I agree; it fits with what we all have experienced in our lives—and that means we are on the right track to the interpretation the author intended. Now, let's go one step further. Putting all of our ideas together, what is this poet saying? (Nodding to Alex.)
Alex:	Well, I'd say life's a kind of circle. We keep going around and around—back to where we've come and then trying to escape to where we've been—maybe that's one kind of vulnerability—like it said in the dictionary.
Teacher:	That's good thinking, Alex. Bobby, because we began with you, I'll let you have the final word.
Bobby:	I think Alex got it, because now I understand why the author thinks we're all fools. We're like a dog going in circles chasing our tails,

| | always wanting what we don't have. That explains the first and the last line, doesn't it? Because we are human, we are vulnerable to always " . . . wanting what is not." Yes, so we're mortal fools. I get it. |
| **Teacher:** | Very good. Now, let's think for a moment about the four steps we just went through to understand this poem. I will repeat them slowly while you write them down. They will become your guide for reading the rest of the poems we study. |

Notice how this teacher contributed something to each of the four components of self-directed learning.

First, she provided the learners with a mental strategy for learning—in this case a framework of four easy-to-follow steps for interpreting poetry. These steps were sufficiently familiar and practical enough to be followed by almost any student, regardless of ability or experience. Notice that they were not just divisions of the task but steps that ultimately *force learners to go beyond the content presented* to find their own meaning and understanding, based on personal experience and individual thinking. In other words, there were no wrong answers with this strategy—only answers that could be improved to raise the learner onto the next rung of the learning ladder.

Second, the strategy provided wasn't just routinely given to the learners by listing its steps on the board; the steps were *illustrated in the context of a real problem.* The application was real world and typical of other examples to which they would be asked to apply the strategy.

Third, the learners were invited to become *participants in the learning,* not just passive listeners waiting to be told what to do. By using a question-and-answer dialogue to provide a structure for the learners' opinions and experiences, students became an active part of the process by which new knowledge was being generated. They were, in a sense, their own teachers without knowing it. This was made possible through the format of an unscripted discussion, which removed any fear of producing a wrong response that might have prevented some learners from participating.

And fourth, note that as the lesson evolved, more and more of the most important conclusions were provided by the students, not the teacher. The highest level of interpretation with which the lesson ended came almost entirely from the summarizing remarks of students. By the end of the lesson, the teacher's role was more that of a monitor and codiscussant than of an information provider; that role had been assumed by the students themselves as they actively applied each of the steps given earlier in the lesson.

Now let's look more closely at some of the invisible mental strategies that learners can actually use to acquire meaning and understanding from text.

METACOGNITION

One invisible strategy for self-directed learning is metacognition. **Metacognition** refers to mental processes that assist learners to reflect on their thinking by internalizing, understanding, and recalling the content to be learned. They include thinking skills such as self-interrogation, self-checking, self-monitoring, and analyzing, as well as memory aids (called *mnemonics*) for classifying and recalling content.

Metacognitive strategies are most easily conveyed to learners through a process called **mental modeling** (G. Duffy, Roehler, & Herrmann, 1988). This involves using instructional techniques whereby learners increasingly accept responsibility for their own learning by implementing and monitoring a previously modeled way of thinking. Mental modeling involves three important stages (G. Duffy & Roehler, 1989):

1. Show students the reasoning involved.
2. Make students conscious of the reasoning involved.
3. Focus students on applying the reasoning.

These steps usually are carried out through verbal statements that walk learners through the process of attaining a correct solution. They begin with *verbal markers* such as the following:

> Now, I will show you how to solve this problem by talking out loud as I go through it, identifying exactly what is going on in my mind.
>
> Think about each decision I make, where I stop to think, and what alternatives I choose—as though you are making the same decisions in your own mind.

Notice that the teacher is not giving the learner the mechanics of getting a right answer: do step A, then B, then C. More importantly, the teacher is providing an actual live demonstration of the mental procedures that may lie behind the routine completion of a problem.

Research on what makes a good demonstration (Gage & Berliner, 1992; Good & Brophy, 1995) indicates that skilled demonstrators of mental procedures do the following:

- *Focus the learners' attention.* They begin their demonstration only when their learners' attention is focused on them. Then, they direct students' attention to the thinking or reasoning skill they want them to learn.
- *Stress the value of the demonstration.* They briefly and concisely point out why their learners should observe what they are about to demonstrate. They relate the thinking skill to the content to be learned.
- *Talk in conversational language while demonstrating.* They back up to cover unfamiliar concepts and repeat actions when needed, use analogies to bridge content gaps, and use examples to reinforce learning. They then probe for understanding.
- *Make the steps simple and obvious.* They break complex actions into simple steps that can be followed one at a time. They point out what to do next and then describe the action as it is being performed by thinking out loud while acting.
- *Help learners remember the demonstration.* They go slow ("Stop me if I'm going too fast"), exaggerate certain actions ("Now I'll ask myself a question"), highlight distinctive features ("Notice where I pause"), and give simple memory aids to help learners retain what they've seen and heard.

These mental procedures help students to internalize, recall, and then generalize problem solutions to different content at a later time. You do not just convey information according to the preceding steps but actually demonstrate the decision-making process as it occurs within your own thoughts. By contrast, the mechanical memorization of steps rarely helps learners to solve similar problems in other contexts or allows content to be recalled when the present topic has lost its immediate importance (no exam in sight or homework due).

You then monitor the process as it occurs in the learner, provide feedback, and adjust the complexity and flow rate of content as needed. This leads to a second important concept for self-directed learning called mediation.

TEACHER MEDIATION

On-the-spot adjustments to content flow and complexity that you make to accommodate idiosyncratic learning needs are called teacher mediation. Your role during **teacher-mediated learning** is to adjust the instructional dialogue to help students restructure their learning and move them closer to the intended outcome. In other words, the interactive dialogue you provide helps learners construct their *own* meanings from the content. This aids retention and the generalization of the reasoning process to other contexts.

The knowledge and skills that learners are to acquire are not given to them in the form of end products. Instead, you provide the cognitive stimulation at just the proper times for them to acquire the end products through their own reasoning. The need for adjustment of flow and content seldom can be anticipated. It requires mediation—your on-the-spot judgment of what new information would bring a learner's response to the next level of refinement of which the learner is capable at that moment. This next level reflects the content difficulty and behavioral complexity from which the student can most benefit at that moment.

The Zone of Maximum Response Opportunity

This level of content difficulty and behavioral complexity is the learner's **zone of maximum response opportunity.*** It is the zone of behavior that, if stimulated by you, will bring a learner's response to the next level of refinement. Thus, your response directed at the zone of maximum response opportunity must be at or near the learner's current level of understanding but also designed to lift the learner's following response to the next higher level. Your directed response need not elicit the correct answer, because the learner at that precise moment may be incapable of benefiting from it. It should, however, encourage the learner to refine an initially crude response.

Here are two classroom dialogues in which the first teacher hits the zone of maximum response opportunity, but the second misses it:

---

*The zone of maximum response opportunity is called the "zone of proximal development" by Vygotsky (Kozulin, 1990).

Teacher:	When you see a proportion, such as ⅘ (writes it on board), think of the number on top as "what is" and the number on the bottom as "what could be." Think about a box of cereal that you make your breakfast from. If I wrote the proportion of cereal in the box as ¾ (writes it on board), I would say to myself, the full box is equal to the number 4—that's the "could be" part. But this morning, after I fixed my breakfast, what's left is only the number 3, which is the "what is" part. That's how I can tell the box is still pretty full, because the number for "what is" is close to the number for "what could be."
	Now, Johnny, explain to me what it means when it says on a label that the proportion of vitamin C for one 4-ounce glass of orange juice is ½ the minimum daily requirement.
Johnny:	I'm not sure.
Teacher:	OK, what words can we use to describe the number on top?
Johnny:	You said it's "what is."
Teacher:	What does that mean?
Johnny:	I guess it's how much vitamin C is really in the glass.
Teacher:	And, now for the bottom.
Johnny:	You said the bottom is "what could be." Does that mean that it's all you need?
Teacher:	Yes, it does—good. Now, think of another example—one of your own—in which something was less than it could have been.
Johnny:	Well, I finished Ms. Enro's social studies test before the end of the period.
Teacher:	And how long was the period?
Johnny:	Umm, about 40 minutes, I guess.
Teacher:	Using our words, what would you call that part of the problem?
Johnny:	"What could be." OK, I get it. Then, the time I actually took is what really happened? Yeah, I finished the test in about 20 minutes.
Teacher:	So, how would you express that proportion in numbers?
Johnny:	It would be 20, for "what is," over 40, for "what could be." The top is half of the bottom, so I guess one glass of orange juice gives you half the vitamin C you need in a day.
Teacher:	OK. Let's retrace the steps you just followed for another problem. . . .

Now let's imagine that Johnny relives this episode in another classroom. After the same introductory remarks, Johnny is asked the identical question:

| Teacher: | Now, Johnny, explain to me what it means when it says on a label that the proportion of vitamin C for one 4-ounce glass of orange juice is ½ the minimum daily requirement. |

Johnny:	I'm not sure.
Teacher:	Look, if the number 1 is on the top and the number 2 is on the bottom, it must mean the top is less than the bottom. Right?
Johnny:	Right.
Teacher:	So, if the top number represents what is and the bottom number what could be, then "what is" is one half less than "what could be." And, that can only mean the glass contains half of the minimum daily requirement of vitamin C. Got it?
Johnny:	Yep.

Well, maybe he does and maybe he doesn't. Notice in the first example that, by retracing the mental steps for Johnny to recall, the teacher hit Johnny's zone of maximum response opportunity because his prior understanding and response were taken into account in moving the dialogue forward, closer to the intended goal of the lesson. It provided a peg with which Johnny lifted himself onto the next rung of the learning ladder.

The second teacher simply provided the right answer. This gave Johnny no opportunity to construct *his own* response by using the mental steps provided and thereby derive a process to use for independently arriving at other right answers in similar circumstances. The first teacher focused on developing for the learner a process of reasoning—a line of thinking—that would give the content its own individual meaning and yet be consistent with the intended goal of the lesson.

Through classroom dialogues such as these, you can encourage your learners to construct their own meanings and interpretations, for example, to substitute their own unique constructions for what is and what could be, and to share them with others through discussion and classroom dialogue. Such diversity among self-directed learners activates their unique learning histories, specialized abilities, and personal experiences, thus engaging them in the learning process.

Hitting the Zone of Maximum Response Opportunity

The zone of maximum response opportunity is particularly important in self-directed learning, because you can rarely provide the most appropriate response to each learner at all times. This is the key difference between individualized learning (e.g., programmed instruction) and self-directed learning. In individualized learning, the content writer anticipates the most probable errors and provides remedial or alternative learning routes (called *branching*) for all learners, regardless of their zones of maximum response opportunity. Because the instruction assumes that relatively homogeneous groups of individual learners will work through the content, the same types of errors must be anticipated for all learners. In some cases the remedial steps or alternative branching provided may fall within a learner's zone of maximum response opportunity, but in some cases it may not.

Diversity among self-directed learners can be activated by teacher interaction and the gentle interplay that taps the learner's zone of maximum response opportunity and provides appropriate steppingstones to higher levels of learning.

Because self-directed learning almost always occurs during a student response–teacher reaction sequence, it affords the opportunity to more accurately aim your spoken or written reaction at the learner's zone of maximum response opportunity. However, a variety of teacher reactions can fall within the learner's zone of maximum response opportunity with equal effect. After all, your target is not a point but a zone that in some instances may be as broad as the outfield in a major league ballpark.

In this broad field, a hit is a hit, whether it falls in left field, center field, or right field, as long as it is within the appointed zone. This is an important point, because aiming your reaction to a student response too sharply—to a fixed point like lower center field—may so restrict your response that it will exclude the learning history, specialized abilities, and personal experiences of the learner. And, it may not consider your own content knowledge, specialized abilities, and instructional style. Figure 8.1 illustrates the zone of maximum response opportunity for a lesson in reading.

Thus, the concept of a zone affords both you and your students some latitude within which to construct and to create meanings and understandings that consider the unique needs of both. In this manner, self-directed learning promotes a gentle interplay between the minds of learner and teacher, pulling and pushing each other in a student response–teacher reaction sequence designed to help the learner climb to the next rung of the learning ladder.

Figure 8.1 The zone of maximum response opportunity for a reading lesson.

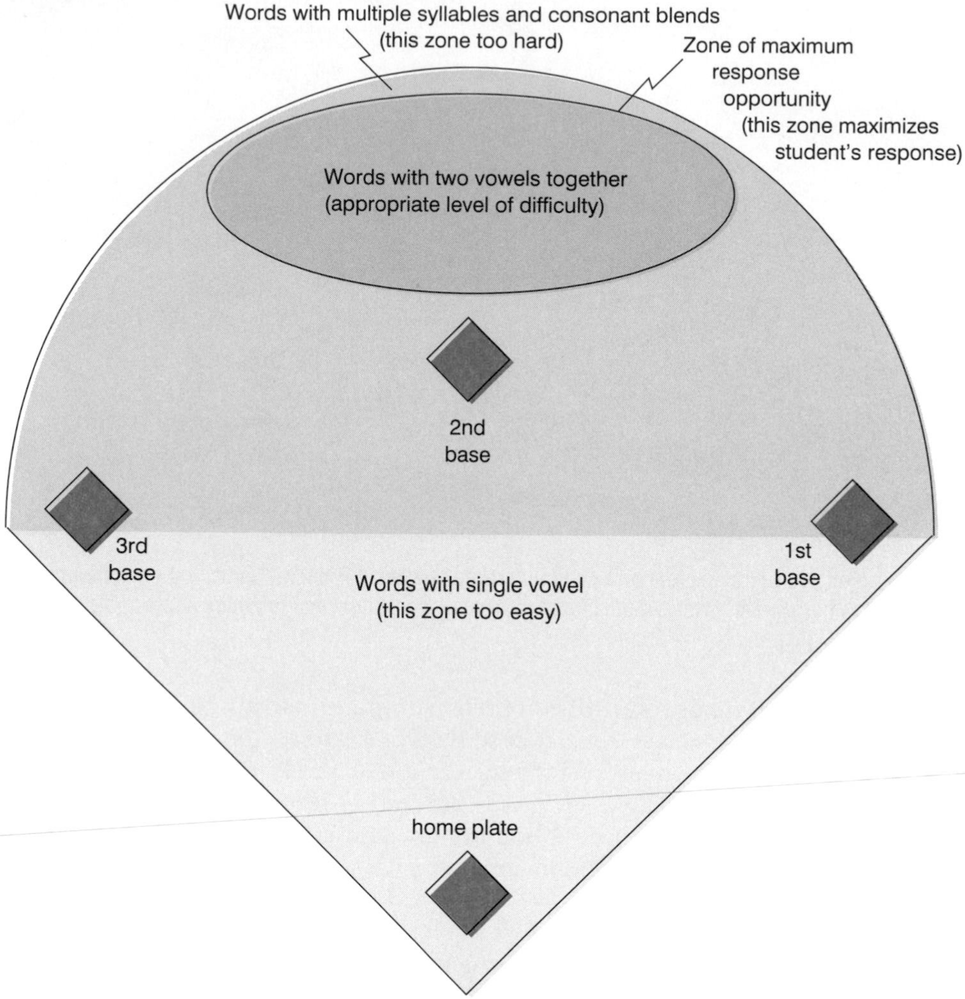

Words with multiple syllables and consonant blends
(this zone too hard)

Zone of maximum
response
opportunity
(this zone maximizes
student's response)

Words with two vowels together
(appropriate level of difficulty)

2nd
base

3rd
base

1st
base

Words with single vowel
(this zone too easy)

home plate

FUNCTIONAL FAILURE (STUDENT ERRORS)

Another concept important to self-directed learning is *functional failure.* Student errors play an important role in the gentle interplay between learner and teacher. If your reaction promotes an inaccurate and meaningless response, the interplay may not be so gentle, at least not in the learner's mind. But, if your reaction creates (or even intentionally promotes) a student response that is inaccurate *but* meaningful, interplay returns to a gentler state.

The latter condition describes a class of student errors called **functional errors.** Whether these errors are unexpected or are planted by you, they enhance the learner's understanding of content. Functional errors provide a logical stepping-stone for climbing to the next rung of the ladder, which may eliminate an erroneous thought process from ever occurring again in the learner's mind. For example, such an error may be necessary so the student will not arrive at the right answer for the wrong reason, thereby compounding the mistake in other contexts.

Consider the following dialogue in which a student error becomes a functional steppingstone to the next level of understanding:

Teacher:	As you recall from yesterday, we were studying the reasons behind the Civil War. Does anyone recall under what president of the United States the Civil War began?
Alexis:	Our book says Jefferson Davis.
Teacher:	Well, it so happens Jefferson Davis was a president at the time. But, that's not the right answer. Now, how do you think Jefferson Davis could be *a* president, but not *the* president of the United States at the time of the Civil War?
Alexis:	Well, maybe at the start of the war there were two presidents, Jefferson Davis and someone else.
Teacher:	As a matter of fact, there were two presidents, but only one could be President of the United States.
Alexis:	Well, if he wasn't President of the United States he must have been president of the other side.
Teacher:	But, do you recall the name of the government that represented the other side?
Alexis:	Yeah, now I remember. It was the Confederacy. It was Lincoln who was the President of the North—which must have been called the United States—and Jefferson Davis, who must have been the President of the South, called the Confederacy. I guess I got confused with all the different names.

Even though the student response was incorrect, this teacher's reaction fell within the zone of maximum response opportunity, because from it directly followed a more correct response. Notice also how the teacher encouraged the learner to supply the answer, using her previous mistake as an aid to obtaining the correct answer. This strategy actually led to information that went beyond the question itself—to putting Jefferson Davis in geographic perspective and in correctly naming the governments representing both North and South.

But, what if this teacher had made a less thoughtful reaction, encouraging not only another inaccurate response but, worse, a blind alley not useful for refining or extending the student's initial response? What might such a reaction look like?

Teacher:	Does anyone recall under what President of the United States the Civil War began?
Alexis:	Our book says Jefferson Davis.

Teacher:	I said President of the United States, not President of the Confederate States of America. See the difference?
Alexis:	I guess so.
Teacher:	Well, OK. Then, let's go on to Mark.

The interplay here becomes considerably less gentle, as the specter of failure is left hanging over the learner, and the teacher has no easy way out of this awkward ending.

Self-directed learning requires considerable **anticipatory teaching.** This means you respond to the learner at the learner's current level of understanding, to promote a student response, correct *or* incorrect, that is functional for moving to the next rung of understanding on the way to the intended goal of the lesson. This is why scripted approaches to instruction (like programmed instruction), although useful in certain contexts, cannot replace the gentle interplay between student response and teacher reaction, supported by the classroom dialogue and group discussion methods of self-directed learning.

RECIPROCAL TEACHING

One way you can apply self-directed learning in your classroom is with a strategy called **reciprocal teaching** (Palincsar & Brown, 1989; Rosenshine & Meister, 1994). Reciprocal teaching provides opportunities to explore the content to be learned via classroom dialogue. At the center of reciprocal teaching are group discussions in which you and your students take turns as leader in discussing the text.

Slavin (1990a) observed that most classroom discussions amount to little more than recitation of facts by students with the aid of question-and-answer sequences in which all or most of the answers are known. This leaves little opportunity for students to construct their own meaning and content interpretation so they can attain higher levels of understanding. In practice, many classroom discussions promote little meaningful dialogue that actually helps students struggle with the adequacy of their ideas and opinions on their way to arriving at acceptable solutions. More often, these discussions are driven by text content, with rapid-fire questions that stay close to the facts as presented in the text.

Reciprocal teaching is a strategy to make such a typical discussion into a more productive and self-directed learning experience. It accomplishes this through four activities: predicting, questioning, summarizing, and clarifying. These unfold into the following sequence, described by Palincsar and Brown (1989):

- *Predicting*—Discussion begins by generating predictions about the content to be learned from the text, based on
  a. Its title or subheading in the text
  b. The group's prior knowledge or information pertaining to the topic
  c. Experience with similar kinds of information

Following the group's predictions about what they expect to learn from the text, the group reads and/or listens to a portion of it.

- *Questioning*. The teacher chooses one individual to lead a discussion of each portion of the text that is read. Afterward, the discussion leader asks questions about the information. Students respond to the questions and raise additional questions.
- *Summarizing*. The discussion leader then summarizes the text, and the teacher invites other students to comment or elaborate on the summary.
- *Clarifying*. If points in the text were unclear (e.g., concepts or vocabulary), they are discussed until clarity is achieved. In this case, students may make more predictions and reread portions of the text for greater clarity.

The following dialogue (based on Palincsar & Brown, 1989) illustrates the four activities of predicting, questioning, summarizing, and clarifying that comprise reciprocal teaching:

Teacher: (Reading from text.) "The pipefish change their color and movements to blend with their surroundings. For example, pipefish that live among green plants change their color to a shade of green to match the plants."

Claire: (Leading the discussion.) One question that I had about this paragraph is: What is special about the way the pipefish looks?

Teacher: (Clarifying.) Do you mean the way that it is green?

Andy: (Elaborating.) It's not just that it's green, it's that it's the same color as the plants around it, all around it.

Claire: (Continuing.) Yes, that's it. My summary of this part tells how the pipefish looks and that it looks like what is around it. My prediction is that this is about its enemies and how it protects itself and who the enemies are.

Monty: (Adding to the summary.) They also talked about how the pipefish moves . . .

Keith: (Rejoining.) It sways back and forth . . .

Andy: (Adding.) . . . along with the other plants.

Teacher: (Questioning.) What do we call it when something looks like and acts like something else? The way we saw the insect called a *walking stick* yesterday? We clarified this word when we talked about the walking stick.

Angel: Mimic.

Teacher: That's right. We said we would say that the pipefish mimics the . . .

Students: (Together.) . . . plants.

Teacher: OK! Let's see if Claire's predictions come true. (Class turns to the text.)

Notice in this discussion how the teacher supports student participation in the dialogue. The teacher's aim is to engage as many students as possible in the learning process by providing reactions to student responses that are in their zones of maximum response opportunity. This is accomplished by elaborating on student responses and allowing ample opportunity for students to participate in the dialogue, from their perspective (R. Mayer & Wittrock, 1996). This gives the teacher ample data upon which to form a reaction that is within their zone of maximum response opportunity.

As the discussion continues, more responsibility for reading and developing the dialogue is given over to the students until, over time, the teacher becomes more of an advisor—or coach—who refines responses instead of providing them. At that point, more and more of the discussion represents the internalization of the text by the students, who now express it through their unique learning histories, specialized abilities, and experiences.

The ultimate goal of reciprocal teaching is to sufficiently engage students in the learning process so that they become conscious of their reasoning process. This occurs through their own and other students' modeling, and the teacher's modeling of that process, and is refined in the context of classroom dialogues. This requires your continuous attention to the ongoing dialogue and to the meanings students are deriving from the text so you can continually adjust the instructional content to meet your learners' current level of understanding.

As students gradually accept the shift in responsibility from teacher to student, you reduce the amount of explaining, explicitness of cues, and prompting that may have marked the earlier part of the lesson. Figure 8.2 indicates some classroom activities that can guide the gradual shift of responsibility from teacher to learner during self-directed learning.

Palincsar and Brown (1989) summarize the teacher's role during reciprocal teaching in the following list:

- The teacher and students share responsibility for acquiring the strategies employed in reciprocal teaching.
- The teacher initially assumes major responsibility for teaching these strategies ("thinks aloud" how to make a prediction, how to ask a question, how to summarize, how to clarify), but gradually transfers responsibility to the students for demonstrating use of the strategies.
- The teacher expects all students to participate in the discussion and gives all students the opportunity to lead it. The teacher encourages participation by supporting students through prompting, providing additional information, or raising/lowering the demand on students so that learners will achieve meaningful responses.
- Throughout each self-directed lesson, the teacher consciously monitors how successfully comprehension is occurring and adjusts the content as needed to the zone of maximum response opportunity.

Figure 8.2 Shifting responsibility from teacher to learners.

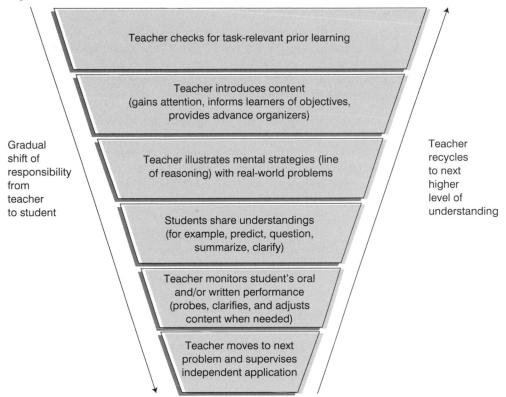

Gradual shift of responsibility from teacher to student

Teacher recycles to next higher level of understanding

Teacher checks for task-relevant prior learning

Teacher introduces content (gains attention, informs learners of objectives, provides advance organizers)

Teacher illustrates mental strategies (line of reasoning) with real-world problems

Students share understandings (for example, predict, question, summarize, clarify)

Teacher monitors student's oral and/or written performance (probes, clarifies, and adjusts content when needed)

Teacher moves to next problem and supervises independent application

SOCIAL DIALOGUE VERSUS CLASS DISCUSSION

As the preceding dialogues demonstrated, classroom conversation between teacher and students is central to self-directed learning. Verbal interactions within a classroom are vastly different from those occurring outside of it. In many classrooms, verbalizations are adult dominated, leaving students with little alternative but to respond to teacher requests for facts and information. These traditional teaching settings may offer few opportunities for students to elaborate or comment on the topic at hand.

However, self-directed learning strategies use classroom dialogue differently. Instead of verbalizations intended to confirm the teacher's authority, classroom dialogue is purposefully guided to gradually shift responsibility to the learner. The teacher scaffolds, building the dialogue layer by layer, each time increasing the challenge to the learner to think independently of earlier constructions provided by the teacher.

Scaffolding must be done carefully to keep the challenge within the learner's zone of maximum response opportunity. This requires the following:

- Your close monitoring of the learner's response
- Your awareness of the learner's current functioning level (e.g., familiarity with the task)
- Your awareness of the understanding level the learner can attain at the moment (based on, e.g., past learning performance)

Attention to these details lets you scaffold the cognitive demands placed on the learner. You do so to increasingly shift the learner from responding to textual material to internalizing its meaning by elaborating, extending, and commenting on it.

As we have seen, the strategy of reciprocal teaching uses group discussion and rotating discussion leaders to achieve this goal. It does so not just by getting students to talk, as do many traditional discussions, but by getting them to expose and elaborate the *processes* by which they are learning the content. The clear articulation and rehearsal of these mental strategies (1) guide the learner in subsequent performances and (2) help you adjust the flow and level of prompts, cues, and questions to hit inside the zone of maximum response opportunity.

THE ROLE OF INNER SPEECH

As we have seen, an important aspect of classroom dialogue in self-directed learning is the increasing responsibility it places on the learner for creating original verbalizations in the form of comments, elaborations, and extensions. These verbalizations, if properly scaffolded, are believed to create an inner speech within the learner (L. Resnick & Klopfer, 1989; Simmons, 1995; Vygotsky, 1962). This **inner speech** ultimately leads to private internal dialogue that takes the place of the teacher's prompts and questions and self-guides the learner through similar problems.

As the responsibility for unique and original productions beyond the text gradually shifts to the learner, the learner increasingly acquires the ability to speak internally, modeling the same line of reasoning and mimicking the same types of questions, prompts, and cues used by the teacher at an earlier stage. In other words, the verbal interactions that the teacher increasingly asked of the learner become internalized in a form of private speech used by the learner in the absence of direct teacher involvement.

The teacher's role now turns to one of monitoring. The teacher prompts and cues only when necessary to keep students on track. Ultimately, it is hoped that by internalizing the scaffold verbalizations of the teacher and recalling them at will in private dialogue, students become their own teachers, mimicking the logic and reasoning process modeled by the teacher. Self-direction can be stimulated by many different techniques in addition to reciprocal teaching, including many forms of cooperative and group learning.

The role of inner speech in guiding the behavior of both children and adults is central to self-directed learning strategies.

Outward verbalizations by the learner, if properly scaffolded, can be turned into inner speech that eventually replaces the teacher's prompts and self-guides the learner through similar problems.

SAMPLE DIALOGUES OF SELF-DIRECTED LEARNING

Let's look at three classroom dialogues that exhibit characteristics of self-directed inquiry. In different teaching contexts, these dialogues illustrate the following:

- How a teacher models the process by which meaning and understanding can be derived from textual material.
- How questions, prompts, and cues can be used to scaffold responses, gradually shifting the responsibility for learning to the student.
- How the teacher thereafter can monitor student responses for continued understanding.

First, let's look at a fourth-grade classroom in which Ms. Koker is teaching reading. We'll observe how she models the process by which meaning and understanding can be derived from text. Our discussion begins with Ms. Koker reading an excerpt from a short story to the class from the daily reader:

Ms. Koker:	(Reading.) "Some of the coldest climate on earth occurs in the northern parts of Alaska. In this land, a small but hardy group of Native Americans lives and prospers in small villages where hunting and fishing is a way of life. This small group of villagers. . . . "
Debbie:	(Interrupting.) Ms. Koker, I don't know what the word *hardy* means.
Ms. Koker:	What do you think it means, Debbie? (Asking her to make a prediction.)
Debbie:	Well, something that's hard—like, maybe, ice.
Ms. Koker:	Let's see if you are right. Let's think of some other words that might mean almost the same thing as *hard*. (Introducing the idea of synonyms.)

Tim:	Something that's hard is strong.
Mickey:	Yeah, and it also lasts a long time.
Ann:	If you're strong, you can't be hurt.
Ms. Koker:	OK, now let's see if any of these ideas fit with the sentence, "In this land a small but hardy group of Native Americans lives and prospers in small villages where hunting and fishing is a way of life." What do you think, Tim? (Encouraging the idea of fitting synonyms into the text to clarify meaning.)
Tim:	Well, if we took the word *hardy* out and put in the word *strong*, I think it would mean the same thing.
Ms. Koker:	What do you think, Barbara?
Barbara:	It makes sense, because when you're strong you can't be hurt—say by all the cold up north—and then you live a long time. (Summarizing.)
Mickey:	But, how do we know they live a long time, just because they're strong? (Asking for clarification.)
Ms. Koker:	That's a good point; we really don't know that yet, so what do you think? (Calling for a prediction again.)
Tina:	I think they won't live as long as us because of all the cold weather.
Ms. Koker:	So, how do you think they stay warm? Let's read on to see.

Notice that Ms. Koker was modeling a strategy for deriving meaning from text. To accomplish this, she introduced the idea of synonyms, by asking Debbie what she thought the word *hardy* meant and then by asking her students to insert the synonym into the text to check its appropriateness. Thus, she was conveying a model—a mental strategy—that students can use time and again, unaided by the teacher, whenever they encounter an unknown word.

Next, let's observe Mr. Willis's junior high science class to see how he uses questions, prompts, and cues to encourage self-direction. In the following discussion, Mr. Willis is teaching a fundamental law of physics by providing questions and reactions that are scaffolded to his learners' zones of maximum response opportunity:

Mr. Willis:	Here you see a balloon, a punching bag, and a tire pump. Watch carefully as I let the air out of the balloon (lets air out), punch the bag (punches it), and press down on the pump handle (pushes handle). What did you notice about all three actions? Bobby?
Bobby:	You got tired. (Class laughs.)
Mr. Willis:	You're right, especially when I did the punching and pumping. (Reaching to Bobby's current level of understanding:) Yes, you saw a reaction in me; I got tired. What other action did you see?
Bobby:	The balloon flitted across the room.
Mr. Willis:	And, what else?

Bobby:	The punching bag moved forward—and, well the pump handle went down and then a little up.
Mr. Willis:	You saw several reactions, didn't you. What were they?
Bobby:	Something happened to the object you were playing with and . . . well . . . I guess something else was going on too.
Mr. Willis:	Anita, what did you see in all three cases?
Anita:	Movement in two directions, I think.
Mr. Willis:	What were the movements?
Anita:	Well, for the balloon, it went forward, but also it pushed the air backward . . . over your face. And, for the punching bag, it went forward . . . umph (mimics the sound) . . . and stopped. I don't know what other movement there was.
Mr. Willis:	(Pushing to the next higher level of understanding.) Think about what happened both after *and* before I punched the bag. To help you, write on the top of a piece of paper the words *before* and *after.* Now, write down what you saw in each of these three instances—the balloon, the punching bag, and the pump. Let's all take a minute to do this.
Anita:	(After about a minute.) Now I remember. The punching bag came back to hit your hand again. That was the second movement.
Mr. Willis:	(Checking for understanding among the others.) And, what about the tire pump? Michael, you have your hand up.
Michael:	When you pushed the pump handle down to inflate the tire, it came back up a little.
Mr. Willis:	Yes, in each case, there were two identifiable movements, which we will call an *action* and a *reaction.* Now, let's check to see if this is true for some other movements by identifying on your paper the action and reactions associated with the following. I'll say them slowly so you have time to write:

> The space shuttle taking off from Cape Canaveral
>
> An automobile moving down the street
>
> A gunshot
>
> A football being kicked over a goalpost

Notice how Mr. Willis used questions targeted to his students' current level of understanding. This allowed them to respond in some meaningful way, which gave him the opportunity to build on an earlier incomplete response to reach the next higher level of understanding. For example, Mr. Willis used Bobby's first crude response, aided by the prompt "What other action did you see?" to introduce the concept of action followed by a reaction. Each time the questioning turned to a new student, Mr. Willis targeted his question, prompt, or cue higher but still within the learners' zone of maximum response opportunity.

Also, the idea of thinking through a solution on paper—called *think sheets*—kept students actively engaged in working through their responses. At the same time, it provided a strategy from which they might more easily derive actions and reactions for the new problems presented at the end of the dialogue. Mr. Willis's use of questions, prompts, and cues at various levels of difficulty kept this class moving through the lesson with increasingly more sophisticated responses.

Now, let's look in on a third classroom. Mrs. LeFluir is teaching Spanish to a high school class not just by altering the level of questioning, as did Mr. Willis, but by altering the tasks from which learners experience the application of content first hand. Without realizing it, Mrs. LeFluir's class is experiencing the difference between **declarative knowledge**—knowledge intended for oral or verbal regurgitation—and **procedural knowledge**—knowledge intended to be used in some problem-solving or decision-making task:

Mrs. LeFluir:	Today, we will study the gender of nouns. In Spanish all nouns are either masculine or feminine. Nouns ending in *o* are generally masculine, and those ending in *a* are generally feminine. Tisha, can you identify the following nouns as either masculine or feminine? (Writes on board.)
	libro
	pluma
	cuaderno
	gramática
Tisha:	(Correctly identifies each.)
Mrs. LeFluir:	Now, let's see how you identified each of the words and what each word means.
Tisha:	Well, I followed the rule that if it ends in an *o* it will be masculine but if it ends in an *a* it will be feminine. I think the words are book, pen, notebook, and grammar.
Mrs. LeFluir:	Good. Now for the next step, you've all used indefinite articles *a* and *an* many times in your speaking and writing. In Spanish the word *un* is used for *a* or *an* before a masculine noun, and *una* is used for *a* or *an* before a feminine noun. In Spanish the article is repeated before each noun. Now, using the vocabulary words on the board, let's place the correct form of the indefinite article in front of each word. (Shifting the task demand:) Why don't you take the first one, Ted?
Ted:	It would be *un libro*.
Mrs. LeFluir:	Mary.
Mary:	*Una pluma.*
Mrs. LeFluir:	Bob and Mike, take the next two.
Bob:	*Un cuaderno.*
Mike:	*Una gramática.*

Mrs. LeFluir:	OK. Now, we are ready to put our knowledge to work. I will give you a sentence in English, and you translate it into Spanish, being sure to include the correct form of the indefinite article. (Shifting the task demand again:) For this you will need to remember your vocabulary from last week. If you need to, look up the words you forgot. Mark, let's start with you. Come up to the board and write, "Do you want a book?"
Mark:	(Writes on board) *Desea usted un libro?*
Mrs. LeFluir:	Good. And how did you decide to use *un* instead of *una?*
Mark:	The noun ended in *o.*
Mrs. LeFluir:	(Continues with three other examples.)

> Do you need grammar?
>
> Do you want to study a language?
>
> Do you need a notebook?

(After the students respond, she shifts the task demand again by moving to the following activity:) Now, read each sentence on the transparency and write down the correct form of the indefinite article that goes before the noun. (Shows transparency.)

> Yo necesito _____ gramática.
>
> Nosotros estudiamos _____ lengua.
>
> Necesita Tomás _____ libro?
>
> Es _____ pluma?

(After the students respond, she moves to a final activity and yet another task demand:) Now for the following sentences, I will speak in English, and I want you to repeat the same sentence entirely in Spanish. Be sure, once again, to include the correct form of the indefinite article.

Notice in this episode the different activities required of the students and how they differ in cognitive complexity. Mrs. LeFluir gradually changed the demands on her learners by shifting the tasks to which they were to respond. Her lesson began by asking only for the simple regurgitation of rules (declarative knowledge) but ended by engaging students in oral delivery of the kind that might be required in ultimately having a conversation in Spanish (procedural knowledge). She gradually shifted her tasks from declarative to procedural *in small enough degrees* to ensure that all her students, or at least most of them, could follow.

This process also conveyed a language-learning model that will be helpful in subsequent contexts by providing a learning strategy that flows from memorization of rules and vocabulary, through completion and fill-in, to oral delivery. Notice that this sequence was completed even for this elementary lesson. This tells the learners that oral and written delivery, and not the regurgitation of rules, is the end goal to which all previous learning must contribute and toward which they must strive in their own individual learning and practice.

The systematic varying of task demands within a unit comprises an **activity structure.** Activity structures are most effective for self-directed learning when they vary the demands or problems being placed on the learner in ways that gradually require the learner to assume responsibility for learning the content at a higher level of understanding. The following list indicates some of the steps in teaching self-directed inquiry to individual learners:

Steps in Teaching Self-Directed Inquiry to Individual Learners

- Provide a new learning task, and observe how the student approaches it (e.g., reading a short selection in a history text that will be the basis for an essay exam).
- Ask the student to explain how she or he approaches the task of learning the textual information—for example, in preparation for the exam.(This helps the student analyze her or his own cognitive approach.)
- Describe and model a more effective procedure for organizing and accomplishing the task. For example, explain and demonstrate how to use the study questions at the end of the selection to help focus reading; highlight the main ideas in each paragraph of the selection with a fluorescent marker; write outline notes of key points on a separate sheet or on note cards as a study guide for later review. This gives the student new strategies for cognitively organizing the learning task.
- Provide the student with another, similar learning task for practicing the new cognitive strategies. Observe as the student proceeds with the task, giving reminders and corrective feedback.
- Model self-questioning behavior as you demonstrate analysis of a similar problem. For example, "What are the key questions you will need to answer?" or "What is the main idea in this paragraph?" Write such questions on a small card for the student to use as a reminder.
- Provide another opportunity for the student to practice the skills using self-direction, decreasing your role as monitor.
- Check the result of the learning task by questioning for comprehension and asking the student to recall the specific learning strategies used.

OTHER COGNITIVE STRATEGIES

When you use a mental strategy to help you learn on your own, you have learned what psychologists call a **cognitive learning strategy.** Cognitive learning strategies are general methods of thinking that improve learning across a variety of subject areas. They accomplish this by helping the learner to retain incoming information (called *reception*), recall task-relevant prior knowledge (called *availability*), and build logical connections among incoming knowledge (called *activation*). These strategies (Goetz, Alexander, & Ash, 1992) include

- Mnemonics (memory aids)
- Elaboration/organization (note taking)
- Comprehension-monitoring strategies
- Problem-solving strategies
- Project-based strategies

Let's take a look at each of these.

Mnemonics

Cognitive psychologists such as Bruner (1966) and Ausubel (1968) advocate that teachers organize their lessons around a limited set of powerful ideas, called *key understandings* and *principles* (Brophy, 1992). Nevertheless, they recognize that all learners will have to learn facts as well in order to grasp the major ideas. These may be number facts, dates, names, rules, classifications, and so on. Bradstad and Stumpf (1982) describe several strategies that can aid the mental organization and retention of such facts.

Jingles or Trigger Sentences.   Jingles or trigger sentences can cue sequential letters, patterns, or special historical dates. For example, most music students learn some variation of the sentence, "Every Good Boy Does Fine," to recall the musical notes EGBDF on the lines of a music treble staff. "Spring forward, fall back" helps one remember which way to adjust clocks at the spring and autumn time changes. And, many schoolchildren learn that "In fourteen hundred and ninety-two, Columbus sailed the ocean blue." Such devices also can be used for recalling the steps of a mental strategy.

Narrative Chaining.   Narrative chaining is the process of weaving a list of key words you wish to remember into a brief story. For example, if you need to memorize the life cycle of a butterfly in sequence, including the key stages of egg, larva, pupa, and adult, you could invent a narrative such as the following:

> *This morning I cooked an egg for breakfast, but I heated it so long that it looked like molten lava from a volcano. A pupil from a nearby school stopped by, and when he saw my egg-turned-lava, he yelled, "I'm just a pupil! You're the adult! Couldn't you cook an egg better than that?"*

In this case, *lava* and *pupil* sound enough like *larva* and *pupa* to trigger memory of the correct words in the life cycle sequence.

Number Rhyme or Peg Word.   A number-rhyme or peg-word mnemonic system uses words that rhyme with a sequence of numbers as a basis for developing imaginative mental pictures that assist in memorizing a set of other, less related words.

Using the life cycle of the butterfly as an example again, you might employ the number-rhyme system this way:

one-sun   Imagine a big, fried *egg* hanging in the sky overhead in place of a brightly shining sun.

two-stew	Imagine a bubbling stew erupting from a gigantic volcano under the fried egg, drying to form molten *lava*.
three-sea	Imagine a tiny, screaming *pupil* afloat on a swirling, angry sea where the hot lava sizzles as it meets the seawater.
four-door	Imagine a golden door in the side of the volcano that is opened by a gentle, helpful *adult* who reaches out to pull the pupil from the sea near the lava that was heated by the egglike sun.

Chunking.   Chunking, or grouping bits of information into sets of five to seven discrete pieces, also can assist in memorization. If this is combined by chunking the data into logical categories, the information is then doubly processed in a mental framework for improved recall. A common example is memorizing a grocery list by splitting it into logical categories (dairy products, vegetables, beverages, etc.) of several items each. Teaching students to employ such mental organizers gives them creative alternatives by which to manipulate ideas and information and retain mental strategies for learning, thus internally reinforcing their own learning.

Elaboration/Organization (Note Taking)

Elaboration involves teaching learners how to build internal connections between new knowledge and existing knowledge. Organization entails showing your learners how to order and systematize new information so that they can remember it and use it efficiently (R. E. Mayer, 1987). The most practical way to help your learners elaborate and organize new knowledge is to teach them how to take notes (Goetz et al., 1992).

Note taking can improve information processing in several ways. It enhances reception by prompting learners to attend better to what they are hearing or seeing. Furthermore, note taking assists activation by helping learners make internal connections among information and building a network of external connections with information in memory. You can give your learners several suggestions to help them take notes:

- Read the text before the lesson. This provides advance organizers for the new information.
- Watch for signals that indicate important information (gestures, key words, cues to the organization of the information).
- Write down the big ideas, not isolated facts. Try to be selective and not write down everything.
- When needed, use a more free-form outline format, called *webbing*, using pictures, arrows, and code letters. See Figure 8.3 for an example of webbing.
- Write down examples and questions as you listen.
- Leave blanks or some other prompt to indicate what you missed.
- Review your notes as soon as possible.

Figure 8.3 Webbing.

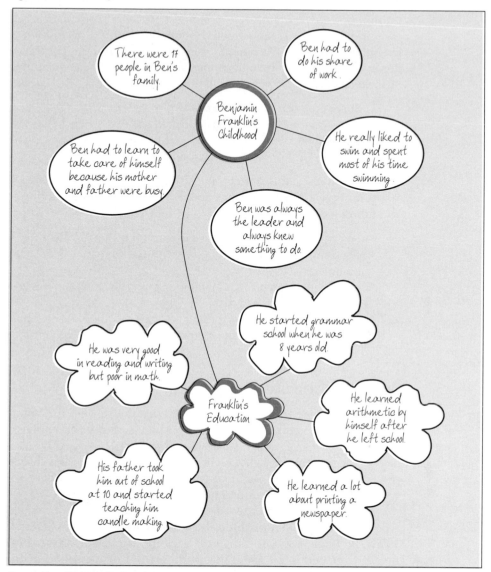

Source: From "Cooperative Learning Strategies," by D. F. Dansereau, in, *Learning and Study Strategies: Issues in Assessment, Instruction and Evaluation* (pp. 103–120), edited by C. F. Weinstein, E. T. Goetz, and P. A. Alexander, 1988, San Diego: Academic Press. Copyright 1988 by Academic Press. Reprinted by permission.

Comprehension Monitoring

Comprehension monitoring is a strategy wherein students learn to evaluate their own understanding by frequently checking their own progress during the course of a lesson. A. L. Brown (1980) used a strategy based on the reciprocal teaching method described earlier for helping poor as well as good readers understand. Teachers modeled for learners the following three skills:

1. Survey the text, and *make predictions* about what it says.
2. *Ask questions* about the main idea of the text as it is being read.
3. Become aware of unclear passages by *monitoring one's own understanding,* asking: "Do I understand what I just read?"

Learners who used this strategy increased their reading comprehension from 50% to 80% after only 4 weeks of instruction. Comprehension monitoring strategies have in common the following skills:

- Setting goals: "What do I have to do?" "Why am I doing this?"
- Focusing attention: "What am I supposed to read?" "What activity must I complete?"
- Self-reinforcement: "Great, I understand this. Keep up the good work." "This strategy really works."
- Coping with problems: "I don't really understand this. I should go back and read it again." "That's a simple mistake. I can fix that."

Problem-Solving Strategies

Cognitive learning strategists recommend that the school curriculum in most subject areas be organized around real-life problems that learners work on for days or weeks. According to some, we now have curricula isolated by disciplines (algebra, biology, geography, etc.) that identify lists of topics, facts, and skills to be covered by the end of a semester. Such curricula typically place learners in a relatively passive role and encourage rote or nonmeaningful learning.

As an alternative to this approach, growing numbers of educators advocate a type of learning called **problem-based learning** (Blumenfeld et al., 1991; Verduin, 1996). Problem-based learning organizes the curriculum around loosely structured problems (Goetz et al., 1992) that learners solve by using knowledge and skills from several disciplines. Recall that we introduced this general approach to unit planning in Chapter 4 under the topic of interdisciplinary thematic units.

To benefit from problem-based learning, however, learners must know how to problem solve. Since problem solving is a cognitive learning strategy in which few learners receive systematic instruction, teachers increasingly will be called on to teach this skill to their learners.

There are many systems for solving problems that you may teach to learners (R. E. Mayer, 1987). These methods are generalizable to all curriculum areas and to a variety of problems, whether they are well-defined problems (e.g., the word problems typically seen in math curricula) or ill-defined problems with no single answer, with many solution paths, and for which the nature of the problem shifts as learners work on them.

One such problem-solving system is called IDEAL (Bransford & Steen, 1984). IDEAL involves five stages of problem solving:

1. *I*dentify the problem. Learners must first know what the problem or problems are before they can solve them. During this stage of problem solving, learners ask themselves if they understand what the problem is and if they have stated it clearly.

2. *D*efine terms. During this stage, learners check that they understand what each word in the problem statement means.

3. *E*xplore strategies. At this point in the IDEAL process, learners compile relevant information and try out strategies to solve the problem. This can involve options such as drawing diagrams, working backward to solve a math or reading comprehension problem, or breaking complex problems into manageable units.

4. *A*ct on the strategy. Once learners have explored a variety of strategy options, they now use one.

5. *L*ook at the effects. During this final stage, learners ask themselves whether they have come up with an acceptable solution.

The following sample dialogue shows how a fifth-grade teacher taught her learners to use IDEAL.

Teacher:	Today we're going to think a little more about the greenhouse problem. Remember what we talked about yesterday. The PTA is giving us money to build a greenhouse, but we have a problem about how we can get the flowers and vegetable plants to grow inside a house when they're supposed to grow outside.
Student 1:	First the letter I. You identify the problem.
Teacher:	And what do we do when we identify a problem?
Student 2:	We read the problem and try to figure out what we're supposed to answer or solve.
Teacher:	OK. I'll try to identify one of the problems with the greenhouse and then ask one of you to do the same. One of the problems I see: how the plants get food. Anybody else?
Student 3:	I see a problem: What about when it gets cold?
Teacher:	So, what's the problem?
Student 3:	Well, it's how do you make sure they have the right temperature to live?
Teacher:	Good? What was another thing we talked about when you think about problems?
Student 4:	Letter D? You define any words you don't understand in the problem.
Teacher:	Why is this important?

Student 4:	Well, you want to make sure you really understand the problem. Sometimes we use words and think we know what they mean, but we really don't. So D reminds us to make sure we really know what we mean when we define the problem.
Teacher:	Good. I'll give you an example, then you give me one. What is a greenhouse? Are we all agreed on this?
Student 5:	And right temperature. What's that mean?
Teacher:	Great. Now what's the third thing we do when we think about solving a problem?

Teachers who incorporate cognitive strategies into their lessons have two broad goals: (1) Enhance learner acquisition of knowledge (declarative, procedural, metacognitive) and (2) enhance cognitive processes (reception, availability, activation). Teachers accomplish these goals when they design instruction that helps learners when they are studying and participating in lessons. Teachers further increase the likelihood of achieving these two cognitive goals when they teach cognitive learning strategies (mnemonics, elaboration/organization, comprehension monitoring, and problem solving) to their students.

Project-Based Strategies

Phyllis Blumenfeld and her colleagues (Blumenfeld et al., 1991) propose that teachers who build their instruction around projects provide learners with an environment ideally suited for the self-directed inquiry. But they must do this in ways that ensure learners that their success depends on factors they control. Project-based learning (1) stresses to learners the importance of the learning process and not just the product, (2) helps them set goals, and (3) uses instructional groupings to promote cooperation.

Project-based learning makes extensive use of theories of intrinsic motivation in designing its comprehensive approach to classroom teaching and learning (Deci, Vallerand, Pelletier, & Ryan, 1991; Schunk, 1991; Weiner, 1986).

Project-based learning asserts that intrinsic motivation is not a feature of learning tasks, a disposition of learners, or the sole responsibility of teachers. Rather, intrinsic motivation is marshaled, generated, and sustained in a learning environment where the teacher and students recognize that each of these elements has a necessary role to play, though each alone is not sufficient. Let's examine project-based learning and see how it promotes self-directed inquiry through intrinsic motivation.

The Role of Tasks in Project-Based Learning

Project-based learning assigns a critical role in the development of intrinsic motivation to the nature of the classroom learning task. It asks the question "What kinds of tasks are most likely to induce and support learner interest, effort, and persistence?"

Project-based learning advocates the use of projects as the most appropriate vehicles for engaging learners. Projects have two essential components: (1) They are built around a central question or problem that serves to organize and energize classroom activities, and (2) they require a product or outcome to successfully answer the question or resolve the problem.

Projects challenge learners with important (often real-world) problems and usually require them to draw on several diverse skill areas to solve them. A third-grade project, for example, built around the problem of nonrecyclable garbage, can involve the skills of reading, research, data gathering, data analysis, hypothesis generating, and problem solving.

Projects may be built around issues of current societal concern or questions of more historical or purely intellectual interest. Good projects have these critical characteristics:

- They are of extended duration (require several weeks to complete).
- They link several disciplines (e.g., involve math, reading, writing skills).
- They allow for a variety of solutions (the focus should be as much on process as product).
- They involve the teacher as coach, and require small group collaboration to complete.

They must also (1) present a real-world, authentic challenge, (2) allow for learner choice and control, (3) be doable—capable of being carried out within the time and resource limitations of the student and classroom, (4) require collaboration, and (5) produce a concrete result. Let's look more closely at each of these characteristics:

Present a challenge. Your projects will meet this important ingredient when they offer learners an authentic, sometimes novel, and always challenging problem or question to investigate, resolve, and report on. This is in contrast to worksheets, exercise books, end-of-chapter question answering, and other routine tasks, which may take up most of the academic time of learners (Doyle, 1983; Goodlad, 1984; Sizer, 1985).

Allow for learner choice and control. Effective projects allow learners options regarding modes of investigation (reading, interviewing, observing, controlled experimentation), styles of reporting (written reports, audiotapes or videotapes, visual displays), solutions to problems, or types of products or artifacts to develop.

Be doable. Learners will persevere and expend high amounts of effort if they see results. Similarly, they are more likely to believe that they can see a project through to a successful conclusion (self-efficacy) if it is time limited, requires readily available resources, and includes points along the way where they can receive positive feedback, make revisions, and generate further products.

Require collaboration. Intrinsic motivation is nurtured in classrooms that allow learners to meet their social needs. This theory points out how learners acquire beliefs about their own capabilities from observing others. Projects that cannot be completed unless a small group of learners adopt different but essential roles are ideal vehicles for incorporating the principles of these motivational theories.

Result in a concrete product. Products that give learners concrete goals to work toward are more likely to sustain intrinsic motivation. Moreover, products and the process involved in producing them allow for performance-based assessment. This type of assessment allows learners to see the connection between what they do in class and what their grades are based on. This provides a greater sense of control over their grades, and it better meets their needs for autonomy than grades based on paper-and-pencil tests alone.

The Role of the Learner in Project-Based Learning

Educators have urged school reforms that engage learners in "hands-on" learning activities as the best way to develop self-directed learning. Project-based learning recognizes that learners will acquire important knowledge and skills from projects only if they (1) attribute their success to effort, (2) believe that they can accomplish the goals of the project, and (3) perceive themselves as competent. Project-based learning also recognizes that learners are more likely to perceive themselves as competent if they have the prior knowledge, prerequisite skills, and learning strategies necessary for completing the projects before they begin.

The Role of the Teacher in Project-Based Learning

Project-based learning recognizes that the teacher is the last piece in the intrinsic motivational puzzle. The teacher's unique role in project-based learning is that of the supporter of intrinsic motivation. Consequently, Blumenfeld and her colleagues (1991) urge teachers to support their learners' interest, effort, and achievement through the following:

- Avoid statements implying that innate ability is all that is required to complete a project.
- Focus learners' attention both on the process of completing the project and on the end product.
- Make encouraging statements to learners.

PROMOTING THE GOALS OF SELF-DIRECTED LEARNING IN THE CULTURALLY DIVERSE CLASSROOM

The work of Palincsar and Brown (1989) and Bowers and Flinders (1991) have underscored two important dimensions of the teacher's role in modifying classroom dialogue to foster the goals of self-directed learning in the culturally diverse classroom. One of these is that of *teacher mediation*—on-the-spot adjustments made by the teacher to extend or refocus a student response to move the learner to the next rung of the learning ladder. The second dimension is *mental modeling*—the active demonstration of strategies by which students can better learn and retain the content taught.

These results have been applied to the culturally diverse classroom through various forms of social interaction that encourage students to construct their own meanings and interpretations and revise and extend them under the guidance of the teacher. As we have seen, among the techniques for promoting the concept of teacher mediation are reciprocal teaching (Palincsar & Brown, 1989) and problem-based learning (Blumenfeld et al., 1991). In both of these strategies, the teacher elicits student responses at the student's current level of understanding based on personal experiences with assumptions about, and predictions from, the content to be taught.

Some strategies that can promote self-directed instruction in a culturally diverse classroom follow:

1. Pose challenging problems. Focus the problem so the learner must make key decisions about what is important for a solution. This feeling of responsibility and control over the inquiry is important if the learner is to become engaged and see the learning as truly self-directed.

2. Choose learning activities that allow freedom of choice and include interests. By letting students pursue and investigate some topics of their own, choosing and constructing their own meanings and interpretations, you will be making them participants in the design of their own learning.

3. Plan instruction around group activities during self-directed instruction. This is when learners are the most capable of picking up ideas from others and creating from them new and unusual variations that can be applied during self-directed learning.

4. Include real-life problems that require problem solving. Let learners become actual investigators in solving real-world dilemmas. This will force them to place newly acquired knowledge and understandings in a practical perspective and to increase the problem-solving challenge.

5. In testing, draw out knowledge and understanding using content that is compatible with their culture and culturally familiar to them. Use assessments that make the student go beyond knowing and remembering facts by asking your learners to explain, analyze, compare, contrast, hypothesize, infer, adopt, and justify as a means of indicating that they can construct in their own words the meaning of what you are teaching.

With these and similar self-directed approaches to learning, you will be able to support the participation of all your learners in the dialogue of the classroom. Your aim should be to engage as many students as possible in the learning process by providing reactions to student responses that are in their zones of maximum response opportunity. This can be accomplished by the following:

1. Adjust the flow and complexity of content to meet individual learner needs.

2. Offer ample opportunity for all students to participate in the dialogue *from their perspective.*

3. Provide cognitive strategies with which they can better learn and remember the content taught.

Finally, ask yourself these questions to check on the success of your efforts:

• Has my instruction been focused within my learners' zones of maximum response opportunity? Are learners bored because they have already mastered these skills, or are they frustrated because the skills are beyond what they can be expected to learn?

- Has my instruction been too solitary? Have I met my learners' social learning needs by allowing for sufficient conversation, public reasoning, shared problem solving, and cooperative projects that reproduce the culture in which they spend the most time?
- Have I been expecting learners to acquire knowledge that is incompatible with their cultures? Do I use instructional methods that are culturally unfamiliar, irrelevant, or contradictory?

SUMMING UP

This chapter introduced you to strategies for self-directed learning. Its main points were as follows:

1. Self-directed learning is an approach to teaching and learning that actively engages students in the learning process for the purpose of acquiring outcomes at higher levels of cognitive complexity.

2. Self-directed learning involves the following sequence of activities:
   - Provide information about when and how to use mental strategies for learning.
   - Illustrate how the strategies are to be used in the context of real problems.
   - Provide students the opportunity to restructure content in terms of their own ways of thinking and prior understandings.
   - Gradually shift the responsibility for learning to students through activities (exercises, dialogues, discussions) that engage them in increasingly complex patterns of thought.

3. *Metacognition* is a strategy for self-directed learning that assists learners in internalizing, understanding, and recalling the content to be learned.

4. Metacognitive strategies include self-interrogation, self-checking, self-monitoring, and techniques for classifying and recalling content, called *mnemonics*.

5. Metacognitive strategies are taught through mental modeling in which learners are "walked through" the process of attaining a correct solution. Mental modeling includes the following:
   - Illustrate for students the reasoning involved.
   - Make them conscious of it.
   - Focus learners on the application of the reasoning illustrated.

6. *Teacher mediation* is the teacher's on-the-spot adjustment of content flow rate and complexity to accommodate the individual learning needs of the student.

7. The role of teacher mediation is to adjust the instructional dialogue as needed to help learners restructure what they are learning according to each learner's unique abilities, learning history, and personal experiences.

8. A *zone of maximum response opportunity* represents the level of content difficulty and behavioral complexity from which the learner can most benefit at the moment a response is given.

9. The zone of maximum response opportunity is reached through a classroom dialogue in which the teacher provides reactions to student responses that activate the unique learning history, specialized ability, and personal experience of each learner. From these unique characteristics, learners can acquire individual meanings and interpretations of the content.

10. Functional errors are incorrect or partially correct answers made by the learner that can enhance the meaning and understanding of

content and provide a logical steppingstone for climbing onto the next rung of the learning ladder.

11. Reciprocal teaching provides opportunities to explore the content to be learned via group discussion.

12. Reciprocal teaching involves a type of classroom dialogue in which the teacher expects students to make predictions, ask questions, summarize, and clarify when learning from text.

13. Reciprocal teaching involves a sequence of activities, which include the following:
   • The initial class discussion generates predictions about the content to be learned from text.
   • Read and/or listen to a portion of the text.
   • Choose a discussion leader who asks questions about the text of other students, who then respond with questions of their own.
   • The discussion leader summarizes the text, and the teacher invites other students to comment or elaborate.
   • The teacher clarifies any unresolved questions and rereads portions of text for greater clarity, if needed.

14. The teacher's role during reciprocal teaching is to gradually shift the responsibility for learning to the students by reducing the amount of explaining, explicitness of cues, and prompting that may have marked earlier portions of the lesson.

15. During reciprocal teaching, the teacher's role is to do the following:
   • Jointly share the responsibility for learning with the students.
   • Initially assume responsibility for modeling how to make a prediction, how to ask a question, how to summarize, and how to clarify, but then transfer responsibility to students for demonstrating use of these strategies.
   • Encourage all students to participate in the classroom dialogue by prompting, providing additional information, and/or altering the response demand on students.

   • Monitor student comprehension, and adjust the rate and complexity of information as needed.

16. In self-directed learning, the teacher scaffolds—builds the dialogue within a discussion step by step—each time increasing the challenge to the learner to think independently of earlier constructions. Scaffolding must occur to the appropriate degree for each learner response to keep the challenge within the learner's zone of maximum response opportunity.

17. During self-directed learning, inner (private) speech helps the learner elaborate and extend the content in ways unique to the individual. As responsibility for learning beyond the text gradually shifts to the learner, the learner's inner-speech ability increases, modeling the same reasoning and using similar questions, prompts, and cues used by the teacher at an earlier stage.

18. The following are steps for teaching self-directed inquiry to individual learners:
   • Provide a new learning task, and observe how the student approaches it.
   • Ask the student to explain how he or she would learn the content (e.g., preparing for an exam).
   • Describe and model a more effective procedure for organizing and learning the content (e.g., using study questions, notes, or highlighting key features in the text).
   • Provide another, similar task on which the student can practice the strategies provided.
   • Model self-questioning behavior during the task to ensure the learner follows the strategies correctly (e.g., "Did I underline the key words?").
   • Provide other opportunities for the student to practice, decreasing your role as a monitor.
   • Check the result by questioning for comprehension and use of the strategies taught.

19. Other cognitive strategies can be helpful for organizing and remembering new material during self-directed learning:

- Mnemonics
- Elaboration/organization (note taking)
- Comprehension monitoring
- Problem solving

20. Problem-based learning is an approach to learning that organizes instructional tasks around loosely structured or ill-defined problems that learners solve by using knowledge and skills from several disciplines.

21. Project-based learning is an approach to learning that promotes intrinsic motivation by organizing instruction around tasks that are most likely to induce and support learner interest, effort, and persistence.

22. Classroom dialogue can be modified to foster the goals of self-directed learning in a culturally diverse classroom in the following ways:
    - Adjust the flow and complexity of content.
    - Offer ample opportunity for all to participate.
    - Teach cognitive strategies.

FOR DISCUSSION AND PRACTICE

Questions marked with an asterisk are answered in Appendix B. See also *Bridges: An Activity Guide and Assessment Options,* which accompanies this text.

*1. Identify two purposes for engaging your students in self-directed learning. In which content areas that you will be teaching will these purposes most apply?

*2. What are four unique teaching functions associated with self-directed learning. Which order do you think might be most important for their success?

*3. What is *metacognition?* What can metacognitive strategies accomplish in your classroom?

*4. What are the three stages of mental modeling? Give an example of each stage using subject matter content with which you are familiar.

5. Provide an example of a verbal marker in your content area that would alert learners that you are about to begin mental modeling.

*6. During demonstration, what specific outcomes can mental modeling help your students acquire?

*7. What is your role during teacher-mediated learning? How would this role differ from teacher lecture or student recitation?

*8. In your own words, describe the *zone of maximum response opportunity*. Then, using the natural language of the classroom, write a short teacher–student dialogue that hits the zone of maximum response opportunity.

9. Give an example of a student response–teacher reaction that illustrates the concept of functional failure. Explain why in your example the student's response would not promote any further learning.

*10. What is the purpose of reciprocal teaching? With what content or during which activities would you most likely use reciprocal teaching in your classroom?

*11. Explain the sequence of activities that would normally occur during reciprocal teaching.

*12. What should be your most important goal in promoting classroom dialogue during self-directed learning?

*13. What is the purpose of inner (private) speech during self-directed learning? Do you recall ever having used inner speech to increase your learning? In what setting?

14. Create a brief excerpt from a classroom dialogue to show what a scaffolded dialogue would look like in your teaching area. Be sure to choose an example that is at your learner's current level of understanding and content that the learner can benefit from at the moment based on past learning.

*15. Describe the difference between declarative knowledge and procedural knowledge. Provide an example of each.

16. Think of an example of an activity structure in your subject area or grade level that varies task demand. How would you vary the task for those learners unable to respond to the increase in complexity?

*17. What steps would you follow in order to teach self-directed learning skills to an individual learner? What student behavior might make you decide to take the extra time to teach these skills?

*18. Describe four cognitive strategies for organizing and remembering new material. Considering your subject matter or grade level, which of these do you think you would find most useful?

9 Cooperative Learning and the Collaborative Process

This chapter will help you answer the following questions:
1. What must I do to plan a cooperative learning activity?
2. What roles can I assign to group members?
3. What are some of the ways I can reward good group performance?
4. What are some collaborative skills I can teach my learners?
5. How can I promote the goals of cooperative learning in the culturally diverse classroom?

n Chapter 8 you saw how self-directed learning could promote higher forms of thinking with the aid of metacognitive strategies. In this chapter, you will see how these same outcomes can be extended and reinforced through various forms of peer collaboration. You will learn how self-directed and cooperative learning share the complementary objectives of engaging students in the learning process and promoting higher thought processes and more authentic behaviors required in the world of work, family, and community.

OUTCOMES OF COOPERATION

What good are critical thinking, reasoning, and problem-solving skills if your learners cannot apply them in interaction with others? Cooperative learning activities instill in learners important behaviors that prepare them to reason and perform in an adult world (Fillmore & Meyer, 1992). Let's consider some of these behaviors.

Attitudes and Values

Adult learners form their attitudes and values from social interaction. Although we learn much about the world from books, magazines, newspapers, and audiovisual media, most of our attitudes and values are formed by discussing what we know or think with others. In this manner we exchange our information and knowledge with that of others who have acquired their knowledge in different ways. This exchange shapes our views and perspectives. It turns cold, lifeless facts into feelings, and then to attitudes and values that guide our behavior over longer periods of time.

Our attitudes and values are among the most important outcomes of schooling, because they alone provide the framework for guiding our actions outside the classroom, where there may be no formal sources of knowledge to fall back on. Cooperative learning is important in helping learners acquire from the curriculum the basic cooperative attitudes and values they need to think independently inside and outside of your classroom.

Prosocial Behavior

During close and meaningful encounters among family members, models of **prosocial behavior** are communicated. Children learn right from wrong implicitly through their actions and the actions of others that come to the attention of adult family members. These adults are quick to point out the effects of these actions on family, friends, and the community.

With the decreasing presence of adults in the homes of working parents, the classroom becomes an important vehicle for bolstering home and community values. Cooperative learning brings learners together in adultlike settings which, when carefully planned and executed, can provide appropriate models of social behavior (Stevens & Slavin, 1995a). As a teacher, one of your most important roles will be to promote and model positive social interactions and relationships within your classroom (Abruscato, 1994; Zehm & Kottler, 1993).

Alternative Perspectives and Viewpoints

It is no secret that we form our attitudes and values by confronting viewpoints contrary to our own. Our likes and dislikes come from our exposure to alternatives we could not have thought of on our own, given the limitations of our immediate context and experience. These alternatives—some of which we adopt, some we borrow from, and some we reject—are the raw material from which we form our own attitudes and values.

Confronted with these alternatives, we are forced into an objectivity necessary for thinking critically, reasoning, and problem solving. In other words, we become less self-centered. Depending on the merits of what we see and hear, we grow more open to exchanging our feelings and beliefs with those of others. This active exchange of viewpoints and the tension it sometimes creates within us form the catalyst for our growth. Cooperative learning provides the context or meeting ground where many different viewpoints can be orchestrated, from which we form more articulate attitudes and values of our own.

Integrated Identity

One of the most noticeable outcomes of social interaction is its effect on how we develop our personalities and learn who we are. Social interaction over long periods forces us to see ourselves—our attitudes, values, and abilities—in many different circumstances. The main result is that inconsistencies and contradictions in who we are—or think we are—cannot be hidden, as might be the case in a single interaction or small number of social interactions.

If we say and think one way in one situation, and say and think another way in another situation, we cannot help but notice our own inconsistency and wonder why it exists. We attempt to resolve such contradictions, to clarify what we really believe and to believe what we really say. Our personality becomes more coherent and integrated and is perceived by others as a more forceful and confident projection of our thoughts and feelings. Over time, repeated social interactions reduce the contradictions until our views become singular and consistent and we achieve an integrated identity.

Cooperative learning can be the start of stripping away the irrelevant, overly dramatic, and superficial appendages that mask our deepest thoughts and feelings. Thus we begin to gain an integrated sense of self.

Higher Thought Processes

If all of the preceding benefits of cooperative learning were not enough, the fact that it has been linked to increases in the academic achievement of learners at all ability levels is another reason for its use (Stevens & Slavin 1995a, 1995b). As noted, cooperative learning actively engages the student in the learning process and seeks to improve the critical thinking, reasoning, and problem-solving skills of the learner (Bramlett, 1994; Megnin, 1995; Webb, Trooper, & Fall, 1995). Critical thinking cannot occur outside a context of attitudes and values, prosocial behavior, alternative perspectives, and an integrated identity. Cooperative learning provides the ingredients for higher thought processes to occur and sets them to work on realistic and adultlike tasks.

These higher thought processes—required for analyzing, synthesizing, and decision making—are believed to be stimulated more by interaction with others than by books and lectures, which typically are not interactive. Books and lectures may be useful for teaching knowledge, comprehension, and application, but they seldom are sufficient to bring about the private, inner speech required for thinking critically, reasoning, and problem solving in real-life settings. These behaviors require interaction with others as well as oneself to unleash the motivation required for thinking and performing in complex ways. Therefore, it should be no surprise that some of the behaviors in the Higher-Order Thinking and Problem-Solving Checklist in Appendix C include cooperative behaviors.

The model of cooperative learning we have been discussing thus far is illustrated in Figure 9.1.

COMPONENTS OF A COOPERATIVE LEARNING ACTIVITY

In the rest of this chapter, you will see how to organize your classroom for cooperative learning. In planning a cooperative learning activity, you need to decide on the following:

1. The type of interactions you will have with your students
2. The type of interactions your students will have with one another
3. The task and materials you will select

Figure 9.1 Model of cooperative learning.

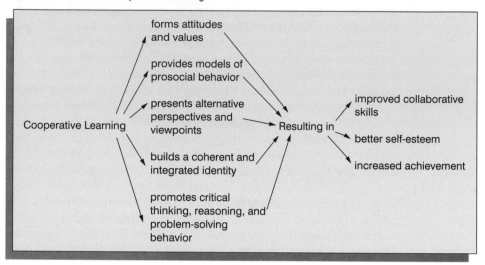

4. Role expectations and responsibilities you will assign

These four aspects are discussed in the following sections.

Teacher–Student Interaction

One purpose of teacher–student interaction during cooperative learning is to promote independent thinking. Much like student response–teacher reaction sequences during self-directed inquiry, exchanges between you and your learners in the cooperative classroom focus on getting learners to think for themselves, independently of the text. To accomplish this goal, you model and collaborate with learners in much the same way as in the self-directed classroom. This should come as no surprise, as the goals of cooperative and self-directed inquiry are complementary.

However, the way you establish teacher–student interaction during cooperative learning is different from self-directed learning. In self-directed inquiry, the interaction usually is one on one, with verbal messages directed to individuals one at a time and adjusted to their zones of maximum response opportunity. On the other hand, cooperative learning occurs in groups that share a common purpose and task, so you must broaden interactions to fit the zone of maximum response opportunity that is common to most group members. Your goal is to help the *group* become more self-reflective and aware of its own performance.

"Think about that some more," "Why not check with the reference at the learning center?" and "Be sure you've followed the guidelines I've given you," are frequent expressions you will address to a group of four or five learners assigned a specific task. Your role is to intervene at critical junctures and then to retreat, allowing the group to grapple with the new perspective or information given. In this manner, you monitor and collaborate with the group during brief but focused interventions, keeping them on course and following a productive line of reasoning.

Student–Student Interaction

Interaction among students in cooperative learning groups is intense and prolonged. Unlike self-directed inquiry, in cooperative learning groups, students gradually take responsibility for *each other's* learning. The effect may well be the same as in self-directed learning. Again, this is why cooperative and self-directed learning may be used as complementary learning strategies, with one reinforcing the skills acquired in the other.

During cooperative learning, the feedback, reinforcement, and support come from student peers in the group, as opposed to coming from you. Student–student interaction constitutes the majority of time and activity during cooperative learning, unlike the modest amount of direct student–student interaction that occurs in the self-directed classroom. Groups of four or five, working together in the physical closeness promoted by a common task, encourage collaboration, support, and feedback from the closest, most immediate source—one's peers. An essential ingredient of cooperative learning is each learner's desire to facilitate the task performance of fellow group members.

Task Specialization and Materials

Another component of cooperative learning is the task to be learned and the materials that comprise a cooperative learning activity structure. Cooperative learning tasks are preplanned activities; they are timed, completed in stages, and placed within the context of the work of others. This promotes the sharing of ideas and/or materials and the coordination of efforts among individuals. The choice of task and supporting materials is important to promote meaningful student–student interaction.

Cooperative learning typically uses **task specialization,** or "division of labor," to break a larger task into smaller subparts on which separate groups work. Eventually, these efforts come together to create the whole, and thus each member of the class has contributed. Therefore, each group may be asked to specialize, focusing its efforts on a smaller yet meaningful part of some larger end product for which the entire class receives credit. Groups may even compete against one another with the idea of producing a better part or higher quality product than other groups. However, the purpose is not the competition that produces the final product, but the *cooperation* within groups that the competition promotes.

Cooperative task structures have the goal of dividing and specializing the efforts of small groups of individuals across a larger task whose outcome depends on the sharing, cooperation, and collaboration of individuals within groups.

Role Expectations and Responsibilities

Proper assignment of roles is important to the success of cooperative learning activities. In addition to groups being assigned specialized tasks, individuals often are assigned specialized roles to perform within their groups. Some roles are *group leader*, *researcher*, *recorder*, and *summarizer*.

The success of a cooperative learning activity depends on your communication of role expectations and responsibilities and modeling them when necessary. This is another reason why cooperative learning has little resemblance to loosely formed discussion groups; not only must you divide labor among learners and specialized tasks, but you also must designate roles that foster the orderly completion of a task.

If someone's duties are unclear, or a group's assignment is ambiguous, cooperative learning quickly degenerates into undisciplined discussion, in which there may be numerous uninvolved and passive participants. Uninvolved and passive participants are individuals who successfully escape sharing anything of themselves. This defeats the purpose of cooperative learning, for if a group produces an outstanding report but only a few students have contributed to it, the group as a whole will have learned no more than if each member had completed the assignment alone. Worst of all, the critical thinking, reasoning, and problem solving that are so much a part of the shared effort of a cooperative learning activity will not have occurred.

ESTABLISHING A COOPERATIVE TASK STRUCTURE IN YOUR CLASSROOM

Now let us put to work in your classroom the four components of cooperative learning: teacher–student interaction, student–student interaction, task specialization and materials, and role expectations and responsibilities. Establishing a **task structure** for a cooperative learning activity involves five specific steps:

1. Specify the goal of the activity.
2. Structure the task.
3. Teach and evaluate the collaborative process.
4. Monitor group performance.
5. Debrief.

1. Specifying the Goal

The goal of a cooperative learning activity specifies the product and/or behaviors that are expected at the end of the activity. The outcome can take different forms:

- Written group reports
- Higher individual achievement on an end-of-activity test
- Oral performance, articulating the group consensus
- Enumeration of critical issues
- Critique of an assigned reading
- List of bibliographic references

To ensure the desired outcome, your job is to identify the outcome, check for understanding, and set a cooperative tone. Each of these steps is described in the following subsections.

Identify the Outcome.   Teachers must clearly articulate the form of the final product or performance from the beginning. For each of the outcomes just listed, you should illustrate the style, format, and length of the product that will constitute acceptable group work. For a written report, you might write on the board the acceptable length and format and display a sample report to guide group efforts. In each case, you must give your students signs of acceptable progress or milestones to be achieved and, where possible, examples of a successfully completed final product.

Following clear specification of the goal, you must place it in the context of past and future learning. Organize the content so that students will attach meaning and significance to it and see it in terms of their own experience. Typically, statements like "Remember when we had trouble with . . . " or "Next week we will need these skills to . . . " sufficiently highlight the importance of the impending activity.

Check for Understanding.   Next, check for understanding of the goal and your directions for achieving it. Using a few average and high performers as a steering group, ask for an oral regurgitation of your goal and directions. The entire class can benefit from hearing them again, and you can correct them if needed. Because groups typically expend so much effort during a cooperative learning activity, misinterpretation of the goal and your directions for attaining it can severely affect classroom morale.

In self-directed learning, one individual can be led astray by poorly understood directives. But in cooperative learning, entire groups, not just occasional individuals, can wander off the path, leaving a significant portion of your classroom working toward the wrong goal. Having one member of each group restate the goal and your directions for attaining it is time well spent.

Set a Cooperative Tone.   Your final task in introducing the goal of your cooperative learning activity is to set a tone of cooperation.

Students customarily begin cooperative learning activities as they have begun thousands of school activities before—as individuals competing against individuals. This competitive style has been ingrained in us from earliest childhood. It may be difficult for some of your learners to get the competitive spirit out of their blood, because it has become so much a part of their schooling.

Your job at the start of a cooperative learning activity is to set the tone: "two heads are better than one." Other phrases such as "united we stand, divided we fall," or "work together or fail together," can remind groups of the cooperative nature of the enterprise. You could ask each group to choose or create a group motto (e.g., "all for one and one for all") that provides a distinctive identity and reminds students that collaboration, not competition, is the goal.

Your role also must be one of cooperation, and this too must be communicated at the outset. "I am here to help . . . to answer your questions . . . to be your assistant . . . your consultant . . . your information provider. . . . " These reassuring comments can lift your classroom from the realm of competition and into the world of cooperation.

2. Structuring the Task

The structure of the task is what separates just any group activity from a cooperative learning activity. Group discussions have tasks, but they often are so generally defined (discuss the facts, raise issues, form a consensus) that they rarely allow for the division of labor, role responsibilities, collaborative efforts, and end products that promote critical thinking in a cooperative learning activity.

In structuring a cooperative learning task, you must decide several factors in advance:

- How large will the groups be?
- How will group members be selected?
- How much time will be devoted to group work?
- What roles, if any, will you assign to group members?
- What incentives/rewards will you provide for individual and group work?

Let's look at alternatives for each of these factors and how you can choose among them.

Group Size.   How many in the group? Group size is one of your most important decisions. Although influenced by the size of your class, the number of individual learners assigned to groups has far-reaching consequences for the following:

Division of labor, often overlooked when structuring tasks, is critical to the success of group learning. Allowing students to analyze the task and identify divisions of labor can foster metacognitive growth and higher-order thinking.

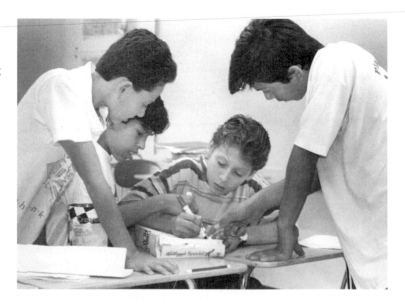

- The range of abilities within a group
- The time required for a group to reach consensus
- The efficient sharing of materials within a group
- The time needed to complete the end product

Each of these four factors will be altered by the number of members assigned to groups. This is why, when subtasks are comparable, group sizes should be made approximately equal.

The most efficient group size for attaining a goal in the least time is four to six members (E. Cohen, 1994; Johnson, Johnson, & Holubec, 1994; Slavin, 1990b). Thus, in a class of 25 to 30 students, about five or six groups should be formed. Smaller groups make monitoring of group performance more difficult, because the number of times you can interact with each group is reduced accordingly. On the other hand, groups of seven or eight generally argue more, reach consensus later, have more difficulty sharing limited materials (e.g., a reference that must be shared), and take longer to complete the final product.

Thus, the rule of thumb is to compose groups of four or five members for single-period activities and slightly larger groups (of five or six) when the activity stretches over more than a class period, requiring greater task complexity and role specialization.

Group Composition.   Whom will you select for each group? Unless the task specifically calls for specialized abilities, you will form most groups heterogeneously, with a representative sample of all the learners in a class. Therefore, you will assign to groups a mix of higher/lower ability, more verbal/less verbal, and more task-oriented/less task-oriented learners. This diversity usually contributes to the collaborative process by creating a natural flow of information from those who have it to those who need it. Surprisingly, it also promotes the transmission of alternative perspectives and viewpoints that often sends the flow of information in unexpected and desirable directions.

Groups within a classroom generally should reflect the composition of the community outside it. This composition confronts learners with differences as well as similarities to provide the motivation for dialogue, the need for sharing, and the natural division of interests and abilities needed to get the job done.

It also is important that groups not only represent a diversity of talents, interests, and abilities but that typically nonengaged students be represented across groups. Social scientists long have observed that the pressure from peers working together often pulls in even recalcitrant and passive learners, sweeping them up in the excitement of some larger goal. This is especially true if they are deprived of the support of other passive or inactive participants.

Johnson and Johnson (1991) provide additional suggestions for forming groups:

1. Identify isolated students who are not chosen by any other classmates. Then, build a group of skillful and supportive students around each isolated learner.

2. Randomly assign students by having them count off; place the ones together, the twos together, and so forth. If groups of 5 are desired in a class of 30, have students count off by 6.
3. To build constructive relationships between majority and minority students, between children with and without disabilities, and between boys and girls, use heterogeneous groups with students from each category.
4. Share with students the process of choosing group members. First, you select a member for a group, then that member selects another, and so on, alternating between your choice and students' choices until the group is complete.

One approach to drawing nonengaged learners into the cooperative activity is to structure the task so that success depends on the active involvement of all group members. Structuring the task reduces the problems of active and passive uninvolvement. **Active uninvolvement** is when a group member talks about everything but the assigned goal of the group. **Passive uninvolvement** is when a student doesn't care and becomes a silent member of the group. Here are ways you can structure a cooperative task to increase the likelihood that all group members will be actively involved:

- Request a product that requires a clearly defined division of labor to generate (e.g., looking up new words, writing a topic sentence, preparing a chart, finding examples, etc). Then assign specific individuals to each activity at the start of the session.
- Within groups, form pairs that are responsible for looking over and actually correcting each other's work/contribution.
- Chart the group's progress on individually assigned tasks, and encourage poor or slow performers to work harder to improve the group's overall progress. (A wall chart may be all that is needed.)
- Purposefully limit the resources given to a group, so that individual members must remain in personal contact to share materials and complete their assigned tasks (e.g., one dictionary or hand calculator to share).
- Make one stage of the required product contingent on a previous stage that is the responsibility of another person. This way, encouragement will be given or help provided by group members to those not performing adequately, so that they can complete their contribution.

Time on Task. How much time should you allot for group work? This obviously depends on task complexity (e.g., single class period or multiple periods), but you must make some more refined estimates as well. You need to determine the time to devote to group work and the time to devote to all groups coming together to share their contributions. This latter time may be used for group reports, a whole-class discussion, debriefing to relate the work experiences of each group to the end product, or some combination.

Group work can easily get out of hand in the excitement, controversy, and natural dialogue that can come from passionate discussions. This requires you to place limits on each stage of the cooperative learning activity, so that one stage does not eclipse time from another and leave the task disjointed and incomplete in your learners' minds.

Most time naturally will be devoted to the work of individual groups, where the major portion of the end product is being completed. This normally will consume 60% to 80% of the time devoted to the cooperative learning activity. The remaining time must be divided among individual group presentations and/or whole-class discussion that places the group work into the perspective of a single end product.

If you plan both group reports and a whole-class discussion for the same day, be aware that the whole-class discussion probably will get squeezed into a fraction of the time required to make it meaningful. To avoid this, schedule group discussions or debriefings for the following class day, so that class members have ample time to reflect on their group reports and to pull together their own thoughts about the collaborative process, which may or may not have occurred as intended. Fifteen or twenty minutes at the beginning of class the next day usually provides students the proper distance to meaningfully reflect on their experiences the day before.

Role Assignment.   What roles should you assign to group members? As you saw, division of labor within and across groups is an important dimension of cooperative learning that is not shared by most group discussion methods. This task specialization, and the division of labor it often requires, promotes the responsibility and idea sharing that marks an effective cooperative learning activity. Teachers can encourage the acceptance of individual responsibility and idea sharing in a cooperative learning experience by role assignments within groups and sometimes by task specialization across groups. Teachers use these roles and responsibilities to complement group work and to interconnect the groups.

Some of the more popular **cooperative student role** functions that teachers can assign within or across groups are suggested by Johnson and Johnson (1991):

1. *Summarizer*. Paraphrases and plays back to the group major conclusions to see if the group agrees and to prepare for (rehearse) the group's contribution before the whole class.
2. *Checker*. Checks controversial or debatable statements and conclusions for authenticity against text, workbook, or references. Ensures that the group will not be using unsubstantiated facts or be challenged by more accurate representations of other groups.
3. *Researcher*. Reads reference documents and acquires background information when more data are needed (e.g., may conduct an interview or seek a resource from the library). The researcher differs from a checker in that the researcher provides critical information for the group to complete its task, while the checker certifies the accuracy of the work in progress and/or after it has been completed.
4. *Runner*. Acquires anything needed to complete the task: materials, equipment, reference works. Far from a subservient role, this requires creativity, shrewdness, and even cunning to find the necessary resources, which may also be diligently sought by other groups.

5. *Recorder*. Commits to writing the major product of the group. The recorder may require individuals to write their own conclusions, in which case the recorder collates, synthesizes, and renders in coherent form the abbreviated work of individual group members.

6. *Supporter*. Chosen for his or her upbeat, positive outlook, the supporter praises members when their individual assignments are completed and consoles them in times of discouragement (e.g., if proper references can't be found). Keeps the group moving forward by recording major milestones achieved on a chart for all the class to see, identifying progress made, and encouraging efforts of individuals, particularly those who may have difficulty participating or completing their tasks.

7. *Observer/Troubleshooter*. Takes notes and records information about the group process that may be useful during whole-class discussion or debriefing. Reports to a class leader or to you when problems appear insurmountable for a group or for individual members.

Typically, any one of the preceding role functions also could serve as a group leader. However, because each of these roles entails some form of leadership, the formal designation of leader may not be necessary. This has the desirable effect of making all role functions more equal and eliminating an authority-based structure that can lead to arguments and disunity among members who may see themselves as more or less powerful than others. Also, be sure to explain and model the specific duties entailed in each of these roles before assigning them.

In addition to these specific role functions assigned to individual group members, there are other responsibilities for all group members to perform. You may wish to provide students with the following reminders by writing them on the board or in a handout before a cooperative learning activity:

- Ask other group members to explain their points clearly whenever you don't understand.
- Be sure to check your answers and those of others in your group against references or the text.
- Encourage members of your group to go farther, to expand on their points to surpass previous accomplishments and expectations.
- Let everyone finish what they have to say without interrupting, whether you agree or disagree.
- Don't be bullied into changing your mind, if you really don't want to.
- Criticize ideas, not individuals.

Providing Reinforcement and Rewards.   Besides deciding on group composition, size, time, and the individual responsibilities of group members, you need to establish a system of reinforcement and reward to keep your learners on task and working toward the goal. The following are among the reinforcement strategies that have been used effectively with cooperative learning activities:

- Grades: individual and group
- Bonus points
- Social responsibilities
- Tokens or privileges
- Group contingencies

Grades—the familiar type used in competitive learning—can be used to reinforce and reward the behavior of individuals and groups during cooperative learning. However, use of individual grades in the context of cooperative learning should stress the importance of individual effort in achieving *the group goal.* For this reason, cooperative learning grades usually incorporate both individual performance (quality and/or extensiveness of work toward accomplishing the group goal) and the thoroughness, relevance, and accuracy of the group product. Each individual's grade can be in two separate parts or can be a composite grade that combines his or her own plus the group's effort. Individuals can rate each other on a five-point scale measuring the active involvement of each teammate in the group process, the average of which could be a score for individual effort. Sample scales for measuring group and individual effort are illustrated in Figure 9.2.

Teachers may also use other types of grades as rewards:

1. Average the individual scores to determine the group grade.
2. Assign all group members the average of the highest (or lowest) half of the members' scores.
3. Average an individual's score with the group score (e.g., average an individual score of 4 with a group score of 5: 4 + 5 = 9, divided by 2 = 4.5).
4. Add points to the group score for each active participant within the group (or subtract points from the group score for each nonparticipant).

Another reinforcement technique you can use in partnership with grades is bonus points, earned on the basis of how many group members reach a preestablished level of performance by the end of their group's activity. You might devise a group quiz (or take it from the text or workbook) and then assign an expected score for each individual member, which could vary according to ability or task. Those obtaining or exceeding their expected score would earn their group a bonus point.

Figure 9.2 Sample scales for evaluating individual and group effort in a collaborative activity.

1. How active was _____ in helping the group attain its final product?

_____ very active
_____ fairly active
_____ somewhat active
_____ not too active
_____ not active at all

2. How complete (or accurate, or useful, or original) is this group's final product?

_____ very complete
_____ fairly complete
_____ somewhat complete
_____ not too complete
_____ not complete at all

Another popular form of reinforcement during cooperative learning includes rewarding individual efforts with desirable social responsibilities, such as granting the high performer the first pick of group role next time (observer, supporter, checker, etc.). Also, you can employ tokens or privileges to motivate individuals and group members. You might give the highest-performing group independent study time, trips to the learning center, or use of special materials and/or resources. You could accord these same privileges for high-performing individuals within groups.

Finally, teachers frequently have used group contingencies to motivate and reinforce members during cooperative learning. You may choose one of three ways of rewarding the group based on the performance of its individuals:

1. Average-performance contingency, in which all members are graded or reinforced based on the average performance of all group members.
2. High-performance group contingency, in which the highest quarter of the group is the basis for grades, reinforcements, or privileges.
3. Low-performance group contingency, in which the lowest quarter of the group is the basis for individual grades or other forms of reinforcement.

3. Teaching and Evaluating the Collaborative Process

Another responsibility you have during cooperative learning is teaching the collaborative process. Most learners lack the collaborative skills needed to benefit from many cooperative learning activities. Therefore, you need to identify collaborative behaviors, place them in proper sequence, and demonstrate them. Just as self-directed learning strategies must be modeled, so must collaborative behaviors.

At the heart of collaborative skills is the ability to exchange thoughts and feelings with others at the same conceptual level. Students need to feel comfortable in communicating their ideas, beliefs, and opinions to others in a timely and efficient manner. Johnson and Johnson (1991) suggest some important sending skills and some of the ways you can encourage them:

1. *Teach how to communicate one's own ideas and feelings.* Encourage use of *I* and *my* to let students know it is *their* ideas and feelings that make the collaborative process work. Let students know that their personal experiences—events observed, problems encountered, people met—are valued information they can use to justify their own ideas and feelings.
2. *Make messages complete and specific.* Indicate that, along with the message being sent, there should be a frame of reference, perspective, or experience that led to the content of the message. For example, "I got this idea while traveling through a Pueblo Indian reservation in southern Colorado during our vacation last summer." Or, "I heard the President speak, and his main point reminded me of . . . or, "I read this newspaper article, and it led me to believe some things about.. . . . "
3. *Make verbal and nonverbal messages congruent.* Establish a serious tone in which hidden meanings or snide remarks are not acceptable. Indicate that voice and body language always are to reinforce the message being conveyed

and that communicating serious information comically or overdramatizing will confuse both the message and the listener.

4. *Convey an atmosphere of respect and support.* Indicate that all students can contribute information, ideas, feelings, personal experiences, and reactions without fear of ridicule. Make clear that unsupportive behaviors ("You're crazy if you think . . . ") are not allowed. Make clear that cooperation rests on sharing both emotional and physical resources, receiving help, dividing responsibility, and looking out for one another's well-being.

5. *Demonstrate how to assess whether the message was properly received.* Instruct your learners in how to ask for interpretive feedback from listeners. Ask them to use phrases such as "What do you think about what I said?" "Does what I said make sense?" "Can you see what I'm trying to say?" The more listeners are asked to paraphrase the message, the more the sender is sure the message has been received as intended.

6. *Teach how to paraphrase another's point of view.* Most learners will want to agree or disagree with the speaker without checking to see if they have the full intent of the message. Make it known that before one can be either critical or supportive of another's viewpoint, it must be paraphrased to the satisfaction of the sender. Teach the following rules of paraphrasing:
   a. Restate the message in your own words, not those of the speaker.
   b. Introduce your paraphrased remarks with phrases such as "It seems to me you're saying . . . " "If I understand you, you believe that . . . " "From what I heard you say, your position is. . . . "
   c. During the paraphrasing, avoid any indication of approval or disapproval. For example, let it be known that responses such as "I disagree with you" or "I think you're right" should not be part of the paraphrased response, for its sole purpose is to determine whether the message has been accurately received.

7. *Demonstrate how to negotiate meanings and understandings.* Often one's understanding of a message must be corrected or fine tuned, because the message was ambiguous, incomplete, or misinterpreted. This means that paraphrases often must be recycled to a greater level of understanding, sometimes for the benefit of both sender and receiver. This requires tactful phrases from the sender such as "What I mean to say is . . . " "What I forgot to add was . . . " or "To clarify further. . . . " It also requires tactful phrases from the receiver, such as "What I don't understand is . . . " "Can you say it some other way?" This approach is indispensable for refining the message and ensuring more accurate interpretation. Sender and receiver each must provide a graceful means for the other to correct misperceptions of what was said or heard, without emotional injury to either.

8. *Teach participation and leadership.* Communicate the importance of the following:
   a. Mutual benefit: What benefits the group will benefit the individual.
   b. Common fate: Each individual wins or loses on the basis of the overall performance of group members.

    c. Shared identity: Everyone is a member of a group, emotionally as well as physically.

    d. Joint celebration: Receiving satisfaction in the progress of individual group members

    e. Mutual responsibility: Being concerned for underperforming group members

4. Monitoring Group Performance

To establish a cooperative learning structure, you must observe and intervene as needed to assist your learners in acquiring their group's goal. Your most frequent monitoring functions will be telling students where to find needed information, repeating how to complete the task, exhibiting the form of the product to be produced (in whole or part), and/or modeling for a group the process to be used in achieving the group goal. Your role is critical in keeping each group on track. Thus, your constant vigilance of group performance is necessary to discover problems and trouble spots before they hamper group progress.

One goal of your monitoring activity should be to *identify when a group needs assistance*. One common need will be to repeat or remind the group of its goal.

A teacher's role as monitor during group work includes identifying when additional resources may be needed by a group, redirecting group work in more productive directions, and providing emotional support to encourage commitment to the task.

Groups easily become disengaged or sidetracked or will invent new and perhaps more interesting goals for themselves. Typically, you will move from group to group at least once at the beginning of a cooperative activity, repeating the task and the goal just to be certain each group understands it.

A second goal of your monitoring activity should be to *redirect groups* that have discussed themselves into a blind alley. The heat of discussion and debate frequently distracts groups from productive thought, raising issues that may be only marginally relevant to accomplishing the group goal. Key to your monitoring is your ability to recognize when a group is at a difficult juncture. A group might pursue an avenue of fruitless discussion and waste valuable time, when a different avenue could set their course productively toward an attainable goal. Your close vigilance and direction of group work can make the difference between aimless talk and productive discussion.

A third monitoring activity you will perform during cooperative learning is to *provide emotional support and encouragement* to overwhelmed and frustrated group members. Not all group members will gladly accept their individual assignments, nor will all groups accept their designated goal. Your encouragement and support can instill the confidence some will need to complete a task they may be unsure of and that may not be of their own choosing.

5. Debriefing

Your feedback to the groups on how well they are collaborating is important to their progress in acquiring collaborative skills (Weissglass, 1996). You can accomplish **debriefing** and evaluation at the end of the collaborative activity:

1. Openly talk about how the groups functioned. Ask students for their opinions. What were the real issues that enhanced or impeded each group (a) in producing the product and (b) in completing the process?
2. Solicit suggestions for improving the process and avoiding problems so that higher levels of collaboration can be reached.
3. Get viewpoints of predesignated observers. You might assign one or two individuals to record instances of particularly effective and ineffective group collaboration and to report to the full class at the time of the debriefing.

Group members also can rate each other's collaborative skills during debriefing. Individual group members could receive their ratings privately while group averages could be discussed during the debriefing session to pinpoint strengths and deficiencies.

Figure 9.3 is a scale for rating collaborative skills of group members. It can be used (1) by group members to rate each other, (2) by a group member (e.g., an observer) assigned the task of rating group members, or (3) by you, the teacher. Use this scale as a checklist. On it, note the presence or absence of each skill for each group member by placing a checkmark in the appropriate box. Use *NA* (not applicable) for skills that do not apply for a given role or task. If you wish, instead of listing the names of group members, assign each member a number to keep the ratings anonymous. The whole group then could be assigned one point for each check placed on the scale, and the "winning" group could be given a reward to special recognition.

Figure 9.3 Checklist scale for rating collaborative skills of group members.

Collaborative Skills	Names of Group Members				
Provides knowledge and information to help group's progress					
Is open and candid to whole group with personal feelings					
Provides individual assistance and support to group members who need it					
Evaluates contributions of others in a nonjudgmental, constructive manner					
Shares physical resources—books, handouts, written information—for group to use					
Accurately paraphrases or summarizes what other group members have said					
Gives recognition to other group members when key contributions are made					
Accepts and appreciates cultural, ethnic, and individual differences					

Here is a summary of some obstacles to debriefing and how you can structure your cooperative learning activity to promote evaluation and feedback (based on D. Dishon & O'Leary, 1984):

1. *There is not enough time for debriefing.* For many reasons (announcements, assemblies, ensuing lessons), teachers often believe they do not have the time to evaluate and gather feedback about the cooperative activity. Try the following:
   a. Do quick debriefing by asking the class to tell how well their groups functioned. You can do this by asking a question, such as "Did each group have enough time?" Then, have students indicate agreement or disagreement by answering *yes,* hand in air; *don't know*, arms folded; or *no*, hands down. You can ask and respond to two or three questions in a minute or so.

     b. Do debriefing during the cooperative activity, or have the class complete a questionnaire or checklist at home pertaining to how well their group functioned.

2. *Debriefing stays vague.* When students conclude, "We did OK," "We did a good job," or "Everyone was involved" several times, you know that the feedback is not specific enough. Try the following:

     a. Give the group specific written questions to be answered about their group's functioning.

     b. Identify key events or incidents that occurred during the collaborative process for which students must indicate their comfort or satisfaction.

     c. Use student observers so that specific events indicating effective and ineffective group functioning are recorded.

3. *Students stay uninvolved in debriefing.* Occasionally there are groups whose members consistently stay uninvolved in the debriefing process. Try the following:

     a. Ask for a written report from the group, reporting the strengths and weaknesses of their group's functioning.

     b. Use questionnaires that require completion by everyone.

     c. Assign a student the job of debriefer for the group.

     d. Have each member sign a statement summarizing how their group functioned.

     e. Give bonus points for good debriefing reports.

4. *Written debriefing reports are incomplete.* Some groups may hand in incomplete debriefing reports. Try the following:

     a. Have group members read and sign each other's debriefing reports to show that each has been checked for accuracy and completeness.

     b. Give bonus points for completeness.

5. *Students use poor collaborative skills during debriefing.* When group members do not listen carefully to each other, when they are afraid to contribute to the debriefing process, or when the discussion becomes divisive, try the following:

     a. Assign specific roles for the debriefing.

     b. Have one group observe the debriefing of another group and discuss the results.

TEAM-ORIENTED COOPERATIVE LEARNING ACTIVITIES

Recent research indicates that teams of heterogeneous learners can increase the collaborative skills, self-esteem, and achievement of individual learners (Slavin, 1993). Four **team-oriented cooperative learning** techniques have been particularly successful in bringing about these outcomes: Student Teams—Achievement Division, Teams-Games-Tournaments, Jigsaw II, and Team-Assisted Individualization. A brief summary of these follows, based on the work of Slavin (1993).

Student Teams—Achievement Division

In Student Teams—Achievement Division (STAD), the teacher assigns students to four-or-five-member learning teams. Each team is as heterogeneous as possible to represent the composition of the entire class (boys/girls, higher achieving/lower achieving, etc.).

Begin the cooperative learning activity by presenting new material via lecture or discussion and providing worksheets of problem sets, vocabulary words, questions, and such from which students can review the main points of the lecture or discussion. When your lecture, explanation, or introduction is complete, team members study your worksheets, quizzing each other. They work in pairs or in small groups in which team members discuss the worksheet content, clarifying difficult or confusing points among themselves and raising questions of you, when necessary.

Before team members begin, give one member of each group or pair the answers to all the questions or problems on the worksheet, and assign this member the task of checking the written or oral responses of others. Allow team members sufficient time for everyone to complete the problems or questions on the worksheet (make the worksheet concise to encourage this).

After the teams have had sufficient time to practice with the worksheet and answer key, give individuals a written quiz over the material in which team members may not help one another. Score the quizzes immediately, and form individual scores into team scores (e.g., by averaging all, top half, or bottom half). Determine the contribution of individual students by how much each student's quiz score exceeds her or his past quiz average or exceeds a preset score based on each student's learning history. This way, while the entire group receives a score based on each individual member's performance, individual learners also receive an improvement score based on the extent to which their individual score exceeds past performance or a preestablished standard that recognizes their learning history.

During STAD, you act as a resource person and monitor group study activities to intervene when necessary to suggest better study techniques ("Why not choose partners now, and quiz each other on the questions you've been discussing?").

Research shows that, during STAD, learners gain a sense of camaraderie and helpfulness toward fellow team members, pursue self-directed learning and rehearsal strategies modeled by the teacher, and become self-motivated through having some control over their own learning.

Teams-Games-Tournaments

A cooperative learning activity closely related to STAD is the use of Teams-Games-Tournaments (TGT). TGT uses the same general format as STAD (four-to-five-member groups studying worksheets). However, instead of individually administered quizzes at the end of a study period, students play academic games to show their mastery of the topic studied.

Jigsaw II

In the cooperative learning activity called Jigsaw II, you assign students to four-to-six member teams to work on an academic task that is broken into several subtasks, depending on the number of groups. You assign students to teams and then assign a unique responsibility to each team member. For example, assign each student within each team a section of the text to read. Then, give each team member a special task with which to approach the reading. Assign one team member to write down and look up the meanings of any new vocabulary words. Assign another to summarize or outline the main points in the text. Assign another the job of identifying major and minor characters, and so on.

When all team members have their specific assignments, break out from their original group all team members having the same assignment (e.g., finding and defining new vocabulary words) to meet as expert groups to discuss their assignment and to share their conclusions and results. Once in an expert group, members may assist each other by comparing notes (e.g., definitions) and identifying points overlooked by other group members. When all the expert groups have had the opportunity to share, discuss, and modify their conclusions, return them to their respective home groups. Each member then takes turns teaching their teammates about their respective responsibility.

Jigsaw II heightens interest among group members because the only way other team members can learn about the topics to which they were not assigned is to listen to the teammate who received that assignment. After all the experts make their presentation to the team, attempting to teach the group what they learned from their expert group, give individual quizzes to assess how much they have learned. As in STAD, you can assign both an overall group score as well as individual improvement score based on past performance. These scores become the basis for team and individual rewards for the highest scorers.

Team-Assisted Individualization

One of the newest cooperative learning activities is Team-Assisted Individualization (TAI), which combines some of the characteristics of individualized and cooperative learning. Although originally designed for elementary and middle school mathematics classes, TAI can be used with any subject matter and grade level for which some individualized learning materials are available (e.g., programmed or self-paced texts). In TAI, you start each student working through the individualized materials at a point designated by a placement test or previous learning history. Thus, students may work at different levels depending on the heterogeneity of abilities in the classroom.

Give each student a specified amount of content to work through (e.g., pages, problem sets, questions and answers) at his or her own pace. Also, assign each learner to a team selected to represent all ability levels and, therefore, individuals who enter the individualized materials at different levels of complexity. Heterogeneity within the teams is important, because you then ask each team member to have their work checked by another teammate. Checkers are expected to have completed portions of the materials that are more advanced than others. Have as many group members as possible assume the role of checker. When necessary, give the checkers answer sheets.

Have student monitors give quizzes over each unit, and score and record the results on a master score card. Base team scores on the average number of units completed each week by team members and their scores on the unit quizzes.

Reward those teams that complete a preset number of units with a minimum average quiz score (e.g., with certificates, independent study time, learning center privileges). Assign one student monitor (rotate this assignment frequently) to each team to manage the routine checking, distribution of the individualized materials, and administering and recording the quizzes.

Because TAI uses individualized materials, it is especially useful for teaching heterogeneous classes that afford you few opportunities for whole-class instruction and little time to instruct numerous small groups who may have diverse learning needs.

Overview of Team-Oriented Cooperative Learning Activities

Similarities and differences among the four cooperative learning methods are summarized in Table 9.1.

Table 9.1 Similarities and differences among four cooperative learning activities.

Student Teams–Achievement Division (STAD)	Team-Games Tournament (TGT)	Jigsaw (II)	Team-Assisted Individualization (TAI)
1. Teacher presents content in lecture or discussion	1. Teacher presents content in lecture or discussion	1. Students read section of text and are assigned unique topic	1. Students are given diagnostic test/exercise by student monitor to determine placement in materials
2. Teams work through problems/questions on worksheets	2. Teams work through problems/questions on worksheets	2. Students within teams with same topic meet in "expert groups"	2. Students work through assigned unit at their own pace
3. Teacher gives quiz over material studied	3. Teams play academic games against each other for points	3. Students return to home group to share knowledge of their topic with teammates	3. Teammate checks text against answers and student monitor gives quiz
4. Teacher determines team average and individual improvement scores	4. Teacher tallies team points over four-week period to determine best team and best individual scorers	4. Students take quiz over each topic discussed	4. Team quizzes are averaged and number of units completed are counted by monitor to create team scores
		5. Individual quizzes are used to create team scores and individual improvement scores	

Many different forms of cooperative learning have been successfully used in classrooms of all grade levels and subject matter. Some of the most successful cooperative learning activities, however, have come from the ingenuity and creativity of individual teachers who, with little formal preparation, devise a group activity to promote social interaction when the subject they are teaching encourages cooperative outcomes. Although many versions of cooperative learning can be devised from the preceding four, as an effective teacher, you should seize the opportunity to create a cooperative learning experience whenever content goals lend themselves to promoting collaborative skills. This, in turn, can increase your learners' self-esteem, critical thinking, and problem-solving abilities.

PROMOTING THE GOALS OF COOPERATIVE LEARNING IN THE CULTURALLY DIVERSE CLASSROOM

One of the first things you will notice during cooperative learning activities is the variety of learning styles among your students. The variety you will observe in your students' independence, persistence, and flexibility during cooperative learning will be influenced, to some extent, by the predominant cultures and ethnicities in your school and classroom.

For example, C. Bennett (1990) points out how interactions among students and between students and teacher are influenced by learning styles that are modified by their culture. Cushner, McClelland, and Safford (1992) indicate how being a member of a subculture, minority, or ethnic group can enhance the nature of interpersonal relationships within a classroom by increasing its cohesiveness, informality, interpersonal harmony, and cooperation. Also, Bowers and Flinders (1991) provide examples of how the noise level, use of classroom space, turn taking, and negotiation can vary among social classes and ethnicities to create different but equally productive learning climates when properly managed and matched to cultural expectations.

In Chapter 2 we saw that learners could be distinguished on the basis of the cognitive processes they used to learn and whether they were presented a task *in a way that allowed them the opportunity to use their preferred learning style.* Two of the learning styles that have been frequently studied are field independence and field dependence (Wakefield, 1996; Woolfolk, 1997).

Field-Independent Learner	**Field-Dependent Learner**
Focuses on global issues	Focuses on details
Seeks out guidance	Enjoys independence
Prefers to work with others	Prefers to work alone
Prefers organization to be provided by teacher	Prefers to organize by him or herself
Likes to cooperate	Likes to compete

The implications of field independence and field dependence for cooperative learning have been related to students' need for structure. Hunt (1979) identified characteristics of students who need more or less structure to maximize their opportunity to learn. Some of his characteristics, which have implications for how to plan a cooperative learning activity, follow:

Those needing more structure:

- Have shorter attention spans, like to move through material rapidly.
- Are reluctant to try something new, and don't like to appear wrong.
- Tend not to ask many questions.
- May need reassurance before starting a task.
- Want to know facts before concepts.
- Usually give only brief answers.

Those needing less structure:

- Like to discuss and argue.
- Want to solve problems with a minimum of teacher assistance.
- Dislike details or step-by-step formats.
- Are comfortable with abstractions and generalities.
- Emphasize emotions and are open about themselves.
- Tend to make many interpretations and inferences.

Hunt (1979) goes on to suggest specific ways teachers can orient their cooperative activities to promote particular learning styles. Try these suggestions:

During cooperative learning, some learners may benefit more and adapt better to a task orientation that is less structures and more field dependent. Recent findings (Hunt, 1979) suggest that some task orientations, such as cooperative learning, may be more appropriate for some groups. Research also suggests that some of today's objectives—such as interdisciplinary thematic units and objectives pertaining to integrated bodies of knowledge—may require cooperative and collaborative activities to achieve their goals.

For students who require more structure:

- Have definite and consistent rules.
- Provide specific, step-by-step guides and instructions.
- Make goals and deadlines short and definite.
- Change pace often.
- Assess problems frequently.
- Move gradually from group work to discussion.

For students who require less structure:

- Provide topics to choose from.
- Make assignments longer, with self-imposed deadlines.
- Encourage the use of resources outside the classroom.
- Devote more time to group assignments with teacher serving as a resource.
- Use and encourage interest in the opinions and values of others.
- Provide opportunity for extended follow-up projects and assignments.

Little is known about how these aspects of a teacher's task orientation relate to specific groups of learners during cooperative learning. Hill (1989), however, suggests that some cultural and ethnic groups tend to benefit more and adapt better to a task orientation that is less structured and more field dependent. For example, cooperative learning has been shown to increase the school success of Hispanic students (Losey, 1995). These and other authors provide alternatives to the notion that the most effective task orientation for the teacher is always to stand in front of the classroom, lecturing or explaining to students seated in neatly arranged rows, who are assumed to have little or no expectations about or experiences with the content being taught. Recent findings suggest that not only may some task orientations, such as cooperative learning, be more appropriate for some groups but some of today's objectives (especially interdisciplinary objectives and objectives pertaining to integrated bodies of knowledge) may *require* cooperative and collaborative activities to achieve their goals.

SUMMING UP

This chapter introduced you to strategies for cooperative learning. Its main points were as follows:

1. Critical thinking, reasoning and problem-solving skills are of little use if they cannot be applied in cooperative interaction with others.
2. Self-directed and cooperative learning share the complementary objectives of engaging students in the learning process and promoting higher (more complex) patterns of behavior.

3. Cooperative learning activities can instill the following in your learners:
   - Attitudes and values that guide the learner's behavior outside of the classroom
   - Acceptable forms of social behavior that may not be modeled in the home
   - Alternative perspectives and viewpoints with which to think objectively
   - An integrated identity that can reduce contradictory thoughts and actions

- Higher thought processes

4. Planning for cooperative learning requires decisions pertaining to the following:
   - Teacher–student interaction
   - Student–student interaction
   - Task specialization and materials
   - Role expectations and responsibilities

5. The primary goal of teacher–student interaction during cooperative learning is to promote independent thinking.

6. The primary goal of student–student interaction during cooperative learning is to encourage the active participation and interdependence of all members of the class.

7. The primary goal of task specialization and learning materials during cooperative learning is to create an activity structure whose end product depends on the sharing, cooperation, and collaboration of individuals within groups.

8. The primary goal of assigning roles and responsibilities during cooperative learning is to facilitate the work of the group and to promote communication and sharing among its members.

9. Establishing a cooperative task structure involves five steps:
   a. Specify the goal of the activity.
   b. Structuring the task
   c. Teach the collaborative process.
   d. Monitor group performance.
   e. Debrief.

10. The goal of a cooperative activity may take different forms, such as the following:
    - Written group reports
    - Higher individual achievement
    - An oral performance
    - An enumeration or listing
    - A critique
    - Bibliographic research

11. You have four responsibilities in specifying the goal of a cooperative activity:
    - Illustrate the style, format, and length of the end product.
    - Place the goal in the context of past and future learning.
    - Check for understanding of the goal and directions given for achieving it.
    - Set a tone of cooperation, as opposed to competition.

12. Structuring the cooperative learning task involves the following decisions:
    - How large the groups will be
    - How group members will be selected
    - How much time will be devoted to group work
    - What roles group members will be assigned
    - What incentives will be provided for individual and group work

13. Generally, the most efficient size for a group to reach the desired goal in the least amount of time is four to six members.

14. Unless a group task specifically calls for specialized abilities, groups should be formed heterogeneously—or with a representative sample of all learners in the class.

15. Methods for selecting group members include the following:
    a. Ask students to list peers with whom they would like to work.
    b. Randomly assign students to groups.
    c. Choose matched opposites: minority/majority, boy/girl, with/without disabilities, and so on.
    d. Share with students the process of choosing group members (e.g., teacher selects first, then person selected chooses another, etc.).

16. An actively uninvolved group member is one who talks about everything but the assigned goal of the group; a passively uninvolved group member is one who doesn't care about the work of the group and becomes silent.

17. Methods for discouraging active and passive uninvolvement include the following:
    - Request a product requiring division of labor.
    - Form pairs that oversee each other's work.
    - Chart group progress on individually assigned tasks.
    - Purposefully limit group resources to promote sharing and personal contact.
    - Require a product that is contingent on previous stages that are the work of others.

18. Group work should entail 60% to 80% of the time devoted to a cooperative activity, the

remainder being devoted to whole-class discussion and debriefing.

19. Division of labor within a group can be accomplished with role assignments. The following are some of the most popular:
    - Summarizer
    - Checker
    - Researcher
    - Runner
    - Recorder
    - Supporter
    - Observer/troubleshooter

20. The following are among the types of reinforcement strategies that can be used with cooperative learning activities:
    - Individual and group grades
    - Bonus points
    - Social responsibilities
    - Tokens or privileges
    - Group contingencies

21. Teaching the collaborative process involves showing your learners how to do the following:
    - Communicate their own ideas and feelings.
    - Make messages complete and specific.
    - Make verbal and nonverbal messages congruent.
    - Convey respect and support.
    - Assess if the message was properly received.
    - Paraphrase another's point of view.
    - Negotiate meanings and understandings.
    - Actively participate in a group, and assume leadership.

22. During the monitoring of group performance, the teacher's role is to see that each group remains on track, to redirect group efforts when needed, and to provide emotional support and encouragement.

23. During debriefing, there are several ways to gather feedback in a whole-class discussion about the collaborative process:
    - Openly talk about how the groups functioned during the cooperative activity.
    - Solicit suggestions for how the process could be improved.
    - Obtain the viewpoints of predesignated observers.

24. Desirable outcomes have been documented for four popular team-oriented cooperative learning activities:
    - Student Teams—Achievement Division (STAD)
    - Teams-Games-Tournaments (TGT)
    - Jigsaw II
    - Team-Assisted Individualization (TAI)

FOR DISCUSSION AND PRACTICE

Questions marked with an asterisk are answered in Appendix B. See also *Bridges: An Activity Guide and Assessment Options,* which accompanies this text.

*1. What two complementary objectives do self-directed and cooperative learning share? Can you think of an instance in which self-directed learning might occur within the context of a cooperative group?

*2. Identify five specific outcomes of cooperation. Which will be the most important for your classroom?

*3. What three general outcomes can result from these more specific outcomes? Which will be the most important for your classroom?

*4. Identify the four most important components of a cooperative learning activity and one critical decision that you will have to make pertaining to each. Which will be the most difficult decision?

*5. What five steps will be required for establishing a cooperative task structure in your classroom? To which step will you devote the most (a) planning time and (b) classroom time?

*6. What end products or behaviors should you require at the end of a cooperative learning activity? Which product or behavior do you think presents the biggest challenge for evaluation and assessment?

*7. Approximately how large should a cooperative learning group be to reach a specified goal in the least amount of time? Can you think of a situation in which the cooperative learning group could be smaller or larger and still function effectively?

*8. What methods can you use for selecting members of a cooperative group? Can you think of an advantage of using one method over another?

*9. What are three methods for minimizing passive and active uninvolvement in a cooperative learning activity? In your opinion, which method is best for drawing nonengaged learners into the cooperative activity?

*10. Identify the student role functions suggested by D. Johnson and Johnson (1991) that can be assigned to group members. Briefly describe their responsibilities, and add any additional role functions that might be suited to the goals of your classroom.

*11. In what five ways could you reinforce and reward group members for appropriate performance? Create one specific example of each that would be practical within your classroom.

*12. When combining individual and group work into a single score, what options are available for weighting an individual's work and the work of the group to which the individual belongs differently?

*13. D. Johnson and Johnson (1991) identify eight sending skills. Provide an example of how you would teach each of them, in a sentence or two, by using classroom dialogue.

*14. What are three activities that can be performed during a cooperative learning activity to monitor and, when necessary, improve group performance?

*15. What activities can be used to debrief your class after a cooperative learning activity? Which would you prefer to use in your classroom?

*16. D. Dishon and O'Leary (1984) identify five obstacles to debriefing and several approaches for dealing with each of them. For each obstacle, identify from among the options the one you would first try to improve the debriefing process.

17. Describe two of Slavin's (1993) team-oriented cooperative learning activities with respect to the structure of the activity to be performed, the work of the teams, your role as teacher, and procedures for team scoring and recognition. Choose the two that you would be most willing to try in your classroom.

10 Classroom Management

This chapter will help you answer the following questions:

1. What can I do during the first weeks of school to get my learners to trust one another and feel as members of a group?
2. What can I teach my learners to help them discuss and resolve group conflicts on their own?
3. How do I get my class to develop group norms?
4. What types of classroom rules will I need?
5. How might I use the social organization of my classroom to bridge cultural gaps?

For most teachers, confronting some sort of behavior problem is a daily occurrence. These problems may include simple infractions of school or classroom rules, or they may involve more serious events, including disrespect, cheating, obscene words and gestures, and the open display of hostility.

It is important that the management of your classroom begin with developing trusting relationships with your students. Without mutual feelings of trust and respect, you will be unable to assume the role of an instructional leader in your classroom. To accomplish this, we will discuss how you can

1. Design an orderly workplace that promotes your academic goals.
2. Develop rules for the workplace that create group norms that students respect and follow.
3. Adapt in the face of unproductive rules, routines, and procedures.
4. Maintain a workplace that fosters feelings of belonging and group solidarity.
5. Know how to seek help from other school professionals and from parents.

EARNING TRUST AND BECOMING A LEADER—THE OLD-FASHIONED WAY

According to social psychologists (French & Raven, 1959; Raven, 1974), to establish yourself as an effective leader, you will have to gain your students' trust and respect the old-fashioned way; you'll have to earn it. But how? French and Raven provide a way of looking at how you earn respect by asking the question, "How do you achieve social power?" They identify five types of **social power** or leadership a teacher can strive for: *expert* power, *referent* power, *legitimate* power, *reward* power, and *coercive* power.

Expert Power

Certain individuals become leaders because others perceive them as experts. Successful teachers have *expert power*. Their students see them as competent to explain or do certain things and as knowledgeable about particular topics. Such influence is earned, rather than conferred by virtue of having a particular title. Teachers with expert power explain things well, show enthusiasm and excitement about what they teach, and appear confident and self-assured before their classes.

New teachers often find it difficult to establish leadership through expert power. Even though they are knowledgeable and competent in their field, uncertainty and inexperience in front of a group may make them appear less so. Students are attuned to body language suggesting lack of confidence and indecision and may test the competence and challenge the authority of teachers who appear not to be in command of their subject.

Referent Power

Students often accept as leaders teachers they like and respect. They view such teachers as trustworthy, fair, and concerned about them (Goodlad, 1984). The term *referent power* describes leadership earned in this way. Ask any group of junior high or high school students about why they like particular teachers, and invariably they describe the teachers they like as "fair," "caring," and "someone you can talk to." Without referent power, even teachers with expert power may have their authority challenged or ignored.

One often hears teachers say that they would rather be respected than liked, as if these two consequences were mutually exclusive. Research by Soar and Soar (1983) suggests that teachers can be both respected and liked: Teachers who were both respected and liked were associated with greater student satisfaction and higher achievement. Glasser (1986) emphasizes that students' needs for belonging in a classroom will more likely be met by a teacher who is perceived as both warm and competent.

Legitimate Power

Some roles carry with them influence and authority by their very nature. Police officers, presidents, and judges exert social power and leadership by their very titles. Influence in such cases may be conferred by the role itself rather than depend on the nature of the person assuming the role. Savage (1991) refers to this type of power as *legitimate power,* and, unlike expert and referent power, it may not be earned. Teachers possess a certain degree of legitimate power. Our society expects students to give teachers their attention, respect them, and follow their requests. Most families also stress the importance of listening to the teacher. Every new teacher begins her or his first day of class with legitimate power.

Legitimate power, therefore, gives the new teacher some breathing room during the first few weeks of school. Most students will initially obey and accept the authority of new teachers by virtue of their position of authority. However, building classroom leadership solely through legitimate power may be like building a house on a foundation of sand. Teachers should use their legitimate power to establish referent and expert power.

Reward Power

Individuals in positions of authority are able to exercise *reward power* in relation to the people they lead. These rewards can take the form of privileges, approval, or more tangible compensation, such as money. To the extent that students desire the rewards conferred by teachers, teachers can exert a degree of leadership and authority. There are, however, few rewards available to teachers and a great number of rewards available to students without the aid of a teacher. Students who don't care much about good grades or teacher approval are difficult to lead solely by exerting reward power, since students can attain outside of school much of what is reinforcing to them. In such cases some teachers resort to using tangible reinforcers such as access to desired activities, objects, and even food. In this chapter, you will learn that reward power can be an effective tool in the classroom but cannot substitute for referent and expert power.

Coercive Power

Through state and local government, teachers are allowed to act *in loco parentis*, that is, in place of the parent. Consequently, within limits, schools can punish students who defy the authority or leadership of the teacher by such techniques as suspension or expulsion, denial of privileges, or removal from the classroom. Teachers who rely on such techniques to maintain social power in their classroom are using *coercive power*. The use of coercive power may stop misbehavior for a time, but this will sometimes be at the cost of developing trust and meeting student needs. Over-reliance on coercive power has the danger of increasing attitudes that may lead to antagonism and disengagement from the learning process.

Using Power

While each of the preceding sources of power, when properly used, is a legitimate tool for managing the classroom, teachers, especially new teachers, should work quickly to achieve expert and referent power. You can achieve expert power by keeping up to date with developments in your teaching field, completing in-service and graduate programs, attending seminars and workshops, and completing career ladder and mentoring activities provided by your school district. From your very first day in the classroom, you can exhibit referent power by giving your students a sense of belonging and acceptance.

STAGES OF GROUP DEVELOPMENT

Social psychologists, such as Schmuck and Schmuck (1992) and Johnson and Johnson (1996), believe that the sources of social power you acquire are important for guiding your learners through the process of group development. They believe that every successful group passes through a series of **stages of development** during which it has certain tasks to accomplish and concerns to resolve. The way the group accomplishes these tasks and resolves these concerns determines the extent to which you can effectively and efficiently manage the group and accomplish the goals of your classroom. Mauer (1985) describes these stages:

Stage 1, **forming**: Resolving concerns about acceptance and responsibilities

Stage 2, **storming**: Resolving concerns about shared influence

Stage 3, **norming**: Resolving concerns about how work gets done

Stage 4, **performing**: Resolving concerns about freedom, control, and self-regulation

Stage 1: Forming

When learners come together at the start of the school year, they usually are concerned about two issues: (1) finding their place in the social structure and (2) finding out what they are expected to do. Schutz (1958) identifies this first issue as concerns about inclusion, or group membership.

During the first several days of class, learners (and teachers) naturally ask, "How will I fit in?" "Who will accept or reject me?" "What do I have to do to be respected?" At this time, a phenomenon called *testing* takes place (Froyen, 1993). Learners engage in specific actions to see what kind of reaction they get from teachers and peers. At this stage of group formation, learners are curious about one another. They want to know where other class members live, who their friends are, what they like to do, and where they like to go. As students learn more about one another, they begin to see how and with whom they fit in. Putnam and Burke (1992) urge teachers to engage in activities during the first few weeks of school to help learners trust one another and feel as members of a group.

Social psychologists caution teachers that there is a tendency during the first stage of classroom group development to concentrate almost exclusively on concerns about work and rules to the exclusion of concerns about inclusion. They warn that learners who have unresolved fears about acceptance by their teacher and where they fit in the peer group will find it difficult to concentrate on academic work without first developing trust and feeling as valued members of a group (Schmuck & Schmuck, 1992).

Table 10.1 lists questions you can ask to promote group development during the forming stage.

Table 10.1 Important questions about group development.

Stage 1: Forming	Stage 2: Storming	Stage 3: Norming	Stage 4: Performing
1. Are there activities for everyone to get to know about one another?	1. Are conflicts openly recognized and discussed?	1. Is there a process for resolving conflict?	1. Can this group evaluate its own effectiveness?
2. Has everyone had a chance to be heard?	2. Can the group assess its own functioning?	2. Can the group set goals?	2. Can the group and individuals solve their own problems?
3. Do learners interact with a variety of classmates?	3. Are new and different ideas listened to and evaluated?	3. Can learners express what is expected of them?	3. Does the group have opportunities to work independently and express themselves through a medium of their own choosing?
4. Do learners and teachers listen to one another?	4. Are the skills of all members being used?	4. Is there mutual respect between teacher and learners?	4. Can individuals evaluate themselves and set goals for personal improvement?
5. Have concerns and/or fears regarding academic and behavioral expectations been addressed?	5. Do all learners have an opportunity to share leadership and responsibility?	5. What happens to learners who fail to respect norms?	5. Is the group prepared to disband?

Source: From Richard A. Schmuck and Patricia A. Schmuck, *Group Processes in the Classroom,* 6th edition. Copyright © 1992 Wm. C. Brown Communications, Inc., Dubuque, Iowa. Reproduced with permission of The McGraw-Hill Companies.

Stage 2: Storming

The goal of the forming stage of group development is to help learners feel secure and perceive themselves as members of a classroom group. Healthy group life at this stage occurs if learners have accepted the teacher as their leader, made some initial commitment to follow rules and procedures, and agree to respect other members of the class.

During the storming stage of group development, they begin to test the limits of these commitments (Froyen, 1993). This limit testing may take the form of amiable challenges to academic expectations (homework, classwork, tests, etc.) and rules in order to establish under what conditions they do and do not apply. Learners may question seating arrangements, homework responsibilities, seatwork routines, and so on. Social psychologists refer to these amiable challenges to teacher authority and leadership as examples of **distancing behavior**. They occur in any group where a leader initially establishes authority by virtue of his or her position rather than through competence or credibility. This distancing behavior represents reservations learners have at this stage of group development about the commitments they made during the forming stage to class expectations and group participation.

A second type of amiable limit testing, which often accompanies distancing behavior, is called **centering**. Centering occurs when learners question how they will personally benefit from being a group member. Their behavior can be described with the question, "What's in it for me?" The questions they ask and assertions they make reflect a preoccupation with fairness. They are quick to notice favoritism toward individual members of the group.

These distancing and centering conflicts arising between teachers and learners and among learners are a natural part of group development. Social psychologists caution teachers about overreacting at this stage. During these types of conflicts, you will need to monitor compliance with rules and procedures but be willing to reconsider those that may not be working.

Glasser (1986) and Putnam and Burke (1992) urge teachers to have class discussions centering around group conflict resolution. They recommend that teachers instruct their learners on how to problem solve using the following guide:

1. *Problem agreement*. The teacher gets all members of the class to agree that there is a problem and that they will work together to solve it.
2. *State the conflict*. The teacher states concisely what the conflict is and assures all learners that they will have the opportunity to state their perspective.
3. *Identify and select responses*. Teachers and learners brainstorm and record solutions to the problem. They assess the short- and long-term consequences of the solutions and discard those that have negative consequences.
4. *Create a solution*. The class discusses and records a solution that all basically agree will resolve the conflict.
5. *Design and implement a plan*. The class discusses and works out the details of when, where, and how to resolve the conflict.
6. *Assess the success of the plan*. The students identify information they can gather to determine the success of the plan. The teacher identifies checkpoints to evaluate how the class is doing. When the conflict is resolved, the whole class discusses the value of the problem-solving process.

Table 10.1 lists questions you can ask to promote group development during the storming stage.

Stage 3: Norming

The security learners develop at the forming stage provides them with a safe foundation to challenge teacher authority during the storming stage. Skilled leadership during the storming stage assures learners that they will be listened to, treated fairly, and allowed to share power and influence. This assurance leads them during the norming stage to accept both academic expectations, procedures, and rules for the group and the roles and functions of the various group members.

Norms are shared expectations among group members regarding how they should think, feel, and behave. Social psychologists view norms as the principal regulators of group behavior (Zimbardo, 1992). They may take the form of either written or unwritten rules that all or most of the group voluntarily agree to follow. A classroom group has norms when learners, for the most part, agree on what is and is not socially acceptable classroom behavior.

Norms play an important role in governing behavior in the classroom. But their role differs from that of rules and procedures. Norms are more personally meaningful than rules, as seen in the following examples:

It's OK to be seen talking to the teacher.

Learners in this class should help one another.

We're all responsible for our own learning.

We shouldn't gloat when one of our classmates gives the wrong answer.

We need to respect the privacy of others.

The most important thing for this class is learning.

Social psychologists believe that positive norms serve several important functions in the classroom (Froyen, 1993; Putnam & Burke, 1992; Schmuck & Schmuck, 1992).

- Norms orient group members to which social interactions are and are not appropriate and then regulate these interactions. When norms are present, learners can anticipate the ways others will behave in the classroom and also how they are expected to behave.
- Norms create group identification and group cohesiveness (Zimbardo, 1992). Social psychologists believe that the process of group formation begins when its members agree to adhere to the norms of the group. This process begins during the forming stage of group development and ends during the norming stage.
- Norms promote academic achievement and positive relationships among class members. Academic and social goals are more likely to be achieved in classrooms with consistent norms. For example, peer group norms represent one of the most important influences on school performance (Schmuck & Schmuck, 1992).

Group norms, whether in support of a teacher's goals or opposed to them, begin to develop on the first day of school during the forming stage of group development. Zimbardo (1992) identifies two basic processes by which norms develop: **diffusion** and **crystallization**. Diffusion takes place as learners first enter a group or class. They bring with them expectations acquired from experiences in other classes, from other group memberships, and experiences growing up. As learners talk and mingle with each other during breaks and recess, they communicate with one another. Their various expectations for academic and social behavior are diffused and spread throughout the entire class. Eventually, as learners engage in a variety of activities together, their expectations begin to converge and crystallize into a shared perspective of classroom life.

You should do all you can to influence the development of norms that support your classroom goals. It is important that you know how to positively influence the development of class norms and to identify and alter existing ones. Here are some suggestions for developing, identifying, and altering group norms:

- Explain to the class the concept of a *group norm*. Draw up a list of norms with the class and, over time, add and delete norms that either help or impede the work of the group.
- Conduct discussions of class norms, and encourage learners to talk among themselves about them. Glasser (1986) suggests discussing with students ideas on how the class might be run, problems that may interfere with the group's performance, and needed rules and routines.
- Appoint or elect a class council to make recommendations for improving class climate and productivity. Have the group assess whether the norms are working.
- Provide a model of the respect, consistency, and responsibility for learning that you want your learners to exhibit.

Healthy group development at the norming stage is characterized by group behavior primarily focused on academic achievement.

Stage 4: Performing

By the time the group has reached the fourth developmental stage, learners feel at ease with one another, know the rules and their roles, accept group norms, and are familiar with the routine of the classroom. The principal concern for the group at this stage is establishing its independence.

Just as the storming stage of development was characterized by a testing of limits, the performing stage is characterized by learners wanting to show that they can do some things independently of the teacher. Social psychologists urge teachers to encourage the desire for independence at this stage by focusing less on classroom control and more on teaching the group how to set priorities, budget its time, and self-regulate.

The performing stage ends when the school year or semester ends. Thus, this stage represents a time of transition. Assuming all four stages of development have been successfully completed, learners will have developed relationships with one another and with their teacher through which they may manage themselves with the guidance and direction of the teacher. For this transition to successfully occur, however, you will need to establish a classroom climate in which group development can flourish through all four stages.

ESTABLISHING AN EFFECTIVE CLASSROOM CLIMATE

Classroom climate is the atmosphere or mood in which interactions between you and your students take place. Your classroom climate is created by the manner and degree to which you exercise authority, show warmth and support, encourage com-

One aspect of an effective learning climate is the physical or visual arrangement of the classroom. This arrangement is a matter of choice that can be altered to create just the right climate for your learning objectives.

petitiveness or cooperation, and allow for independent judgment and choice. The climate of your classroom is your choice, just as are your instructional methods.

This section introduces two related aspects of an effective classroom climate: the **social environment**, meaning the interaction patterns you promote in the classroom, and the **organizational environment**, meaning your physical or visual arrangement of the classroom. Both are your choice, and you can alter them to create just the right climate.

The Social Environment

The social environment of your classroom can vary from *authoritarian*, in which you are the primary provider of information, opinions, and instruction, to *laissez-faire*, in which your students become the primary providers of information, opinions, and instruction. Between these extremes lies the middle ground in which you and your students *share responsibilities*: students are given freedom of choice and judgment under your direction. Many variations are possible.

For example, a group discussion might be a colossal failure in a rigid authoritarian climate, because the climate clues students that their opinions are less important than yours, that teacher talk and not student talk should take up most of the instructional time, and that the freedom to express oneself spontaneously is your right but not theirs. In a more open atmosphere, this same attempt at discussion might well be a smashing success, because the classroom climate provides all the ingredients of a good discussion—freedom to express one's opinion, high degree of student talk, and spontaneity.

The social atmosphere you create, whether authoritarian, laissez-faire, or somewhere between, is determined by how you see yourself: Are you a commander-in-chief who carefully controls and hones student behavior by organizing and providing all the learning stimuli? Or, are you a translator or summarizer of the ideas provided by students? Or, are you an equal partner with students in creating ideas and problem solutions? Consider the effects of each climate and how you can create it.

The effective teacher not only uses a variety of teaching strategies but also creates a variety of classroom climates. However, your ability to create a certain climate is as important as your ability to *change* the climate when the objectives and situation demand. Although early research in social psychology tried to identify the type of climate most conducive to individual behavior (Lippitt & Gold, 1959), the results suggest that different climates have both their advantages and disadvantages, depending on the intended goal.

Because goals change from lesson to lesson and week to week, so too must your classroom climate that supports the goals. When the goals change but your classroom climate does not, the stage is set for off-task, disruptive, and even antagonistic behavior among your students.

Competitive, Cooperative, or Individualistic.

We have already examined several ways you can vary your authority, and that of your students, in accordance with your objectives. These variations correspond not only with how much you relinquish your authority and therefore your control of the learning process, but also how competitive, cooperative, or individualistic you wish the interactions among members of your class to be. These three conditions are illustrated in Table 10.2. You can see in the table that, as you shift classroom climate from competitive to cooperative to individualistic, you relinquish control over the learning process until, in the individualistic mode, students have almost sole responsibility for judging their own work.

Applying the Three Climates.

In addition to encouraging the proper climate for a given instructional activity, you must decide whether each climate can be applied to the full class, to groups, and to individuals with equal effectiveness. For example, as shown in Figure 10.1, it is not necessary to conduct all group discussions in a cooperative climate.

Although some cells in Figure 10.1 may be more popular than others, various arrangements of students and climates are possible, depending on your instructional goals. Your job is to ensure that the degree of authority you impose matches your instructional goal (e.g., the expression of student opinion you allow, the amount of time you devote to student talk, and the spontaneity with which you want your students to respond).

Table 10.2 Three types of classroom climate.

Social climate	Example activity	Authority vested in students	Authority vested in teacher
Competitive: Students compete for right answers among themselves or with a standard established by the teacher. The teacher is the sole judge of the appropriateness of a response.	Drill and practice	None	To organize the instruction, present the stimulus material, and evaluate correctness of responses
Cooperative: Students engage in dialogue that is monitored by the teacher. The teacher systematically intervenes in the discussion to sharpen ideas and move the discussion to a higher level.	Small and large group discussion	To present opinions, to provide ideas, and to speak and discuss freely and spontaneously	To stimulate the discussion, arbitrate differences, organize and summarize student contributions
Individualistic: Students complete assignments monitored by the teacher. Students are encouraged to complete the assignment with the answers they think are best. Emphasis is on getting through and testing one's self.	Independent seatwork	To complete the assignment with the best possible responses	To assign the work and see that orderly progress is made toward its completion

The Organizational Environment

In addition to arranging the social climate of your classroom, you also must arrange the physical climate. It goes without saying that a classroom should be attractive, well lighted, comfortable, and colorful. But, aside from a colorful bulletin board and neatness, you may have very little influence over the external features of your classroom. Attempts to improve these external conditions always are worth a try, but do not be surprised if your repeated requests are in vain. It is not unusual for teachers to bring their own essential items, such as a clock, bookcase, file cabinet, rug, or pedestal stool to the classroom at the beginning of the year and take them home again for the summer.

What may be more important than these items, however, is the way the internal features of your classroom (desks, chairs, tables) are arranged. Students quickly get

Figure 10.1 Targets for three types of classroom climates.

	Competitive	Cooperative	Individualistic
Full Class	Students compete with other students by having the correct answer when it's their turn.	Students are allowed to call out hints or clues when a student is having difficulty finding the right answer.	The entire class recites answers in unison.
Groups	Subgroups compete against each other as opposing teams.	Subgroups work on different but related aspects of a topic combining their results into a final report to the class.	Each subgroup completes its own assigned topic which is independent of the topics assigned the other subgroups. No shared report is given to the class.
Individual	Individuals compete with each other by having to respond to the same question. The quickest most accurate response "wins."	Pairs of individuals cooperate by exchanging papers, sharing responses, or correcting each other's errors.	Individuals complete seat work on their own without direct teacher involvement.

used to and accept the external features of a classroom, good or bad. But the internal arrangement of the classroom will affect your students every day of the school year.

The most flexible furniture arrangement places your desk at the front of the room and aligns the student desks in rows. Although it may seem strange to associate this traditional format with flexibility, it is most flexible because you can use it to create competitive, cooperative, or individualistic environments, although not always with equal effectiveness. This fact, plus the difficulty of rearranging classroom furniture every time a change in social climate is desired, makes the traditional classroom arrangement almost as popular today as it was 50 years ago.

There are times, however, when you should change the arrangement to encourage a more cooperative, interactive, and group-sharing climate. Such a classroom arrangement has many variations that depend on the external features of the classroom and available furniture.

The important thing is the deliberate attempt to get people together. The barriers to interpersonal sharing and communication that sometimes result from the rigid alignment of desks can be avoided by a more informal, but still systematic, furniture arrangement. Because this arrangement suggests that interpersonal communication and sharing are permitted, increased interpersonal communication and sharing will undoubtedly occur, whether you desire it or not.

By grouping four or five student desks together, you expect more expression of student opinion, increased student talk, and greater spontaneity in student responses. This emphasizes the important notion that *the social climate created by your words and deeds always should match the organizational climate created by the physical arrangement of your classroom.*

Of course, changing the internal arrangement of a classroom from time to time for the sake of variety is refreshing. You might compromise by maintaining the basic nature of the formal classroom but, space permitting, setting aside one or two less formal areas (e.g., a learning center or group discussion table) for times when instructional goals call for interpersonal communication and sharing.

Establishing Rules and Procedures

Establishing **rules and procedures** to reduce the occurrence of classroom discipline problems will be one of your most important classroom management activities (Emmer et al., 1997, Evertson, 1995, 1997; Evertson & Harris, 1992). These rules and procedures, which you should formulate before the first school day, are your commitment to applying the ounce of prevention to avoid having to provide a pound of cure.

Teachers need different types of rules and procedures for effectively managing a classroom; these fall into four basic categories:

- Rules related to academic work
- Rules related to classroom conduct
- Rules that must be communicated your first teaching day
- Rules that can be communicated later, at an appropriate opportunity

The top half of Figure 10.2 identifies rules commonly needed the very first day of class, either because students will ask about them or because events are likely to

Figure 10.2 Classroom rules related to conduct and work.

	Rules related to classroom conduct	Rules related to academic work
Rules that need to be communicated first day	1. where to sit 2. how seats are assigned 3. what to do before the bell rings 4. responding, speaking out 5. leaving at the bell 6. drinks, food, and gum 7. washroom and drinking privileges	8. materials required for class 9. homework completion 10. makeup work 11. incomplete work 12. missed quizzes and examinations 13. determining grades 14. violation of rules
Rules that can be communicated later	15. tardiness/absences 16. coming up to desk 17. when a visitor comes to the door 18. leaving the classroom 19. consequences of rule violation	20. notebook completion 21. obtaining help 22. notetaking 23. sharing work with others 24. use of learning center and/or reference works 25. communication during group work 26. neatness 27. lab safety

arise requiring their use. Notice that these rules are divided into seven conduct rules and seven work rules. For the elementary grades, it is best that you present them orally, *and* provide a handout, *and* post them for later reference by the students. In the lower grades, learners can forget oral messages quickly—or choose to ignore them if there is no physical representation of the rule as a constant reminder. In the later elementary grades and junior high, your recital of the rules while students copy them into their notebooks may be sufficient. For high school students, simply hearing the rules may be sufficient, as long as they are posted for later reference.

Not all "first-day" rules are equally important, and other rules may have to be added as special circumstances require. But rules about responding and speaking out, making up work, determining grades, and violation of due dates are among the most important. It is in these areas that confusion often occurs on the very first day. Figure 10.3 shows some of the issues you must consider in these four rule areas.

A few moments of thought before these issues are raised in class can avoid embarrassing pauses and an uncertain response when a student asks a question. You may want to identify alternative issues for the remaining rule areas in Figure 10.2 and to extend those just listed to your own grade level.

The bottom half of Figure 10.2 identifies areas for which rules can be communicated as the situation arises. Some are specific to a particular situation (e.g., safety during a lab experiment, notebook completion, obtaining help) and are best presented in the context to which they apply. They will be more meaningful and more easily remembered *when a circumstance or event applies to the rule and thus aids*

Figure 10.3   Rules to establish on the first day of class.

Responding, speaking out	*Determining grades*
• Must hands be raised?	• What percentage will quizzes and tests contribute to the total grade?
• Are other forms of acknowledgement acceptable (e.g., head nod)?	• What percentage will class participation count?
• What will happen if a student speaks when others are speaking?	• When will notification be given of failing performance?
• What will you do about shouting or using a loud voice?	• How much will homework count?
Makeup work	*Violation of rules*
• Will makeup work be allowed?	• What happens when repeated violations occur?
• Will there be penalties for not completing it?	• Where can a student learn the due dates if absent?
• Will it be graded?	• What penalties are there for copying another person's assignment?
• Whose responsibility is it to know the work is missing?	• Will makeup work be required when a due date is missed?

in its retention. Many other rules in these areas, however, are likely to be needed in the first few days or weeks of school (e.g., tardiness/absences, leaving at the bell, note taking). Even though you may not communicate these rules on the first day of school, they usually are required so soon afterward that you must compose a procedure for them before your first class day.

Some of the most troublesome behaviors in this category include students getting out of their seats, communicating during group work, completing in-class assignments early, and violating rules. Issues to be considered for these behaviors include those shown in Figure 10.4.

Here are several general suggestions for creating classroom rules:

- Specify only necessary rules. There are four reasons to have rules, and each should reflect at least one of these purposes:

    Enhance work engagement and minimize disruption

    Promote safety and security

    Prevent disturbance to others or other classroom activities

    Promote acceptable standards of courtesy and interpersonal relations

- Make your rules consistent with the classroom climate you wish to promote. As a beginning teacher, now is the time to recognize your values and preferences for managing your classroom. Articulate your personal philosophy of classroom management, and have your class rules reflect it. For example, do you want your classroom climate to emphasize independent judgment, spontaneity, and risk taking, or do you want it to emphasize teacher-initiated exchanges, formal classroom rules, and teacher-solicited responses?

Figure 10.4 Rules that teachers should establish before the first day of class.

Getting out of seat

- When is out-of-seat movement permissible?
- When can a student come to the teacher's desk?
- When can reference books or learning centers be visited?
- What if a student visits another?

Communicating during group work

- Can a student leave an assigned seat?
- How loudly should a student speak?
- Who determines who can talk next?
- Will there be a group leader?

Early completion of in-class assignments

- Can work for other classes or subjects be done?
- Can a newspaper or magazine be read?
- Can the next exercise or assignment be worked on?
- Can students rest their heads on their desks?

Rule violation

- Will names be written on the board?
- Will extra work penalties be assigned?
- Will you have after-class detention?
- When will a disciplinary referral be made?

- Don't establish rules that you can't enforce. A rule that says "No talking," or "No getting out of your seat," may be difficult to enforce when your personal philosophy continually encourages spontaneity, problem solving, and group work. Unfairness and inconsistency may result in applying rules you do not fully believe in.
- State your rules at a general enough level to include a range of specific behaviors. The rule "Respect other people's property and person" covers a variety of problems, such as borrowing without permission, throwing objects, and so on. Similarly, the rule "Follow teacher requests" allows you to put an end to a variety of off-task, disruptive behaviors that no list of rules could anticipate or comprehensively cover. However, be careful not to state a rule so generally that the specific problems to which it pertains remain unclear to your learners. For example, a rule stating simply, "Show respect," or "Obey the teacher," may be sufficiently vague to be ignored by most of your learners and unenforceable by you. If you follow this suggestion and the preceding one, you should have about four to six classroom rules.

Unless you clearly communicate your rules and apply them consistently, all your work in making them will be meaningless. Consistency is a key reason why some rules are effective while others are not. Rules that are not enforced or that are not applied consistently over time result in a loss of prestige and respect for the person who has created the rules and has the responsibility for carrying them out.

Following are the most frequently occurring reasons why a particular rule is not applied consistently (Emmer et al., 1997):

1. The rule is not workable or appropriate. It does not fit a particular context or is not reasonable, given the nature of the individuals to whom it applies.
2. The teacher fails to monitor students closely, and consequently, some individuals violating the rule are caught while others are not.
3. The teacher does not feel strongly enough about the rule to be persistent about its enforcement and thus makes many exceptions to the rule.

Keep in mind that minor deviations to a rule may not be worth your effort to respond when (1) it would provide an untimely interruption to your lesson or (2) it is only momentary and not likely to recur. However, when problems in applying a rule persist over time, either increase your vigilance or adjust the rule to allow more flexibility in your response (e.g., coming up to the desk without permission for help may be acceptable, but coming up just to talk may not).

PROBLEM AREAS IN CLASSROOM MANAGEMENT

A primary purpose of effective classroom management is to keep learners actively engaged in the learning process. Active engagement means getting learners to work with and act on the material presented, as evidenced by carefully attending to the material, progressing through seatwork at a steady pace, participating in class discussions, and being attentive when called on. This section describes four events that are particularly crucial for keeping students actively engaged in the learning process: *monitoring students, making transitions, giving assignments*, and *bringing closure to lessons*. Following are some effective classroom management practices in each of these areas.

Monitoring Students

Monitoring is the process of observing, mentally recording, and, when necessary, redirecting or correcting students' behaviors. Monitoring occurs when you look for active, alert eyes during discussion sessions; faces down and directed at the book or assignment during seatwork; raised hands during a question-and-answer period; and, in general, signs that indicate that learners are participating in what is going on. These signs of engagement (or their absence) indicate when you need to change the pace of your delivery, the difficulty of the material, or even the activity itself.

Kounin (1970) used the word *with-it-ness* to refer to a teacher's ability to keep track of many different signs of engagement at the same time. Kounin observed that one of the most important distinctions between effective and ineffective classroom managers is the degree to which they exhibit withitness. Effective classroom managers who exhibited withitness were aware of what was happening in all parts of the classroom and were able to see different things happening in different parts of the room at the same time. Furthermore, these effective classroom managers were able to *communicate this awareness to their students*.

There are several simple ways to increase your withitness and the extent of your students' active engagement in the learning process. One way is to increase your physical presence through eye contact. If your eye contact is limited to only a portion of the classroom, you effectively lose withitness for the rest of the classroom. It is surprising to note that a great many beginning teachers consistently do the following:

Talk only to the middle-front rows.

Talk with their backs to the class when writing on the chalkboard.

Talk while looking toward the windows or ceiling.

Talk while not being able to see all students due to other students' blocking their view.

In each of these instances, you see only a portion of the classroom, and *the students know that you see only a portion of the classroom*. Your eye contact that covers all portions of the classroom is one of the most important ingredients in conveying a sense of withitness.

A second ingredient for improving withitness is learning to monitor more than one activity at a time. Here, the key not only is to change your eye contact to different parts of the room but also to change your focus of attention. For example, progress on assigned seatwork might be the focus of your observations when scanning students in the front of the class, but potential behavior problems might be your focus when scanning students in the back of the class.

You should switch back and forth from conduct-related observations to work-related observations at the same time you change eye contact. However, a great impediment to such switching is a tendency to focus exclusively on one student who is having either conduct- or work-related problems. Once other students realize you are preoccupied with one of their peers, problems with other students in other parts of the classroom may be inevitable.

Making Transitions

Another problem area is transitions. It is difficult to keep students' attention during a transition from one instructional activity to another. Moving the entire class from one activity to another in a timely and orderly manner can be a major undertaking. Problems in making these transitions often occur for two reasons: (1) learners are not ready to perform the next activity (or may not even know what it is), and (2) learners have unclear expectations about appropriate behavior during the transition.

When students are uncertain or unaware of what is coming next, they naturally become anxious about their ability to perform and to make the transition. This is the time when transitions can get noisy, with some students feeling more comfortable clinging to the previous activity than changing to the next. The beginning of the school year is a time of noisy transitions as students fumble to find the proper mate-

One approach to moving the entire class from one activity to another in a timely and orderly manner is to communicate clearly the actual divisions in time between activities.

rials (or guess which ones are needed) and to find out what is expected of them next. They will not rush headlong into a new activity, for fear they will not like it or will be unable to do well.

In this sense, transitions are as much psychological barriers as they are actual divisions between activities. Students must adjust their psychology for the next activity, just as they must adjust their books and papers. You can help in their adjustment by telling them the daily routine you expect of them. This routine becomes second nature after a few weeks, but it deserves special attention during the first days of school. This is the time for you to describe these daily activities and the order in which they will occur (e.g., 10 minutes of lecture, 15 minutes of questions and answers, 15 minutes of seatwork, and 10 minutes of checking and correcting).

Figure 10.5 provides some suggestions for addressing the problems that occur during transitions.

Giving Assignments

Another crucial time for effective classroom management is when you are giving or explaining assignments. This can be a particularly troublesome time because it often means assigning work that at least some students will not be eager to complete. Grunts and groans are common student expressions of distaste for homework or other assignments that must be completed outside of the regular school day. At times like these, outbursts of misbehavior are most likely to occur.

Evertson and Emmer (1982) found that one difference between effective and ineffective classroom managers was the manner in which they gave assignments, particularly homework. The difference was attributed to several simple procedures that were commonplace among experienced teachers but not among inexperienced teachers.

One procedure was to attach assignments directly to the end of an in-class activity. By doing so, the teacher avoided an awkward pause and even the need for a transition, because the assignment was seen as a logical extension of what already was taking place.

By contrast, imagine how you might feel being given an assignment under these conditions:

Teacher A: I guess I'll have to assign some homework now, so do problems 1 through 10 on page 61.

Teacher B: For homework, do the problems under Exercise A and Exercise B— and be sure all of them are finished by tomorrow.

Teacher C: We're out of time, so you'll have to finish these problems on your own.

In each of these assignments, there is a subtle implication that the homework may not really be needed or that it is being given mechanically or as some sort of punishment. Why this homework is being assigned may be a complete mystery to most stu-

Figure 10.5   Addressing problems that occur during transitions.

Problems	Solutions
Students talk loudly at the beginning of transitions.	It is difficult to *allow* a small amount of talking and *obtain* a small amount. So, establish a no-talking rule during transitions.
Students socialize during the transition, delaying the start of the next activity.	Allow no more time than is necessary between activities (e.g., to close books, gather up materials, select new materials).
Students complete assignments before the scheduled time for an activity to end.	Make assignments according to the time to be filled, not the exercises to be completed. Always assign more than enough exercises to fill the allotted time.
Students continue to work on the preceding activity after a change.	Give five-minute and two-minute warnings before the end of any activity and use verbal markers such as "Shortly we will end this work," and "Let's finish this up so that we can begin . . . " Create definite beginning and end points to each activity, such as "OK, that's the end of this activity; now we will start . . . " or "Put your papers away and turn to . . . "
Some students lag behind others in completing the previous activity.	Don't wait for stragglers. Begin new activities on time. When a natural break occurs, visit privately with students still working on previous tasks to tell them that they must stop and change. Be sure to note the reason they have not finished (e.g., material too hard, lack of motivation, off-task behavior).
You delay the beginning of the activity to find something (file cabinet keys, materials, roster, references, etc.).	Be prepared—pure and simple! Always have the materials you need in front of you at the start of the activity.

dents, because none of the teachers mentioned either the in-class activities to which the homework presumably relates or the benefits that may accrue from the assignment. Students expect and appreciate knowing why an assignment is made before they are expected to do it.

Now consider these assignments again, this time with some explanations added:

Teacher A: Today we have talked a lot about the origins of the Civil War and some of the economic unrest that preceded it. But some other types of unrest also were responsible for the Civil War. These will be impor-

	tant for understanding the real causes behind this war. Problems 1 through 10 on page 61 will help you understand some of these other causes.
Teacher B:	We have all had a chance now to try our skill at forming possessives. As most of you have found out, it's a little harder than it looks. So let's try Exercises A and B for tonight, which should give you just the right amount of practice in forming possessives.
Teacher C:	Well, it looks like time has run out before we could complete all the problems. The next set of problems we will study requires a lot of what we have learned here today. So, complete the rest of these tonight, to see if you've got the concept. This should make the next lesson go a lot smoother.

Keep in mind that effective classroom managers give assignments that immediately follow the lesson or activities to which they relate, that explain which in-class lessons the assignment relates to, and that avoid any *unnecessary* negative connotations (e.g., "finish them all," "be sure they are correct," "complete it on time"), which may make your assignment sound more like a punishment than an instructional activity.

It is also important that you convey assignments in a manner that motivates your students to complete them. Table 10.3 summarizes five different ways in which you can convey assignments positively and motivate your learners to continue engaging in the activity at a high level of involvement.

Finally, it is always a good idea to display prior assignments somewhere in your classroom so that students who have missed an assignment can conveniently look it up without requiring your time to remember or find an old assignment. A simple 2-foot square sheet of art board, divided into days of the month and covered with plastic to write on, can be a convenient and reusable way of communicating past assignments on a monthly basis.

Bringing Closure

Another time for effective classroom management is when you are bringing a lesson to its end. This is a time when students sense the impending end of the period and begin in advance of your close to disengage themselves from the lesson. It is a time when noise levels increase and students begin to fidget with books, papers, and personal belongings in anticipation of the next class or activity.

Closing comments also should serve a double purpose—not only ending the lesson but also keeping students actively engaged in the lesson until its very end by reviewing, summarizing, or highlighting its most important points. *Closure*, therefore, is more than simply calling attention to the end of a lesson. It means keeping the momentum of a lesson going by reorganizing what has gone before into a unified body of knowledge that can help students remember the lesson and place it into perspective. Following are ways you can keep your learners actively engaged at the end of your lessons and help them retain what you have taught.

Table 10.3 Some motivators and their appropriate use.

Motivator	Use phrases such as . . .	Motivator	Use phrases such as . . .
Using praise and encouragement	You've got it.	Accepting diversity	That's not the answer I expected, but I can see your point.
	Good work.		
	Good try.		
	That was quick.		That's not how I see it, but I can understand how others might see it differently.
Providing explanations	The reason this is so important is . . .		
			This is not something I'm familiar with. Where did you get that idea?
	We are doing this assignment because . . .		
	This will be difficult, but it fits in with . . .		That is not a word I've heard before. Tell us what it means.
	Experience has shown that without these facts the next unit will be very difficult.		All homework completed means five extra points.
Offering to help	Should you need help, I'll be here.	Emphasizing reinforcement and reward	If you get a *C* or better on all the tests, I'll drop the lowest grade.
	Ask if you need help.		
	I'll be walking around; catch me if you have a problem.		Those who complete all the exercises on time can go to the learning center.
	Don't be afraid to ask a question if you're having trouble.		If you have a *C* average, you get to choose any topic for your term paper.

Combining or Consolidating Key Points.   One way of accomplishing closure is by combining or consolidating key points into a single overall conclusion. Consider the following:

Teacher: Today we have studied the economic systems of capitalism, socialism, and communism. We have found each of these to be similar in that some of the same goods and services are owned by the government. We have, however, found them different with respect to the *degree* to which various goods and services are owned by the government: The least number of goods and services are owned by a government under capitalism, and the most goods and services are owned by a government under communism.

This teacher is drawing together and highlighting the single most important conclusion from the day's lesson. The teacher is doing so by expressing the highest-level generalization or conclusion from the lesson without reference to any of the details that were necessary to arrive at it. This teacher consolidated many different bits and pieces by going to the broadest, most sweeping conclusion that could be made, capturing the essence of all that went before.

Summarizing or Reviewing Key Content. Another procedure for bringing closure to a lesson is by summarizing or reviewing key content. The teacher reviews the most important content to be sure everyone understands it. Obviously, not all of the content can be repeated in this manner, so some selecting is in order, as illustrated by the following:

Teacher: Before we end, let's look at our two rules once again. Rule 1: Use the possessive form whenever an *of* phrase can be substituted for a noun. Rule 2: If the word for which we are denoting ownership already ends in an *s*, place the apostrophe after, *not* before, the *s*. Remember, both these rules use the apostrophe.

Now the teacher is consolidating by summarizing, or touching on each of the key features of the lesson. The teacher's review is rapid and to the point, providing students with an opportunity to fill in any gaps about the main features of the lesson.

Providing a Structure. Still another method for closing consists of providing learners with a structure by which they can remember key facts and ideas without an actual review of them. With this procedure, the teacher reorganizes facts and ideas into a framework for easy recall, as indicated in this example:

Teacher: Today we studied the formulation and punctuation of possessives. Recall that we used two rules: one for forming possessives wherever an *of* phrase can be substituted for a noun and another for forming possessives for words ending in *s*. From now on, let's call these rules the *of rule* and the *s rule*, keeping in mind that both rules use the apostrophe.

By giving students a framework for remembering the rules (the *of rule* and *s rule*), the teacher organizes the content and indicates how it should be stored and remembered. The key to this procedure is giving a code or symbol system whereby students can more easily store lesson content and recall it for later use.

Notice that in each of the previous dialogues, the teacher accomplished closure by looking back at the lesson and reinforcing its key components. In the first instance, the teacher accomplished this by restating the highest-level generalization that could be made; in the second, by summarizing the content at the level at which it was taught; and in the third, by helping students to remember the important categories of information by providing codes or symbols. Each of these closings has the potential of keeping your learners engaged when the main part of your lesson has ended. Endings to good lessons are like endings to good stories: they keep you engaged and in suspense and leave you with a sense that you have understood the story and can remember it long afterward.

LEARNER DIVERSITY AND CLASSROOM MANAGEMENT

A number of authors have studied the effects of various styles of classroom management and the engagement of their learners. For example, E. Hall (1977) found a connection between spatial distance and classroom order. The greater the spatial distance between teacher and student, the more some students became passive listeners and engaged in off-task behavior. As the teacher moved closer to students, communication tended to become more interactive, with more students following the wishes of the teacher. Hall observed that standing closer to individual students can promote compliance to classroom rules, since students will be drawn into nonverbal forms of communication, such as eye contact and changes in voice and body movement, that send a message of involvement.

Similarly, Scollon (1985) found the use of space can communicate a sense of social power, which can promote engagement *or* unengagement. For example, Bowers and Flinders (1991) report a case of a teacher who moved from student to student, checking work while on a swivel chair with casters. In this manner the teacher was able to elicit more spontaneous and relaxed student responses, resulting in greater student involvement and compliance with classroom rules. This was especially so among students who, by virtue of their language, culture, or ethnicity, did not wish to be spotlighted in the traditional teacher-dominated manner.

Other research has studied the compatibility of various classroom management techniques with the culture and ethnicity of the learner. Tharp and Gallimore (1989), D. Dillon (1989), and Bowers and Flinders (1991) present convincing arguments that different cultures react differently to nonverbal and verbal classroom management techniques that use space and distance (called *proximity control*), eye contact, warnings, and classroom arrangement (e.g., cooperative vs. competitive). Furthermore, they cite numerous examples of how teachers of different cultures interpret disruptive behaviors of children differently.

For example, facial expressions during a reprimand have been found to communicate different messages concerning the importance of the reprimand (H. Smith, 1984). Research by D. Dillon (1989) has pointed out that many actions of teachers may diminish engagement among minority students and/or build resentment because their actions are culturally incongruent. One of Dillon's suggestions is that teachers examine their own value and belief systems to become more aware how different they may be from their students and use the social organization of the classroom to bridge cultural gaps:

- Establish an open, risk-free classroom climate where students can experience mutual trust and confidence.
- Plan and structure lessons that meet the interests and needs of students.
- Implement lessons that allow all students to be active learners through activities and responsibilities that are congruent with the learners' cultures.

These are important considerations in understanding the culture and ethnicity of your classroom and establishing a culturally sensitive classroom management system.

Another classroom management challenge that you are likely to face in keeping your class engaged is the learner who is at risk academically. Academically at-risk learners can be among those who are most often off-task and disengaged. Students **at risk** for their academic performance are those who have difficulty learning at an average rate from the instructional resources, texts, workbooks, and learning materials that are designated for the majority of students in the classroom. These students need special instructional pacing, frequent feedback, supplemental instruction, and/or modified materials, all administered under conditions sufficiently flexible to keep them actively engaged in the learning process.

Learners who are at risk for poor academic performance usually are taught in one of two possible instructional arrangements: (1) a class composed mostly of average-performing students or (2) a class specifically designated for lower-performing students. The latter classes sometimes are part of a **track system** in which different sections of math, English, science, social studies, and so on are allocated for lower-performing, average, and higher-performing students. It is estimated that 80% of secondary schools and 60% of elementary schools use some form of tracking (O'Neil, 1992).

The desirability and fairness of various tracking systems, however, are being extensively debated (Gamoran, 1992; Mansnerus, 1992; Slavin, 1991a). The argument typically offered in favor of tracking is that it allows schools to better differentiate instruction by giving high achievers the challenge and low achievers the support they need to learn. Opponents argue that (1) tracking is undemocratic in that it separates learners into homogeneous groups unrepresentative of the world outside the classroom, and (2) recent research has indicated that it fails to increase learner achievement beyond what can be expected to occur in heterogeneous classrooms (Kavale, 1990; Skirtic, 1991; Slavin, 1987, 1990a).

Whether you meet at-risk learners in a regular class or in a tracked class, keeping at-risk learners engaged may require more than the usual variation in presentation methods (e.g., direct, indirect), classroom climate (e.g., cooperative, competitive), and instructional materials (e.g., practice activities, learning centers). Some characteristics of these learners that place them at risk for school failure and/or behavioral problems are their deficiency in basic skills (reading, writing, mathematics), their difficulty in dealing with abstractions, and their sometimes unsystematic or careless work habits, which may require instruction in note taking, listening, and organization skills. When these learning strategies are not provided as part of your instruction, the result can be a performance below the child's potential to learn, beginning a cycle of deficiencies that promotes poor self-concept, misbehavior, and disinterest in school—all of which have contributed to a particularly high dropout rate for this type of learner (Patterson, De Baryshe, & Ramsey, 1989; Walker & Sylwester, 1991).

Some instructional strategies that can help you keep at-risk learners engaged in your classroom follow:

- *Develop lessons around students' interests, needs, and experiences.* This will help heighten the attention of at-risk learners and actively engage them in the learning process. Design some instructional lessons with their specific interests or experiences in mind. Oral or written auto-biographies at the beginning of the year, or simple inventories in which students indicate their hobbies, jobs, and unusual trips or experiences can provide the basis for lesson plans, projects, and assignments that allow learners to construct their own meanings from direct experience and the interactions they have with others around them.
- *Encourage oral as well as written expression.* For at-risk learners, many writing assignments go unattempted or are begun only half-heartedly because these learners recognize that their written product will not meet minimal writing standards. Consider an audio- or videotaped assignment at the beginning of school; this has the advantage of avoiding spelling, syntax, and writing errors at a crucial time.
- *Provide study aids.* Study aids alert students to the most important problems, content, or issues. They also eliminate irrelevant details that at-risk learners can study in the belief that they are important. Example test questions or a list of source topics for possible questions can help focus student effort.
- *Teach learning strategies.* Learning strategies (Chapter 8) are general methods of thinking that improve learning across a variety of subject areas. They accomplish this by enhancing the way information is received, placed in memory, and activated when needed. You can increase the engagement of your at-risk learners by teaching elaboration/organization (e.g., note taking and outlining), comprehension and monitoring (e.g., setting goals, focusing attention, self-reinforcement), and problem-solving strategies (e.g., vocal and subvocal rehearsal).

PLANNING YOUR FIRST DAY

If your first class day is like that of most teachers, it will include some or all of these activities:

- Keeping order before the bell
- Introducing yourself
- Taking care of administrative business
- Presenting rules and expectations
- Introducing your subject
- Closing

Because your responses in these areas may set the tone in your classroom for the remainder of the year, let's consider your first-day planning in more detail to see how you can prepare an effective routine.

Before the Bell

As the sole person responsible for your classroom, your responsibility extends not just to when your classes are in session but to whenever school is in session. Consequently, you must be prepared to deal with students before your classes begin in the morning, between classes, and after your last class has ended—or anytime you are in your classroom. Your first class day is particularly critical in this regard, because your students' before-class peek at you will set in motion responses, feelings, and concerns that may affect them long after the bell has rung. Following are a few suggestions that can make these responses, feelings, and concerns positive ones:

1. To provide a sense of withitness (defined earlier in this chapter), stand near the door as students enter your classroom. In this way, you will come in direct contact with each student and be visible to them as they take their seats. Your presence at the doorway, where students must come in close contact with you, will encourage an orderly entrance (and exit) from the classroom. Remember, your class starts when the first student walks through your classroom door.

2. Have approximately four to six rules, divided between conduct and work, clearly visible on the chalkboard, bulletin board, overhead, or in the form of a handout already placed on each student's desk. You may want to prepare rules for the areas shown in the upper half of Figure 10.3 that you feel will be most critical to your classes during the first few days of school. You can formally introduce these rules later, but they should be clearly visible as students enter your class the first day.

3. Prepare a brief outline of your opening day's routine. This outline should list all the activities you plan to perform that day (or class period), in the order in which you will perform them. You can make a cue card for yourself. You can use a simple 4-by-6-inch index card to remind yourself:
   - Greet students and introduce yourself (5 minutes)
   - Take roll (5 minutes)
   - Fill out forms (10 minutes)
   - Assign books (15 minutes)
   - Present rules (10 minutes)
   - Introduce course content (0 to 10 minutes)
   - Remind students to bring needed materials (2 minutes)
   - Close (3 minutes)

In the elementary grades, this schedule easily can be amended to include an introduction to the entire day.

Let's look briefly at several of these activities for your first day.

Introducing Yourself

Introduce yourself by giving your name and something special about yourself, such as an area of interest or expertise. Your personality will, and should, unfold in small degrees during the first few weeks of school. There is no need to rush it. However, a small glimpse of the kind of person you are outside of the classroom often is a nice touch for students, who would like to see you as a friend as well as a teacher. A short comment about your interests, hobbies, or special experiences—even family or home life—often is appreciated by students, who at the end of this first day will be struggling to remember just who you are.

Administrative Business

Your first opportunity to meet your students up close will be while taking the roll. This is when you may want to turn the tables and have your students not only identify themselves but indicate some of their own interests, hobbies, or special experiences, especially as they may related to some of the things you will be teaching.

Your other administrative duties at this time can be considerable, and in some cases can consume most of the remainder of the class period at the upper grades and a full hour or more in the lower grades. Filling out forms requested by the school and school district, checking course schedules, guiding lost students to their correct rooms, and accepting new students during the middle of the class may all be part of your duties this first class day.

Rules and Expectations

Plan to devote some time to discussing your classroom rules and your overall expectations about both conduct and work. This is the time to remove student uncertainties and let your learners know what to expect. There is no better way to begin this process than by referring to the conduct and work rules that you either have posted for all to see or have handed out.

Introducing Your Subject

Although time may not permit you to present much content on the first day, we offer several tips for presenting content during your first lessons.

1. Begin teaching to the whole class. This is a time when not all of your students will be eager to participate in group work or seatwork or be relaxed enough to meaningfully contribute to inquiry or problem-solving type assignments. Effective indirect and self-directed instruction formats depend on the trust and confidence that students acquire from their experience with you over time. They will be acquiring this trust and confidence during your first days and weeks in the classroom.

2. During your initial days in the classroom, choose content activities that you believe everyone can successfully complete. At this time, you will not yet know the difficulty level most appropriate for your learners, so use this time to gradually try out the types of tasks and activities you eventually will ask your learners to perform, beginning with those from which you expect the most student success.

Closure

Have a definite procedure for closing in mind (e.g., a preview of things to come, instructions to follow for tomorrow's class, a reminder of things to bring to class). Begin closing a full 3 minutes before the bell is to ring. End with a note of encouragement that *all* of your students can do well in your grade or class.

SUMMING UP

This chapter introduced you to motivation and classroom management. Its main points were as follows:

1. Five types of social power or leadership that a teacher can strive for are expert power, referent power, legitimate power, reward power, and coercive power.

2. Four stages in which a successful group passes through are forming, storming norming, and performing.

3. *Distancing* is a type of amiable limit testing in which group members challenge academic expectations and rules in order to establish under what conditions they do or do not apply.

4. *Centering* is a second type of amiable limit testing in which learners question how they will personally benefit from being a group member.

5. Two basic processes by which norms develop are *diffusion* and *crystallization*. The former occurs when different academic and social expectations held by different members are spread throughout the group. The latter occurs when expectations converge and crystallize into a shared perspective.

6. Classroom climate refers to the atmosphere or mood in which interactions between you and your students take place. A classroom climate can be created by the social environment, which is related to the patterns of interaction you wish to promote in your classroom, and by the organizational environment, which is related to the physical or visual arrangement of the classroom.

7. The social climate of the classroom can extend from authoritarian (in which you are the primary provider of information, opinions, and instruction) to laissez faire (in which your students become the primary providers of information, opinions, and instruction).

8. Your role in establishing authority in the classroom and the social climate can vary. You can adopt different roles, including the following:
   - Commander-in-chief, who carefully controls and hones student behavior by organizing and providing all the stimuli needed for learning to occur
   - Translator or summarizer of ideas provided by students
   - Equal partner with students in creating ideas and problem solutions

9. The social climate of your classroom also can vary, depending on how competitive, cooperative, or individualistic you wish the interac-

tions among class members to be. Differences among these include extent of opportunities for students to express opinion, time devoted to student talk, and spontaneity with which your students are allowed to respond.

10. Organizational climate pertains to the physical or visual arrangement of the classroom and is determined by the positioning of desks, chairs, tables, and other internal features of a classroom.

11. The degree of competition, cooperation, and individuality in your classroom are a result of the social and organizational climate you create.

12. Rules can be divided into those that relate to one or more of four distinct areas:
    • Academic work
    • Classroom conduct
    • Information you must communicate your first teaching day
    • Information you can communicate later

13. Rules can be communicated orally, on the board, on a transparency, or in a handout. Rules for the early elementary grades should be presented orally, provided as a handout, and posted for reference. Rules for the elementary grades and junior high school may be recited and copied by students. Rules for high school may be given orally and then posted.

14. The following suggestions will help you develop classroom rules:
    • Make rules consistent with your climate.
    • Don't make rules that can't be enforced.
    • Specify only necessary rules.
    • State rules generally enough to include different but related behaviors.

15. Your inability to enforce a rule over a reasonable period of time is the best sign that you need to change the rule.

16. Monitoring students, making transitions, giving assignments, and bringing closure are four particularly troublesome areas of classroom management.

17. *Withitness* is a form of monitoring in which you are able to keep track of many different signs of student engagement at the same time.

18. You can convey assignments positively and motivate learners in the following ways:
    • Use praise and encouragement.
    • Provide explanations.
    • Offer to help.
    • Accept diversity.
    • Emphasize reward, not punishment.

19. Problems during transitions most frequently occur when learners are not ready to perform the next activity and do not know what behavior is appropriate during the transition.

20. Homework assignments should be given immediately following the lesson or activities to which they relate and without negative connotations.

21. Closing statements should gradually bring a lesson to an end by combining or consolidating key points into a single overall conclusion, by summarizing or reviewing key content, or by providing a symbol system whereby students can easily store and later recall the contents of the lesson.

22. You may use the following methods to bridge cultural gaps in the classroom:
    • Establish an open, risk-free climate.
    • Plan lessons that meet student interests and needs.
    • Allow for activities and responsibilities congruent with learners' cultures.

FOR DISCUSSION AND PRACTICE

Questions marked with an asterisk are answered in Appendix B. See also *Bridges: An Activity Guide and Assessment Options,* which accompanies this text.

*1. Describe in your own words the two types of social power beginning teachers should most quickly achieve. How would you achieve each?

*2. Imagine a group of learners similar to the classroom in which you will teach. Using specific examples of student behavior, identify the four stages of group development you will help your students through in order for them to function as a cohesive group.

3. Using examples of student classroom dialogue, illustrate the group behaviors of distancing and centering.

*4. What is meant by the diffusion and crystallization of norms? In what order can you expect these two basic processes of norm development to occur?

*5. What are three roles that communicate different levels of authority that you can assume in your classroom? How will expression of student opinions, proportion of student talk to teacher talk, and spontaneity of response change as a function of each of these three roles?

*6. Provide some example classroom activities that would result in (a) a competitive, (b) a cooperative, and (c) an individualistic classroom climate.

7. Draw three diagrams of the internal features of a classroom, each illustrating how to promote one of the three classroom climates in question 6.

8. Identify four academic rules and four conduct rules that you believe will be needed your first day of class. Write out a rule for each of these eight areas, exactly as you might show it to your students on a handout or transparency on the first day of class.

*9. Identify two rules whose retention might be aided if they were communicated in the context of a circumstance or incident requiring the rule. Describe each circumstance or incident.

*10. State three guidelines for developing effective classroom rules. Identify four rules that, in your opinion, follow these guidelines.

*11. Identify a practical strategy for deciding when you should revise or eliminate a rule. Which type of rule, academic or conduct, do you feel would need to be revised most?

12. Explain in your own words what *withitness* means. Give an example from your own experience of when you displayed withitness, and when you did not but should have. What were the consequences for you personally of each event?

*13. What are four teaching practices that can help avoid misbehavior during a transition? Which do you feel you would use the most?

*14. What are two ways discussed in this chapter that out-of-class assignments can be made more meaningful and accepted by your students? What other ways can you think of?

*15. Identify three ways you can bring a lesson to an end that can help students to organize the lesson in retrospect. Which one(s) best fits the grade or subject matter you will be teaching? Why?

16. What information about yourself would you feel comfortable communicating to your students on the first day of class? In what order might you present the information?

*17. If you were teaching in a culturally diverse or heterogeneous classroom, in what ways would you try to bridge the different cultures or social classes to form a productive and cohesive classroom?

C H A P T E R

11 Classroom Order and Discipline

This chapter will help you answer the following questions:

1. What is an effective classroom management plan?
2. What behaviors do effective classroom managers possess?
3. Which is more effective in changing the behavior of learners: rewards or punishment?
4. How do I plan a parent–teacher conference?
5. What is culturally responsive classroom management?

*A*nyone who reads the newspaper, listens to candidates running for public office, attends school board meetings, or overhears conversations in the teachers' lounge quickly realizes that classroom order and discipline are among education's most frequently discussed topics. Inability to control a class is one of the most commonly cited reasons for dismissing or failing to reemploy a teacher, and beginning teachers consistently rate classroom discipline among their most urgent concerns (Elam, Rose, & Gallup, 1996).

In Chapter 10, you learned about setting the tone for a manageable classroom. In this chapter, you will learn more specific techniques for preventing disruptive behaviors and managing an effective learning environment.

SYSTEMS OF CLASSROOM MANAGEMENT

Approaches to dealing with classroom management can be grouped into three traditions. One tradition emphasizes the critical role of communication and problem solving between teacher and students. This approach is called the *humanist tradition* of classroom management (Ginott, 1972; Glasser, 1986, 1990). The second tradition comes from the field of *applied behavior analysis*. This approach to classroom management emphasizes behavior modification techniques and reinforcement theory applied to the classroom (Alberto & Troutman, 1986; Canter, 1989; F. C. Jones, 1987). The third approach is the most recent, emphasizing the teaching skills involved in organizing and managing instructional activities and in presenting content and is called the *classroom management tradition* (Emmer et al., 1997; Evertson, 1997; Doyle, 1986; Kounin, 1970). This third approach, more so than the humanistic and applied behavior analysis traditions, underscores the critical role of prevention in managing classroom behavior. In this chapter we will briefly summarize the main features of these traditions, point out how they are used in the classroom, and show how the best features of each can be combined into a single approach. To begin, let's identify six criteria of an effective classroom management plan:

1. *Establish positive relationships among all classroom participants.* A positive, supportive classroom environment that meets students' needs for building trusting relations is a necessary foundation for managing an orderly classroom. In the previous chapter, we saw some of the ways you can build trusting relations.

2. *Prevent attention-seeking and work-avoidance behavior.* Time devoted to managing the classroom should be directed to engaging students in the learning process and preventing behaviors that interfere with it. Engagement and prevention include both arrangement of physical space and the teaching of rules for working in this space. In the previous chapter, we saw the importance of classroom climate and provided some guidelines and examples for teaching classroom rules.

3. *Quickly and unobtrusively redirect misbehavior once it occurs.* Most classroom problems take the form of minor off-task and attention-seeking behaviors. Techniques for coping with these events should not cause more disruption than the behavior itself.

4. *Stop persistent and chronic misbehavior with strategies that are simple enough to be used consistently.* Management systems that require responses to every act of positive or negative behavior may not be sufficiently practical to be implemented consistently in today's busy classrooms.

5. *Teach self-control.* Students should be allowed the opportunity to exercise internal control before the teacher imposes external control. When external controls are imposed, they should be implemented with plans for fading them out.

6. *Respect cultural differences.* Verbal and nonverbal techniques for redirecting disruptive behavior do not mean the same thing to all cultural groups. Likewise, systematic strategies involving rewards and consequences can violate important cultural norms.

Now, let's learn something about each of our three approaches to classroom management. As you read about them, see how each meets these criteria.

THE HUMANIST TRADITION IN CLASSROOM MANAGEMENT

The principles underlying the humanist tradition come from the practice of clinical and counseling psychology. It is called *humanist* because it focuses primarily on the inner thoughts, feelings, psychological needs, and emotions of the individual learner. Humanist approaches emphasize the importance of allowing the student time to develop control over his or her behavior rather than insisting on immediate behavioral change or compliance. Teachers using humanist approaches hope to achieve these ends through interventions stressing the use of communication skills, an understanding of student motives, private conferences, individual and group problem solving, and the exercise of referent and expert power.

Ginott's (1972) cooperation through congruent communication (also called the communication skills approach) and Glasser's (1990) cooperation through individual and group problem solving (also called cooperative learning and reality therapy) are examples of the humanist tradition. While each emphasizes a different area of skill that the effective classroom manager should possess, they essentially represent two sides of the same coin.

Ginott's Congruent Communication

The cardinal principle underlying Ginott's (1972) **congruent communication** skills approach is that learners are capable of controlling their own behavior if only teachers would allow them to do so. Teachers foster this self-control by allowing learners to choose how they wish to change their own behavior and how the class will be run. In addition, they help their students to deal with their inner thoughts and feelings through the use of effective communication skills.

The use of communication skills is the primary vehicle for influencing learners' self-esteem, which, in turn, is the primary force underlying acceptable behavior. Therefore, this tradition tries first and foremost to influence student behavior by enhancing student self-esteem. According to the proponents of this approach, congruent communication is the vehicle for promoting self-esteem.

Teachers have many opportunities during the school day to engage their students in congruent communication, usually during private conferences with students who misbehave. However, such communication also can go on during problem solving with the whole class. At such times, teachers communicate congruently when they do the following:

1. *Express "sane" messages.* Sane messages communicate to students that their behavior is unacceptable, but they do so in a manner that does not blame, scold, preach, accuse, demand, threaten, or humiliate. Sane messages describe what should be done rather than scold what was done. "Rosalyn, we are all supposed to be in our seats before the bell rings," in contrast to, "Rosalyn you're always gossiping at the doorway and coming late to class."

2. *Accept rather than deny feelings.* Teachers should accept the feelings of students about their individual circumstances rather than argue about them. If a student complains, "I have no friends," the teacher should accept the student's feeling of isolation and identify with the student, such as by saying, "So, you're feeling that you don't belong to any group," rather than by trying to convince the student that he or she has misperceived the social situation.

3. *Avoid the use of labels.* When talking to students about what they do well or poorly, teachers should avoid terms such as *lazy, sloppy,* and *bad attitude,* as well as *dedicated, intelligent,* or *perfectionist.* Instead, teachers should describe, in purely behavioral terms, what they like or don't like about stu-

dents. "You have a lot of erasures and white-outs on your homework," versus, "Your homework is sloppy." "You form your letters correctly," versus, "You are a good writer."

4. *Use praise with caution*. Ginott believes that many teachers use praise excessively and manipulatively to control student behavior rather than to acknowledge exceptional performance. They use praise judgmentally ("Horace, you are a good student"), confuse correctness with goodness (referring to a student who completes work with a minimum of mistakes as a "good child"), praise students performing minimally acceptable behavior as a way of influencing other students ("I like the way Joan is sitting in her seat"), and praise so often that the statements lose all significance and aren't even heard by the students. Ginott urges teachers to use praise only to acknowledge exceptional performance and in terms that separate the deed from the doer, for example, "That essay showed a great deal of original thought and research."

5. *Elicit cooperation*. Once a teacher and student have identified behavioral concerns, Ginott encourages teachers to offer them alternatives to solving the problem rather than using coercive power to tell them what to do. "Cooperate, don't legislate," is a convenient maxim to remember this point.

6. *Communicate anger*. Teachers are people, too. They get frustrated and angry just as anyone else. Ginott believes that teachers should express their feelings through the use of "I messages" instead of "you messages." The former focuses on your feelings about the behavior or situation that angered you ("You talked when the guest speaker was lecturing, and *I feel* very unhappy and embarrassed by that"). The latter puts the focus on the students and typically accuse and blame ("You were rude to the guest speaker"). "I messages" should be used when you own the problem, that is, when you are the one who is angry or upset.

If you were to resolve a classroom management problem using the humanist tradition, you might have an open discussion with your students to draw their attention to the problem. Then, you would invite their cooperation in developing mutually agreed rules and consequences. Finally, as problems arise, you would have individual conferences with your students during which you would use the preceding steps 1 through 6 to engage them in congruent communication.

Glasser's Cooperative Learning

Glasser (1990) points out that effective classroom managers create a learning environment where students want to be, develop mutually agreed standards of behavior that students must follow to remain in this environment, and conduct problem-solving conferences with those who violate the standards. Glasser advocates **cooperative learning** as a way to make the classroom a place learners want to be. Glasser believes classrooms emphasizing cooperative learning motivate all children to engage in learning activities. He believes whole-group instruction, in which students compete with one another for limited rewards, inevitably causes 50% of the students to be bored, frustrated, inattentive, or disruptive.

According to Glasser (1990), one response to disruptive behavior is discussing the problem with the student. During that time, you stress the importance of right choices and accept no excuses for wrong ones.

For Glasser (1990), dealing with disruptive students is straightforward, given a classroom where students experience belonging, power, and freedom—in other words, a classroom the learner would regret leaving. Faced with a student who persists in violating classroom rules the group believes are essential, Glasser states that the teacher should hold a brief, private conference with the student during which the student recalls the rules, and the teacher describes the disruptive behavior, asserts the need for following such rules, and makes clear the consequence for not obeying the rules, for example, removal from the room until the learner chooses to follow the rules. Glasser cautions teachers not to accept excuses from students for why they can't control their own behavior. He disagrees with teachers who use socioeconomic or sociocultural conditions as scapegoats or excuses for learners not making the right choices. For Glasser, there can be no excuse for disrupting an environment designed to meet learners' needs. Furthermore, when faced with removal from such an environment, Glasser believes students will choose, and will not need to be forced, to behave.

Glasser (1990) has a clear directive for you as you begin to manage your classroom: Begin building a more friendly workplace based on principles of cooperative learning. He has specific recommendations:

- Develop with your students rules for the workplace.
- Get support from school administrators for having an area to which disruptive students can be removed.
- Have private conferences with disruptive students during which you stress the importance of right choices and accept no excuses for wrong ones.
- Follow through when students must be removed, but always allow them the opportunity to return when they choose to follow class rules.

THE APPLIED BEHAVIOR ANALYSIS TRADITION IN CLASSROOM MANAGEMENT

The tradition of applied behavior analysis in classroom management is closely linked with Skinner's (1953) theory of learning called *behaviorism*, or *operant conditioning*. The techniques underlying the practice of behavior modification derive from this theory. Applications of behavior modification to changing socially important behaviors in the fields of education, business, and the social sciences has been called *applied behavior analysis* (Baer, Wolf, & Risley, 1968). To introduce both the strengths and weaknesses of this tradition, we first review the components of behavior modification that have resulted from this approach.

Behavior Modification

Behavior modification, as its name implies, focuses on changing or modifying behavior. Behavior is something a person does that is seen, heard, counted, or captured, say, in a snapshot or a home video.

Figure 11.1 summarizes some of the most important concepts of behavior modification. As Figure 11.1 indicates, when you want to teach a new behavior or make an existing behavior occur more frequently (e.g., spell more words correctly), you must follow the behavior with some type of reinforcement. Reinforcement can be both positive and negative. **Positive reinforcement** occurs when a desired stimuli or reward you provide after a behavior increases its frequency of occurrence. **Negative reinforcement** occurs when the frequency of a behavior is increased by ending or terminating some painful, uncomfortable, or aversive state. In other words, the actions you take to turn off an annoying sound (shut the radio off), or relieve a headache (aspirin), or end a frustrating experience (walk away) will likely be repeated again (learned) the next time you experience a similar source of annoyance, discomfort, or frustration.

Negative reinforcement refers to escape or avoidance learning to strengthen the behavior, not simply to the application of discomfort or punishment. Thorndike (1913), for example, used negative reinforcement to teach cats how to escape a puzzle box. To get out of the box, the cat had to pull a cord hanging from the top of the

Figure 11.1 The process of behavior modification.

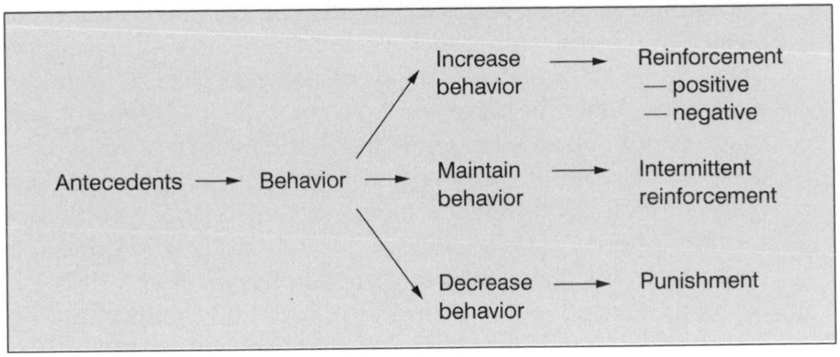

box. As soon as the cat succeeded, the door opened and it escaped. The next time the cat was placed in the same box, the cat pulled the cord because it had learned how to escape to avoid the uncomfortable condition.

The reason negative reinforcement is important in the classroom is that learners often experience events they want to avoid: boring or difficult work, a scolding, requests to do something they don't want to do, or to stop doing something they want to continue. For example, when a shy student learns that when she doesn't look at the teacher the teacher stops calling on her, then the not-looking-at-the-teacher behavior becomes negatively reinforced. Or, when a learner makes distracting sounds during a lecture to get the teacher to send him out of the room, the teacher negatively reinforces the making-of-annoying-sounds behavior. Or, when some learners don't pay attention to get the teacher to stop the lesson, their not-paying-attention behavior becomes negatively reinforced. In other words, the teacher has taught these learners to pursue certain behaviors to escape or avoid an unpleasant condition.

As these examples illustrate, a teacher may inadvertently fall into the trap of "negative reinforcement" that learners unconsciously set. In fact, some psychologists believe that more inappropriate behavior is learned through negative than positive reinforcement, that is by learning what it takes to avoid or escape something undesirable than by being rewarded for doing something appropriate (positive reinforcement) (Iwata, 1987).

When you are satisfied with a particular behavior and how frequently it occurs, *intermittent reinforcement* can be applied to maintain the behavior at its present level. For example, consider a student who at the start of the school year was consistently late and unprepared for class, but now is beginning to arrive on time. You can maintain this behavior by reinforcing the student on a random or intermittent schedule, for example, every second day, every fourth day, or on randomly selected days. This procedure is called intermittent reinforcement. An example of intermittent reinforcement is putting tokens into a slot machine long after your last win or fishing in the same spot long after your last nibble.

Behavioral antecedents are events (or stimuli) that are present when you perform a behavior that elicit or set off the behavior. Antecedents can be *sounds* (e.g., a noisy room influences students to become more noisy, an insult from a peer influences you to give an insult back, or the tone of voice in a teacher's demand influences a child to argue back), *sights* (the teacher raises finger to lips to indicate silence or flips the light switch on and off), *people* (the principal walks in, and everyone gets quiet), *materials* (math worksheets elicit a groan), or *places* (the auditorium elicits different behaviors from the principal's office). Behaviorists believe that much of our behavior has come under the control of antecedents (called *antecedent control*) because of the repeated pairing of reinforcers or punishers following the behavior with environmental stimuli (sounds, sights, people, and materials).

Applications of these principles to schools have produced a variety of systems or procedures for changing a student's behavior. Some of these procedures involve ignoring disruptive behavior and immediately reinforcing positive behavior. The assumption underlying these procedures is that disruptive students may have learned misguided ways of satisfying their needs for recognition. These disruptive behaviors will become less frequent when they learn that they will only gain recognition and rewards (receive positive reinforcement) when they behave well.

Other systems are built on the assumption that children learn desired behavior most efficiently when adults immediately punish inappropriate behavior and immediately reward appropriate behavior. The authors of these systems believe that behavior will improve more rapidly when adults use both timely punishment and timely reward rather than either punishment or reinforcement alone. These systems routinely involve such punishment procedures as time-out, where the teacher immediately removes the student to an area where he or she can experience no reinforcement of any kind following a disruptive act; response cost, where the teacher removes a students' privilege or reinforcer, contingent on disruptive behavior (also called *fines*); or overcorrection, where students not only make amends for what they did wrong but also go beyond it by contributing something positive. For example, a student who defaces a desk not only must clean the desk he wrote on but must clean every other desk in the room as well. Or, a student who insults another student apologizes to that student *and* to the whole class.

Although specific approaches may vary, if you were to invite an applied behavior analyst to help you with a behavior problem, he or she would likely suggest the following steps for improving a learner's behavior:

- Identify both the inappropriate behavior you wish to change *and* the appropriate behavior you want to take its place.
- Identify the antecedents to both the inappropriate and appropriate behavior (e.g., influential peer), and make necessary changes in the classroom environment (e.g., change seating arrangement) to prevent the former from occurring and to increase the likelihood of the latter.
- Identify the student's goal or purpose behind the inappropriate behavior (e.g., attention seeking), and discontinue actions on your part (or those of peers) that satisfy this purpose.
- Establish procedures for reinforcing the appropriate behavior that you want to replace the inappropriate behavior.
- Use punishment only as a last resort.

THE CLASSROOM MANAGEMENT TRADITION

Throughout much of the latter half of this century, classroom discipline was focused on the question of how best to respond to student misbehavior. The humanist and the applied behavior analysis approach to classroom management shared the spotlight about equally during this period. As shown in the previous sections, both of these traditions are primarily *reactive* rather than preventive systems of classroom management. That is, they tend to emphasize solutions to misbehavior after rather than before it occurs. The 1970s and 1980s, however, provided another approach to classroom management that framed the question of classroom order and discipline, not in terms of reaction, but in terms of prevention. This approach was based on classroom research that examined what effective teachers do to prevent misconduct and what less effective teachers do to create it.

Some of this research involved observation and analysis of both experienced and inexperienced teachers while they taught. The major conclusion of this research was that more effective and less effective classroom managers can be distinguished more by what they do to *prevent* misbehavior than how they respond to misbehavior. In this section we will explain how the researchers came to this conclusion and the characteristics of effective classroom managers they found. But, first, let's look at one study of classroom management and how it was conducted.

Emmer, Evertson, and Anderson (1980) recruited 27 third-grade teachers in eight elementary schools into a year-long observation study. Using the average rate of student engagement and student off-task behavior obtained after the first 3 weeks of school, the researchers classified the teachers into two groups, one consisting of the more effective managers and the other consisting of the less effective managers. Those teachers who were categorized as more effective classroom managers had significantly higher student engagement rates (more students actively engaged in the goals of the lesson) and significantly lower student off-task behavior (fewer reprimands and warnings) throughout the school year. Then, Emmer et al. used observation data pertaining to the classroom management procedures of these teachers during the first 3 weeks of school to compare the two groups.

During the first 3 weeks of school, observers gathered several types of information on each of the teachers, including room arrangement, classroom rules, consequences of misbehavior, response to inappropriate behavior, consistency of teacher responses, monitoring, and reward systems. In addition, observers counted the number of students who were on task or off task at 15-minute intervals to determine the extent to which students were attending to the teacher.

The more effective managers established themselves as instructional leaders early in the school year. They worked on rules and procedures until students learned them. Instructional content was important for these teachers, but they also stressed group cohesiveness and socialization, achieving a common set of classroom norms. By the end of the first 3 weeks, these classes were ready for the rest of the year.

In contrast to the more effective managers, the less effective managers did not have procedures well worked out in advance. This was most evident among the first-year teachers being observed. For example, the researchers described one new teacher who had no procedures for using the bathroom, pencil sharpener, or water fountain, and as a result, the children seemed to come and go, complicating the teacher's instructional tasks.

The poorer managers, like the better managers, had rules, but there was a difference in the way the rules were presented and followed up. In some cases, the rules were vague: "Be in the right place at the right time." In other cases, they were introduced casually without discussion, leaving it unclear to most children when and where a rule applied.

The poorer managers were also ineffective monitors of their classes. This was caused, in part, by the lack of efficient routines for pupil activities. In other cases this was the result of teachers removing themselves from the active surveillance of the whole class to work at length with a single child. A major result of the combination of vague and untaught rules and poor procedures for monitoring and establishing routines was that students were frequently left without sufficient guidance to direct their own activities.

One further characteristic of the less effective managers was that the consequences of good behavior and inappropriate behavior were either not in evidence in those classrooms or were not delivered in a timely manner. For example, sometimes teachers issued general criticisms that failed to identify a specific offender or a particular event. Some of these teachers would frequently threaten or warn children but not follow through, even after several warnings. This tended to allow children to push the teacher to the limits, causing more problems. Others issued vague disciplinary messages ("You're being too noisy") that were not adequately focused to capture the attention of any one child or subgroup of children to whom they were intended. It was easy to see how deficiencies in the areas of rules, establishment of routines, monitoring, and praise and reward structure negatively affected the overall management and organization of the classroom. Most of the time these deficiencies became windows of opportunity that prompted a wider range of pupil misconduct, off-task behavior, and disengagement from the goals of the classroom. After only a few weeks had elapsed in the less effective managers' classrooms, undesirable patterns of behavior and low teacher credibility tended to become established that persisted throughout the school year.

From this and related studies of classroom management (Evertson, 1995; Evertson & Emmer, 1982; Tauber, 1990), we learn that effective classroom managers possess three broad classes of effective teaching behaviors:

- They devote extensive time before and during the first few weeks of school to planning and organizing their classroom to minimize disruption and enhance work engagement.
- They approach the teaching of rules and routines as methodically as they approach teaching their subject area. They provide their students with clear instructions about acceptable behavior and monitor student compliance with these instructions carefully during the first few weeks of school.
- They inform students about the consequences for breaking rules and enforce these consequences consistently.

As you can see, the classroom management tradition is essentially a preventive approach. It has a lot to say about how to ensure that behavior problems do not occur. But it offers few immediate solutions after the problem has occurred, since it emphasizes planning in anticipation of problems, not their resolution afterward. You will need a comprehensive plan incorporating elements of all three traditions to make your classroom a positive environment for learning.

AN INTEGRATED APPROACH TO CLASSROOM MANAGEMENT

All three approaches to classroom management have their advantages and limitations. While each has made a significant contribution to our understanding of an effective classroom manager, teachers do not need to select one tradition over another. In fact, the research conducted by Emmer et al. (1980), Evertson and Emmer (1982), and Doyle (1986) has shown that effective classroom managers are able to blend together the best parts of different approaches. Let's look at some of the ways effective teachers have been able to accomplish this.

Low-Profile Classroom Control

Leriche (1992) and Rinne (1984) have used the concept of **low-profile classroom control** to refer to coping strategies used by effective teachers to stop misbehavior without disrupting the flow of a lesson. These techniques are effective for "surface behaviors" (J. Levin & Nolan, 1991), which represent the majority of disruptive classroom actions. Examples of surface behaviors are laughing, talking out of turn, passing notes, daydreaming, not following directions, combing hair, doodling, humming, tapping, and so on. They are labeled **surface behaviors** because they are the normal developmental behaviors that children find themselves doing when confined to a small space with large numbers of other children. They do not indicate some underlying emotional disorder or personality problem. However, they can disrupt the flow of a lesson and the work engagement of others if left unchecked.

Figure 11.2 depicts the components of low-profile classroom control. Low-profile control for dealing with surface misbehavior is actually a set of techniques that requires *anticipation* by the teacher to prevent problems *before they occur; deflection* to redirect disruptive behavior that is *about to occur*; and *reaction* to unobtrusively stop disruptions immediately *after they occur*. Let's look at each of these.

Anticipation.   Alert teachers have their antennae up to sense changes in student motivation, attentiveness, arousal level, or excitability, as these changes are or are about to happen. They are aware that, at certain times of the year (before and after holidays), or week (just before a major social event), or day (right after an assembly or physical education class), the readiness of the class for doing work will be different from what usually can be expected. Skilled classroom managers are alert not only to changes in the groups' motivational or attention level but also to changes in specific individuals, which may be noticed as soon as they enter class.

Figure 11.2 Characteristics of low-profile control.

Anticipation	Deflection	Reaction
Lower Profile ◄	►	Higher Profile
• Scanning	• Proximity	• Warning
• Pick up the pace	• Eye contact	• Loss of privileges
• Remove temptation	• Prompting	• "Time out"
• Boost interest	• Name dropping	• Removal
• Change seating arrangements	• Peer recognition	• Detention

At these times *anticipation* involves scanning back and forth with active eyes to quickly size up the seriousness of a potential problem and head it off before it emerges or becomes a bigger problem. For example, you may decide to pick up the pace of the class to counter some perceived lethargy in the class after a 3-day weekend or remove magazines or other objects that may distract attention from the individual or group before a long holiday. Some teachers maintain a reserve of activities likely to boost the interest of their students during times when it is difficult to stay focused on normal day-to-day activities. Others boost interest by forcing themselves to be more positive or eager in the face of waning student enthusiasm, for example, by raising and lowering the pitch of their voice and moving to different parts of the room more frequently. At other times it may be necessary to quickly change seating arrangements to minimize antagonisms when arguments between students occur. Anticipation involves not only knowing what to look for but also where and when to look for it. It also involves having a technique ready, no matter how small, for changing the environment quickly and without notice to your students to prevent the problem from occurring or escalating.

Deflection. As noted, good classroom managers sense when disruption is about to occur. They are attuned to verbal and nonverbal cues that in the past have preceded disruptive behavior. The applied behavior analysts would call these behavioral cues *antecedents* or *precursors*. They take the form of a glance, an abruptly closed textbook, sitting and doing nothing, squirming, asking to be excused, ignoring a request, a sigh of frustration, or a facial expression of annoyance or anger. Although not disruptive by themselves, these behaviors may signal that more disruptive behavior is about to follow.

Some teachers can detect the significance of these antecedents and deflect them by simply moving nearer to the student who may be about to misbehave, thus preventing a more disruptive episode from occurring. Other teachers may make eye contact with the learner combined with certain facial expressions, for example, raising of eyebrows or slight tilt of the head, to communicate a warning. Both these techniques effectively use nonverbal signals to deflect a potential problem. But verbal signals are also effective. Verbal deflection techniques include *prompting*, where the teacher reminds the class of the rule or says, "We are all supposed to be doing math, now"; *name dropping*, when the target student's name is inserted into the teacher's explanation or lecture, as in, "Now if Angela were living in Boston at the time of the Boston Tea Party, she might have . . . "; and *peer recognition*, in which the teacher notices a peer engaged in appropriate behavior and acknowledges this to the class. As potential for the problem to escalate increases, the effective manager shifts from nonverbal to verbal techniques to keep pace with the seriousness of the misbehavior that is about to occur.

Reaction.   Anticipation and deflection can efficiently and unobtrusively prevent actions from disrupting the flow of a lesson. They allow students the opportunity to correct *themselves*, thus fostering the development of self-control. However, the classroom is a busy place, and you will have many demands on your attention, which may make a behavior difficult to anticipate or to deflect.

When disruptive behavior occurs that you cannot anticipate or unobtrusively redirect, your primary goal should be to end the disruptive episode as quickly as possible. Effective classroom managers, therefore, must at times react to a behavior by providing a warning or an incentive to promote positive self-control. Your reaction requires first that you have included among your class rules a rule that corresponds with the behavior in question and the consequences for violating the rule. Glasser (1990) points out that an effective consequence for breaking a rule is temporary removal from the classroom—provided that your classroom is a place where that student wants to be—or loss of privileges, school detention, loss of recess, or other activity that the learner would miss.

When disruptive behavior occurs, your anticipation-deflection-reaction would be similar to the following:

1. As soon as a student disrupts, acknowledge a nearby classmate who is performing the expected behavior, "Carrie, I appreciate how hard you are working on the spelling words." Then, wait 15 seconds for the disruptive student to change his or her behavior.

2. If the disruption continues say, "Carlos, this is a warning. Complete the spelling assignment and leave Carrie alone." Wait 15 seconds.

3. If the student doesn't follow the request after this warning, say, "Carlos, you were given a warning. You must now leave the room for 5 minutes (*or* you must stay inside during lunch or cannot go to the resource center today). I'll talk to you about this during my free period."

Dealing with Persistent Disruptive Behavior

The low-profile techniques of anticipation, deflection, and reaction when used skillfully should promote lesson flow. Occasionally, when these techniques do not work for a particular student or group of students, it may be a signal that the needs of the student are not being met. When disruptive behavior persists and you have assured yourself that you have taken low-profile steps to deal with it, you may need to increase the intensity of your involvement in responding to the problem.

Responses to Misbehavior

There are many responses at your disposal for dealing with misbehavior. You may choose to ignore an infraction if it is momentary and not likely to recur (e.g., when students jump out of and back into their seats to stretch their legs after a long assignment). At the other extreme, you may call an administrator to help resolve the problem. Between these extremes are many alternatives; listed here in order of increasing severity:

- Look at the student sternly.
- Walk toward the student.
- Call on the student to provide the next response.
- Ask the student to stop.
- Discuss the problem with the student.
- Assign the student to another seat.
- Assign punishment, such as a writing assignment.
- Assign the student to detention.
- Write a note to the student's parents.
- Call the student's parents.

These alternatives vary in severity from simply giving the student a look of dissatisfaction to involving parents in resolving the problem. More important than the variety these alternatives offer, however, is your ability to *match the correct response to the type of misbehavior that has occurred*. One of the most difficult problems you will encounter in effectively maintaining classroom discipline will be deciding on a response that is neither too mild nor too severe (Sugai, 1996).

Although all rule violations consistently must receive some response, the severity of the consequence can and should vary according to the nature of the violation and the frequency with which such a violation has occurred in the past. If you respond too mildly to a student who has violated a major rule many times before, nothing is likely to change. If you respond too severely to a student who commits a minor violation for the first time, you will be unfair. Flexibility is important in the resolution of different discipline problems and must take into account *both the context in which the violation occurs and the type of misbehavior that has occurred*.

Here is some general advice for dealing with mild, moderate, and severe misbehavior:

- Mild misbehaviors like talking out, acting out, getting out of seat, disrupting others, and similar misbehaviors deserve a mild response, *at first*. But if they occur repeatedly, a moderate response may be appropriate. In unusual cases, such as continual talking that disrupts the class, a severe response may be warranted.

- Moderate misbehaviors like cutting class, abusive conduct toward others, fighting, and use of profanity deserve a moderate response, *at first*. But if these behaviors become frequent, a severe response may be warranted.
- Severe misbehaviors like cheating, plagiarism, stealing, and vandalism deserve a severe response. But don't try to handle major incidents of vandalism, theft, incorrigible conduct, and substance abuse in your classroom. Immediately bring these to the attention of school administrators.

Table 11.1 presents responses you can make to mild, moderate, and severe misbehavior.

Reinforcement Theory Applied in the Classroom

Clearly, there are multiple ways to use your authority in managing discipline problems (you alone decide the consequence; you have students share in the responsibility; you choose the consequence from alternatives provided by the student) and multiple levels of response severity (from a stern glance to calling parents). But still more options exist. In this section you will learn how learners respond to reward and to punishment, why they respond to them differently, and how you can use them effectively in your classroom.

Reinforcement theory states that behavior can be controlled by the consequences that immediately follow it. The word *controlled* means that the consequences of a particular behavior can change the likelihood that the behavior will recur. Consider the following:

Event	Consequence	Future Event
You start going to the library to study.	Your test grades go up.	You begin going to the library more often.
You go to a new restaurant.	You get lousy service.	You never go there again.
You give your boyfriend or girlfriend a word of encouragement before a big test.	He or she gives you a kiss and a hug.	You give a word of encouragement before every big test.

When the consequence following a behavior changes the probability of that behavior's occurrence (test grades go up; you don't go there again; you get more kisses and hugs), reinforcement has occurred.

In your classroom, many events and their consequences will demonstrate the effects of reinforcement—whether you intend it or not. You may be surprised to learn that you are unintentionally increasing the frequency of some misbehaviors in your classroom through reinforcement. How can this happen? Consider another sequence of behaviors that, unknown to you, may occur in your classroom:

Table 11.1 Examples of mild, moderate, and severe misbehaviors and some alternative responses.

Misbehaviors	Alternative Responses
Mild misbehaviors	**Mild responses**
Minor defacing of school property or property of others	Warning
Acting out (horseplaying or scuffling)	Feedback to student
Talking back	Time out
Talking without raising hand	Change of seat assignment
Getting out of seat	Withdrawal of privileges
Disrupting others	Afterschool detention
Sleeping in class	Telephone/note to parents
Tardiness	
Throwing objects	
Exhibiting inappropriate familiarity (kissing, hugging)	
Gambling	
Eating in class	
Moderate misbehaviors	**Moderate responses**
Unauthorized leaving of class	Detention
Abusive conduct toward others	Behavior contract
Noncompliant	Withdrawal of privileges
Smoking or using tobacco in class	Telephone/note to parents
Cutting class	Parent conference
Cheating, plagiarizing, or lying	In-school suspension
Using profanity, vulgar language, or obscene gestures	Restitution of damages
Fighting	Alternative school service (e.g., clean up, tutoring)
Severe misbehaviors	**Severe responses**
Defacing or damaging school property or property of others	Detention
Theft, possession, or sale of another's property	Telephone/note to parents
Truancy	Parent conference
Being under the influence of alcohol or narcotics	In-school suspension
Selling, giving, or delivering to another person alcohol, narcotics, or weapons	Removal from school or alternative school placement
Teacher assault or verbal abuse	
Incorrigible conduct, noncompliance	

Event	Consequence	Future Event
Johnny cheats on a test.	He gets a good grade.	Johnny plans to cheat again.
Mary passes a note to her boyfriend.	Her boyfriend is able to pass a note back.	Mary buys a special pad of perfumed paper for writing more notes in class.
Bobby skips school.	He earns $5 helping a friend work on a car.	Bobby plans to skip again the next time his friend needs help.

In each instance an undesirable behavior was reinforced (with a good grade, a returned note, $5). In each case the probability of recurrence increased because the consequence was desirable. In these examples, there is nothing you could have done, because your vigilance cannot be perfect: You didn't know about the cheating, note, or that school was missed for the wrong reason. But here are some ways you may unwittingly reinforce undesirable behaviors, which you *can* do something about:

- A student complains incessantly that her essay was graded too harshly. To quiet her, you add a point to her score. Reinforced, she complains after every essay for the rest of the year.
- Parents complain to you about their child's poor class participation grade. You start calling on the student more often, probing and personally eliciting responses. Reinforced, the student believes she no longer needs to volunteer or raise her hand.
- A student talks back every time you call on him, so you stop calling on him. Reinforced, he does the same in his other classes, to be left alone.

In each of these cases, the link connecting the behavior, the consequence, and the students' perception of the consequence might not be immediately apparent to you. Nevertheless, reinforcement of an undesirable behavior occurred.

The problem in each instance was that you chose to remove the misbehavior in a way that rewarded the student, thereby actually reinforcing the misbehavior. Notice that in each case you considered the consequence of your actions *only from your own point of view* (e.g., quieting an annoying student, preventing a parent from calling back, avoiding an ill-mannered student), without realizing that your actions *reinforced* the very behavior you wished to discourage.

Now that you see how reinforcement theory works, here are some guidelines for making it work not against you but for you.

Rewards and Reinforcement.   Many types of rewards and reinforcement are available to increase the probability of a desirable response. A reward or reinforcement can be *external*, delivered by some other person, or *internal*, provided by the learner himself or herself. Here are some familiar external rewards commonly found in the classroom:

- Verbal or written praise
- Smile, a head nod
- Special privileges (e.g., visit to the learning center, library, etc.)
- Time-out of regular work to pursue a special project (e.g., lab experiment)
- Permission to choose a topic or assignment
- Getting to work in a group
- Extra points toward grade
- "Smiley face" stickers on assignments
- Note to parents on top of a test or paper
- Posting a good exam or homework for others to see
- Special recognitions and certificates (e.g., "most improved," "good conduct award," "neatest," "hardest worker," etc.)

Not all of these external rewards may be equally reinforcing, however. Some learners may disdain verbal praise; others will have no desire to visit the library or learning center. Some students like to be called on; others may be too shy and dislike the added attention. A reinforcement for one student may be completely irrelevant to another.

Educators have sometimes been criticized for creating a generation of learners who are hooked on artificial or extrinsic rewards in order to learn and behave in classrooms (de Charms, 1976). This has led to an increased interest in the use of internal rewards, also called **natural reinforcers**. An internal (natural) reward or reinforcer is one that is naturally present in the setting where the behavior occurs.

Some learners are naturally reinforced by learning to write, read, color, answer questions, play sports, solve equations, answer textbook questions, and write essays. But some are not. Many learners may require external reinforcers to begin to engage in certain classroom activities they do not find naturally reinforcing. For such chil-

Rewards consistent with the goals of your classroom and matched to student interests keep learners engaged in the learning process and responding at high rates of success.

dren, external reinforcers have an important role to play: They (1) allow you to shape and improve the behaviors you desire through the use of positive reinforcement and (2) enable you to transfer their control over the learner's behavior to natural reinforcers. This transfer from external to internal control is called **operant conditioning** (Horcones, 1992). Over the past decade, researchers have developed strategies for transferring the control of extrinsic reinforcers to that of natural reinforcers:

Step 1: Select the target behavior.   This could be forming letters correctly, solving multiplication problems, drawing geometric figures, bisecting angles, writing compositions, or whatever is appropriate.

Step 2: Identify the natural consequences of the selected behavior.   For example, writing on a piece of paper produces many natural consequences: a scratching sound, the formation of letters, the filling up of a page, the gradual wearing away of a pencil point. Writing an essay has similar natural consequences but, in addition, produces sentences that express thoughts, ideas, images, and so on.

Step 3: Choose intrinsic consequences.   From your list of natural consequences, select those likely to be reinforcing to the person and relevant to the purpose of the activity. For example, the formation of the letters is a more appropriate consequence to focus on than the scratching sound on the paper or the filling up of the page.

Step 4: Identify those consequences the learner may more easily notice. The more conspicuous the consequence to the learner, the easier it will be to condition this as a natural reinforcer. For example, the shape of a printed word is a conspicuous consequence of correct handwriting and may serve as a natural reinforcer. Likewise, writing a complete thought, coming up with an answer that matches that in the back of the textbook, or the feeling you get when something is finished can all serve as natural reinforcers.

Step 5: Design your lessons in such a way that you make conspicuous the occurrence of natural consequences.   Rather than focusing only on the right answer to a problem, point out and describe for the learner the sequence involved. In general, focus on how something was done, not just on the end result. Some learners may not notice or direct their attention to the natural consequences of their work. By setting up instructional conditions to do this, you allow for natural reinforcers to acquire power over behavior.

Step 6   Select appropriate backup reinforcers.   To transfer the power an extrinsic reinforcer has over behavior to a natural consequence, you must select extrinsic or backup reinforcers. These reinforcers should have educational value, be available in your classroom, and, ideally, involve you in the reinforcing activity (Horcones, 1991).

Step 7   Condition the natural reinforcer.   Have your learners engage in the behavior. As soon as possible, give informational feedback, pointing out the natural consequences that you hope will become natural reinforcers. Immediately, give the backup reinforcers. Gradually, remove these reinforcers from the learning setting but continue to point out and illustrate the natural consequences of what the learner did. Gradually, point out the natural consequences less and less. Deliver and intermittently pair the backup reinforcers with the natural reinforcers.

Punishment

Punishment is used to decrease the probability or likelihood that a behavior will occur. For example, you can try to keep Daniel in his seat either (1) by giving him an extra assignment every time he is out of his seat or (2) by giving him a trip to the reading center for every 30 minutes he stays in his seat. In the first instance, you are giving Daniel a *punishment* to encourage him to do what's expected, and in the second you are giving him a *reward* to achieve this same end. Punishment creates an avoidance response to an undesirable behavior. On the other hand, a reward encourages a desirable behavior to recur by dispensing something pleasant or rewarding immediately after the desirable behavior.

But rewards and punishments generally are not equally effective in promoting a desired behavior. Given two choices to keep Daniel in his seat—the punishment of extra homework, or reward of something interesting to work on—the reward usually will be more successful. Here are several reasons:

Punishment does not guarantee that the desired response will occur. The extra homework may indeed keep Daniel in his seat the next time he thinks of moving about, but it by no means ensures that he will pursue the truly desired behavior, which is to perform some meaningful instructional activity while he is there. Instead, he can daydream, write notes to friends, or even pull Rebecca's hair. All succeed in keeping him from being punished again for getting out of his seat. Punishment in the absence of rewards can create other undesired behaviors.

The effects of punishment usually are specific to a particular context and behavior. This means that extra homework is not likely to keep Daniel in his seat when a substitute teacher arrives, because it was not *that* teacher who assigned the punishment. Also, *that* punishment is not likely to deter Daniel from pulling Rebecca's hair, because the punishment was associated only with keeping him in his seat. Punishment rarely keeps one from misbehaving beyond the specific context and behavior to which it was most closely associated.

The effects of punishment can have undesirable side effects. If extra homework is truly an aversive for Daniel—if it is a highly undesirable and painful consequence in his eyes—he may decide never to risk leaving his seat again, even to ask for your assistance or to use the rest room. Daniel may decide to take no chances about leaving his seat and not even to trust his own judgment about when an exception to the rule may be appropriate.

Punishment sometimes elicits hostile and aggressive responses. Although any single punishment is unlikely to provoke an emotional response, students receive punishment in various forms all day long, both at school and at home. If your punishment is the "straw that breaks the camel's back," do not be surprised to observe an emotional outburst that is inconsistent with the amount of punishment rendered.

This is not sufficient reason to avoid assigning punishment when it is needed, but it is reason to use it sparingly and in association with rewards.

The punishment can become associated with the punisher. If you use punishment consistently as a tool for increasing the likelihood that a desirable behavior will occur, you may lose the cooperation you must have for managing your classroom effectively. With this cooperation gone, you will find that the vital link for making management techniques work is gone. *Plan not to solve every discipline problem by using punishment*; otherwise, the punishment could become more strongly associated with you than the desired behavior you wish to encourage.

Punishment that is rendered to stop an undesired *behavior, but that is not immediately associated with the* desired *behavior, seldom has a lasting effect.* If the desired behavior is not clear to your students at the time you administer punishment, then they will see the punishment only as an attempt to hurt and not as an attempt to encourage the desired behavior.

Warnings. Warnings can prevent minor problems from intensifying to where punishment is the only recourse. For the misbehaviors listed as mild in Table 11.1, it is not unusual to provide several warnings before dispensing some kind of consequence. However, after two or three warnings, you should assign some type of consequence, because waiting longer reinforces the student's belief that you are not serious about the misbehavior. This undermines the integrity of the rule being violated and your credibility, as well.

Corporal Punishment. Absent from the common forms of punishment listed in Table 11.1 is any form of corporal punishment, such as paddling a student. Such punishment, although permissible in some school districts when administered by a specifically designated school authority, has not proven particularly effective in deterring misbehavior.

A reason is that the heightened emotion and anxiety on the part of the student (and the administrator) at the time of the punishment often prevent rational discussion of the appropriate behavior that the punishment is supposed to encourage. In addition, corporal punishment easily can provoke aggression and cause hostility in both students and parents. This can outweigh any immediate benefit that might accrue from the punishment.

Generally, you should not have physical contact with a student, because such contacts are easily misunderstood. This applies whether the contact is to administer punishment or, in the case of older students, is a reward (patting a student for doing a good job) or assistance (placing your arm around a student in times of high anxiety). Although your own judgment, the situation, and age of the student will be your best guides, the only clear exception is a situation requiring your immediate assistance. Examples of such situations are breaking up a fight to prevent physical injury, curtailing the movement of a student who is hurting another, or restraining a student from self-injury. At such times, you should call an administrator as quickly as possible.

THE PARENT–TEACHER DISCIPLINARY CONFERENCE

When a major infraction of a school or classroom rule has occurred, more effective than any form of corporal punishment is the parent–teacher conference. This is your opportunity to inform one or both parents of the severity of the misbehavior and for eliciting their active help in preventing it. Without the support of the student's family in providing the appropriate rewards and punishment at home, there is little chance that interventions at school will have a lasting effect in deterring the misbehavior (Rotter, Robinson, & Fey, 1987).

Being grounded for the week, having to be in at a certain time, completing extra study time in the quiet of one's bedroom, or performing extra chores around the house *always will have more impact than any aversive that can be administered during the school day*, as long as these family aversives are administered with a complete understanding of the desired behavior (Rich, 1987).

Notifying parents that a conference is desired usually is your responsibility, if the request for a conference is the result of a specific problem in your classroom. This notification should consist of a call or letter expressing to the parent or guardian the following:

1. Purpose of the conference, including a statement of the joint goal of supporting the student's success in school
2. Statement or comment pointing out the integral role of the parent in the discipline management process (this may include a citation from any state or school policy regarding such matters)
3. Possible dates, times, and location of conference
4. A contact person and phone number, if the parent is unable to reach you directly

If you request a conference with the student's parents by phone, be sure to ask the parent to record the date, time, location, and contact person for the conference at the time of the call.

During the conference you should do the following:

- Try to gain the parents' acknowledgment of the problem and their participation in the discipline management process.
- Present a plan of action for addressing the problem at home and at school.
- Identify follow-up activities (e.g., note home each week indicating progress, immediate phone call if problem should recur, a review of the situation at the next parent–teacher night).
- Document what took place at the conference, including the agreements and disagreements.

Conducting the Parent Conference

In addition to these general guidelines, during the parent conference, you will be expected to talk plainly, listen, and use "I messages" (Swap, 1987).

Plain Talk.   New teachers—particularly when they first meet parents or address them at group meetings—rely on familiar jargon, terms such as *norms, developmental needs, heterogeneous grouping, cognitive skills, higher-order thinking,* which may mean little to some parents. Jargon, however familiar to you, will diminish rather than increase your credibility with parents.

Listen.   Listening is your most important communication skill. Parents, particularly when they are upset, want to be heard. One of the most frequent complaints leveled by parents against teachers is that they don't listen (Gordon, 1974). The Appalachian Educational Laboratory (Shalaway, 1989) offers the following list of hints for you to become a good listener:

1. Maintain eye contact: Face the speaker and lean forward slightly.
2. Nod or give other noninterrupting acknowledgments.
3. When the speaker pauses, allow him or her to continue without interrupting. Wait to add your comments until the speaker is finished.
4. Ignore distractions, such as others seeking your attention.
5. Check your understanding by summarizing the essential aspects of what the speaker tried to say or the feeling he or she tried to convey.
6. Ask for clarification when necessary.

Gordon (1974) refers to this last skill as *active listening*. It is particularly valuable during reactive parent conferences or conferences requested by parents who are upset over something they perceive that you said or did. Such conferences can be emotionally charged. Teachers typically take a defensive or aggressive posture when confronted by an angry parent. Rather than listen to what the parents have to say—regardless of how inaccurate it may seem—the teacher follows the parents' statement with a denial, or a defensive statement, or a refusal to talk further.

Gordon (1974) believes that active listening, in which the listener provides feedback to the speaker on the message heard and the emotion conveyed, opens doors to further communication by letting the speaker know that she or he was being understood and respected. Active listening is an essential communication skill to be used with the parents of learners and the learners themselves. But it is a difficult skill to learn. It requires the ability to concentrate on what someone is saying even when you strongly object to what is being said. Like any skill, it must be practiced before it can be used naturally and automatically.

Use "I Messages" to Express Your Feelings.   Particularly when you are upset about the actions of a learner or the words and actions of a parent, it is important to clearly communicate your feelings. However, the way to do this is not by criticizing or blaming (with a "you message") but rather by describing (1) what you find offensive ("When you . . . " or "When your . . . "), (2) the feeling or emotion you experience when the offensive condition occurs ("I feel"), and (3) a statement of the reason for the feeling ("because"). For example, "When Amanda talks back to me, her behavior is disruptive to the entire class, and that makes me angry because I have to take time away from all the other students in the class to deal with her." This message focuses on your reaction to the problem rather than on what the child said or did. It opens up positive avenues to further communication.

Evaluating the Parent Conference

Following the conference, summarize what was said and agreed on, and make a list of any actions to be taken by you or the parent. Make follow-up calls, send notes, and follow through on whatever you committed yourself to. Finally, take a moment to reflect on how well you communicated with the parents and achieved your goals and what you might change or do differently next time you have a parent conference. This moment of reflection will be one of the most important aids to sharpening your parent conferencing skills.

THE INFLUENCE OF HOME AND FAMILY ON CLASSROOM BEHAVIOR PROBLEMS

Finally, it is important to note that some of the discipline problems you will face in your classroom have their origin at home. Living in a fast-paced, upwardly mobile society has created family stresses and strains that our grandparents could not have imagined. Their lives while growing up were not necessarily any easier than yours or your students', but they were most assuredly different, particularly in the intensity and rapidity with which children today experience developmental stages and life cycle changes.

For example, by some estimates, boys and girls are maturing earlier than they did 50 years ago. This means that they come under the influence of the intense emotions of sex, aggression, love, affiliation, jealousy, and competitiveness far earlier than our own parents probably did. Teachers in the elementary grades are no longer surprised by the depth of understanding and ability of young students to emulate the media's attractively packaged images of adult behavior and lifestyles, especially as they relate to clothes, relationships, and dominance.

Although not often recognized, these generational differences sometimes are even more difficult for parents to accept than for you, the teacher. This often leads to major conflicts at home that surface in your classroom as seemingly minor but persistent misbehaviors. You can have little influence over home conflicts, except to understand that they originate in the home and not in your classroom.

There will be times when no amount of reward or punishment will work, because the source of the problem is within the home and may be far more serious than you suppose—including marital discord, verbal or physical abuse, competition among brothers and sisters, financial distress, and divorce. One or more of these family disturbances could be occurring in the families of some of your students.

These are not trivial burdens for students, especially when combined with the social and academic demands of school, the uncertainties of a future job or education, and the tension that school-age children always feel between youth and adulthood (Erikson, 1968). If a problem persists and your rewards and punishments are to no avail, you must consider the possibility that such a family problem may be occurring. Although there is no easy way to know what is happening in the lives of your students at home, many students welcome the opportunity to reveal the nature of these problems, *when they are asked*. For some it will be just the opportunity they have sought to shed some of the emotional burden these events are creating in their lives.

It is not your role to resolve such problems, but knowing the reason they are occurring may explain why your rewards and punishments may not be working. Knowing the reason also can help you decide whether to refer the problem to other professionals who are in a position to help, such as a social worker, counselor, or school psychologist.

CULTURALLY RESPONSIVE CLASSROOM MANAGEMENT

One of the most interesting and encouraging advances in the understanding of classroom management is the emerging field of **culturally responsive teaching** and behavior management. As we saw in previous chapters, the writings and research of Tharp and Gallimore (1989), D. Dillon (1989), and Bowers and Flinders (1991) present convincing arguments that different cultures react differently to nonverbal and verbal behavior management techniques, including proximity control, eye contact, warnings, and classroom arrangement. Furthermore, they cite numerous examples of how teachers of one culture interpret disruptive behaviors of children differently from those of another culture. Therefore, it is important to be aware that many of the behavioral management techniques presented in this and the previous chapter may be culturally sensitive and that the effective classroom manager matches not only the technique he or she uses with the situation but also with the cultural history of the learner.

If the research supporting culturally responsive teaching has yet to provide explicit prescriptions for teaching culturally different learners, what does it tell us about better understanding students in multicultural classrooms?

The traditional method of conducting classroom research is to study large groups of teachers, classify their teaching methods, give learners achievement tests, and try to find relationships between achievement test scores and particular teaching practices. D. Dillon (1989), however, used a different approach. She studied one teacher, Mr. Appleby, and his class for a year using a research method called *microethnography*. Her study, published in the *American Educational Research Journal*, provided valuable insights into what a teacher can do to create a classroom where culturally different learners experience academic and personal success.

Dillon (1989) concludes that Appleby's effectiveness as a classroom teacher was due to his ability to assume the role of "translator and intercultural broker" between the middle-class culture of the school and the lower-class African American culture of his students. As a cultural broker and translator, Appleby was thoroughly knowledgeable about the backgrounds of his learners and, as a result, was able to bridge the differences between school and community/home cultures.

With this cultural knowledge, Appleby created a classroom with three significant attributes:

1. He created a social organization where teacher and learners knew one another, trusted one another, and felt free to express their opinions and feelings.
2. He taught lessons built around the prior knowledge and experiences of his learners. Because of his knowledge of his learners' background, he was familiar with their knowledge, skills, and attitudes toward the content. This knowledge allowed him to represent the subject matter in ways that encouraged his students to link it with what they already knew and felt.
3. He used instructional methods that allowed learners to actively participate in lessons, to use the language and sociolinguistic patterns of their culture, and to use the language and social interaction patterns both he and his learners were familiar with.

Dillon (1989) concludes that what teachers need to know in order to teach successfully in multicultural classrooms has more to do with knowing the values, socialization practices, interests, and concerns of their learners than with knowing about presumed learning style preferences and cognitive styles and the do's and don'ts of teaching learners with these traits. Rather, Dillon believes that the cultural knowledge teachers such as Appleby have about their learners allows them to represent subject matter content in ways that are meaningful to students, to develop lessons that gain their active participation, and to create social organizations in the classroom within which learners feel free to be themselves.

SUMMING UP

This chapter introduced you to some concepts and techniques for maintaining classroom order and discipline. Its main points were as follows:

1. Most classroom discipline problems are low intensity, continuous, and unconnected with any larger, more serious event.
2. The humanist tradition of classroom management focuses on the inner thoughts, feelings, psychological needs, and emotions of the individual learner. Humanist approaches emphasize the importance of allowing the student time to control his or her own behavior.
3. Ginott's "sane messages" communicate to students that their behavior is unacceptable but in a manner that does not blame, scold, or humiliate.

4. Glasser's cooperative learning emphasizes building a more friendly workplace that the learner would regret leaving for misbehavior, if told to do so.
5. The humanist tradition focuses on developing rules, getting support from school administrators, holding private conferences with students, and following through when students must be removed from the classroom.
6. The applied behavior analysis tradition of classroom management applies the techniques of operant conditioning to change socially important behaviors.
7. Behavior modification focuses on changing or modifying behavior by following a behavior with some type of reinforcement.

8. Positive reinforcement occurs when a desired stimuli or reward is provided after a desired behavior to increase its frequency.

9. Negative reinforcement occurs when a painful, uncomfortable, or aversive state is terminated to increase the frequency of a desired behavior.

10. *Antecedents* are events or stimuli present when you perform a behavior that elicits or sets off the behavior, such as sounds, sights, or people.

11. The applied behavior analysis tradition focuses on identifying the appropriate and inappropriate behavior, identifying antecedents that could trigger these behaviors, the student's goal for the misbehavior, and procedures for reinforcing the appropriate behavior.

12. The classroom management tradition frames the question of classroom order and discipline, not in terms of reaction, but in terms of prevention.

13. The classroom management tradition focuses on planning and organizing the classroom, teaching rules and routines, and informing students of the consequences of breaking the rules.

14. Low-profile classroom control refers to coping strategies used by effective teachers to stop misbehavior without disrupting the flow of a lesson.

15. Three ways to apply your authority in dealing with misbehavior are as follows:
    - You alone judge what occurred and what the punishment should be.
    - You provide some alternative forms of punishment from which the student must choose.
    - You select a punishment from alternatives that the students provide.

16. The level of severity with which you respond to a misbehavior should match the misbehavior that has occurred.

17. The idea behind reinforcement theory is that any behavior can be controlled by the consequences that immediately follow it. When the consequences that follow a behavior change the probability of the behavior's recurrence, reinforcement has occurred.

18. Some misbehaviors that occur in classrooms are unintentionally increased through reinforcement, in which case the probability of the misbehavior increases because a consequence that follows the misbehavior is perceived as desirable by the student.

19. Both rewards and punishment can increase the probability of a behavior, although punishment without reward is rarely effective.

20. Punishment in the absence of rewards tends to be less effective in increasing the probability of a desired behavior for the following reasons:
    - Punishment does not guarantee that the desirable response will occur.
    - The effects of punishment are specific to a particular context.
    - The effects of punishment can spread to undesirable behavior.
    - Punishment can create hostile and aggressive responses.
    - Punishment can become associated with the punisher.

21. After two or three warnings, a punishment should be assigned.

22. Corporal punishment is rarely effective in deterring misbehavior.

23. One feature of the parent–teacher conference that accounts for its effectiveness is the involvement of the parent in eliminating the misbehavior.

FOR DISCUSSION AND PRACTICE

Questions marked with an asterisk are answered in Appendix B. See also *Bridges: An Activity Guide and Assessment Options,* which accompanies this text.

*1. What are six criteria for developing an effective classroom management plan? Which, in your opinion, will be the easiest to achieve in your classroom, and which will be the most difficult?

*2. Describe what Ginott calls "sane messages," and provide an example at your grade level using teacher dialogue.

*3. Using an example of teacher dialogue, provide an example of an "I message" to communicate your anger to a student.

*4. What are several specific recommendations Glasser would have you do as you begin to manage your classroom? Which do you feel is (are) the most important?

*5. How might you use both positive and negative reinforcement to stop a student from repeatedly talking? Use an example of each to make your point.

*6. Describe time-out and response cost. What would be a classroom situation in which you would use each of these?

*7. According to research studies of classroom management, what are three broad classes of preventative classroom management techniques? List the three in order of least to most difficult to implement at your grade level.

8. Create a brief teacher–student dialogue that describes a low-profile anticipation–deflection–reaction sequence directed to a child who leaves a seat without permission.

*9. In what ways can you use your authority to assign consequences to a student for misbehaving? Which would you feel most comfortable using?

10. For the following misbehaviors, identify a consequence that reflects the severity of the offense. Do not use the same response more than once.
- Talking back
- Cutting class
- Eating in class
- Jumping out of seat
- Sleeping in class
- Acting out
- Obscene gesturing
- Selling or using drugs
- Fighting

11. What reward would you give to get a student to do each of the following?
- Homework
- Stop talking
- Stop talking back
- Turn in assignments on time
- Be on time for class
- Remember to bring pen and pencil
- Not talk without raising hand

*12. What steps would you follow to transfer the control from an extrinsic reinforcer to that of a natural reinforcer? Identify a reinforcer at your grade in which you might follow these steps.

*13. Identify five reasons why punishment is rarely effective in the absence of rewards. Looking back at your own school days, which seems the most true for you?

*14. Using a specific example in the classroom, under what two conditions is the use of punishment most effective?

*15. What are the two objectives for having a parent–teacher conference discussed in this chapter? What might be some others?

16. In your own words, what is meant by culturally responsive classroom management? Provide an example of how you would respond in a culturally responsive manner to a student who failed to complete a homework assignment. What might a culturally unresponsive reply be in this situation?

12 Assessing Learners: Objective and Essay Tests

This chapter will help you answer the following questions:

1. How can I be sure that my tests cover what I teach?
2. What is the difference between a norm-referenced and a criterion-referenced test?
3. What are the advantages and disadvantages of different objective test formats?
4. How can I grade essay tests fairly?
5. How will I know if my tests measure what I say they measure?

*S*ome of your strongest childhood and adolescent memories probably include taking tests in school. For that matter, test taking probably is among the most vivid memories of your college experience. If you are like most people who have spent many years in school, you have strong or mixed feelings about tests. In this and the following chapter, we will try to dispel some of the discomfort you might feel about tests and show how they can be effective tools in your classroom.

NORM-REFERENCED AND CRITERION-REFERENCED TESTS

To evaluate your learners' progress, what type of information do you need? That depends on your purpose. Testing can provide two types of information:

1. A student's place or rank compared to other students is revealed by a **norm-referenced test** (NRT), so named because it compares a student's performance to that of a norm group (a large, representative sample of learners). Such information is useful when you need to compare a learner's performance to that of others at the same age or grade level.
2. A student's level of proficiency in or mastery of a skill or set of skills is revealed by a **criterion-referenced test** (CRT), so named because it compares student performance with an absolute standard called a *criterion* (such as 75% correct). Such information helps you decide whether a student needs more instruction to acquire a skill or set of skills.

Figure 12.1 illustrates when to use NRTs and CRTs. As the figure indicates, you should identify the type of information needed *before* selecting a particular test.

Unfortunately, some teachers know little more about a student after testing than they did before. In our technically oriented society, test scores sometimes have become ends in themselves, without the interpretation of them that is essential for

Figure 12.1 Relationship of the purpose of testing and information desired to the type of test required.

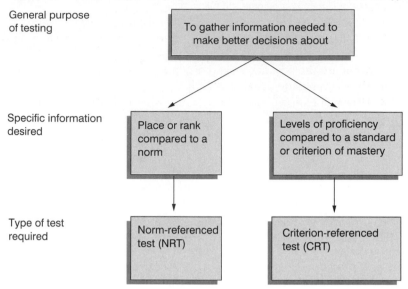

improvement of the learner. In such cases teachers, parents, and others may be quick to denounce a test, often suggesting that such abuse of testing proves that test data are useless. In reality, it may only indicate that the teacher who selected the test either failed to identify the specific information needed *before* administering the test or failed to carefully match the test to this purpose.

A similar situation can occur when existing test data are inappropriately used or interpreted. An example is the following situation, in which counselor John is checking his records when sixth-grade teacher Mary taps on his door:

Mary:	I just stopped by to see you about Danny. He's been in remedial classes for the last 5 years, and now he'll be in my class this year. Mrs. Rodrigues had him last year, and she said you have all the test information on him.
John:	Yeah. In fact, I was just reviewing his folder. Danny's Math Cluster score on the Woodstock-Johnson is at the sixth percentile, and his Reading Cluster is at the first percentile. Good luck with him!
Mary:	Boy, he sure is low. I guess that's why he's been in the remedial classroom for so long.
John:	You've got it!
Mary:	Well, really that's about what I was expecting. What about his skill levels?
John:	What do you mean?
Mary:	You know, his academic skill levels.

John:	Oh, his grade levels! Umm, let's see. . . . His math grade equivalent is 2.6, and his reading grade equivalent is even lower, 1.7.
Mary:	Well . . . that's not really what I need to know. I know he's way below grade level, but I'm wondering about his skills—specific skills, that is. You know, like what words he can read, what phonetic skills he has, if he can subtract two-digit numbers with regrouping . . . things like that.
John:	(Becoming a bit irritated.) Mary, what more do you need than what I've given you? Don't you know how to interpret these scores?
Mary:	(Stung and frustrated.) John, I *do* know what those scores mean, but they only compare Danny to other students. I'm not interested in that. I want to know what he *can* and *can't* do, so I can begin teaching him at the proper skill level.
John:	(Shaking his head.) Look, he's at first-grade level in reading and second-grade level in math. Isn't that enough?
Mary:	But, what level of mastery has he demonstrated?
John:	Mastery? He's years behind! He has mastered very little.

It appears there is a communication gap between Mary and John. John has conveyed a lot of test information to Mary, yet she doesn't seem to get much out of it. John is frustrated, Mary is frustrated, and little that will help Danny has been accomplished. What is the problem?

The problem appears to be John's. Mary's questions refer to competencies or mastery of skills. Referring to Figure 12.1, we can conclude that she was interested in information about Danny's *level of proficiency*. But John's answers refer to test performance compared to other students, which means information about Danny's *rank compared to others*. Answers to Mary's questions can come only from a test designed to indicate whether Danny exceeded some standard of performance taken to indicate mastery of some skill.

If a test indicated that Danny could subtract two-digit numbers with regrouping, Mary would say that he had mastered this skill if, for example, 80% or more correct was the criterion for mastery. In other words, he would have exceeded the standard of 80% mastery of subtraction of two-digit numbers with regrouping. Recall that a CRT is designed to measure whether a student has mastered a skill, where the definition of mastery depends on an established level or criterion of performance.

But the information John provided was normative or comparative. Danny's grade-equivalent scores allow decisions only involving comparisons between his performance and that of the typical or average performance of learners in a norm group. Danny's grade-equivalent score of 1.7 in reading indicates that his reading ability equals that of the average first grader after seven months in the first grade. It says nothing about which words he knows, nor does it give any information about the process he uses to read new words or how long it takes him to comprehend what he reads or learn the meaning of new words. All this score indicates is that his ability to read is well below that of the average fifth grader and equivalent to that of an average first grader after 7 months of school.

Grade-equivalent scores and other scores obtained from norm-referenced tests thus allow only general, comparative decisions, not decisions about mastery of specific skills.

Comparing Norm-Referenced and Criterion-Referenced Tests

As you may have guessed, CRTs must be specific to yield information about individual skills. This is both an advantage and a disadvantage. With a specific test of individual skills, you can be relatively certain that your students have either mastered or failed to master the skill in question. However, the major disadvantage is that many CRTs would be necessary to make decisions about the multitude of skills taught in the average classroom.

The NRT, on the other hand, tends to be general. It measures a variety of specific and general skills at once but cannot measure them thoroughly. Thus, with NRT results, you are not as sure as you would be with CRT results that your students have mastered the individual skills in question. On the other hand, NRT results give you an estimate of ability in a variety of skills much faster than you could achieve with a large number of CRTs. Because of this tradeoff in the uses of criterion-referenced and norm-referenced measures, there are situations in which each is appropriate. Determining the appropriateness of a given type of test depends on your purpose in testing.

The appropriateness of a given type of test depends on the purpose of testing. Criterion-referenced tests (CRTs) measure specific skills related to lesson objectives or unit content, while norm-referenced tests (NRTs) measure skills related to general categories of achievement and aptitude.

THE TEST BLUEPRINT

In Chapter 3 we discussed writing objectives at different levels of behavioral complexity. In this chapter, we will introduce the test blueprint. A **test blueprint** matches test items to your objectives. The test blueprint ensures that you do not overlook details essential to a good test. More specifically, it ensures that a test will sample learning across the range of (1) content areas covered by your instruction and (2) the cognitive and/or affective processes you consider important. It ensures that your test will include a variety of items that tap different levels of cognitive complexity. Figure 12.2 illustrates a test blueprint for a unit on elementary school mathematics.

A test blueprint is constructed according to the following procedure:

Figure 12.2   Test blueprint for a unit on subtraction without borrowing.

Content Outline	Knowledge	Comprehension	Application	Total	Percent
1. The student will discriminate the subtraction sign from the addition sign.	1			1	4%
2. The student will discriminate addition problems from subtraction problems.	2			2	8%
3. The student will discriminate correctly solved subtraction problems from incorrectly solved subtraction problems.		4		4	16%
4. The student will solve correctly single-digit subtraction problems.			6	6	24%
5. The student will solve correctly subtraction problems with double-digit numerators and single-digit denominators.			6	6	24%
6. The student will solve correctly double-digit subtraction problems.			6	6	24%
Total	3	4	18	25	
Percent	12%	16%	72%		100%

1. Classify each instructional objective according to the behaviors described in Chapter 3.
2. Record the number of items to be constructed for each objective in the cell corresponding to its behavioral category.
3. Total the items for each instructional objective, and record the number in the *total* row.
4. Total the number of items falling into each behavior, and record the number at the bottom of the table.
5. Compute the column and row percentages by dividing each total by the number of items in the test.

Constructing a test blueprint before preparing a test ensures that you have adequately sampled the content area and have accurately matched test items to your instructional objectives.

OBJECTIVE TEST ITEMS

Your test blueprint may call for objective test items. Objective test items have one of four formats: true–false, matching, multiple-choice, and completion (short answer). Stiggins (1994) prefers the term *selected response* for these formats to emphasize that it is the system by which these formats are *scored* that is objective, not the selection of content that they measure. In this section we will consider characteristics of each format that can make your objective, or selected response, test items more effective.

Your first decision after completing the test blueprint will be to choose a format, or a combination of formats, for your test. The way you wrote the objectives may have predetermined the format, but in many instances you will have a choice among several item formats. For example, consider the following objectives and item formats:

True–False Items

True–false items are popular because they are quick and easy to write, or at least they seem to be. True–false items really do take less time to write than good objective items of any other format, but *good* true–false items are not so easy to prepare.

As you know from your own experience, every true–false item, regardless of how well or poorly written, gives the student a 50% chance of guessing correctly, even without reading the item. In other words, on a 50-item true–false test, we would expect individuals who were totally unfamiliar with the content being tested to answer about 25 items correctly. Fortunately, ways exist to reduce the effects of guessing:

1. Encourage *all* students to guess when they do not know the correct answer. Because it is virtually impossible to prevent certain students from guessing, encouraging all students to guess should equalize the effects of guessing. The

test scores will then reflect a more or less equal guessing factor *plus* the actual level of each student's knowledge. This also will prevent test-wise students from having an unfair advantage over nontest-wise students.

2. Require revision of statements that are false. In this approach, provide space at the end of the item for students to alter false items to make them true. Usually, the student first is asked to underline or circle the false part of the item and then to add the correct wording, as in these examples:

T   Ⓕ   High-IQ children <u>always</u> get high grades in school

     <u> tend to </u>

T   Ⓕ   Panama is <u>north</u> of Cuba

     <u> south </u>

T   Ⓕ   <u>September</u> has an extra day during leap year.

    <u> February </u>

With this strategy, full credit is awarded only if the revision is correct. The disadvantage of such an approach is that more test time is required for the same number of items, and scoring time is increased.

Here are some suggestions to keep in mind when writing true–false test items:

1. Tell students clearly how to mark *true* or *false* (e.g., circle or underline the T or F) before they begin the test. Write this instruction at the top of the test, too.
2. Construct statements that are definitely true or definitely false, without qualifications. If the item is true or false based on someone's opinion, then identify the opinion's source as part of the item. For example, "According to the head of the AFL-CIO, workers' compensation is below desired standards."
3. Keep true and false statements at approximately the same length, and be sure that there are approximately equal numbers of true and false items.
4. Avoid using double-negative statements. They take extra time to decipher and are difficult to interpret. For example, avoid statements such as, "It is not true that addition cannot precede subtraction in algebraic operations."
5. Avoid terms denoting indefinite degree (e.g., *large, long time, regularly*) or absolutes (*never, only, always*).
6. Avoid placing items in a systematic pattern that some students might detect (e.g., True–True–False–False, TFTF, and so on).
7. Don't take statements directly from the text without first making sure that you are not taking them out of context.

Matching Items

Like true–false, matching items are a popular and convenient testing format. Just like good true–false items, however, good matching items are not easy to write. Imagine you are back in your ninth-grade American history class, and the following matching item shows up on your test:

- *Directions:* Match A and B

A	B
1. Lincoln	a. President during the twentieth century
2. Nixon	b. Invented the telephone
3. Whitney	c. Delivered the Emancipation Proclamation
4. Ford	d. Only president to resign from office
5. Bell	e. Black civil rights leader
6. King	f. Invented the cotton gin
7. Washington	g. Our first president
8. Roosevelt	h. Only president elected for more than two terms

See any problems? Compare the problems you identify with the descriptions of faults that follow.

Homogeneity. The lists are not homogeneous. Column A contains names of presidents, inventors, and a civil rights leader. Unless specifically taught as a set of related individuals or ideas, this is too wide a variety for a matching exercise.

Order of Lists. The lists are reversed: Column A should be in place of column B, and column B should be in place of column A. As the exercise is now written, the student reads a name and then has to read through all or many of the more lengthy descriptions to find the answer, a much more time-consuming process. It also is a good idea to introduce some sort of order—chronological, numerical, or alphabetical—to your list of options. This saves the student time.

Easy Guessing. Notice that there are equal numbers of options and descriptions. This increases the chances of guessing correctly through elimination. If there are at least three more options than descriptions, the chance of guessing correctly is reduced to one in four.

Poor Directions. The instructions are much too brief. Matching directions should specify the basis for matching:

- Column A contains brief descriptions of historical events. Column B contains the names of U.S. presidents. Indicate who was president when the historical event took place by placing the appropriate letter to the left of the number in column A.

Multiple Correct Responses. The description "president during the twentieth century" has three defensible answers: Nixon, Ford, and Roosevelt. And, did you mean Henry Ford, inventor of the Model T automobile, or Gerald Ford? Always include first and last names to avoid ambiguities. Here is a corrected version of these matching items:

- *Directions:* Column A describes events associated with U.S. presidents. Indicate which name in Column B matches each event by placing the appropriate letter to the left of the number in Column A. Each name may be used only once.

Column A	Column B
___ 1. Only president not elected to office.	a. Abraham Lincoln
___ 2. Delivered the Emancipation Proclamation.	b. Richard Nixon
	c. Gerald Ford
___ 3. Only president to resign from office.	d. George Washington
___ 4. Only president elected for more than two terms.	e. Franklin Roosevelt
	f. Theodore Roosevelt
___ 5. Our first president.	g. Thomas Jefferson
	h. Woodrow Wilson

Notice that we now have complete directions, more options than descriptions, and homogeneous lists (all items in Column A are about U.S. presidents and all the items in Column B are names of presidents), and we have made the alternatives unambiguous.

Suggestions for Writing Matching Items

1. Keep short and homogeneous both the descriptions list and the options list. They should fit together on the same page. Title the lists to ensure homogeneity (e.g., Column A, Column B).
2. Make sure that all the options are plausible *distracters* (wrong answer choices) for each description to ensure homogeneity of lists.
3. The descriptions list should contain the longer phrases or statements, while the options should consist of short phrases, words, or symbols.
4. Number each description (1, 2, 3, etc.), and letter each option (a, b, c, etc.).
5. Include more options than descriptions, or some that match more than one, or both.
6. In the directions, specify the basis for matching and whether options can be used more than once.

Multiple-Choice Items

Another popular item format is the multiple-choice question. Multiple-choice tests are more common in high school and college than in elementary school. Multiple-choice items are unique among objective test items because they enable you to measure higher-level cognitive objectives. When writing multiple-choice items, be careful not to give away answers by inadvertently providing students with clues in the following ways.

Stem Clue.   The statement portion of a multiple-choice item is called the *stem*, and the answer choices are called *options* or *response alternatives*. A stem clue occurs when the same word or a close derivative occurs in both the stem and an option, thereby clueing the test taker to the correct answer. For example:

- The free-floating structures within the cell that synthesize protein are called _____.
  - a. chromosomes
  - b. lysosomes
  - c. mitochondria
  - d. free ribosomes

In this item the word *free* in the option is identical to *free* in the stem. Thus, the wise test taker has a good chance of answering the item correctly without mastery of the content being measured.

Grammatical Clue.   Consider this item:

- U.S. Grant was an _____.
  - a. president
  - b. man
  - c. alcoholic
  - d. general

Most students would pick up on the easy grammatical clue in the stem. The article *an* eliminates options a, b, and d, because "*an* man," "*an* president," or "*an* general" is ungrammatical. Option c is the only one that forms a grammatical sentence. A way to eliminate the grammatical clue is to replace *an* with *a/an*. Similar examples are *is/are, was/were, his/her*, and so on. Alternatively, place the article (or verb, or pronoun) in the options list:

- Christopher Columbus came to America in _____.
  - a. a car
  - b. a boat
  - c. an airplane
  - d. a balloon

Redundant Words/Unequal Length.   Two very common faults in multiple-choice construction are illustrated in this item:

- When 53 Americans were held hostage in Iran, _____.
  - a. the United States did nothing to free them.
  - b. the United States declared war on Iran.
  - c. the United States first attempted to free them by diplomatic means and later attempted a rescue.
  - d. the United States expelled all Iranian students.

The phrase "the United States" is included in each option. To save space and time, add it to the stem: "When 53 Americans were held hostage in Iran, the United States _____." Second, the length of options could be a giveaway. Multiple-choice item writers have a tendency to include more information in the correct option than in the incorrect options. Test-wise students know that the longer option is the correct one more often than not. Avoid making correct answers more than one and one-half times the length of incorrect options.

All of the Above/None of the Above.   In general, use "none of the above" sparingly. Some item writers use "none of the above" only when no clearly correct option is presented. However, students catch on to this practice and guess that "none of the above" is the correct answer without knowledge of the content being measured. Also, at times it may be justified to use multiple correct answers, such as "both a and c" or "both b and c." Again, use such options sparingly, because inconsistencies can easily exist among alternatives that logically eliminate some from consideration. Avoid using "all of the above," because test items should *encourage* discrimination, not discourage it.

Higher-Level Multiple-Choice Questions

A good multiple-choice item is the most time-consuming type of objective test item to write. Unfortunately, most multiple-choice items also are written at the knowledge level in the taxonomy of educational objectives. As a new item writer, you will tend to write items at this level, but you need to write some multiple-choice items to measure *higher*-level cognitive objectives as well.

First, write some of your *objectives* to measure comprehension, application, analysis, or evaluation. This ensures that your items will be at the higher-than-knowledge level. Consult Appendix C and Chapter 3 for examples of higher-order thinking and problem-solving behavior. Following are some suggestions to make your higher-level multiple-choice questions more authentic.

Use Pictorial, Graphical, or Tabular Stimuli.   Pictures, drawings, graphs, and tables require the student to think at least at the application level in the taxonomy of educational objectives and may involve even higher cognitive processes. Also, such stimuli often can generate several higher-level multiple-choice items rather than just one.

Use Analogies to Show Relationships Among Terms.   To answer analogies correctly, students must not only be familiar with the terms but also be able to *understand* how the terms relate to each other. For example:

- Physician is to humans as veterinarian is to _____.
  - a. fruits
  - b. animals
  - c. minerals
  - d. vegetables

Require Application of Principles or Procedures.   To test whether students comprehend the implications of a procedure or principle, have them use the principle or procedure with new information, or in a novel way. This requires them to do more than just follow the steps in solving a problem. It has them demonstrate an ability to go beyond the context within which they originally learned a principle or procedure. Consider this example, from a division lesson that relied on computation of grade-point averages as examples:

- After filling his car's tank with 18 gallons of gasoline, Mr. Watts said to his son, "We've come 450 miles since the last fill-up. What kind of gas mileage are we getting?" Which of the following is the best answer?
  a. 4 miles per gallon
  b. 25 miles per gallon
  c. Between 30 and 35 miles per gallon
  d. It can't be determined from the information given.

Suggestions for Writing Multiple-Choice Items

1. Be sure that there is one and only one correct or clearly best answer.
2. Be sure all wrong-answer choices ("distracters") are plausible. Eliminate unintentional grammatical clues, and keep the length and form of all the answer choices equal. Rotate the position of the correct answer from item to item randomly.
3. Use negative questions or statements only if the knowledge being tested requires it. In most cases it is more important for the student to know what the correct answer *is* rather than what it is not.
4. Include three to five options (two to four distracters plus one correct answer) to optimize testing for knowledge rather than encouraging guessing. It is not necessary to provide additional distracters for an item simply to maintain the same number of distracters for each item.
5. Use the option "none of the above" sparingly and only when all the answers can be classified unequivocally as wrong.
6. Avoid using "all of the above." It usually is the correct answer and makes the item too easy for students who have only partial information.

Completion Items

Like true–false items, completion items are relatively easy to write. The first tests constructed by classroom teachers and taken by students often are completion tests. Like items of all other formats, there are good and poor completion items. Here are some suggestions for completion items:

1. Require a single-word answer or a brief, definite statement. Avoid items so indefinite that they may be logically answered by several terms:
   Poor Item: World War II ended in _____.

   Better Item: World War II ended in the year _____.
2. Be sure the item poses a problem. A direct question often is better than an incomplete statement because it provides more structure for an answer:
   Poor Item: What do you think about a main character in the story "Lilies of the Field?"

Better Item: The main character in the story "Lilies of the Field" was

_____.

3. Be sure the answer is factually correct. Precisely word the question in relation to the concept or fact being tested. For example, can the answer be found in the text, workbook, or class notes taken by students?
4. Omit only key words; don't eliminate so many elements that the sense of the content is impaired:

Poor Item: The _____ type of test item usually is graded _____ than the _____ type.

Better Item: The multiple-choice type of test item usually is graded more objectively than the _____ type.

5. Word the statement so the blank is near the end. This prevents awkward sentences.
6. If the problem requires a numerical answer, indicate the units in which it is to be expressed (e.g., pounds, ounces, minutes).

Advantages and Disadvantages of Objective-Item Formats

Table 12.1 summarizes the advantages and disadvantages of each of the preceding objective-item formats.

ESSAY TEST ITEMS

In this section, we will explain what an essay item is, describe the two major types, and provide suggestions for writing them. In essay items, the student supplies, rather than selects, the correct answer. It demands that the student compose a response, often extensive, to a question for which no *single* response or pattern of responses can be cited as correct to the exclusion of all others. The accuracy and quality of such a response often can be judged only by a person skilled in the subject area.

Like objective test items, essay items may be well constructed or poorly constructed. The well-constructed essay item tests complex cognitive skills by requiring the student to organize, integrate, and synthesize knowledge, to use information to solve novel problems, or to be original and innovative in problem solving. The poorly constructed essay item may require the student to do no more than recall information as it was presented in the textbook or lecture. Worse, the poorly constructed essay item may not inform the learner what is required for a satisfactory response.

Extended Response Items

An essay item that allows the student to determine the length and complexity of a response is called an **extended response essay item.** This type of essay is most useful at the analysis, synthesis, or evaluation levels of cognitive complexity. Because of the length of this type of item and the time required to organize and express the

Table 12.1 Advantages and disadvantages of various objective-item formats.

Advantages	Disadvantages

True-False Tests

Advantages	Disadvantages
Tend to be short, so more material can be covered than with any other item format; thus, use T–F items when extensive content has been covered.	Tend to emphasize rote memorization of knowledge (although complex questions sometimes can be asked using T–F items).
Faster to construct (but avoid creating an item by taking statements out of context or slightly modifying them).	They assume an unequivocally true or false answer (it is unfair to make students guess at your criteria for evaluating the truth of a statement).
Scoring is easier (tip: provide a "T" and "F" for them to circle, because a student's handwritten "T" or "F" can be hard to decipher).	Allow and may even encourage a high degree of guessing (generally, longer examinations compensate for this).

Matching Items

Advantages	Disadvantages
Simple to construct and score.	Tend to ask trivial information.
Ideal for measuring associations between facts.	Emphasize memorization.
Can be more efficient than multiple-choice questions because they avoid repetition of options in measuring association.	Most commercial answer sheets can accommodate only five options, thus limiting the size of a matching item.
Reduce the effects of guessing.	

Multiple-Choice Tests

Advantages	Disadvantages
Versatile in measuring objectives, from the knowledge level to the evaluation level.	Time consuming to write.
Since writing is minimal, considerable course material can be sampled quickly.	If not carefully written, can have more than one defensible correct answer.
Scoring is highly objective, requiring only a count of correct responses.	
Can be written so students must discriminate among options varying in correctness, avoiding the absolute judgments of T–F tests.	
Reduce effects of guessing.	
Amenable to statistical analysis, so you can determine which items are ambiguous or too difficult (see Kubiszyn & Borich, 2000, Chapter 8).	

Completion Tests

Advantages	Disadvantages
Question construction is relatively easy.	Encourage a low level of response complexity.
Guessing is reduced because the question requires a specific response.	Can be difficult to score (the stem must be general enough to not communicate the answer, leading unintentionally to multiple defensible answers).
Less time is needed to complete than multiple-choice items, so more content can be covered.	Very short answers tend to measure recall of specific facts, names, places, and events instead of more complex behaviors.

response, the extended response item is sometimes better as a term-paper assignment or take-home test. The extended response essay often is of value in assessing communication ability as well as in assessing achievement. For example:

- Compare and contrast the presidential administrations of George Bush and Ronald Reagan. Consider economic, social, and military policies. Avoid taking a position in support of either president. Your response will be graded on objectivity, accuracy, organization, and clarity.

Restricted Response Items

An essay item that poses a specific problem for which the student must recall proper information, organize it in a suitable manner, derive a defensible conclusion, and express it within the limits of the posed problem is called a **restricted response essay item**. The statement of the problem specifies response limitations to guide the student in responding and to provide evaluation criteria for scoring. For example:

- List the major similarities and differences between U.S. participation in the Korean War and World War II, being sure to consider political, military, economic, and social factors. Limit your answer to one page. Your score will depend on accuracy, organization, and conciseness.

When Should You Use Essay Questions?

Although each situation must be considered individually, some lend themselves to essay items. For example:

1. The instructional objectives specify high-level cognitive processes; they require supplying information rather than simply recognizing information. These processes often cannot be measured with objective items.
2. Only a few tests or items need to be graded. If you have 30 students and design a test with six extended response essays, you will spend a great deal of time scoring. Use essays when class size is small, or use only one or two essays in conjunction with objective items.
3. Test security is a consideration. If you are afraid test items will be passed on to future students, it is better to use an essay test. In general, a good essay test takes less time to construct than a good objective test.

Following are some learning outcomes for which essay items may be used:

- Analyze relationships
- Arrange items in sequence
- Compare positions
- State necessary assumptions
- Identify appropriate conclusions
- Explain cause-and-effect relations
- Formulate hypotheses

- Organize data to support a viewpoint
- Point out strengths and weaknesses
- Produce a solution to a problem
- Integrate data from several sources
- Evaluate the quality or worth of an item, product, or action
- Create an original solution, arrangement, or procedure

Suggestions for Writing and Using Essay Items

1. Have clearly in mind what mental processes you want the student to use before starting to write the question. Refer to the mental processes in Appendix C and those required at the various levels in the taxonomy of educational objectives for the cognitive domain (e.g., compare and contrast, create alternatives, make choices among). If you want students to analyze, judge, or think critically, determine what mental processes involve analysis, judgment, or critical thinking.

   Poor Item: Criticize the following speech by our President.

   Better Item: Consider the following presidential speech. Focus on the section dealing with economic policy, and discriminate between factual statements and opinion. List these statements separately, label them, and indicate whether each statement is or is not consistent with the President's overall economic policy.

2. Write the question to clearly and unambiguously define the task to the student. Tasks should be explained (1) in the overall instructions preceding the test items and/or (2) in the test items themselves. Include instructions for the type of writing style desired (e.g., scientific vs. prose), whether spelling and grammar will be counted, and whether organization of the response will be an important scoring element. Also, indicate the level of detail and supporting data required.

   Poor Item: Discuss the value of behavioral objectives.

   Better Item: Behavioral objectives have enjoyed increased popularity in education over the years. In your text and in class, the advantages and disadvantages of behavioral objectives have been discussed. Take a position for or against the use of behavioral objectives in education, and support your position with at least three of the arguments covered in class or in the text.

3. Start essay questions with such words or phrases as *compare, contrast, give reasons for, give original examples of, predict what would happen if,* and so on. Do not begin with such words as *what, who, when,* and *list,* because these words generally lead to tasks that require only recall of information.

   Poor Item: List three reasons behind America's withdrawal from Vietnam.

   Better Item: After more than 10 years of involvement, the United States withdrew from Vietnam in 1975. Speculate on what would have happened if America had *not* withdrawn at that time and had *not* increased significantly its military presence above 1972 levels.

4. A question dealing with a controversial issue should ask for, and be evaluated in terms of, the presentation of evidence for a position, rather than the position taken. It is not defensible to demand that a student accept a specific conclusion or solution, but it is reasonable to appraise how well he or she has learned to use the evidence on which a specific conclusion is based.

Poor Item: What laws should Congress pass to improve the medical care of all citizens in the United States?

Better Item: Some feel that the cost of all medical care should be borne by the federal government. Do you agree or disagree? Support your position with at least three logical arguments.

5. Avoid using optional items. That is, require all students to complete the same items. Allowing students to select 3 of 5, 4 of 7, and so forth decreases the uniformity of the test across all students, which will decrease your basis for comparison among students.

6. Establish reasonable time and/or page limits for each essay item to help the student complete the entire test and to indicate the level of detail you have in mind. Indicate such limits either in the statement of the problem or close to the number of the question.

7. Restrict the use of essays to those learning outcomes that cannot be satisfactorily measured by objective items.

8. Be sure each question relates to an instructional objective. Check your test blueprint to see if the content of the essay item is represented.

Advantages and Disadvantages of the Essay Item

Here are several advantages:

- To the extent that instructional objectives require the student to organize information to solve a problem, analyze and evaluate information, or perform other high-level cognitive skills, the essay test is an appropriate assessment tool.
- Although essay tests are relatively easy to construct, do not construct the items haphazardly. Consult your behavioral objectives blueprint, identify only the topics and objectives that can best be assessed by essays, and build items around those—and only those.
- If developing communication skills is an instructional objective, you can test it with an essay item. However, this assumes that you have spent time teaching communication pertinent to the course area, including special vocabulary and writing styles, as well as providing practice with arguments for and against controversial points.
- Because no options are provided, the student must supply rather than select the proper response, reducing guessing.

Here are several disadvantages:

- It is tedious for you to wade through pages and pages of student handwriting. Also, it is difficult not to let spelling and grammatical mistakes influence grading or to let superior communication abilities cover up for incomplete comprehension of facts.
- It is difficult to maintain a common set of criteria for all students. Two persons may disagree on the correct answer for any essay item; even the same person will disagree on the correctness of one answer read on two separate occasions.
- Fewer essay items can be attempted than with objective items. Also, students become fatigued faster with essay items than with objective items.
- It is no secret that longer essays tend to be graded higher than short essays, regardless of content! As a result, students may bluff.

The first two limitations—time required for grading and maintaining consistent objectivity—are serious disadvantages. Fortunately, there are some ways to make the task of scoring essays more manageable and reliable.

Scoring Essays

As mentioned, essays are difficult to score consistently across individuals. That is, the *same* essay answer may be given an A by one scorer and a B or C by another scorer. Or, the same answer may be graded A on one occasion, but B or C on another occasion by the *same* scorer! As disturbing and surprising as this may seem, these conclusions are supported by research findings (Coffman, 1972). What can you do to avoid such scoring problems?

Write Good Essay Items.   Poorly written questions are one source of scorer inconsistency. Questions that do not specify response length are another. In general, long (e.g., three-page) essay responses are more difficult to score consistently than restricted essay responses (say, one page). This is due to student fatigue and subsequent clerical errors, as well as a tendency for grading criteria to vary from response to response, or for that matter, from page to page, or even paragraph to paragraph within the same response.

Use Several Restricted Response Items.   Rather than a single extended response item, use several restricted response items. Writing good items and using restricted response essays will help improve essay scoring. However, as mentioned, extended response essays sometimes are desirable or necessary. When they are, use a predetermined scoring scheme

Use a Predetermined Scoring Scheme.   All too often, teachers grade essays without having specified in advance what they are looking for in a "good" answer. If you do not specify the criteria beforehand, your scoring consistency will be greatly reduced. If these criteria are not readily available (written down) for scoring each question, the criteria themselves may change (you may grade harder or easier after a number of papers, even if the answers do not change). Or, your ability to keep these criteria in mind will be influenced by fatigue, distractions, frame of mind, and so on. Because we all are human, we all are subject to these factors.

Some Criteria for Scoring Higher-Level Essay Items

Following are several criteria that are useful in scoring higher-level essay items.

Content.   Although essays are used less to measure factual knowledge than thinking processes, the content of an essay can and should be scored specifically for its precision and accuracy, in addition to its organization and use (and tell your students if you are doing so).

Organization.   Does the essay have an introduction, body, and conclusion? If you are looking for these characteristics, let the students know that you will be scoring for organization. Beyond these three general organizational criteria, you may want to develop specific criteria for your class. For example: Are recommendations, inferences, and hypotheses supported? Is it apparent which supporting statements go with which recommendation? Do progressions and sequences follow a logical or chronological development? You also should decide on a spelling and grammar policy, and develop these criteria, alerting the students *before* they take the test.

Process.   If your essay item tests at the application level or above, the most important criteria for scoring are those that reflect the extent to which the process has been carried out. Each process (application, analysis, synthesis, and evaluation) results in a solution, recommendation, or decision, or some reasons to justify or support the final decision, and so on. Thus, the process criteria should assess both the adequacy of the solution or decision and the reasons behind it.

Accuracy/Reasonableness.   Will it work? Have the correct analytical dimensions been identified? You ultimately must decide what is accurate, but be prepared for unexpected, yet accurate, responses.

Completeness/Internal Consistency.   Does the essay deal adequately with the problem presented? Again, your judgment will weigh heavily, but points should be logically related and cover the topics as fully as required.

Originality/Creativity.   Again, it is up to you to recognize the unexpected and give credit for it. That is, expect some students to develop new ways of conceptualizing questions, and award credit for such conceptualizations when appropriate.

Tell students about any or all of the preceding criteria. Once they know how you are going to score the test, they can prepare better and more defensible responses. Figure 12.3 illustrates a scheme for scoring essays with the preceding criteria, which can be easily modified to include other criteria and definitions.

Figure 12.3 Example scoring scheme for an essay test.

Content

1	2	3	4	5
Very limited investigation. Little or no material related to facts.		Some investigation and attention to the facts are apparent.		Extensive investigation. Good detail and attention to the facts.

Organization

1	2	3	4	5
Very little organization of ideas. Presentation is confusing and hard to follow.		Some organization of ideas, but logical order needs to be improved.		Good organization. Ideas logically connected and built on one another.

Process

1	2	3	4	5
Very little justification or support of ideas. Final solution or decision unsubstantiated.		Some justification and support of ideas. Final solution or decision needs greater substantiation.		Good justification and support of ideas. Final solution or decision well substantiated.

Accuracy

1	2	3	4	5
Very little attention to the facts. Misread or ignored the data.		Some attention to the facts. Interpretation of the data needs to be improved.		Good attention to the facts. Accurately interpreted the data.

Completeness

1	2	3	4	5
Very little focus on detail. Ideas are superficial and incomplete.		Some attention to detail. Greater focus and attention to detail needed.		Good attention to detail. Ideas are thorough and complete.

Originality

1	2	3	4	5
Response lacks originality. Nothing new or creative.		Some originality. Greater creativity needed.		Response is original and creative. Many novel and unexpected ideas.

PACKAGING THE TEST

After all the care and work you put into developing good test items, follow through and package the test properly for the sake of your learners and your own professionalism. As you study the following guidelines, you probably will recall seeing every one of them violated at some time on tests you have taken. Start off right by attending to these details.

Guidelines for Packaging

Group Together All Items of Similar Format.   If you have all true–false items grouped together, all completion items together, and so on, then students will not have to shift gears and adjust to new formats. This enables them to cover more items than if you mixed item formats throughout the test. Also, by grouping items of a given format together, you will only need to give one set of directions for each type of format—another timesaver.

Arrange Test Items from Easy to Hard.   Arranging test items according to level of difficulty will enable more students to answer the first few items correctly, thereby building confidence and hopefully reducing test anxiety.

Space the Items for Easy Reading.   Provide enough blank space between items so that each is distinctly separate from others. When items are crowded together, students may inadvertently perceive a word, phrase, or line from an adjacent item as being part of the item they are focused on.

Keep Items and Options on the Same Page.   Few things aggravate a test taker more than having to turn the page to read the options for multiple-choice or matching items, or to complete reading a true–false or completion item. To avoid this, do not begin an item at the bottom of the page unless you will have at least an inch left *after completing* the item. Not only does this eliminate carrying over items onto the next page, it also minimizes the likelihood that the last line or two of the item will be cut off when you photocopy the test.

Position Illustrations Near Descriptions.   Place diagrams, maps, or other supporting material immediately above the item or items to which they refer. In other words, if items 9, 10, and 11 refer to a map of South America, locate the map above items 9, 10, and 11—not between 9 and 10 or between 10 and 11 and not below them. Also, if possible, keep any such stimuli and related questions on the same page to save the test taker time.

Check Your Answer Key for Randomness.   Be sure the correct answers follow a random pattern. Avoid true–false patterns such as TFTF or TTFF and multiple-choice patterns such as DCBADCBA. At the same time, see that your correct answers are distributed about equally between true and false and among multiple-choice options.

Determine How Students Record Answers. Decide whether your students will record their answers on the test paper or on a separate answer sheet. In the lower elementary grades, it is best for students to record answers on the test papers. In the upper elementary and secondary grades, separate answer sheets can facilitate scoring accuracy and reduce scoring time. Also, in the upper grades, learning to complete separate answer sheets familiarizes students with the process they will use when taking standardized tests.

Provide Space for Name and Date. Be sure to include a blank on your test booklet and/or answer sheet for the student's name and the date. If you think this is unnecessary, you have never graded a pile of unsigned papers from young children, wondering who they belong to! It is *not* always evident to a nervous test taker that a name should be included on the test. Students are much more likely to put their names on tests if space is provided.

Check Test Directions. Check your directions for each item format to be sure they are clear. Directions should specify all of the following:

1. The numbers of the items to which the directions apply
2. How to record answers
3. The basis on which to select answers
4. Criteria for scoring

Proofread the Test. Proofread for typographical and grammatical errors, and correct them before reproducing the test. Having to announce corrections to the class just before or during the test wastes time and will disturb the test takers' concentration.

Before reproducing the test, it's a good idea to check off these steps. The checklist in Figure 12.4 can be used for this purpose.

VALIDITY, RELIABILITY, AND ACCURACY

Test results are useful only if they are valid, reliable, and accurate. These terms are defined as follows:

1. *Validity.* Does the test measure what it is supposed to?
2. *Reliability.* Does the test yield the same or similar scores consistently?
3. *Accuracy.* Does the test approximate an individual's true level of knowledge, skill, or ability?

Types of Validity

A test is **valid** if it measures what it says it is supposed to measure. For instance, if it is supposed to be a test of third-grade arithmetic ability, it should measure third-grade arithmetic skills, not fifth-grade arithmetic skills and not reading ability. If it is

Figure 12.4   Test assembly checklist.

Test Assembly Checklist

Check each statement to see whether it applies to your test.

	Yes	No
1. Are items of similar format grouped together?	☐	☐
2. Are items arranged in order of difficulty from easy to hard?	☐	☐
3. Are items properly spaced?	☐	☐
4. Are items and options on the same page?	☐	☐
5. Are diagrams, maps, and supporting material above designated items and on the same page with items?	☐	☐
6. Are answers random?	☐	☐
7. Have you decided whether an answer sheet will be used?	☐	☐
8. Are blanks for name and date included?	☐	☐
9. Have you checked the directions for clarity and completeness?	☐	☐
10. Have you proofread the test for errors?	☐	☐

supposed to be a measure of ability to write behavioral objectives, it should measure that ability, not the ability to recognize poor objectives.

Clearly, if test results will be used to make any kind of decision and if the test information is to be useful, it is essential that the test be valid. There are several ways of deciding whether a test is sufficiently valid to be useful. The three methods most often used are *content validity, concurrent validity*, and *predictive validity*.

Content Validity.   The content validity of a test is established by examining its contents. The teacher inspects test questions to see whether they correspond to what should be covered. This is easiest when the test is measuring achievement, where it may be fairly easy to specify what to include. It is more difficult if the concept being tested is a personality or aptitude trait, because it can be difficult to specify beforehand what a relevant question would look like.

A test sometimes can look valid but measure something different from what is intended, such as guessing ability, reading level, or skills that learners may have acquired before the instruction. Content validity is, therefore, a minimum requirement for a useful test but does not guarantee a valid test.

Concurrent Validity.   To establish concurrent validity, you must administer an established test at the same time as the new test you have designed. Unlike content validity, concurrent validity yields a numerical value in the form of a correlation coefficient, called a validity coefficient (see Kubiszyn & Borich, 2000, Chapter 14).

The teacher administers both the new test and the established test to a group of students and then finds the relationship—the correlation—between the two sets of test scores. If there exists an established test (criterion) with which the new test can be compared and in which people have confidence, concurrent validity provides a good method of estimating the validity of a test.

Predictive Validity.   Predictive validity refers to how well the test predicts some future behavior of the examinee that is representative of the test's content. This form of validity is particularly useful for aptitude tests, which attempt to predict how well the test taker will do in some future setting. Predictive validity also yields a numerical index, also in the form of a correlation coefficient. This time, however, it is the relationship between the test and some future behavior that is being measured.

All three methods for determining validity—content, concurrent, and predictive—assume that some criterion exists external to the test that can be used to anchor or validate it. In the case of content validity, it is the instructional objectives that provide the anchor or point of reference; in the case of concurrent validity, it is another well-accepted test measuring the same thing; and in the case of predictive validity, it is some future behavior or condition that we are attempting to predict.

Types of Reliability

The **reliability** of a test refers to the consistency with which it yields the same rank or score for an individual taking the test several times. In other words, a test is reliable if it consistently yields the same, or nearly the same, ranks among all individuals over repeated administrations during which we would not expect the trait being measured to have changed.

There are several ways to estimate the reliability of a test. The three basic methods most often used are called *test-retest, alternative form*, and *internal consistency*.

Test-Retest.   Test-retest is a method of estimating reliability that is exactly what its name implies. The teacher gives the test twice to the same individuals, and determines the relationship—or correlation—between the first set of scores and the second set of scores.

Alternate Form.   If two equivalent forms of a test are available, the teacher can use both to estimate the reliability of the test. The teacher administers both to a group of students and determines the relationship (correlation) between the two sets of scores. Because the two forms have different items but equivalent content, this estimate eliminates the problems of memory and practice involved in test-retest estimates of reliability. Large differences in a student's score on two forms of a test that supposedly measures the same behavior would indicate an unreliable test. To use this method of estimating reliability, two equivalent forms of the test must be available, and the teacher must administer them under conditions as nearly equivalent as possible and at approximately the same time.

Internal Consistency. If the test measures a single basic concept, then it is reasonable to assume that people who get one item right will more likely get other, similar items right. In other words, items ought to be related or correlated with each other, and the test ought to be internally consistent. If this is the case, then the reliability of the test can be estimated by the internal-consistency method. (Specific numerical procedures for determining the internal consistency of a test and other methods of measuring reliability are in Kubiszyn & Borich, 2000.)

Here are some tips and cautions about interpreting reliability coefficients:

- Higher coefficients will result from heterogeneous groups than from homogeneous groups. Groups comprising very different types of individuals (e.g., at-risk and gifted, older and younger, motivated and unmotivated learners) will result in higher reliabilities than more homogeneous groups.
- Scoring reliability limits test reliability. If tests are scored unreliably, error is introduced that will limit the reliability of the test. A test cannot have reliability higher than the reliability of the scoring.
- All other factors being equal, the more items included in a test, the higher the test's reliability.
- Reliability tends to decrease as tests become too easy or too difficult.

Typically, validity coefficients for a test are lower than reliability coefficients. Acceptable validity coefficients for a test generally range between .60 and .80 or higher, while acceptable reliability coefficients generally range from .80 to .90 or higher. The maximum coefficient obtainable for either validity or reliability is 1.0. **Test accuracy** is in part a combined measure of validity and reliability and in part determined by how well the test content matches the prevailing general educational curriculum.

MARKS AND MARKING SYSTEMS

After you have administered your test, you will have to score it and assign marks. Often, the type of symbol a teacher uses to represent a mark is determined at the school or district level, for example, A–F, E–G–S–P–U (Excellent–Good–Satisfactory–Poor–Unsatisfactory), or a numerical marking system. However, the classroom teacher often has considerable flexibility in determining how to assign these marks to learners. You may have considerable control over *how* you decide who gets an A or B or 75 or 80. **Marks and grading systems** are based on comparisons, usually comparisons of students with one or more of the following:

- Other students
- Established standards

- Aptitude
- Actual vs. potential effort
- Actual vs. potential improvement

Comparison with Other Students

The expression "grading on the curve" means that your grade or mark depends on how your achievement compares with the achievement of other students in your class. Sometimes districts or schools encourage grading on the curve by specifying the percentages of students who will be assigned various grades.

The main advantage of such a system is that it simplifies marking decisions. The student either is in the top 10% or doesn't get an A. There is no deliberation or agonizing over what cutoff scores should determine whether students get this grade or that. However, this type of marking system fails to consider differences in the overall ability level of the class. Regardless of achievement, in such a system some students always will get As, and some always will get Fs.

Comparison with Established Standards

In the marking system that uses comparison with established standards, it is possible for any student to get an A or F or any grade between. Achievements of individual students are unrelated to other individual students. All that is relevant is whether a student attains a defined standard of achievement or performance. We labeled this approach *criterion-referenced* earlier in this chapter. In such a system, letter grades may be assigned, based on the percentage of test items answered correctly, as this distribution illustrates:

Grade	Percentage of Items Answered Correctly
A	85
B	75
C	65
D	55
F	Less than 55

In theory, this system makes it possible for all students to obtain high grades if they put forth sufficient effort (assuming that the percentage cutoffs are not unreasonably high). Also, grade assignment is simplified; a student either has correctly answered 75% of the items or has not. As with the comparison with other students method, there is no deliberating or agonizing over assigning grades. Also, teachers who work to improve their teaching effectiveness can observe improvement in grades with the passage of time.

As you might expect, such a system also has its drawbacks. Establishing a standard for each grade attained is no small task, and what is reasonable for an A may vary from school to school and from time to time, as a result of ability levels, the content being taught, and curriculum changes.

Comparisons with other students, established standards, aptitude, effort, and improvement all can be the basis for assigning grades. Ultimately, you must decide the balance of approaches to use that best fits the goals of the classroom and school.

Comparison with Aptitude

Aptitude is another name for potential or ability. In such systems, students are compared neither to other students nor to established standards. Instead, they are compared to themselves. That is, marks are assigned depending on how closely to their potential they are achieving. Thus, students with high aptitude or potential who are achieving at high levels would get high grades, because they would be achieving at their potential. Those with high aptitude and average achievement would get lower grades, because they would be achieving below their potential.

But students with average aptitude and average achievement also would get high grades, because they would be considered to be achieving at their potential. Thus, the same grade could mean very different things in terms of absolute achievement.

Comparison of Achievement with Effort

Systems that compare achievement with effort are similar to those that compare achievement with aptitude. Students who get average test scores but have to work hard to get them are given high marks. Students who get average scores but do not have to work hard to get them are given lower grades. The advantage cited for grading on effort is that it motivates slower or turned-off students. However, it also may turn off brighter students, who quickly see such a system as unfair.

Comparison of Achievement with Improvement

Such systems compare the amount of improvement between the beginning and end of instruction. Students who show the most progress get the highest grades. An obvious problem occurs for the student who does well on a test at the beginning of the instruction, called the *pretest*, because improvement for this student is likely to be less than for a student who does poorly on the pretest.

Which marking system should you choose? Most now agree that comparisons with established standards would best suit the primary function of marking, which is to provide feedback about academic achievement. Once standards are established, comparisons among schools and students may be more easily made. In reality, many schools and districts have adopted multiple marking systems, such as assigning separate grades for achievement and effort or achievement, effort, and improvement. As long as the achievement portion of the grade reflects *only* achievement, such systems are appropriate.

STANDARDIZED TESTS

So far, we have limited our discussion to teacher-constructed tests. However, many teachers also are required at least once a year to administer *standardized* tests, evaluate their results, and interpret them to curious and sometimes concerned parents.

Standardized tests are developed by test-construction specialists, usually with the assistance of curriculum experts, teachers, and school administrators, to determine a student's performance level relative to others of similar age and grade. These tests are *standardized* because they are administered and scored according to *specific* and *uniform* (standard) procedures.

When schools use standardized tests, administrators can more easily and confidently compare test results from different students, classes, schools, and districts than is the case with different teacher-made tests. For the most part, schools use standardized tests for comparative purposes. This is quite different from the purposes of teacher-made tests, which are to determine pupil mastery or skill levels, to assign grades, and to provide specific feedback to students and parents. Table 12.2 compares standardized and teacher-made tests on several important dimensions.

The results of standardized tests are reported as percentile ranks. Percentile ranks enable you to determine how a student's performance compares with others of the same grade or age. Keep in mind two points when interpreting percentile ranks:

Table 12.2   A comparison of standardized and teacher-made achievement tests.

Dimension	Standardized Achievement Tests	Teacher-Made Achievement Tests
Learning outcomes and content measured	Measures general outcomes and content appropriate to the majority of U.S. schools. These tests of general skills and understanding tend not to reflect specific or unique emphasis of local curricula.	Well adapted to the specific and unique outcomes and content of a local curriculum; adaptable to various sizes of work units, but tend to neglect complex learning outcomes.
Quality of test items	Quality of items generally is high. Items are written by specialists, pretested, and selected on the basis of results from quantitative item analysis.	Quality of items is often unknown. Quality is typically lower than standardized tests due to limited time available to the teacher.
Reliability	Reliability is high, commonly between .80 and .95, and frequently above .90 (highest possible is 1.0).	Reliability is usually unknown, but can be high if items are carefully constructed.
Administration and scoring	Procedures are standardized; specific instructions are provided.	Uniform procedures are possible, but usually are flexible and unwritten.
Interpretation of scores	Scores can be compared to norm groups. Test manual and other guides aid interpretation and use.	Score comparisons and interpretation are limited to local class or school situation. Few if any guidelines are available for interpretation and use.

1. Percentile ranks often are confused with *percentage correct*. In using percentile ranks, be sure you communicate that a percentile rank of, for example, 62 means that the individual's score was *higher* than 62% of all the people who took the test (called the *norming sample*). Or, you can say that 62% of those who took the test scored *lower* than this individual. (Commonly, a score at the 62nd percentile is misinterpreted to mean that the student answered only 62% of the items correctly. But realize that a score at the 62nd percentile might be equivalent to a B or a C, whereas a score of 62% likely would be an F.)

2. Equal differences between percentile ranks do *not* necessarily indicate equal differences in achievement. In a grade of 100 pupils, the difference *in achievement* between the 2nd percentile and 5th percentile is substantial, whereas the difference between the 47th and 50th percentile is negligible. Interpretation of percentile ranks must take into consideration that percentiles toward the extreme or end points of the distribution tend to be spread out (like a rubber band), while percentiles toward the center tend to be compressed.

NEW TRENDS IN STANDARDIZED TESTING

Standardized testing has undergone criticism in recent years (Elliott & Shapiro, 1990; Stiggins, 1994; Ysseldyke & Marston, 1990). This criticism has centered on three questions concerning the relevance of standardized tests:

1. How much does classroom learning depend on the skills measured by a standardized test?
2. Are these tests fair to learners from diverse cultures and ethnic backgrounds?
3. Do such tests provide information useful for making instructional decisions in the classroom?

Consideration of these questions has led to alternative approaches to and revisions in the construction of standardized tests. Underlying these alternative approaches and revisions are four assumptions that are likely to guide the development of standardized tests in the future. Let's look at them briefly.

Learning Is a Process

The standardized testing tradition sought to measure the outcomes of learning (facts, concepts, principles, generalizations, etc.) by making assumptions about, but not actually measuring, the processes involved in achieving these outcomes. For example, the standardized approach assumed that learning could be measured by systematically recording its effects, that repeated measurement of the effects would overcome any imprecision in the measures themselves, and that the amount of learning acquired could be known through relative (comparison with other students) rather than absolute measurement. *New approaches to standardized tests are likely to record both the effect (what was learned) and the process (how it was learned). In other words, the cognitive processes employed to attain the effect will be as important as the test scores themselves.*

Learning Ability Can Be Improved

The standardized testing approach originated at a period in our history when we believed that ability to learn was inherited, fixed, and largely immutable. These beliefs exerted strong influence on the construction and interpretation of standardized tests. We now know that some types of learning ability can be enhanced and that many skills can be instrumental in doing so. *New approaches to standardized testing are likely to be based on the modifiability of learning ability and the identification of specific learning abilities that can be changed through instruction.*

Learning Occurs in a Social Context

Many tests derived from the standardized approach view learning as a largely private act. The results of such tests have been used to place learners in programs emphasizing homogeneous groups or tracks, or into instructional programs emphasizing self-

New approaches to standardized tests are likely to record both the effect (what was learned) and the process (how it was learned). In other words, the cognitive processes employed to attain the effect will be as important as the test scores themselves.

paced or mastery learning. But classrooms by their very nature are social settings, and most learning takes place in a social context. Consequently, since learning is an inherently social act, new approaches to standardized testing are likely to take into account that teachers and groups of peers interact to affect the process of learning. *One goal of standardized testing in the future may be to include the measurement of children's learning in the context of cooperative groups and the naturally occurring dialogue of the classroom.*

Learning Assessment Should Have Instructional Validity

One of the fundamental problems with the use of standardized tests in the classroom has been that they do not identify the instructional processes that can help learners remove learning deficits. This has been called the instructional validity of a test (Bergan & Dunn, 1976; Tombari & Borich, 1999). The assessment of learning should not only reliably identify learning deficits but also point the way to resolving them. To meet this standard of test validity, standardized tests in the future may have to do more than present evidence of content, concurrent, and predictive validity. *They would have to show evidence that school-based programs can remediate the learning deficits they uncover.*

SUMMING UP

This chapter introduced you to some techniques for evaluating student learning. Its main points were as follows:

1. A test that determines a student's place or rank among other students is called a norm-referenced test (NRT). This type of test conveys information about how a student performed compared to a large sample of pupils at the same age or grade.

2. A test that compares a student's performance to a standard of mastery is called a criterion-referenced test (CRT). This type of test conveys information about whether a student needs additional instruction on some skill or set of skills.

3. The major advantage of an NRT is that it covers many different content areas in a single test; its major disadvantage is that it is too general to be useful in identifying specific strengths and weaknesses tied to individual texts or workbooks.

4. The major advantage of a CRT is that it can yield highly specific information about individual skills or behaviors. Its major disadvantage is that many such tests would be needed to make decisions about the many skills or behaviors typically taught in school.

5. A test blueprint is a graphic device that matches the test items to be written with the content areas and levels of behavioral complexity taught. The test blueprint helps to ensure that a test samples learning across (1) the range of content areas covered and (2) the cognitive and/or affective processes considered important.

6. Objective test item formats include the following:
   * True–false
   * Matching
   * Multiple choice
   * Completion or short answer

7. Two methods for reducing the effects of guessing in true–false items are (1) to encourage all students to guess when they do not know the answer and (2) to require revision of statements that are false.

8. In constructing matching items:
   * Make lists homogeneous, representing the same kind of events, people, or circumstances.
   * Place the shorter list first, and list options in chronological, numbered, or alphabetical order.
   * Provide approximately three more options than descriptions to reduce the chance of guessing correctly.
   * Write directions to identify what the lists contain, and specify the basis for matching.
   * Closely check the options for multiple correct answers.

9. Avoid the following flaws when writing multiple-choice items:
   * Stem clues in which the same word or a close derivative appears in both the stem and an option.
   * Grammatical clues in which an article, verb, or pronoun eliminates one or more options from being grammatically correct.
   * The same words are repeated across options that could have been provided only once in the stem.
   * Response options are of unequal length, indicating that the longer option may be correct.
   * The use of "all of the above," which discourages response discrimination, or "none of the above," which encourages guessing.

10. Suggestions for writing higher-level multiple-choice items include use of the following:
    * Pictorial, graphical, or tabular stimuli
    * Analogies that demonstrate relationships among items

• Previously learned principles or procedures

11. The following are suggestions for writing completion items:
    • Require a single-word answer.
    • Pose the question or problem in a brief, definite statement.
    • Check to be sure that an accurate response can be found in the text, workbook, or class notes.
    • Omit only one or two key words.
    • Word the statement so the blank is near the end.
    • If the question requires a numerical answer, indicate the units in which the answer is to be expressed.

12. An *extended response* essay item allows the student to determine the length and complexity of a response.

13. A *restricted response* essay item poses a specific problem for which the student must recall and organize the proper information, derive a defensible conclusion, and express it within a stated time or length.

14. Essay items are most appropriate when (1) the instructional objectives specify high-level cognitive processes, (2) relatively few test items (students) need to be graded, and (3) test security is a consideration.

15. Suggestions for writing essay items include the following:
    • Identify beforehand the mental processes that you want to measure (e.g., application, analysis, decision making).
    • Identify clearly and unambiguously the task to be accomplished by the student.
    • Begin the essay question with key words, such as *compare, give reasons for, predict*.
    • Require presentation of evidence for controversial questions.
    • Avoid optional items.
    • Establish reasonable time and/or page limits.
    • Restrict the use of essay items to those that cannot easily be measured by multiple-choice items.
    • Relate each essay question to an objective on the test blueprint.

16. The following are suggestions for increasing consistency and accuracy when scoring essay items:
    • Specify the response length.
    • Use several restricted response essay items instead of one extended response item.
    • Prepare a scoring scheme in which you specify beforehand all ingredients necessary to achieve each of the grades that could be assigned.

17. Some suggestions for packaging the test are as follows:
    • Group together all items of similar format.
    • Arrange test items from easy to hard.
    • Space items for easy reading.
    • Keep items and options on the same page.
    • Position illustrations near descriptions.
    • Check the answer key.
    • Determine beforehand how students are to record the answers.
    • Provide space for name and date.
    • Check test directions for clarity.
    • Proofread the test.

18. Validity refers to whether a test measures what it says it measures. Three types of validity are content, concurrent, and predictive.

19. *Content* validity is established by examining a test's contents. *Concurrent* validity is established by correlating the scores on a new test with the scores on an established test given to the same set of individuals. *Predictive* validity is established by correlating the scores on a new test with some future behavior of the examinee that is representative of the test's content.

20. Reliability refers to whether a test yields the same or similar scores consistently. Three types of reliability are test-retest, alternative form, and internal consistency.

21. *Test-retest* reliability is established by giving the test twice to the same individuals and correlating the first set of scores with the second. *Alternative form* reliability is established by giving two parallel but different forms of the test to the same individuals and correlating the two sets of scores. *Internal*

consistency reliability is established by determining the extent to which the test measures a single basic concept.

22. Accuracy refers to whether a test approximates an individual's true level of knowledge, skill, or ability.

23. Marks are based on comparisons, usually comparisons of students with one or more of the following:
    • Other students
    • Established standards
    • Aptitude
    • Actual versus potential effort
    • Actual versus potential improvement

24. Standardized tests are developed by test-construction specialists to determine a student's performance level relative to others of similar age and grade. They are *standardized* because they are administered and scored according to specific and uniform procedures.

25. The following assumptions are likely to guide the development of standardized tests in the future:
    • Learning is a process.
    • Learning ability can be improved.
    • Learning occurs in a social context.
    • Learning assessment should have instructional validity.

FOR DISCUSSION AND PRACTICE

Questions marked with an asterisk are answered in Appendix B. See also *Bridges: An Activity Guide and Assessment Options,* which accompanies this text.

*1. Identify the characteristics of a norm-referenced and criterion-referenced test and the decisions for which each is best suited.

*2. What two instructional dimensions are measured by a test blueprint?

*3. Identify four formats for objective test items, and give two advantages and two disadvantages of each.

*4. What would be four things to avoid in writing good multiple-choice test items? Which do you feel would be the hardest to avoid?

*5. What three devices may be used to prepare multiple-choice questions at higher levels of cognitive complexity? Prepare an example of a multiple-choice item using one.

*6. Contrast the characteristics of extended response and restricted response essay items. Prepare an example of each in your teaching field.

*7. Identify the reasons for preparing an essay as opposed to an objective test discussed in this chapter. Can you find any other reasons for using an essay test?

*8. Describe three advantages and three disadvantages of essay items.

What, in your opinion, is the biggest advantage and biggest disadvantage?

*9. What is a "scoring scheme" for an essay item? Construct a scoring scheme for each of the essay items you prepared in question 6.

*10. Identify six possible criteria for scoring higher-level essay items. What percentage weight of 100 would you assign to each?

*11. Identify 10 guidelines for packaging a test. Which do you feel would be most likely to be overlooked in the hectic pace of test preparation?

*12. Describe the concepts of validity, reliability, and accuracy using a recent test you have taken. Were you aware of the reliability and validity of the test? If not, did you know where you might obtain this information?

*13. What three methods may be used to determine the validity of a test? Give an example of what information each would provide for a test given in your classroom.

*14. What three methods may be used for determining the reliability of a test? Give an example of what information each would provide for a test given in your classroom.

*15. Provide an approximate range for an acceptable validity and acceptable reliability coefficient. What is the maximum possible size of a validity or reliability coefficient?

*16. Identify five procedures for assigning marks and one advantage and one disadvantage of each. Which approach or combination of approaches would you prefer to use in your classroom?

*17. What is a standardized test? Name two you have taken most recently.

*18. What does a percentile rank indicate for a given individual? What two points should be kept in mind in interpreting a percentile rank?

13

Assessing Learners: Performance and Portfolio Assessment

This chapter will help you answer the following questions:

1. What is a performance test?
2. How are some teachers conducting performance assessments?
3. What types of tasks should I select for a performance test?
4. How do I score a performance test?
5. What is a student portfolio?
6. How can I combine performance test grades with other classroom grades?

Some skills—particularly those involving independent judgment, critical thinking, and decision making—are best assessed with performance tests and portfolios. Although traditional paper and pencil tests currently represent the principal means of assessing these more complex cognitive outcomes, in this chapter we will study other ways of measuring them in more authentic contexts.

PERFORMANCE TESTS: DIRECT MEASURES OF COMPETENCE

Performance tests use direct measures of learning, rather than indicators that simply suggest that cognitive, affective, or psychomotor processes have occurred. In the field of athletics, diving and gymnastics are examples of performances judges rate directly. Their scores are pooled and used to decide, for example, who earns a medal, who wins first, second, third, and so on, or who qualifies for district or regional competition.

Teachers can use performance tests to assess **complex cognitive processes**, as well as attitudes and social skills in academic areas such as science, social studies, or math. When doing so, they establish situations that allow them directly to observe and to rate learners as they analyze, problem solve, experiment, make decisions, measure, cooperate with others, present orally, or produce a product. These situations simulate real-world activities, as might be expected in a job, in the community, or in various forms of advanced training, for example, in the military, a technical institute, on-the-job training, or college.

Performance tests also allow teachers to observe achievements, habits of mind, ways of working, and behaviors of value in the real world that conventional tests may miss, and they do so in ways that an outside observer would be unaware that a "test" is going on. Performance tests can include observing and rating learners during a dialogue in a foreign language, or when learners conduct a science experiment, edit a composition, present an exhibit, work with a group of other learners to design a student attitude survey, or use equipment. In other words, the teacher observes and evaluates student abilities to carry out complex activities that also are used and valued outside the classroom.

Performance Tests Can Assess Processes and Products

Performance tests can be assessments of processes, products, or both. For example, at the Darwin School in Winnipeg, Manitoba, teachers assess the reading processes of each student by noting the percentage of words read accurately during oral reading, the number of sentences read by the learner that are meaningful within the context of the story, and the percentage of story elements the learner can talk about in his or her own words after reading.

At the West Orient school in Gresham, Oregon, fourth-grade learners assemble a portfolio of their writing products. These portfolios include rough as well as final drafts of poetry, essays, biographies, and self-reflections. Several math teachers at Twin Peaks Middle School in Poway, California, require their students to assemble math portfolios, which include the following products of their problem-solving efforts: long-term projects, daily notes, journal entries about troublesome test prob-

Teachers at the Darwin School in Winnipeg, Canada, assess the reading processes of each student by noting the percentage of words read accurately during oral reading, the number of sentences the learner reads that are meaningful within the context of the story, and the percentage of story elements the learner can talk about in her or his own words after reading.

lems, written explanations of how they solved problems, and the problem solutions themselves.

In the Aurora, Colorado, Public Schools, teachers assess social studies learning processes and products by having learners engage in a variety of projects built around the following question: "Based on your study of Colorado history, what current issues in Colorado do you believe are the most important to address, what are your ideas about the resolutions of those issues, and what contributions will you make toward the resolutions?" (Pollock, 1992). Learners answer these questions in a variety of ways involving individual and group writing assignments, oral presentations, and exhibits.

Performance Tests Can Be Embedded in Lessons

The preceding examples of performance tests involve performances occurring outside the context of a lesson and completed at the end of a term or during an examination period. Many teachers use performance tests as part of their lessons. In fact, some proponents of performance tests hold that the ideal performance test is a good teaching activity (Shavelson & Baxter, 1992). Viewed from this perspective, a well-constructed performance test can serve as a student learning experience as well as an assessment.

For example, Figure 13.1 illustrates a performance activity and assessment that was embedded in a unit on electricity in a general science class (Shavelson & Baxter, 1992). During the activity, the teacher observes and rates the learners on the method they used to solve the problem, the care with which they measured, the manner of recording results, and the correctness of the final solution. This type of assessment provides immediate feedback on how learners are performing, reinforces hands-on teaching and learning, and underscores for learners the important link between teaching and testing. In this manner, it moves the instruction toward higher-order and more authentic behavior.

Other examples of lesson-embedded performance tests might include observing and rating the following as they actually happen: typing, preparing a microscope slide, reading out loud, programming a calculator, giving an oral presentation, determining how plants react to certain substances, designing a questionnaire or survey, solving a math problem, developing an original math problem and a solution for it, critiquing the logic of an editorial, or graphing information.

Performance Tests Can Assess Affective and Social Skills

Teachers across the country are using performance tests not only to assess higher-level cognitive skills but also noncognitive outcomes such as self-direction, ability to work with others, and social awareness (Redding, 1992). This concern for the affective domain of learning reflects an awareness by educators that the skilled performance of complex tasks involves more than the ability to recall information, form concepts, generalize, and problem solve. It also involves habits of mind, attitudes, and social skills.

Figure 13.1 Sample performance activity and assessment.

HANDS-ON ELECTRIC MYSTERIES INVESTIGATION

Find out what is in the six mystery boxes A, B, C, D, E, and F. They have five different things inside, shown below. Two of the boxes will have the same thing. All of the others will have something different inside.

Two batteries:

A wire:

A bulb:

A battery and a bulb:

Nothing at all:

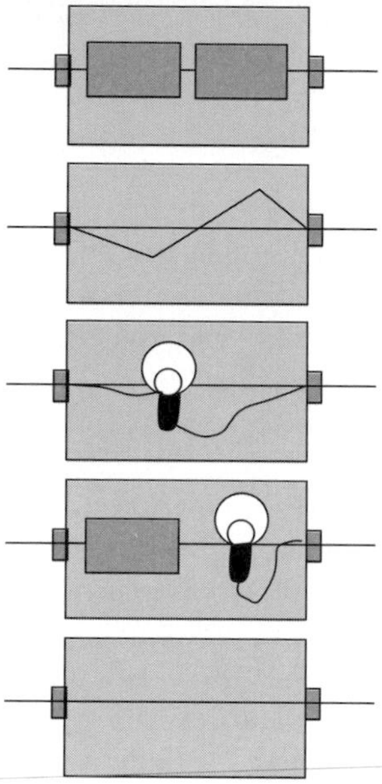

You can use your bulbs, batteries, and wires any way you like. Connect them in a circuit to help you figure out what is inside.

When you find out what is in the box, fill in the spaces on the following pages.

Box A: Has _____ inside.

Draw a picture of the circuit that told you what was inside **Box A**.

How could you tell from your circuit what was inside **Box A**.

_____

_____

_____

Do the same for Boxes B, C, D, E, and F.

_____

_____

Source: From Shavelson, R. J., & Baxter, G. P. What we've learned about assessing hands-on science. *Educational Leadership,* 1992, 49(8), p. 22. Alexandria, VA: Association for Supervision and Curriculum Development. Copyright © 1992 by ASCD. Used with permission.

The Aurora public school system in Colorado has developed a list of learning outcomes and their indicators for learners in kindergarten through twelfth grade. These are shown in Figure 13.2. For each of these 19 indicators, a four-category rating scale serves as a guide for teachers who are unsure of how to define "assumes responsibility" or "demonstrates consideration." While observing learners during performance tests in social studies, science, art, or economics, teachers are alert to recognize and rate those behaviors that suggest that learners have acquired the outcomes.

Teachers in the Aurora Public Schools are encouraged to use this list of outcomes when planning their courses. They first ask themselves, What key facts, con-

Figure 13.2 Learning outcomes of Aurora Public Schools.

Source: From Curriculum Report, Aurora Public Schools, Aurora, Colorado, 1993, p. 11.

A Self-Directed Learner

1. Sets priorities and achievable goals.
2. Monitors and evaluates progress.
3. Creates options for self.
4. Assumes responsibility for actions.
5. Creates a positive vision for self and future.

A Collaborative Worker

6. Monitors own behavior as a group member.
7. Assesses and manages group functioning.
8. Demonstrates interactive communication.
9. Demonstrates consideration for individual differences.

A Complex Thinker

10. Uses a wide variety of strategies for managing complex issues.
11. Selects strategies appropriate to the resolution of complex issues and applies the strategies with accuracy and thoroughness.
12. Accesses and uses topic-relevant knowledge.

A Quality Producer

13. Creates products that achieve their purpose.
14. Creates products appropriate to the intended audience.
15. Creates products that reflect craftsmanship.
16. Uses appropriate resources/technology.

A Community Contributor

17. Demonstrates knowledge about his or her diverse communities.
18. Takes action.
19. Reflects on his or her role as a community contributor.

cepts, and principles should all learners remember? In addition, they try to fuse this subject area content with the five district outcomes by designing special performance tests. For example, a third-grade language arts teacher who is planning a writing unit might choose to focus on indicators 8 and 9 to address district outcomes related to "collaborative worker," indicator 1 for the outcome of "self-directed learner," and 13 for the outcome, "quality producer." She would then design a performance assessment that allows learners to demonstrate learning in these areas. She might select other indicators and outcomes for subsequent units and performance tests.

Performance tests represent an addition to the testing practices reviewed in the previous chapter. Paper and pencil tests are the most efficient, reliable, and valid instruments available for assessing knowledge, comprehension, and some types of application. But, when it comes to assessing complex thinking skills, attitudes, and social skills, performance tests can, if properly constructed, do a better job. On the other hand, if not properly constructed, performance assessments can have some of the same problems with authenticity, scoring efficiency, reliability, and validity as traditional approaches to testing. Tombari and Borich (1999) and Stiggins (1994) emphasize that performance assessments of affect must adhere to the same standards of evaluation and scoring as assessments of achievement, or the results may prove too subjective and inferential to be of value. This chapter will guide you through a process that will allow you to properly construct performance tests in your classroom.

DEVELOPING PERFORMANCE TESTS FOR YOUR LEARNERS

As mentioned in the previous section, performance assessment has the potential to improve both instruction and learning. However, teachers must resolve both conceptual and technical issues associated with the use of performance tests before they can effectively and efficiently use this form of assessment. This section discusses four steps to consider in planning and designing a performance test. We will identify the tasks around which you may base performance tests and how to score these tasks. Also, we will suggest how to improve the reliability of performance test scoring, including evaluation of portfolios.

Step 1: Deciding What to Test

The first step in developing a performance test is to create a list of performance objectives that specifies the knowledge, skills, attitudes, and indicators of the outcomes that will be the focus of your instruction.

You should ask three general questions when deciding what to teach:

1. What knowledge or content (i.e., facts, concepts, principles, rules) is essential for learner understanding of the subject matter?
2. What intellectual skills are necessary for the learner to use this knowledge or content?
3. What habits of mind or attitudes are important for the learner to successfully perform with this knowledge or content?

Instructional objectives that come from answering question 1 are usually measured by traditional paper and pencil tests. Objectives derived from answering questions 2 and 3, although often assessed with objective or essay-type questions, can be more authentically assessed with performance tests. Thus, your assessment plan for a unit should include both paper and pencil tests to measure mastery of content and performance tests to assess skills and attitudes. Let's see what objectives for these latter outcomes might look like.

Performance Objectives in the Cognitive Domain.   Designers of performance tests usually ask the following questions to help guide their initial selection of objectives:

- What kinds of essential tasks, achievements, or other valued competencies am I missing with paper and pencil tests?
- What accomplishments of those who practice my discipline (historians, writers, scientists, mathematicians) are valued but left unmeasured by conventional tests?

Typically, these questions identify two categories of performance skills:

1. Skills related to acquiring information
2. Skills related to organizing and using information

Figure 13.3 presents a list of skills useful for acquiring, organizing, and using information. As you study this list and the higher-order thinking and problem-solving behaviors in Appendix C, consider which you might use as a basis for a performance test in your area of expertise.

The following are sample objectives for performance tests derived from a consideration of the performance skills described in Figure 13.3.

1. Write a summary of a current controversy drawn from school life, and tell how a courageous and civic-minded American you have studied might decide to act on the issue.
2. Draw a physical map of North America from memory, and locate 10 cities.
3. Prepare an exhibit showing how your community responds to an important social problem of your choosing.
4. Construct an electrical circuit using wires, a switch, a bulb, resistors, and a battery.
5. Describe two alternative ways to solve a mathematics word problem.
6. Identify the important variables that accounted for recent events in our state, and forecast the direction they might take.
7. Design a freestanding structure in which the size of one leg of a triangular structure must be determined from the other two sides.
8. Program a calculator to solve an equation with one unknown.
9. Design an exhibit showing the best ways to clean up an oil spill.
10. Prepare a presentation to the city council using visuals requesting increased funding to deal with a selected problem in our community.

Performance Objectives in the Affective and Social Domains.   Performance assessments not only require curriculum to teach thinking skills but also to develop positive dispositions and habits of mind. **Habits of mind** include such behaviors as constructive criticism, tolerance of ambiguity, respect for reason, and appreciation for the significance of the past. Performance tests are ideal vehicles for assessing positive attitudes toward learning, habits of mind, and social skills (e.g., cooperation, sharing,

Figure 13.3　Skills for acquiring, organizing, and using information.

Skills in Acquiring Information	Skills in Organizing and Using Information
Communicating explaining modeling demonstrating graphing displaying writing advising programming proposing drawing **Measuring** counting calibrating rationing appraising weighing balancing guessing estimating forecasting **Investigating** gathering references interviewing using references experimenting hypothesizing	**Organizing** classifying categorizing sorting ordering ranking arranging **Problem Solving** stating questions identifying problems developing hypotheses interpreting assessing risks monitoring **Decision Making** weighing alternatives evaluating choosing supporting defending electing adopting

and negotiation). The following are key questions to ask when including affective and social skills in your list of performance objectives:

- What dispositions, attitudes, or values characterize successful individuals in the community who work in my academic discipline?
- What are some of the qualities of mind or character traits of good scientists, writers, reporters, historians, mathematicians, musicians, and others?
- What will I accept as evidence that my learners have or are developing these qualities?
- What social skills for getting along with others are necessary for being successful as a journalist, weather forecaster, park ranger, historian, economist, mechanic, and so on?

- What evidence will convince my learners' parents that their children are developing these skills?

Following are examples of attitudes, or habits of mind, that could be the focus of a performance assessment in science, social studies, and mathematics.

In science (from Loucks-Horsley et al., 1990, *Elementary School Science for the '90's*, p. 41):

- Desiring knowledge. Viewing science as a way of knowing and understanding.
- Being skeptical. Recognizing the appropriate time and place to question authoritarian statements and self-evident truths.
- Relying on data. Explaining natural occurrences by collecting and ordering information, testing ideas, and respecting the facts that are revealed.
- Accepting ambiguity. Recognizing that data are rarely clear and compelling, and appreciating the new questions and problems that arise.
- Willingness to modify explanations. Seeing new possibilities in the data.
- Cooperating in answering questions and solving problems. Working together to pool ideas, explanations, and solutions.
- Respecting reason. Valuing patterns of thought that lead from data to conclusions and, eventually, to the construction of theories.
- Being honest. Viewing information objectively, without bias.

In social studies (from Parker, 1991, *Renewing the Social Studies Curriculum*, p. 74):

- Understanding the significance of the past to their own lives, both private and public, and to their society.
- Distinguishing between the important and inconsequential to develop the discriminating memory needed for a discerning judgment in public and personal life.
- Preparing to live with uncertainties and exasperating, even perilous, unfinished business, realizing that not all problems have solutions.
- Appreciating the often tentative nature of judgments about the past, and thereby avoiding the temptation to seize on particular lessons of history as cures for present ills.

In mathematics (from Willoughby, 1990, *Mathematics Education for a Changing World*, p. 62):

- Appreciating that mathematics is a discipline that helps solve real-world problems.
- Seeing mathematics as a tool or servant rather than something mysterious or mystical to be afraid of.
- Recognizing that there is more than one way to solve a problem.

Once you have completed step 1, you will have identified the important knowledge, skills, and attitudes that will be the focus of your instruction and assessment. The next step is to design the task or context in which you will assess these outcomes.

Step 2: Designing the Assessment Context

First, and most obviously, you must identify and define the directly observable performance that will tell you whether you have achieved your instructional objectives. The purpose of step 2 is to create an authentic task, simulation, or situation that will allow learners to demonstrate their acquired knowledge, skills, and attitudes. Ideas for these tasks may come from newspapers, reading popular books, or interviews with professionals as reported in the media (e.g., an oil tanker runs aground and creates an environmental crisis; a drought occurs in an underdeveloped country, causing famine; a technological breakthrough presents a moral dilemma). The tasks should center on issues, concepts, or problems important to your subject matter. In other words, they should be the same issues, concepts, and problems that professionals in the field face everyday.

Here are some questions to get you started on step 2, suggested by Wiggins (1992):

- What does the doing of mathematics, history, science, art, writing, and so forth look and feel like to professionals who make their living working in these fields in the real world?
- What are the projects and tasks performed by these professionals that can be adapted to school instruction?
- What are the roles—or habits of mind—that these professionals acquire that learners can re-create in the classroom?

The tasks you create may involve debates, mock trials, presentations to a city commission, reenactments of historical events, science experiments, job responsibilities (e.g., a travel agent, weather forecaster, park ranger), or other scenarios. Regardless of the specific context, they should present the learner with an authentic challenge.

For example, consider the following social studies performance test item (adapted from Wiggins, 1992).

> *You and several travel agent colleagues have been assigned the responsibility of designing a trip to China for 12- to 14-year-olds. Prepare an extensive brochure for a month-long cultural exchange trip. Include itinerary, modes of transportation, costs, suggested budget, clothing, health considerations, areas of cultural sensitivity, language considerations, and other information necessary for a family to decide if they want their child to participate.*

Notice that this example presents learners with (1) a hands-on exercise or problem to solve that produces (2) an observable outcome or product (typed business letter, a map, graph, piece of clothing, multimedia presentation, poem, etc.), such that the teacher (3) can observe and assess not only the product but also the process used to get there.

Designing the content for a performance test involves equal parts inspiration and perspiration. While there is no formula or recipe to follow that guarantees a valid performance test, the following criteria can help you in revising and refining the task (Resnick & Resnick, 1991; Wiggins, 1992).

Make clear the requirements for task mastery but not the solution itself. While your tasks should be complex, learners should not have to question whether they are finished or whether they have provided what you want. They should, however, have to think long and hard about how to complete the task. As you refine the task, make sure you can visualize what mastery of the task looks like and identify the skills you can infer from it.

The task should represent a valid sample from which you can make generalizations about the learner's knowledge, thinking ability, and attitudes. What performance tests lack in breadth of coverage, they make up in depth. In other words, they get you to observe a lot of behavior in a narrow domain or skill. Thus, the type of tasks you choose should be complex enough and rich enough in detail to allow you to draw conclusions about transfer and generalization to other tasks. Ideally, you should be able to identify about 8 to 10 important performance tasks for an entire course of study (one or two a unit) that assess the essential performance outcomes you wish your learners to achieve (Shavelson & Baxter, 1992).

The task should be complex enough to allow for multimodal assessment. Most assessment tends to depend on the written word. Performance tests, however, are designed to allow learners to demonstrate learning through a variety of modalities. In science, for example, you could make direct observations of students while they investigate a problem using laboratory equipment, have students give oral explanations of what they did, require them to record procedures and conclusions in notebooks, prepare an exhibit of their project, and solve short-answer paper and pencil problems. This **multimodal assessment** will be more time-consuming than a multiple-choice test only, but it will provide unique information about your learners' achievement untapped by other assessment methods. Shavelson and Baxter (1992) have shown that performance tests allow teachers to draw different conclusions about a learner's problem-solving ability than do higher-order multiple-choice tests or restricted response essay tests that ask learners to analyze, interpret, and evaluate information.

The task should yield multiple solutions where possible, each with costs and benefits. Performance testing is not a form of practice or drill. It should involve more than simple tasks for which there is one solution. Performance tests should be, in the words of L. B. Resnick (1987), nonalgorithmic (the path of action is not fully specified in advance) and complex (the total solution cannot be seen from any one vantage point) and should involve judgment and interpretation.

The task should require self-regulated learning. Performance tests should require considerable mental effort and place high demands on the persistence and determination of the individual learner. The learner should be required to use cognitive strategies to arrive at a solution rather than depend on coaching at various points in the assessment process.

Figures 13.4 to 13.6 illustrate performance assessments containing most of these design considerations.

Figure 13.4   Performance assessment: Math.

Joe, Sarah, José, Zabi, and Kim decided to hold their own Olympics after watching the Olympics on TV. They needed to decide what events to have at their Olympics. Joe and José wanted a weightlifting and frisbee toss event. Sarah, Zabi, and Kim thought a running event would be fun. The children decided to have all three events. They also decided to make each event of the same importance.

One day after school they held their Olympics. The children's mothers were the judges. The mothers kept the children's scores on each of the events.

The children's scores and rankings for each of the events are listed below:

Child's Name	Frisbee Toss	Weightlifting	50-Yard Dash
Joe	40 yards (3)	205 pounds (1)	9–5 seconds (5)
José	30 yards (4)	170 pounds (2)	8–0 seconds (2)
Kim	45 yards (2)	130 pounds (4)	9–0 seconds (4)
Sarah	28 yards (5)	120 pounds (5)	7–6 seconds (1)
Zabi	48 yards (1)	140 pounds (3)	8–3 seconds (3)

Answer the question, "Who Won the Olympics?" and give an explanation of how you arrived at your answer (4 points). Sample responses:

Student A

Who would be the all-round winner?   *Zabi*

Explain how you decided who would be the all-round winner. Be sure to show all your work.

I decided by how each person came in, and that's who won $\boxed{2}$

Student B

Who would be the all-round winner?   *Zabi*

Explain how you decided who would be the all-round winner. Be sure to show all your work.

I wrote in order all the rankings from first place to fifth place. Then I averaged them, and whoever had the least amount, won. $\boxed{3}$

Student C

Who would be the all-round winner?   *Zabi*

Explain how you decided who would be the all-round winner. Be sure to show all your work.

Zabi got one first and two thirds. I counted 3 points for every first place they got and 2 points for second place and 1 point for third place. Zabi got the most points. $\boxed{4}$

Source: Adapted from Blumberg, E., Epstein, M., MacDonald, W., & Mullis, I., 1986. *A pilot study of higher-order thinking skills assessment techniques in science and mathematics (Final Report).* Princeton, NJ: National Assessment of Educational Process. Adapted with permission.

Figure 13.5   Performance assessment: Communication.

Source: From Redding, N. Assessing the Big Outcomes, *Educational Leadership,* May, 1992, p. 49. Alexandria, VA: Association for Supervision and Curriculum Development. Copyright © 1992 by ASCD. Used with permission.

1. You are representing an ad agency. Your job is to find a client in the school who needs photos to promote his/her program. (Examples: the Team Mothers' program, the fine arts program, Student Congress.)

2. Your job is to research all the possibilities, select a program, learn about that program, and then record on film the excitement and unique characteristics that make up the program you have selected. Your photos will be used to advertise and stimulate interest in that area.

3. Previsualize how you will illustrate your ideas by either writing descriptions or by drawing six of your proposed frames. Present these six ideas to your instructor (the director of the ad agency) before you shoot.

Figure 13.6   Performance assessment: History.

Source: From Wiggins, G., Creating Tests Worth Taking, In *Educational Leadership,* May, 1992, p. 28. Alexandria, VA: Association for Supervision and Curriculum Development. Used with permission.

You and your colleagues (groups of 3 or 4) have been asked to submit a proposal to write a U.S. history textbook for middle school students. The publishers demand two things: that the book hit the most important things, and that it be interesting to students. Because of your expertise in 18th-century American history, you will provide them a draft chapter on the 18th century, up to but not including the Revolution, and "field-tested" on some middle school students. They also ask that you fill in an "importance" chart with your response to these questions:

1. Which event, person, or idea is more important in this time period, and why?

2. Which of three sources of history—ideas, people, events—is most important?

You will be expected to justify your choices of "most important" and to demonstrate that the target population will likely be interested in your book.

Step 3: Specifying the Scoring Rubrics

One of the principal limitations of performance tests is the time required to score them reliably. Just as these tests require time and effort on the part of the learner, they demand similar commitment from teachers when scoring them. True–false, multiple-choice, and fill-in tests are significantly easier to score than projects, portfolios, or performances. In addition, these latter accomplishments force teachers to make difficult choices over how to weigh in the final score affective qualities such as effort, participation, and attitude.

Given the challenges confronting teachers who use performance tests, there is a temptation to limit the scoring criteria to those performance qualities that are easiest to rate, rather than those most important for doing an effective job. Wiggins (1992) cautions teachers that resorting to scoring what is easiest or least controversial can turn a well-thought-out and authentic performance test into a bogus one. Thus, your goal when scoring performance tests is to do justice to the time spent developing them and the effort expended by students taking them. You can accomplish this by developing carefully articulated scoring systems, called **rubrics**.

By giving careful consideration to rubrics, you can develop a scoring system that minimizes the arbitrariness of your judgments while holding learners to high standards of achievement. Let's look at some important considerations for developing rubrics for a performance test.

Develop rubrics for a variety of accomplishments. In general, performance tests require four types of accomplishments from learners:

- Products: Poems, essays, charts, graphs, exhibits, drawings, maps, etc.
- Complex cognitive processes: Skills in acquiring, organizing, and using information (see Figure 13.3)
- Observable performance: Physical movements as in dance, gymnastics, or typing; oral presentations; use of specialized procedures as when dissecting a frog, bisecting an angle, or following a recipe
- Attitudes and social skills: Habits of mind, group work and recognition skills

As this list suggests, the effect of your teaching may be realized in a variety of ways. The difficulty in scoring some of these accomplishments should not be a deterrent to your attempts to measure them. Kubiszyn and Borich (2000), Shavelson and Baxter (1992), Stiggins (1994), and Sax (1989) have shown that performance measures can be scored reliably, depending on the care with which they are developed and the training of those doing the scoring.

Choose a scoring system best suited for the type of accomplishment you want to measure. In general, teachers use three categories of rubrics when scoring performance tests: checklists, rating scales, and holistic scoring. Each has certain strengths and limitations, and each is more or less suitable for scoring products, cognitive processes, performances, or attitudes and social skills.

Checklists.   Checklists contain lists of behaviors, traits, or characteristics that can be scored as either present or absent. They are best suited for complex behaviors or performances divisible into a series of clearly defined, specific actions. Dissecting a frog, bisecting an angle, balancing a scale, making an audiotape recording, or tying a shoe are behaviors requiring sequences of actions that may be clearly identified and listed on a checklist. Checklists are scored on a yes/no, present or absent, 0 or 1 point basis and also should provide the opportunity for observers to indicate that they had no opportunity to observe the performance. Some checklists also include frequent mistakes that learners make when performing the task. In such cases, a score of +1 may be given for each positive behavior, −1 for each mistake, and 0 for no opportunity to observe. Figure 13.7 shows a checklist for using a microscope.

Figure 13.7   Checklist for using a microscope.

No opportunity to observe	Observed	
☐	☐	Wipes slide with lens paper
☐	☐	Places drop or two of culture on slide
☐	☐	Adds few drops of water
☐	☐	Places slide on stage
☐	☐	Turns to low power
☐	☐	Looks through eyepiece with one eye
☐	☐	Adjusts mirror
☐	☐	Turns to high power
☐	☐	Adjusts for maximum enlargement and resolution

Rating Scales.   Teachers typically use rating scales for those aspects of a complex performance that do not lend themselves to yes/no or present/absent type judgments. The most common form of rating scale assigns numbers to categories of performance. Figure 13.8 shows a rating scale for judging elements of writing in a term paper. This scale focuses the rater's observations on certain aspects of the performance (accuracy, logic, organization, style, etc.) and assigns numbers to five degrees of performance.

Most numeric rating scales use an analytical scoring technique called **primary trait scoring** (Sax, 1989). This type of rating requires that the test developer first identify the salient characteristics or primary traits of greatest importance when observing the product, process, or performance. Then, for each trait, the developer assigns numbers (usually 1 to 5) representing degrees of performance.

Figure 13.9 displays a numerical rating scale using primary trait scoring to rate problem solving (Szetela & Nicol, 1992). In this system, problem solving is subdivided into the three primary traits of understanding, solving, and answering the problem. Points are assigned to certain aspects or qualities of each trait. Notice how the designer of this rating scale identified characteristics of both effective and ineffective problem solving.

Usually, two key questions are addressed when planning scoring systems for rating scales using primary trait scoring (Wiggins, 1992):

1. What are the most important characteristics that show a high degree of the trait?
2. What errors most justify achieving a lower score?

Figure 13.8   Rating scale for themes and term papers that emphasizes interpretation and organization.

Quality and accuracy of ideas

1	2	3	4	5
Very limited investigation; little or no material related to the facts.		Some investigation and attention to the facts are apparent.		Extensive investigation; good detail and representation of the facts.

Logical development of ideas

1	2	3	4	5
Very little orderly development of ideas; presentation is confusing and hard to follow.		Some logical development of ideas, but logical order needs to be improved.		Good logical development; ideas logically connected and build on one another.

Organization of ideas

1	2	3	4	5
No apparent organization. Lack of paragraphing and transitions.		Organization is mixed; some of the ideas are not adequately separated from others with appropriate transitions.		Good organization and paragraphing; clear transitions between ideas.

Style, individuality

1	2	3	4	5
Style bland and inconsistent, or "borrowed."		Some style and individuality beginning to show.		Good style and individuality; personality of writer shows through.

Wording and phrasing

1	2	3	4	5
Wording trite; extensive use of clichés.		Some word choices awkward.		Appropriate use of words and phrasing work to sharpen ideas.

Answering these questions can prevent raters from assigning higher or lower scores on the basis of performance that may be trivial or unrelated to the purpose of the performance test, such as the quantity rather than quality of a performance. One advantage of rating scales is that they focus the scorer on specific and relevant aspects of a performance. Without the breakdown of important traits, successes, and relevant errors provided by these scales, a scorer's attention may be diverted to aspects of performance unrelated to the purpose of the performance test.

Holistic Scoring.   Holistic scoring is used when the rater is more interested in estimating the overall quality of the performance and assigning a numerical value to that

Figure 13.9 Analytic scale for problem solving.

Understanding the problem

0 — No attempt
1 — Completely misinterprets the problem
2 — Misinterprets major part of the problem
3 — Misinterprets minor part of the problem
4 — Complete understanding of the problem

Solving the problem

0 — No attempt
1 — Totally inappropriate plan
2 — Partially correct procedure but with major fault
3 — Substantially correct procedure with major omission or procedural error
4 — A plan that could lead to a correct solution with no arithmetic errors

Answering the problem

0 — No answer or wrong answer based upon an inappropriate plan
1 — Copying error, computational error, partial answer for problem with multiple answers; no answer statement; answer labeled incorrectly
2 — Correct solution

Source: From Szetela, W., & Nicol, C. Evaluating problem solving in mathematics. *Educational Leadership,* 1992, 49(8), p. 42. Alexandria, VA: Association for Supervision and Curriculum Development. Copyright © 1992 by ASCD. Used with permission.

quality than in assigning points for including or omitting a specific aspect of performance. Holistic scoring is typically used in evaluating extended essays, term papers, and some artistic performances, such as dance or musical creations.

For example, a rater might decide to score an extended essay question or term paper on an A to F rating scale, in which case, it would be important for the rater to have a model paper that exemplifies each score category. After having created or selected these models from the set to be scored, the rater again reads each paper and then assigns it to one of the categories. A model for each category (A to F) helps to ensure that all the papers assigned to a given category are of comparable quality.

Holistic scoring systems can be more difficult to use for performances than for products. For the former, some experience in rating the performance, for example, dramatic rendition, oral interpretations, debate, may be required. In these cases, audio- or videotapes from past classes can be helpful as models representing different categories of performance.

Combining Scoring Systems. As suggested, good performance tests require learners to demonstrate their achievements through a variety of primary traits, for example, cooperation, research, and delivery. You may therefore need to combine several ratings from checklists, rating scales, and holistic impressions to arrive at a total assessment. Figure 13.10 shows how scores across several traits for a current events project might combine to provide a single performance score.

Comparing the Three Scoring Systems. Each of the three scoring systems—checklists, rating scales, and holistic scoring—has its particular strengths and weaknesses. Table 13.1 evaluates each scoring system as suitable for a given type of performance, according to the following criteria:

Figure 13.10 Combined scoring rubric for current events project (17 total points).

Checklist (Assign 1 or 0 points)   Total Points (5)

_____ Interviewed 4 people

_____ Cited current references

_____ Typed

_____ No spelling errors

_____ Included title and summary page

Rating Circle numbers which best represent quality of the presentation.
       Total Points (9)

Persuasiveness

1	2	3
Lacks enthusiasm	Somewhat unanimated	Highly convincing

Delivery

1	2	3
Unclear, mumbled a lot	Often failed to look at audience, somewhat unclear	Clear, forceful delivery

Sensitivity to audience

1	2	3
Rarely looked at or noticed audience	Answered some questions, not always aware when audience didn't understand	Encouraged questions, stopped and clarified when saw that audience didn't understand

Holistic Rating Total Points (3)

What is your overall impression of the quality of the project?

1	2	3
Below Average	Average	Clearly outstanding

Table 13.1 The strength of three performance-based scoring systems according to five measurement criteria.

	Ease of Construction	Scoring Efficiency	Reliability	Defensibility	Feedback	Performance Most Suitable For
Checklists	low	moderate	high	high	high	procedures
Rating Scales	moderate	moderate	moderate	moderate	moderate	attitudes, products, social skills
Holistic Scoring	high	high	low	low	low	products and processes

1. *Ease of construction.* Refers to the time involved in coming up with a comprehensive list of the important aspects or traits of successful and unsuccessful performance. Checklists, for example, are particularly time consuming, while holistic scoring is not.
2. *Scoring efficiency.* Refers to the amount of time required to score various aspects of the performance and sum these scores into an overall score.
3. *Reliability.* The likelihood of two raters independently coming up with a similar score; or the likelihood of the same rater coming up with a similar score on two separate occasions.
4. *Defensibility.* Refers to the ease with which you can explain your score to a student or parent who challenges it.
5. *Quality of feedback.* Refers to the amount of information the scoring system gives to learners or parents about the strengths and weaknesses of the performance.

Limit the number of points the assessment or component is worth to what can be reliably discriminated. For example, 25 points assigned to a particular product or procedure assumes that the rater can discriminate 25 degrees of quality. When faced with more degrees of quality than can be detected, a typical rater may assign some points arbitrarily, reducing the reliability of the assessment.

On what basis should you assign points to a response on a performance test? On the one hand, you want a response to be worth enough points to allow you to subtly differentiate response quality. On the other hand, you want to avoid assigning too many points to a response that does not lend itself to complex discriminations. Thus, assigning 1 or 2 points to a math question requiring complex problem solving would not allow you to differentiate among outstanding, above average, average, and poor responses. On the other hand, assigning 30 points to this same answer would seriously challenge your ability to distinguish a rating of 15 from a rating of 18. Two considerations can help you make decisions about the size and complexity of a rating scale.

The first is that you may prepare a scoring model wherein the rater specifies the exact performance—or examples of acceptable performance—that corresponds with each scale point. The ability to successfully define distinct criteria can determine the number of scale points that are defensible. The second consideration is that, although it is customary for homework, paper and pencil tests, and report cards to use a 100-point (percent) scale, scale points derived from performance assessments do not need to add up to 100. In a following section, we will indicate how to assign marks to performance tests and how to integrate them with other aspects of an overall grading system (e.g., homework, paper and pencil tests, classwork, etc.), including portfolios.

Step 4: Specifying Testing Constraints

Should performance tests have time limits? Should learners be allowed to correct their mistakes? Can they consult references or ask for help from other learners? If these questions were asked of a multiple-choice test, most test developers would respond negatively without much hesitation. But, performance tests confront the designer with the following dilemma: If performance tests are designed to confront learners with real-world challenges, why shouldn't they be allowed to tackle these challenges as real-world people do?

In the world outside of the classroom, mathematicians make mistakes and correct them, journalists write first drafts and revise them, weather forecasters make predictions and change them. Each of these workers can consult references to help them solve problems and consult with colleagues. Why, then, shouldn't learners who are working on performance tests that simulate similar problems be allowed the same working (or testing) conditions? But, even outside the classroom, professionals have constraints on their performance, such as deadlines, limited office space, outmoded equipment, and so on. So, how does a teacher decide which conditions to impose during a performance test? Before examining this question, let's look at some of the typical conditions imposed on learners during tests. Wiggins (1992) includes the following among the most common forms of **testing constraints**:

1. *Time.*   How much time should a learner have to prepare, rethink, revise, and finish a test?
2. *Reference material.*   Should learners be able to consult dictionaries, textbooks, notes, and so on as they take a test?
3. *Other people.*   May learners ask for help from peers, teachers, experts, and others as they take a test or complete a project?
4. *Equipment.*   May learners use computers, calculators, and the like to help them solve problems?
5. *Prior knowledge of the task.*   How much information about what they will be tested should learners receive in advance?
6. *Scoring criteria.*   Should learners know the standards by which the teacher will score the assessment?

Wiggins (1992) recommends that teachers take an "authenticity test" to decide which of the preceding constraints to impose on a performance assessment. His authenticity test involves answering the following questions:

1. What kinds of constraints authentically replicate the constraints and opportunities facing the performer in the real world?
2. What kinds of constraints tend to bring out the best in apprentice performers and producers?
3. What are the appropriate or authentic limits one should impose on the availability of the six resources listed here?

Indirect forms of assessment, by the nature of the questions asked, require numerous constraints during the testing conditions. Allowing learners to consult reference materials or ask peers for help during multiple-choice tests would significantly reduce their validity. Performance tests, on the other hand, are direct forms of assessment in which real-world conditions and constraints play an important role in demonstrating the competencies desired.

PORTFOLIO ASSESSMENT

There is another type of performance assessment that is more than a one-time picture of what a learner has accomplished. Its principal purpose is to tell a story of a learner's growth in proficiency, long-term achievement, and significant accomplishments in a given academic area. It is called *portfolio assessment*. A portfolio is a planned collection of learner achievement that documents what a student has accomplished and the steps taken to get there. The collection represents a collaborative effort among teacher, learner, and parent to decide on portfolio purpose, content, and evaluation criteria. The portfolio is a measure of deep understanding like the performance demonstrations covered earlier. But, in addition, it shows growth in competence and understanding across the term or school year (Frazier & Paulson, 1992).

A portfolio is based on the idea that a collection of a learner's work throughout the year is one of the best ways to show both final achievement and the effort put into getting there. You are already familiar with the idea of a portfolio. Painters, fashion designers, artisans, and writers assemble portfolios that embody their best work. Television and radio announcers compile video- and audiotaped excerpts of their best performances that they present when interviewing for a job. A portfolio is their way of showing what they can really do.

Classroom portfolios serve a similar purpose. They show off a learner's best writing, artwork, science projects, historical thinking, or mathematical achievement. But they also show the steps the learner took to get there. They compile the learner's best work. But they also include the works-in-progress: the early drafts, test runs, pilot studies, or preliminary trials. Thus, they are an ideal way to assess final mastery, effort, reflection, and growth in learning that tell the learner's story of achievement.

The idea of a classroom portfolio has gained considerable support and momentum. Many school districts use portfolios and other types of exhibitions to help motivate effort and show achievement and growth in learning. While the reliability and validity of a classroom teacher's judgments are always a matter of concern, they are less so when the teacher has multiple opportunities to interact with learners and numerous occasions to observe their work and confirm judgments about their capabilities.

Rationale for the Portfolio

We believe that a portfolio's greatest potential is for showing teachers, parents, and learners a richer array of what students know and can do than paper and pencil tests and other snap-shot assessments. If designed properly, portfolios can show a learner's ability to think and problem solve, to use strategies and procedural-type skills, and to construct knowledge. But in addition, they also tell something about a learner's persistence, effort, willingness to change, skill in monitoring his or her own learning, and ability to be self-reflective or metacognitive Hebert (1992). So, one purpose for a portfolio is to give a teacher information about a learner that no other measurement tool can provide.

There are other reasons for using portfolios. Portfolios also provide a means to communicate to parents and other teachers the level of achievement that a learner has reached. Report card grades give us some idea of this. But portfolios supplement grades by showing parents, teachers, and learners the supporting evidence.

Portfolios are not an alternative to paper and pencil tests, essay tests, or performance tests. Each of these tools possesses validity for a purpose not served by a different tool. If you want to assess a learner's factual knowledge base (as discussed in Chapter 12), then objective-type tests are appropriate. If you are interested in a snapshot assessment of how well a learner uses a cognitive strategy, there are ways to do this that don't involve the work required for portfolio assessment. But, if you want to

Portfolios tell a story. They answer the student's question "What have I learned during this period of instruction, and how have I put it into practice?"

assess both achievement and growth in an authentic context, portfolios are a tool that you should consider.

Now let's get started building a portfolio for your teaching area.

Step 1: Deciding on the Purposes for a Portfolio

Have your learners think about their purpose in assembling a portfolio. Having learners identify for themselves the purpose of the portfolio is one way to increase the authenticity of the task. However, your learners' purposes for the portfolio (e.g., getting a job with the local news station) won't necessarily coincide with yours (e.g., evaluating your teaching). So, be clear about your purposes at the outset of portfolio design.

Classroom level purposes that portfolios can achieve include

- Monitoring student progress
- Communicating what has been learned to parents
- Passing on information to subsequent teachers
- Evaluating how well something was taught
- Showing-off what has been accomplished
- Assigning a course grade

Step 2: Identifying Cognitive Skills and Dispositions

Portfolios, like performance assessments, are measures of deep understanding and genuine achievement. They can measure growth and development of competence in areas like knowledge construction (e.g., knowledge organization), cognitive strategies (analysis, interpretation, planning, organizing, revising), procedural skills (clear communication, editing, drawing, speaking, building), metacognition (self-monitoring, self-reflection), as well as certain dispositions—or habits of mind—like flexibility, adaptability, acceptance of criticism, persistence, collaboration, and desire for mastery. Throughout this text you have had practice in specifying different types of cognitive learnings, identifying aspects of these learning types, and in planning to assess them. Apply this same practice to specifying what you want to know about your learners from their portfolios. As part of your teaching strategy, you will want to discuss these outcomes with your learners.

Step 3: Deciding Who Will Plan the Portfolio

When deciding who will plan the portfolio, consider what's involved in preparing gymnasts or skaters for a major tournament. The parent hires a coach. The coach, pupil, and parent plan together the routines, costumes, practice times, music, and so on. They are a team whose sole purpose is to produce the best performance possible. The gymnast or skater wants to be the best that he or she can be. They also want to please their parents and coach and meet their expectations. The atmosphere is charged with excitement, dedication, and commitment to genuine effort.

This is the atmosphere you are trying to create when using portfolios. You, the learner, and parents are a team for helping the student improve writing, or math reasoning, or scientific thinking and to assemble examples of this growing competence. Learners want to show what they can do and to verify the trust and confidence that you and their family have placed in them. The portfolio is their recital, their tournament, their competition.

The principal stakeholders in the use of the portfolio are you, your learners, and their parents. Therefore, involve parents by sending home an explanation of portfolio assessment, and ask that parents and students discuss its goals and content.

Step 4: Deciding Which Products to Put in the Portfolio and How Many Samples of Each Product

When determining what and how much to include in the portfolio, you must make two key decisions: ownership and your portfolio's link with instruction. *Ownership* refers to your learners' perception that the portfolio contains what they want it to. You have considered this issue in step 3. By involving learners and their parents in the planning process, you enhance their sense of ownership. You also do this by giving them a say in what goes into the portfolio. The task is to balance your desire to enhance ownership with your responsibilities to see that the content of the portfolio measures the cognitive skills and dispositions that you identified in step 3.

Both learners and their parents need to see that your class instruction focuses on teaching the skills necessary to fashion the portfolio's content. You don't want to require products in math, science, or social studies that you didn't prepare learners to create. If it's a writing portfolio, then your instructional goals must include teaching skills in writing poems, essays, editorials, or whatever your curriculum specifies. The same holds for science, math, geography, or history portfolios. Thus, in deciding what you would like to see included in your learners' portfolios, you will have to ensure that you only require products that your learners were prepared to develop.

The most satisfactory way to satisfy learner needs for ownership and your needs to measure what you teach is to require certain categories of products that match your instructional purposes and cognitive outcomes and to allow learners and parents to choose the samples within each category. For example, you may require that an eighth-grade math portfolio contain the following categories of math content (Lane, 1993):

1. Number and operation, in which the learner demonstrates the understanding of the relative magnitude of numbers, the effects of operations on numbers, and the ability to perform those mathematical operations
2. Estimation, in which the learner demonstrates understanding of basic facts, place value, and operations; mental computation; tolerance of error; and flexible use of strategies
3. Predictions, in which learners demonstrate abilities to make predictions based on experimental probabilities; to systematically organize and describe data; to make conjectures based on data analyses; and to construct and interpret graphs, charts, and tables

Learners and their parents would have a choice of which assignments to include in each of the categories listed. For each sample the learner includes a brief statement about what it says about his or her development of mathematical thinking skills.

Another example could be a high school writing portfolio. The teacher requires that the following categories of writing be in the portfolio: persuasive editorial, persuasive essay, narrative story, autobiography, and dialogue. Learners choose the samples of writing in each category. For each sample they include a cover letter that explains why they chose this sample and what the sample shows about the learner's development as a writer.

You will also have to decide how many samples of each content category to include in the portfolio. For example, do you require two samples of persuasive writing, one of criticism, three of dialogue? Shavelson, Gao, and Baxter (1991) suggest that at least eight products or tasks over different topic areas may be needed to obtain a reliable estimate of performance from portfolios. You should make this decision after eliciting suggestions from your students.

Step 5: Building the Portfolio Rubrics

In step 2 you identified the major cognitive skills and dispositions that your portfolio will measure. In step 4 you specified the content categories that your portfolio will contain. Now, you must decide what good, average, and poor performance look like for each entry in the portfolio and the portfolio as a whole.

You already have experience at this earlier in this chapter. You will follow the same process here. For each cognitive learning outcome for each category of content in your portfolio, list the primary traits or characteristics that you think are important. Next, construct a rating scale that describes the range of student performance that can occur for each trait. Figures 13.11 and 13.12 show how this was done for the essay writing content area.

Figures 13.13 and 13.14 show examples from a math portfolio under the content category of problem solving. The teacher wants to measure the cognitive outcomes of knowledge base, cognitive strategies, communication, and reflection.

Once you design rubrics for each entry in the portfolio, you next design scoring criteria for the portfolio as a whole product. Some traits to consider when developing a scoring mechanism for the entire portfolio are thoroughness, variety, growth or progress, overall quality, self-reflection, flexibility, organization, and appearance. Choose among these traits or include others, and build 5-point rating scales for each characteristic.

Thus, the key to step 5 is to do the following:

1. For each cognitive skill and disposition in each content area, build your scoring rubrics.
2. Put these on a form that allows you to include ratings of early drafts.
3. Prepare a rating for the portfolio as a whole.

Figure 13.11   Essay portfolio rating form.

___ First Draft
___ Second Draft
___ Final Draft

To Be Completed by Student:

1. Date submitted: _____

2. Briefly explain what this essay says about you. _____

   _____

3. What do you like best about this piece of writing? _____

   _____

4. What do you want to improve on the next draft? _____

   _____

5. If this is your final draft, will you include this in your portfolio and why? _____

   _____

   _____

To Be Completed by Teacher:

Rating	Description

1. Quality of Reflection

   5   States very clearly what he or she likes most and least about the essay. Goes into much detail about how to improve the work.

   4   States clearly what he or she likes and dislikes about the essay. Gives detail about how to improve the work.

   3   States his or her likes and dislikes but could be clearer. Gives some detail about how the work will be improved.

   2   Is vague about likes and dislikes. Gives few details about how the essay will be improved.

   1   No evidence of any reflection on the work.

2. Writing Conventions

   5   The use of writing conventions is very effective. No errors are evident. These conventions are fluid and complex: spelling, punctuation, grammar usage,sentence structure.

   4   The use of writing conventions is effective. Only minor errors are evident. These conventions are nearly all effective: punctuation, grammar usage, sentence structure, spelling.

   3   The use of writing conventions is somewhat effective. Errors don't interfere with meaning. These conventions are somewhat effective: punctuation, grammar usage, sentence structure, spelling.

   2   Errors in the use of writing conventions interfere with meaning. These conventions are limited and uneven: punctuation, grammar usage, sentence structure, spelling.

Figure 13.11 *Continued*

Rating	Description
1	Major errors in the use of writing conventions obscures meaning. Lacks understanding of punctuation, grammar usage, sentence structure, spelling.

3. Organization

5	Clearly makes sense.
4	Makes sense.
3	Makes sense for the most part.
2	Attempted but does not make sense.
1	Does not make sense.

4. Planning (1st draft only)

5	Has clear idea of audience. Goals are very clear and explicit. An overall essay plan is evident.
4	Has idea of audience. Goals are clear and explicit. Has a plan for the essay.
3	Somewhat clear about the essay's audience. Goals are stated but somewhat vague. Plan for whole essay somewhat clear.
2	Vague about who the essay is for. Goals are unclear. No clear plan evident.
1	Writing shows no evidence of planning.

5. Quality of Revision (2nd draft only)

5	Follows up on all suggestions for revision. Revisions are a definite improvement.
4	Follows up on most suggestions for revision. Revisions improve on the previous draft.
3	Addresses some but not all suggested revisions. Revisions are a slight improvement over earlier draft.
2	Ignores most suggestions for revision. Revisions made do not improve the earlier draft.
1	Made only a minimal attempt to revise if at all.

Sum of ratings: _____

Average of ratings: _____

Comments: _____

_____

_____

Figure 13.12   Essay summative rating form (attach to each completed essay).

Student _____

	Draft 1		Draft 2		Final Draft
Criteria	Rating	Criteria	Rating	Criteria	Rating
Reflection	_3_	Reflection	_4_	Reflection	_3_
Conventions	_3_	Conventions	_4_	Conventions	_4_
Organization	_4_	Organization	_5_	Organization	_5_
Planning	_4_	Revision	_4_	Revision	_3_
Average	_3.5_	Average	_4.25_	Average	_3.75_

Teacher: Comments on final essay development _____

_____

_____

Student: Comments on final essay development _____

_____

_____

Parent: Comments on final essay development _____

_____

_____

Included in portfolio: ____ Yes
                          ____ No

Step 6: Developing a Procedure to Aggregate All Portfolio Ratings

For each content category that you include in the portfolio, learners will receive a score for each draft and the final product. You will have to decide how to aggregate these scores into a final score or grade for each content area and then the portfolio as a whole. Figures 13.12 and 13.14 are examples of a summative rating form in two content areas (essay and math) for one student. You will have one of these summative rating forms for each content area identified in step 4. Thus, if you want a writing portfolio to include five areas of content (persuasive writing, dialogue, biography, criticism, commentary), you will have five summative rating forms, each of which rates drafts and final product.

As you can see in Figure 13.12, the teacher averaged the ratings for the two preliminary drafts and the final one. The next step is to develop a rule or procedure for combining these three scores into an overall score. One procedure would be to

Figure 13.13   Math problem-solving portfolio rating form.

Content Categories:

√   Problem solving   Problem _____ 1
_____ Numbers and operations   √ 2
_____ Estimation   _____ 3
_____ Predictions

To Be Completed by Student:

1.   Date submitted: _____

2.   What does this problem say about you as a problem solver? _____

_____

_____

3.   What do you like best about how you solved this problem? _____

_____

_____

4.   How will you improve your problem solving skill on the next problem? _____

_____

_____

To Be Completed by Teacher:

   Rating   *Description*

1. Quality of Reflection

   5   Has excellent insight into his or her problem-solving abilities and
              clear ideas of how to get better.
   4   Has good insight into his or her problem-solving abilities and
              some ideas of how to get better.
   3   Reflects somewhat on problem-solving strengths and needs. Has
              some idea of how to improve as a problem solver.
   2   Seldom reflects on problem-solving strengths and needs. Has lit-
              tle idea of how to improve as a problem solver.
   1   Has no concept of him- or herself as a problem solver.

2. Mathematical Knowledge

   5   Shows deep understanding of the problems, math concepts, and
              principles. Uses appropriate math terms and all calculations are
              correct.
   4   Shows good understanding of math problems, concepts, and
              principles. Uses appropriate math terms most of the time. Few
              computational errors.
   3   Shows understanding of some of the problems, math concepts,
              and principles. Uses some terms incorrectly. Contains some
              computation errors.

Figure 13.13   *Continued*

Rating	Description
2	Errors in the use of many problems. Many terms used incorrectly.
1	Major errors in problems. Shows no understanding of math problems, concepts, and principles.

3. Strategic Knowledge

Rating	Description
5	Identifies all the important elements of the problem. Reflects an appropriate and systematic strategy for solving the problem; gives clear evidence of a solution process.
4	Identifies most of the important elements of the problem. Reflects an appropriate and systematic strategy for solving the problem and gives clear evidence of a solution process most of the time.
3	Identifies some important elements of the problem. Gives some evidence of a strategy to solve the problem, but the process is incomplete.
2	Identifies few important elements of the problem. Gives little evidence of a strategy to solve the problem, and the process is unknown.
1	Uses irrelevant outside information. Copies parts of the problem; no attempt at solution.

4. Communication

Rating	Description
5	Gives a complete response with a clear, unambiguous explanation; includes diagrams and charts when they help clarify explanation; presents strong arguments that are logically developed.
4	Gives good response with fairly clear explanation, which includes some use of diagrams and charts; presents good arguments that are mostly but not always logically developed.
3	Explanations and descriptions of problem solution are somewhat clear but incomplete; makes some use of diagrams and examples to clarify points, but arguments are incomplete.
2	Explanations and descriptions of problem solution are weak; makes little, if any, use of diagrams and examples to clarify points; arguments are seriously flawed.
1	Ineffective communication; diagrams misrepresent the problem; arguments have no sound premise.

Sum of ratings: _____

Average of ratings: _____

Comments: _____

_____

_____

Figure 13.14 Math problem-solving summative rating form (attach to problem-solving entries).

Student _____

Problem 1		Problem 2		Problem 3	
Criteria	Rating	Criteria	Rating	Criteria	Rating
Reflection	3	Reflection	4	Reflection	3
Knowledge	2	Knowledge	3	Knowledge	3
Strategies	2	Strategies	2	Strategies	2
Comm.	2	Comm.	2	Comm.	2
Average	2.25	Average	2.75	Average	2.5

Teacher: Comments on problem-solving ability and improvement: _____

_____

_____

Student: Comments on problem-solving ability and improvement: _____

_____

_____

Parent: Comments on problem-solving and improvement: _____

_____

_____

_____

compute a simple average of three scores. This method gives equal importance in the final score to the drafts and final product. Another procedure is to assign greatest importance to the final product, lesser importance to the second draft, and least importance to the first draft.

This is called weighting. If and how you weight scores is up to you. You might seek input from learners and parents, but there is no hard-and-fast rule about whether or which products in an area should be given more weight.

If you should decide to assign different importance or weight to the products in a content area, then do the following:

1. Decide on the weight in terms of a percentage, for example, first draft counts 20%, second draft counts 30%, and final draft counts 50% of final score. Make sure the percentages add up to 100%.

2. Take the average score for each product, and multiply that by the weight. In our example as shown in Figure 13.12, this would involve the following calculations:

$$\text{Draft 1: } 3.50 \times 0.2 = 0.7$$
$$\text{Draft 2: } 4.25 \times 0.3 = 1.3$$
$$\text{Final: } \quad 3.75 \times 0.5 = 1.9$$

3. Add up these products (.7 + 1.3 + 1.9), and you get an overall score of 3.9 for the content area of essay writing. We will consider the meaning of this value shortly. (Had you not weighted, the average score would have been 3.8.)

Follow this same procedure for each content area. If you have five content areas in the portfolio, you will have five scores. Let's say that these are

Content Area	Score
Essay	3.9
Dialogue	4.0
Criticism	2.5
Biography	3.8
Commentary	2.0

The next step is to decide how to aggregate these scores. Again, you can choose to weight or not to weight. You may decide to involve learners and their parents in this decision. If you decide not to weight, then the average rating for all the content areas is 3.2 (rounded to the nearest decimal).

Finally, assign a rating to the portfolio as a whole. Let's say that the rating came out to be a 4.5. Now you must decide how to include this rating in the overall portfolio grade. If you take an unweighted average, you assign as much importance to that one rating as you did all the separate content ratings. That's probably not a good idea. Your average grade of 3.9 for the portfolio areas taken separately is a more reliable rating than your one rating of 4.5 for the whole portfolio. So, we recommend that you assign more weight to the former score than the latter—let's say 90% versus 10%, which produces a final grade of

$$3.9 \times 0.9 = 3.51$$
$$4.5 \times 0.1 = 0.45$$

Final Grade = 3.51 + .45 = 3.96 (vs. 4.2 if you had you not weighted).

Now, let's consider what 3.96 (or 4.0 rounded) means in terms of the quality of the overall portfolio. The value 4.0 is a measurement. It is a number that reflects the performance of the learner. But, how good is a 4.0 in indicating the competence of the learner? Making this decision involves evaluation.

Here is one way to assign meaning to our measurement of 4.0. Schools usually assign the following values to grades:

Grading Schemes	Meaning
90–100, A or E	Outstanding
80–89, B or S+	Above average
70–79, C or S	Average
60–69, D or S-	Below average
Below 60, F or N	Failure, not at standard, etc.

When using 5-point rating scales, we usually consider 3 as average, 1 as below standard, and 5 outstanding. Similarly, if you use a 7-point scale, a 3.5 is average, ratings between 1 and 2 are below standard, and ratings between 6 and 7 are outstanding. So, one way to assign value to a 4.0 would be to link the traditional grading systems and their conventional meanings to scores on the rating scale. Pick a range of rating scale values that corresponds to a letter or numerical grade in your school, and link the two:

Average Rating	Grade
1.0–1.9	F, 50–59
2.0–2.5	D, 60–69
2.6–3.6	C, 70–79
3.6–4.3	B, 80–89
4.4–5.0	A, 90–100

If we use the preceding chart, a 4.0 would represent a grade of B, a numerical grade somewhere from 80 to 89, or a grade of Satisfactory + (S+). Or, decide that a B gets a grade of 85, B- gets a grade of 80, and B+ a grade of 89. Making these decisions before you begin grading the portfolios, and evaluating each portfolio using the same criteria help minimize subjectivity.

Step 7: Determining the Logistics

Just a few details are left.

Time Lines.   Your learners and their parents need to know exact dates when things are due. Point this out to your learners. This reinforces in your learner's minds the link between your teaching and what's required in the portfolio. Be prepared to revise some of your requirements. You may find that there's not enough time in the school year and not enough hours in a week for you to read all the drafts and products and get them back to your learners in a timely fashion.

How Products Are Turned in and Returned.   Decide how you want your learners to turn in their products. At the start of class? Placed in an "in" basket? Secured in a folder or binder? Returned in an "out" basket? How will late assignments be handled? How do absent learners submit and get back assignments? Will there be penalties for late assignments?

Where Final Products Are Kept.   Decide where the final products will be stored. Will it be the learners' responsibility to keep them safely at home? Or, do you want to store them so that they can be assembled easily for a final parent conference and passed on to other teachers? Remember that the products may include video- or audio-tapes, so a manila folder might not work. You may need boxes, filing cabinets, or closets.

Who Has Access to the Portfolio?.   Certainly you, learners, and parents have a right to see what's in it. But do other students, current and future teachers, or administrators? You might want learners (and their parents) to help make these decisions, since it is their portfolio and their story.

Plan a Final Conference

Plan to have a final conference at the end of the year or term with individual learners and, if possible, their parents to discuss the portfolio and what it says about your learners' development and final achievement. Your learners can be responsible for conducting the conference, with a little preparation from you on how to do it. This final event can be a highly motivating force for your learners to produce an exemplary portfolio.

PERFORMANCE TESTS AND REPORT CARD GRADES

Performance tests require a substantial commitment of teacher time and learner engagement. Consequently, a teacher who decides to use them should ensure that the performance test grade has substantial weight in the 6-week or final report card grade. Here are two approaches to designing a grading system that includes performance assessments:

The first approach to scoring quizzes, tests, homework assignments, performance assessments, and so on is to score each on the basis of 100 points. Computing the final grade simply involves averaging the grades for each component, multiplying these averages by the weight assigned, and adding these products to determine the total grade. Figure 13.15 provides examples of three formulae for accomplishing this. These methods require that you assign 0 to 100 points to everything you grade.

The second approach is to use a percentage of total points system. With this system, you decide individually how many points each component of your grading system is worth. You may want some tests to be worth 40 points, some 75, and so on, depending on the complexity of the questions and the performance desired. Likewise, some of your homework assignments may be worth 10 points, some 5 points, and some 15 points. With such a system, there is no need to have every homework assignment, test, or class assignment worth 100 points or the same number of points. Following are the procedures involved in setting up such a grading scheme for a 6-week grading period.

Grading Formula Example #1   ("One, Two, Three Times Plan")

Homework and Classwork: All grades for homework and classwork are totaled and averaged. The average grade will count once.

Homework and classwork grades followed by the average:
84, 81, 88, 92, 96, 85, 78, 83, 91, 79, 89, 94 = 1040 ÷ 12 = 86.6 = 87 average

Quizzes: All of the quizzes are totaled and averaged. This average grade will count two times.

Quiz grades followed by the average:
82, 88, 80, 91, 78, 86 = 505 ÷ 6 = 84.2 = 84 average

Tests and Major Projects: All of the tests and major projects are totaled and averaged. This average grade will count three times.

Test and major project grade followed by the average:
81, 91, 86 = 258 ÷ 3 = 86 average

The six weeks grade is computed as follows:
87 (one time) + 84 + 84 (two times) + 86 + 86 + 86 (three times) = 513 ÷ 6 = 85.5 = 86 as the grade

Grading Formula Example #2   ("Percentages Plan")

A teacher determines a percentage for each area. For example, homework and classwork count 20% of the grade; quizzes count 40% of the grade; and tests and major projects count 40% of the grade.

Using the same scores as listed above, a student's grade is computed as follows:
20% of the 86.6 for homework and classwork is 17.3; 40% of the 84.2 for quizzes is 33.7; and 40% of the 86 for tests and major projects is 34.4.

The six weeks grade is: 17.3 + 33.7 + 34.4 = 85.4 = 85. (The average is different because the "weight" put on each area varies in the two examples.)

Grading Formula Example #3   ("Language Arts Plan")

A language arts teacher determines that the publishing, goal meeting, journal, and daily process grades each count one fourth (25%) of the six weeks grade.

A language arts grade is computed as follows:

The publishing grade is issued only at the end of the six weeks = 88

The goal meeting grade is issued only at the end of the six weeks = 86

The journal grades are: 82 + 92 + 94 + 90 + 88 + 86 = 532 ÷ 6 = 88.7 = 89

The daily process grades are : 78 + 82 + 86 + 94 + 94 + 91 = 525 ÷ 6 = 87.5 = 88

The six weeks grade is: 88 + 86 + 89 + 88 = 351 ÷ 4 = 87.75 = 88

Performance tests require a substantial commitment of teacher time and learner engagement. Consequently, a teacher who decides to use them should ensure that the performance test grade has substantial weight in the 6-week or final report card grade.

Step 1: Identify the components of your grading system, and assign each component a weight.   A *weight* is the percentage of total points a particular component carries. Components and example weights for a 6-week grading plan are shown here:

Component	Weight (%)
Homework	15
Objective tests	20
Performance tests	20
Portfolio	20
Classwork	15
Notebook	10
	100

Step 2: Record in your grade book the actual points earned out of the possible points.   Leave a column for totals (see Figure 13.16). As you can see, each component and each separate assignment has varying numbers of points earned out of the total number of points possible. Assign possible points for the components based on the complexity of the required performance, the length of the assignment, your perception of your ability to assign reliable ratings, and so on.

Figure 13.16 Sample grade recording sheet, first 6 weeks.

Component	Homework							Objective Tests			Performance Tests			Portfolio	Classwork						Notebook
Dates	8/20	9/7	9/14	9/20	9/28	10/6	Total	9/17	10/7	Total	9/23	10/8	Total	10/7	9/2	9/6	9/14	9/23	10/5	Total	10/8
Cornell	10/10	8/10	14/15	10/10	8/15	0/10	50/70	20/30	25/30	45/60	15/20	18/20	33/40	18/20	9/10	7/15	10/10	9/10	4/5	39/50	5/10
Rosie	10/10	5/10	12/15	8/10	12/15	8/10	55/70	15/30	20/30	35/60	20/20	19/20	39/40	15/20	8/10	14/15	0/10	10/10	5/5	37/50	8/10

Step 3: Total the actual points earned for each component, and divide this by the possible points. The results represent the percentage of points earned for each particular component. Thus, in our example from Figure 13.16, Cornell and Rosie earned the following total points:

	Cornell	Rosie
Homework	50/70 = 71%	55/70 = 79%
Objective Tests	45/60 = 75%	35/60 = 58%
Performance Tests	33/40 = 83%	39/40 = 98%
Portfolio	18/20 = 90%	15/20 = 75%
Classwork	39/50 = 78%	37/50 = 74%
Notebook	5/10 = 50%	8/10 = 80%

Step 4: Multiply each of these percentages by the component weights assigned. Then, sum these products.

	Cornell	Rosie
Homework	71 × .15 = 10.6	79 × .15 = 11.8
Objective Tests	75 × .20 = 15	58 × .20 = 11.6
Performance Tests	83 × .20 = 16.6	98 × .20 = 19.6
Portfolio	90 × .20 = 18	75 × .20 = 15
Classwork	78 × .15 = 11.7	74 × .15 = 11.1
Notebook	50 × .10 = 5	80 × .10 = 8
Sum Totals	76.9	77.1

Step 5: Record the 6-week grade. Record this either as a letter grade (A = 90% to 100%, B = 80% to 89%, C = 70% to 79%, etc.) or as the percentage itself, depending on your school's marking system.

A FINAL WORD

Performance and portfolio assessments create challenges that differ from those of objective and essay tests. Performance grading requires greater use of judgment than do true–false or multiple-choice questions. These judgments can become more reliable if (1) the performance to be judged (process and product) is clearly specified, (2) the ratings or criteria used in making the judgments are determined beforehand, and (3) two or more raters independently grade the performance and an average taken.

Using video- or audiotapes can enhance the validity of performance assessments when direct observation of performance is required. Furthermore, performance assessments need not take place at one time for the whole class. Learners can be assessed at different times, individually or in small groups. For example, learners can rotate through classroom learning centers (Shalaway, 1989), and you may assess them when you feel they are acquiring mastery.

Finally, don't lose sight of the fact that performance assessments are meant to serve and enhance instruction rather than being simply an after-the-fact test given to assign a grade. When tests serve instruction, they can be given at a variety of times and in as many settings and contexts as instruction requires. Some performance assessments can sample the behavior of learners as they receive instruction, and some may occur within ongoing classroom activities rather than consume extra time during the day.

SUMMING UP

This chapter introduced you to performance-based assessment. Its main points were as follows:

1. Performance tests use direct measures of learning that require learners to analyze, problem solve, experiment, make decisions, measure, cooperate with others, present orally, or produce a product. Performance tests not only can assess higher-level cognitive skills but also noncognitive outcomes, such as self-direction, ability to work with others, and social awareness.

2. Paper and pencil tests are most efficient, reliable, and valid for assessing knowledge, comprehension, and some types of application. When properly constructed, performance tests are most efficient, reliable, and valid for assessing complex thinking, attitudes, and social skills.

3. Three questions to ask when deciding what to test with a performance assessment are the following:
   - What knowledge or content is essential for learner understanding?
   - What intellectual skills are used?
   - What habits of mind or attitudes are important?

4. Two categories of performance skills in the cognitive domain are (1) skills related to acquiring information and (2) skills related to organizing and using information.

5. The four steps to constructing a performance assessment are (1) deciding what to test, (2) designing the assessment context, (3) specifying the scoring rubrics, and (4) specifying the testing constraints.

6. Some questions to ask in designing the performance assessment context are (1) what does the doing of math, history, and so on

look and feel like to professionals, (2) what projects and tasks are performed by these professionals, and (3) what roles—or habits of mind—do professionals assume?

7. A good performance assessment includes a hands-on exercise or problem, an observable outcome, and a process that can be observed.

8. *Rubrics* are scoring standards composed of model answers, which are used to score performance tests. They are samples of acceptable responses against which the rater compares a student's performance.

9. Primary trait scoring is a type of rating that requires that the test developer first identify the most relevant characteristics or primary traits of importance.

10. A performance test can require four types of accomplishments from learners: Products, complex cognitive processes, observable performance, and attitudes and social skills. These performances can be scored with checklists, rating scales, or holistic scales.

11. Checklists contain lists of behaviors, traits, or characteristics that can be scored as either present or absent. They are best suited for complex behaviors or performances that are divisible into a series of clearly defined, specific actions.

12. Rating scales assign numbers to categories representing different degrees of performance. They are typically used for those aspects of a complex performance, such as attitudes, products, and social skills, that do not lend themselves to yes/no or present/absent type judgments.

13. Holistic scoring estimates the overall quality of a performance by assigning a single

numerical value to represent a specific category of accomplishment. It is used for measuring both products and processes.

14. Constraints to decide on when constructing and administering a performance test are amount of time allowed, use of reference material, help from others, use of specialized equipment, prior knowledge of the task, and scoring criteria.

15. A portfolio is a planned collection of learner achievement that documents what a student

has accomplished and the steps taken to get there.

16. Two approaches to combining performance grades with other grades are (1) to assign 100 total points to each assignment that is graded and average the results and (2) begin with an arbitrary total and then determine the percentage of points each component is worth.

FOR DISCUSSION AND PRACTICE

Questions marked with an asterisk are answered in Appendix B. See also *Bridges: An Activity Guide and Assessment Options,* which accompanies this text.

*1. Compare and contrast some of the reasons given to explain why we give conventional tests with those given to explain why we give performance assessments.

*2. In your own words, explain how performance assessment can be a tool for instruction in your classroom.

*3. Using an example from your teaching area, explain the difference between a direct and an indirect measure of behavior. Which was used the most when you were in school?

4. Describe some habits of mind that might be required by a performance test in your teaching area. How did you learn about the importance of these attitudes, social skills, and ways of working?

*5. Describe how at least two school districts have implemented performance assessments. Indicate the behaviors they assess and by what means they are measured.

6. Would you agree or disagree with the statement that "an ideal performance test is a good teaching activity?" With a specific example in your teaching area, illustrate why you believe as you do.

7. State at least two learning outcomes and how you would measure them in your classroom to indicate that a learner is (a) self-directed, (b) a collaborative worker, (c) a complex

thinker, (d) a quality producer, and (e) a community contributor.

*8. Describe what is meant by a *scoring rubric*. In what way, if any, does a scoring rubric differ from a scoring scheme, as described for essay tests in the previous chapter?

9. In your own words, how would you answer a critic of performance tests who says they do not measure generalizable thinking skills outside the classroom and can't be scored reliably? Support your answer with examples.

10. Identify for a unit of instruction several attitudes, habits of mind, and/or social skills that would be important when using the content you are teaching outside the classroom.

11. Create a performance test of your own choosing that (1) requires a hands-on problem to solve, (2) results in an observable outcome, and (3) involves observable processes used by learners to achieve the outcome. Use the five criteria by Wiggins (1992) and Resnick and Klopfer (1989) as your guide.

12. For the performance assessment in question 11, describe and give an example of the accomplishments—or rubrics—you would look for in scoring the assessment.

13. For this same assessment, compose a checklist, rating scale, holistic scoring method, or a combination, by which you could evaluate a learner's performance. Explain why you chose the scoring system you did.

14. For the performance assessment in question 11, describe the constraints you would place

on your learners pertaining to time to prepare for and complete the activity; references they may use; people they may consult, including other students; equipment allowed; prior knowledge about what is expected; and points or percentages you would assign to various degrees of their performance.

15. Develop a portfolio rating form and summative rating form for the entries in your portfolio using Figures 13.11 to 13.14 as a guide. Be sure to include definitions for all the scale alternatives (e.g., 1 to 5) being rated, as illustrated in Figure 13.11.

16. Describe the procedure you will use to aggregate scores for all the portfolio ratings. By providing hypothetical ratings for the entries on your rating form, indicate with actual numbers and averages how you will (a) calculate weights, (b) take the average score for each entry, (c) add up all the entries to get an overall score, and (d) assign a grade symbol (e.g., A to F) to the average score.

17. Imagine you have to arrive at a final grade composed of homework, objective tests, performance tests, portfolio, classwork, and notebook, which together you want to add up to 100 points. Compose a grading scheme that indicates the weight, number, individual points, and total points assigned to each component. Indicate the percent and total number of points required for the grades A through F.

Teacher Concerns Checklist

Francis F. Fuller and Gary D. Borich
The University of Texas at Austin

DIRECTIONS: This checklist explores what teachers are concerned about at different stages of their careers. There are no right or wrong answers, because each teacher has his or her own concerns.

On the following page are statements of concerns you might have. Read each statement, and ask yourself: WHEN I THINK ABOUT TEACHING, AM I CONCERNED ABOUT THIS?

- If you are *not concerned*, or the statement does not apply, write *1* in the box.
- If you are *a little concerned*, write *2* in the box.
- If you are *moderately concerned*, write *3* in the box.
- If you are *very concerned*, write *4* in the box.
- And if you are *totally preoccupied* with the concern, write *5* in the box.

① Not concerned ② A little concerned ③ Moderately concerned
④ Very concerned ⑤ Totally preoccupied

☐ 1. Insufficient clerical help for teachers.
☐ 2. Whether the students respect me.
☐ 3. Too many extra duties and responsibilities.
☐ 4. Doing well when I'm observed.
☐ 5. Helping students to value learning.
☐ 6. Insufficient time for rest and class preparation.
☐ 7. Not enough assistance from specialized teachers.
☐ 8. Managing my time efficiently.
☐ 9. Losing the respect of my peers.
☐ 10. Not enough time for grading and testing.
☐ 11. The inflexibility of the curriculum.
☐ 12. Too many standards and regulations set for teachers.
☐ 13. My ability to prepare adequate lesson plans.
☐ 14. Having my inadequacies become known to other teachers.
☐ 15. Increasing students' feelings of accomplishment.
☐ 16. The rigid instructional routine.
☐ 17. Diagnosing student learning problems.
☐ 18. What the principal may think if there is too much noise in my classroom.
☐ 19. Whether each student is reaching his or her potential.
☐ 20. Obtaining a favorable evaluation of my teaching.
☐ 21. Having too many students in a class.
☐ 22. Recognizing the social and emotional needs of students.
☐ 23. Challenging unmotivated students.
☐ 24. Losing the respect of my students.
☐ 25. Lack of public support for schools.
☐ 26. My ability to maintain the appropriate degree of class control.

☐ 27. Not having sufficient time to plan.
☐ 28. Getting students to behave.
☐ 29. Understanding why certain students make slow progress.
☐ 30. Having an embarrassing incident occur in my classroom for which I might be judged responsible.
☐ 31. Not being able to cope with troublemakers in my classes.
☐ 32. That my peers may think I'm not doing an adequate job.
☐ 33. My ability to work with disruptive students.
☐ 34. Understanding ways in which student health and nutrition problems can affect learning.
☐ 35. Appearing competent to parents.
☐ 36. Meeting the needs of different kinds of students.
☐ 37. Seeking alternative ways to ensure that students learn the subject matter.
☐ 38. Understanding the psychological and cultural differences that can affect my students' behavior.
☐ 39. Adapting myself to the needs of different students.
☐ 40. The large number of administrative interruptions.
☐ 41. Guiding students toward intellectual and emotional growth.
☐ 42. Working with too many students each day.
☐ 43. Whether students can apply what they learn.
☐ 44. Teaching effectively when another teacher is present.
☐ 45. Understanding what factors motivate students to learn.

This instrument was revised with the assistance of John Rogan, Western Montana University.

The following items on the Teacher Concerns Checklist represent the dimensions of Self, Task, and Impact:

Self	*Task*	*Impact*
2	1	5
4	3	15
8	6	17
9	7	19
13	10	22
14	11	23
18	12	29
20	16	34
24	21	36
26	25	37
28	27	38
30	31	39
32	33	41
35	40	43
44	42	45

You can complete the concerns instrument at the beginning and again at the end of your student teaching or field observation experience, noting any changes in the three areas of concern over time.

To determine your score, total the number of responses in each of the three categories of concern: self, task, and impact. The higher your score in a category (of a maximum 75 per category), the more you are identified with that stage of concern. Also, by summing responses to items in each category and dividing by the number of items completed, you may compute an average rating for each of the three areas.

The sum of the scores for each of the three areas of concern (maximum = 75) can be recorded in the following format, shown here with some example data:

Stage	Beginning	End	Change
Self	60	45	− 15
Task	45	60	+ 15
Impact	15	30	+ 15

This example profile indicates a shift of concern from self to task and from self to impact. This is typical of student teachers who spend about a semester in a field experience. Smaller shifts following this same pattern are not uncommon, however, after a semester of in-school observation without practice teaching. Larger shifts, particularly from task to impact, are frequently noted for beginning in-service teachers during their first 2 to 3 years of teaching.

SUGGESTED READING

Borich, G. (1992). *Clearly outstanding: Making each day count in your classroom* (Chapter 8). Boston: Allyn & Bacon.

Borich, G. (1999). *Observation skills for effective teaching* (3d ed., Chapter 5). Upper Saddle River, NJ: Merrill/Prentice Hall.

Borich, G. (1995). *Becoming a teacher: An inquiring dialogue for the beginning teacher*. Bristol, PA: Falmer Press Ltd.

Fuller, F. F. (1969). Concerns of teachers: A developmental conceptualization. *American Educational Research Journal, 6,* 207–226.

Fuller, F., Brown, O., & Peck, R. (1966). *Creating climates for growth.* Austin: University of Texas, Research and Development Center for Teacher Education. (ERIC Document Reproduction Service No. ED 013 989)

Fuller, F., Pilgrim, G., & Freeland, A. (1967). *Intensive individualization of teacher preparation.* Austin: University of Texas, Research and Development Center for Teacher Education. (ERIC Document Reproduction Service No. ED 011 603)

Hall, G. E., & Hord, S. M. (1987). *Change in schools: Facilitating the process.* Ithaca: State University of New York Press.

Hord, S. M., Rutherford, W. L., Huling-Austin, L., & Hall, G. E. (1987). *Taking charge of change.* Alexandria: Association for Supervision and Curriculum Development.

Rogan, J., Borich, G., & Taylor, H. (1992). Validation of the stages of concern questionnaire. *Action in Teacher Education, 14*(2), 43–49.

Rutherford, W. L., & Hall, G. E. (1990). *Concerns of teachers: Revisiting the original theory after twenty years.* Paper presented at the annual meeting of the American Educational Research Association, Boston. (Available from W. Rutherford, College of Education, The University of Texas at Austin, Austin, TX 78712)

Answers to Chapter Questions

These are answers to questions marked (*) in the "For Discussion and Practice" sections of the text chapters. Answers are not supplied for questions that lack the asterisk.

Chapter 1

1. 1, 2, 1 (or 2), 1 (or 2), 2, 3, 2, 3, 2 (or 1), 3, 2, 3, 3.

3. *Lower SES:*

   Individualization: Supplement standard curriculum with media and specialized material.

   Teacher affect: Provide warm and encouraging climate.

   Higher SES:

   Thinking and decision making: Pose and require questions that encourage associations, generalizations, and inferences.

   Classroom interaction: Encourage interactions in which students take responsibility for their own learning.

Chapter 2

1. a. Match instructional methods to individual learning needs.

   b. Understand the reasons behind the school performance of individual learners.

2. Environmentalists believe that differences in IQ scores among groups can be attributed to social class or environmental differences. Hereditarians believe that heredity rather than the environment is the major factor determining intelligence.

3. By some estimates, social competence may account for about 75% of school learning, leaving only about 25% to the influence of intelligence. If the influence of socioeconomic status on learning could be removed, differences in IQ among learners could be expected to become smaller.

4. Factors that would be more predictive of school learning than general IQ would be specialized abilities such as those suggested by Thurstone and Gardner and Hatch, which may include verbal intelligence (English), spatial intelligence (art), and interpersonal intelligence (social studies, drama).

8. Get students to talk about themselves; reward unique talents.

9. a. state
   b. trait
   c. trait
   d. trait
   e. state
   f. trait
   g. trait
   h. state but also trait
   i. trait
   j. trait but also state

11. Form heterogeneous groups composed of members of different peer groups. Conduct a group discussion of class norms.

13. Front half/back half

    Girls/boys

    More able/less able

    Nonminority/minority

14. Spread interactions across categories of students.

    Select students randomly.

    Pair students.

    Code class notes.

Chapter 3

1. a, g, a, g, a, g, a, g, g, g.
3. (a) Tie general aims and goals to specific classroom strategies that will achieve those aims and goals. (b) Express teaching strategies in a format that allows you to measure their effects on your learners.
4. The behavior is observable, it is measurable, and it occurs in a specifiable period of time.
5. The observable behavior, conditions under which it is to be observed, and level of proficiency at which it is to be displayed.
6. Teachers tended to focus their concerns on self and task, sometimes to the exclusion of their impact on students.
7. Because action verbs truly point toward the goal of achieving the desired behavior and observing its attainment.
8. A, O, A, A, A, O, O, O.
9. The circumstances under which the behavior is to be displayed.
10. By establishing the setting under which the behavior will be tested, which guides them in how and what to study.
11. The extent to which the conditions are similar to those under which the behavior will have to be performed in the real world.
12. The level of proficiency at which the behavior must be displayed.
14. (1) b, (2) a, (3) b, (4) e, (5) f.

Chapter 4

1. Knowledge of aims and goals, knowledge of learners, knowledge of subject matter content and organization, knowledge of teaching methods, and tacit knowledge.
2. By the way in which individual lessons are sequenced and build on one another to produce a unified whole.
3. Hierarchy helps us see the relationship between individual lesson outcomes and the unit outcome. It also helps us identify lessons that are not too big or too small, but that are just right. Teachers use task-relevant prior learning to identify the proper sequence of lessons needed to teach the unit outcome.
4. Both help us picture the flow and sequence of a lesson plan.

5. Cognitive: analysis, synthesis, evaluation. Affective: valuing, organization, characterization. Psychomotor: precision, articulation, naturalization.
6. They represent smaller, more detailed portions of content.
8. The former must show hierarchy and sequence; the latter does not.
9. Ability grouping, peer tutoring, learning centers, review, and follow-up materials.
11. Gain attention, inform the learner of the objective, stimulate recall of prerequisite learning, present the stimulus material, elicit the desired behavior, provide feedback, assess the behavior.
12. Present the stimulus material.
13. Assess the behavior.
14. Elicit the desired behavior.
15. Provide feedback: immediate and nonevaluative. Assess the behavior: delayed and evaluative.

Chapter 5

1. Type 1: facts, rules, action sequences. Type 2: concepts, patterns, abstractions. Type 1 outcomes generally apply to the knowledge, comprehension, and application levels, while Type 2 outcomes generally apply to the analysis, synthesis, and evaluation levels.
2. Knowledge acquisition: facts, rules, action sequences. Inquiry or problem solving: concepts, patterns, and abstractions.
3. Full-class instruction; questions posed by the teacher; detailed and redundant practice; one new fact, rule, or sequence mastered before the next is presented; arrangement of classroom to maximize drill and practice.
4. Cognitive: recall, describe, list. Affective: listen, attend, be aware. Psychomotor: repeat, follow, place.
5. (a) Disseminate information that is not readily available from texts or workbooks in appropriately sized pieces. (b) Arouse or heighten student interest. (c) Achieve content mastery.
6. a. Have students correct each other's work.
   b. Have students identify difficult homework problems.

c. Sample the understanding of a few students who represent the range of students in the class.

d. Explicitly review the task-relevant information necessary for the day's lesson.

7. Part–whole, sequential, combinatorial, comparative.

8. Rule–example–rule.

9. To create a response, however crude, that can become the basis for learning.

10. It is used to help convert wrong or partially correct answers to right answers by encouraging the student to use some aspects of the answer given in formulating the correct response.

11. a. Correct, quick, and firm: Acknowledge correctness and either ask another question or move on.

b. Correct but hesitant: Acknowledge correctness and review steps for attaining correct answer.

c. Incorrect but careless: Acknowledge incorrectness and immediately move on.

d. Incorrect due to lack of knowledge: Acknowledge incorrectness and then, without actually giving the student the answer, channel student's thoughts in ways that result in a correct answer.

14. Review key facts, explain steps required, prompt with clues or hints, walk student through a similar problem.

15. 60% to 80%. Reduce content coverage, increase opportunities for practice and feedback.

16. To form action sequences. They should increasingly resemble applications in the real world.

17. Keep contacts to a minimum, on the average of 30 seconds; spread contacts across most students, avoiding concentrating on a few students.

18. About 95%.

19. Gradually increase the coverage and depth of weekly reviews until time for a comprehensive monthly review arrives.

Chapter 6

1. Inquiry, discovery, and a problem.

2. Type 1: facts, rules, and action sequences. Type 2: concepts, patterns, and abstractions.

3. The learner indirectly acquires a behavior by transforming stimulus material into a response or behavior that differs (a) from the stimulus used to present the learning and (b) from any previous response emitted by the learner.

4. It is not generally efficient or effective for attaining outcomes at the higher levels of complexity involving concepts, patterns, and abstractions.

5. Unitization: the learning of individual facts or rules. Automaticity: putting the facts or rules together in an action sequence and being able to execute the sequence rapidly and automatically. Example: learning to read.

6. Generalization: classifying apparently different stimuli into the same category on the basis of criterial attributes. Discrimination: distinguishing examples of a concept from nonexamples. Example: learning the meaning of *democracy*.

7. a. Type 1
   b. Type 2
   c. Type 1
   d. Type 2
   e. Type 2
   f. Type 1
   g. Type 2
   h. Type 2
   i. Type 1
   j. Type 2

8. Our memories would become overburdened trying to remember all possible instances of the concept; also, instances of the concept could easily be confused with noninstances.

11. *Induction:* the process of thinking in which a set of specific data is presented or observed and a generalization or unifying pattern is drawn from the data. *Deduction:* the process of thinking in which the truth or validity of a theory is tested in a specific instance.

12. Stating a theory, forming a hypothesis, observing or collecting data, analyzing and interpreting the data, making a conclusion.

14. Criterial: lesson clarity, instructional variety, task orientation, engagement in the learning

process, moderate-to-high success rate. Non-criterial: number of credit hours attained, degree held, number of in-service workshops attended, college grades, years of teaching experience.

15. a. Provide more than a single example.
    b. Use examples that vary in ways that are unimportant to the concept.
    c. Include nonexamples of the concept that also include important dimensions of the concept.
    d. Explain why nonexamples are nonexamples, even though they have some of the same characteristics as examples.

16. *Direct instruction:* to elicit a single right answer or reveal level of understanding. *Indirect instruction:* to help the student search for and discover an appropriate answer with a minimum of assistance.

17. Questions that present contradictions, probe for deeper responses, extend the discussion, and pass responsibility back to the class.

18. Student-centered or unguided discovery learning. In indirect instruction, student ideas are used as means of accomplishing the goals of the prescribed curriculum.

19. (a) Encourage students to use examples and references from their experience. (b) Ask students to draw parallels and associations from things they already know. (c) Relate ideas to students' interests, concerns, and problems.

20. In direct instruction, nearly all instances of the facts, rules, and sequences are likely to be encountered during instruction. This is not true during indirect instruction, so student self-evaluation is essential.

21. Orienting students, providing new or more accurate information, reviewing and summarizing, adjusting the flow of information to more productive areas, and combining ideas and promoting compromise.

22. a. direct
    b. direct
    c. indirect
    d. indirect
    e. direct
    f. direct
    g. direct
    h. indirect
    i. indirect
    j. indirect
    Both models might be used for topics c, d, h, and j.

Chapter 7

1. A question that actively engages a student in the learning process.

2. Structuring, soliciting, reacting.

3. 80%.

4. As high as 80%; as low as 20%.

5. Interest- and attention-getting, diagnosing and checking, recall of specific facts or information, managerial, encourage higher-level thought processes, structure and redirect learning, allow expression of affect.

6. *A convergent question* has only a single or small number of correct responses. *A divergent question* has no single best answer and generally has multiple answers; however, divergent questions can have wrong answers.

8. If the learner previously has seen and memorized an answer to this question.

9. If the learner arrived at the solution by other than simple recall and memorization, perhaps by reasoning $2 + 2 + 2 + 2 = 8$, which is the same as 2 multiplied by 4.

10. Such questions are unlikely to affect standardized achievement but are likely to increase the learner's analysis, synthesis, and evaluation skills.

16. The time the teacher waits for a student to respond to a question. Generally, beginning teachers should work to increase their wait time.

17. Raising overly complex questions, not being prepared for unusual answers, not knowing the behavioral complexity of the response desired from a question, providing answers to questions before students can respond, using questions as a form of punishment.

Chapter 8

1. (a) To actively engage them in the learning process. (b) To help them acquire reasoning, critical thinking, and problem-solving skills.

2. a. Provide when and how to use mental strategies.
   b. Illustrate how the strategies are to be used.

c. Encourage learners to go beyond the information given.

d. Gradually shift the responsibility for learning to the student.

3. *Metacognition* refers to the mental processes used by the learner to understand the content being taught. *Metacognitive strategies* are procedures that assist learners in internalizing, understanding, and recalling the content to be learned.

4. (a) Illustrate the reasoning involved. (b) Make students conscious of it. (c) Focus learners on the application of the reasoning illustrated.

6. Mental modeling can help students internalize, recall, and generalize problem solutions to different content at a later time.

7. During mediation, the teacher helps students restructure what they are learning to move them closer to the intended outcome.

8. The zone of maximum response opportunity is the content difficulty and behavioral complexity from which the student can most benefit at the moment.

10. Reciprocal teaching provides opportunities to explore the content to be learned via group discussion.

11. a. Ask what students think they will learn from the text. Read from the text.

b. Choose a discussion leader to ask questions regarding the text.

c. Ask the discussion leader to summarize the text, and invite comments.

d. Discuss points that remain unclear, invite more predictions, and reread the text if needed.

12. To gradually shift the responsibility for learning to the student through scaffolded discussion.

13. To model the same line of reasoning and the same types of questions, prompts, and cues used by the teacher at an earlier stage.

15. Declarative knowledge is intended only for oral and verbal regurgitation. Procedural knowledge is used in some problem-solving or decision-making task.

17. a. Provide a new learning task.

b. Ask the student to explain how he or she will complete the task (e.g., learn the content).

c. Provide another learning task on which the student can try out the new approach.

d. Model self-questioning behavior for the student as the new material is being learned.

e. Provide a third opportunity for practice, decreasing your role as monitor.

f. Check the result by questioning for comprehension.

18. a. Jingles or trigger sentences

b. Narrative chaining

c. Number rhyme or peg word

d. Chunking

Chapter 9

1. (a) Engaging students in the learning process. (b) Promoting higher—more complex—patterns of thought.

2. a. Attitudes and values.

b. Prosocial behavior.

c. Alternative perspectives and viewpoints.

d. Integrated identity.

e. Higher thought processes.

3. a. Improved collaborative skills.

b. Better self-esteem.

c. Increased achievement.

4. a. Teacher–student interaction.

b. Student–student interaction.

c. Task specialization and materials.

d. Role expectations and responsibilities.

5. a. Specify the goal.

b. Structure the task.

c. Teach the collaborative process.

d. Monitor group performance.

e. Debrief.

6. Written group reports, test achievement, oral performance, enumeration of issues, critique, reference list.

7. 4 or 5 members.

8. a. Ask students to list peers.

b. Randomly assign students.

c. Purposefully form groups heterogeneously.

d. Share with students the selection process.

9. (a) Request a product that requires a clearly defined division of labor. (b) Form pairs within groups that have the responsibility of looking over and correcting each other's work. (c) Visually chart group's progress on individually assigned tasks.

10. a. Summarizer
    b. Checker
    c. Researcher
    d. Runner
    e. Recorder
    f. Supporter
    g. Observer/troubleshooter
11. a. Grades—individual and group
    b. Bonus points
    c. Social responsibilities
    d. Tokens or privileges
    e. Group contingencies
12. Forming a ratio, with a score for individual effort on top and a score for the group to which the individual belongs on the bottom.
13. a. Communicate one's own ideas and feelings.
    b. Make messages complete and specific.
    c. Make verbal and nonverbal messages congruent.
    d. Convey an atmosphere of respect and support.
    e. Assess whether the message was properly received.
    f. Paraphrase another's point of view.
    g. Negotiate meanings and understandings.
    h. Participate and lead.
14. (a) Repeat or remind group of its assigned role. (b) Redirect group's effort to more productive area. (c) Provide emotional support and encouragement.
15. (a) Openly talk about how the groups functioned. (b) Solicit suggestions for how the process could be improved. (c) Get viewpoints of predesignated observers.
16. a. Not enough time for group debriefing.
    b. Debriefing stays vague.
    c. Students stay uninvolved.
    d. Written reports are incomplete or messy.
    e. Students exhibit poor collaborative skills.

Chapter 10

1. Expert and referent power. By keeping up with developments in your field and giving your students a sense of belonging and acceptance.
2. Forming, storming, norming, and performing.
4. Diffusion occurs when different academic and social expectations held by different members are spread throughout the group. Crystallization occurs when expectations converge and crystallize into a shared experience. Diffusion precedes crystallization.
5. Sole provider of information (commander-in-chief), translator or summarizer of student ideas, and equal partner with students in creating ideas and problem solutions; student opinion, student talk, and spontaneity will increase from the former to the latter.
6. a. Drill and practice
   b. Group discussion
   c. Seatwork
9. Visitor at the door; safety concerning equipment.
10. Make rules consistent with your classroom climate. Make rules that can be enforced. State rules generally enough to include specific behaviors.
11. When the rule cannot be consistently reinforced over a reasonable period of time.
13. a. Allow no talking.
    b. Allow no more time than is absolutely necessary.
    c. Make arrangements according to time to be spent, not exercises to be completed.
    d. Give a 5-minute and a 2-minute warning.
14. Give reasons for the assignment, and give the assignment immediately following the content presentation to which it is related.
15. (a) Restate highest-level generalization. (b) Summarize key aspects of content taught. (c) Provide codes or symbols for remembering the content.
17. Establish an open risk-free climate. Plan lessons that match student interests and needs. Allow for activities and responsibilities congruent with the learners' cultures.

Chapter 11

1. a. Establish positive relationships.
   b. Prevent attention seeking and work avoidance.
   c. Quickly and unobtrusively redirect misbehavior.
   d. Stop persistent and chronic misbehavior.
   e. Teach self-control.
   f. Respect cultural differences.

2. Sane messages communicate to students that their behavior is unacceptable in a manner that does not blame, scold, or humiliate.

3. "I messages" focus on your feelings about the behavior or situation that angered you.

4. a. Develop classroom rules.
   b. Get support from school administrators for an area to which disruptive students can be moved temporarily.
   c. Hold private conferences with disruptive students.
   d. Follow through by giving students an opportunity to return to the classroom.

5. *Positive:* Give a reward immediately following a desirable behavior. *Negative:* End an uncomfortable state when a desirable behavior occurs.

6. *Time-out:* Remove a student to an area where he or she can receive no reinforcement. *Response cost:* Remove a reinforcer or privilege contingent on disruptive or inappropriate behavior.

7. (a) They devote extensive time to organizing their classroom to minimize disruption and enhance work engagement. (b) They methodically teach rules and routines and monitor their compliance. (c) They inform students of the consequences for breaking the rules and enforce the consequences.

9. (a) You alone can be the judge of what occurred, what the proper punishment is, and whether the punishment has been met. (b) You provide alternative forms of punishment from which the student must choose. (c) You select a punishment from alternatives provided by the student.

12. a. Select the target behavior.
    b. Identify natural consequences of the target behavior.
    c. Choose from among the natural consequences those most likely to be reinforcing.
    d. Identify from these the natural consequences most easily noticed by the learner.
    e. Design lessons that make the natural consequence conspicuous to the learner.
    f. Select appropriate backup reinforcers.

g. Condition the natural reinforcer by having learners engage in the behavior.

13. a. Punishment does not guarantee that the desirable behavior will occur.
    b. The effects of punishment are specific to a particular context and behavior.
    c. The effects of punishment can spread to desirable behaviors
    d. Punishment can elicit hostile and aggressive responses.
    e. Punishment can become associated with the punisher.

14. When the desired behavior is made clear at the time of the punishment and when used in conjunction with rewards.

15. (a) Gain support of the parent for assuming some of the responsibility for the discipline management process. (b) Design a plan of action for addressing the problem at home and at school.

Chapter 12

1. *NRTs* compare a student's performance to the performance of a large sample of pupils (called the norm group) representative of those being tested. It is useful when you need to compare a learner's performance to that of others of the same age or grade level. *CRTs* compare a student's performance to a standard of mastery called a criterion. It is useful when we wish to decide if a student needs more instruction in a certain skill or area of content.

2. (a) Level of cognitive complexity. (b) Area of instructional content.

3. a. True–False
   b. Matching
   c. Multiple-choice
   d. Completion or short answer

4. a. Stem clues.
   b. Grammatical clues.
   c. Redundant words/unequal response length.
   d. Use of "all of the above"/"none of the above."

5. (a) Pictorial, graphical, or tabular stimuli. (b) Analogues that demonstrate relationships among terms. (c) Application of previously learned principles or procedures.

6. *Extended response:* Allows student to determine the length and complexity of a response. It is most useful when the problem provides little or no structure and outcomes at the synthesis and evaluation levels are desired. *Restricted response:* poses a specific problem for which the student must recall proper information, organize it, derive a defensible conclusion, and express it within the limits of the problem. It is most useful when the problem posed is structured and when outcomes at the application and analysis levels are desired.

7. (a) Higher-level cognitive processes have been taught. (b) Class size is small. (c) Test security is a consideration.

8. *Advantages:* They require students to use higher-level cognitive processes, some topics and objectives are best suited for them, and they can measure communication skills pertinent to a subject area. *Disadvantages:* They are tedious to read and score, may be influenced by communication skills of the learner, and may involve some degree of subjectivity on the part of the scorer.

9. A guide written in advance, indicating the criteria or components of an acceptable answer.

10. a. Content
    b. Organization
    c. Process
    d. Accuracy/reasonableness
    e. Completeness/internal consistency
    f. Originality/creativity

11. a. Group similar items together.
    b. Arrange items from easy to hard.
    c. Properly space items.
    d. Keep items and options on same page.
    e. Place illustrations near descriptive material.
    f. Check for randomness.
    g. Decide how students will record answers.
    h. Provide space for name.
    i. Check directions for clarity.
    j. Proofread the test.

12. *Validity:* Does the test measure what it is supposed to measure? *Reliability:* Does the test yield the same or similar scores consistently? *Accuracy:* Does the test approximate an individual's true level of knowledge, skill, or ability?

13. (a) Content, (b) concurrent, (c) predictive.

14. (a) Test–retest, (b) alternate form, (c) internal consistency.

15. *Validity,* approximately .60–.80 or higher. *Reliability,* approximately .80–.90 or higher. The maximum possible size of a validity or reliability coefficient is 1.0.

16. Comparisons with
    a. Other students
    b. Established standards
    c. Aptitude
    d. Actual versus potential effort
    e. Actual versus potential improvement

17. A test constructed by specialists to determine a student's level of performance relative to other students of similar age and grade.

18. That the student's score associated with the percentile rank was higher than the scores of that percentage of individuals in the norming sample—or that in the norming sample the percent indicated scored lower than this individual.
    a. It is not the percent of correct answers.
    b. The extreme or end points of a percentile distribution tend to be spread out, while percentiles toward the center tend to be compressed, making comparisons between the same number of points at different portions of the scale difficult.

Chapter 13

1. Conventional tests are given to provide data on which to base grades, indicate how much has been learned, make decisions about instructional placement, talk to parents about, and help others make employment decisions. Performance assessments are given to stimulate higher-order thinking in the classroom and simulate real-world activities.

2. By refocusing the curriculum on thinking, problem solving, and student responsibility for learning.

3. An indirect measure, such as knowledge shown in a multiple-choice test, will only suggest that something has been learned. A direct measure, such as a problem-solving activity, requires that what has been learned

can be applied and exhibited in the context of a real-world problem.

5. For example, the Darwin School records percentage of words read accurately during oral reading, number of sentences read with understanding, and number of story elements learners can talk about on their own. The West Orient School requires portfolios of poetry, essays, biographies, and self-reflections.

8. Scoring rubrics are model answers against which a learner's performance is compared. They can be a detailed list of what an acceptable answer must contain or a sample of typical responses that would be acceptable.

C

Higher-Order Thinking and Problem-Solving Checklist

Check each column below indicating (a) the extent to which your curriculum *requires* students to achieve the following outcomes and (b) the extent to which *you are teaching* your students to achieve these outcomes.

Assign the number 5 to each checkmark under "Great Extent," a 4 to "Fair Extent," a 3 to "Some Extent," a 2 to "A Little," and a 1 to "Not at All." Subtract your assigned values for the Degree of Implementation column from the Degree of Importance column for each behavior to arrive at your highest priorities.

Some Higher-Order Thinking and Problem-Solving Behaviors	Degree of Importance — Does your curriculum require students to achieve the following? (Check one)					Degree of Implementation — Are you teaching your students to achieve the following? (Check one)				
	To a Great Extent	To a Fair Extent	To Some Extent	A Little	Not at All	To a Great Extent	To a Fair Extent	To Some Extent	A Little	Not at All
1. Form a mental or symbolic representation of a given problem.										
2. Search one's long term memory for what is already known about a problem and different ways to solve it.										
3. Analyze and identify the components of an argument.										
4. Judge the credibility of evidence.										
5. Catch fallacies and contradictions.										
6. Make value judgments.										

491

	To a Great Extent	To a Fair Extent	To Some Extent	A Little	Not at All	To a Great Extent	To a Fair Extent	To Some Extent	A Little	Not at All
7. Identify the similarities and differences among various elements of a problem.										
8. Understand the relationship of each element of a problem to the whole problem.										
9. Gather information or evidence to solve a problem using inductive or deductive reasoning										
10. Apply given rules or heuristics to reach a conclusion.										
11. Identify criteria for judging the adequacy of a position or conclusion.										
12. Present evidence of how well a solution or position meets various criteria.										
13. Judge the adequacy of a conclusion or solution.										
14. Compare a problem to problems encountered previously.										
15. Compose drafts and tryouts in attempts to solve a problem.										
16. Examine the adequacy of strategies used to reach a solution.										
17. Distinguish the most important elements of a problem.										
18. Organize a conclusion about a problem in a logical fashion.										
19. Identify criteria for evaluating a problem solution.										
20. Draw a diagram that depicts all the forces impacting a problem.										

	To a Great Extent	To a Fair Extent	To Some Extent	A Little	Not at All	To a Great Extent	To a Fair Extent	To Some Extent	A Little	Not at All
21. Apply given logical or mathematical operations to a problem to generate new knowledge.										
22. Summarize, orally and in writing, what is read.										
23. Ask questions of self about ideas one is unsure of.										
24. Predict what will occur next in a sequence of events.										
25. Find corroborating evidence from among different data sources.										
26. Place an interpretation of a problem in the context of prevailing circumstances.										
27. Evaluate and revise what is written.										
28. Reformulate to make a problem more manageable.										
29. Change the structure of a problem from the one originally given.										
30. Compensate for an adjustment by making an equal and opposite adjustment.										
31. Plan/conduct a controlled experiment to test one's prediction.										
32. Explain the reasons or theory behind a hypothesis or prediction.										
33. Clearly communicate the results of what was observed in written and oral format.										
34. Draw a conceptual map or picture that shows what was learned or observed.										

	To a Great Extent	To a Fair Extent	To Some Extent	A Little	Not at All	To a Great Extent	To a Fair Extent	To Some Extent	A Little	Not at All
35. Consult experts, magazines, encyclopedias, newspapers, scientific journals, etc., for new information.										
36. Demonstrate independence and autonomy in completing a project or demonstration.										
37. Construct and interpret graphs charts, and tables.										
38. Make reasonable conjectures based on analysis of data.										
39. Meaningfully praise the performance of others.										
40. Accurately summarize what others have said.										
41. Provide assistance to others when asked.										
42. Ask for feedback when needed.										
43. Change viewpoint to match the facts.										
44. Listen attentively to others.										
45. Use a constructive tone when responding to others.										
46. Share and take turns.										
47. Set goals that are achievable within a specific span of time.										
48. Consult a variety of knowledge sources to achieve deep understanding.										
49. Realistically evaluate one's own performance.										
50. Keep a record of one's own progress toward important goals.										
51. Ignore distractions that interfere with goal attainment.										
52. Help keep others on task.										

References

Abruscato, J. (1994). Boost your students' social skills with this 9 step plan. *Learning 22*(5), 60–61, 66.

Alberto, P., & Troutman, A. (1986). *Applied behavior analysis for teachers: Influencing student performance* (2nd ed.). Upper Saddle River, NJ: Merrill/Prentice Hall.

American Association for the Advancement of Sciences. (1993). *Benchmarks for science literacy: Project 2061.* New York: Oxford University Press.

Anderson, J. R. (1990). *Cognitive psychology and its implications* (4th ed.). San Francisco: W. H. Freeman.

Anderson, L., & Block, J. (1987). Mastery learning models. In M. J. Dunkin (Ed.), *International encyclopedia of teaching and teacher education* (pp. 58–67). New York: Pergamon.

Anderson, L., Evertson, C., & Brophy, J. (1982). *Principles of small group instruction in elementary reading*. East Lansing: Michigan State University, Institute for Research on Teaching.

Anderson, L., Stevens, D., Prawat, R., & Nickerson, J. (1988). Classroom task environments and students' risk-related beliefs. *The Elementary School Journal, 88,* 181–296.

Anderson, M. G. (1992). The use of selected theater rehearsal technique activities with African-American adolescents labeled "Behaviorally Disordered." *Exceptional Children, 59,* 132–140.

Aschlbacher, P. R. (1991). Humanitas: A thematic curriculum. *Educational Leadership, 49*(2), 9–16.

Atkinson, M. L. (1984). Computer-assisted instruction: Current state of the art. *Computers in the Schools, 1,* 91–99.

Atwood, V., & Wilen, W. (1991). Wait time and effective social studies instruction: What can research in science education tell us? *Social Education 55,* 179–181.

Ausubel, D. P. (1968). *Educational psychology: A cognitive view*. New York: Holt, Rinehart & Winston.

Baer, D. M., Wolf, M. M., & Risley, T. R. (1968). Some current dimensions of applied behavior analysis. *Journal of Applied Behavior Analysis, 1,* 91–97.

Bandura, A. (1977). *Social learning theory.* Upper Saddle River, NJ: Prentice Hall.

Bandura, A. (1986). *Social foundations of thought and action: A social cognitive theory*. Upper Saddle River, NJ: Prentice Hall.

Bangert, R., Kulik, J., & Kulik, C. (1983). Individualized systems of instruction in secondary schools. *Review of Educational Research, 53,* 143–158.

Banks, J. *Teaching strategies for ethnic studies: 6th edition*. Needham, MA: Allyn & Bacon, 1997.

Barnes, J. (1987). Teaching experience. In M. J. Dunkin (Ed.), *International encyclopedia of teaching and teacher education* (pp. 608–611). New York: Pergamon.

Bartz, K., & Levine, E. (1978). Child rearing by black parents: A description and comparison to Anglo and Chicano parents. *Journal of Marriage and the Family, 40,* 709–719.

Beane, J. A. (1991). Sorting out the self-esteem controversy. *Educational Leadership, 49,* 25–30.

Bellack, A., Kliebard, H., Hyman, R., & Smith, F. (1966). *The language of the classroom*. New York: Teachers College Press.

Bennett, C. (1990). *Comprehensive multicultural education: Theory and practice* (2nd ed.). Boston: Allyn & Bacon.

Bennett, N., & Desforges, C. (1988). Matching classroom tasks to students' attainments. *The Elementary School Journal, 88,* 221–224.

Bennett, N., Desforges, C., Cockburn, A., & Wilkinson, B. (1981). *The quality of pupil learning experiences: Interim report.* Lancaster, England: University of Lancaster, Centre for Educational Research and Development.

Bereiter, C., & Englemann, S. (1966). *Teaching disadvantaged children in the preschool.* Upper Saddle River, NJ: Prentice Hall.

Bergan, J. R., & Dunn, J. A. (1976). *Psychology and education: A science for instruction.* New York: Wiley.

Berliner, D. (1979). Tempus educare. In P. Peterson & H. Walberg (Eds.), *Research on teaching: Concepts, findings, and implications* (pp. 120–135). Berkeley, CA: McCutchan.

Berliner, D., & Biddle, B. (1995). *The manufactured crisis: Myth, fraud, and the attack on America's public schools.* New York: Addison-Wesley.

Bettencourt, E., Gillett, M., Gall, M., & Hull, R. (1983). Effects of teacher enthusiasm training on student on-task behavior and achievement. *American Educational Research Journal, 20,* 435–450.

Beyer, B. (1992). Teaching thinking: An integrated approach. In W. Keefe & H. Walberg (Eds.), *Teaching for thinking.* Reston, VA: National Association of Secondary School Principals.

Beyer, B. (1995). *Critical thinking.* Bloomington, IN: Phi Delta Kappa Educational Foundation, Fastback No. 385.

Bloom, B. (1981). *All our children learning.* New York: McGraw-Hill.

Bloom, B., Englehart, M., Hill, W., Furst, E., & Krathwohl, D. (1984). *Taxonomy of educational objectives: The classification of educational goals. Handbook I: Cognitive domain.* New York: Longman Green.

Blumenfeld, P. C., Soloway, E., Marx, R. W., Krajcik, J. S., Guzdial, M., & Palincsar, A. (1991). Motivation project-based learning: Sustaining the doing, supporting the learning. *Educational Psychologist, 26,* 369–398.

Borich, G. (1993). *Clearly outstanding: Making each day count in your classroom.* Boston: Allyn & Bacon.

Borich, G. (1999). *Observation skills for effective teaching* (3rd ed.). Upper Saddle River, NJ: Merrill/Prentice Hall.

Borich, G., & Tombari, M. (1997). *Educational psychology: A contemporary approach* (2nd ed.). New York: Longman.

Bowers, C., & Flinders, D. (1991). *Culturally responsive teaching and supervision: A handbook for staff development.* New York: Teachers College Press.

Boyer, E. (1993, March). *Making the connections.* Address presented at the meeting of the Association for Supervision and Curriculum Development, Washington, DC.

Bradstad, B., & Stumpf, S. (1982). *A guidebook for teaching study skills and motivation.* Boston: Allyn & Bacon.

Bramlett, R. (1994) Implementing cooperative learning: A field study evaluating issues of school-based consultants. *Journal of School Psychology 32*(1), 67–84.

Bransford, J. D., & Steen, B. (1984). *The IDEAL problem solver.* New York: Freeman.

Bronfenbrenner, V. (1989). Ecological systems theory. In R. Vasta (Ed.), *Annals of child development* (Vol. 6, pp. 187–251). Greenwich, CT: JAI Press.

Brophy, J. (Ed.). (1989). *Advances in research on teaching* (Vol. 1). Greenwich, CT: JAI Press.

Brophy, J. (1992). Probing the subtleties of subject-matter teaching. *Educational Leadership, 49*(7), 4–8.

Brophy, J. (1996). *Teaching problem students.* New York: Guilford Press.

Brophy, J., & Evertson, C. (1976a). *Learning from teaching: A developmental perspective.* Boston: Allyn & Bacon.

Brophy, J., & Evertson, C. (1976b). *Process–product correlations in the Texas Teacher Effectiveness Study: Final report* (Research Report 74–4). Austin: University of Texas, Research and Development Center for Teacher Education. (ERIC Document Reproduction Service No. ED 091 094)

Brophy, J., & Good, T. (1986). Teacher behavior and student achievement. In M. C. Wittrock (Ed.), *Handbook of research on teaching* (3rd ed., pp. 328–375). Upper Saddle River, NJ: Merrill/Prentice Hall.

Brown, A. L. (1980). Metacognitive development and reading. In R. J. Spiro, B. C. Bruce, & W. F. Brewer (Eds.), *Theoretical issues in reading comprehension: Perspectives from cognitive psychology, linguistics, artificial intelligence, and education* (pp. 453–481). Hillsdale, NJ: Erlbaum.

Brown, G., & Edmondson, R. (1984). Asking questions. In E. Wragg (Ed.), *Classroom teaching skills* (pp. 97–119). New York: Nichols.

Brown, G., & Wragg, E. (1993). *Questioning*. London: Routledge.

Browne, D. A. (1984). WISC-R scoring patterns among Native Americans of the northern plains. *White Cloud Journal, 3,* 3–16.

Bruner, J. S. (1966). *Toward a theory of instruction*. New York: W. W. Norton.

Bullough, R. V. (1989). *First-year teacher: A case study*. New York: Teachers College Press.

Burden, P. (1986). Teacher development: Implications for teacher education. In J. Raths and L. Katz (Eds.), *Advances in teacher education* (Vol. 2). Norwood, NJ: Ablex.

Buzan, T. (1994). *The mindmap book*. New York: Dutton

Cabello, B., & Terrell, R. (1994). Making students feel like family: How teachers create warm and caring classroom climates. *Journal of Classroom Interaction, 29,* 17–23.

Calfee, R. (1986, April). *Those who can explain teach*. Paper presented at the annual meeting of the American Educational Research Association, San Francisco.

Campbell, B., Campbell, L., & Dickinson, D. (1996). *Teaching and learning through multiple intelligences*. Boston: Allyn & Bacon.

Canning, C. (1991). What teachers say about reflection. *Educational Leadership, 48*(6), 69–87.

Canter, L. (1976). *Assertive discipline: A take-charge approach for today's educator*. Seal Beach, CA: Canter and Associates.

Canter, L. (1989, September). Assertive discipline. More than names on the board and marbles in a jar. *Phi Delta Kappan,* pp. 57–61.

Carlson, C. (1992). Single parenting and stepparenting: Problems, issues and interventions. In M. J. Fine & C. Carlson (Eds.), *The handbook of family–school intervention: A systems perspective* (pp. 188–214). Boston: Allyn & Bacon.

Cassidy, J., & Asher, S. R. (1992). Loneliness and peer relations in young children. *Child Development, 63,* 350–365.

Christenson, S. L., Rounds, T., & Franklin, M. J. (1992). Home–school collaboration: Effects, issues and opportunities. In S. L. Christenson & J. C. Conoley (Eds.), *Home–school collaboration: Enhancing children's academic and social competence*. Silver Spring, MD: National Association of School Psychologists.

Chuska, K. (1995). *Improving classroom questions: A teacher's guide to increasing student motivation, participation and higher-level thinking*. Bloomington, IN: Phi Delta Kappa Educational Foundation.

Clark, C., & Peterson, P. (1986). Teachers' thought processes. In M. R. Wittrock (Ed.), *Handbook of research on teaching* (3rd ed., pp. 255–296). Upper Saddle River, NJ: Merrill/Prentice Hall.

Cochran, M., & Dean, C. (1991). Home–school relations and the empowerment process. *Elementary School Journal, 91,* 261–270.

Coffman, W. E. (1972). On the reliability of ratings of essay examinations. *NCME Reports on Measurement in Education, 3*(3).

Cohen, E. (1994). Restructuring the classroom: Conditions for productive small groups. *Review of Educational Research, 64*(1), 1–35.

Cohen, R. A. (1969). Conceptual styles, cultural conflict and nonverbal tests of intelligence. *American Anthropologist, 71,* 828–856.

Cooper, J. O., Heron, T. E., & Heward, W. L. (1987). *Applied behavior analysis*. Upper Saddle River, NJ: Merrill/Prentice Hall.

Corey, S. (1940). The teachers out-talk the pupils. *School Review, 48,* 745–752.

Corno, L., & Snow, R. (1986). Adapting teaching to individual differences among learners. In M. C. Wittrock (Ed.), *Handbook of research on teaching* (3rd ed., pp. 605–629). Upper Saddle River, NJ: Merrill/Prentice Hall.

Costa, A., & Lowery, L. (1989). *Techniques for teaching thinking*. Pacific Grove, CA: Midwest Publications.

Council for Basic Education. (1996). *What teachers have to say about teacher education*. New York: Council for Basic Education.

Covington, M., & Omelich, C. (1987). "I knew it cold before the exam": A test of the anxiety blockage hypothesis. *Journal of Psychology, 79,* 393–400.

Cronbach, L., & Snow, R. (1977). *Aptitudes and instructional methods.* New York: Irvington/Naiburg.

Cushner, K., McClelland, A., & Safford, P. (1992). *Human diversity in education: An integrative approach.* New York: McGraw-Hill.

Dahllof, U., & Lundgren, U. P. (1970). *Macro- and micro-approaches combined for curriculum process analysis: A Swedish educational field project.* Goteborg, Sweden: University of Goteborg, Institute of Education.

Dann, E. (1995). *Unconsciously learning something: A focus on teaching questioning.* (ERIC Document Reproduction Service No. ED 389 618)

de Charms, R. (1976). *Enhancing motivation: Change in the classroom.* New York: Irvington.

Deci, E., Vallerand, R., Pelletier, L., & Ryan, R. (1991). Motivation and education: The self-determination perspective. *Educational Psychologist, 26,* 325–346.

Delgado-Gaitan, C. (1991). Involving parents in the schools: A process of empowerment. *American Journal of Education, 100*(1), 20–46.

Delgado-Gaitan, C. (1992). School matters in the Mexican-American home: Socializing children to education. *American Educational Research Journal, 29*(3), 495–516.

Devin-Sheehan, L., Feldman, R. S., & Allen, V. L. (1976). Research on children tutoring children: A critical review. *Review of Educational Research, 46,* 355–385.

Dillard, J. L. (1972). *Black English: Its history and usage in the United States.* New York: Random House.

Dillon, D. (1989). Showing them that I want them to learn and that I care about who they are: A microethnography of the social organization of a secondary low-track English reading classroom. *American Educational Research Journal, 26,* 227–259.

Dillon, J. (1990). *The practice of questioning.* New York: Routledge.

Dillon, J. (1995). Discussion. In L. W. Anderson (Ed.), *International encyclopedia of teaching and teacher education* (2nd ed., pp. 251–255). Tarrytown, NY: Elsevier Sciences.

Dillon, J. T. (1988a). *Questioning and discussion: A multidisciplinary study.* Norwood, NJ: Ablex.

Dillon, J. T. (1988b). *Questioning and teaching: A manual of practice.* New York: Teachers College Press.

Dishon, D., & O'Leary, P. (1984). *A guidebook for cooperative learning.* Kalamazoo, MI: Learning Publications.

Dishon, T. J., Patterson, G. R., Stoolmiller, M., & Skinner, M. L. (1991). Family, school and behavioral antecedents to early adolescent involvement with antisocial peers. *Developmental Psychology, 27,* 172–180.

Dochy, F., & Alexander, P. (1995). Mapping prior knowledge: A framework for discussion among researchers. *European Journal of Psychology Education, 10*(3), 225–242.

Douglas, M. (1975). *Implicit meaning.* London: Routledge and Kegan Paul.

Dowaliby, F., & Schumer, H. (1973). Teacher-centered versus student-centered mode of college classroom instruction as related to manifest anxiety. *Journal of Educational Psychology, 64,* 125–132.

Doyle, W. (1983). Academic work. *Review of Educational Research, 53,* 159–200.

Doyle, W. (1986). Classroom organization and management. In M. Wittrock (Ed.), *Handbook of research on teaching* (3rd ed., pp. 392–431). Upper Saddle River, NJ: Merrill/Prentice Hall.

Duffy, G., & Roehler, L. (1989). The tension between information-giving and mediation: Perspectives on instructional explanation and teacher change. In J. Brophy (Ed.), *Advances in research on teaching* (Vol. 1, pp. 1–33). Greenwich, CT: JAI Press.

Duffy, G., Roehler, L., & Herrman, B. (1988). Modeling mental processes helps poor readers become strategic readers. *The Reading Teacher, 41*(8), 762–767.

Duffy, T., & Jonassen, D. (1992). *Constructivism and the technology of instruction: A conversation.* Hillsdale, NJ: Erlbaum.

Dunkin, M., & Biddle, B. (1974). *The study of teaching.* New York: Holt, Rinehart & Winston.

Dunn, R., & Griggs, S. (1995). *Multiculturalism and learning styles: Teaching and counseling adolescents.* Westport, CT: Praeger.

Eisner, E. (1969). Instructional and expressive educational objectives: Their formulation and use in curriculum. In W. Popham, E. Eisner, H. Sullivan, & L. Tyler (Eds.), *Instructional objectives: AERA monograph series on curriculum evaluation*, No. 3 (pp. 1–18). Chicago: Rand McNally.

Eisner, E. (1998). *The enlightened eye: Qualitative inquiry and the enhancement of educational practice*. Upper Saddle River, NJ: Merrill/Prentice Hall.

Elam, S., Rose, L., & Gallup, A. (1996). The 28th annual Phi Delta Kappa/Gallup poll of the public's attitudes toward the public schools. *Phi Delta Kappan, 78*(1), 41–59.

Elbaz, A. (1983). *Teacher thinking: A study of practical knowledge*. New York: Nichols.

Elliot, S. N., & Shapiro, E. S. (1990). Intervention techniques and programs for academic performance problems. In T. B. Gutkin & C. R. Reynolds (Eds.), *The handbook of school psychology* (2nd ed., pp. 637–662). New York: Wiley.

Emmer, E., Evertson, C., & Anderson, L. (1980). Effective classroom management at the beginning of the school year. *The Elementary School Journal, 80*(5), 219–231.

Emmer, E., Evertson, C., Clements, B., & Worsham, M. (1997). *Classroom management for secondary teachers*. Upper Saddle River, NJ: Prentice Hall.

Englemann, S. (1991). Teachers, schemata, and instruction. In M. M. Kennedy (Ed.), *Teaching academic subjects to diverse learners* (pp. 218–234). New York: Teachers College Press.

Englemann, S., & Carnine, D. (1982). *Theory of instruction: Principles and applications*. New York: Irvington.

Epstein, J. L. (1987). Toward a theory of family–school connections: Teacher practices and parent involvement. In K. Hurrelmann, F. Kauffman, & F. Losel (Eds.), *Social interventions: Potential and constraints* (pp. 121–136). New York: De Gruyter.

Erikson, E. (1968). *Identity, youth and crises*. New York: W. W. Norton.

Evertson, C. (1995). Classroom rules and routines. In L. Anderson (Ed.), *International encyclopedia of teaching and teacher education* (2nd ed., pp. 215–219). Tarrytown, NY: Elsevier Science.

Evertson, C. (1997) *Classroom management for elementary teachers: 4th edition*. Needham, MA: Allyn & Bacon.

Evertson, C., & Emmer, E. (1982). Effective management at the beginning of the school year in junior high classes. *Journal of Educational Psychology, 74*, 485–498.

Evertson, C., & Harris, H. (1992). What we know about managing classrooms. *Educational Leadership, 49*(7), 74–78.

Fielding, G., Kameenui, E., & Gerstein, R. (1983). A comparison of an inquiry and a direct instruction approach to teaching legal concepts and applications to secondary school students. *Journal of Educational Research, 76*, 243–250.

Fillmore, L., & Meyer, L. (1992). The curriculum and linguistic minorities. In P. Jackson (Ed.), *Handbook of research on curriculum.* New York: Macmillan.

Fisher, C. W., et al. (1978). *Teaching and learning in the elementary school: A summary of the Beginning Teacher Evaluation Study. Beginning Teacher Evaluation Study Report VII-I.* San Francisco: Far West Laboratory for Research & Development.

Flanders, N. (1970). *Analyzing teacher behavior.* Reading, MA: Addison-Wesley.

Franklin, M. E. (1992). Culturally sensitive instructional practices for African-American learners with disabilities. *Exceptional Children, 59*, 115–122.

Frazier, D. M., & Paulson, F. L. (1992). How portfolios motivate reluctant learners. *Educational Leadership, 49*(8), 62–65.

French, J., Jr., & Raven, B. (1959). The bases of social power. In D. Cartwright (Ed.), *Studies in social power* (pp. 150–168). Ann Arbor: University of Michigan Press.

Froyen, L. A. (1993). *Classroom management: The reflective teacher-leader* (2nd ed.). Upper Saddle River, NJ: Merrill/Prentice Hall.

Fuller, F. (1969). Concerns of teachers: A developmental conceptualization. *American Educational Research Journal, 6*, 207–226.

Gage, N. (1976). A factorially designed experiment on teacher structuring, soliciting and reacting. *Journal of Teacher Education, 16*, 35–38.

Gage, N., & Berliner, D. (1992). *Educational psychology* (5th ed.). Chicago: Rand McNally.

Gagné, E., Yekovich, C., & Yekovich, F. (1993). *The cognitive psychology of school learning.* Boston: Little, Brown.

Gagné, R., & Briggs, L. (1979). *Principles of instructional design.* New York: Holt, Rinehart & Winston.

Gagné, R., & Briggs, L. (1992). *Principles of instructional design* (4th ed.). New York: Holt, Rinehart & Winston.

Galambos, S. J., & Goldin-Meadow, S. (1990). The effects of learning two languages on levels of metalinguistic awareness. *Cognition, 34,* 1–56.

Gall, M. (1984). Synthesis of research on questioning in recitation. *Educational Leadership, 42*(3), 40–49.

Gallimore, R., Tharp, R. G., Sloat, K., Klein, T., & Troy, M. E. (1982). *Analysis of reading achievement test results for the Kamehameha Early Education Project: 1972–1979* (Tech. Rep. No. 102). Honolulu: Kamehameha Schools/Bishop Estate.

Gamoran, A. (1992). Synthesis of research: Is ability grouping equitable? *Educational Leadership, 50*(2), 11–13.

Gamoran, A. (1993). Alternative uses of ability grouping in secondary schools: Can we bring high-quality instruction to low-ability classes? *American Journal of Education, 102,* 1–22.

Garcia, R. L. (1991). *Teaching in a pluralistic society: Concepts, models, strategies* (2nd ed.). New York: HarperCollins.

Gardner, H., & Hatch, T. (1989). Multiple intelligences go to school. *Educational Researcher, 18*(8), 4–10.

Gardner, J. F., & Chapman, M. S. (1990). *Program issues in developmental disabilities* (2nd ed.). Baltimore: Paul H. Brookes.

Garger, S., & Guild, P. (1984). Learning styles: The crucial differences. *Curriculum Review, 23,* 9–12.

Ginott, H. G. (1972). *Teacher and child: A book for parents and teachers.* Upper Saddle River, NJ: Merrill/Prentice Hall.

Glasser, W. (1986). *Control theory in the classroom.* New York: Harper & Row.

Glasser, W. (1990). *Quality school: Managing students without coercion.* New York: Harper & Row.

Glover, J., & Corkill, A. (1990). The implications of cognitive psychology for school psychology. In T. B. Gutkin & G. Reynolds (Eds.), *The handbook of school psychology* (2nd ed.). New York: John Wiley.

Goetz, E. T., Alexander, P. A., & Ash, M. J. (1992). *Educational psychology: A classroom perspective.* Upper Saddle River, NJ: Merrill/Prentice Hall.

Good, T. (1979). Teacher effectiveness in the elementary school. *Journal of Teacher Education, 30,* 52–64.

Good, T., & Brophy, J. (1987). *Looking in classrooms* (5th ed.). New York: Addison-Wesley Longman.

Good, T., & Brophy, J. (1995). *Contemporary educational psychology* (5th ed.). New York: Longman.

Good, T., & Brophy, J. (1997). *Looking in classrooms* (7th ed.). New York: Longman.

Good, T., & Grouws, D. (1979). Teaching effects: A process-product study in fourth-grade mathematics classrooms. *Journal of Teacher Education, 28,* 49–54.

Good, T., & Grouws, D. (1987). Increasing teachers' understanding of mathematical ideas through inservice training. *Phi Delta Kappan, 68,* 778–783.

Good, T., & Stipek, D. (1983). Individual differences in the classroom: A psychological perspective. In G. D. Fenstermacher & J. I. Goodlad (Eds.), *Individual differences and the common curriculum: 82nd yearbook of the National Society for the Study of Education, Part 2* (pp. 9–43). Chicago: University of Chicago Press.

Goodlad, J. (1984). *A place called school.* New York: McGraw-Hill.

Gordon, T. (1974). *Teacher effectiveness training.* New York: Peter H. Wyden.

Grabe, M., & Grabe, C. (1996). *Integrating technology for meaningful learning.* Boston: Houghton Mifflin.

Grant, C. A. (1991). Culture and teaching: What do teachers need to know? In M. M. Kennedy (Ed.), *Teaching academic subjects to diverse learners* (pp. 237–256). New York: Teachers College Press.

Grave, M. E., Weinstein, T., & Walberg, H. J. (1983). School-based home instruction and learning: A quantitative analysis. *Journal of Educational Research, 76*(6), 351–360.

Greenwood, C. R., Delguardi, J. C., & Hall, R. V. (1984). Opportunity to respond and student academic achievement. In W. L. Heward, T. E. Heron, D. S. Hill, & J. Trap-Porter (Eds.), *Focus on behavior analysis in education* (pp. 58–88). Upper Saddle River, NJ: Merrill/Prentice Hall.

Gullickson, A. R., & Ellwein, M. C. (1985). Post-hoc analysis of teacher-made tests: The goodness of fit between prescription and practice. *Educational Measurement: Issues and Practice, 4*(1), 15–18.

Hakuta, K., Ferdman, B. M., & Diaz, R. M. (1987). Bilingualism and cognitive development: Three perspectives. In S. Rosenberg (Ed.), *Advances in applied psycholinguistics: Volume 2. Reading, writing, and language learning* (pp. 284–319). New York: Cambridge University Press.

Hall, E. (1977). *Beyond culture*. Garden City, NY: Anchor.

Hall, R. V., Delguardi, J., Greenwood, C. R., & Thurston, L. (1982). The importance of opportunity to respond in children's academic success. In E. B. Edgar, N. G. Haring, J. R. Jenkins, & C. G. Pious (Eds.), *Mentally handicapped children: Education and training* (pp. 107–140). Austin, TX: PRO-ED.

Hansford, B., & Hattie, J. (1982). The relationship between self and achievement/performance measures. *Review of Educational Research, 52,* 123–142.

Harrow, A. (1972). *A taxonomy of the psychomotor domain: A guide for developing behavioral objectives*. New York: David McKay.

Hartup, W. W. (1989). Social relationships and their developmental significance. *American Psychologist, 44,* 120–126.

Haynes, H. (1935). *The relation of teacher intelligence, teacher experience and type of school to type of questions*. Unpublished doctoral dissertation, George Peabody College for Teachers, Nashville, TN.

Hebert, E. A. (1992). Portfolios invite reflection from students and staff. *Educational Leadership, 49*(8), 58–61.

Henderson, R. W. (1980). Social and emotional needs of culturally diverse children. *Exceptional Children, 46,* 598–605.

Henderson, R. W., Swanson, R. A., & Zimmerman, B. J. (1974). Inquiry response induction in preschool children through televised modeling. *Developmental Psychology, 11*(4), 523–524.

Herrnstein, R., & Murray, C. (1994). *The bell curve: Intelligence and class structure in America*. New York: Free Press.

Hess, R. D., & Shipman, V. C. (1965). Early experience and the socialization of cognitive modes in children. *Child Development, 36,* 869–886.

Hester, J. (1994). *Teaching for thinking: A program for school improvement through critical thinking across the curriculum*. Durham, NC: Carolina Academic Press.

Hill, H. (1989). *Effective strategies for teaching minority students*. Bloomington, IN: National Educational Service.

Hilliard, A. (1976). *Alternatives to IQ testing: An approach to the identification of gifted minority children*. Final report. Sacramento Division of Special Education, California State Department of Education. (ERIC Document Reproduction Service No. ED 147 009)

Hilliard, A. (1992). The pitfalls and promises of special education practice. *Exceptional Children, 59*(2), 162–172.

Hodgkinson, H. (1988). *All one system: Demographics of education, kindergarten through graduate school*. Washington: The Institute for Educational Leadership.

Horcones, J. (1991). Walden Two in real life: Behavior analysis in the design of the culture. In W. Ishag (Ed.), *Human behavior in today's world*. New York: Praeger.

Horcones, J. (1992). Natural reinforcement: A way to improve education. *Journal of Applied Behavior Analysis, 25*(1), 71–76.

Hunkins, F. (1989). *Teaching thinking through effective questioning*. Boston: Christopher-Gordon.

Hunt, D. (1979). Learning style and student needs: An introduction to conceptual level. In *Student learning styles: Diagnosing and prescribing programs*. Reston, VA: National Association of Secondary School Principals.

Hunter, M. (1982). *Mastery teaching*. El Segundo, CA: Instructional Dynamics.

Hyerle, D. (1995–1996). Thinking maps: Seeing is understanding. *Educational Leadership 53*(4), 85–89.

Iwata, B. A. (1987). Negative reinforcement in applied behavior analysis: An emerging technology. *Journal of Applied Behavior Analysis, 20,* 361–387.

Jackson, P. (1968). *Life in classrooms.* New York: Holt, Rinehart & Winston.

Jensen, A. (1969). How much can we boost IQ and scholastic achievement? *Harvard Educational Review, 39*(1), 1–123.

Johnson, D., & Johnson, R. (1991). *Learning together and alone* (3rd ed.). Upper Saddle River, NJ: Prentice Hall.

Johnson, D., & Johnson, R. (1996). Cooperative learning and traditional American values: An appreciation. *NASSP Bulletin* 80(579), 63–65.

Johnson, D. W., Johnson, R. T., & Holubec, E. J. (1994). *The new circles of learning: cooperation in the classroom.* Alexandria, VA: ASCD.

Jones, F. C. (1987). *Positive classroom discipline.* New York: McGraw-Hill.

Jones, K. (1995). *Simulations: A handbook for teachers and trainers.* East Brunswick, NJ: Nichols.

Kagan, D., & Tippins, D. (1992). The evolution of functional lesson plans among twelve elementary and secondary student teachers. *Elementary School Journal, 92*(4), 477–489.

Kaplan, A. (1964). *The conduct of inquiry.* San Francisco: Chandler.

Kavale, K. A. (1990). Effectiveness of special education. In T. B. Gutkin & C. R.Reynolds (Eds.), *The handbook of school psychology* (2nd ed., pp. 870–900). New York: Wiley.

Kendall, F. E. (1983). *Diversity in the classroom: A multicultural approach to the education of young children.* New York: Teachers College Press.

Kendon, A. (1981). *Nonverbal communication, interaction, and gesture.* The Hague: Mouton.

Kennedy, M. (Ed.). (1991). *Teaching academic subjects to diverse learners.* New York: Teachers College Press.

Kerchoff, A. C. (1986). Effects of ability grouping in British secondary schools. *American Sociological Review, 51,* 842–858.

Knight, G. P., & Kagan, S. (1977). Acculturation of prosocial and competitive behaviors among second- and third-generation Mexican-American children. *Journal of Cross-Cultural Psychology, 8,* 273–284.

Kounin, J. (1970). *Discipline and group management in the classroom.* New York: Holt, Rinehart & Winston.

Kozulin, A. (1990). *Vygotsky's psychology: A biography of ideas.* Cambridge: Harvard University Press.

Krabbe, M., & Polivka, J. (1990, April). *An analysis of students' perceptions of effective teaching behaviors during discussion activity.* Paper presented at the annual meeting of the American Educational Research Association, Boston.

Krathwohl, D., Bloom, B., & Masia, B. (1964). *Taxonomy of educational objectives. The classification of educational goals. Handbook II: Affective domain.* New York: David McKay.

Kubiszyn, T., & Borich, G. (2000). *Educational testing and measurement: Classroom application and practice* (6th ed.). New York: Wiley.

Kulik, J. A., & Kulik, C. C. (1984). Effects of accelerated instruction on students. *Review of Educational Research, 54,* 409–425.

La Berge, D., & Samuels, S. (1974). Toward a theory of automatic information processing in reading. *Cognitive Psychology, 6,* 293–323.

Lambert, N. M. (1991). Partnerships of psychologists, educators, community-based agency personnel, and parents in school redesign. *Educational Psychologist, 26,* 185–198.

Lane, S. (1993, Summer). The conceptual framework for the development of a mathematics performance assessment instrument. *Educational Measurement: Issues and Practice*, pp. 16–23.

Lazear, D. (1992). *Teaching for multiple intelligences.* Fastback No. 342. Bloomington, IN: Phi Delta Kappa Educational Foundation.

Lein, L. (1975). "You were talkin' though, oh yes, you was." Black American migrant children: Their speech at home and school. *Council on Anthropology and Education Quarterly, 6*(4), 1–11.

Leler, H. (1983). Parent education and involvement in relation to the schools and to parents of school-aged children. In R. Hoskins & D. Adamson (Eds.), *Parent education and public policy* (pp. 141–180). Norwood, NJ: Ablex.

Leriche, L. (1992). The sociology of classroom discipline. *The High School Journal, 75*(2), 77–89.

Levin, H. (1986). *Educational reform for disadvantaged students: An emerging crisis*. Washington: National Education Association.

Levin, J., & Nolan, J. F. (1991). *Principles of classroom management: A hierarchical approach*. Upper Saddle River, NJ: Prentice Hall.

Levine, D., & Havinghurst, R. (1984). *Society and education* (6th ed.). Boston: Allyn & Bacon.

Levis, D. S. (1987). Teachers' personality. In M. J. Dunkin (Ed.), *Encyclopedia of teaching and teacher education* (pp. 585–588). New York: Pergamon.

Lightfoot, S. (1983). *The good high school*. New York: Basic Books.

Lindsley, O. R. (1991). Precision teaching's unique legacy from B. F. Skinner. *Journal of Behavioral Education, 1,* 253–266.

Lindsley, O. R. (1992). Why aren't effective teaching tools widely adopted? *Journal of Applied Behavior Analysis, 25*(1), 21–26.

Linney, J. A., & Vernberg, E. (1983). Changing patterns of parental employment and the family-school relationship. In C. D. Hayes & S. Kamerman (Eds.), *Children of working parents: Experiences and outcomes* (pp. 73–99). Washington, DC: National Academy Press.

Lippitt, R., & Gold, M. (1959). Classroom social structure as a mental health problem. *Journal of Social Issues, 15,* 40–58.

Losey, K. (1995). Mexican American students and classroom interaction: An overview and critique. *Review of Educational Research, 65*(3), 283–318.

Loucks-Horsley, S., Kapiton, R., Carlson, M. D., Kuerbis, P. J., Clark, P. C., Melle, G. M., Sachse, T. P., & Wolten, E. (1990). *Elementary school science for the '90s*. Alexandria, VA: Association for Supervision and Curriculum Development.

Luiten, J., Ames, W., & Aerson, G. (1980). A meta-analysis of advance organizers on learning and retention. *American Educational Research Journal, 17,* 211–218.

Lysakowski, R., & Walberg H. (1981). Classroom reinforcement and learning: A quantitative synthesis. *Journal of Educational Research, 75,* 69–77.

Mansnerus, L. (1992, November 1). Should tracking be derailed? *Education Life. New York Times Magazine,* pp. 14–16.

Martin, P. (1995). Creating lesson blocks: A multi-discipline team effort. *Schools in the Middle, 5*(11), 22–24.

Martinello, M., & Cook, G. (1994). *Interdisciplinary inquiry in teaching and learning*. Upper Saddle River, NJ: Merrill/Prentice Hall.

Marx, R., & Peterson, P. (1981). The nature of teacher decision-making. In B. Joyce, C. Brown, & L. Peck (Eds.), *Flexibility in teaching: An excursion into the nature of teaching and training*. New York: Longman.

Marx, R., & Walsh, J. (1988). Learning from academic tasks. *The Elementary School Journal, 88*(3), 207–219.

Mauer, R. E. (1985). *Elementary discipline handbook: Solutions for the K–8 teacher*. West Nyack, NY: The Center for Applied Research in Education.

Mayer, R., & Wittrock, M. (1996). Problem-solving transfer. In Berliner & R. Calfee (Eds.), *Handbook of educational psychology* (pp. 47–62). New York: Macmillan.

Mayer, R. E. (1987). *Educational psychology: A cognitive approach*. Boston: Little, Brown.

McDonald, J., & Czerniak, C. (1994). Developing interdisciplinary units: Strategies and examples. *School Science and Mathematics, 94*(1), 5–10.

McKenzie, R. (1979). Effects of questions and test-like events on achievement and on-task behavior in a classroom concept learning presentation. *Journal of Educational Research, 72,* 348–350.

Medrich, E. A., Roizen, J. A., Rubin, V., & Burkley, S. (1982). *The serious business of growing up: A study of children's lives outside school*. Berkeley: University of California Press.

Megnin, J. (1995) Combining memory and creativity in teaching math. *Teaching PreK-8, 25*(6), 48–49.

Messick, S. (1995). Cognitive styles and learning. In L. Anderson (Ed.), *International encyclopedia of teaching and teacher education* (2nd ed., pp. 387–390). Tarrytown, NY: Elsevier Science.

Michaels, S., & Collins, J. (1984). Oral discourse styles: Classroom interaction and the acquisition of literacy. In D. Tannen (Ed.), *Coherence in spoken and written discourse*. Norwood, NJ: Ablex.

Mitchell, R. (1992). *Testing for learning: How new approaches to evaluation can improve American schools*. New York: Free Press.

Moore, K. (1992). *Classroom teaching skills* (2nd ed.). New York: McGraw-Hill.

National Center for Education Statistics. (1993a). *The condition of education 1993*. Washington, DC: U.S. Department of Education, Office of Educational Research and Improvement.

National Center for Education Statistics. (1993b). *Youth indicators 1993: Trends in the well-being of American youth*. Washington, DC: U.S. Department of Education, Office of Educational Research and Improvement.

National Commission on Excellence in Education. (1983). *A nation at risk: The imperative for educational reform*. Washington, DC: U.S. Department of Education.

National Commission on Excellence in Education. (1983). *A Nation at risk: The imperative for educational reform*. Washington, DC: U.S. Department of Education.

National Council for the Social Studies. (1994). *Expectations of excellence: curriculum standards for social studies*. Washington, DC: National Council for the Social Studies.

National Council of Teachers of English. (1996). *Standards for the English language arts*. Urbana, IL: National Council of Teachers of English and International Reading Association.

National Council of Teachers of Mathematics. (1995). *Assessment standards for school mathematics*. Reston, VA: National Council of Teachers of Mathematics.

National Research Council. (1996). *National science education standards 1995*. Washington, DC: National Academy Press.

O'Neil, J. (1992). On tracking and individual differences: A conversation with Jeannie Oakes. *Educational Leadership, 50*(2), 18–21.

Oser, F. (1986). Moral education and values education: The discourse perspective. In M. Wittrock (Ed.), *Handbook of research on teaching* (3rd ed., pp. 917–941). Upper Saddle River, NJ: Merrill/Prentice Hall.

Padilla, A. M., Lindholm, K. J., Chen, A., Duran, R., Hakuta, K., Lambert, W., & Tucker, G. R. (1991). The English-only movement: Myths, reality, and implications for psychology. *American Psychologist, 46,* 120–130.

Palincsar, A. (1987). *Discourse for learning about comprehending text*. Paper presented at the National Reading Conference, St. Petersburg Beach, FL.

Palincsar, A., & Brown, A. (1989). Classroom dialogues to promote self-regulated comprehension. In J. Brophy (Ed.), *Advances in research on teaching* (Vol. 1, pp. 35–71). Greenwich, CT: JAI Press.

Parker, W. C. (1991). *Renewing the social studies curriculum*. Alexandria, VA: Association for Supervision and Curriculum Development.

Patterson, G. R., DeBarsyshe, B. D., & Ramsey, E. (1989). A developmental perspective on antisocial behavior. *American Psychologist, 44,* 329–335.

Paul, R. (1990). *Critical thinking*. Rohnert Park, CA: Center for Critical Thinking and Moral Critique, Sonoma State University.

Piaget, J. (1977). Problems in equilibration. In M. Appel & L. Goldberg (Eds.), *Topics in cognitive development: Vol. 1. Equilibration: Theory, research and application* (pp. 3–13). New York: Plenum.

Piestrup, A. (1973). *Black dialect interference and accommodation of reading instruction in first grade* (Monograph No. 4). Berkeley, CA: University of California, Language Behavior Research Laboratory.

Polanyi, M. (1958). *Personal knowledge*. Chicago: University of Chicago Press.

Pollock, J. E. (1992). Blueprints for social studies. *Educational Leadership, 49*(8), 52–53.

Porter, A. (1993). School delivery standards. *Educational Researcher, 22,* 24–30.

Posner, G. (1987). Pacing and sequencing. In M. J. Dunkin (Ed.), *Encyclopedia of teaching and teacher education* (pp. 266–271). New York: Pergamon.

Putnam, J., & Burke, J. B. (1992). *Organizing and managing classroom learning communities*. New York: McGraw-Hill.

Rallis, S., Rossman, G, Phlegar, J., & Abeille, A. (1995). *Dynamic teachers: leaders of change.* Thousand Oaks, CA: Corwin Press.

Ramirez, M., & Castaneda, A. (1974). *Cultural democracy: Biocognitive development and education.* New York: Academic Press.

Raven, B. H. (1974). The comparative analysis of power and power preference. In J. T. Tedeschi (Ed.), *Perspectives on social power* (pp. 172–198). Chicago: Aldine.

Redding, N. (1992). Assessing the big outcomes. *Educational Leadership, 49*(8), 49–53.

Redfield, D., & Rousseau, E. (1981). A meta-analysis of experimental research on teacher questioning behavior. *Review of Educational Research, 51,* 237–245.

Resnick, L., & Klopfer, L. (Eds.) (1989). *Toward the thinking curriculum: Current cognitive research.* Arlington, VA: Association for Supervision and Curriculum Development.

Resnick, L. B. (1987). *Education and learning to think.* Washington, DC: National Academy Press.

Resnick, L. B., & Resnick, D. P. (1991). Assessing the thinking curriculum: New tools for educational reform. In B. R. Gifford and M. C. O'Connor (Eds.), *Future assessments: Changing views of aptitude, achievement and instruction.* Boston: Kluwer.

Reynolds, M. C. (Ed.). (1989). *Knowledge base for the beginning teacher.* New York: Pergamon.

Rich, D. (1987). *Teachers and parents: An adult-to-adult approach.* Washington: National Education Association.

Richmond, G., & Striley, J. (1994). An integrated approach. *The Science Teacher, 61*(7), 42–45.

Rinne, C. (1984). *Attention: The fundamentals of classroom control.* Upper Saddle River, NJ: Merrill/Prentice Hall.

Risner, G., Skeel, D., & Nicholson, J. (1992). A closer look at textbooks. *Science and Children, 30*(1), 42–45, 73.

Rist, R. (1970). Student social class and teaching expectations: The self-fulfilling prophecy in ghetto education. *Harvard Educational Review, 40,* 411–451.

Roberts, P., & Kellough, R. (1996). *A guide for developing interdisciplinary thematic units.* Upper Saddle River, NJ: Merrill/Prentice Hall.

Rogan, J., Borich, G., & Taylor, H. P. (1992). Validation of the stages of concern questionnaire. *Action in Teacher Education, 14*(2), 43–49.

Rogoff, B. (1990). *Apprenticeship in thinking: Cognitive development in social context.* New York: Oxford University Press.

Rohrkemper, M., & Corno, L. (1988). Success and failure on classroom tasks: Adaptive learning and classroom teaching. *The Elementary School Journal, 88*(3), 298–312.

Rosenshine, B. (1971). *Teaching behaviors and student achievement.* London: National Foundation for Educational Research in England and Wales.

Rosenshine, B. (1983). Teaching functions in instructional programs. *The Elementary School Journal, 83,* 335–351.

Rosenshine, B. (1986). Synthesis of research on explicit teaching. *Educational Leadership, 43*(7), 60–69.

Rosenshine, B., & Meister, C. (1992). The use of scaffolds for teaching higher-level cognitive strategies. *Educational Leadership, 49*(7), 26–33.

Rosenshine, B., & Meister, C. (1994). Reciprocal teaching: A review of the research. *Review of Educational Research, 64,* 479–530.

Rosenshine, B., & Stevens, R. (1986). Teaching functions. In M. C. Wittrock (Ed.), *Handbook of research on teaching* (3rd ed., pp. 376–391). Upper Saddle River, NJ: Merrill/Prentice Hall.

Rotter, J., Robinson, E., & Fey M. (1987). *Parent–teacher conferencing.* Washington: National Education Association.

Rowe, M. B. (1986, January-February). Wait time: Slowing down may be a way of speeding up. *Journal of Teacher Education, 23,* 43–49.

Rowe, M. B. (1987). Wait time: Slowing down may be a way of speeding up. *American Educator, 11*(1), 38–43, 47.

Ryan, K. (1992). *The roller coaster year: Essays by and for beginning teachers.* New York: HarperCollins.

Sacks, S. R., & Harrington, C. N. (1982, March). *Student to teacher: The process of role transition.* Paper presented at the meeting of the American Educational Research Association, New York.

Savage, T. (1991). *Discipline for self-control*. Upper Saddle River, NJ: Prentice Hall.

Sax, G. (1989). *Principles of educational and psychological measurement and evaluation* (3rd ed.). Belmont, CA: Wadsworth.

Scarr, S. (1981). Testing for children: Assessment and the many determinants of intellectual competence. *American Psychologist, 36*(10), 1159–1166.

Schmuck, R., & Schmuck, P. (1992). *Group processes in the classroom* (6th ed.). Dubuque, IA: William C. Brown.

Schunk, D. H. (1991). Self-efficacy and academic motivation. *Educational Psychologist, 26,* 207–232.

Schutz, W. (1958). *FIRO: A three dimensional theory of interpersonal behavior*. New York: Holt, Rinehart & Winston.

Scollon, R. (1985). The machine stops: Silence in the metaphor of malfunction. In D. Tannen & M. Saville-Troike (Eds.), *Perspectives on silence*. Norwood, NJ: Ablex.

Shade, B. J. (1982). Afro-American cognitive style: A variable in school success. *Review of Educational Research, 52,* 219–244.

Shalaway, L. (1989). *Learning to teach*. Cleveland, OH: Edgell Communications.

Shavelson, R. J., & Baxter, G. P. (1992). What we've learned about assessing hands-on science. *Educational Leadership, 49*(8), 20–25.

Shavelson, R. J., Gao, X., & Baxter, G. (1991). *Design theory and psychometrics for complex performance assessment*. Los Angeles: UCLA Center for Research on Evaluation, Standards and Student Testing.

Shulman, L. S. (1992). Toward a pedagogy of cases. In J. H. Shulman (Ed.), *Case methods in teacher education* (pp. 72–92). New York: Teachers College Press.

Simmons, P. (1995). Metacognitive strategies: Teaching and assessing. In L. Anderson (Ed.), *International Encyclopedia of teaching and teacher education:* (2nd ed., pp. 481–485). Tarrytown, NY: Elsevier Science, Inc.

Singer, H., & Donlon, D. (1982). Active comprehension problem-solving schema with question generation for comprehension of complex short stories. *Reading Research Quarterly, 17,* 116–186.

Sizer, T. (1985). *Harace's compromise: The dilemma of the American high school*. Boston: Houghton & Mifflin.

Skinner, B. F. (1953). *Science and human behavior*. Upper Saddle River, NJ: Merrill/Prentice Hall.

Skirtic, T. (1991). The special education paradox: Equity as the way to excellence. *Harvard Educational Review, 61*(2), 148–206.

Slavin, R. (1987). Ability group and student achievement in elementary schools: A best evidence synthesis. *Review of Educational Research, 57,* 273–336.

Slavin, R. (1990a). Achievement effects of ability grouping in secondary schools: A best evidence synthesis. *Review of Educational Research, 60,* 471–499.

Slavin, R. (1990b). *Cooperative learning*. Upper Saddle River, NJ: Prentice Hall.

Slavin, R. (1991a). Are cooperative learning and untracking harmful to the gifted? *Educational Leadership, 48,* 68–71.

Slavin, R. (1991b). *Educational psychology: Theory into practice*. Upper Saddle River, NJ: Prentice Hall.

Slavin, R. (1993). *Student team learning: An overview and practical guide*. Washington, DC: National Education Association.

Slavin, R., Sharan, S., Kagan, S., Hertz-Lazarowitz, R., Webb, C., & Schmuck, R. (1985). *Learning to cooperate, cooperating to learn*. New York: Plenum.

Sleeter, C., & Grant, C. (1991). *Race, class, gender, and disability in current textbooks*. New York: Routledge & Chapman.

Smilansky, M. (1979). *Priorities in education: Preschool, evidence and conclusions*. Washington, DC: World Bank.

Smith, B., & Meux, M. (1970). *A study of the logic of teaching*. Champaign, IL: University of Illinois.

Smith, G. (1995). *Understanding grammar*. New York: City Press.

Smith, H. (1984). State of the art of nonverbal behavior in teaching. In A. Wolfgang (Ed.), *Nonverbal behavior: Perspectives, applications, intercultural insights*. New York: Hogrefe.

Soar, R., & Soar, R. (1983). Context effects in the learning process. In D. C. Smith (Ed.), *Essen-*

tial knowledge for beginning educators (pp. 156–192). Washington, DC: American Association of Colleges of Teacher Education.

Spielberger, C. (Ed.) (1966). *Anxiety and behavior*. New York: Academic Press.

Stallings, J., & Keepes, B. (1970). *Student aptitudes and methods for teaching beginning reading: A predictive instrument for determining interaction patterns. Final report* (Project No. 9-1-099, Report OEG-9-70-0005). Washington, DC: U.S. Department of Health, Education and Welfare, Office of Education, Bureau of Research.

Steffe, L., & Gale, J. (Eds.). (1995). *Constructivism in education*. Hillsdale, NJ: Erlbaum.

Sternberg, R. (1989). *The triarchic mind: A new theory of human intelligence*. New York: Penguin.

Sternberg, R. (1994). *Thinking and problem solving*. San Diego: Academic Press.

Sternberg, R. (1995). *The nature of insight*. Cambridge, MA: MIT Press.

Stevens, R., & Slavin, R. (1995a). The cooperative elementary school: Effects on students' achievement, attitudes and social relations. *American Educational Research Journal, 32*(2), 321–351.

Stevens, R., & Slavin, R. (1995b). Effects of a cooperative learning approach in reading and writing on academically handicapped and non-handicapped students. *Elementary School Journal, 95*(3), 241–262.

Stevenson, C., & Carr, J. (Eds.). (1993). *Integrated studies in the middle grades*. New York: Teachers College Press.

Stiggins, R. J. (1994). *Student-centered classroom assessment*. Upper Saddle River, NJ: Merrill/Prentice Hall.

Sugai, G. (1996, fall–winter). UO and public schools design just-in-time learning approaches to find solutions to rising student discipline problems. *Education Matters, 3*(1), 10–11.

Swap, S. (1987). *Enhancing parental involvement in schools*. New York: Teachers College Press.

Szetela, W., & Nicol, C. (1992). Evaluating problem solving in mathematics. *Educational Leadership, 49*(8), 42–45.

Tamir, P. (1995). Discovery learning and teaching. In L. Anderson, (Ed.), *International encyclopedia of teaching and teacher education* (2nd ed., pp. 149–155). Tarrytown, NY: Elsevier Science.

Tannen, D. (1986). *That's not what I meant!* New York: Morrow.

Tauber, R. (1990). *Classroom management from A to Z*. Chicago: Holt, Rinehart & Winston.

Teddlie, C., & Stringfield, S (1993). *Schools make a difference: Lessons learned from a 10-year study of school effects*. New York: Teachers College Press.

Tharp, R. G. (1989). Psychocultural variables and constants: Effects on teaching and learning in schools. *American Psychologist, 44,* 349–359.

Tharp, R. G., & Gallimore, R. (1989). *Rousing minds to life: Teaching, learning and schooling in social context*. New York: Cambridge University Press.

Thorndike, R. L. (1913). *The psychology of learning (Educational Psychology II)*. New York: Teachers College Press.

Thurstone, L. (1947). *Primary mental abilities, Form AH*. Chicago: Science Research Associates.

Tobin, K. (1987). The role of wait-time in higher cognitive level learning. *Review of Educational Research, 57,* 69–95.

Tombari, M., & Borich, G. (1999). *Authentic assessment in the classroom: Practice and applications*. Upper Saddle River, NJ: Merrill/Prentice Hall.

Turnbull, A. P., & Turnbull, H. R. (1986). *Families, professionals and exceptionality*. Upper Saddle River, NJ: Merrill/Prentice Hall.

Tyler, R. W. (1934). *Constructing achievement tests*. Columbus: Ohio State University Press.

Tyler, R. W. (1974). Considerations in selecting objectives. In D. A. Payne (Ed.), *Curriculum evaluation: Commentaries on purpose, process, product*. Lexington, MA: D. C. Heath.

Valencia, R. (1997). *The evolution of deficit thinking*. London: Falmer Press.

Vasta, R. (1976). Feedback and fidelity: Effects of contingent consequences on accuracy of imitation. *Journal of Experimental Child Psychology, 21,* 98–108.

Verduin, J. (1996). *Helping student develop investigative problem solving and thinking skills in a cooperative setting*. Springfield, IL: Charles C. Thomas, 1996.

Vygotsky, L. (1962). *Thought and language*. Cambridge, MA: MIT Press.

Wakefield, J. (1996). *Educational psychology: Learning to be a problem solver*. Boston: Houghton Mifflin.

Walberg, H. (1986). Syntheses of research on teaching. In M. C. Wittrock (Ed.), *Handbook of research on teaching* (3rd ed., pp. 214–229). Upper Saddle River, NJ: Merrill/Prentice Hall.

Walberg, H. (1991). Productive teaching and instruction: Assessing the knowledge base. In H. Waxman & H. Walbert (Eds.), *Effective teaching: Current research*. Berkeley, CA: McCuchan.

Walker, H., & Sylwester, R. (1991). Where is school along the path to prison? *Educational Leadership,* pp. 14–16.

Watson-Gegeo, K. A., & Boggs, S. T. (1977). From verbal play to talk story: The role of routines in speech events among Hawaiian children. In S. Ervin-Tripp & C. Mitchell-Kernan (Eds.), *Child discourse* (pp. 67–90). New York: Academic Press.

Webb, N., Trooper, J., & Fall, R. (1995) Constructive activity and learning in collaborative small groups. *Journal of Educational Psychology, 87*(34), 406–423.

Weiner, B. (1986). *An attribution theory of motivation and emotion.* New York: Springer-Verlag.

Weisner, T., Gallimore, R., & Jordan C. (1988). Unpackaging cultural effects on classroom learning: Native Hawaiian peer assistance and child-generated activity. *Anthropology and Education Quarterly, 19,* 327–353.

Weissglass, J. (1996). Transforming schools into caring learning communities. *Journal for a Just and Caring Education, 2*(2), 175–189.

Wiggins, G. (1992). Creating tests worth taking. *Educational Leadership, 49*(8), 26–34.

Wilen, W. (1991). *Questioning skills for teachers* (3rd ed.). Washington, DC: National Education Association.

Willoughby, S. S. (1990). *Mathematics education for a changing world*. Alexandria, VA: Association for Supervision and Curriculum Development.

Wood, W. (1992). The stock market game: classroom use and strategy. *Journal of Economic Education, 23*(3), 236–246.

Woolfolk, A. (1997). *Educational psychology* (7th ed.). Needham, MA: Allyn & Bacon.

Wyne, M., & Stuck, G. (1982). Time and learning: Implications for the classroom teacher. *The Elementary School Journal, 83,* 67–75.

Yelon, S. (1996). *Powerful principles of instruction*. White Plains, NY: Longman.

Young, V. H. (1970). Family and childhood in a Southern Georgia community. *American Anthropologist, 72,* 269–288.

Ysseldyke, J. E., & Marston, D. (1990). The use of assessment information to plan instructional interventions: A review of the research. In T. B. Gutkin & C. R. Reynolds (Eds.), *The handbook of school psychology* (2nd ed., pp. 663–684). New York: Wiley.

Zahorik, J. (1987). Reacting. In M. J. Dunkin (Ed.), *Encyclopedia of teaching and teacher education* (pp. 416–423). New York: Pergamon.

Zakariya, S. (1987). How to keep your balance when it comes to bilingual education. *The American School Board Journal, 6,* 21–26.

Zehm, S., & Kottler, J. (1993). *On being a teacher: The human dimension.* Thousand Oaks, CA: Corwin Press.

Zimbardo, P. G. (1992). *Psychology and life*. New York: HarperCollins.

Zimmerman, B. (1989). A social cognitive view of self-regulated academic learning. *Journal of Educational Psychology, 81,* 329–339.

Author Index

Subject Index